Commentary on 1&2 Corinthians

OTHER BOOKS BY FRED FISHER

A Composite Gospel
Christianity Is Personal
The Purpose of God and the Christian Life
Prayer in the New Testament
Jesus and His Teachings
Falling Walls: Study of Reconciliation
Paul and His Teachings

Commentary on

1&2

Corinthians

Fred Fisher

WORD BOOKS, Publisher
Waco, Texas

COMMENTARY ON 1 AND 2 CORINTHIANS

Library of Congress catalog card number: 74–27486
Printed in the United States of America

CONTENTS

1 Corinthians

INTRODUCTION

1 Corinthians

1 Corinthians is one of the most interesting and important books in our New Testament. It is interesting because it gives us insight into the life and problems of a church in New Testament times. In our study of it we will take our place in the meetings of the church, sense the problems of a church facing life in a pagan world, understand the thoughts of people only recently converted to Christ, and share the dreams of Christians who sought the higher life. In all of this we may be instructed for our own Christian life.

1 Corinthians is important in its own peculiar way. It is not, like the Gospels, a source of knowledge of the life and teachings of Jesus, but its message is based on the work of Christ. It is not, like Acts, a history of New Testament times, but it supplements the material in Acts by giving us insight into the life of a New Testament church. It is not, like Romans, a treatment of great Christian doctrines, but it shows how doctrines apply to life. It is important because it reveals how the problems of the Christian life may be solved according to Christian principles.

THE CITY OF CORINTH

It could only have happened at Corinth. At least this is the impression one gains after studying Paul's correspondence with the church at Corinth against the background of the city itself.

Corinth was a unique city in the Roman empire—unique in its wickedness, in its commerce, in its religion, in its population, in its life.

The wickedness of the city was a byword in the ancient world. "To live like a Corinthian" was the phrase used to describe loose and immoral conduct. A church located in such a bed of iniquity was bound to be affected by its surroundings, and there is evidence in Paul's letters that this was actually true.

The commerce of the city was by the sea. Located between two gulfs, the Gulf of Corinth and the Saronic Gulf, the chief business of Corinth was the transport of goods from ships anchored in one gulf to ships anchored in the other. Sometimes, it seems, the smaller ships were hauled on log rollers across the three-and-a-half-mile isthmus which separated them. A church located in such a situation would need to bear witness to Christ in a multitude of languages; this perhaps explains the gift of tongues about which Paul wrote in 1 Corinthians 12 and 14.

The religion of the city was the worship of gods of sensual pleasure and self-indulgence. The chief goddess seems to have been Aphrodite Pandemos, a Greek version of the Phoenician Astarte. In old Corinth there had been a thousand priestesses associated with the temple worship. Sexual intercourse was an integral part of the religious worship of this goddess. We do not know that there were so many priestesses in Paul's day, but we cannot doubt that religion was one of the debasing factors in the life of the city. A Christian church in such surroundings would be tempted in many ways. Paul's discussion of the Christians' contact with the worshipers of the pagan gods reveals the presence of such problems in the church at Corinth.

The population of Corinth was mixed and fluctuating. It was the least Greek of all the Greek cities and the least Roman of all the Roman cities. The permanent citizens were an admixture of Italians, Greeks, and Jews. The passing throngs were seamen, merchants, and travelers from over the world. Extreme wealth and extreme poverty lived as neighbors in Corinth. Slavery was extensive, and slaves possibly composed as much as three-fourths of its population. The classes of people who composed the congregation (cf. 1 Cor. 1:26–28) reflect the population of the city.

The life of Corinth was one of continuing activity and constant pursuit of pleasure and amusement. The Isthmian Games had their headquarters here and furnished an illustration for Paul (cf. 1 Cor. 9:24–27). Gladiatorial battles were first introduced into Greece in this city. There is no evidence of a strong philosophical tradition in the city, but there is evidence of a pseudo-intellectuality which corrupted the powers of the people to think (cf. 1 Cor. 2:1–5).

The main life of Corinth, as in all Greek cities, was to be found in the *agora* (the market place). Here the business of the city was conducted; here the populace met to argue and debate; here was the *bema* (the judgment seat) where political matters were settled. It was here that Paul probably preached often and where the Christians met the people to whom they bore witness.

THE CHURCH AT CORINTH

The congregation at Corinth was young in the Christian faith. When Paul wrote this letter, Christianity had existed in the city not more than six years. There were some, but not many, men of substance and education. Most of the members were of the lower classes of society; perhaps a majority were slaves. Some were Jews, but most were Gentiles coming from a background of pagan religion and Corinthian immorality and licentiousness.

One wonders how a church could be formed in such surroundings and of such people, and once formed, how it could survive. One of the evidences of the grace of God is that the Corinthian church was formed and that it did survive. It is little wonder that its continuing life was filled with peril, heartache, difficulties, differences of opinion, encroachments of old habits and ways of life, fluctuation in loyalties, instability of character, and extremes in both doctrine and practice. Such was certainly the case in Corinth, as Paul's correspondence abundantly shows. But this very diversity of problems, though it must have caused the great apostle untold anguish of heart, has benefited all subsequent generations of Christians. It called into being the correspondence which is the outstanding example in the New Testament of the way in which Christ transforms men and their habits and the gospel finds meaningful application to both religious and social behavior.

PAUL'S PRIOR RELATIONS WITH THE CORINTHIANS

To discuss the authorship of this epistle would be superfluous, for there is no doubt that Paul was the author. However, a knowledge of his prior relations with this church is important to our understanding of the epistle.

Paul was the founder of the church at Corinth. This is quite clear from the account in Acts (18:1–17); it is also expressly stated in this epistle. Paul reminded the Corinthians of the nature of his message (1 Cor. 15: 1–3) and the manner of his preaching (1 Cor. 2:1–5) while he was with them. He claimed to have been the one who laid the foundation of the church "According to the commission of God given to me" (1 Cor. 3:10). He insisted that he alone was the father of the church, saying, "For though you have countless guides in Christ, you do not have many fathers. For I became your father in Christ Jesus through the gospel" (1 Cor. 4:15).

Paul had maintained contact with the church since leaving them. Ephesus was not far from Corinth, and there was constant traffic between the two cities. Only a week or two would have sufficed for a visit or an exchange of letters. Our records are probably not complete at this point, but they do furnish proof of continued contact. A previous letter from Paul is mentioned in 1 Corinthians 5:9: "I wrote to you in my letter." A letter from them is mentioned: "Now concerning the matters about which you wrote" (1 Cor. 7:1). A visit from certain members of the congregation, perhaps bearers of their letter, are named—Stephanas, Fortunatus, and Achaicus (1 Cor. 16:17–18). A report from some members of Chloe's household is mentioned (1 Cor. 1:11). Possibly these were slaves of an aristocratic lady named Chloe and were members of the congregation. Another report is mentioned, but the one making the report is not named: "It is actually reported that there is immorality among you" (1 Cor. 5:1). Chapter 6 reveals an intimate knowledge of the life of the Corinthians and deals with problems not mentioned in their letter. Paul's answers to their questions (chaps. 7–15) reveal a greater knowledge than it is likely they reported in their letter to him.

The relationship between the Corinthians and Paul had been intimate, loving, and based on a mutual regard. Paul did not speak, in this letter, to people who did not know him or about conditions which he knew only secondhand. The letter itself emanates an aura of fatherly concern as well as, at times, of apostolic sternness.

THE DATE OF 1 CORINTHIANS

1 Corinthians was written not earlier than A.D. 55 and not later than A.D. 57. It is even possible to know the time of year—it was spring. This knowledge is based on 1 Corinthians 16:5–9, where Paul told of his

plans to visit Corinth after passing through Macedonia but insisted that he intended to remain in Ephesus until Pentecost (i.e., seven weeks after Easter by our calendar).

The data on which the conclusion as to the year of writing is based are as follows:

1. Paul was brought before Gallio at Corinth probably near the end of his stay there (cf. Acts 18:1–12), though it is stated that he stayed "many days longer" (Acts 18:18). From information gained from an ancient inscription found at Delphi, it is possible to date the tenure of Gallio as proconsul within a year of A.D. 52. It could have been during 51–52 or during 52–53. This confluence of data makes this one of the most certain of all New Testament dates.

2. When Paul left Corinth "after . . . many days longer" (Acts 18:18), he took Priscilla and Aquila with him to Ephesus and left them there. They fell in with a brilliant young preacher, Apollos. Having corrected his theology, they shortly sent him with letters of recommendation to Corinth, where he was of great service to the Corinthian brethren (cf. Acts 18:24–28).

3. Paul, meantime, visited Antioch in Syria, spending some time with the Christians there. Then he returned to Ephesus by way of the churches he had founded on his first missionary journey.

4. His ministry in Ephesus lasted approximately two and a half years from the time of his arrival.

Now if we assume, as Paul's statement of his travel plans in 1 Corinthians 16:5–9 would certainly justify, that this letter was written near the close of his stay in Ephesus, the first statement in this section would be certain.

If we allow one year from the time of Paul's departure from Corinth until his return to Ephesus and two years and six months for his stay at Ephesus, 1 Corinthians was written somewhat less than four years after Paul's departure. If we take A.D. 53 as the date of his appearance before Gallio, the latest possible date, 1 Corinthians would have been written in 57 or late 56. If we take A.D. 51 as the date of his appearance before Gallio, the earliest possible date, the letter would have been written in A.D. 55. To be more exact than this is impossible on the basis of our present data.

The important matter for interpretation is not the exact date but the understanding that the Christians at Corinth had been Christians for only a short time—six years at the most. This fact explains why a church would be faced with so many problems, especially in the absence of stable leadership.

OUTLINE

1 Corinthians

I. INTRODUCTION (1:1–9)
   1. The Church at Corinth Addressed and Greeted (1:1–3)
   2. Thanksgiving for the Spiritual Gifts of the Corinthians (1:4–9)
II. REPROOF OF DISSENSIONS IN THE CHURCH AT CORINTH (1:10—4:21)
   1. Dissensions Had Arisen in the Church (1:10–12)
   2. Their Dissensions Violated the Duty of Complete Devotion to Christ (1:13–17)
   3. Their Dissensions Were Based on a Misunderstanding of the Gospel (1:18—2:5)
      (1) The gospel was not a human wisdom but a divine power (1:18–25)
      (2) Reception of the gospel, a divine gift (1:26–31)
      (3) Paul's method of preaching dictated by the nature of the gospel (2:1–5)
   4. Their Dissensions Were Based on a Misunderstanding of the Source of True Wisdom (2:6—3:4)
      (1) True wisdom from God (2:6–13)
      (2) True wisdom discerned only by spiritual men (2:14–16)
      (3) True wisdom still hidden from the Corinthians because they were behaving like ordinary men (3:1–4)
   5. Their Dissensions Were Based on a False Estimation of Apostles and Teachers (3:5—4:5)
      (1) Apostles and teachers belonged to God and worked together in his field (3:5–9)
      (2) Apostles and teachers were builders of the church and responsible to God for their work (3:10–15)
      (3) Apostles and teachers faced destruction if they destroyed God's church (3:16–17)
      (4) Apostles and teachers ministered for the enrichment of the Corinthians (3:18–23)
      (5) Apostles and teachers were stewards of God (4:1–5)
   6. Paul's Appeal for Unity in the Church at Corinth (4:6–21)
      (1) His remarks were made for their benefit (4:6–7)
      (2) Their feeling of self-sufficiency was self-deception (4:8–13)
      (3) Paul's appeal for unity was made as the father of the church (4:14–21)

[13]

VI. INSTRUCTIONS CONCERNING ORDER IN CHURCH
SERVICES (11:2–34)
1. Women Should Be Veiled (11:2–16)
2. The Lord's Supper Should Be Observed Properly (11:17–34)
 (1) Their practice was sinful (11:17–22)
 (2) The purpose of the Supper was remembrance of the Lord
 (11:23–26)
 (3) Each member was responsible for self-examination in this
 matter (11:27–32)
 (4) The Supper should be an orderly fellowship service (11:
 33–34)
VII. INSTRUCTIONS CONCERNING SPIRITUAL GIFTS (12:1—
14:40)
1. Diversity and Purpose of Spiritual Gifts (12:1–31)
 (1) Need for spiritual understanding (12:1–3)
 (2) The Holy Spirit, the source of all gifts (12:4–11)
 (3) The church, a spiritual organism (12:12–13)
 (4) All gifts functions of the one body (12:14–26)
 (5) Mutual service, not uniformity, the Christian's aim (12:
 27–31)
2. Love—the Supreme Gift (13:1–13)
 (1) Love gives meaning to all other gifts (13:1–3)
 (2) Love is the most Christian of all gifts (13:4–7)
 (3) Love is one of the enduring gifts (13:8–13)
3. The Superiority of Prophecy over Tongues (14:1–25)
 (1) Prophecy edifies the church (14:1–5)
 (2) Tongues do not edify others (14:6–12)
 (3) Prophecy enables the outsider to understand (14:13–19)
 (4) Prophecy is serviceable in evangelism (14:20–25)
4. Order in the Church Services (14:26–40)
 (1) Conforming to God's character should be the aim of church
 services (14:26–33a)
 (2) Women should keep silence in the church services (14:
 33b–36)
 (3) Paul's instructions were a command of the Lord (14:37–
 40)
VIII. TEACHINGS ABOUT THE RESURRECTION OF THE DEAD
(15:1–58)
1. The Certainty of the Resurrection (15:1–34)
 (1) Resurrection an essential part of the gospel (15:1–11)
 (2) The resurrection of Christ insures the resurrection of believers (15:12–20)
 (3) The resurrection essential to the fulfillment of God's purpose for the world (15:21–28)
 (4) Hope for the resurrection gives meaning to Christian devotion (15:29–34)
2. The Nature of the Resurrection Body (15:35–57)
 (1) Having continuity with, but different from, the present body
 (15:35–41)

COMMENTARY

1 Corinthians

I. INTRODUCTION (1:1–9)

Paul followed the usual custom of a first-century letter writer in the salutations of his letters. The custom was to give the name of the writer, the addressee(s), then a greeting. However, it was Paul's custom to give a distinctively Christian character to these common elements of letter writing, as he did in addressing the church at Corinth. First, in giving his own name, he laid special stress on his apostleship, that is, his right to speak for Jesus Christ (vs. 1). Second, he addressed the church at Corinth but laid stress on its dedication to Jesus Christ (vs. 2). Third, he greeted them with a combination of the common Jewish and Greek greetings but identified these as coming from "God our Father and the Lord Jesus Christ" (vs. 3). Finally, he wrote a prayer for the church but made it primarily a thanksgiving for what God had given them (vss. 4–9). Both the prayer and the salutation reflected the problems in the church at Corinth and prepared the way for their solution.

1. The Church at Corinth Addressed and Greeted (1:1–3)

In his salutation Paul, whether purposely or not, drew an interesting parallel between himself and the church at Corinth. His apostleship was due to divine call; so was their sainthood. He was an apostle of Christ; they were sanctified in Christ Jesus. He was an apostle by the will of God; they were a church of God.

Verse 1: This verse introduces the writer of the letter.

Paul: There can be little doubt that Paul was the author of this letter. He had founded the church at Corinth (cf. Acts 18:1–18); he had continued his relationship to them by writing a letter (cf. 1 Cor. 5:9); they had written him a letter of inquiry about disputed matters (1 Cor. 7:1); he had had at least one group of visitors from Corinth during his stay at Ephesus (1 Cor. 1:11). Thus Paul was familiar with the Corinthian church and they with him.

Called: refers to Paul's experience on the road to Damascus when God had called him to his vocation (cf. Acts 9:1–19). *Called* was a dynamic word for Paul. It meant more than "invited"; it meant the effective act of God by which one was brought to obedience.

The will of God: an act of God which is dictated by his own choice. By this expression Paul repudiated any thought of merit on his part. He did not speak as one who deserved to speak, but as one who had been *called* to speak.

[17]

An apostle: a commissioned messenger who spoke for another. The New Testament sense of the word arises from the verb rather than the noun. In common Greek usage the noun could refer to anything that was sent—for example, a bill of lading—or to the act of sending. There is no evidence of the word referring to an authorized religious or political messenger. With the verb the case is different. The verb was used for the sending of a messenger for a specific purpose. It was from the verbal form that the New Testament writers developed the unique Christian conception of *apostle.* In the New Testament it never refers to a thing sent or to the act of sending, but to the person who is sent. Though Christian usage has tended to limit the title to the Twelve and Paul, it was used in a much wider way in the New Testament. It could be employed of any person sent on a particular mission and was most often used of a man who had a divine commission to preach. There seems to have been a method in Paul's use of the title. When he wrote to churches where his authority was not in question or in which no major problems existed, he did not use the title (cf. Phil. 1:1; 1 Thess. 1:1; Philemon 1); but when he wrote to a church or churches where his authority might be questioned or where a serious problem existed, he introduced himself as an apostle (cf. Rom. 1:1; Gal. 1:1; Col. 1:1; 2 Cor. 1:1). Its use here was purposeful.

Christ Jesus: the Master for whom Paul spoke. Paul meant to say that the instructions which he was to give in this letter expressed the mind of Christ.

Our brother Sosthenes: may or may not have been the ruler of the synagogue at Corinth who was beaten before the tribunal of Gallio (cf. Acts 18:17). However, despite the fact that some deny this identification, it is the most plausible reason for including him in the greetings to the church at Corinth. If it was the same Sosthenes, he had subsequently been converted and become Paul's coworker. His inclusion in the greetings does not mean, of course, that he was in any sense the coauthor of the letter. Some have thought he was the amanuensis (secretary) to whom Paul dictated the letter. But including him in the greeting does not necessarily indicate this; it was not Paul's custom to include his secretaries in his greetings in other letters.

Verse 2: From his self-characterization Paul turned to a description of the church at Corinth. He said three things about it: it belonged to God; it was consecrated; and it was composed of saints.

The church: the local congregation of God's people (this was Paul's invariable use of the word in his recognized epistles). The Greek word here translated *church* meant an assembly of people. Its most common use in the Greek world was for the city council, a political body. It is probable that Paul was responsible for introducing the word into Christian usage to distinguish Christian groups from the Jewish synagogues and the pagan religious societies. At any rate, it became the dominant term in Greek-speaking congregations. To distinguish it from the various political churches, it was necessary always to include implicitly or explicitly some other term such as: "of God" or "of Christ." Christians today have lost the original meaning of the word to such an extent that a building, a denomination, or the universal spiritual fellowship of Christians may be called a church. We must remember that in Paul's usage the word always referred to the people as a congregation that belonged to God and functioned as a body of Christ.

Of God: identifies the owner of the church at Corinth. Paul wished at the beginning to remind the church that it was a divine institution, bound by its very nature to do all things for the glory of God. The church's primary concern was God and his good pleasure.

Sanctified: belonging to God. This word, also translated "consecrated," does not refer to moral or ethical character but to ownership. To say that one is consecrated is to say that he belongs to God. For Paul to say that a church was consecrated meant that it belonged to God. Of course, ownership by God had ethical implications, but the ethical implications were not the primary concern.

In Christ Jesus: dynamic union with *Christ Jesus.* This was one of Paul's unique expressions to describe what it meant to be a Christian. The related expressions, in Christ Jesus, in Christ Jesus our Lord, and in Christ, occur sixty-eight times in Paul's epistles (ten times in 1 Corinthians) and only four times in the rest of the New Testament. Each expression means the same as the others; they all speak of salvation as vital and dynamic union with Christ Jesus. There is no way in which this can be explained to the unbeliever; to him it is an enigma. Paul was saying that the Corinthians existed as God's people by reason of their union with Christ.

Called to be saints: rather, "saints by reason of a divine call." Just as Paul was an apostle because God moved in grace to make him one, the Corinthians were *saints* (i.e., Christians) because God had moved in grace to make them such. The word *saints* has been changed in Christian usage from the New Testament meaning. Today we think of a saint as one who is peculiarly righteous. In the New Testament all Christians were called *saints*. Paul addressed the Corinthians as *saints* even though he believed that many of them were "still of the flesh" and "behaving like ordinary men" (cf. 3:3). The Greek word is the adjective form (used here as a noun) of the same word which was translated "consecrated." Thus, in New Testament language *saints* were simply God's people. It is interesting that the word was never used in the singular; there was always the thought of fellowship involved in it.

Together with all those who in every place call on the name of our Lord Jesus Christ: That is, all who invoked in prayer the name of Jesus Christ were considered to be saints along with the Corinthian Christians. These words do not mean that the letter was addressed to all Christians generally. The particularity of the letter and its application only to the congregation at Corinth are beyond question. Furthermore, these words do not mean that some believers were not enrolled in the communion of the church. This is a modernization of the New Testament which has no basis in historical fact. *Saints* is the New Testament way of expressing the concept which in modern days is called "the universal spiritual church," an expression which had its origin in the writings of Zwingli in Reformation times. But the term does denote a valid New Testament idea, namely, that all Christians are brothers because they belong to God. Therefore, Paul did not add this phrase to include others in his salutations, but to define the meaning of sainthood. In doing so, he reminded the Corinthians that they were not the only Christians in the world.

Both their Lord and ours: expresses the basis of Christian brotherhood. It is not horizontal, i.e., based on a fellow feeling among men. It is vertical, i.e., based on a common devotion to the same Master.

Verse 3: This was Paul's usual salutation, uniting the common Greek and Jewish salutations, but giving them deeper spiritual meaning.

Grace: God's unmerited favor on unworthy men, which accounts for all spiritual gifts. The Greeks used the verbal form in greeting one another, but to them it was little more than our English greeting, "hello." Paul took the word and gave it a new Christian meaning.

Peace: wholeness of life, the result of *grace.* This was the usual greeting of the Jews, one to another. Already it had taken on the deeper meaning which Paul adopted. However, the word was Christianized by looking on it as a gift of *grace* through the Lord Jesus Christ.

From God our Father and the Lord Jesus Christ: The single preposition shows that in granting peace by grace, the Father and his Son act as co-equals.[1] Though Paul was not aware of the questions which led to the ancient doctrine of the Trinity, his language at this point is consistent with that doctrine.

God our Father: the distinctively Christian designation for God. It goes back to the consciousness and teaching of Jesus. The Christian concept of God must always begin here.

The Lord: the Christian understanding of *Jesus Christ.* In modern language the word *Lord* is usually made, at least in our thinking, a part of the compound name for our Savior. In the New Testament this is never so. The earliest Christian confession seems to have been, "Jesus is Lord." The dynamic meaning of *Lord* is always to be assumed in New Testament writings. When we remember that this was the title of the master of slaves and carried with it the thought that Christians were slaves of Christ, we sense something of its meaning. It means that the Christian is to recognize that Jesus Christ is the Master of his life.

2. Thanksgiving for the Spiritual Gifts of the Corinthians (1:4–9)

Paul began a letter which would contain much criticism and harsh censure with a prayer of thanksgiving. He wished to set his criticism in its proper context, a context of love under the lordship of Christ. He took nothing away from the sharpness of his reprimands by this beginning. Rather, he directed the Corinthians' eyes to the grace of God and, in doing so, clarified the danger against which the congregation must be guarded. Their sin was their misuse and misapplication of grace. By reminding them of the grace of God, his criticism and teaching were placed in the context of faith and made to be an expression of love for them.

Verse 4: I give thanks to God always: The Greek verb is in the present tense, pointing to habitual action. *Always* is, of course, hyperbolic. Paul

[1] Le P. E.-B. Allo, *Saint Paul Première Épître Aux Corinthiens* (Paris: Librairie Le-coffre, 1956), says that the Father and Jesus are thus placed on the same level as givers of the grace, p. 4. Hereafter referred to as Allo.

meant that he made a habit of thanking God for them whenever he prayed.

The grace of God: an ellipsis which means the gifts of God's grace. Paul reminded them, thereby, that their gifts were not due to their own intelligence or merit. They were truly gifts.

Which was given you in Christ Jesus: rather, by reason of your union with *Christ Jesus. In Christ Jesus* suggests a relation so personal and unique that one is identified with Christ, that Christ is reincarnated in one (cf. Gal. 2:20). Christ becomes the true ego of the Christian.

Verse 5: Paul identified the gifts and endowments which God had given to the Corinthians.

That: introduces a specification of what was meant by *the grace of God.*

In every way: should be taken with "speech" and "knowledge." Thus it was in every kind of speech and knowledge that they had been enriched.

You were enriched: points to the past action of God but does not imply that these gifts had since been lost.

In him: stands for "in Christ Jesus" in verse 4.

With all speech and all knowledge: defines the sphere in which the enrichment had taken place. *With* translates the Greek preposition *en,* here meaning "in the sphere of." *All . . . all* translates the Greek particle which, when used in the singular and without the article, means *every kind of. Speech* may have special reference to the gift of tongues (cf. 1 Cor. 12 and 14) but was not confined to that. It included all kinds of witnessing to Jesus. *Knowledge* was religious knowledge, the opposite of the human wisdom which Paul condemned.

Verse 6: Even as: rather, "inasmuch as." This verse gives the human cause of their enrichment. *As* (Greek, *kathos*) suggests that the preaching and enrichment were concurrent.[1]

The testimony to Christ: the testimony which Paul had borne to Christ.

Confirmed: rather, "established." That is to say, the testimony of Christ had taken root in their hearts and led them to faith in Christ. This does not refer to miracles but to their reception of the Holy Spirit through the preaching of Paul. Their own experience had confirmed the truth of his testimony (cf. 1 Cor. 15:1).

Verse 7: So that: introduces the result of God's gifts.

You are not lacking: not impoverished in anything. This phrase expressed the quest of the Corinthians, with which Paul would later deal, to find additional benefits in human wisdom or oratory. He reminded them that the gifts of God did not leave them impoverished; they did not need to supplement them from other sources.

Spiritual gift: means a gift granted by the Holy Spirit. *Spiritual* does not describe the kind but the source of the gift (cf. 1 Cor. 12:4–11).

As you wait for the revealing of our Lord Jesus Christ: Paul looked on the life of the congregation as a life of expectant waiting. *Wait* translates a word which means "eager expectation." *The revealing of our Lord Jesus Christ* is the final revelation of Christ in glory at his second coming (cf.

---

[1] C. K. Barrett, *A Commentary on the First Epistle to the Corinthians* (New York and Evanston: Harper & Row, Publishers, © 1968). Hereafter referred to by the last name of the author, Barrett.

Rev. 1:7). The Christian expectation of this event was more immediate than it is in our day.

Verse 8: Will sustain: same Greek word as that translated *confirmed* in verse 6. Their continued confirmation of the truth of Christian teaching rested in the activity of Jesus Christ, not in the questions and debates of the groups in Corinth.

To the end refers to the second coming of Christ at the end of the age.

Guiltless: rather, "unimpeachable." The word comes from the law court. Paul's use of it here inferred that the coming of Christ would mean the judgment of the world, and that the Corinthians, by reason of the continuing work of Christ, would be free from any charge.

The day of our Lord Jesus Christ: is an old Testament phrase adapted to Christianity. *The day of the Lord* is the day of final judgment.

Verse 9: God is faithful: he can be depended on. The whole hope of the world rests upon the fidelity of God to his own self and to his promises.

You were called: at the time of conversion.

Fellowship of his Son: rather, "fellowship with his Son," i.e., participation in his sonship (cf. 1 Tim. 1:1). Sonship, for the Christian, is adopted sonship; but it introduces us to all the privileges of Christ so that we may be called "fellow heirs with Christ" (cf. Rom. 8:17). In a sense, this puts God under obligation to preserve his children and explains why Paul began the verse with: *God is faithful.*

Jesus Christ our Lord: Jesus Christ who is *our Lord.*

II. REPROOF OF DISSENSIONS IN THE CHURCH
AT CORINTH (1:10—4:21)

Before taking up the matters of dispute in the church concerning which they had written Paul (1 Cor. 7:1—15:58), the apostle dealt with some problems of which he had knowledge from other sources. The first of these was the matter of dissension in the church. What this consisted of and the way in which Paul sought to solve the problem is the concern of this section.

First, Paul stated the problem and gave his source of information about it (1:10–12). Next, he pointed out that the dissensions, when carried to their logical conclusions, violated the Corinthians' duty of complete devotion to Christ (1:13–17). Then follows a lengthy discussion of the bases of the dissensions. They were based on a misunderstanding of the nature of the gospel (1:18—2:5), on a misunderstanding of the source of true wisdom (2:6—3:4), and on a false estimation of the place of apostles and teachers in the Christian religion (3:5—4:5). Paul followed this with a stirring appeal to the Corinthians to have done with dissension, sometimes speaking ironically, sometimes harshly, and sometimes with tenderness (4:6–21).

Before we turn to an exegesis of the passage, we must seek to understand the nature and extent of the trouble at Corinth. The pertinent hints from the section itself are as follows:

"I appeal to you, brethren . . . that there be no dissensions among you" (1:10).

"It has been reported . . . that there is quarreling among you, my brethren" (1:11).

"What I mean is that each one of you says, 'I belong to Paul,' or 'I belong to Apollos,' or 'I belong to Cephas,' or 'I belong to Christ' " (1:12).

"For while there is jealousy and strife among you, are you not of the flesh, and behaving like ordinary men?" (3:3).

"If any one among you thinks that he is wise in this age, let him become a fool that he may become wise" (3:18).

"I have applied all this to myself and Apollos for your benefit, brethren, that you may learn by us to live according to scripture, that none of you may be puffed up in favor of one against another" (4:6).

"Some are arrogant, as though I were not coming to you" (4:18).

Add to this some remarkable lexical facts in this section:

[23]

Foolishness (*mōria*), found nowhere else in the New Testament, occurs five times in this passage (1:18, 21, 23; 2:14; 3:19).

Fool, the related word, is found four times (1:25, 27; 3:18; 4:10).

The wise (*sophos*), found only twenty times in the New Testament, sixteen in Paul's letters, is found ten times in this passage (1:19, 20, 25, 26, 27; 3:10, 18, 19, 20).

Wisdom (*sophia*), found fifty-one times in the New Testament, twenty-eight times in Paul's writings, is found sixteen times in this passage (1:17, 19, 20, 21, 22, 24, 30; 2:1, 4, 5, 6, 7, 13; 3:19).

Wise and *wisdom* are used seventeen times in the sense of human wisdom, nine times in the sense of divine wisdom or wisdom from God.

Add to this evidence the facts that the dissensions, as such, are not mentioned in any other part of the letter, that Paul did not take sides in the dispute, and that the tone of the passage is peaceable, with no evidence that Paul thought the dissensions had become dangerous to the gospel itself.

From the tone of Paul's language, we may rule out any idea of false doctrine as the basis of dissension. This section is in marked contrast to Paul's language in Galatians. We would suppose that the spirit of fatherly reprimand which marks his words could not have been possible had the errors of the church centered in false doctrine.

From the fact that the so-called parties are mentioned only in this section of his letter, we can assume that the trouble had not brought about any real factions in the church. Certainly there were not four opposing communities of Christians in Corinth.[1]

From the absence of any reference to distinctly Jewish beliefs after 1:24, we may assume that this was not a matter of the Judaizing doctrines or of a Jewish-Gnostic sect. What Paul said in these chapters would be of interest to Jewish Christians, it is true. However, the whole passage suggests problems that had arisen by pagan people's bringing into their Christian life some of the standards which they had had before their conversion.

The trouble is called *dissensions* (1:10) and *quarreling* (1:11). The Greek word behind *dissensions* is *schismata,* from which we get our English word "schism." However, the word does not seem to have had its modern meaning in Paul's day. John used the same word in three passages (John 7:43; 9:16; 10:19). In each case the word signified a difference of opinion among the people about Jesus, some thinking he had a demon, others thinking otherwise. Paul also used the same word in two other passages in this letter (11:18; 12:25). In both of these passages the thought seems to have been about differences of opinion, in one passage concerning the Lord's Supper, in the other concerning the relative importance of spiritual gifts. We should conclude that the word does not refer to rival camps but to diverse opinions.

---

[1] Munck decides after a thorough study of the evidence that this was a church without factions. He sees the trouble as simply cliques who had ignorantly changed the gospel into another version of Hellenistic wisdom. This led to a misunderstanding of the gospel, the Christians' leaders, and their own position with which Paul dealt in these chapters. (Johannes Munck, *Paul and the Salvation of Mankind,* translated by Frank Clarke [Richmond, Virginia: John Knox Press, 1959], pp. 151–154. Hereafter referred to by the last name of the author, Munck.)

The Greek word behind *quarreling* is *eris,* from which we get our English adjective "eristic." The English meaning, "argumentative, controversial," preserves the basic meaning of the Greek word. From Paul's explanation in 1:13, it would seem that these quarrelings were more in the nature of bickerings over minor points of view rather than debate over central issues.

If we add to this study our information about the use of *wisdom* and *foolishness* in this passage, we begin to get a picture, not of philosophical debate, but of sophistry. The Corinthians, accustomed to the pseudo-intellectuality of their city, had come to look on the gospel as a system of wisdom, upon the preachers of the gospel as orators, and upon themselves as wise men. The thing that was valued, in their sight, was not the content of the gospel message but the eloquence or cleverness with which it was presented. They were not aware of the danger involved in this view, but Paul saw that it was a deadening influence upon their Christian growth and maturity. *Sophistry* is defined as "unsound or misleading but clever, plausible, and subtle argument or reasoning." This English definition describes very closely the quality that the Corinthians had come to value more highly than the gospel itself. This estimate of the trouble in Corinth is strengthened by Paul's description of the members of the church as "men of the flesh" . . . "babes in Christ" . . . "behaving like ordinary men" . . . "merely men." Surely stronger language would have been forthcoming if the danger had been that of heresy or of schism in the modern sense of the word.

1. Dissensions Had Arisen in the Church (1:10–12)

In these verses Paul revealed the source of his knowledge and defined the nature of the dissensions at Corinth. His definition is not complete and to the modern scholar is somewhat unclear. We may be sure that the Corinthians knew of what he was speaking.

Verse 10: Paul began the section with a strong appeal to the church for unity. The RSV fails to translate a Greek particle which implied a contrast between the praise suggested in the previous paragraph and the reproof to which he now turned.

I appeal: translates a Greek word with many shades of meaning, ranging from entreaty to exhortation. It is used 109 times in the New Testament, 54 times in Paul's epistles, and 24 times in his two epistles to the Corinthians. It always suggests an attempt to change the mind, "whether from sorrow to joy (consolation), or severity to mercy (entreaty), or wrong desire to right (admonition or exhortation)." [1] The last meaning is the one used here. Paul hoped to change the Corinthians from a wrong course of action to a right one.

Brethren: reminded them of their spiritual kinship with him.

By the name of our Lord Jesus Christ: the ground of the appeal. Paul had already used the name of Christ nine times in the opening paragraph. Here he made it the basis of his exhortation. By using it, he reminded them that they existed under a common lordship of Christ and that the exhorta-

---

[1] Archibald Robertson and Alfred Plummer, *A Critical and Exegetical Commentary on the First Epistle of St. Paul to the Corinthians,* Second Edition (Edinburgh: T. & T. Clark, 1914), p. 9. Hereafter referred to as ICC.

tion of Paul was meant to promote the reign of Christ in their lives. In Paul's writings "Lord" is always a title; *Jesus Christ* is a compound proper name.

That all of you agree: literally, that you all speak the same thing. There is a definite relation between this verse and the spiritual gifts with which the congregation had been enriched—speech and knowledge (cf. vs. 5). Their knowledge had degenerated into a barren intellectualism, their speech into a babel of tongues. The source of their schism was the abuse of the very gifts that God had bestowed to enable them to give effective witness to Christ.

Dissensions: See the introduction to this section for a discussion of this word and the nature of the dissensions in Corinth.

But that you be united in the same mind and the same judgment: The cure for dissensions must be unity, not only in speech but in the underlying cause of speech. *Mind* means the frame of mind which should belong to men who are Christians. It is the human intellect under the guidance of the Holy Spirit. *Judgment* is closer to our word "opinion." It refers to the judgment about the correctness of a point at issue. *United* means to be in perfect harmony. It does not mean uniformity of thought, which is impossible, but unity of thought.

Verse 11: It has been reported to me by Chloe's people: gives the source of Paul's information. It came by oral report rather than by letter from them. *Chloe's people* probably means slaves belonging to an Ephesian lady named Chloe. Perhaps she had visited Ephesus; and the slaves, members of the congregation at Corinth, had reported the state of affairs to Paul.

Quarreling: dissension comes into the open. Their differences had found a tongue.

Verse 12: What I mean is: introduces Paul's explanation of what he meant by *dissensions* and *quarreling.*

Each one of you: implies that the quarreling had infected the whole church. We need not press the language so far as to say that there were no exceptions. But if there were exceptions, they were insignificant.

Says: The Greek present tense indicates a habit of action.

"I belong to Paul": The exact meaning of the expression is vague. Literally translated, the Greek says: "As for me, I am of Paul." It is uncertain whether this meant *I belong to Paul,* or "Paul is my leader," or whether it was a name given to a party, or a claim of allegiance to Paul. It is probable that the dissensions had arisen first. Then *Paul, Apollos,* and *Cephas* had been claimed by various members as supporters of their views. The thing that Paul condemned was the dissension itself, not the men or the views of the men who were championed. He showed no partiality for the group that claimed him, nor any respect for the group that claimed Christ as their leader. All groups were equally wrong in the spirit with which they tried to support their claims.

Apollos: the gifted orator from Alexandria. He had been instructed in the faith by Priscilla and Aquila when they met him at Ephesus. Later he was given letters of recommendation to introduce him to the Christians of Achaia (Acts 18:24–28).

Cephas: a nickname given to Simon by Jesus (cf. John 1:42). *Cephas* is the Aramaic word for rock; *Peter* is the Greek word. There is no solid evidence that he had ever been to Corinth, but he was held in high respect by all Christians. His name was certainly known. However, all attempts to make Paul and Peter leaders of opposing forces in early Christianity have failed.

"I belong to Christ": an enigma in this list. Many solutions have been offered. Some say that it was Paul's answer to the other cries and represents his stand. If so, it would not indicate a group which used this as their rallying cry. Others say it referred to another teacher named Chrestos. We hear of a prominent leader at Corinth who claimed that he belonged to Christ and Paul did not (2 Cor. 10:7).[1] However, the evidence would favor the conclusion that this was entirely unrelated to the situation to which Paul addressed himself in this verse. It is more likely that the cry, *I belong to Christ,* was made by some members of the congregation who prided themselves on their spirituality and refused to acknowledge the leadership of any man. Such loyalty to Christ is good when it is based on the right spirit. But in Corinth it seems to have been a manifestation of the party spirit on the same level as that shown by the other cries.

2. Their Dissensions Violated the Duty of Complete Devotion to Christ (1:13–17)

Paul's first reply to the party spirit which had led to dissensions in Corinth was couched in three rhetorical questions which showed the folly of the party spirit (vs. 13). He followed this with a statement that he himself had not baptized many of the Corinthians (vss. 14–17). He used himself as the example, but what he said about himself would have applied equally well to Apollos or Cephas.

Is Christ divided?: The presence of the parties in Corinth implied that Paul, Apollos, and Cephas each represented a partial revelation of Christ, i.e., Christ had been divided. To claim one man over against the others would mean to accept what Christ had revealed of himself through that one man and reject what he had revealed through the others. Such a conclusion was ridiculous. Thus the party spirit itself was ridiculous.

Was Paul crucified for you? Or were you baptized in the name of Paul?: The presence of the parties could lead to another conclusion, that is, the substitution of the human leaders for Christ himself. To do so would ascribe to *Paul* the redemptive significance of Christ. That Paul was not crucified for them and that they had not been baptized with reference to his name was quite evident. Therefore, the party spirit which logically implied this idea stood discredited.

Verses 14–16: Taking up the idea of baptism, Paul asserted that he had not even baptized people in Corinth, with only a few exceptions. Now he was thankful that this had been true. There was no reason for anyone to think that they were baptized in his name.[2] Paul was not demeaning those

---

[1] ICC sees this as the probable explanation of the so-called Christ party.

[2] Taylor overtranslates verse 15, but in the right direction: "For now no one can think that I have been trying to start something new, beginning a 'Church of Paul.'" (Kenneth N. Taylor, *Living Letters,* Wheaton, Ill.: Tyndale House, Publishers, © 1962.)

who did baptize. What he said applied to this particular case. No doubt, in other places he had often baptized his converts.

Verse 17: This is a transition verse. The first part continues the discussion of baptism. The second part, though grammatically connected with the first part, introduces the thought that occupied Paul's mind in the rest of this section: the gospel is not a philosophy but a message.

Christ did not send me to baptize: negative statement of his primary commission. Paul did not mean to say that baptism was unimportant in the Christian life, but that it was not of primary importance. Baptism is not a part of the gospel that tells men of God's redemptive act in Christ, but a part of the application in Christian living of the meaning of the gospel.

But to preach the gospel: translates a single Greek word meaning "to evangelize."

Not with eloquent wisdom: literally, not with wisdom of speech. These are philosophical terms describing the aim of the orator. Paul's aim was not that of the professional rhetorician—to impress his audience with the wise choice of words. He was concerned with the substance of his message.

Be emptied of its power: be made unreal. Paul was convinced that the real cause of salvation was to be found in the cross. To substitute a system of ideas, or even to proclaim the cross in such terms as to call attention to the form of expression, would lead to an emptying of the cross. It would be like mistaking the theory of atomic energy for atomic energy itself.

3. Their Dissensions Were Based on a Misunderstanding of the Gospel (1:18—2:5)

In this section Paul asserted that the gospel was not a human wisdom but a divine power (1:18–25), that the reception of the gospel was a divine gift (1:26–31), and that his own method of preaching had been dictated by the nature of the gospel (2:1–5).

(1) The gospel was not a human wisdom but a divine power (1:18–25)

The Corinthians had been regarding the gospel as a kind of human philosophy. Paul pointed out that this way of looking at the gospel robbed it of its divine dynamic. This was proved by the fact that those who were perishing regarded the gospel as foolishness. Those who were being saved found it to be a divine power. Paul began his argument by asserting that the message of the cross was irrational in the opinion of Greek philosophers and unacceptable to the Jewish wise men.

Verse 18: The word of the cross: the message with the cross at its center. The King James Version is misleading in this paragraph because it translates *word* (message) as "preaching." Paul was not talking about the act of preaching, but about the message preached. *The word of the cross* is in direct contrast to *eloquent wisdom* in verse 17. The Greek makes the contrast more striking. *Eloquent wisdom* is literally "wisdom of word." *The Cross* was Paul's word to summarize the whole suffering of Christ. The word is used infrequently in other New Testament writings. It describes the death of Christ in terms of utmost humiliation.

Folly: completely irrational or nonsense.

To those who are perishing: those who had not accepted the salvation offered by the gospel. The Greek verb is in the present tense, distributive in sense, signifying that the unsaved were perishing one by one.

To us who are being saved: those who had experienced and were experiencing (one by one) the reality of salvation. The Greek present tense does not denote process here but distribution; thus, one by one they were being saved.

It is the power of God: God's way of getting salvation accomplished. The Greek word *dunamis* is the word from which the English word "dynamite" comes. Paul meant to say that the gospel message was the dynamic of God in salvation. There was a sharp contrast in the way the gospel appeared to the two different classes of men. The unsaved judged the gospel from the standpoint of human wisdom and found it to be foolishness. The saved judged it from the standpoint of their experience and found it to be power. This contrast continues in our day. There are those who insist that the gospel should be made palatable to modern man. They forget that the gospel has never been palatable to man. It is good, of course, to preach the gospel in modern terms, but we must always be sure that it is the gospel which we preach.

Verse 19: This verse quotes Isaiah 29:14 from the Septuagint (Greek) version of the Old Testament. In its original setting the words constituted a threat to Israel "Because this people draw near with their mouth/and honor me with their lips,/while their hearts are far from me" (Isa. 29:13). However, Paul's application to the Corinthian situation was justified. The way of God's action is the same in all situations—spiritual blindness is the judgment on spiritual rebellion. Paul meant that the ways of God run contrary to the wisdom and cleverness of men and will cancel them.

It is written: Paul's usual way of introducing Old Testament quotations.

I will destroy the wisdom of the wise: states a general principle which Paul adopted and adapted to the situation in Corinth. Human wisdom is always impotent to meet the spiritual needs of men.

Cleverness: translates a word which could be translated in English by "common sense." It is necessary in the mind that is dominated by the Holy Spirit (Col. 1:9). The absence of it is fatal in any mind (Rom. 1:21). However, to rely upon it as the sole arbiter of truth is equally fatal. This was what Paul meant to make clear.

Verse 20: Starting from the Old Testament quotation, Paul asked four rhetorical questions to point up the application of the Scripture to the current situation.

Where is the wise man?: The mere asking of the question implied that God had shown him up as foolish. There was nowhere in the world where the *wise man* was to be found who had a solution for the predicament of men in sin. *Wise man* is a general term which includes the following two.

The scribe: the Jewish interpreter of the law. While the term may have had a general meaning for any learned man, it is more likely that Paul had the Jewish *scribe* in mind.

The debater: correctly describes the Greek philosopher as one who delighted in discussion and dispute.

Of this age: belonging to this present sinful age, characteristic of men who were alienated from God.

Has not God made foolish the wisdom of the world?: a rhetorical question demanding an affirmative answer. *Made foolish* means to show it up in its true colors. Man's answers to man's problems are foolish, moronic; they will not work. The meaning of this passage is expanded in Romans 1:21-22: "For although they knew God they did not honor him as God or give thanks to him, but they became futile in their thinking and their senseless minds were darkened. Claiming to be wise, they became fools." *God* showed them to be foolish by bringing the true answer to man's need —the gospel. It works. *The world* is the New Testament word used to describe the men of the world as opposed to the men of God. *The wisdom* that God showed in its true colors was the wisdom that belonged to this world, that is concerned with the things of earth.

Verse 21: This verse states the way in which God had shown the folly of the world's wisdom. He accomplished through the message of the cross what men could not achieve through the exercise of wisdom—salvation for the believer.

For since: introduces the main thought of the verse.

In the wisdom of God: probably the working out of God's wise purpose which was meant to lead the world to recognize the limits of man's wisdom. Some have taken it to mean the revelation of God's wisdom, diffused through nature (cf. Rom. 1:18-32). The order of the words and the context is in favor of the interpretation given above.

The world did not know God through wisdom: expresses the ultimate failure of human wisdom which falls short of the knowledge of God. Philosophy has never been able to discover God. Since the knowledge of God is the supreme need of men, philosophy (*wisdom*) has failed. *The world* is, of course, a figure of speech for the men of the world.

It pleased God: speaks of the sovereign will of God. Paul did not mean that God's actions were arbitrary. He knew that they had a reason. But the reason could be found only in the mind of *God.*

Through the folly of what we preach: good translation, not "the folly of preaching" (KJV). This is the message of the cross which is *folly* only in the sense that it seems so to men. What we preach translates a single Greek word, *kērugma,* which comes from a verb meaning "to herald" or "to proclaim." It stands in the New Testament as a virtual synonym for *gospel.* Here it is obvious that Paul had in mind the "word of the cross" (vs. 18).

Those who believe: placed at the end of the verse for emphasis. The word *believe* meant far more in the New Testament times than the English word does in our day. It did not so much point to an action of the intellect as to an action of the will. It did not mean "to accept a thing as true" but to surrender one's life to that which was true. Thus, in Christian usage it meant the surrender of one's life to Christ as Lord as a matter of trusting committal. In modern terms it would be to give one's allegiance' to Christ as the ruler of one's life.

Verse 22: For: the same Greek word which was translated "since" in verse 21. It should have been so translated here, for this verse does not refer back to verse 21 but looks forward to verse 23. It forms a kind of protasis for the conclusion drawn there. The two verses, however, are an expansion of the thought of verse 21. *The world* is divided up into its constituent parts—as Paul viewed the world—the *Jews* and the *Greeks*. The two verses explain, with reference to the peculiar characteristics of each group, why the gospel had not been accepted by them.

Jews demand signs: miracles as evidence of the truth of Christianity. *Jews,* generally speaking, were matter-of-fact people. In their tradition certain *signs* and wonders had been specified to be worked out by the Messiah when he came. The Gospels give evidence that the Jews often asked Jesus to show signs of his authority. The absence of an article with "Jews" shows that Paul was speaking of them in general terms, describing the characteristics of their religious quest, rather than as individuals. *Demand* is in the present tense, pointing to a habit, and should be translated "keep on asking for."

Greeks seek wisdom: The Greeks were concerned with speculative philosophy. Their great heroes were men of thought—Plato, Aristotle, Socrates. They were proud of their culture and looked down on the rest of the world as composed of barbarians. Though this wisdom had largely degenerated in New Testament times into superficial sophistries, they still remained proud of their so-called wisdom. Since the gospel offered no rational explanation of the universe, no logical system of thought, they had no use for it. As the *Jews* kept on asking for signs, so the Greeks kept on seeking for *wisdom.*

Verse 23: But we: strongly contradictory to the foregoing. *We* for our part. By this Paul probably meant to include the other apostles and teachers, especially the ones which had been claimed by the rival groups.

Preach: keep on proclaiming or heralding (note Greek present tense).

Christ crucified: Christ in the character of one who had been *crucified.* Notice that it was not the cross which they preached, nor the fact of crucifixion. It was Christ who was proclaimed as Savior and Lord. But it was Christ in his character as one who had been crucified (note the Greek perfect tense). Paul believed that the power of God to save came from the death of Christ on the cross. The language of the New Testament is interesting here. They did not preach Christ as the risen one; they proclaimed the resurrection as a fact. They did not preach the cross as a fact; they preached Christ as the crucified one. The center of gravity in the gospel is just here. The historical act of Christ in dying for the sins of men accomplished redemption and led to his resurrection and enthronement as the Lord of all believers.

A stumbling-block to Jews: To the Jews the cross was the real barrier to their acceptance of the gospel. They had expected a victorious Messiah; they were offered a crucified one. The offense of the cross was in the union of the concept of the Messiah with that of the Suffering Servant. *Stumbling-block* is a word derived from the trigger of a trap or snare. It was a graphic metaphor for men who were caught in the trap of their own prejudices and prevented from seeing the truth.

Folly to Gentiles: All non-Jews were Gentiles. Folly is the opposite of reason. Thus, to them, the message of Christ crucified was one which failed to give a rational explanation of the power of the gospel. They refused to believe it because it transcended human wisdom; they thought it contradicted reason.

Verse 24: This verse expresses the meaning of the gospel message to those who are Christians.

But to those who are called: believers. *Called* was Paul's word for the dynamic call of God which led to the response of faith. The *called* were those who had accepted Christ and were Christians. This is a different meaning of the word than that found in the Gospels. There it simply means those who are invited to salvation.

Both Jews and Greeks: The characteristic traits and suspicions of both groups of men were overcome by the call of God.

Power of God: God's way of meeting the needs of men.

Wisdom of God: God's way of answering men's questions.

Verse 25: This sentence summarizes the thought of this section (vss. 18–25). The reason the saved see in the crucified one the power and wisdom that comes from God is that the gospel has proved stronger and wiser than anything human. It saves men; this the world's wisdom and might have failed to do.

For the foolishness of God is wiser than men: Paul took the position of the objector, admitting that the gospel was seemingly foolishness. But what appeared to be foolishness when judged by the wisdom of men turned out to be wiser than anything that man's wisdom could devise.

And the weakness of God is stronger than men: follows the same form and has the same meaning as the previous clause. Here, Paul substituted *weakness* and *stronger* for *foolishness* and *wiser*. In both expressions Christ as the crucified one, i.e., the gospel, is the immediate antecedent. *Foolishness* and *weakness* are not abstract terms to be taken generally. The context shows that they have reference to the gospel. This is true in spite of the fact that the neuter adjective in Greek may be used as an abstract noun.

(2) Reception of the gospel, a divine gift (1:26–31)

Paul pointed to the composition of the congregation and used this to prove that the call of God could not possibly have been based on wisdom. Therefore, the call of God must be based entirely on the grace of God.

Verse 26: In this verse Paul appealed to the congregation to consider its composition to show that it was God's power which was effective. The three groups mentioned were the upper-class groups of that day. They had no real middle class. *Consider your call* was an admonition to look at the kind of people which had been called to salvation. Paul's readers would find that this group included neither the educated, the politically powerful, nor the aristocrats. *Wise according to worldly standards* describes educated men as well as philosophers. *Powerful* describes men of rank and political influence. This class of people rejected Christianity at first. Forty years later Paul could not have made this statement. This is one of the indications of the relevance of this epistle to a particular time and situation.

Noble birth refers to the aristocrats. Roman society was composed primarily of the upper and lower classes.

Verse 27: God chose: used three times in verses 27–28. The Greek verb is in the middle voice, indicating that *God chose* for himself, as his part, men from the lower classes.

What is foolish . . . what is weak: men who are uneducated and hold no position of power or influence.

To shame the wise . . . to shame the strong: that is, to show the superiority of God's grace to education and power or influence. God's wisdom, at its lowest point, is greater than man's wisdom at its best; God's power, at its weakest, is stronger than man's power at its highest level.

Verse 28: Low and despised: would be the tax-collectors and sinners in Jewish society, some of whom God had chosen for salvation. Paul was still speaking of men in the lower classes who composed the membership of the congregation. Perhaps in the Corinthian society the *low* would be the illegitimate or low-born, and the *despised* would be a synonym for the same groups.

Even things that are not: slaves who had no independent existence in society apart from their masters. The form of the Greek indicates that this should read, "those who are considered as not being by men."

To bring to nothing things that are: following the analogy of the previous statement, this would mean that God brought to nothing those who were considered important and meaningful in human society. The purpose involved is, of course, secondary. The primary purpose, from Paul's viewpoint, was expressed in the next verse.

Verse 29: Here is expressed the ultimate aim of God's acts of grace. Whatever approach Paul took to the gospel, it silenced all human claims on God (cf. Rom. 3:27; Phil. 3:3–7).

Verse 30: He is the source: constitutes the climax of Paul's statement in this section. He was anxious to show that the Corinthians' salvation was not based upon anything human—not merit, education, class, or influence. It was solely and entirely an act of God's unmerited favor upon them. The connection of this thought to the total section is apparent. If men were what they were by the grace of God, what basis was there for the party spirit? How could one claim superiority over the other?

Your life in Christ Jesus: "your being made alive by reason of your union with Christ Jesus."

Our wisdom . . . righteousness . . . sanctification . . . redemption: expressions which are synonymous for the content of the Christian blessings. The idea is not that Christ Jesus is the source of these blessings, but that he is the blessing itself. *Wisdom* is true understanding as opposed to false wisdom. *Righteousness* is acceptance with God as his children. *Sanctification* ("consecration") is the act of God in making us his own. *Redemption* is the purchase price paid for the release of a slave or captive. Paul heaped up his common words for salvation in this verse. It is not wise to attempt a sharp distinction in meaning. Each comprises the entirety of Christian salvation from different viewpoints. The important thing in the verse is that *Christ* is these things to men. From the viewpoint of the Old Testament, Christ fulfills the offices of the prophet, the priest, the scribe, and the king.

Verse 31: This verse concludes the section and repeats in scriptural language the thought of verse 29.

Boast: exult in one's possessions or privileges. Since God's power and wisdom were manifested in the congregation through the spiritual privileges and possessions of the Christians, received entirely by grace, any boasting should be in that, not in superficial and insignificant differences that would have meaning only in human eyes.

The Lord: Jesus Christ. In the Old Testament *Lord* is a title for God; in the New Testament it is a title for Christ. Though Paul was quoting the Old Testament, he meant *Lord* to be taken for Christ here.

(3) Paul's method of preaching dictated by the nature of the gospel (2:1–5)

This section illustrates the main thrust of 1:18–31, i.e., that the power of the gospel does not depend on the preacher or upon the intelligence of the hearer. There was a remarkable correspondence between the minister and the gospel. The gospel was the foolish thing of God; the preacher did not preach in "lofty words or wisdom" (vs. 1). The gospel was the weak thing of God; the preacher came "in weakness and in much fear and trembling" (vs. 3). The gospel was the power of God; the preaching was a "demonstration of the Spirit and power" (vs. 4).

It is popularly supposed that Paul's decision rested on his failure at Athens (Acts 17:32–34); that, having failed when he attempted a philosophical presentation of the gospel, he, when he came to Corinth, renounced this method of presentation. This idea seems wrong to me on two counts. First, his presentation to Athens was never finished; we have only the introduction to a proposed sermon. Thus, it is impossible to say with certainty that he would have continued in a philosophical vein. Second, his ministry in Athens was not a total failure; it resulted in the winning of some converts.

It is more likely that Paul's choice of method at Corinth was based on the pseudo-intellectuality of the Corinthians. He knew of their delight in things philosophical, their liking for eloquence and rhetoric. Therefore, he determined not to make a play for their acceptance on these grounds. He knew that the gospel's power could be hindered if the words of the preacher, rather than the content of the message, became the prominent factor. This is a lesson that some modern preachers might do well to learn.

Verse 1: Paul turned from the Corinthians to himself. Even as their humble station in life showed that the reception of the gospel was by grace, so his method of preaching the gospel showed that it was a divine power.

When I came to you: points to his first visit when he had first preached the gospel to the Corinthians. The fact that the gospel had come to the Corinthians reminded them that it was not a native growth. Christianity was a new beginning, not a correction of their own thinking. *I* is emphatic in the Greek. Paul meant to shift their attention from their reception of the gospel to his preaching of it.

I did . . . come proclaiming: His action from the first was to proclaim, i.e., to announce as a herald. The use of the word *preaching* was deliberate. He meant that he had not come to discuss, to argue, to persuade, but to proclaim. Since the gospel was not a system of philosophy or logic but a statement of God's action in Christ, the proper action of its messenger was proclamation.

The testimony of God: The text is questionable at this point. The better attested text seems to be *mystery* instead of *testimony.*[1] In either case, it is the message which he preached, but there is a slight difference of emphasis. If *testimony* is correct, it is the *testimony* to *God,* i.e., to his redemptive action in Christ. God thus becomes the object of the noun. If mystery is the correct reading, it is the mystery from God, i.e., the mystery that God reveals. In this case, God is the source. *Mystery* was a word which Paul borrowed from the mystery religions which were popular in Greece. In their use it meant religious secrets which were known only to the initiated. Paul changed its meaning. To him it meant the truth formerly unknown, but now made known to all believers.

Not . . . in lofty words or wisdom: describes Paul's preaching on its negative side. He did not attempt to demonstrate his superiority in these matters. *Lofty,* i.e., superior, modifies both *words* and *wisdom.* Paul did not make any high pretensions with respect to either. *Words* in the plural refers to his manner of speaking. *Wisdom* refers to a philosophical system. Paul used neither of these as instruments of his proclamation. His additional statements in this paragraph reveal that his reason was to be found in the nature of the gospel.

Verse 2: This verse describes the preaching of Paul positively from the standpoint of its content.

For I decided: points to a definite time of decision (note the past tense). Paul implied that he knew very well what would have captivated the Corinthians and deliberately rejected that as a method of preaching. The Greek word, *krinō,* means "to judge." Paul's determination was based on what he judged to be fitting to the occasion.

To know nothing: to have no other message. This is a hyperbolic statement. He did not literally mean that he erased all else from his mind so that this was all he knew. He meant that he had deliberately decided to make known or to preach only this.

Except Jesus Christ and him crucified: the message of the gospel in its most repelling aspect. He did not proclaim Jesus Christ as a great teacher, example, or leader; he proclaimed him as the one who had been crucified. *Crucified* is a perfect participle in the Greek, pointing to a completed action with permanent results. To the Jews this message would be repelling because of the shame of dying on the cross. Crucified ones were considered to be accursed of God (Gal. 3:13). To the Greeks this message would be offensive because to say that by the crucifixion of Christ salvation came was folly (1 Cor. 1:23).

---

[1] This reading is slightly preferred by *The Greek New Testament,* edited by Kurt Aland, Matthew Black, Bruce M. Metzger, and Allen Wikgren. Published by The American Bible Society, © 1966. Hereafter referred to as, The Greek New Testament.

This is the enduring scandal of the cross. To announce salvation in terms that requires a man to admit his unworthiness and helplessness and rely upon the sacrifice of Christ offends men of all ages. Men like to think that they are good, that they can attain their own salvation. The simple truth is that they cannot. Only God can save. The cross is his way of saving. Though it may appear to be folly to men, those who believe find it to be the power of God.

Verse 3: Paul remembered that his entrance into Corinth was attended by a feeling of personal insufficiency.

Weakness: a general term to describe the contrast between the preacher and the gospel which he preached. In Paul's case, it could have included his "thorn . . . in the flesh" (cf. 2 Cor. 12:7), his poor personal appearance which led his enemies in Corinth later to say, "His letters are weighty and strong, but his bodily presence is weak, and his speech of no account" (2 Cor. 10:10). Possibly, also, there was a memory of the poor reception of the gospel at Athens and the deadly hostility of the Jews at Thessalonica (Acts 17:5, 13). Furthermore, he had been quite aware of the appalling wickedness of the city of Corinth. There had certainly been enough to make him come in weakness to them.

And in much fear and trembling: the emotional counterparts of a feeling of weakness. The combination of *fear* and *trembling* was not rare in Paul's writing (cf. 2 Cor. 7:15; Eph. 6:5; Phil. 2:12). The addition of *trembling* gives depth to *fear*. Of course, Paul was not talking of cowardice on his part. The *fear and trembling* came from an understanding of the importance of the task and the difficulties that awaited him. Most preachers understand the words of Paul here. They express a feeling that is common to men who undertake to speak the gospel to men in every age. Often this feeling is a prelude to the experience of the power of God in one's ministry.

Verse 4: My speech: my manner of presentation.

My message: the content of the preaching.

Not in plausible words of wisdom: touch of irony in which he disclaimed the practice of that which was highly valued in Corinth—the art of persuading people without instructing them.

But in demonstration of the Spirit and power: the power which comes from the Holy *Spirit*. Paul was saying that the Holy Spirit took his weak words and converted them into spiritual power. The Greek word behind *demonstration* is found only here in the New Testament. It can have two meanings: (1) a display of something or (2) demonstration in the sense of logical proof. The second meaning applies here. Paul meant that his preaching was an undeniable proof of the power that came from the Holy Spirit. There is no doubt that the Spirit of God was meant here. The ancient heathen demanded proof of the Christian religion; modern heathens do, also. The only real proof is in the effect of the gospel in the lives of men.

Verse 5: Paul stated the purpose which he had in mind when he preached as he did, reminding them again of his main thought in the previous sections which made disunity in the church without basis.

That: introduces a purpose clause.

Your faith: your acceptance of the gospel and surrender to the lordship of Christ.

In the wisdom of men: the rational understanding that is purely human. Paul recognized that the gospel was essentially irrational when judged by the logic of the human mind. He made no attempt to make it rational.

The power of God: God is the true originator of faith; he produces faith in men; he, and he alone, can. Paul knew this and so he had sought, in the manner of his preaching, to avoid any other suggestion or to lead men to think that faith could be based elsewhere. The previous paragraph ended with an admonition to boast in Christ; this paragraph ends with a suggestion to trust in God.

4. Their Dissensions Were Based on a Misunderstanding of the Source of True Wisdom (2:6—3:4)

Like most great preachers, Paul had overstated his case against wisdom in the previous section. He had seemed to indicate that wisdom of any kind was bad. He did not mean that. He turned in this section to a discussion of the kind of wisdom which was good—divine wisdom. Yet, this divine wisdom is different from the "wisdom of men" in two ways: first, it comes to men by way of revelation rather than discovery, and, second, it can be apprehended only by spiritual men. These two thoughts were the concern of Paul in chapter 2. The last paragraph in the section deals with the inability of the Corinthians to comprehend this true wisdom (3:1–4).

(1) True wisdom from God (2:6–13)

Two thoughts are present in this paragraph: The gospel is indeed a wisdom of God but known only to Christians (2:6–9); the gospel is a revelation from God (2:10–13).

Verse 6: This verse defines the kind of wisdom which Paul preached.

Yet: adversative conjunction introducing a correction of what has been said about wisdom.

Among the mature: in the company of developed Christians. *Mature* translates a Greek word which the King James Version usually translated by the word "perfect." The English word "perfect" denotes an absoluteness which is not found in the Greek word. The Greek word really means that of which the parts are fully developed. Paul usually used the word in contrast with "babes" or "children." The contrast in this passage is found in 3:1–4, where the Corinthians are designated variously as "men of the flesh," "babes in Christ," and "ordinary men." Thus, Paul meant the fully developed Christian by his use of the term, not those who were without any flaw. I doubt that there is any allusion to the mystery religion's use of the term to describe those who were initiated into the secrets of the inner circle.[1]

---

[1] Wilckens insists, to the contrary, that this is a term taken over from the Stoic philosophy. (Ulrich Wilckens, *Weisheit und Torheit* [Tübingen: J.C.B. Mohr, 1959], pp. 53–54. Hereafter referred to as Wilckens.)

We do impart: literally, "we continue to speak." *We* is more than an editorial *we;* it deliberately joined Paul with the other apostles and was a subtle rebuke of the dissensions in Corinth. The people might be divided; the apostles and teachers were not. *Impart* translates the word for speaking. It simply describes the act of speaking, and should not be pressed to denote a kind of utterance distinct from preaching.

Wisdom: [1] is in the emphatic position in the Greek and rules the thought of the whole paragraph. *Wisdom* is without the article in Greek, emphasizing the quality of the word. It might be translated "a kind of wisdom" or "that which has the quality of wisdom." The main question is: What did Paul mean by this? That is to say, did he mean a kind of esoteric truth which was more than the simple gospel, or did he mean the gospel itself?

The commentators are divided on this point. Some, insisting rightly, that the idea of a lower and higher teaching found its development in Christianity at a later date and pointing to the fact that Paul has already called Christ crucified "the wisdom of God" (1:24), insist that Paul meant nothing more than the gospel. If so, its nature as *wisdom* would depend entirely on the apprehension of the hearers. To some it would be *wisdom;* to others it would fall short of this. Other commentators point out that Paul preached the gospel to all alike and insist that something more is meant by *wisdom.* However, none take this to be an esoteric truth, distinct from the gospel. Rather, they take it to mean the gospel with all its implications for the understanding of God's redemptive purpose, the nature of God, and the destiny of man.[2]

This latter solution seems best. Paul certainly made a difference in the way and the extent in which he preached to different hearers. An example of his preaching to unbelievers and babes in Christ can be found in 1 Corinthians 15:3–5. This preaching consisted of a simple witness to the saving power of Christ and a call to decision. An example of his preaching of this same gospel in its wider implications can be found in Romans 8:26–39. This kind of preaching was not an esoteric lore to be communicated only to the initiated; it was a preaching of the wider implications of the gospel which demanded the exercise of the human faculties under the guidance of the Holy Spirit to understand. The point was that this was a *true wisdom* in contrast to the sophistry and *false wisdom* of the world.

Although it is not a wisdom of this age: belonging to this transitory age in which we live.

Or of the rulers of this age: Three opinions have been expressed about the meaning of this expression. Some, from ancient times, have taken it as a reference to the demonic powers of evil which rule the men of the world (cf. Eph. 2:2). Others, also from ancient times, have taken it as a reference

---

[1] ICC points out that the germ of this idea is found in 1:24 and 30. Christ crucified is to the called a wisdom of God.

[2] Craig thinks that the word involves the eschatological aspects of redemption, including: the coming of Christ, the hardening of the Jews, and the indwelling Christ. (Exegesis of 1 Cor. by C. T. Craig in *The Interpreter's Bible,* George Arthur Buttrick, ed. [New York: Abingdon-Cokesbury Press, 1953], Vol. X., p. 37. Hereafter referred to as IB.)

to the Jewish and Roman rulers who put Christ to death (cf. vs. 8). Some have combined the two conceptions, taking it to refer to the Jewish and Roman rulers conceived as instruments of the demonic powers. Against the idea that demonic powers enter into this verse in any way is the fact that they were never in the New Testament thought of as responsible for the crucifixion of Christ. This is an idea which arose in later Christian thought, but it has no foundation in the New Testament. The earliest explanation for the cross was: "this Jesus, delivered up according to the definite plan and foreknowledge of God, you crucified and killed by the hands of lawless men" (Acts 2:23). The more mature Christian explanation was: "God was in Christ reconciling the world to himself" (2 Cor. 5:19). Therefore, it seems that Paul had in mind only the human rulers of this *age*. Perhaps these find a further identification in the "wise," the "powerful," and the "noble" (cf. 1:26).

Who are doomed to pass away: translates a present participle in the Greek which means that *the rulers of this age* were actually in the process of coming to nothing. The purpose of God in choosing the "foolish," the "weak," the "low and despised," and "things that are not" (cf. 1:27–28) was already coming to pass.

Verse 7: This verse clarifies what Paul meant by the *wisdom* which he preached to the developed Christians.

We impart a secret and hidden wisdom of God: an understanding of reality which finds its source in *God* and is unattainable by human thought. *Secret* (literally, "in a mystery") was Paul's word for that which had been *hidden* in the past but was now made known by the revelation of God. It was *secret* and *hidden* only in the sense that men, in their wisdom, were unable to discover it. It was now an "open secret" known by all Christians.

Which God decreed before the ages for our glorification: explains why it has come to light for the first time. Its hiddenness in the past was due to the all-wise purpose of God; he had *decreed* that it be so. This does not mean that God's purpose had no basis; it means that its basis was found only in *God*. *Before the ages* shows that God's decree does not in any way rest on human merit. *For our glorification* defines the ultimate aim of the purpose of God and the results of the wisdom that comes from him. The wisdom of the world leads to destruction, ends in a mystery, and leaves men in misery. The wisdom of God leads to salvation, reveals the mystery of life, and brings men to glory, i.e., true Christian happiness.

Verse 8: This pivotal verse proves from history the point of the previous statement and at the same time prepares the reader for the following verses.

Rulers of this age: the earthly rulers or powers. In this case, Caiaphas and Annas, the high priests, and Pilate, the Roman ruler, would be particularly in mind. Some commentators take this to refer to the spiritual rulers of darkness or to earthly rulers as the instruments of demonic powers. While this is possible, Paul's language is best understood in its purely historical sense (see comment on vs. 6).

They would not have crucified the Lord of glory: Their act in crucifying him showed the inability of the human mind to understand or recognize the wisdom of God.

Lord of glory: one of the loftiest titles for Jesus to be found in the writings of Paul. Jesus is the *Lord* to whom *glory* belongs as a peculiar characteristic. This very phrase occurs in the book of Enoch for God himself. Kindred phrases are: "the Father of glory" (Eph. 1:17), "the God of glory" (Acts 7:2), and the "King of glory" (Ps. 24:7). Paul did not hesitate to attribute to Jesus a characteristic which could be predicated only of God. This says much concerning Paul's belief in the deity of Jesus of Nazareth and his doctrine of the incarnation.

Verse 9: This verse should not be read with verse 10; it is the climax of verses 6–8. It is apparently a quotation from Scripture, but its origin is doubtful. Verbal similarities are found in Isaiah 64:4: "From of old no one has heard or perceived by the ear, no eye has seen a God besides thee, who works for those who wait for him." Perhaps Paul had this in mind; and when considered in the whole context, his purpose was not alien to the quotation.

As it is written: Paul's usual way of introducing Scripture. Paul had a habit of making his point, then quoting an Old Testament passage to confirm it. His purpose was not so much to prove his point, but to show that the gospel was a fulfillment of the promises to Israel.

What no eye has seen nor ear heard: The gospel is not found in visible creation, though it had a historical manifestation on the cross—no eye has seen it. The gospel is not found in a theological system taught by the master to his pupils, though its coming creates a new understanding of theological truth—no ear has heard it.

Nor the heart of man conceived: The gospel is not the creation of the imagination and desires of men, though it creates a new dream of perfection for believers. *Heart* in the New Testament stands for the whole of man's inner life. It does not stand for the seat of emotions, as with us. In this passage Paul used *eye, ear,* and *heart* to express his thought that there was no means of apprehension open to man which would make known to him the wonderful things which God purposed.

What God has prepared for those who love him: refers to the hidden mystery of verse 7. *Prepared* implies the careful planning and minute pains which God took in creating the gospel of Christ. *Those who love him* means those whose lives are dominated by their allegiance to God (cf. Rom. 8:28).

Verse 10: This verse should not be read with verse 9, as the punctuation in the rsv suggests. It is the beginning of a new thought—that the mystery of God, the hidden wisdom which men could not attain, has come by a divine revelation through the Holy Spirit and is imparted by Spirit-led men.

While most translators and commentators seem to connect verse 10 with verse 9 and make the revelation in question a revelation of truth, I cannot agree. It seems to me that Paul was saying that God had made a revelation of himself in Christ. A revelation, both in the Old Testament and in the New, was primarily an event *plus* the Spirit-led interpretation. The event itself was not revelation until the interpretation of the event was made known to men by the Spirit. This fits exactly what is true of the gospel of Jesus Christ. There was first the event—the work and ministry and person of Jesus. Then came the interpretation—the message of the apostles who were led by the Spirit.

God has revealed: literally, "God has made a revelation." The thought is not that God had revealed a fact, i.e., what he had prepared for those who love him. It is rather that God had revealed himself in the person of Jesus Christ, who is the wisdom of God incarnate. *Revealed* is seldom, if ever, used in the New Testament to describe a disclosure of some truth; it usually, if not always, has a personal orientation.

To us: Most commentators take this to refer to the "mature" (vs. 6) or to "those who love him" (vs. 9), but if the foregoing discussion of *revealed* is correct, it must refer to the apostles, to the "we" of verse 6. The revelation came to and through the Spirit-led apostles, and God appointed them to interpret the Christ event. From them it was imparted to the Christians as a whole by way of teaching and preaching.

Through the Spirit: by means of the Holy Spirit. In the New Testament, as in the Old, the Holy Spirit is the means by which God acts in the lives of men. The exact metaphysical relations between the Father, the Son, and the Holy Spirit are difficult if not impossible to define. It is certainly impossible to distinguish in the human experience between the acts of God, of Jesus, and of the Holy Spirit. Seldom are the three united in the New Testament language; never is any attempt made to distinguish between them. While the classical doctrine of the Trinity seems to be the best human solution to the problems raised by the data of the New Testament, we must always remember that the metaphysical relations between the members of the Trinity are impossible to define.

In function the case is different. God the Father is regarded as the supreme source of all blessings. God the Son, Jesus Christ, is regarded historically as the incarnation of God and continually as the Lord and Master of Christians for the glory of God. God the Holy Spirit is regarded as the mediator of God's presence and blessings. The work of the Spirit, while it can be experienced by all Christians, must ever remain a mystery or an enigma which is beyond human explanation.

Up to this point, Paul had emphasized the action of God in history through Jesus Christ; now he turned to emphasize the action of God in experience through the Holy Spirit.

For the Spirit searches everything, even the depths of God: explains why it is that the Spirit can interpret the meaning of the coming of Christ. *Searches* is a metaphorical expression. It does not mean that the Spirit seeks knowledge, as men do when they search; the idea is rather that he penetrates all things to their roots and thus knows the meaning of all things. His knowing extends even to the depths of God. This, also, is a metaphor from the sea, referring to the unfathomable (to the human mind) purposes of God (cf. Rom. 11:33–36).

Verse 11: This verse is an analogy to show that the things of God must be revealed by the Holy Spirit. He alone has inside information.

For what person knows a man's thoughts except the spirit of the man which is in him?: a rhetorical question meant to express the fact that no person can come to know what another person thinks. He alone knows. *The spirit of the man which is in him* expresses, in terms of Paul's understanding of man, what we mean by the inner self.

So also no one comprehends the thoughts of God except the Spirit of

God: expresses the conclusion from the analogy. Remember that this is an analogy, having to do only with the fact of the Spirit's authentic knowledge. Paul was not saying that the Holy Spirit had the same relation to the Father as man's spirit had with him, that is, that they were identical. However, he did imply the full deity of the Spirit.

Verse 12: This verse is a further explanation of verse 10; it tells how God had made a revelation to the apostles.

Now we: is emphatic in the sentence and means the apostles as a whole.

Not the spirit of the world: There is no need to think that Paul had in mind some definite spirit, i.e., such as the demonic powers. This is a negative definition of the Holy Spirit: he is not a *spirit* which is inherently *of the world.* This repeats in negative form what was said in verses 10 and 11 of the Holy Spirit.

But the Spirit which is from God: a positive identification of the Holy Spirit as coming from God. This also implies the distinctiveness of the Spirit as a person. Just as the Son was sent out from God, so was the Spirit, each to accomplish his proper function in redemption.

That: introduces the purpose for which the Christians had received the Spirit.

We might understand: refers to a recognition of the nature of the blessings.

The gifts bestowed on us by God: literally, "the things which were graciously bestowed on us." Some interpreters take this to be the blessings which Christians possess already through faith. Others, more correctly, make it refer to the contents of the mystery bestowed in the coming of Christ. The plural indicates that this phrase refers to the various aspects of the meaning of that one gift. This may seem an overly subtle distinction, but it seems to be necessary to maintain the consistency of the passage.

Verse 13: This verse is one of the most difficult in the letter to interpret in its details. Its central thrust, however, is clear. In the preceding verses Paul had spoken of two things: the content of the gospel and the speaking of the gospel. He had asserted that the knowledge of the content came by a revelation from God through the Holy Spirit. Now he asserted that the speaking of the message was also dependent on the work of the Holy Spirit.

We: again the apostles are meant.

Impart: properly, "speak." The Greek present tense indicates continual action. Thus, "we keep on speaking" is the full meaning.

In words: the proper vehicle of speech. The gospel must be verbalized. This is one of the major problems of preaching and witnessing. It is difficult to find words to express that which goes beyond the wisdom of men to understand. In a sense, the message can never be told, at least not fully. But it must be told. How to tell it is the question.

Not taught by human wisdom: a denial that even the words come from human wisdom, that is, the wisdom of which Paul spoke in chapter 1.

But taught by the Spirit: The source of the words used in witnessing is the Holy Spirit. The method of receiving these words is expressed by the word *taught.* It is noteworthy that Paul did not say *dictated.* One of the continuing debates in theological circles is the debate about the method of inspiration, especially of the Bible. While this verse does not speak for the whole Bible, it suggests what is true for the whole Bible. It suggests that the very terms, the thought patterns, and the turns of phrase were taught by the Holy Spirit. I do not see how one can avoid calling this verbal inspiration. This is, in fact, the only kind of inspiration possible. But it does not mean dictation. The apostles were more than mere stenographers, taking down the words of the Holy Spirit as he dictated them. They were preachers who maintained their own personality in their preaching. What Paul said was that the Holy Spirit penetrated their personality and taught them to express themselves as they did.

Interpreting spiritual truths to those who possess the Spirit: a possible translation but one which is much debated. *Interpreting* translates a Greek word which originally meant "to combine by judicious selection." It is translated "interpreting" in the Greek version of the Old Testament only with reference to dreams and visions (cf. Gen. 40:8, 22; Dan. 5:12). The implications of this background do not fit into Paul's thought here. Though other translations (i.e., adapting, matching, explaining, comparing) have been suggested, it seems better to let the word have its normal meaning here, i.e., judiciously combining. *Spiritual truths (pneumatika)* and *those who possess the Spirit (pneumatikois)* are an attempt to translate the same Greek word repeated in this phrase but in a different grammatical case. The question is the gender of the Greek word in its second use—is it masculine or neuter? Competent and able exegetes have not been able to agree. The phrase could read: "interpreting [or adapting, matching, explaining, comparing, or combining] spiritual truths [or things or words] to spiritual men [or with spiritual things or with spiritual truths]." The RSV translation hides Paul's play on words, which would literally read, if we adopt "combining" as the proper translation: "combining spiritual with spiritual." On this basis I am inclined to adopt the meaning expressed by T. C. Edwards, i.e., that spiritual truths are combined together to make a consistent and systematic whole.[1]

This interpretation fits the context well and leaves the introduction of the hearers of the gospel until the next verse. If we do not press this idea too far and try to make Paul into a systematic theologian in the modern sense, this interpretation would do no violence to the facts of Paul's ministry. However, we must not be dogmatic, nor must we lose sight of the central thrust of the verse, which is quite clear, in debate over the details of interpretation which are not.

(2) True wisdom discerned only by spiritual men (2:14–16)

In this section Paul disclosed the further fact that the message which is a divine revelation must be discerned by men who are led by the Spirit of God.

Verse 14: explains why spiritual truths are not universally accepted. They cannot be understood.

The unspiritual man: is the natural man, i.e., man apart from any divine influence. Though Paul called the weak Christian unspiritual in 3:1, the

---

[1] Thomas Charles Edwards, *A Commentary on the First Epistle to the Corinthians* (London: Hodder and Stoughton, 1903). This is one of the best commentaries on this epistle. I will refer to it hereafter by the name of the author, T. C. Edwards.

form of the Greek word there is different. The Greek word here is *psuchikos,* an adjective derived from a noun (*psuchē*), which is usually translated "soul" in the New Testament. It denotes natural man at his best. But the best is not enough. Paul had introduced a new dimension to human life, something higher than man at his best. It is the dimension of Spirit leadership which heightens the faculties of man beyond that which they can achieve by themselves. Spirit leadership does not dehumanize; it leads to the fulfillment of the human in man. The natural man is not, in a way, fully human. His humanity has been corrupted by the power of sin. His ability to comprehend spiritual realities has been destroyed.

Does not receive: a general word with as many meanings in Greek as in English. Here it means "he rejects."

The gifts of the Spirit of God: that is, the gifts which come from the Spirit of God. *Gifts* is a justifiable translation, though the Greek has only "the things of the Spirit of God." *Gifts* reminds us of the phrase in verse 12: "the gifts bestowed on us by God." They come from the Spirit of God in the sense that his work enables man to understand and appropriate them.

For they are folly to him: explains why the natural man rejects the message. It appears to him to be utter nonsense.

And he is not able to understand them: points to the complete inability of man, without the aid of the Spirit of God, to know the real meaning of the gospel.

Because they are spiritually discerned: that is, discerned under the guidance and with the help of the Holy Spirit. *Discerned* translates a Greek word which means to investigate or examine judiciously with a view to full apprehension. The use of it here suggests that the methods and approaches to learning spiritual truths require spiritual faculties and processes. "In forensic use always the examination into facts and evidence is a preliminary to judgment, not the judgment itself." [1]

Paul did not mean to deny to natural man the ability to hear the gospel and be led by the Spirit to faith. He meant to deny man's ability to investigate it so as to form a judicious decision concerning its truth.

Verse 15: From the inability of the natural man, Paul turned to the equipment of the spiritual man.

The spiritual man: the man whose life is dominated by the Holy Spirit. Paul used the word *spiritual* here in contrast to the natural man of verse 14, but in other places in contrast to the *fleshly* man. For him, the word had ethical as well as religious meaning.

Judges: investigates or examines. The same Greek word as the one translated "discerned" in verse 14.

All things: not only the things of the Spirit but the things that belong to natural life as well. Paul deliberately widened the scope by this expression. He meant that the spiritual man is equipped by his possession of the Holy Spirit—or, perhaps better, because he is possessed by the Holy Spirit—to investigate and come to a judicious opinion about the relative worth of all things.

---

[1] R. St. John Parry, *The First Epistle of Paul the Apostle to the Corinthians* (Cambridge at the University Press, 1957). Hereafter referred to by the last name of the author, Parry.

But is himself to be judged by no one: rather, "he is discerned by no one." Paul repeated the same expression as above, but now asserted that no one (i.e., among natural men) could investigate and know the spiritual man himself. I take this to mean that the unregenerate man is never able to understand the motives and viewpoints of the regenerate man who is dominated by the Holy Spirit. Just as the truths of God remain a mystery to the natural man, so does the man of God.

Verse 16: This verse continues the thought of verse 15. The equipment of the spiritual man to investigate all things rests in the fact that he has the mind of Christ.[1] Quoting from Isaiah 40:13 (which he also quoted in Rom. 11:34), Paul insisted that no man had ever known the mind of the Lord; that is, no man could be his instructor. Perhaps there is a reference as well to the inability of the natural man to investigate the spiritual man since he partakes of the mind of God, but the main concern is with the ability of the spiritual man to investigate all things.

We: is again emphatic and may encompass only the apostles as above; it is more likely, however, that the word now is widened to include the man of verse 15, i.e., spiritual man.

The mind of Christ: perhaps, "we think like Christ." More likely, *mind* is a synonym for Spirit. Thus, *the mind of Christ* is the Holy Spirit. Certainly Paul did not mean the mind only as an intellectual matter. The reasoning of Paul rested on the assumption that Christ had the mind of God. For man to have the mind of Christ is to have the mind of God. Thus, the spiritual man is led of the Spirit to have *the mind of Christ.* This is what makes him what he is in contrast to what he once was.

(3) True wisdom still hidden from the Corinthians because they were behaving like ordinary men (3:1–4)

This paragraph recalls us to the trouble in Corinth. Paul had seemingly digressed in his discussion of true wisdom; now, he showed the connection between the two. The paragraph falls into two sections of thought: first, he pointed out why he did not speak of wisdom during his first visit to Corinth (vss. 1–2); second, he explained why he still could not speak to them of the true wisdom (vss. 3–4).

Verse 1: This verse is a historical reference to Paul's first visit to Corinth.

But I: placed in the emphatic position in the sentence. It introduces a discussion of Paul's treatment of the Corinthians.

Brethren: a common metaphor for fellow Christians.

Could not address you as spiritual men: The inability of Paul rested on the state of their maturity as Christians. He could not then follow the course of preaching he mentioned in 2:6, "Yet among the mature we do impart wisdom." They had not been ready for it because they were not yet spiritual men; i.e., they had not matured to the point where their lives were dominated by the Holy Spirit (cf. 2:14–16). The Corinthians had

---

[1] Schlatter states that this becomes the clear and certain measuring stick whereby we can recognize the leadership of the Holy Spirit and distinguish it from all other rules. (D. Adolf Schlatter, *Die Korintherbriefe* [Stuttgart: Calwer Vereinsbuchhandlung, 1928].)

been beginners in those days and could not be treated as spiritual. Paul's teaching had to be suited to their needs.

But as men of the flesh: The King James Version has "as unto carnal." "Carnal" is an exact rendering of the Greek adjective, but the modern connotation of "carnal" is too strong for the context. The RSV translation, "men of the flesh," is scarcely better. Paul did not mean to imply that they were sinful, but that they had hardly begun to grow as Christians; they still had to be dealt with on the merely natural plane of life. Notice that he avoided the word used in 2:14 for the unconverted man, a word which is in direct antithesis to *spiritual*. They had not been unspiritual, wholly devoid of the influence of the Holy Spirit. They had been Christians, but Christians barely. Their ways of thinking were still dominated by the habits of their pre-Christian life. No blame was attached to this. It was quite natural. It did explain why Paul had taught as he did.

As babes in Christ: a metaphor which explains what Paul meant by *men of the flesh*. Spiritual life is analogous to physical life. It begins with birth and comes to full maturity only slowly. Nevertheless, this expression shows that Paul thought of them as being Christian. They were *in Christ,* i.e., in vital union with him.

Verse 2: The first part of the verse continues Paul's discussion of the spiritual stature of the Corinthians at his first visit. The last part turns sharply to their stature at the time he wrote the letter.

I fed you with milk: continues the metaphor of babes in Christ. Paul described his preaching and instruction on that first occasion as being concerned with the basic principles of the gospel.

Solid food: another metaphor, in contrast to *milk*. Paul meant the true wisdom which is the subject of this section.

For you were not ready for it: the reason why he had fed them with milk rather than solid food.

And even yet you are not ready: introduces the rebuke of Paul. They should have been ready, but they were not. *Ready* here, as in the previous phrase, means able to receive it. It was not that they did not want it; they did. Their problem was that they had not grown as Christians ought to grow. There is nothing more attractive than a young baby; there is nothing more repulsive than an old baby. This is just as true in the spiritual realm as in the natural.

Verse 3: This verse tells why they were not ready.

For you are still of the flesh: Did Paul mean the same here by *of the flesh* as he did in verse 1 by *men of the flesh?* The same Greek word, but with a different ending, is used. In classic Greek the ending used in verse 1 signifies that which is composed of the material, *flesh*. In the two instances in this verse, the ending signifies that which is characterized by an affinity to the material, *flesh*. The problem is: Did Paul use these words in the classical sense? Some say yes; others say no. The change of the form in the immediate context, would, it seems to me, be purposeful. Thus, I believe the apostle used these words with a meaningful distinction. Ethically speaking, the first usage (in vs. 1) was more serious than the second and third (in vs. 3). The first would mean that they were still dominated by human frailties and aims and could not help it. The second would indicate some spiritual progress, but not enough. They were still too much under the influence of merely human concerns. They had not yet achieved the growth to spiritual maturity which would enable Paul to address them as spiritual men. Paul did not blame them for their condition at the first; he did blame them for their lack of growth.[1]

For while there is jealousy and strife among you, are you not of the flesh, and behaving like ordinary men: the proof of their spiritual immaturity. The *jealousy and strife* were discussed in 1:11–12. *Behaving like ordinary men* defines more fully what Paul meant by being *of the flesh.* It meant for the Christian to be undistinguishable from the sinner in aim, purpose, and behavior. Such a condition is all too often true in our churches today, and we need not be surprised that it was true in the Corinthian church.

Verse 4: This verse is an argument by interrogation. It repeats 1:12 with an important difference. In this verse, and the rest of the chapter, only Paul and Apollos are mentioned. Since they were personal friends, Paul could not be accused of animosity toward Apollos. He might have been considered antagonistic toward Peter. Since he was getting ready to say some things about the leaders themselves which might be taken as derogatory, though they were not meant to be, he purposely mentioned only the name of his friend.

5. Their Dissensions Were Based on a False Estimation of Apostles and Teachers (3:5—4:5)

The thought that runs throughout this section is that the apostles and teachers were agents through whom God was working to accomplish his purpose of redemption. Paul made this explicit in a discussion of himself and Apollos (3:5–9). However, this did not mean that the human agents were without responsibility for their labor. They would suffer loss if their building was inadequate and of wrong materials (3:10–15). They would be destroyed if they destroyed God's temple—the church (3:16–17). It did mean that they were not to be glorified by the Corinthians. Rather, the Corinthians were to consider them as ministers who ministered for the enrichment of the church; in this sense they belonged to the church rather than the church belonging to them (3:18–23). However, this part of their ministry was not the whole of it. They also belonged to God and were answerable to him (4:1–5).

(1) Apostles and teachers belonged to God and worked together in his field (3:5–9)

The central thrust of this paragraph is that it was God who accomplished the salvation of the Corinthians. Therefore, they were "God's field"; i.e., they belonged to God. Human agents did indeed labor in the field, but

---

[1] Leon Morris, *The First Epistle of Paul to the Corinthians* (Grand Rapids, Mich.: Wm. B. Eerdmans Publishing Company, 1958), p. 63. Hereafter referred to by the last name of the author, Morris.

they were merely instruments through whom God did his work. Paul used the metaphor of the field throughout the paragraph.

Verse 5: defines the essential function of the agents of God.

What then is Apollos? What is Paul?: two rhetorical questions which Paul meant to answer for them. *What* is used rather than "who," purposefully. Paul meant to define function rather than identity. Perhaps there is a touch of disdain in the use of the neuter pronoun. The questions are philosophical in form, leading up to a definition.

Servants: translates the Greek word from which we get the English word "deacon." Contrasted with slaves in the ancient society, servants were day laborers, paid by the master and doing his work as directed. Perhaps our English word "agents" would be more adequate. Paul meant that in the work of evangelizing the Corinthians and building the church, he and Apollos were acting as agents of God.

Through whom you believed: points to the work of founding and building the church at Corinth.

As the Lord assigned to each: can be taken in three ways: (1) as the Lord gave to each his task,[1] (2) as the Lord gave to each his converts,[2] or (3) as the Lord gave faith to each convert. The following verse would indicate that the first interpretation is correct. Thus Paul drew the mind of the Corinthians away from what he and Apollos did to what the Lord did. *The Lord* is to be taken as a reference to Christ Jesus.

Verse 6: Introducing the metaphor of the field or garden, Paul spoke of the ministry of himself and Apollos and the power of God.

I planted: a metaphor of the field pointing to both the priority in time and the preeminence in importance of his ministry.

Apollos watered: the same metaphor recognizing the importance and necessity of the ministry of Apollos.

But God gave the growth: In the Greek there is a significant change of verb tenses. In speaking of the work of the agents, Paul used a simple past tense. In speaking of the work of God, Paul used a progressive past tense, the Greek imperfect. It indicated that God was giving the growth simultaneously with the work of his agents. The work of God belongs to an entirely different class than the work of men. He did what men could not do. They could place the seed in the ground and water the young shoots. Only God could cause growth. Remember that Paul was talking about the spiritual growth of the Corinthians, though what he said was true also in the natural world.

Verse 7: In verses 7–8, Paul drew three inferences from what he had said. The first inference is that he who plants and he who waters is nothing.

So: introduces the series of inferences.

Neither he who plants nor he who waters is anything: Paul meant that they counted for nothing in the success of the work. He did not mean to disdain the part in the work of God played by his agents; he meant to deny that any praise was due to them for the success of the work. The statement is relative rather than absolute. When compared to the work of God, the work of the agents amounted to nothing.

---

1 So Edwards and Allo.
2 So ICC.

But only God: God alone was due praise for the success of the work.

Who gives the growth: states the reason why God alone was to be thanked. The Greek is an articular participle and may be translated "the one causing the growth."

Verse 8: states the second and third inferences from the fact that God gives the growth.

He who plants and he who waters are equal: the second inference. *Equal* translates the Greek word which is ordinarily rendered "one." Paul meant that they were indistinguishable so far as aim and purpose were concerned. They were in the same category; they were fellow workers. As a result, it was unchristian to set them over against one another as rivals. They played on the same team.

And each shall receive his wages according to his labor: introduces the third inference and a corrective for the previous clause. In this sense, they were not necessarily equal. However, their inequality was for the eyes of God to see and for him alone. He would be the one to pay them their wages. What are the wages of the Christian minister? Christ defined them as participation in his joy (Matt. 25:21). Thus we could say that every servant of God will participate in the joy of Christ to the extent to which he labors. *His,* a possessive adjective, might better be translated "his own." *Labor* is a strong word in the Greek, stronger than our words for work and labor. It really means to toil and suggests not only the energy spent in the work but the weariness and exhaustion that come as a result.

Verse 9: This verse summarizes and restates the thought of the paragraph.

For: takes up the thought of the first clause in verse 8. Paul and Apollos were one in the sense that they were fellow workmen.

We are fellow workers for God: that is, *fellow workmen* who belong to *God.* It is difficult to translate the Greek so as to bring out the right meaning. The King James Version, "labourers together with God," seems to imply a cooperation between God and men. This implication is foreign to the context and, indeed, to the whole teaching of the New Testament. The RSV is better. *For God* would mean in God's service and would suggest both the identity of the workmen and the distinctness of responsibility. However, *God* in the possessive case is repeated three times in this verse, each time with emphasis. The same meaning should be given in each instance. Since "belonging to God" is the only meaning that fits the last two instances, it should be adopted here as well.[1] A literal translation of the verse would read: "God's fellow workmen we are; God's field, God's building you are."

God's field: continues the agricultural metaphor. Not only did Paul and Apollos belong to God, but the Corinthians did also. This follows from what had been said above. They did not belong to Paul, Cephas, or Apollos; they belonged to God. This showed how foolish it was for them to have divisions of opinion based on allegiance to human leaders.

God's building: shifts the metaphor to prepare for the next paragraph. T. C. Edwards' suggestion that the *field* represents the individual Chris-

---

[1] Furnish concludes that the emphasis is on the equality of the apostles (V. P. Furnish, "Fellow Workers in God's Service," *Journal of Biblical Literature,* Dec., 1961, pp. 264–370. Hereafter referred to by the last name of the author, Furnish.)

tians and the *building* represents the church is not well founded. Paul made no such distinction. The church was the Christians, and Paul made no distinction between them as individuals and as a corporate unity.

(2) Apostles and teachers were builders of the church and responsible to God for their work (3:10-15)

What has been said above about the efficiency of God does not relieve the religious leaders of their responsibility. The foundation which is Christ has been laid (vss. 10-11). The teaching of those who build on the foundation must be of equally good material (vs. 12). The work of each preacher will be judged by its results; and the reward will be apportioned, not only according to the toil (vs. 8), but also according to the soundness of the building (vss. 13-15).

Verse 10: Paul took up the figure of the building, introduced in verse 9, and applied it to his own work and the work of his successors.

The commission: literally, "the grace." In stating that his ability was due to the special grace of God, Paul removed any tinge of boastfulness from what he said. This grace was not the general grace of apostleship, but the special grace of founding churches where no one else had laid the foundation (cf. Rom. 15:19-20).

Skilled: based on the Greek word which is usually translated "wise." *Skilled* seems to have been the original meaning of the word. Aristotle defined it as one who was skilled in his particular art.

Master builder: foreman in the modern sense. The term is a translation of the Greek word from which we get the English word "architect." However, in ancient usage it referred, not to the architect or planner, but to the superintendent of the work. The same term is used of Bezalel (cf. Exod. 35:32), who with the assistance of others built the ancient Tabernacle. Paul meant to say in this context that God was the architect and planner of the church at Corinth, but Paul the builder who carried out the actual building. The idea of a foreman with assistants need not be pressed, although he did have helpers.

Paul said that his work of proclaiming the gospel in Corinth was the laying of the *foundation* of the church. *A foundation* (RSV) gives the wrong impression; he was not speaking of one foundation among many. The absence of the article in Greek emphasizes the quality of his work. Thus: "I laid that which alone has the quality of being foundation."

Another man was not a reference to Apollos, but to any other teacher who might arise in Corinth. This teacher, whoever he might be, is conceived of as continuing the building on the foundation which Paul laid. These subsequent builders were to be held responsible for the work they did. Therefore Paul warned them to take care.

How he builds: primarily, the materials with which he builds (cf. vs. 12), that is, the substance of his preaching. But this does not exclude a thought of the manner of his preaching and leadership.

Verse 11: In this verse Paul insisted that it was impossible for another teacher to lay another, different, foundation for the church than the one he had laid.

Can: should be given the full force. It was absolutely impossible for any other teacher to lay another foundation for the church at Corinth. It is likewise true that any church must be founded upon Jesus Christ. A society of men which does not have this foundation is not a church in the true meaning of the word.

Which is Jesus Christ: explains the nature of the foundation. This verse helps us to understand Matthew 16:18, where Christ is reported to have said, "On this rock I will build my church." Christ is himself the "rock." But in what way? Paul explained this more fully in 1 Corinthians 15:1–3. His first message was that of the crucified and risen Lord. This was the way he laid the foundation of the church at Corinth. Thus, the teaching is that the redemptive work of Christ, the heart of the gospel message, is the foundation on which each church must stand. This relates a church to the historical Jesus, just as its continuing life under the leadership of the Spirit relates it to the living Christ. Neither is complete without the other. Modern theologians who would belittle the significance of the historical Jesus find no foundation for their ideas in the New Testament.

Than that which is laid: The present tense in the Greek stresses the fact that the foundation which he once laid still stands. This is a stronger assertion than the one in verse 10. Christ is the continuing foundation.

Verse 12: This verse explains what Paul meant by the admonition in verse 10, "Let each man take care how he builds upon it." Two groups of materials, one abiding, the other temporary, are mentioned. We need not try to make something special of each individual material mentioned. The materials represent the substance of the teaching, the doctrines taught. The contrast is not so much between that which is true and that which is false as it is between that which is meaningful and that which is inadequate. It is possible to preach the truth in a one-sided, warped, or watered-down way so that it does not have the power to give spiritual sustenance to the hearer. This seems to have been the danger in Corinth.

The New Testament itself gives examples of various ways in which the Christian message can be presented inadequately. 1 John counteracts an interpretation of the gospel which led to immorality and licentiousness. Galatians combats a type of teaching which was one-sided and led to positive error. 1 Corinthians is concerned with a type of teaching which led to philosophical speculation, thus losing sight of the essential substance of the gospel. It was this last type which was immediately in the mind of Paul, but modern preachers need to take warning from the other examples as well.

Precious stones: should be taken as marble or some other kind of costly building stones rather than in the sense of jewels.

Verse 13: This verse forms the conclusion of the sentence beginning in verse 12. It sets forth the future testing of each man's work.

Each man's work will become manifest: The worth and character of each man's work will come to light.

The Day: when Christ shall come again and the world shall be judged (cf. 1 Thess. 5:4; Heb. 10:25; 2 Tim. 4:8). *Day,* a technical term in the Old Testament for the coming of God's judgment, is correctly capitalized in the RSV.

Will disclose it: will openly declare it.

Because it will be revealed with fire: reflects the description of the judgment day in 2 Thess. 1:7–8: "when the Lord Jesus is revealed from heaven with his mighty angels in flaming fire." The function of the fire in. this statement is to reveal to men that the day of the Lord has come.

The fire will test what sort of work each one has done: will prove the character of the work by destroying the perishable and purifying the enduring. Wood, hay, stubble will be destroyed. Gold, silver, precious stones will endure. So it is that every man who has built an enduring superstructure on the foundation of Christ will have his work vindicated, but every man who has not so built will see his work destroyed.

Verse 14: If the work which any man has built on the foundation survives: if the fire shows that it is enduring in quality. Remember that we are dealing here with figurative language. The thought is that of enduring the judgment of God.

He will receive a reward: get paid for his work. The reward is not, of course, material but spiritual. It is sharing in the joy of the Lord over the accomplishments of the ministry, a consciousness of a job well done.

Verse 15: If any man's work is burned up: shown to be inadequate by the judgment.

He will suffer loss: He will be fined as well as losing his expected profit. He cannot share in the joy of the Lord, nor have a consciousness of a job well done.

Though he himself will be saved: Eternal salvation is not based on man's work but on the mercy and grace of God. This statement reveals that Paul believed that the local teachers in Corinth, who are in mind throughout the passage, were truly Christians. He appreciated their sincerity and zeal. He doubted their wisdom as builders of a church. While he warned them of the consequences of inadequate work, he did not threaten them with eternal damnation.

But only as through fire: as men rushing through the flames to escape the burning building. The figure is graphic but not to be taken literally.

(3) Apostles and teachers faced destruction if they destroyed God's church (3:16–17)

The thought moves on from the building of God to the temple of God, from the man whose work will be destroyed though he is saved to the man who will be destroyed with his work. The thought in this section is not of the teacher who builds inadequately on the true foundation, but of the teacher who by his teaching corrupts and thus destroys the church. The implications of the passage for the unity of the church are apparent.

Verse 16: This is a rhetorical question which lays the foundation for the conclusion in verse 17.

Do you not know: This form of question expects an affirmative answer. Thus: "You do know, do you not?" Paul appealed to a teaching which he had no doubt given to them orally.

You are God's temple: an important definition of the relation of the church at Corinth with God. *You* must be limited to the addressees of the letter. Paul was not speaking of the church universal, but of the assembly of saints at Corinth. *Temple* is the word for the inner sanctuary, God's dwelling place, not the whole temple building. It is singular and without the article. A paraphrase would read: "You have the character of being a sanctuary of God." Paul used this word figuratively in four passages (here and in 2 Cor. 6:16 and Eph. 2:21 of the church; in 1 Cor. 6:19 of the individual Christian). He was never guilty of the modern heresy of calling a church building a temple of God. His use of the word indicates the radical shift of the center of gravity in New Testament religion as over against Old Testament religion. God does not dwell in houses made by human hands, but in human hearts and lives.

God's Spirit dwells in you: proof that they were indeed the temple of God and an indication that the Holy Spirit is a divine person. The first was purposeful; the second, incidental. *Dwells* is in the present tense and indicates a continuous reality. The pagan temple was inhabited by an *image* of God, the Jewish temple by a *symbol* of his presence, the Christian temple by God himself.

Verse 17: If any one destroys God's temple: The form of the conditional clause indicates that Paul considered this as a reality. Someone was in the process of destroying the temple. Again we must think that he had in mind those who were changing the gospel into a speculative system of worldly wisdom. By preaching this idea men were in the process of rendering inoperative the church in its function as a church. Thus they were guilty of destroying the temple.

God will destroy him: not only his work, as in verse 15, but the man as well. The warning of judgment is made impressive by the repetition of the same verb, *destroy.* The punishment fits the offense.

For God's temple is holy: Thus, to destroy it is the worst sacrilege. *Holy* here, as always, refers to God's ownership, though ethical connotations are never excluded.

And that temple you are: repetition for emphasis of the teaching of verse 16.

(4) Apostles and teachers ministered for the enrichment of the Corinthians (3:18-23)

Paul turned from the doom of the destroyer to the danger that threatened division in the church. It was rooted in the adulation of worldly wisdom which permeated both the church and its local leaders and threatened to rob them of the true riches which belonged to them through the ministry of the apostles and teachers. The Corinthians thought that they were wise men, that they had the wisdom to judge the message of God. Paul, therefore, advised anyone who thought he was wise to become a fool, that he might be truly wise (vs. 18). Quoting from two Old Testament passages (Job 5:13 and Ps. 94:11), he pointed out that all the wisdom of the world ends in futility (vss. 19-20). Finally, he pointed out that the ministry of all the apostles and teachers belonged to the entire church. They were rich indeed, if only they would stop impoverishing themselves by limiting their loyalty to Christ as they adhered to one teacher or another (vss. 21–23).

Verse 18: Let no one deceive himself: could refer to verses 16–17, but probably introduces what is to follow. However, the connection is close. The form of the prohibition in Greek is the present tense, which implies that some were actually doing it. The danger which threatened the church was that many, possibly all, of the church members were practicing a self-deception with respect to the entire subject of this section—that of Christian teachers and the kind of work they did. The singular, *no one,* appeals to each individual member personally. Anyone who looked upon the teachers as men of worldly wisdom made himself unfit to receive the true wisdom of God.

If any one among you thinks that he is wise in this age: defines the form of the threatened self-deception. The question is: Does the expression *any one among you* point to a teacher who was not really one of them or to any particular member of the church? Though some commentators have made much of the use of this expression rather than "any one of you," it seems to me that the distinction is too nicely drawn. *Thinks he is wise* does not mean, "seems to be wise in the sight of others." The warning was to men who had a mistaken notion of their own wisdom. The point was that the Corinthians, in setting themselves up as judges over the teachers, were in danger of coming to a false estimation of their own wisdom. *In this age* defines wisdom as being that wisdom which the world values, but which Paul had already said was folly with God. In the Greek text, *among you* and *in this age* are written side by side. It would seem to point to a deliberate contrast. What is good *in this age* is not to be brought into the church fellowship. There it is bad.

Let him become a fool: graphic way of saying, "Let him become humble enough to learn." He is to renounce any imagined wisdom which he has and come to God as one without any wisdom.

That he may become wise: a play on words. He thinks he is *wise;* let him become a *fool;* he will be made *wise. Wise* points to the wisdom which comes from God, that is, "to have all the riches of assured understanding and the knowledge of God's mystery, of Christ, in whom are hid all the treasures of wisdom and knowledge" (Col. 2:2–3).

Verse 19: This verse repeats the thought found in 1:26–31.

For the wisdom of this world is folly with God: points to two standards of judgment. The *wisdom of this world* is the passing wisdom which belongs to this present world. In the affairs of men it may have some validity. When judged by the standard of God, it is stupidity, *folly. With God* means alongside of God or from the viewpoint of God. It is folly because it is concerned only with things which are material, temporal, passing; it ignores the spiritual reality of man's being. For the Christian this wisdom is never to be the ruling standard of life.

For it is written: Paul's usual way of introducing Scripture.

He catches the wise in their craftiness: a quotation from Job 5:13 which does not follow exactly the Septuagint; it is probably Paul's own translation from the Hebrew. *Catches* means to grasp in the hand, lay hands on. *Craftiness* comes from a word which originally meant readiness to do anything; it came to mean the versatile cleverness of a man who is ready for any and all work if it is bad enough. The bad sense predominates in biblical literature. The word is applied to the subtlety of the devil in deceiving Eve (2 Cor. 11:3) and to the methods of teachers who deceive immature Christians with false doctrines (Eph. 4:14). Paul had been accused of using such craftiness (2 Cor. 12:16) and claimed that he had renounced it (2 Cor. 4:2). Obviously, for Paul it had the meaning of the use of subtle but false reasoning for the purpose of misleading. Its use here may suggest that after his departure other teachers had come to Corinth who were promoters of the church's sophistry.

Verse 20: And again: continues the quotations from the Old Testament.

The Lord knows that the thoughts of the wise are futile: a quotation from Psalm 94:11 with *wise* substituted for "man." In the quotation *the Lord* refers to God, not to Christ. Nothing is hidden from him; he knows both the contents and the futility of man's thoughts. *Thoughts* translates a word which means reasonings or disputations (cf. Phil 2:14). *Futile* means empty of real result, fruitless. It suggests that nothing of permanent value is ever accomplished by worldly wisdom. It concerns only what passes away.

Verse 21: This verse is coordinate with 1:31. The Christian is not to glory in anything except in the Lord.

So: inferential conjunction pointing to the conclusion of what is taught in the Scriptures.

Let no one boast: prohibition in the present tense which means to "stop boasting." They had been doing it; this was the root of their trouble; they must stop it.

Of men: Greek, "in men," in antithesis to "in the Lord." This would include any men, themselves or others. They were not to boast in their own wisdom nor in the wisdom of their teachers. The admonition is general, but the next verse indicates that Paul still had in mind their stubborn overestimation of himself, Apollos, and Peter.

For all things are yours: the reason why they were not to boast in men. To boast in individual leaders was to limit their understanding of Christianity to what that particular leader had to give. This kind of self-limitation was really a kind of self-impoverishment. The fact of the matter was that their new relationship with Christ had opened up to them the whole universe. This statement by Paul reminds us of his other statement in Romans 8:32: "He who did not spare his own Son but gave him up for us all, will he not also give us all things with him?"

Many commentators have pointed out the similarity between this assertion of Paul and the claim of the Stoic to self-sufficiency. It is doubtful that there is any direct borrowing of terms from the Stoics, and there is certainly a vast difference between the concept of Paul and the concept of the Stoics. The Stoics thought of self-sufficiency (mastery over the world and the circumstances of life) as the special possession of the wise man. Paul did not accept that evaluation. The Stoics thought of self-sufficiency as a human achievement, based on a strict program of self-discipline. Paul thought of it as the gift of God. The Stoic thought of

his self-sufficiency as a thing which would free him, not only from dependence on other men, but also from concern for other men. Paul thought
of it as the thing which would equip Christians for creative involvement
in the problems of all men. Any attempt to make Paul a Christian Stoic
must fail; the two systems of life were entirely different and mutually
exclusive.

Verse 22: This verse makes a list of the things which Paul included in
his assertion in verse 21.

Whether Paul or Apollos or Cephas: teachers in whom they had
boasted.[1] The emphasis lies in the fact that the teachers were *all* theirs.
The Corinthians had been limiting themselves to one or the other. Paul
asserted that all of the teachers were the slaves, the possessions, of the
Corinthians. To choose one when all were theirs would be self-impoverishment. We need not press the figure too far. Of course, the teachers were
first of all slaves of Christ, but they were ministers to the Corinthians.
Their task was to enrich them. Each had his own peculiar gift to share.
What Paul meant was that the Corinthians were to take all that each had
to offer. We have seen the same tendency in modern church members
and students who make an idol out of a particular preacher or teacher.
When they do, they can no longer see the good that is in other preachers
and teachers. They limit their understanding of Christianity.

Notice that Paul omitted Christ from this list of their rallying cries
(1:12). Christ cannot be said to be the possession of any man. Rather,
the Christian assertion is that we are possessed of him.

Or the world: either the created order or the society of men. Perhaps
what Paul had in mind was life in the world, which would include both
creation and society. The Christian, just because he is a Christian, sees
the world in a way in which no sophist can ever see it. He sees the hand
of God in the sunshine, in the beauties of nature, in the bountiful supply
of his physical needs. In this way the world nurtures and strengthens his
Christian life and becomes his in a peculiar way. The Christian sees the
struggles of society, the battles of life, even the evils in a new way. Society
becomes the arena in which the character of Christ is wrought out in
him. Because he meets the difficulties of life in the strength of the Lord,
he finds life in the world a way of Christian growth and maturity. He is
no longer the victim of the surrounding influences of the world; he is
victor in Christ. This statement reminds us of the saying of Christ:
"the meek . . . shall inherit the earth" (Matt. 5:5). I would assign the
same meaning to each statement.

Or life or death: represents on the one hand that which man clings to
and on the other that which man dreads. Perhaps they are half-personified
here in Paul's thought.

To the Christian the nature of each is changed. *Life* becomes life in
Christ, a sort of foretaste of the heavenly experience. In Christ life is

---

[1] Thrall points out that since the apostles were servants of the church, they belonged to the church. This means that the Corinthians did not belong to them or owe
them discipleship. (Margaret E. Thrall, *The First and Second Letters of Paul to the
Corinthians* [Cambridge: At the University Press, 1965]. Hereafter referred to by
the last name of the author, Thrall.)

given a new dimension that is unknown to the sophist or the unbeliever. In some ways the Christian's existence on earth is the same as before; in every important way it has been changed. The Christian alone lives the true authentic life on earth, for his life is an other-worldly existence even in this world. *Death* also changes its meaning for the Christian. No longer is it the feared enemy of life, the dreaded end of existence, or the herald of eternal damnation. It becomes a gateway into the fuller experience of life. This does not mean that the Christian does not shrink from the experience of death; he does. It does mean that he no longer looks upon it as his enemy, nor does he mourn his dead Christian friends as do those who have no hope (cf. 1 Thess. 4:13).

Or the present or the future: continuing existence in the world. It is possible that the *future* includes the heavenly life, but it is more likely that Paul thought of it as continued life here. Notice that Paul did not mention the past; it is gone. It no longer belongs to the Christian. But the *present* and the *future* are his in a way in which they do not belong to the unbeliever. Perhaps we can sum up this section by saying that time is a challenge and a responsibility. This reminds us of the saying of Paul in another context where the meaning of "wise" is different than it is in this context: "Look carefully then how you walk, not as unwise men but as wise, making the most of the time, because the days are evil" (Eph. 5:15–16).

All are yours: sums up the list, and what an impressive list it is!

Verse 23: Lest the Corinthians would again be tempted to boast, Paul moved from their opportunities to their responsibilities.

And you are Christ's: states both the reason why all things were theirs and the responsibility that they had to Christ. The reason they had mastery over the universe was that they were incorporated into Christ. It was by virtue of their union with him that they were made victors over life instead of victims of it. Further, they had the responsibility of using their mastery for his glory.

And Christ is God's: completes the series of ownerships that Paul had mentioned. The apostles and teachers were theirs—theirs to use. They were Christ's—Christ's to use. Christ was God's—God's to use. This statement has nothing to do with Paul's concept of the equality of Christ with God. He had made it perfectly clear in other passages that he considered them as equal. But in the redemptive program of God, there is a system of subordination. God sent Christ to be man's redeemer; Christ sent his apostles, even as God had sent him; the apostles had called the Corinthians to faith. Nowhere is there any suggestion of inferiority or superiority of one over the other. Thus we are to take Paul's thought in a limited sense. In all that pertained to his redemptive work, Christ was the agent of God, sent by him, anointed by him, sustained by him through prayer, raised by him from the grave, exalted by him to his own right hand.

(5) Apostles and teachers were stewards of God (4:1–5)

This section closes as it began (3:5) with an admonition to the Corinthians to have the right attitude toward apostles and teachers, ministers of the church. Since they belonged to God, the judgment (i.e., the estimation of their value) belonged to God. The Corinthians were therefore reprimanded for daring to set up worldly standards of judgment. Paul set forth first the fact that ministers were stewards of God (vs. 1). Then he pointed out that the primary requirement for stewards among men, and therefore before God, was that they be found trustworthy (vs. 2). Following this logically, he asserted that the judgments of men had no weight with those who belonged to God (vss. 3–4). This included even the consciousness of the man himself. He then admonished the Corinthians to stop judging at all, but to leave this to God, who will judge all men (vs. 5).

Verse 1: This verse presents the primary premise on which the rest of the paragraph hinges.

This is how one should regard us: sets forth the duty of the Corinthians. The emphasis in the admonition lies on *us,* that is, the ministers of the new covenant (2 Cor. 3:6), whether it be apostles or local teachers of the church. *Regard* comes from a Greek word which means to reckon. Perhaps our English word "rate" would fit the sense. The ministers were not to be rated as leaders of a party or as spokesmen of a new wisdom.

Originally the word *servant* was used for the underrower in the galley ships. It came to mean one who did anything under the authority of another person; hence, the idea is that of "underlings." Paul used the word only here, but we find it in Luke 1:2 for "ministers of the word." In later church life this same Greek word came to be almost a technical term for subdeacon.

Christ was the authority under which the teachers were serving. They were the "underlings" of Christ. He, and he alone, is the Lord of the church. Paul constantly repeated this fact in this section, not only because it was the fundamental belief of the church, but because the Corinthians by their bickerings had tended to elevate the apostles and teachers to places of lordship.

And stewards of the mysteries of God: defines further the character in which the ministers were servants of Christ. They were *stewards,* a translation of a compound Greek word, meaning literally "law of the house." It referred in society to a slave who had been given charge of the master's establishment, assigning to the other slaves their particular tasks. In relation to his master, the steward was a slave, but, in relation to his fellow slaves, he was the overseer or foreman. The two-sided emphasis need not be pressed in this verse. Paul's thought was that the apostles and teachers had been entrusted with the property of the master; they had no independent status.

The property over which they had been made overseers was the *mysteries of God. Mysteries* probably stands here for revealed truths. It was a word which was commonly used in the pagan religions for hidden truths which the initiated gained by a program of discipline. Paul adopted the term from the mystery religions but gave it a new content. It was no longer hidden truth, but revealed truth. However, the word is pertinent since the truth now revealed was once hidden. Paul spoke of it in 2:7: "But we impart a secret and hidden wisdom of God, which God decreed before the ages for our glorification." Paul used the word often, but it is in the plural only here.

Possibly, the idea of distribution to others led to his use of the plural. *Of God* defines the source of the mysteries. They come by revelation, not by discovery of men.

Verse 2: Continuing the metaphor of the steward, Paul pointed out the primary requisite for the position.

Moreover: better translation, "here." The meaning is that here on this earth, in the common affairs of men, what is to follow is true. This verse is a part of the figure of speech.

It is required of stewards that they be found trustworthy: defines the primary demand of a master for the slave who was elevated to this dignified office. Other demands might be made upon him, such as intelligence, and industry, but trustworthiness was the primary demand. *Trustworthy* means reliable, so that his master might rely upon him to carry out his business and not to steal. While the statement in this context seems to be a part of the figure of speech, its enlargement to include the duty of the steward of God is justified. *Required* translates a Greek word which means "seeks." The idea is that the master with a number of slaves kept seeking among them for men to be stewards who were trustworthy. Likewise, God keeps seeking men on whom he can rely to whom to entrust the gospel.

Verse 3: This verse begins the application of the figure of speech to the judgment of the apostles and teachers.

But with me: Paul narrowed his consideration to himself, leaving out the others; he could not speak for them.

It is a very small thing that I should be judged by you: points to the insignificance, in Paul's mind, of the judgment that the Corinthians would make about him in relation to his stewardship. Paul did not mean that he did not want the good opinion of the Corinthians. I am sure that he shared the common human desire to be well thought of by others. However, in relation to his stewardship of the gospel, this was the least of his worries. *Judged* is the same Greek word here as in 2:15. The leading idea is that of sifting, examining, or investigating. Paul did not count it important that men were investigating him to see if he measured up to some human standard of excellence. Since they had no jurisdiction over him, their findings would be of no consequence.

Or by any human court: literally, "or by any human day." The idea is not the same as if he had said, "by any man." The expression is a technical term for a day of judgment set by constituted authorities. Thus the RSV translation, *court,* is justified though it is not literal. Since in Paul's mind the human courts represented the "rulers of this age, who are doomed to pass away" (2:6), their investigation would have no bearing on his stewardship.

I do not even judge myself: a step further. One is perhaps most dis-qualified to investigate himself impartially. Nonetheless, many undertake to do just this. Certainly the inability of one to give a true estimate of his faithfulness in performing his stewardship of God should be self-evident. Paul denied that he submitted his case to his own investigation. This accounts for the fact that he never undertook to defend himself against false charges with a claim of faithful stewardship.

Verse 4: This verse carries forward the idea of self-judgment.

I am not aware of anything against myself: introduces a hypothetical case. It is not a declaration of a clear conscience. The better a man is, the more conscious he is of his failings in this matter. Paul often confessed that he was not perfect. But for the sake of the argument, to show the futility of self-judgment, he introduced a hypothesis. The clause should read: "Even though I am not aware of anything against myself."

But I am not thereby acquitted: the conclusion from the supposition above. He meant that even if he could come before God with a clear conscience, not knowing anything against himself, this would not mean that he would be acquitted. *Acquitted* is a common Pauline word which is usually translated "justified." Here it does not have the evangelical meaning that it usually does with Paul. It has the common meaning of Greek society. It means that a man stands before the judge, is tried, and is pronounced guiltless. But, even in a human court, this pronouncement must come from the judge. In God's tribunal, it must come from God. Just as the accused criminal is not acquitted simply because he pleads "not guilty," so the steward of God is not proved innocent of violating his trust simply because he knows nothing against himself.

It is the Lord who judges me: gives the reason for the futility of self-judgment. *The Lord* is Christ here, as it usually is with Paul except in scriptural quotations. This takes up again the idea that the ministers are underlings of Christ (vs. 1). *Judges* is still based on the Greek word which means to investigate to see if there is any ground for indictment.

Verse 5: This verse gives the conclusion, in the Corinthians' case, of the hypothetical case which Paul had proposed.

Therefore: introduces the practical conclusion from what has been said in the form of an admonition to the Corinthians.

Do not pronounce judgment: literally, "stop judging anything." The Corinthians had been guilty, not only of investigating but of pronouncing *judgment* on their teachers. *Judgment* is not the same word as in verse 4. It means here to pronounce sentence. The admonition to stop judging pointed to the Corinthians' habit in their rallying cries, "I belong to Paul," of pronouncing judgment upon their teachers, both the one they followed and the ones they rejected.

Before the time: the appointed time of judgment, the day of the Lord. The word for *time* in this passage has no exact English equivalent. In this passage it really means the proper time; in other passages it can have the meaning of appropriate or seasonable time for something to happen.

Before the Lord comes: defines the time of the previous phrase. Paul had no doubt that the Lord, Jesus Christ, would come. The time of his coming was and is in doubt. I personally doubt that the common idea that the early churches constantly expected the coming of the Lord is based on fact. However, the fact of his coming was never in doubt nor forgotten. Nor should it be doubted or forgotten in our age, even though it has been long delayed.

Who will bring to light the things now hidden in darkness: states one qualification of the Lord to act as judge when he comes. He will *bring to light* or, perhaps, "illumine" the things which men cannot see and consider when they presume to pass judgment. *Darkness* may be only a part of the figure here, but it could have its usual meaning of evil things. If so, Paul was suggesting that the evil things in both the Corinthians and their teachers remained hidden now, but would be brought to light when Christ would act as the judge.

And will disclose the purposes of the heart: explanatory of the previous clause. The hidden things are the *purposes* that lie hidden in the heart. *Disclose* means to make manifest for all to see. In the Lord's judgment, as in human courts, two things are required to give accurate judgment—a full knowledge of the facts and full insight into the motives. One or the other is often lacking in human courts; both will be present in full in the court of the Lord. The word for "purpose" is usually reserved for the purpose of God; only here is it used to mean the motives of men.

Then every man will receive his commendation from God: supposes that the verdict will be favorable. *Commendation* means the due praise, the merited approval. This was in direct contrast to the lavish praise that the Corinthians were guilty of heaping upon their favored teacher. Paul did not speak of those who might be worthy of blame. The subjects of this paragraph are the teachers: Paul, Cephas, and Apollos. Paul never implied by the slightest innuendo that any of these had been guilty of misconduct in the state of affairs at Corinth. He already had spoken of other teachers who might suffer loss or even be destroyed (cf. 3:12–17). *Will receive . . . from God* seems to say that even the merited praise would be a gift of grace from God.

6. Paul's Appeal for Unity in the Church at Corinth (4:6–21)

His argument over, Paul turned to the appeal to put his admonitions into practice. His appeal took three forms: (1) He reminded the Corinthians that he had applied the principles to himself and Apollos for their benefit (4:6–7). (2) In an ironical outburst he condemned their feeling of self-sufficiency (vss. 8–13). (3) As the father of the church, he appealed to and warned the church to seek unity in its affairs (vss. 14–21).

(1) His remarks were made for their benefit (4:6–7)

In this paragraph Paul revealed the secret of his argument. It was for their benefit. If any doubt had arisen about the unity of Paul and Apollos, these verses would have settled it.

Verse 6: I have applied: comes from the Greek word which means to change the form or shape of, hence, to say one thing while another is meant. Paul meant that his remarks might have been taken as a depreciation of Apollos. This was not so. His target had been other teachers who had violated their trust. This same Greek word was often used by Greek and Latin writers to imply a rhetorical form in which a speaker or writer veiled his allusion to his intended target. Thus, what Paul meant was that he had applied these things to himself and Apollos by way of allusion. He left it to the Corinthians to understand about whom he had been speaking.

All this: what he had written in the previous chapters.

To myself and Apollos: the two whose names had been most frequently used in his argument against bickerings in the church.

For your benefit: that they might learn a general lesson from what he had said. The words are not contained in the Greek text but are justified by the context.

Brethren: This term reminded them of the common allegiance of Paul and his readers to Christ. *Brethren* was a common figurative expression for fellow Christians.

That you may learn by us to live according to scripture: literally, "that you might learn in our case not to go beyond what stands written" (i.e., in your opinion of men). This seems to be, in form, a proverbial saying, but its source has never been found. The word for *scripture* here was Paul's usual word for introducing an Old Testament quotation (perfect tense: what has been written). Yet, there is no Old Testament passage which corresponds to the thought in this verse, and Paul had not made much use of the Old Testament in his arguments, none when he was talking of the relation of ministers to their task. Lenski has suggested that it refers to the clause which follows,[1] but Paul's usual way of doing that was to use the epistolary aorist or past tense rather than the perfect tense, as here. On the other hand, the term was used in social affairs for a contract or commission. If it is taken in this sense, in a figurative way, it would mean that the Corinthians were not to go beyond the commission given to the apostles. If we may assume, and I think it probable, that there were already written passion narratives current among the churches, this could very well refer to the Christian writings rather than the Old Testament Scriptures. In all of them, as is well known, the commission of Christ to the apostles after his resurrection plays a prominent part. Of four suggestions—Old Testament Scriptures, the present context, the technical sense, the Christian writings—I would have to favor the last, without being dogmatic.

That none of you may be puffed up in favor of one against another: defines what Paul meant by living *according to scripture.* This would be true, no matter which alternative is taken in interpreting that saying. The saying has been given two different turns of thought in translations: (1) that in championing your favorite teacher you may not be puffed up against your fellow church member; (2) that no one should boast of one teacher at the expense of another.[2] The RSV translation is almost literal, but it does not tell which interpretation is to be preferred. In the light of the context, it would seem that the second is to be preferred. Their misdemeanor was headed up in their championing of one teacher and the consequent depreciation of the others. If this were not justified in the case of Paul and Apollos, it certainly would not be justified in any other case. Yet, the fact that Paul had just said that his application of this to himself and Apollos was by way of allusion would seem to argue in favor of the first. Conse-

---

[1] R. C. H. Lenski, *The Interpretation of St. Paul's First and Second Epistle to the Corinthians* (Columbus, Ohio: Wartburg Press, © 1946). Hereafter referred to as Lenski.

[2] This is the interpretation given by Edwards and ICC.

quently, I would favor this one as the correct interpretation. This also fits best with the verb *be puffed up*. The idea is that one was *puffed up* with conceit concerning his own wisdom as a self-appointed judge of the teachers.

Verse 7: This verse would seem to argue in favor of the interpretation given in the preceding clause. Paul rebuked self-conceit.

For who sees anything different in you?: half-sarcastic address to the man who was puffed up. *Sees anything different* really means to distinguish something superior in another. The idea is that the feeling of superiority which characterized the Corinthians was self-assumed and presumptuous.

What have you that you did not receive?: shows why their feeling of superiority was false. They had nothing which they had not received from God. True, it had come to them through the apostles and teachers, but it was nevertheless the gift of God. No merit could be claimed by the recipients. When Paul had found them, they had been poverty-stricken and without status even in the community, let alone in the spiritual realm.

If then you received it: an assumption which is to be taken as axiomatic. They had received it; this no one could deny.

Why do you boast as if it were not a gift?: a rhetorical question giving the conclusion of the fact assumed. The play on words in the original is obscured by the translation. *As if it were not a gift* is literally "as if you had not received it." If they had merited the gospel, if they had invented it, if it had arisen by their own achievement, they might very well boast of it. But since none of this was true, since they had received the gospel, since it was a gift of God, they had no reason to boast.

(2) Their feeling of self-sufficiency was self-deception (4:8–13)

In a rare outburst of sarcasm, Paul continued his thought of verse 7. Not only had the Corinthians forgotten that all they had was from God; they had also forgotten the sacrifices of the apostles in bringing it to them. Not only had they forgotten the sacrifices of the apostles; they had also forgotten their own need for continued growth. Paul began with an ironical series of questions about their present attainments (vs. 8), continued with a description of the apostles as condemned men (vs. 9), followed with a series of sharp comparisons between the imagined superiority of the Corinthians and the real position of the apostles (vs. 10), and let this merge into a description of the apostolic labors, apparently general in nature but actually autobiographical (vss. 11–13).

Verse 8: This verse is a derisive rebuke of the imagined self-sufficiency of the Corinthians. The first three parallel exclamations are without any connective word. They are heaped up in swift succession. Some interpreters have taken the statements as questions, but this spoils the irony. It is true that the original Greek text was not punctuated, that editors have had to furnish the punctuation marks. It seems to me that the RSV translators have caught the nature of the verse with their exclamation marks. Some interpreters have also taken this passage to be addressed not to the church as a whole but to a group of local teachers which are supposed to have arrived in Corinth after Paul and Apollos left. It is true that some such group of teachers must have arisen in the church or come in from outside; but their figures, to say the least, are indefinable in this whole passage against dissension. Paul softened the irony somewhat in verse 14, where it is quite apparent that he was addressing the church as a whole. I think it is best to look upon this passage as including the entire church, though, of course, there would have been exceptions.

Already: introduces each of the first two statements. Either it points to the contrast between the *already* and the yet to come or to the contrast between the imagined state of the Corinthians and the actual state of the apostles. Much is to be said in behalf of the first interpretation, but the parallel, *without us,* in the third statement would argue for the second interpretation. The point is that while the apostles were still far from perfection and satisfaction, the Corinthians had come to imagine that they were already perfect.

Filled: comes from the metaphor of eating and means to be filled to the full, to have enough and more than enough. *Glutted* would be an English equivalent.

Become rich . . . have become kings: expressions which were common among the Stoics. The Stoics thought that a wise man was a king. Perhaps Paul used this background to deepen the sarcasm of his remarks. He would have been saying that their imagined sufficiency was like that of the unbeliever.

Without us: not "without our help," but "without our having achieved such eminence." Apart from the very men which had made their enrichment possible, the Corinthians imagined that they had achieved riches and kingship.

And would that you did reign: expresses a wish that their imagined reign were a reality. The form of the Greek in this clause marks it as an exclamation to express a wish as to what might have happened but has not, or what might happen but is not expected. If this whole verse is governed by the thought of the fullness of the messianic reign at the second coming of Christ, which is doubtful, this would be an expression of Paul's hope for that event. If my interpretation is correct, it would simply be a continuation of the taunt of Paul.

So that we might share the rule with you: expresses the idea that the triumph of the Corinthians would be the triumph of Paul and the other apostles. This should be taken, I think, as a continuation of the irony. This form of language is extremely hard to interpret exactly. We find it very seldom in the Scriptures. Its interpretation is always governed, in Scripture or in ordinary speech, by the situation. Since the situation of the Corinthian church is open to question, the interpretation must remain, in some degree, open to question.

Verse 9: This verse contains a description of the apostles as condemned men. The background is the Roman victory procession in which the victorious general led his captives in review before the populace. At the end of the procession came the captured princes and kings who were condemned to die in the arena.

For I think: states the case as it seemed to Paul. It was in contrast to the kingship that would be theirs if the Corinthians really did reign.

That God has exhibited us apostles as last of all: an interesting application of the metaphor of the victor. God is the victor who has overcome
and leads his captives in procession. At the end of the procession (*last of
all*) come the *apostles,* who form the ignominious finale. Paul used the
plural, *apostles,* to avoid claiming the position for himself alone.

Like men sentenced to death: reflects the custom of public execution
or the spectacle in the arena. There men fought against beasts or other
men to the death as the crowning scene in the day's spectacle.

Because we have become a spectacle to the world: answers to "I think"
and gives the basis for his opinion. *Spectacle* comes from the Greek word
theatron, from which we get our English word "theater." Obviously Paul
thought that he and the other apostles had actually become a spectacle for
the world to see. But in what sense did he think this? As a Roman citizen,
Paul would not have been cast into the arena. He must therefore have had
some metaphorical meaning in mind. Some have suggested that he had
in mind the Stoic saying: "The wise man at war with fortune is a spectacle
for God and man." This is highly unlikely. The Stoic saying smacks of
egotism; Paul was thinking of humiliation. Perhaps his thought was of the
mobs, the imprisonments, the beatings, the perils which he had suffered
in his apostolic labors. It would not take too great a flight of the imagination to compare these to the spectacle in the arena.

To angels and to men: defines the two classes of spectators who make
up the world. *Angels* were mentioned because they were said to have an
interest in the affairs of men and because they could see more of the
apostolic sufferings than men could.

Verse 10: This verse has a series of three contrasts between the condition
of the apostles and that of the Corinthians. It may be regarded as detailed
illustrations of the thought in verses 8–9. With a combination of earnestness
and irony, Paul described the ways the apostles were spectacles while the
Corinthians were kings.

We are fools for Christ's sake: recalls the thought of 1:18 ff. The gospel
which the apostles preached was considered to be folly by the world; the
men who preached it, fools. Paul did not speak hypothetically here. At
Athens he had been laughed at by the philosophers when he mentioned
the resurrection of Christ (Acts 17:32). Festus later called Paul "mad"
when he mentioned the resurrection (Acts 26:24). This ridicule of men
was not burdensome, however, as it was *for Christ's sake.* To suffer for him
who had suffered for them was to be counted as privilege and honor.

But you are wise in Christ: that is, you claim wisdom through your
union with Christ. *Wise* is from a different Greek word than in previous
passages. This word means to be prudent, sensible. Its use here is dictated
by the fact that it is the opposite of "fool." Notice also that here it is *in
Christ,* not *for Christ's* sake. The apostles were accounted fools because
they preached the gospel of Christ. Therefore they were *fools for Christ's
sake.* The Corinthians had made their being in Christ a matter of pride.
Therefore, Paul ironically designated them as *wise in Christ.*

We are weak: that is, without any means of accomplishing our task which
the world considers to be effective. The apostles' methods were, like their
message, without worldly sanction. They used no military power; they

had no political influence; they disdained the use of rhetoric and persuasion. Consequently, when viewed from the world's viewpoint, they were weak.

But you are strong: that is, you imagine yourself to be strong. The tone is ironical. The Corinthians imagined that they were strong because they had come to rely upon worldly wisdom and worldly ways of action. This contrast reflects in a real way a conflict of the ages. The disciples of Christ and the Jews felt that the Kingdom of God was to be established by military might; Christ established it by dying on a cross. In every age men have been tempted to turn from the seemingly weak and ineffective way of service by proclaiming the message and teaching the believers. Today men are urging that the churches enter the arena of political action and social service as ways of promoting the cause of Christ. We must remember that the churches have always been strongest when they relied upon the preaching of the gospel in the power of the Holy Spirit. This power changes men; it also works its social leaven so as to change the world. One of my teachers used to say that the church is the greatest reforming force on earth when it does not try to be a reforming force. He meant that the work of Christ is redemptive in nature; it must be accomplished by means that men think of as ineffective.

You are held in honor: ironical in tone again. Their honor was self-honor. It might lead to worldly acceptance, but on the whole it was ostentatious pretense. The Greek word which is translated *honor* has the idea of glitter and show with a suggestion of pretense.

But we in disrepute: considered as outlaws, criminals, or men condemned to death. Again Paul shifted from irony to earnestness when he turned from the egotism of the Corinthians to the realities of the condition of the apostles.

Verse 11: This verse begins a series of illustrations which extends through verse 13, proving the truth of what was said in verse 10 about the apostles. First, that the apostles were fools in the eyes of men was proved by their suffering hardships for Christ. This the world would take for fanaticism or folly (vs. 11). Second, that the apostles were weak in the eyes of the world was proved by their refusal to retaliate against persecution (vs. 12). Third, that the apostles were without honor in the eyes of the world was proved by the world's maltreatment of them (vs. 13).

To the present hour: refers especially to Paul's sufferings in Ephesus, the place from which he wrote this letter. While the Corinthians had been basking in their imagined riches, Paul had been suffering for the gospel in Ephesus.

We: has a primary reference to Paul in these verses. The other apostles were not excluded, but the language is so intimate that it must be thought of as largely autobiographical.

Hunger and thirst: describes a lack of the necessary things for bodily sustenance.

Ill-clad: not naked, but scantily clad. The word occurs nowhere else in the New Testament. In the Greek classics it usually meant to go to war without sufficient arms.

Buffeted: literally, "beaten with the fist." The same Greek word was used by Paul in 2 Corinthians 12:7 when he spoke of his thorn in the flesh as "a messenger of Satan, to harass [buffet] me, to keep me from being too elated." Paul also spoke of "countless beatings" which he had endured (2 Cor. 11:23), though he used a more general word there. Paul's choice of the word here may have been dictated by the fact that it describes the treatment of a slave by his master.

Homeless: a verb which occurs nowhere else in the New Testament. It is reminiscent of the words of Jesus: "Foxes have holes, and birds of the air have nests; but the Son of man has nowhere to lay his head" (Luke 9:58). The apostles were men without any place of their own in which to rest; they were vagrants and were branded as such.

Verse 12: The first part of the verse continues the description of the apostolic way of life which would brand them as fools in the eyes of the world. The second part describes their actions which would brand them as weaklings.

And we labor, working with our own hands: reflects the experience of Paul in Corinth in voluntarily refraining from accepting support from the church (1 Cor. 9:6). In the eyes of the world, for the learned scholar to work as a mechanic marked him as a fool. *Labor* translates a Greek word which emphasizes physical weariness resulting from work.

When reviled, we bless: reflects, perhaps not purposely, the command of Jesus to his disciples (Matt. 5:44). *Reviled* means to be slandered to one's face. Thus the sting of the spoken word is emphasized. *Bless* means literally "to speak a good word to"; but in Christian circles, as in Jewish, it meant to call down a blessing from God.

When persecuted, we endure: may reflect Paul's own career as the persecutor of the church in Jerusalem. At any rate, both Paul and the other apostles had suffered persecution at the hands of the Jews many times. *Endure* means to suffer patiently rather than bravely. It speaks of a type of endurance which would have been scorned by the Greeks, but which in reality reflected the spirit of Christ.

Verse 13: This verse, in the first part, continues the thought of verse 12, and, in the second part, enlarges on the idea of the ill-repute of the apostles in the eyes of the world.

Slandered: translates a Greek word found nowhere else in the New Testament and only once in biblically related material. In 1 Maccabees 7:41, it is used to describe the insults of Rabshakeh, the envoy of Sennacherib. The basic meaning is to use evil words, thus, to speak evil of.

Conciliate: a strange meaning of a common word of the New Testament. The Greek word has many shades of meaning, coming from the basic idea of calling to one side in order to speak privately. The New Testament translations vary from "exhort" to "entreat." None of the common meanings fit into this context. Perhaps Proverbs 15:1 can be taken as the meaning here: "A soft answer turns away wrath." The idea is certainly that of acting mildly in the face of insult. This would be a quality despised by the Greeks as a sign of weakness.

We have become, and are now, as the refuse of the world, the offscouring of all things: an enlarged statement of the ill-repute of the apostles. *Refuse* translates a word which means "that which is scoured or scraped off when cleaning a kitchen vessel." *Offscouring* is a similar word, which literally means "to wipe all around." The use of these words to describe the scapegoat or the condemned criminals reserved by the city of Athens to be thrown into the sea in case of plague or disease is hardly pertinent here. Perhaps the modern term "the scum of the earth" gives the approximate meaning. The idea is certainly not that the apostles were considered as redemptive in their function, but that they were despised and held in the lowest possible disrepute.

(3) Paul's appeal for unity was made as the father of the church (4:14–21)

The paragraph has two divisions: fatherly admonition to the church as a whole (vss. 14–17); stern rebuke of the arrogant few (vss. 18–21).

Verse 14: This verse was intended to mollify the harsh tones of the previous paragraph in which irony and sarcasm had been used.

I do not write this to make you ashamed: refers primarily to the previous paragraph, but is pertinent to all that he had said about dissensions in the church. The root meaning of *ashamed,* in the Greek, is "to turn in" and so to make a person hang his head, either in reverence (Matt. 21:37) or in shame, as here. This statement was meant to decrease the harshness of the last statement.

But to admonish you as my beloved children: stated Paul's purpose in his writing. *Admonish* describes one duty of a father (Eph. 6:4). Basically it means to put in mind of something; it always has a touch of sternness in it, perhaps of blame. *As my beloved children* metaphorically describes Paul's feelings of tenderness and concern for the Corinthians. He did not want them to think that his tirade meant that he had lost his concern for them. *Beloved* describes the love that Paul had for them rather than their love for him.

Verse 15: In this verse Paul established the basis for his admonition, his right to speak. He held a position of preeminence with respect to the Corinthian church.

For though you have countless guides in Christ: a recognition that others had ministered to them in subsidiary ways. It was assumed as true that some had ministered to them, but Paul made his supposition improbable by saying *countless guides. Countless* translates the Greek word *murious,* from which we get our English word "myriads," meaning "tens of thousands."

Guides translates the Greek word, *paidagōgous,* literally, "leaders of the children." The English derivative is "pedagogue," which has led translators to make a serious mistake in translating the word here and in Galatians 3:24. The King James Version has "instructors," and this idea of teaching has dominated English translations. But the Greek pedagogue was not a teacher; he was a slave who was given charge of the moral watch-care over the children. He escorted the children to school and disciplined them when they needed it. He might become attached to the children, be more able and more affectionate than the father, but he could never become the father.

It is doubtful that Paul used the term as a disparagement of other ministers; he used it primarily to set off, from the negative point, his own peculiar relation to the Corinthians. Perhaps there is a hidden allusion to the childishness of the Corinthians, but this is debatable. The thing he was saying was that even though ten thousand others should minister to you, they could not minister in the way in which I have ministered.[1]

You do not have many fathers: the point of emphasis in the verse. *Many* is less than *countless;* yet even it is hyperbolical. The negative statement was meant to emphasize the fact that they had and could have only one father.

For I became your father in Christ Jesus through the gospel: explains the sense in which Paul was the father of the Corinthians. *For I became your father* is literally, "I, even I, have begotten you." In what sense did Paul mean that he had begotten them? The natural answer is to say that he had brought about their conversion; he became their father by leading them to an acceptance of Jesus Christ. But this would not be true of all the Corinthians. Other teachers had followed Paul and had also won converts. He meant that he had become the father of all the Corinthians in some way. Perhaps we find the interpretation of this figure in 3:10. He laid the foundation of the church; thus he was the spiritual father of the whole church, even though some members of it at the time of his writing were not his converts. *In Christ Jesus* defines the sphere of his fatherhood; it was through their coming into union with Christ Jesus that he had become their father. *Through the gospel* is an ellipsis. It means *through* the preaching of *the gospel. I* has the emphatic position in the Greek sentence and receives the stress in a literal translation.

Verse 16: Then: is based on the Greek word for "therefore." Paul was drawing a conclusion based on the assertion in verse 15.

I urge you: a good translation. "Exhort" would be too strong; "beg" would be too weak in this context. The Greek word has many shades of meaning, and the RSV has caught the right one here.

Be: continuous action implied. It is the present tense in Greek. Not only did Paul want them to become like him; he wanted them to continue in his ways.

Imitators: not followers. Christians are to be followers or disciples of Christ, but imitators of those who embody the principles of Christ in their own lives. Paul made much use of this term in this correspondence with the churches (1 Cor. 11:1, "Be imitators of me, as I am of Christ"). Paul did not claim credit for the pattern; Christ had established that. He did claim that he followed the pattern of Christ's life in such a way that the Corinthians could take him as the pattern of their lives, as children pattern themselves after a respected father. He did not specify in what way they were to be imitators of him; the word is left general and undefined.

Me: unstressed in the sentence. Paul did not mean to draw a contrast between himself and other teachers. If the occasion had called for it, he

---

[1] Furnish, contrary to most interpreters, believes that this expression refers to local troublemakers in Corinth.

might have admonished them to be imitators of Apollos as well. What he wanted was for them to leave their childish bickering and dissensions and become mature followers of Christ.

Verse 17: Paul inserted here a note about Timothy, but what he said about him was in harmony with the thought of the passage.

Therefore: translates the Greek words meaning "for this reason." Some good manuscripts have "for this very reason" or "for this same reason." The variant reading only stresses that which is stressed in the words. Paul had sent Timothy for the reason that he wished them to become imitators of him and because he was their father.

I sent: may be epistolary aorist. If so, Timothy would have been the bearer of the letter. However, this does not fit in with the notice in 16:10: "when Timothy comes." It is better to take it as a true past tense and to suppose that Timothy had already been sent on his way. Acts 19:22, in speaking of Paul's stay in Ephesus, says, "And having sent into Macedonia two of his helpers, Timothy and Erastus, he himself stayed in Asia for a while." It is likely then that Timothy had been sent on to Macedonia, with Corinth as his ultimate goal. The fact that Erastus was his traveling companion (cf. Rom. 16:23, where an Erastus is identified as coming from Corinth) strengthens this supposition. It is vain to speculate on the particular mission of Timothy. If we take this verse seriously, Paul himself defined the mission sufficiently.

Timothy, my beloved and faithful child in the Lord: Paul's description of his fellow worker. Like the Corinthians, Timothy was a beloved child; unlike some of them, at least, he was a faithful child. *In the Lord* defines the sphere of the relationship; it was in the realm of the lordship of Christ.

To remind you: implies that they had forgotten the ways of their father and needed to be reminded. The verb is milder than "teach." They did not need to be taught; they had been taught. They did need to be reminded. Their dissensions proved this.

Of my ways in Christ: not Paul's personal actions but his teachings. However, there is an implication in this verse that Paul's own life conformed to his teachings. I think none of us would doubt that. The reference is vague; any details would have had an air of boasting which was itself contrary to Paul's ways.

As I teach them everywhere in every church: Paul's ways and teachings did not change, basically, from church to church. He reminded the Corinthians that they were not the only church nor the perfect church. They were a part of the brotherhood of Christians which encompassed the whole world. No more was required of them than of other churches, but as much was required. *Teach* is in the present tense in the Greek and meant that Paul continued to teach in other churches as he had in Corinth.

Verse 18: introduces the rebuke of the minority who were the seat of the problem in Corinth. Parry believes that the main responsibility lay with local teachers who had come into the church after Paul's departure. This may be a good guess, but the evidence for such teachers is lacking in the material.

Some are arrogant: describes the situation to which Paul wished to address himself. There is no way of knowing whether the *some* were the same ones who boasted of their wisdom (3:18). It seems probable that they were. The use of the indefinite pronoun could mean either that Paul could have named them or that he could not. At least, the Corinthians would have known of whom he spoke. *Arrogant* translates the same Greek word that was translated "puffed up" in 4:6. *Are* is a poor translation; it should be "were." The past tense indicates that Paul was speaking of something of which he had heard. He could not use the present tense because he was ignorant of the state of affairs when he wrote. He did not, however, mean to imply that the trouble was a thing of the past. The idea of "puffed up" is that of prideful boasting.

As though I were not coming to you: They had mistaken the sending of others as a sign that Paul himself was afraid to come and would not come. Paul's aversion to acrimonious debate had been taken as a sign of cowardice. They thought that he dared not come. The Greek is a form of indirect discourse in which Paul quoted what the arrogant ones had been saying. The RSV translation catches the idea perfectly, but it obscures the fact that Paul based his information on a report of what his opponents were saying.

Verse 19: a statement of Paul's intended traveling plans.

But I will come to you soon: From 16:8, we learn that Paul planned to stay at Ephesus until Pentecost and then to visit the Corinthians. When we combine the word *soon* with that information, we can place the time of the writing of this letter shortly before Pentecost. His plans, change of plans, and the resulting accusations against him are discussed in 2 Corinthians 1:15–16 and 23.

If the Lord wills: Paul recognized that his plans were subject to the desire of his Lord, i.e., Christ. There was no doubt about his own intentions.

And I will find out: literally, "I will know." This implies a testing process and the results of the test.

Not the talk of these arrogant people: Paul already knew what they had been saying, but he planned to ignore that. The words proceeded from conceited (puffed up) people and deserved to be ignored. *Arrogant people* translates a perfect participle based on the verb meaning "to be puffed up." The perfect tense implies a continuing state of being, resting on a past completed action. *Talk* translates the Greek word for "word." *Talk* is a good translation of the generic use of the singular.

But their power: not their power to perform miracles (as some commentators have suggested), but their power to transform lives. In 2:4–5, we had an antithesis of "word" and "power" in a different sense. *Power* here would be their participation in the power of the Holy Spirit in their ministry. Paul looked upon this as the primary credentials of a true minister of the gospel.

Verse 20: For: introduces the reason why Paul was concerned with power instead of talk (cf. vs. 19).

Kingdom of God: an expression found often on the lips of Jesus but seldom in the Acts and the Epistles. Paul used it only thirteen times in all his epistles, but it is found five times in this epistle (here; 6:9–10; 15:24, 50). There are three possible meanings for the expression: (1) the future messianic reign of Christ; (2) the present reign of Christ, which is the kingdom in process (cf. 15:25, "for he must reign until he has put all his enemies under his feet"); (3) the inner spiritual reign of God through Christ in the hearts of men, as in Romans 14:17. The last meaning is indicated here. Actually, the three concepts run into one. The spiritual reign is the method by which Christ is putting his enemies down, and this will usher in the final messianic reign. Paul used the term here because of the reference in verse 8, "Without us you have become kings!"

Does not consist in talk: receives the emphasis in this verse by its position at the first of the sentence in Greek. The translation seems to be in error. *Consist in* translates the Greek preposition *en* (in). The literal translation is: "not in word the Kingdom of God." T. C. Edwards insists that this does not mean "consists in" but "is established on." Lenski demurs; he agrees that it does not mean "consists in" but urges that it does mean "accompanied by." Lenski is probably more correct. What Paul had in mind was that talk, and in this case boasting talk, was not the outward sign by which one recognized the reign of God in another man's heart.

But in power: same sense as in verse 19.

Verse 21: What do you wish?: indicates that they had the choice in the matter. The question was not whether Paul would come but how he would come. It is quite clear from the context that he would prefer to come with the gentle spirit of the father rather than as a dispenser of discipline.

Shall I come to you with a rod: defines one way in which he could come. *A rod* is metaphorical; Paul did not mean that he would come armed with a physical weapon to be used for correction or chastisement. In the Greek family the rod was usually carried by the "child leader." Perhaps Paul was offering them the choice between him as a father and as a guide.

Or with love in a spirit of gentleness: describes Paul's preferred way of coming. *A spirit* is not the Holy Spirit, but the inner disposition of the mind. *Gentleness* translates the Greek word which is usually translated "meekness" in the New Testament. *Gentleness* is the meaning of the word when it is used to describe human relations. Paul would have come in love in either case, even if he had come with a rod. T. C. Edwards suggests that the reason *a spirit* does not modify *love* as well as *gentleness* is that love is not a natural disposition but a Christian grace. The spirit of gentleness is always the natural desire of love.

III. CORRECTION OF THREE DANGERS THAT THREATENED THE LIFE AND WITNESS OF THE CHURCH (5:1—6:20)

The central thrust and connecting centrality of this section is somewhat difficult to ascertain. It is clear that Paul dealt with three dangers that threatened the life and witness of the church: the danger of laxity in church discipline (5:1–13); the danger of litigation in pagan courts (6: 1–11); and the danger of licentiousness in the name of liberty (6:12–20).

T. C. Edwards sees the connecting centrality in the supposed fact that "the Corinthians denied or ignored the conception of the Church as the body of Christ." Parry sees the whole section as a discussion of church discipline. Lenski simply calls it "moral delinquences in the congregation." All of these ideas are present in the material, but none of them gives a satisfying explanation of the central thrust of the section.

I suggest that Paul was attempting to correct certain misunderstandings of his own teachings which had led the church to take a permissive attitude toward unchristian practices of its membership. There seems to be little connection between this section and the preceding one. The tone is different; irony is almost entirely laid aside. The style is more formal, slower, and less jerky. All of this is understandable on the assumption that Paul considered himself to be dealing, not with a sharp departure from his own teaching, but with a misunderstanding of it.

Paul had certainly taught that salvation did not depend upon words. Perhaps he had reminded them of the practice of Jesus of companying with sinners. Hence, it is possible that the Corinthians felt they were showing real Christian liberty in overlooking the case of gross immorality in their midst. They did not seem to know that their attitude would offend even the pagan world and destroy the fabric of the church's life. The appeal in chapter 5 was to the church. They were commanded to act to purify their fellowship. There was no suggestion that anyone condoned the man. The problem was that the church did not condemn him. It is entirely possible that they felt they were following the example of Jesus in their refusal to condemn.

Paul had certainly taught them that every Christian was equal and that the rights of each man must be granted to him by other Christians. The Corinthians had translated this to mean that each man must stand up for his rights at any cost. They had failed to see that the granting of rights, not the demanding of them, was the Christian attitude. Paul's appeal in regard to litigation seemed to be to the individuals who were involved in it, not to the church.

[73]

It is difficult to ascertain whether the cry, "All things are lawful for me" (6:12), reflected the teaching of Paul or the cry of men who were licentious. It is not inconceivable that it represented the teaching of Paul with reference to Jewish legalistic restrictions. If so, it would seem that some of the Corinthians had taken this to mean that all actions were lawful, that no restraint was to be placed on the Christian. Paul answered by pointing to the destructive nature of some kinds of action. He did not appeal to law, but to the living out of one's dedication to Christ. His primary principle of ethics was that one's relation to Christ must dictate his practices.

If this suggestion is correct, it would explain why Paul could write later: "I commend you because you remember me in everything and maintain the traditions even as I have delivered them to you" (11:12). They had been maintaining them, but with a misunderstanding of their full implications.

1. The Danger of Laxity in Church Discipline (5:1–13)

Sexual laxity was a mark of first-century life in the Roman Empire; it took a great deal to shock the sensibilities of the pagans. But one of the Corinthian church members had managed to do just that. He was practicing incest by living with his father's wife. Though the Christian teaching had set itself against sexual laxity of any kind, the Corinthians as a whole, though there is no evidence that they condoned the practice, refused to condemn it. Paul rebuked the arrogance of this attitude (vss. 1–2), admonished them to excommunicate the sinning brother (vss. 3–5), and pointed to the danger to the church if the church failed to act (vss. 6–8). Finally, he corrected a false impression which the Corinthians had gained from a former letter and admonished them to practice discipline toward all sinning Christians (vss. 9–13).

(1) Arrogance in the face of gross immorality rebuked (5:1–2)

Verse 1: describes the condition that shocked Paul.

Actually: translates a Greek word of many meanings. It can mean "everywhere," "generally speaking," or "actually." It is difficult to decide whether Paul meant that the report was general in the sense that everybody knew it or that it was assuredly true. Perhaps Paul's sense of shock and outrage is caught by our translation.

It is reported . . . among you: This connection is justified by the Greek. *Among you* modifies the verb *reported.* Paul was saying that the matter was being talked about in the congregation. It was no longer a secret but common knowledge. This fact explains why Paul was so shocked, not so much at the sin, but at the apparent indifference of the church.

That there is immorality: translates a single Greek word which is usually translated "fornication." The Greek word stands for any illicit sexual intercourse. In classical Greek it meant "prostitution." T. C. Edwards suggests that the expression governs all of chapters 5 and 6 in a general way. However, the context does not seem to favor this. Rather, the word might be translated "a case of fornication." Since the Greek word is singular and lacks the article, this translation would be justified.

And of a kind that is not found even among pagans: means that it was of a kind not condoned among pagans. Paul, of course, could not know that such a case could not be found. He spoke hyperbolically to emphasize the seriousness of the sin.

For a man is living with his father's wife: describes the exact nature of the sin. *Is living*—literally, "has"—describes the relation as permanent, not momentary. Lightfoot suggests four things about the relation: (1) that it was lasting, consisting either of concubinage or marriage; (2) that the former husband and father was still living (he refers to 2 Cor. 7:12 for proof of this); (3) that since the crime is called "fornication" instead of "adultery," there had been a divorce or separation, and (4) since no censure is uttered against the woman, it may be inferred that she was not a Christian, but one of those "from without" whom God would judge (vs. 13).[1] This seems to cover the ground thoroughly, though the relation of 2 Corinthians 7:12 to this passage is doubtful.

Verse 2: And you are arrogant!: should be considered as a question and a reference to the previous discussion. Thus, "and are you still puffed up over your imagined wisdom?" *Arrogant* translates the Greek word for "puffed up" which Paul used three times in the previous chapter (4:6, 18, 19). Paul did not mean that the Corinthians were puffed up about the man who was committing incest. He meant that they had been puffed up in their vaunted wisdom and this had caused them to ignore the canker in their midst. The form of the Greek participle stresses the continuing reality of their arrogance.

Ought you not rather to mourn?: a good translation. Instead of continuing to be puffed up, the congregation should have been in a state of mourning. The rhetorical question expects an affirmative answer. *Mourn* is the word which is specially used for mourning the dead, but it is also used in a spiritual sense. Paul used it to express his fears concerning the Corinthians' lack of repentance: "I fear . . . I may have to mourn over many of those who sinned before and have not repented" (2 Cor. 12:21). *You* in both questions is plural: the whole congregation was involved and had a corporate responsibility.

Let him who has done this be removed from among you: a poor translation. The connection is obscured. The passage should read: "Ought you not rather to mourn in order that he who has done this be removed from among you?" The action contemplated should have been the result of their mourning. Our translation makes it appear to be a command of Paul. The point is that removal would have been the natural result of mourning. Some commentators, however, would support the RSV translation as possible. *Removed* meant excommunicated by the action of the church.

---

[1] J. B. Lightfoot, *Notes on the Epistles of St. Paul,* reprint by Zondervan Publishing House, Grand Rapids, Michigan, 1957, originally published in 1895. Hereafter referred to as Lightfoot.

(2) Excommunication of the sinning brother admonished (5:3–5)

This section contains the recommendation of Paul for church action. Notice that he did not command the church to act, nor did he act for it in the way of an authoritative bishop. He admonished them. This says much for the autonomy of the local congregations in the apostolic age.

Verse 3: contains Paul's decision about what the church should do.

I: is in the emphatic position in the Greek, pointing to the sentence as containing the decision of Paul, in contrast to the apparent lack of decision by the congregation.

For though absent in body I am present in spirit: explains Paul's feeling of oneness with the congregation in spite of his physical absence from them.

As if present: indicates what Paul would have said had he been present in the congregation. Paul was dramatically thinking of them as gathering in judgment with himself present, voicing the decision of the congregation on the authority of Jesus Christ. But this was all imagery. The court was not yet in session. The Corinthians had neglected their duty.

I have already pronounced judgment: a part of the imagery which was, alas, far from reality. *Already* meant at once, when he had heard of the matter. *Pronounced judgment* must either be a part of the imagery of Paul, or, if not, means simply that he had decided what ought to be done. There is no hint in the paragraph that Paul considered that he had authority to act for the church.[1] The same Greek word is translated "I decided" in 2:2.

Verse 4: continues the thought of verse 3 in the first part, passing to the action of the congregation in the second part.

In the name of the Lord Jesus: as the representative of the Lord Jesus. "Christ" is added in KJV but is based on a poorer text; its deletion in our translation is justified by the evidence. *In the name of* is most often used in the New Testament with reference to prayer. It means "when acting as the representative of." The connection of this phrase is debated. Some think it should go with what follows; some think it should be connected with what precedes. The decision is entirely subjective, since the thought of the phrase could just as well be the basis of Paul's action as of the church's action.

On the man who has done such a thing: literally, "who has worked out this thus." *Done* translates a word which means to "work out to completion." The Greek which is translated *such a thing* emphasizes both the deed and the manner of doing it. It would indicate that the man had done this wrong quite openly and was unrepentant of his deed.

When you are assembled: shifts the thought to the action of the church. It contemplates their action as a congregation acting as the body of Christ.

And my spirit is present: The congregation was to imagine the presence of Paul and act as they would have acted if he had actually been present.

With the power of our Lord Jesus: The congregation was to act with the power of Christ present also. *With* means "with the help of" here. It contemplates that the congregation would be helped to make the right decision and to enforce it. *Power* is spiritual in nature here.

---

[1] Allo, on the contrary, believes that Paul's sentence was authoritative and irrevocable.

Verse 5: contains the recommended action in this case and the hoped for result.

You are to deliver this man to Satan: In Paul's mind, to be excommunicated from the congregation of Christians was to be delivered *to Satan.* The redeemed society was under the reign of Christ; unredeemed society was under the tyranny of Satan. This man had already placed himself under the power of Satan by his action. Paul recommended that the church deliver him over publicly and formally so that all the world would know where he stood.

This verse has always caused a great deal of difficulty in interpretation. A superficial reading seems to imply that the church was to deliver a man who lived under the lordship of Christ over into another realm where he would live under the power of Satan. This was not the case at all. The church's action would only recognize the true state of affairs in this case; it would inform the pagan world that this man's behavior did not represent the actions of men who lived under Christ's rule. The exact phrase is found in 1 Timothy 1:19–20: "By rejecting conscience, certain persons have made shipwreck of their faith, among them Hymenaeus and Alexander, whom I have delivered to Satan that they may learn not to blaspheme." In both instances, Job 2:6–7 may be in the background: "And the Lord said to Satan, 'Behold, he is in your power; only spare his life.' So Satan went forth from the presence of the Lord, and afflicted Job with loathsome sores from the sole of his foot to the crown of his head." If so, Paul did not contemplate that the man delivered to Satan would resume a normal and peaceful life in pagan society but that he would suffer affliction which might produce repentance. Such a one would be exposed to the malice of Satan, and disaster was certain to follow.

For the destruction of the flesh: describes the purpose of the man's deliverance into the hands of Satan. This expression is difficult for the modern man to understand because he gives a different meaning to *flesh* than Paul did. Our modern idea that man is part flesh and part soul comes from the Greek thought, not the Hebrew, which is reflected in the New Testament. To the Hebrew, these various terms—flesh, body, soul, spirit—were used to describe man in his wholeness from various points of view. "Body" described man as an organized being, living in the world. "Flesh" described man from the standpoint of his frailty, in some writers without any connotation of sinfulness, but in Paul usually with the added idea of man as sinful. To Paul, then, "flesh" was the whole man, the natural man, without any influence of the Spirit of God. While John could write, "The Word became flesh" (John 1:14), Paul could only write, "sending his own Son in the likeness of sinful flesh" (Rom. 8:3). Paul conceived of the flesh as remaining present in the believer even after he had come under the domination of the Holy Spirit. Flesh remained as a constant tempter to sin and an opponent to the work of the Spirit (cf. Gal. 5:17: "For the desires of the flesh are against the Spirit"). Thus, when the Christian sinned, it was because he had yielded to the flesh.

This helps us to understand what Paul meant here. He hoped that the afflictions which Satan would heap upon this man, perhaps even physical sufferings, would destroy the flesh. That is, they would root out of the man's character the fleshly desires which had led him to commit this serious offense.[1] What Paul contemplated was that Satan would unwittingly become the servant of God in bringing the man to repentance and restoration. It is quite clear that Paul meant the church action to be remedial rather than simply punitive.

This interpretation does not meet with universal acceptance among commentators. "It is impossible to understand how Satan could be said to abolish sinful character . . . the expected result of the judgment is the man's doom to disease and death" (Parry). Other commentators would agree, pointing to the fact that Satan was considered to be the cause of disease. However, it seems that the interpretation given takes this into account without making it the whole substance of the expected judgment.

That his spirit may be saved in the day of the Lord Jesus: the ultimate hope of Paul. *The day of the Lord Jesus* is the expected coming of Christ at the end of the world. It is to be a day of judgment, when man's final destiny is pronounced. *Spirit* describes man in his wholeness, not merely as opposite to the flesh but with the added thought of the indwelling of the Holy Spirit. If this is Paul's thought here (it is not universally accepted as being so), he believed the man, in spite of his sinning, to be a Christian. The destruction of the flesh would lead to the resurgence of the spirit so that, at last if not in the present, he would be able to stand in the judgment of God as justified and saved. We are not to suppose that this was Paul's only hope. No doubt he hoped that the man would be led to repentance and restoration to the redeemed society immediately so that not only in the day of judgment but also in the present life his spirit might experience the blessings of the redeemed. Remember that Paul was writing as a pastor, not as a theologian. This verse is not to be taken as contradicting his clear teaching of the perseverance of the saints. He was expressing his hope that the disciplined member would appear among the Lord's people at the judgment day.

(3) Danger of failure to act pointed out (5:6–8)

The impression that Paul could only recommend and the church must act is strengthened in this paragraph. Danger threatened the church if they failed to act. The cancer of sin would spread and infest the whole congregation.

Verse 6: Your boasting is not good: repeats the thought of verse 2. The church was boasting in its vaunted wisdom, while all the time sin was eating away at its vital lifeblood. *Good* is the Greek word which means beautiful or pleasing or fitting. Paul meant that it was not proper for them to boast. *Boasting* translates the passive form of the Greek noun. It was not the act of boasting that was bad, but the thing boasted about.

Do you not know that a little leaven leavens the whole lump?: an axiomatic saying which demands no answer. Of course they knew this to be true. *Little* has the place of emphasis in the proverb and thus implies an

---

[1] Grosheide agrees and points out that it is not Satan who destroys the sinful nature. Such destruction is the result of Satan's work, but is considered to be brought about by God. (F. W. Grosheide, *Commentary on the First Epistle to the Corinthians* [Grand Rapids: Wm. B. Eerdmans Publishing Company, 1953]. Hereafter referred to by the last name of the author, Grosheide.)

argument *a fortiori,* i.e., from the stronger fact to the weaker. It is true that it takes only a little leaven to have such an effect. Thus, if only one sin may infect the whole community, how much more deadly would be the influence of such a sin and the congregation's attitude toward it.

Leaven: i.e., yeast, is a common figure in the New Testament. The chief emphasis is always that of the penetrating power of a small matter so as to influence the greater, for either good or ill. The context must always show whether it represents good or evil. In this case it is quite clear that evil is represented by leaven. But what was the evil that Paul had in mind? It was not the evil of the man's sin; it was the evil of the congregation's attitude. The toleration of the man's sin was apparent concurrence in the sin and would weaken the moral standards of the church. Indifference to evil creates an atmosphere in which more evil is bound to spring up.

Verse 7: The use of the proverb in verse 6 suggested an allegory to Paul's mind which he expanded in verses 7 and 8. The background of the allegory was the Jewish Passover, the celebration of the deliverance of the Jews from the Egyptian captivity (cf. Exod. 12:29–51). One of the prominent elements in that celebration was the eating of unleavened bread. The Jewish family, prior to the time of celebration, would search the house to make sure that no scrap of leavened bread remained. This is the background; but Paul's allegory, as is the case with most allegories, gets mixed up. In his allegory the congregation is both the family and the bread that is used in the festival.

Cleanse out the old leaven: a sharp appeal to rid themselves of the residue of pagan moral judgment which was apparent in their attitude toward the sin in their midst. The act of throwing out the old leaven in the Jewish festival marked Israel's complete break with the life of Egypt. In Paul's figure it represented the complete break of Christians with the pagan life which they had known before conversion. As suggested above, the congregation thought that their attitude was the practice of Christian liberty and had its basis in the teachings of Christ. Paul saw it as a carryover from their pagan background. Paul often used the word "old" to refer to the life of the Christian before his conversion (cf. Rom. 6:6, "We know that our old self was crucified with him so that the sinful body might be destroyed").

That you may be fresh dough: contemplates the church as the unleavened bread. *Fresh* translates the Greek word for that which is absolutely new, not having had previous existence. Its translation as *fresh* conforms to the figure of speech here. The Corinthians' Christian life was to be characterized by an entirely fresh start in life with no trace of pagan customs and ideas.

As you really are unleavened: expresses the true character of the Corinthians. They were in reality a "new creature" (2 Cor. 5:17). Paul wanted them to make their lives conform to the reality of their new character. *As* emphasizes the idea of harmony between what they were and what they were to do.

For Christ, our paschal lamb, has been sacrificed: expands the figure into an allegory. The connection implied by *for* is with the appeal to cleanse out the old leaven. It gives the reason for the necessity to act. In the Jewish family the old leaven had to be thrown out before the slaying of the Passover lamb. In the application the lamb already had been slain, but the old leaven still remained. *Christ* is in the emphatic position in the sentence.

Some commentators take this expression as the reason why they were un-leavened rather than the reason why they were to act. This would call for a comma preceding rather than a period. However, the connection seems to be to the command.

Verse 8: Let us, therefore, celebrate the festival: The congregation is now conceived of as the celebrants of the festival. The Passover feast was pro-longed for seven days in Jewish custom, during which no leavened bread was eaten. The thought is that the entire life of the church is a continual celebration of the festival of Passover. Therefore, it was essential that they not only be truly unleavened in essential character, but that they also should remain so in their lives and attitudes. *Celebrate* is in the present tense in Greek and implies the continuing act of celebration.

Not with the old leaven: describes negatively how the church should con-tinue to celebrate the festival. *Old leaven* continues the thought of verse 7; it stands for pagan practices and attitudes.

The leaven of malice and evil: poor translation in this context. The Greek word which is translated *malice* means "badness in quality"; hence, "wickedness, depravity, malignity." While it may be translated *malice* and though it may be true that Paul usually used it for this vice (Parry), the translation does not fit the context here. The Greek word which is trans-lated *evil* is a synonym for the other one. Perhaps Robertson's suggestion that the two words thus used mean "vicious disposition and evil deed" catches the meaning in this context.[1] The context favors this meaning, since Paul had in mind the sinful act of the Christian brother as well as the attitude of the church. What Paul meant to stress was that life characterized by gross immorality was not the proper way to celebrate the Christian's Passover.

But with the unleavened bread of sincerity and truth: describes from the positive side the proper celebration of the Christian's Passover. *Sincerity* comes, in the Greek, from two words which mean "sun" and "judge." Per-haps the thought is that which can stand the light of the sun. Thus, it would have no alloys, no mixtures which might not be seen in the dim light of the ancient lamps but which would be readily apparent in the sunlight. *Truth* is a common word in Greek as in English. It means that which is open and frank in contrast to that which is hidden or devious. The words are synonyms and describe well the kind of action which should characterize the life of Christians in all ages.

(4) Discipline of all sinning Christians admonished (5:9–13)

Paul had dealt with two matters in his discussion of the case of incest: fellowship with those who openly practiced sin and church action in rela-tion to such people. This paragraph deals with both subjects in a more general way, extending the principles that underlay the discussion of the incestuous man to all Christians who practiced open sin.

---

[1] A. T. Robertson, *Word Pictures in the New Testament*, Vol. IV., *The Epistles of Paul* (New York: Harper and Brothers Publishers, © 1931). Hereafter referred to as Robertson.

Verse 9: refers to a former epistle in which Paul had given instructions concerning association with the wicked.

I wrote to you in my letter: It is surprising that some commentators have denied that this expression refers to a former letter. It seems to me that the language quite clearly refers to a letter which he had written previously. Some have thought to find a portion of this letter in 2 Corinthians 6:14—7:1. Aside from any discussion of the unity of 2 Corinthians, it seems to me that the language of this portion of 2 Corinthians could not possibly fit the description that Paul gave of his letter here. The portion in 2 Corinthians quite clearly dealt with partnership between believers and unbelievers. Paul's former letter dealt only with association with Christian brethren who openly sinned. It is true that the Corinthians seemingly had misunderstood this teaching, but this does not mean that Paul had written one thing and meant another.

Not to associate with immoral men: gives the substance of Paul's former letter which was relevant to the present passage. *Associate with* translates a compound word which means literally, "not to mix yourselves up together with." The same word is used in a similar way in 2 Thessalonians 3:14, "If any one refuses to obey what we say in this letter, note that man, and *have nothing to do with* him." (Italics indicate the translation of the Greek word.) The idea was that the Corinthians were to refuse to have regular fellowship with *immoral men,* i.e., those who lived in sexual sin.

Verse 10: the negative side of Paul's explanation of the real purpose of his former letter.

Not at all meaning: a poor translation of the Greek. It should read, "not meaning altogether." Paul had not meant that they were to cut off all intercourse with the pagan world, at least not absolutely so. Our translation gives the idea that the Christians were not to be at all concerned about fellowship with pagans. I doubt that Paul would have said that. At least, he did not say it here.

The immoral of this world: the sexual offenders who belong to the world of men who ignore God and rebel against his rule. Paul usually meant by *world* human society as distinct from the Christian congregation. *Immoral* throughout this chapter translates the Greek word *pornos,* from which we get our English word "pornography." The word does not mean immoral in the general sense of the term but in the specific sense of improper sexual behavior.

Or the greedy and robbers, or idolaters: widens the application to indicate a principle of action which involves all kinds of flagrant sinners. *Greedy and robbers* are linked together, describing a distinct class of people who are motivated entirely by selfishness. *Idolaters* were quite common in ancient Corinth. Thus the list of Paul includes men who sin against themselves (*immoral,* cf. 6:18), those who sin against society (*greedy and robbers*), and those who sin against God (*idolaters*). Paul's choice was probably dictated by the fact that these were the cardinal vices of the heathen world.

Since then you would need to go out of the world: assumes an impossibility. Paul felt that it was impossible for the Christians to give up all dealings with the unchristian world; this was not what he had meant by his former letter. The ascetic movement in Christian circles, which still influences much of our thinking about Christian behavior, arose much later. In the Middle Ages men came to feel that the only way to live a Christian life was to cut off all contact with sinful men, to withdraw into monasteries. This was not Paul's idea. He felt, as Jesus had taught, that men must live out their Christian lives in the midst of sinful society. This did not involve "no contact"; it did involve "no conformity." Some older commentators gave these words a different twist, one not justified by the Greek. They felt that Paul meant to say, "I did not write you about this because, of course, you know of yourselves to avoid contact with the world."

Verse 11: gives the positive side of Paul's explanation of the meaning of his previous letter.

But rather I wrote to you: a good translation. Some have felt that the past tense here is epistolary and should be translated, "I now write." While the Greek makes this possible, it seems clear from the context that Paul was still speaking of his former letter.

Not to associate: same Greek word as in verse 9, not to have close and regular association.

With any one who bears the name of brother: a fellow Christian, professed or real.

If he is guilty of immorality or greed: same words as in verse 10 but with a different connection. Sexual impurity and covetousness are linked together. This does not mean that *greed* is to be taken as sensuality in this verse, as some commentators think. It means rather that both sins spring from a common source, lack of love for fellowmen. Both the immoral and the greedy look upon their fellows as means to satisfy their own desires, an attitude which is the opposite of Christian love.

Or is an idolater: worships a false god.

Reviler, drunkard: two new classes of sin which are not mentioned in verse 10. *Reviler* means one who makes a habit of abusing the character and reputation of others. The Greek noun is found only here and in 6:10. The verbal form of the word is found in 1 Peter 2:23, where, speaking of Christ, it is said, "When he was reviled, he did not revile in return." *Drunkard* had the same meaning in New Testament times as it does today.

Or robber: has the same meaning as in verse 10.

Not even to eat with such a one: does not refer to eating the Lord's Supper but to social contact. Eating together was one of the ancient signs of friendship. Concerning the sinners of the world, Paul permitted limited contact, such as was necessary for life in the world. Concerning sinning brothers, Paul admonished complete withdrawal—no contact at any level. The reason for this admonition was that men who had professed faith in Christ and then fallen into open sin were traitors to the faith.

Verse 12: lays the basis for Paul's admonition in verse 11.

What have I to do with judging outsiders?: a rhetorical question which expects the answer—"nothing." *Outsiders* describes those who are not in the church fellowship. *Judging* means to "sit in judgment," not necessarily to condemn. The Corinthians should have known that Paul's former letter did not refer to outsiders. The Greek phrase behind *outsiders* is of Jewish origin. Jews applied it to Gentiles; Jesus applied it to Jews who were not his disciples (Mark 4:11); Paul applied it to those who were not Christians, whether Jew or Gentile.

Is it not those inside the church whom you are to judge?: another rhetorical question, but this one expects the answer—"yes." Paul substituted *you* for *I* to include the Corinthians in the responsibility of judging. They had been slack in their duty. While limiting their judgment to the church members, he reminded them that judgment was their duty. The modern application of this teaching is difficult, but there are two times when it seems that a Christian congregation should sit in judgment. (1) When one seeks admittance to the congregation, he must be judged as to his fitness, spiritually, to be a part of the body of Christ. (2) When one continues in open and flagrant sin, he must be disciplined, either by excommunication from the congregation or by winning his repentance so that he may continue to be a part of the body of Christ. For the church to fail to act in either instance is to run the risk of diluting the spiritual quality of the congregation so that it can no longer function in the world as a body of Christ. This does not mean that all church members must be perfect; it does mean that they should be sincere in their pursuit of a truly Christian life.

Verse 13: God judges those outside: continues the idea of responsibility for judgment. God is the one who has the responsibility to judge the unbeliever. That is not the duty of the believer. This statement has the nature of an axiom in New Testament language.

Drive out the wicked person from among you: a quotation from Deuteronomy 22:24, where the removal was to be effected by stoning the wicked ones to death (cf. also Deut. 17:7; 24:7). This does not mean that the congregation at Corinth were to pronounce a sentence of death on their sinning members. It meant that they were to remove them from their congregation. Paul followed his usual custom of appropriating Old Testament language to express his thoughts when possible.

2. The Danger of Litigation in the Pagan Courts (6:1-11)

This is the weakest link in my suggestion that Paul, throughout this section, was correcting misunderstandings of his own teachings. We have no certain knowledge that he had taught them the proper action when disputes concerning property arose between church members. However, my suggestion that litigation arose from the misunderstanding of what human rights involved is possible, though not compelling. Whether this suggestion explains the background or not, the thought of these verses is clear. There had arisen a practice among the Corinthians of taking disputes about property before pagan judges. To Paul this was sinful because: (1) it ignored the responsibility of the church to mediate in disputes between members (vss. 1–6); (2) it led to the use of the courts to defraud one another (vss. 7–8); (3) it ignored the essential unrighteousness of the pagan world (vss. 9–11).

(1) Litigation in pagan courts ignored the responsibility of the church to mediate in disputes between members (6:1-6)

Perhaps the subject had been suggested to Paul by his closing remark in the last chapter. Perhaps Paul had instructed them about the duty of the church in this regard, and they had been lax in carrying out his instructions. At any rate, they seem to have been aware of the proper action, and Paul reminded them of the necessity to carry it out. The discussion, though masterful, does not have the tone of a new teaching.

Verse 1: introduces the matter with the first of a series of rhetorical questions. Paul's argument rested upon knowledge which the Corinthians already had but were not using.

Grievance: literally, "matter," or, in the legal sense, "case." It was the regular technical term for a lawsuit.

Against a brother: justified by the context, though the Greek has only "the other." Paul was certainly dealing with disputes between fellow church members, not with a dispute between a church member and an outsider.

Does he dare: placed first in the Greek sentence for the sake of emphasis. The word expresses a sense of outrage at the impropriety of the action. It corresponds to our expression, "How dare you?"

Before the unrighteous: the unbelievers. The term does have ethical connotations, but this is not the primary emphasis.

Instead of the saints: the believers. *Saints* means "those who belong to God." It is one of the most common terms of the New Testament to designate the believer. T. C. Edwards suggests that the practice of litigation, since it was common among the Greeks, probably had infested the Greek portion of the congregation rather than the Jews. The Jews were in the habit of choosing an arbitrator from among themselves to settle their disputes. In the light of this, it is likely that Paul had mediation in mind rather than a full court session by the congregation. He did not mean that justice was impossible in the pagan courts. His own experience had shown otherwise. The idea was that litigation brought reproach upon the church and therefore should be avoided.

Verse 2: two more rhetorical questions.

Do you not know that the saints will judge the world?: expects an affirmative answer. Paul took it as axiomatic that *the saints will judge the world.*[1] Undoubtedly the Corinthians knew what Paul meant. We do not. Three suggestions have been made by numerous commentators: (1) It means that Christians will condemn the world for its unbelief, as the men of Nineveh will rise up against those who rejected Christ (cf. Luke 11:32); (2) It means that the future will see the time when Christians will be the magistrates of the world; or (3) It means that the saints will share in the future messianic reign of Christ, which will include the task of judging the world. The closest parallel in Jewish literature is in the apocryphal book, Wisdom of Solomon 3:1, 8, NEB: "But the souls of the just are in God's hand. . . . They will be judges and rulers over the nations of the world, and the Lord shall be their king for ever and ever." In the light of this, it would seem that the last interpretation reflects the thought of Paul. If so, the thought is not necessarily that the saints will condemn the world, but rather that they will share in its rule. I prefer to take "rule" in the biblical sense of

---

[1] Cf. H. L. Goudge, *The First Epistle to the Corinthians* (London: Methuen & Co. Ltd., © 1903), p. 444. Hereafter referred to as Goudge.

serving and apply this expression to the present age, but the context forbids. This is one of Paul's expressions, the understanding of which must await the light of the accomplished fact.

And if the world is to be judged by you, are you incompetent to try trivial cases?: explains the immediate application which Paul had in mind. That the saints would judge the world was considered true. Paul's conclusion was based on this fact. The Christians should certainly be competent to judge trivial cases.[1] The Greek indicates that *trivial cases* should be translated "smallest tribunals." The thought is clear. The argument is *a fortiori,* an argument from the stronger assumption to the weaker conclusion.

Verse 3: continues the same argument from another viewpoint.

Do you not know that we are to judge angels?: presents the same difficulty as verse 2. We do not know what Paul meant by judging angels. Probably the same general reference as in verse 2 is in mind. To press the discussion to the extreme of trying to decide whether he meant good angels or bad and in what sense he meant that Christians were to judge them obscures the thought of the verse. It was assumed to be true that Christians will judge angels. The point was: given this, how would anybody dare to imply that they were not competent in smaller affairs?

How much more, matters of this life!: literally, "not to mention material things." Both the context and the Greek word justify this translation. Paul was talking of the common resources of life such as food, clothing, and property. Aristotle used the same Greek word in an active sense to mean "the means of living" (T. C. Edwards). The context makes it clear that Paul was speaking of property disputes rather than disputes that had to do with the living of the Christian life in its wider meaning.

Verse 4: This is a verse which is difficult to interpret with assurance.

If then you have such cases: is indefinite and should be translated, "on those occasions when you have property disputes that require court action." There is a suggestion of surprise on Paul's part that this should ever be true.

Why do you lay them before those who are least esteemed by the church?: The question mark here is a possible punctuation, though the Greek also allows the expression to be taken as an imperative: "Lay them before those who are least esteemed in the church." If the imperative is correct, Paul would have been commanding them to lay their cases before the least esteemed among the Christians. If the RSV is to be preferred, the question reflects their action of laying their cases before the unrighteous, who are further described as being of lesser esteem in the church than the most despised Christian.

A decision is difficult to make. However, on the whole, I would think that the alternative given above is to be preferred to the RSV. *Lay . . . before* really means "to seat as judges." Since pagan magistrates were already seated, the expression would better apply to the appointment of church members as arbitrators. *Least esteemed* is a strange word to be

---

[1] Héring suggests that it was doubly tragic that the church which vaunted itself of wisdom could not find men of judgment among its members. (Jean Héring, *The First Epistle of Saint Paul to the Corinthians,* trans. by A. W. Heathcote and P. J. Allcock [London: The Epworth Press, 1962]).

applied to heathen judges, but it would fit perfectly the attitude of the church as a whole to members of lesser spiritual qualifications. Paul did not, of course, approve the pride which was revealed in their contempt for the brethren, but he recognized it. Both the commentators and translators are divided concerning the proper interpretation of this verse. A good case can be made for both sides. When such is the case, it is better not to be dogmatic. In either case, whichever is correct, the trend of the thought in the section is essentially the same.

Verse 5: I say this to your shame: that is, "to move you to shame." [1] This is an interesting contrast to Paul's statement in 4:14: "I do not write this to make you ashamed, but to admonish you as my beloved children." Obviously Paul thought that the litigation was more serious than their pride in wisdom. The Corinthians' pride in wisdom was motivated by their desire to be more fully Christian. The method followed was wrong; the motives were good. The use of litigation was wrong both as to method and as to motive.

Can it be: catches the implications of the Greek well. Paul was asking if the case had come to be such.

There is no man among you wise enough: no one with sufficient wisdom. The expression is very strong in the Greek, with a suggestion of irony.

To decide between members of the brotherhood: to act as arbitrator [2] in a case between fellow Christians. This expression indicates that Paul had in mind the Jewish practice of disputants choosing fellow Jews to arbitrate their differences. The same practice, he felt, should be followed among Christians.

Verse 6: expresses the practice that existed at Corinth. The punctuation in the RSV is poor. Verse 5 should end with a question mark. Verse 6 should perhaps have an exclamation mark, at least a period. The verse contains two assertions, both of which were painful to Paul.

But: a strong adversative conjunction. Implies that the situation was far different than it should be.

Brother goes to law against brother: Instead of accepting arbitration, they were going to law.

And that before unbelievers: expresses Paul's greatest shock. Instead of referring matters to the church, they were taking their complaints before pagan courts. For shame!

(2) Litigation led to defrauding of one another (6:7-8)

In this paragraph Paul pointed out the evil results in the lives of the Corinthians.

Verse 7: Paul believed that it would have been better to suffer wrong, to be defrauded, than to go to pagan courts.

To have lawsuits at all with one another is defeat for you: The English translation does not catch the intensity of the Greek. Literally translated, the clause would read: "already indeed therefore altogether a falling short with respect to you is because judgments you have with one another." The

---

[1] So Morris.

[2] Edwards suggests this translation.

Greek order is impossible in English, but only the Greek reveals the particles of emphasis added one to the other. There is no need to comment on the first part of the expression; it merely continues and repeats what has been said.

Is defeat for you: is a weak translation of the Greek; much is left out. There are three things which Paul emphasized. First, the very fact of having lawsuits was in itself defeat. Second, this was true "altogether," i.e., no matter what the decision turned out to be or what tribunal sat in judgment. Third, the defeat was with reference to their own spiritual lives. It consisted of a falling short of the spiritual attainment which should have been theirs. The word which is translated *defeat* may mean that or "a defect." The idea is that they suffered loss, not from the decision of the lawsuit, but from the fact of lawsuit. Perhaps the reference was to the matter of disputes which lay behind the lawsuits.[1] However, it seems to me that Paul would not have said this if they had had their disputes arbitrated by fellow Christians. *With one another* should be translated "with yourselves." The Greek pronoun emphasizes the identity of interest rather than reciprocity. The idea is that the Corinthians should have been interested in the same thing—their spiritual development. Instead, they were fighting among themselves while the enemy gained ground; they were tearing themselves apart.

Why not rather suffer wrong? Why not rather be defrauded?: suggests an alternative course of action when disputes arose. Both are in the middle voice in Greek and carry the idea of enduring something as a result of decision. They do not suggest passive nonresistance, but active refusal to resist. Paul felt that the way to real victory was not in demanding one's rights, but in being willing to forego them for the sake of the church.

Verse 8: describes the action which was characteristic of the litigants. One may suppose that this did not apply to all the church, as the pride in wisdom did. Nor was there any thought in Paul's mind of church discipline, as was the case with the immoral man. Here he described the action of some members.

But you yourselves wrong and defraud: So far were they from following the rule suggested by the gospel that they themselves went contrary to it. The verbs are the same as in verse 7, but here they are in the active voice and the present tense. This means that the Corinthians were making a practice of acting unjustly toward their fellow Christians and causing them to suffer deprivation of their property.

And that even your own brethren: expresses a feeling of shock on the part of Paul. It would be bad enough for the church members to act thus against outsiders. The enormity of their sin was that their actions were aimed at those within the church. The use of *your own brethren* stresses the relationship and makes it more personal.

(3) Litigation ignored the essential unrighteousness of the pagan world (6:9–11)

The connection of this paragraph with what goes before is not entirely clear. Paul seemed to be saying to the Corinthians that their litigation

---

[1] Cf. Lenski.

showed an adherence to pagan customs and actions which was inconsistent with their salvation. The paragraph begins with an assertion that the unrighteous shall not share in God's reign (vs. 9*a*), continues with a listing of the most repulsive of pagan sins (vss. 9*b*–10), and closes with the Corinthians' experiences which had separated them from the pagan world (vs. 11). The connection with the foregoing is indicated by the word *unrighteous;* it is built on the same Greek stem as the verbs which were translated "wrong" in verses 7–8.

Verse 9: Do you not know?: introduces a question which expects an affirmative answer. They did know this; Paul had taught it to them.

The unrighteous: a general term which includes all those who are listed in verses 9–10.

Will not inherit: "will not come into full possession of." The word *inherit* is an allusion to the promise given to Abraham (cf. Gal. 3:29). It was used in the Old Testament for the coming of Israel into the Promised Land. Paul adopted it to describe the fullness of Christian blessings (Rom. 8:16–17). According to his theology, all of God's children are his heirs. It is just this that would exclude from the inheritance the *unrighteous.*

The kingdom of God: reflects the central idea in the teaching of Jesus. The term is not frequent in the writings of Paul. Christians had substituted the lordship of Christ for the idea of the reign of God. Paul used the shorter form of the expression, "God's kingdom." The proper noun, *God,* is placed first in order to bring it into sharp contrast with *unrighteousness.*

Do not be deceived: literally, "stop being led astray." The expression implies a fundamental error in the conception of the Corinthians about the meaning of the Christian life. Some Jews held that belief in God was sufficient to insure final redemption regardless of the kind of life one lived. Perhaps the Corinthians had come to feel that their behavior had no bearing on their inheritance. Some who believe in a mechanical perseverance of the saints have trouble with this passage. However, we need to remember that while the New Testament teaches that the final salvation of all true believers is certain, it does not teach that it is automatic. Final salvation demands that the Christian remain a Christian, that he shall not become a man of the world, an unrighteous man. Paul did not believe that they would lose their salvation; he did believe that they needed to be warned against that possibility.

Immoral . . . idolaters . . . adulterers . . . homosexuals: begins the list of the unrighteous, a list which is similar to but longer than the one found in 5:10–11. *Immoral* is the general word for any kind of sexual impropriety. *Idolater* is self-explanatory. *Adulterer* is the technical term to describe sexual intercourse between married people who are not married to each other. *Homosexual* had the same meaning in ancient times as today. RSV seems to have omitted one word from the list, the Greek *malakoi,* which means effeminate. Lenski takes it here to mean a voluptuary. It could mean one who submitted himself to the homosexual.

Verse 10: continues the list of the unrighteous, but the emphasis on those who violate property rights or personal rights.

Thieves . . . greedy . . . drunkards . . . revilers . . . robbers: All of these words have been explained in connection with our comments on 5:10–11.

Will inherit the kingdom of God: repetition for emphasis of the assertion that begins the section (cf. 9*a*).

Verse 11: reminded the Corinthians of their changed status with an implication of the necessity of a changed life.

And such were some of you: pictures the revolution brought about in the lives of people by the preaching of the gospel. The apostles did not find prospects only among the good and kind people of the world; they found them among the most repulsive. *Some* limits the number of the Corinthians who had been involved in these repulsive sins. Certainly the Jewish converts had not practiced them; these were, on the whole, pagan sins. We may assume, as well, that many of the pagans did not engage in these most repulsive sins. *Were* sharply reminded them of their change. They had been, but they were no longer.

But: a strong adversative conjunction which introduces the contrast between the pre-Christian life and the post-Christian reality.

You were washed: a verb used only here and in Acts 22:16, where Paul was commanded: "Rise and be baptized, and wash away your sins, calling on his name." The verb is in the middle voice in Greek and should read, "you had yourselves washed," or "you allowed yourselves to be washed." The idea of personal choice by responsible people is involved. Baptism in the New Testament was considered a symbolic or outward expression of a previous act of God in effectively cleansing one of sins. This seems to be the idea here. While the experiential order was cleansing by God followed by baptism, the order was often reversed in speaking of the experience (cf. Titus 3:5).

You were sanctified: spiritually set aside by the act of God to be his people. The verb is a simple past passive, signifying an act that took place in the past, of which the Corinthians were recipients. In modern theology the ethical consequences of this act have come to the front so that one who is *sanctified* (i.e., consecrated) is thought of as a righteous person. In some cases consecration has been made to mean the growth in Christian character which follows justification. In the New Testament this distinction was not made. Both words—consecration and sanctification—referred to the initial act of God's grace in making one a Christian. Both words are figurative, consecration or sanctification coming from the religious practice of setting aside a day or an object for God's special use. Of course this was, in Christian thinking, a dynamic act of God which changed the center of man's moral character. Thus it had necessary ethical consequences, but the emphasis lay on the dynamic act of God rather than on the results.

You were justified: a synonymous expression, used mainly by Paul in the New Testament. It also refers to the act of God in making men Christians, though the emphasis is slightly different. The term came from the realm of the law. An indicted prisoner who was found innocent of his crime was said to be *justified*. Paul adopted the word but gave it new content. For him it meant that the sinner was forgiven and received into the fellowship of God even though he was in reality guilty. Some theologians have interpreted this in a purely judicial sense, even at times calling God's action a legal fiction. Not so with Paul! God's act was dynamic. The resulting openness of fellowship between God was what led Paul to use the term to describe the Christian experience.

In the name of the Lord Jesus Christ: an expression often connected with baptism (cf. Acts 2:38; 10:48) and with prayer (cf. John 14:14) in the New Testament. Its use here, since it is plainly connected to all three verbs, is somewhat strange. Three explanations of *the name* are possible: (1) It is the revelation of Christ presented in the Word of God.[1] (2) It is the source of the church's authority.[2] (3) It is a circumlocution for the person of Christ. On the whole, the last suggestion seems to fit this context better. If so, the expression would mean the same as Paul's frequently used "in union with Christ." The use of the full title *Lord Jesus Christ* emphasizes the dignity of the person of Jesus Christ who is the Lord.

In the Spirit of our God: the way in which God acted in the lives of the Corinthians to accomplish their spiritual revolution. The emphasis is upon the newness of the life which the Corinthians had. "It is a life in Christ, given in His name: and a life in the Spirit, given by Him and lived in His power" (Parry). Consequently, the new life is to be lived by new principles and characterized by new practices and habits. Paul often spoke of this contrast between the new and the old, using such expressions as "old" and "new" man (cf. Eph. 4:22–24), the works of the "flesh" and the fruits of the "Spirit" (cf. Gal. 5:19–24), and "death" and "resurrection" (cf. Rom. 6:1–6). The use of the names of the Trinity has often been noted by commentators, but this seems to be incidental to the passage.

3. The Danger of Licentiousness in the Name of Liberty (6:12–20)

This section deals with a problem of the first century, but it could have been written in the late twentieth. It deals with the question of sexual freedom or liberty and the relation of faith in Christ to morality. The background of the section is Greek thought which still infected the Corinthians and kept them from seeing the relation of faith to morality. One element in that thought was the belief that the natural processes of life, such as sex, had no moral significance. This was carried to great lengths by the Cynics and infested the early Christian churches in the form of Antinomian Gnosticism (1 John is an outstanding example in the New Testament of a letter written against this heresy). Another element in pagan thought as a whole, which is reflected in this section, was that religion and morality had no relation. Religion, it was felt by the pagans, was an attempt to win the gods over to their side. The gods had no concern with man's normal life, only with his religious offerings.

A further problem, not philosophical, made the problem more acute in Corinth than it might have been in other cities. Corinth was a city of sin. Sexual promiscuity was common; prostitution even entered the temples. The Corinthians were children of their times. No wonder they had difficulty

---

[1] Cf. Lenski.
[2] Cf. Edwards.

in achieving a Christian view of sex and of life. Not only so, but also it seems that the Corinthians had misunderstood the teaching of Paul. They thought that his teaching of Christian liberty was meant to be absolute, without any limitations.

Against this complex of ideas and errors, Paul wrote this section. There is no logical outline of the thought, but several motifs can be discerned in the section: (1) Christian liberty can never be unlimited; it must be limited by consideration of what is good for the individual and what is demanded by Christian dedication. (2) The body and its natural functions have spiritual significance; it should be used for the glory of God. (3) Sexual intercourse with prostitutes destroys man.

Verse 12: states the principle of life which was the guide of licentious people and gives Paul's Christian corrections of it.

"All things are lawful for me": a teaching of Paul, but not in the sense in which the Corinthians were using the saying. They had taken it to mean that the liberty had no limits. Paul meant that men were freed from the legalistic demands of Judaizers. The repetition of the cry shows that at least some of the Corinthians were using it. It may suggest that some of the others were questioning its validity. Paul started out with an acceptance of the truth of the maxim. Of course, in his thought *all things* would not include such things as he had just condemned as the practices of the unrighteous (cf. vss. 9–10). It would include those things which were not sinful in themselves, such as the eating of meat and even sexual intercourse itself. To Paul, these things were good if practiced according to God's teaching and according to the leadership of the Holy Spirit, but evil when they violated human good, human rights, or spiritual principles. Thus, though liberty was real, it was not license.

But not all things are helpful: one limitation on liberty. Liberty is limited by considerations of one's own good. *Helpful* may apply either to the individual or to his fellows. In 1 Corinthians 10:23–30, Paul discussed this same principle. There the emphasis is on the harm done to others by improper actions. In this paragraph the emphasis seems to be on the harm done to self. Harm to self may take two directions. It may bring positive harm by destruction of physical or spiritual powers, or it may harm by hindering growth. Both considerations, according to Paul, should constitute a real limitation on the use of liberty.

But I will not be enslaved by anything: the second limitation on liberty in this passage. Liberty must not be used in such a way as to lose it. *Enslaved* is a good translation of a Greek word which means "come under the power or domination of." In the Greek there is a word play with "lawful" which is lost in the English translation. We may see this if we use "power" in both clauses and translate thus: "All things are within my power, but I will not come under the power of anything." *But* is very emphatic in the clause. *I* is less emphatic, but more so than *anything*. Paul was contrasting what would be true in his case with what was true in the case of some of the Corinthians.

Verse 13: This verse is a correction of the confusion which seems to have existed in Corinth. They had classed in the same category things which were essentially different, i.e., the eating of various foods and the practice of sensuality. Paul made it luminously clear that they did not belong in the same category.

"Food is meant for the stomach and the stomach for food": a statement which is true within a limited scope. What one eats, if he is not a glutton, has no spiritual significance. This principle was enunciated by both Paul and Jesus in four instances: (1) It was true with regard to meat that had been offered to idols (cf. chaps. 8 and 10). (2) It was true with regard to the Mosaic distinction between clean and unclean meats (cf. Mark 7:19). (3) It was true with regard to vegetarianism (Rom. 14:1–4). (4) It was true with regard to the ascetic prohibitions of the Colossian heretics (cf. Col. 2:20–23). Since meat offered to idols occupies so large a place in this letter, Paul may have had these in mind. But we are not to suppose that his remark here was limited only to this subject. The reason is clear. The process of eating and digesting food is a purely physical exercise. God made the food for this purpose; God made the stomach for this purpose. There could be no spiritual significance attached to the process.

And God will destroy both one and the other: states the purely worldly nature of this process. When life on this earth is over, both food and the stomach will no longer exist as we know them.

The body: was quite different from the stomach or even from the sexual organs in the thought of Paul. *Body* was a word which, for Paul, meant man in his total self as existing and operating in the world. Commentators, in discussing this passage, have often been guilty of imposing on the thought of Paul the Greek categories, body and soul. Paul had no such categories. Body was the whole man, the organized man, the man living in this world.[1] It is difficult for any modern man to understand Paul at this point because we are heirs of the Greek way of thinking. Unconsciously, we think of the body merely as a complex of physical organs of various functions which will die and decay in the grave. This was true with Paul when he thought of physical organs, such as the stomach. But when he used the word *body,* he meant very much the same as we mean by the word "self." Thus, in this section we could almost substitute our word "man" for Paul's word *body.* This does not mean that for Paul no distinction existed between "soul" and "body." It does mean that each term was used for the whole of man. "Soul" meant man when viewed as a thinking, feeling, purposeful individual capable of fellowship with God. "Body" meant man when viewed as an acting, organized personality living in the world.

Not meant for immorality: Man is not created for sexual purposes only. Paul was combating a view which was held by some of the Corinthians. They had said that the body was to have its natural functions, that no sin could be attached to doing what was natural. Therefore, they could see no wrong in fornication and felt there should be no limitations on sexual intercourse. The reason that Paul could not agree becomes clear as we go further in the passage. To him the practice of sex did not involve only the sexual organs of man, but the whole man. Man as a person was involved

---

[1] James Moffatt, *The First Epistle of Paul to the Corinthians* (New York and London: Harper and Brothers, Publishers, n.d.). Referred to hereafter as Moffatt.

in the sex act, whether in marriage or out of it. Sex, to him, was not a mere physical transaction. Paul could agree with the Corinthians when the act involved was merely physical, like eating and digesting food. He could not agree with them when this same principle was applied to other acts which were more than physical, like sex acts.

But for the Lord: Man is made for service to the *Lord.* This was Paul's starting point. Man, as an organized being, had a primary relation which was personal and spiritual. He was made for the *Lord,* i.e., Jesus Christ. *For* can either mean "for the service of" or "for fellowship with." Paul's teaching was the same in either case. Whatever man did involved himself, his *body,* which had spiritual significance.

And the Lord for the body: parallel in structure with the previous statement; but something different is implied. The Lord was not created for man; he functions for the good of man. The context suggests that Paul's immediate thought was of the resurrection.

Verse 14: And God raised the Lord: points to the event which is fundamental to Christian theology. Notice that Paul did not say that God raised the body of the Lord, but that he raised the Lord. Resurrection is not merely physical; it affects the whole man. The Lord, by his resurrection, was raised to new dignity and power. While we focus our attention on the bodily aspect of the event, the New Testament focuses its attention on the implications for the person of Christ.

And will also raise us up by his power: the Christian hope for the future. Paul had no doubt about it. Notice that Paul substituted *us* for *body* in this statement. This reveals that, for Paul, *body* was a synonym for self. Again, his emphasis was not upon the mere physical resurrection but upon its implications for the whole man. The Christian will be raised to a new kind of life, like that of his Lord. He should not therefore be motivated by desires for sensual pleasure but by Christian motives in all that he does.

Verse 15: presses on from the general principle to the immediate situation.

Do you not know: should be, "you do know, don't you?" This expression introduces a rhetorical question which demands an affirmative answer. Paul was reminding the Corinthians of a teaching which he had given them, but the implications of which they had not realized. He repeated the teaching so that he might point out its implications.

Your bodies are members of Christ?: united with Christ, so that Christ and the believer are one. This was a favorite thought for Paul. He expressed his own feeling of oneness with Christ in Galations 2:20: "it is no longer I who live, but Christ who lives in me." Though the word "member" is used here, it does not refer to membership in the body of Christ, the church (cf. chap. 12). The contrast here is between *members of Christ* and being *members of a prostitute.*

Shall I therefore take: rather, "take away." The Greek word means to "take away." The thought is that such action would rob Christ of what belonged to him. This stresses the spiritual implications of the act.

The members of Christ: the body which is united with him. The plural is demanded by the context, but Paul did not mean that one could act for all.

And make them members of a prostitute: describes the results of fornication. Verse 16 explains what Paul meant by *make them members. A prostitute* meant the same then as in modern language.

Never!: shows how abominable the suggestion seemed to Paul. *Never* translates a Greek expression in the form of a prayer, "may it not be." Our expressions, "God forbid" and "heaven forbid," express the meaning better than *never.* It was an expression which Paul often used to express his aversion to some idea. It is found thirteen times in Paul's epistles.

Verse 16: explains what Paul meant by making a member of Christ a member of a prostitute.

Do you not know: rather, "you do know, do you not?" The question demands an answer of "yes."

He who joins himself to a prostitute: has sexual intercourse with her. The present tense emphasizes the act of joining; the middle voice emphasizes the fact that it is himself which he joins.

Becomes one body with her: Cohabitation with a woman was held by Paul to be of such nature that it united the two so that they became one person. It was far from being merely a temporary physical union.

For, as it is written, "The two shall become one": an appeal to Scripture to verify his statement. The quotation is taken from Genesis 2:24 from the Greek version of the Old Testament. *As it is written* is a poor translation. The Greek has "it says" or "he says." Probably Paul was quoting Scripture but ascribing it to the author, God. Thus, "he says" would fit the thought better. *"The two shall become one"* is applied in Scripture to legitimate union between man and wife. It may seem odd that Paul would apply it to union with a prostitute. However, in Jewish practice it was the act of sexual intercourse that consummated the marriage. This is also true, I am told, with reference to modern law. The application then is justified. If sexual intercourse is the true mark of marriage, then one who has sexual intercourse with a prostitute is in fact married to her.

Verse 17: But he who is united to the Lord: The same verb is used here as in verse 16. The method of union is, of course, different. While one joins himself to the prostitute by sexual intercourse, one joins himself to the Lord through the exercise of faith.

Becomes one spirit with him: describes the union as an inner, spiritual reality. It would not have been proper for Paul to have said, "becomes one body with him." Since Christ was no longer an earthly person, this would have been impossible. But to say, *becomes one spirit with him,* does not exclude man as an organized being living in the world. It lifts the whole conception to a new plane. Man in his higher spiritual self becomes one with Christ. All of his life, including his lower relations, i.e., his body, are dominated and changed by this new relationship with Christ. *Spirit* should not be taken as the Holy Spirit, but as man himself. The implication of this statement is remarkable. The union of the believer with Christ is no less real than the union of man and wife.

Verse 18: Shun immorality: literally, "flee from immorality." The only defense against this sin is flight. The Christian must avoid the occasion for it if he is to escape.

Every other sin which a man commits is outside the body: a difficult saying. The Greek is inclusive. *Every other sin* is literally, "every sin whatever." If we take *body* in Paul's sense of personality, the sense would be that no other sin would destroy man's personality; it does not unite him with another person so as to destroy his power to serve God. But even this is hard to maintain as true when we consider such sins as murder, suicide, treason, or lying. I think we must let the context limit Paul's thought to such sins as gluttony. The acts which are merely physical and involve only the physical organs are at the root of his discussion (cf. vs. 13). To take this saying out of its context would involve one in the same misunderstanding as the Corinthians. They had taken one of Paul's sayings out of context. Look where it had led them!

But the immoral man sins against his own body: that is, he destroys himself. Paul's meaning is quite clear from the context. He was thinking of man's spiritual capacities, his ability to serve the Lord. By perverting his body, i.e., his life, to lower and base uses, man destroys its use for spiritual ends.

Verse 19: This verse was meant to remind the Corinthians of the true function of man's life on earth. While they should not be brought under the power of anything, they had been brought into subjection to God.

Do you not know: the sixth occurrence in this chapter of this expression. It is also used in four other passages in this epistle (3:16; 5:6; 9:13; 24), but only twice in Paul's other epistles. It is the proper Greek expression to call to remembrance, as something already known, what had been Paul's oral teaching.

Your body is a temple of the Holy Spirit within you: repeats 3:16, but the application here is to the individual believer.[1] *Temple* is the word for the inner sanctuary rather than the outer temple precincts. *The Holy Spirit* is the dynamic presence of God through his Spirit. *Within you* marks the sphere in which the Holy Spirit dwells and acts. The necessary background is the Jewish Temple in Jerusalem. God dwelt in his glory within the sanctuary. From there he acted in forgiving and redeeming his people. In Jewish practice only the high priest was allowed to enter that inner sanctuary, and that only once each year. Paul used this background for his metaphor. God now dwells in the hearts and lives of individual believers as well as being the cohesive force in the congregational fellowship. It is from within the believer that he acts in forgiving and redeeming the world. The sanctity of the human life on earth, i.e., the body, is thus emphasized. That life should not be dedicated to base and lower aims; it should be dedicated to the true aims of the Christian life. This is Paul's thought in this passage.

Which you have from God?: identifies the ultimate source of the Holy Spirit which dwells in the believer.

You are not your own: states the result of the believer's relationship to God. Again it is noteworthy that Paul shifted from *your body* to *you* without any thought of changing the subject. This emphasizes the fact stated

---

[1] Kempthorne, on the contrary, interprets this whole paragraph in relation to 5:1–9, and makes the body to be the church. (R. Kempthorne, "Incest and the Body of Christ: A Study of 1 Corinthians vi. 12–20," *New Testament Studies*, Vol. 14, Apr., 1968, pp. 568–574).

above. To Paul, *your body* and *you* were two ways of saying the same thing. Paul stated this as a fact, but his purpose was much the same as in Romans 6:15–23. He meant for the fact to imply the responsibility of the Corinthians to yield themselves to God for his use.

Verse 20: You were bought with a price: appeals to Christians on the basis of the cost of redemption. *You were bought* is in the past tense; it suggests the once-for-all nature of the payment. *Price* refers to the death of Christ on the cross. It is the purchase price by which Christ became the believers' owner and they became his slaves. It implied that the new owner had absolute rights in the believer's life.

So glorify God in your body: an urgent command which summarizes, in its positive aspects, the goal of the human life on earth. *So* translates a Greek particle which gives emphasis to the urgency of the command. The aorist tense of the Greek verb does the same. The command rings out with all the force of the drill sergeant's on the parade grounds. To *glorify God* means to make his glory manifest to all the world. We cannot add to his glory; we can let men know what it is.

In your body: the end of the genuine text. Later copyists added, "and in your spirit which are God's." The addition probably came after Christians had lost sight of Paul's meaning for *body*. It was an attempt to include the spiritual life of man in the admonition. As has been seen, Paul did that by using the term *body* for the whole man.

IV. DISCUSSION OF THEIR QUESTION CONCERNING MARRIAGE (7:1–40)

With this discussion Paul began his answer to a letter which the Corinthians had written him. It is possible to trace the main outlines of that letter from the phrases used by Paul to introduce his answers: "Now concerning the matters about which you wrote" (7:1); "Now concerning the unmarried" (7:25); "Now concerning food offered to idols" (8:1); "Now concerning spiritual gifts" (12:1). His discussion of women being veiled when they prayed or prophesied contains indications that it also was a response to their letter. Other material in this last part of the letter may or may not have been mentioned in their letter.

The discussion concerning marriage and the unmarried has often led men to believe that Paul was an old bachelor without any sympathy for the problems of the common man. This idea, on closer examination, proves to be a misconception. He actually wrote with a great deal of sympathetic understanding; his remarks here should be compared with other passages in which he mentioned marriage (2 Cor. 11:2; Rom. 7:4; Eph. 5:28–33).

Paul recognized the need for marriage in most cases and gave good advice about the mutual relations of husband and wife (vss. 1–7). Then he discussed the relative merits of the single and the married life (vss. 8–9). While he believed that divorce was contrary to the teachings of Christ (vss. 10–11), he recognized that separation was permissible if a Christian were married to an unbeliever, should the unbeliever want a separation (vss. 12–16); otherwise the marriage should be maintained. Related to the problem, at least to Paul, was the problem of slavery; he advised men not to be overly concerned with changing the outward circumstances of their lives (vss. 17–24). He made his understanding of the relationship of slavery and marriage explicit in regard both to the married and the unmarried (vss. 25–31). He defended his position that being unmarried was preferable in some cases because it freed one from worldly care that might interfere with his devotion to God (vss. 32–35). Then, turning his attention to the unmarried, he discussed the action of the father of a marriageable daughter (vss. 36–38, KJV). (Here my interpretation will differ from the RSV translation.) Finally, he gave instructions concerning the Christian widow, recommending that she should not remarry, but insisting that she marry a Christian if she did (vss. 39–40). There is much in Paul's discussion which is dated; i.e., it relates only to the problems which faced the Corinthians in the first century. But there is much that is permanently valid; i.e., it applies equally well to pressing problems of human life in all ages.

1. Marriage Was Needful to Maintain Moral Order (7:1–7)

This discussion is placed first because it summarizes the central position of Paul in regard to marriage. The rest of the chapter contains modifications and explanations of his position.

Verse 1: Now concerning the matters about which you wrote: refers to the letter which they had written. No doubt it contained questions concerning matters in dispute in the church. However, all attempts to relate particular questions to particular groups have failed to be convincing. It is better to suppose that the questions arose from two sources: the pagan environment of the church at Corinth and the internal life of the developing church.

Well: in this context means "preferable." It comes from a Greek word which primarily refers to the outward form of an act, in contrast to "good" which speaks of an act as essentially good, i.e., beneficial. Other meanings which are well attested in New Testament usage are: (1) "excellent" with regard to that which is well adapted to its ends; (2) "good" in the ethical sense of that which is right, noble, and honorable. The meaning in this passage is debated. Some have taken it to mean that celibacy is a moral and spiritual good and marriage is evil, not necessarily in itself, but in its consequences. This idea is unacceptable in this passage. There is no real justification in this passage for the opinion that Paul looked upon sexual intercourse in marriage as sinful. Others have taken the term to refer to what was prudent in the special circumstances of the Corinthians. Paul did use the same Greek word with this meaning in verse 26: "I think that in view of the impending distress it is well for a person to remain as he is." Yet this meaning does not fit this first use.

We must give the expression in this verse the meaning of "superior." To paraphrase: "Marriage is good; celibacy is better." Paul felt that the Christian's primary aim was the service of God. He further felt that the entangling ties of marriage were a handicap to that service (cf. vss. 32–35). Thus the unmarried state was *well* in the sense that it permitted a person to give his undivided attention to the demands of the Lord's service. We may not agree with Paul; his conclusion may not be true at all times. Paul himself recognized that it was not true for all men even in his times. The remainder of the discussion in this chapter modifies and explains his meaning, but we must not lose sight of the fact that this was his teaching.

To touch a woman: a euphemism for sexual intercourse with a woman. In Paul's teaching this would include the whole idea of marriage. He had already given his opinion of immorality and prostitution in 2 Corinthians 6:12–20. For the unmarried it was positively sinful to touch a woman in this sense. Yet Paul's thought did not involve sexual abstinence within marriage. In modern terms he said, "It is better not to get married."

Verse 2: introduces one reason why celibacy should not be a universal rule.

But because of the temptation to immorality: This translation may be justified by the context, but it is not true to the Greek. There is no word in the Greek for *temptation to.* Literally, the translation should be, "but on account of the fornications." "Fornications," i.e., "immorality," is in the plural in the Greek and refers to the prevalence of the acts of fornication in Corinth. There was no public opinion against such immorality; sexual promiscuity was actually fostered by society, being a part of religion and an attendant evil in slavery. This use of the plural of an abstract noun where we would use the singular was a common practice of the Hebrews. No doubt Paul recognized that the almost universal practice of fornication would lead to temptation, especially for the unmarried. For this reason the RSV insertion of *temptation to* may be justifiable.

Because suggests that the prevalence of fornications was a reason for marriage. Of course, Paul did not think it was the only reason, but he did think it was an important one. Paul did not write a great deal about the philosophy of marriage, so we cannot say that he would agree with modern opinions about the purpose and basis of marriage. Perhaps he would; perhaps he would not. The best thinking about marriage today would insist that mutual love must be its basis and a Christian family its purpose. However good this suggestion may be, it cannot find support from this verse.

Each man should have his own wife: imperative verbal form pointing to duty rather than permission. Literally, "Let each man have his own wife." This expression is an incidental prohibition of polygamy, which was common among the Greeks and not unknown among the Jews. "Such a prohibition was by no means unnecessary at this time, when polygamy was recklessly encouraged by the Jewish rabbis" (Lightfoot).

His own . . . her own: presents an interesting study. The two expressions are translations of different Greek words. *His own* translates a reflexive pronoun. *Her own* translates a possessive adjective. This distinction when speaking of the mutual relations of husband and wife seems to have been characteristic of Paul. Some have suggested that this distinction implied that Paul thought of the wife as being owned by her husband. Though this was the common attitude of the pagan world, it does not seem to have been the opinion of Paul. More likely is the suggestion that the danger of polygamy, i.e., a plurality of wives, was prevalent; but the danger of polyandry, i.e., a plurality of husbands, was not.

Each: appears to be absolute. If so, it would erase the first principle of Paul that celibacy was the preferred state. Later in the chapter, Paul modified this *each* to mean those who could not restrain their sexual impulses (cf. vs. 9).

Verse 3: implements Paul's idea that sexual desire was one reason why marriage was desirable in most cases. He had pointed out in verse 2 that the prevalence of fornication made marriage advisable.

The husband should give to his wife her conjugal rights: refers to the right of normal sexual intercourse. This right (i.e., debt of husband to wife) was contemplated in the original institution of marriage, and Christianity did not disturb it. The implications of Paul's statement in this verse are far reaching. Sex is recognized as a divine gift to men which, when practiced within the will of God, is good. The idea that has been prevalent in

Christian circles that sex is sinful, even within the marriage union, finds no support here. There is no suggestion that sexual intercourse within the marriage relationship must be restricted to the express purpose of pro-creating children. There is certainly no basis for a feeling that asceticism is the superior expression of Christian faith.

Likewise the wife to her husband: makes the debt reciprocal. It is inter-esting in all of Paul's correspondence that when he spoke of the duties of wife to husband, he also spoke of the duties of husband to wife. Though this may seem ordinary in our society, it was revolutionary in his day. More than anything else, the Christian message has served to elevate women to their rightful place as persons.

Verse 4: states the basis for the command in verse 3.

For the wife does not rule over her own body, but the husband does: the first of two exactly parallel statements that define the power of marriage to unite man and wife into one complex personality. *Body* is not to be taken here as the physical self only. As in chapter 6, *body* stands for the whole person. Paul did not conceive of sexual intercourse as a merely physical relation, but as one which involved the whole personality of man or woman. *Rule* translates a word which means "to have authority over." It is in the present tense in Greek, indicating a permanent reality of life. The thought of Paul was that marriage was a permanent union between one man and one woman in which both surrendered their rights to indepen-dence. While Paul spoke with special reference to sexual intercourse, the same principle would apply to all aspects of life.

Such a view of the marriage relation should convince doubters that Paul was not a soured old bachelor. He understood marriage and its meaning; he honored it as being instituted by God and good for men. Though he had come to believe that the special circumstances of his own day made mar-riage a handicap to Christian service, he did not try to force this belief on all men. Since only a relatively few shared his ability to restrain their sexual impulses, his advice to remain unmarried applied only to them.

Further, it is to be noted that this view of marriage was in marked contrast both to Jewish and Greek thought. By the law of Moses, polygamy was permitted under certain limitations. Concubinage was common in Greek life. In each case, to a greater or lesser degree, the woman was looked upon as the tool of man, having no rights of her own. The Christian view of marriage which Paul expressed gives to each partner equal rights and authority and looks upon the two as united in the closest possible way.

Likewise: introduces the second parallel statement, which has the same meaning and implications as the first.

Verse 5: continues the thought of verse 4. Since sexual intercourse is the right of each party of the marriage, they are not to rob each other of that right except in certain instances. Paul laid down four limitations of this general rule. They might interrupt the normal practice of sex (1) by mutual *agreement*, (2) *for a season*, (3) for the purpose of *prayer*, and (4) with the intention of resuming normal relations.

Do not refuse one another: rather, "stop robbing each other." *Refuse* does not catch the full meaning of the prohibition. Paul was speaking of rights. To refuse to grant one his rights is to rob him of his due. The prohibition is in the present tense in Greek, suggesting that they were actually doing this and should stop it. Seemingly, some of the Corinthians had come to the conclusion that sexual intercourse was sinful in itself and must be given up even within the marriage relationship. This verse should be sufficient to show that such an idea is not Christian.

Except perhaps: very tentative exception. Paul did not seem to be sure that abstention from sex in marriage was good under any circumstances. The expression in Greek is made up of four particles. The first two equal the English *except.* The third adds a note of uncertainty to the exception. The fourth tends to further limit the exception to a particular case that is considered possible.

By agreement: the first limitation on abstention. The Greek word is the one from which we get our English word "symphony." So, unless both the husband and wife speak in symphony on the subject, abstention becomes involuntary on the part of one and constitutes a robbery on the part of the other.

For a season: may be merely temporal in significance, but the Greek word connotes the idea of "fitting season." Perhaps the meaning would be "for a particular occasion." If this meaning is adopted, it would be in harmony with the fourth particle used to introduce the exceptions. Thus, abstention was permitted only for a particular occasion. It was not to become a common rule.

That you may devote yourselves to prayer: the third limitation on abstention. "Fasting" is joined to *prayer* in some of the later texts, but the RSV reading is supported by the best Greek texts. *Devote* in the Greek has the primary sense of "have leisure for," and this translation is found in some versions. However, the secondary sense had supplanted the primary in the first century, and the RSV translation is to be preferred (Lightfoot). *Prayer* is a common word in the New Testament; the practice of prayer was and is one of the basic necessities for Christian living. Paul did not refer to special church seasons of prayer but to private devotions. There is no suggestion that prayer cannot be practiced by one who continues the normal marriage relationship.

But then come together again: the fourth limitation on abstention. *But* should not be used. The whole clause is coordinate with the preceding clause and is governed by *that.* Together they should read: "that you may devote yourselves to prayer, and that you may again be the same." The Greek, though not incorrect, is somewhat obscure unless the connection is made. Later copyists changed the text to make it clearer. However, the RSV gives a good meaning for the text as it stands. The idea is that the agreement to abstain from sexual intercourse should not only have a religious purpose, i.e., prayer, but also a purpose to resume the normal marriage relations.

Lest Satan tempt you through lack of self-control: gives the reason why abstention should not be more common and for longer periods. Paul had mentioned the prevalence of sexual immorality in Corinth in verse 2. Now he suggested that the Corinthians might have a lack of self-control. The implication was not that they were especially lewd but that they were human. This is an evidence of Paul's sympathetic understanding of human nature. Human frailty is of such nature that once sexual intercourse has been started, it is difficult to stop. This was especially true in a society where sexual immorality was the rule of the day. This thought has meaning, not only in the context in which Paul used it, but also in any discussion of the rightness or wrongness of premarital sexual experimentation. Paul attributed the temptation to Satan, whom he considered to be the "prince of this age," i.e., the instigator and promoter of the moral standards of men who do not know God.

Verse 6: I say this: It is uncertain whether the expression refers only to what has been said in verse 5 or to the whole discussion of marriage in verses 2–5. If it refers to verse 5 only, the verse would mean that abstention within marriage is not a duty under any circumstances. If it refers to verses 2–5, it would mean that marriage and all of its relations are not to be considered a Christian duty. Most commentators believe that it refers to the whole discussion of marriage. In view of the following verse, this is the more probable conclusion.

By way of concession: literally, "according to understanding." The Greek word which is translated *concession* occurs only here in the New Testament. In common Greek the same word was used in the sense of "pardon." This, however, is a derived sense. In its verbal form the word means to "think the same as someone." In 2 Maccabees 14:31, the noun appearing here is translated "aware." If this is Paul's meaning, the expression would mean that Paul's discussion of marriage was due to his "awareness" of human frailty. He was speaking out of an understanding of their weakness and inability to exercise self-control. This meaning expresses Paul's thought better than *concession. Concession* is subject to the implication that there was a rigid standard which Paul was willing to bend. Paul's discussion reveals no thought of such a standard. To him marriage was a good estate, though he thought that it was better to be unmarried under certain conditions. Parry agrees that the term carries the idea of "consideration as a result of fellow-feeling." Our word "understanding" can carry this thought.

Not of command: literally, "not according to command." Throughout this discussion Paul carefully distinguished between his own advice, which he gave with the belief that he had "the Spirit of God" (cf. vs. 40) and the commands which came from the Lord (cf. vs. 25). This is exactly the contrast in this verse. His discussion of marriage had been an "opinion" which he received from the Holy Spirit and which took into consideration the whole circumstances of the Corinthians' life. It had not been according to a command that came from the Lord. That is, no teaching of Jesus had dealt with this particular problem. *Command* is not to be taken in this verse to mean that Paul felt that he had apostolic authority to order the lives of his converts. Rather, it meant that he was passing on the tradition of the words of Jesus which were looked upon as commands of the living Lord. However, his opinions were not thought of as merely human advice. Since they came from the Holy Spirit, they were to be taken as guidance from God.

Verse 7: expresses Paul's desire for all Christians. In the Greek a connective is used which relates this statement to the previous verse. The sense would be that though Paul thought that marriage was good for most Christians, his desire for all Christians lay in another direction.

That all were as I myself am: able to exercise self-control in sexual matters and thus able to serve the Lord without hindrance. Paul looked upon his self-control as a gift of grace from the Lord, not as a human achievement on his own part.

This verse raises the question of Paul's past. Was he a widower, a divorced man, or a bachelor? Had he ever been married? Much has been written on this subject, and the answer may never be found. In favor of the belief that he had never been married is the fact that no mention is made of wife or children in the New Testament. In favor of the belief that he had been married at one time is his understanding of the married life and the fact that rabbis were required to be married and have children before they could sit in judgment in a capital offense. This stipulation certainly was true in later Judaism and was probably true in New Testament times. Since Paul was a Jewish rabbi and did sit in judgment (cf. Acts 26:10), it is argued that he must have met these requirements. If so, it is certain that his marriage had ended in tragedy. Either his wife and child had died, or they had separated themselves from him when he became a Christian. I am inclined to think that Paul had been married and that his marriage had ended in separation. I would not be dogmatic about this. The rabbinical requirements plus Paul's sympathetic understanding of marriage seem convincing to me.

But each has his own special gift from God: a qualification of his desire. Some commentators think that Paul thought of the unmarried state as the ideal of Christian living. This does not seem to be the case. This clause is an admission that his own special feeling was not decisive in any other life. *Special gift* is a gift of grace, not to be confused with peculiar talents. Paul was speaking with special reference to marriage and celibacy. He regarded his own self-mastery in sexual matters as a special gift of grace. Others had different gifts which did not make self-mastery possible, but which were used in the service of God. Some commentators have made celibacy the gift referred to and have added that marriage is the matching gift. This opinion does not conform to Paul's use of the word "gift" in this letter. To Paul a special gift of grace was something which God gave to enable a man to serve him. He mentioned many in this letter—faith, knowledge, healing, tongues, etc. Here he put the gift of self-mastery in the same category as these other gifts. His reasoning was that this gift freed one from earthly ties, which, in the special circumstances of his day, hindered effective service for God.

One of one kind and one of another: modifies the thought of *his own special gift*. Gifts are not all of the same kind. There is no Greek word for *kind* in this passage. *Kind* is the RSV translation for the Greek "thus . . . thus." Our English word "direction" would be a more accurate translation. The thought is that one man has a gift to serve God in one direction, while another man has another gift to serve God in another direction.

2. Single Bliss Was Preferable; Marriage Was Permissible (7:8-9)

This paragraph reveals exactly the thought of Paul on marriage. From the standpoint of service to God, he thought it was better not to be hindered by wife or family. However, he realized that this was true only with regard to those who were able to exercise self-control.

Verse 8: constitutes the statement of Paul's position.

To the unmarried: could include the widows; but since it is the masculine plural in Greek, the probability is that he was thinking of unmarried men —both bachelors and widowers. Paul spoke later on in the chapter about the situation of unmarried girls (cf. vs. 25). The word could be taken as inclusive of all unmarried people, including bachelors, widowers, maidens, and widows. If so, the special mention of widows would be because of their desolate condition. However, ancient custom gave the choice in marriage only to the men. Widows had more freedom in the matter than single girls.

Widows: women who had lost their husbands through death.

I say: has the emphatic position in the Greek sentence. Logically, it introduces the rest of the chapter, but grammatically it belongs only to this paragraph. The sentence resumes the thought of verse 1. Again Paul was speaking of his opinion and his advice, but he thought he had the leadership of the Holy Spirit (cf. vs. 40).

It is well: the same adjective as in verse 1. He did not say that it was better to be unmarried, but this seems to be the inference from the context. Some think he was making *well* absolute, expressing the Christian ideal. However, the word cannot bear that interpretation by itself, and the context points in the opposite direction.

To remain single as I do: a translation justified by the context. Literally, it is "to remain as I:" Again the question of Paul's status is unanswered. He was one of the unmarried; there is no doubt of that. But whether he was a bachelor or widower or divorced against his will is not stated.

Verse 9: gives the exception to the general rule and the reason for that exception.

If they cannot exercise self-control: literally, "if they do not have power over themselves." The verb is in the present tense, pointing to a state of being. There is no doubt that the self-mastery is limited to the matter of sexual desire.[1]

They should marry: Marriage is the only proper framework in which to have sexual intercourse. Therefore, the Christian who cannot control his desire should marry and satisfy it. Such a statement might seem crass to some, but we must remember that this represents only one aspect of Paul's thought on marriage. Nor should we forget that it is an important aspect of human life.

For it is better to marry than to be aflame with passion: a good translation of this difficult phrase. Literally, it reads "better to marry than to burn." "Burn" seems, by the context, to mean "burn with sexual desire." The verb is in the present tense, indicating a continuous burning. Paul did not have in mind momentary temptations but a long and intense struggle against desire. Such a struggle would be fatal to spiritual growth and might

---

[1] Wendland believes that abstention was not so much a matter of self-control, but of a charismatic gift from God. Heinz-Dietrich Wendland, *Die Briefe an die Korinther* (Göttingen: Vandenhoeck & Ruprecht, 1954). Hereafter referred to by the author's last name, Wendland.

lead to immorality. At any rate, Paul thought it better to marry than to endure the desire and risk the sin.

3. The Married Should Remain Married (7:10–16)

Paul turned in this paragraph to consider the situation of those who no longer had a choice about marriage—the married Christians. First, he stated the general principle, which was based upon the historical teachings of Jesus (vss. 10–11). Second, he gave his own Spirit-led advice to those Christians who were married to unbelievers (vss. 12–16).

(1) The general principle (7:10–11)

It is certain that Paul was talking of Christians who were married to Christians, but the suggestion that he was speaking only to those who had married since they became Christians [1] seems unwarranted. It could just as well be that both husband and wife in many cases had been converted after their marriage. That Paul did not intend his words to be taken universally is shown by the fact that he did not think it his business to judge the outsider (cf. 5:12). These verses do not speak of the treatment of a Christian brother who has disobeyed the commandment of Christ and has divorced his wife, only to marry another. Rather, Paul set up the ideal that should be followed.

Verse 10: To the married: includes only Christians, but both husbands and wives.

I give charge: translates a word which suggests the order of a superior authority. The word is to be contrasted with "I wish" in verse 7. This is not a wish but an order. These are strange words to come from the apostle, but they are immediately modified by the next expression.

Not I but the Lord: explains why Paul spoke with authority. He was passing on orders from the Lord.[2] Jesus, in his teaching, had enunciated the principle of "no divorce" (cf. Mark 10:2–9 and parallel passages). In doing so, he had abrogated the permission to divorce which was included in the law of Moses because of men's "hardness of heart." There is no way of softening this saying to mean that divorce under some circumstances is correct and right. Many people have supposed that Paul used the expression, *not I but the Lord,* as a contrast to his own merely human opinions. This is not the case. He used it to refer to the tradition of the teachings of Jesus. He did not feel that his own opinions were any less inspired and true than the words of Jesus, but he made a careful distinction between what the Lord himself had said and what the Holy Spirit had led Paul to say. This fact contradicts the opinion held in many quarters that early Christians made no effort to distinguish between the historical words of Jesus and the words of Spirit-led Christians. At least, Paul made such an effort, and we may assume that his practice represented the attitude of Christians as a whole.

---

[1] ICC makes this suggestion.
[2] Cf. Wendland.

That the wife should not separate from her husband: The same injunction is given to the husband in verse 11, but a different Greek word is used. However, the Greek language offered a variety of words to indicate separation and divorce, and it is unlikely that a distinction was intended. The surprising thing is that the case of the *wife* should be mentioned first in this doublet. Perhaps this would indicate that there was an actual case at Corinth of which Paul knew, either by report or by mention in their letter.

Verse 11: deals first with a parenthetical discussion of the action of the wife if she does separate from her husband and then states the injunction against the husband.

But if she does: if she separates herself from her husband. The form of *if* indicates the possibility of such a case. If Paul knew of a case that was pending in Corinth, he treated it as if it had not happened.

Let her remain single: The same word is translated "unmarried" in verse 8, thus indicating that a divorced person was considered to be "unmarried." Again Paul was speaking of the Christian ideal. His whole discussion creates problems in our modern churches where so many of the people have had the tragedy of divorce in their lives. Some legalistically minded Christians are prone to treat such people as if they had committed the one unpardonable sin. I do not think that Paul's discussion justifies this attitude. Such people should be treated in the same manner as other Christians who have sinned and repented and are attempting to live a Christian life. They should be forgiven, helped, and encouraged to do the best they can. However, if the ideal is to be carried out, the wife should remain unmarried.

Or else be reconciled to her husband: offers the alternative in the Christian ideal to remaining unmarried.

And that the husband should not divorce his wife: literally, "send her away." This makes the prohibition mutual. Neither Christian wife nor Christian husband should take the initiative in destroying the marriage by which they are joined together in one flesh.

(2) The special case of Christians married to unbelievers (7:12–16)

Having discussed the case of married Christian couples, Paul turned to the situation of mixed marriages, of which there must have been many in Corinth. His primary thought was that Christians should not take the initiative in dissolving such marriages, but that they should not prevent the unbelievers from leaving if they insisted. Paul did not think of modern marriages in which Christians marry unbelievers. He would have been shocked at the thought. In his mind a Christian should never marry except "in the Lord." His discussion concerned the case of those who had first married and then been converted, but whose husband or wife did not share their faith.

Verse 12: states the case of the Christian husband.

To the rest: coordinate with the "unmarried" (vs. 8) and the "married" (vs. 10). Of course the rest included married people but in a different category.

I say: Note the contrast with "I give charge" (vs. 10).

Not the Lord: That is, there was no teaching of Jesus in the tradition which dealt with this special situation.[1] It was only because of this fact and the urgency of the problem that Paul felt compelled to deal with it.

That if any brother has a wife who is an unbeliever: The form of the condition shows that such cases did exist. Paul was not dealing with hypothetical questions, but with reality. *Brother* means fellow Christian. The case, as suggested above, is of conversion after marriage.

And she consents to live with him: somewhat weak translation. The verb *consents* comes from a compound Greek word which means "to think well together." The idea is that of mutual agreement after consideration. The assumption is that the believing husband and the unbelieving wife had discussed the matter and come to a mutual agreement that their marriage should continue, even though she could not share his faith. *To live with him* means to continue to dwell in his house as his wife.

He should not divorce her: That is, "he should not send her away." The Christian brother was not to suppose that it was his duty to take the initiative in dissolving the marriage.

Verse 13: duplicates verse 12 exactly. The only difference is that it was now the woman (i.e., the Christian wife) who was told not to divorce her unbelieving husband.

Verse 14: This verse gives the reason why the Christian wife or husband should not take the initiative in dissolving a marriage with an unbeliever. It is a difficult verse to interpret, and commentators have not generally agreed.

For: indicates that Paul was giving the reason for his previous statements.

The unbelieving husband is consecrated through his wife, and the unbelieving wife is consecrated through her husband: needs to be modified at two points. *Through* should be "in relation to." The Greek is "in the wife . . . in the brother." The thought is that the consecration took place by reason of their marital relation. *Consecrated* is a word usually used of Christians alone, referring to conversion, but this sense does not fit the context. "Consecration" means "to be made holy" in the sense of belonging to God, not in an ethical sense. The thought seems to be that a secondary relation to God was conferred upon the unbelieving spouse, unbelieving though he was, by his union with a believer.

How is that so? The purpose of Paul was not to answer that question. His purpose was to assure the Christian that he or she was not contaminated by marriage with an unbeliever, that it was possible to live a Christian life in such a union. The answer to our question must be stated primarily in negative terms. Paul did not mean that the unbeliever was automatically made a Christian by marriage to a Christian. Perhaps what he meant was that marriage to a Christian created a relationship to God for the unbeliever which, while it fell short of that of a Christian, was certainly far superior to one whose whole life was pagan. Thus, one Christian spouse made the home a Christian home. Perhaps the Corinthians

---

[1] Edwards points out that this does not mean that Paul's instructions were uninspired.

had believed the contrary: that one pagan spouse made the home a pagan home. Paul's purpose was to show that this was not necessarily true.

Otherwise: that is, if the unbeliever were not consecrated by his union with the believer.

Your children: the children of the parents involved, not the children of the congregation.

Would be unclean, but as it is they are holy: a difficult passage. Three opinions [1] have been given concerning Paul's meaning: (1) The children of mixed marriages would be legitimate. (2) The children of mixed marriages would be subject to Christian influence and be led to conversion. (3) The children of mixed marriages were in the covenant and had a right to baptism, the sign of the covenant. Most of these opinions reflect the ecclesiastical beliefs of the commentators in question and are not entirely satisfactory as explanations of Paul's thought. One thing is commonly accepted: "This verse throws no light on the question of infant baptism." [2]

Perhaps the answer may be found by noticing that *holy* is a form of the same Greek word which is translated *consecrated* above. Thus, the holiness of the child is of the same nature as the holiness of the unbelieving spouse. It speaks of a privileged relationship to God, not of a personal element of character. The child of a Christian home is *holy* in the sense that he is related to God through the Christian parent in a way which is not true of the child in a pagan home. Of course, this will inevitably, or should, involve his exposure to Christian influences, teachings, and witness. I would like to think that the thought of Christian influence was in Paul's mind, but it seems too much like reading my thoughts into his mind. Perhaps we must leave the expression without full explanation because we do not have the clue to the background which called forth the discussion. It is probable that Paul was dealing with a real problem that existed in Corinth, and we cannot fully understand the answer without knowledge of the problem.

Verse 15: turns to another aspect of the same situation.

But if the unbelieving partner desires to separate, let it be so: This is the opposite of the case assumed in verses 12–13. The unbelieving partner does not consent to share the home of a believer. He wants to separate himself. The middle voice indicates that the unbeliever takes the initiative rather than the believer. In such a case, he is to be permitted to go.

In such a case: when the unbelieving partner takes the initiative in the separation. Probably several such cases occurred in Corinth. The question would naturally arise concerning the obligation of the Christian.

The brother or sister: metaphors for fellow Christians.

Is not bound: "has not been enslaved." The verb is perfect, pointing to a past act with continuing results. The negative denies that marriage constitutes a permanent enslavement. *Bound* is the verbal form of the Greek noun which means "slave." This whole word group, in the Greek language, was attached to the thought of involuntary servitude. While Paul often used words of this group to define his voluntary servitude to Christ, it is probable

---

[1] These opinions are cited by Edwards from previous commentators.
[2] Cf. ICC.

that the common meaning should prevail here. Thus, it is the ties of
marriage which are in mind. Paul felt that the Christian was not bound by
indissoluble ties to an unbelieving spouse who wished to be separated.
Some have felt that this verse implied a right to remarry (Parry). I doubt
that Paul would have thought so. A Christian whose spouse had left him
would be considered one of the unmarried. It is possible that Paul's own
marital experience is seen in the verse.

For God has called us to peace: The connection of this expression is
debated. Some connect it with the whole discussion (vss. 12 ff.). In this
case, Christian peace would be maintained by mutual agreement to continue
the marriage quite as much as by nonresistance to the breaking of it.
Others, probably with more reason, connect it with the immediate context.
For translates a Greek particle which is usually continuative in significance.
Called is Paul's special word for the dynamic act of God in making one a
Christian. *Called* is in the perfect tense, indicating a present reality based
on a past act. *Peace* describes the condition into which God called men.
Usually, in Paul's language, *peace* meant far more than the absence of
strife. It referred to the general well-being of life. The thought is that the
Christian, by refusing to oppose the separation, may continue his life in
the atmosphere of peace which is his privilege.

A minor textual problem exists in the text. Some texts read "you"
instead of *us.* The manuscript evidence is about evenly divided; perhaps
the internal evidence favors *us.* By that I mean that a later copyist likely
would be more inclined to change *us* to "you" to make it conform to the
context. It would be more difficult to imagine a copyist changing "you" to
us. Since the meaning of the verse is not materially changed in either case,
we need not be overly concerned about it.

Verse 16: This verse is again ambiguous from our viewpoint. It can be
taken as another reason why the separation of the unbelieving spouse
should not be opposed. Thus, Paul's admonition would be against risking
the disruption of peace to maintain the marriage in the hope of bringing
the unbeliever to salvation. On the other hand, it can be taken as a reason
for trying to maintain the marriage if the unbelieving partner is willing (cf.
vss. 12–13). If so, Paul's question would hold out a hope for the salvation
of the unbeliever as a reason for maintaining the marriage. The RSV translation well conserves the ambiguity of the Greek text. Lightfoot's arguments
for the second interpretation are cogent. He doubted that the Corinthian
Christians would have been using such an argument in favor of maintaining the marriage; he also doubted that Paul would have urged the uncertainty of the result as a reason for seeking freedom. On the other hand,
the immediate context calls for the first interpretation. The verse should
then be taken as an attempt to ease the conscience of the Christian who was
faced with the choice of accepting the separation.

Wife . . . Husband: addresses the Christians facing the decision. The
wife is again addressed first. Perhaps this order is based on the fact that
unbelieving husbands would be more likely to want to break up the marriage
than unbelieving wives.

How do you know: The particle implies the extent of knowledge. The
question would be, "How sure are you?" If our interpretation of Paul's

thought is correct, the expression would indicate the improbability of the conversion of a spouse who, purely on religious grounds, wished to depart from a Christian.

Whether you will save your husband: an ellipsis. Paul was not thinking of the wife or husband as actually saving the unbeliever but as being the human agent through whom God would save them.

4. Christians Should Not Be Concerned to Change Their Outward Circumstances (7:17–24)

From this discussion of the unmarried, the married, and mixed marriages, Paul turned to the general principle which applied to marriage as well as to other aspects of the Christian life. Since the Christian's main concern is his relationship with God and his service for Christ, he should not be overly concerned about things in his life which do not have spiritual significance in themselves. Paul was writing with the conviction that "the appointed time" had grown "very short" (vs. 29) and "in view of the impending distress" (vs. 26). Thus, the application of his teachings to a continuing life in the world when the coming of Christ has been long delayed must not be rigid. His principle is valid, but the applications of that principle which Paul made were dictated by his times and by his expectancy as well as by the leadership of the Holy Spirit.

The principle was stated (vs. 17). An application was made to the problem of circumcision (vss. 18–19). The principle was restated in slightly different form (vs. 20). An application was made to the problem of slavery (vss. 21–23). The principle was again restated (vs. 24). If we take the applications of the principle as explanations of it, it may have permanent validity. The principle was that one should "remain in the state in which he was called" (vs. 20). In regard to circumcision, the application was absolute—no change was to be sought or accepted. In regard to slavery, the application was modified—no change was to be sought, but change was to be accepted if offered.

Verse 17: the first statement of the principle. Literally, the verse reads: "Only, to each as the Lord apportioned, each as God has called, thus let him continue to walk." The RSV seeks to smooth out the roughness of the Greek and in so doing prejudices the interpretation.

Let every one lead the life: a justified translation of the Greek, which means "let him continue to walk." "Walk" is a common New Testament metaphor for living a life. *Every one* gathers up the two occurrences of "each." The emphasis is upon individual decision. Paul did not mean to lay down a rigid regulation which men were forced to follow. He meant to state a guiding principle for decisions which men must make.

Which the Lord has assigned to him: literally, "to each as the Lord apportioned." *Assigned* is a poor translation. The Greek verb means "to apportion to one his share in something." What the "something" is, is not stated in this verse. Two possible interpretations are given: (1) The thing apportioned is our situation in life, the circumstances under which our life is to be lived for God. If this is the meaning, the context gives many illustrations of what is meant—unmarried, married, mixed marriage, circumcision, slavery. (2) The thing apportioned is our spiritual gift, the endument by which we are enabled to serve God and by which the direction of our service is defined. If this is the meaning, the larger context of the letter must define what is meant. Tempting as it is to spiritualize Paul's thought, the context forbids it. He was not referring, I think, to one's task in Christianity, one's gifts for service, but to one's situation in life. He regarded this situation as apportioned by the Lord (i.e., Jesus Christ). This interpretation is supported by the next clause, which should be regarded as parallel.

In which God has called him: literally, "each as God called." *Called* is the dynamic call to conversion. God, in Paul, was always the author of this call. *In which* is justified by the fact that the Greek "as" refers to the outward situation of life. Thus, the thought was that God had called a man in his own situation and that this situation was apportioned to him by the Lord even before his call.

This is my rule in all the churches: states that Paul's letter to Corinth was based on his universal practice in the churches. *My rule* (literally, "I ordain") is a military term which means the distribution of the troops for the coming battle. Paul thought of the churches as militant bodies of Christ whose task it was to win the world for their Lord. Thus, he arranged the people in the ranks to take full advantage of their strength.

The reason for Paul's thinking should be obvious. The Christian gospel was a revolutionary message. It taught the equality of all men and women in Christ. It would have been natural for the new converts to transfer this sense of equality to the common situations of life. They would have been prone to take it as a directive to change those situations. Thus women would have thought that the structure of the home should be changed to fit the new situation. Slaves would have thought that they should have freedom. This attitude is understandable, but it would have been fatal to the Christian mission to have changed the gospel into a social force. It always is fatal to Christian witness to make Christianity primarily a social message. Paul recognized this. He counseled restraint. The gospel will work and has worked its social reformations, but it has done so in the manner of leaven rather than by revolution.

Verse 18: applies the general principle to circumcision.

Was any one at the time of his call: when he became a Christian. Another instance of Paul's use of *call* for the act of God which brings one under the lordship of Christ.

Already circumcised: either a Jew or a proselyte Jew. Circumcision was the religious rite which distinguished Jews from all other people. The male Jewish child was circumcised when he was eight days old; the proselyte Jew received circumcision as a part of his initiation. Originally circumcision was the seal of God's promise to Abraham, but many Jews thought it was the guarantee of God's blessings.

Let him not seek to remove the marks of circumcision: Paul believed that circumcision or the lack of it no longer had spiritual significance. Therefore, the Jew who had become a Christian was not to seek to efface the outward evidences of his heritage as a Jew. History tells us that some Jews had actually tried to do this under other circumstances. Renegade

Jews in the time of Antiochus (cf. 1 Macc. 1:15; Josephus, *Antiquities,* XII. V. 1) had done so to avoid being recognized as Jews in gymnastic exercises.[1] We do not know that any Christian Jew had attempted this because of his conversion.

Let him not seek circumcision: Some Christian Jews believed that a Gentile who was converted to Christ must be circumcised in order to enjoy the full benefits of his salvation. This group were called Judaizers. It was concerning this very problem that the Jerusalem Council met (cf. Acts 15; Gal. 2:1–10). Perhaps some of the Corinthians were Judaizers, and the desire for circumcision constituted a minor problem at Corinth. Paul was certain that the rite of circumcision had no spiritual meaning. The Gentile convert was not to seek circumcision.

Verse 19: states the basis for Paul's admonitions in verse 18.

For neither circumcision counts for anything nor uncircumcision: The rite has no significance for the living of the Christian life. The context here is quite different than in Galatians. In Galatia the Gentile converts were being told that they must add circumcision to their faith in order to be saved. To them Paul wrote, "If you receive circumcision, Christ will be of no advantage to you" (Gal. 5:2). To receive circumcision on that basis would amount to a denial of the adequacy of Christ to save. Thus, it would have been a renunciation of faith itself. In Corinth, however, the case seems not to have been the same. If circumcision were urged at all, it was urged on the ground that reception of the rite would add to the quality of Christian character. In dealing with this problem, Paul was much milder. He advised against it on the ground that it did not count for anything.

But keeping the commandments of God: That is, this does count for something in the living of the Christian life. *Keeping* translates an active noun without the article and means the quality of obedience. We keep the commandments of God by obeying them. *Commandments* is also without the article in the Greek. The important distinction between a noun with the article and one without is that the article points to identity. Thus, if Paul had used the article, it would have indicated that he had particular commandments in mind. His use of the word without the article indicates that he had no particular commandments in mind but anything which had the nature or quality of a commandment of God. What he did have in mind were the practical duties of the Christian life which God had commanded. The permanent application of Paul's statement in this verse is important. It would suggest that the one who insists on a particular outward form as essential is wrong. It would also suggest that the one who insists that outward form is wrong is wrong. Outward form in religion has no real spiritual validity in and of itself.

Verse 20: repeats the substance of verse 17 with a slight, but meaningful, modification.

Every one should remain in the state in which he was called: Literally, "Each one in the calling in which he was called, in this let him remain." The RSV translation is justified by the context. Paul's concern was that the Corinthians should realize that their primary business was being Chris-

---

[1] Edwards.

tians. All outward circumstances of life were relatively unimportant. However, the context shows that this principle was not absolute. Paul did not believe that one must remain *in the state,* the outward circumstance of life, in which he became a Christian (cf. vs. 21). He did believe that changing the outward circumstances of life should not become a major concern of the Christian. "The calling in which he was called" should not be taken here as the Christian vocation. The idea is not of the circumstances to which one is called, but the circumstances in which he was called (cf. 1 Cor. 1:26 for another instance of the word in this sense).

Verse 21: an application of this principle to slavery.

Were you a slave when called?: shows that Paul was thinking in verse 20 about the circumstances that one was in when he was called. Slavery was common in Paul's day. Scholars have estimated that the slave population of the Roman Empire constituted as much as one half of the total. Many slaves became Christians (cf. the letter to Philemon).

Never mind: Do not let that be a matter about which to worry. A slave could be a good Christian (Eph. 6:5–8; Col. 3:22). Paul was not approving of slavery as such. He was merely saying that it did not constitute an insurmountable obstacle to the Christian life. This fact has been proved over and over again in history. However, we must not forget that Christianity contained the seed which eventually banished slavery from the civilized world.

But if you can gain your freedom: if the opportunity to be free arises without your making it a matter of major concern.

Avail yourself of the opportunity: literally, "use it rather." Two opposite interpretations have been given to this admonition—"remain a slave" and "accept your freedom." Both interpretations are possible and have their supporters. If the first is accepted, Paul would have been saying that the Christian slave, although he had the opportunity to be free, should remain a slave and make use of that station in the service of God.[1] If the second is accepted, the Christian slave was admonished to accept his freedom and use that to serve God.[2] In this case, this command would be a modification of verse 20.

Though neither the context nor the Greek compels either interpretation, I would be inclined to accept the RSV translation as correct. It is not possible to be dogmatic. One must decide on the basis of what he feels Paul had in mind. This is always dangerous, because our own subjective feelings on the subject of slavery are such that we naturally want to make Paul a supporter of them. Interestingly, Origen took the slavery to refer to marriage and took the clause as recommending liberty.[3] He does not seem to have convinced anyone else that this was Paul's thought.

Verse 22: The connection of this verse is doubtful. It depends on our interpretation of verse 21. It may give the reason why the Christian slave should accept his freedom, or it may state the reason why the Christian slave should not be concerned about his freedom. I would be inclined to

---

[1] Edwards supports this interpretation.
[2] Morris supports this view.
[3] Cf. Lightfoot.

connect it with "never mind," whatever may be the meaning of the second clause in verse 21.

For he who was called in the Lord as a slave is a freedman of the Lord: The Lord has emancipated him in the area of life that really counts. This does not mean that the Lord has freed him from slavery to the Lord, but from slavery to sin (cf. Gal. 5:1). The language suggests the formula of emancipation which was common in ordinary affairs. A slave could purchase his freedom by depositing a price in the temple of his deity. This was done with the consent of the owner and was really a fictitious purchase of the slave by the deity so that human owners would no longer have any authority over him. *Of the Lord* suggests the new ownership that takes primacy over human ownership.

Likewise he who was free when called is a slave of Christ: no longer his own boss but obligated to obey his new spiritual Master in all things. Since this condition applies to most modern Christians, it is well to take notice of its implications. Conversion means surrender to the lordship of Christ, not merely trusting Christ to save us from the consequences of our sins. Too often this fact is ignored by preachers and people alike.

Verse 23: a digression suggested by the language which Paul had been using.

You: is plural. Paul was no longer speaking to the slaves but to the entire congregation.

Were bought with a price: recalls 1 Corinthians 6:20 and applies to all Christians. Both the slave and the free had been bought and existed under new ownership. They belonged to God. The price was the death of Christ on the cross. Sometimes, in the New Testament, his death is considered as the price of man's liberation from sin; sometimes it is considered as the price by which God purchased men and became their owner. Each sense complements the other.

Do not become slaves of men: It is improbable that this admonition is to be taken literally. Paul was not thinking of deliberate bondage in the social sense. It is much more likely that Paul meant: "Do not let men become the rulers of your spiritual lives." The temptation to do this is constant. All Christians are tempted to let some external circumstance, some opinion of their fellowmen, violate God's right to absolute ownership in their lives.

Verse 24: the third repetition of the principle (cf. vss. 17, 20).

With God: the only change in the verse from previous statements. *With* may mean "in the presence of," "in the household of," or "on the side of." Perhaps the last meaning is the true one in this context. It forms a perfect antithesis to the thought of verse 23: "Do not become slaves of men." Paul meant that the Christian's attachment should be with God and not with men. The idea would be that our outward circumstances of life should not be permitted to interfere with our primary devotion to God.

5. Fathers of Virgin Daughters Were Given Advice (7:25–38)

This paragraph is difficult to interpret; and the RSV has compounded that difficulty by its paragraph divisions and its translation, both of which leave much to be desired. First, it is to be noted that the paragraph is about virgins, not the "unmarried" (vs. 25) nor the "betrothed" (vs. 36). The reason for these unhappy translations will be discussed in relation to verses 36–38, but one needs to be aware that the word "virgin" (Greek, *parthenos*) is used a total of six times in this paragraph. The RSV translation is mixed: "unmarried" (vs. 25); "girl" (vss. 28–34); "betrothed" (vss. 36–38). Second, the subject is the same throughout this paragraph, though Paul did not answer the question directly until verses 36–38.

Finally, the difficulty of interpretation is compounded by the supposition that practices which arose much later in Christian history, and were never approved by the main stream of Christianity, were current in Corinth. Some have thought that Paul was discussing the so-called Joseph marriages of later Christianity. In these marriages men and women with a vow of virginity lived together as husband and wife but did not engage in sexual intercourse. At least this was the theory. The practice often turned out to be the opposite. There is no evidence of this kind of arrangement in Corinth. If there had been such a practice, Paul would have condemned it. Paul believed that marriage had as one of its main purposes the satisfaction of sexual impulses. He certainly would not have approved of an arrangement which was sure to fan such impulses to a blaze while demanding that they should not be satisfied.

The thought of the section does have some progress. Paul first pointed to the source of the advice which he was to give (vs. 25). He then discussed the bearing of the "impending distress" on the living of a Christian life (vss. 26–31). Next, he discussed the basis of his opinion of marriage (vss. 32–35). Finally, he answered the question which seemed to have to do with the father's action with regard to virgin daughters who wished to get married (vss. 36–38).

(1) The source of the advice (7:25)

Verse 25: Now concerning: indicates a question of the church posed to Paul.

The unmarried: rather, "the virgins." The use of the article is a further indication that a specific group of virgins was under discussion. It is debated whether Paul meant both women and men. The Greek word is used in Revelation 14:4 in a symbolic sense for those "who have not defiled themselves with women." Thus, it is possible for the Greek word to be used for either sex. However, this does not seem to be the case in this verse. Paul had already discussed the case of the male "unmarried" (cf. vs. 8). In this section he discussed the case of the female virgins.

I have no command of the Lord: certainly excludes a recorded saying of the Lord; may exclude a direct revelation. It is probable that Paul only meant that there was no recorded saying of Jesus dealing with this particular situation.

But I give my opinion: advice based upon considered judgment. Paul was not speaking of a mere personal opinion or preference. On the other hand, he was not speaking of an apostolic opinion which would be based on authority. Somewhere between these two extremes is the meaning of *opinion* here.

As one who by the Lord's mercy is trustworthy: states the basis on which the Corinthians were asked to accept his advice. It was the advice of one who had been a recipient of the Lord's mercy. No doubt, this expression refers to Paul's conversion and appointment to apostleship. The idea involved is that one who has known such mercy can be considered trustworthy. This does not mean so much that his advice was trustworthy but that he himself was faithful to his Lord. A strong reluctance seems to have come over Paul as he faced this problem. He was very careful to prepare the Corinthians for his advice, not only by pointing out the absence of a direct command from the Lord, but by showing some evidence of uncertainty. The advice which follows is not based on moral considerations but on practical considerations. Perhaps this is why Paul was loath to speak with his usual assurance.

(2) The "impending distress" (7:26–31)

This material seems to suggest that Paul considered the coming of Christ imminent, and that the woes which he thought would precede that event were also imminent. He stated this fact and its general implication (vs. 26), went on to a discussion of its implications for marriage (vss. 27–28), and then made a rather obscure application to many areas of life (vss. 29–31).

Verse 26: states the fact of Paul's expectancy and its general application to life.

I think: emphasizes the fact that Paul was speaking of what was expedient rather than of what was right. One needs only to compare this statement with the statement: "This is my rule in all the churches" (vs. 17), to sense the change of tone. In the previous division he laid down with complete assurance a principle of right. Here he expressed, somewhat more than tentatively, his opinion.

In view of the impending distress it is well for a person to remain as he is: leaves out some Greek words which the translators considered redundant. In full the verse reads: "I think therefore this good to be in view of the present [or impending] distress, that good for a man to be thus." The RSV represents an interpretation of each of these elements of the sentence which may or may not be correct. We are not criticizing the RSV for being an interpretation; all translations are. Our discussion must consider the possibilities of the verse.

First, RSV omits the words "this good to be" in the first part of the verse, considering them to be redundant. To this Lightfoot objects. He would take these words to mean, "this is good to begin with." If he is correct, Paul was expressing the fundamental axiom, the starting point of the discussion which followed. This verse would then be parallel with verse 1 of this chapter. Most other commentators do not take notice of this omission. Findlay does, however, agreeing with Lightfoot that the omitted phrase means "good in principle." [1] We are inclined to agree with these two scholars.

---

[1] G. G. Findlay, *St. Paul's First Epistle to the Corinthians*, "The Expositor's Greek Testament," Vol. II, W. Robertson Nicoll, ed., Wm. B. Eerdmans Publishing Company, Grand Rapids, Michigan. Reprint edition. Henceforth referred to as EGT.

Second, *impending distress* literally means "present distress." RSV gives "present" as a marginal reading. However, most scholars recognize *impending* as a possible meaning but with the sense of being imminent, i.e., immediately on the horizon. The question is: Was Paul talking about the troubles attached to marriage, the persecutions which threatened Christians, or the end of the world? Each of these interpretations has been given, but the weight of evidence seems to be in favor of the last. Paul was of the opinion that the end of the world was on the horizon. Perhaps his troubles at Ephesus and other signs of the gathering storm were the basis of his opinion. It was commonly felt that the end of the world would be preceded by distress. Paul felt that his own troubles were a foretaste of that distress. The word occurs in Luke 21:23 in the context of prophecies of the future by Jesus; in other passages it refers to the persecutions of Paul (1 Thess. 3:7; 2 Cor. 6:4; 12:10). We must remember that Paul did not say that the end of the world was near in the sense of a doctrine revealed from God. He expressed it as his opinion. Maybe his words referred only to the coming storm of persecutions.

Finally, we must ask: Does "good for a man to be thus" mean *it is well for a person to remain as he is?* While the expression could be taken in other senses, this translation seems to be correct in this context. Paul was thus recommending that no change be sought in outward status.

Verse 27: applies this thought to marriage.

Are you bound to a wife?: married. *Bound* is a perfect tense of a word meaning "to bind." This is a different word in Greek from the one used in verse 15. The perfect tense speaks of a settled condition.

Do not seek to be free: stop trying to be loosed. The form of the prohibition indicates that they should stop what they were doing. The problem was a real one in Corinth. *Free* means free of the marriage ties.

Are you free from a wife: unmarried. *Free* translates a perfect tense of the verb "to be loosed." The perfect tense indicates a permanent state of freedom from marriage ties. Some have taken it to refer to a man, once married, who was now free either by death or divorce. It may refer to such persons, but it would apply equally well to bachelors.

Do not seek marriage: breaks the parallelism of the first three clauses but expresses the meaning of *bound* and *free*. The translation is literal.

Verse 28: removes any suspicion that Paul might have thought marriage to be sinful.

But if you marry: views marriage as a distinct possibility. *But if* is intensive in the Greek and should read, "but even if." *Marry* is the classical word for marrying. This needs to be kept in mind in view of our discussion in verses 36–38.

You do not sin: literally, "there is no sin in that." Paul did not say that one who married had done "well." However, see verse 38. His statement did take this discussion out of the realm of right and wrong and placed it in the realm of expediency.

And if a girl marries she does not sin: parallel with the previous statement, except that the subject is *girl* (Greek, "virgin").

Yet those who marry will have worldly troubles: makes the advice not to marry the expedient course. *Worldly troubles* has the emphatic position in the clause and translates words which literally mean "tribulations in the flesh." Paul was talking of the ever-present troubles of married life. *Troubles* translates a word which may refer to the tribulations of the last days or in times of persecution. It comes from the Greek word which means "to press together," and was used of pressing the grapes to extract the juice. Our modern word "pressures" would be equivalent but would not carry the sense of impending distress. *Worldly* means "in the flesh." "Flesh" usually had for Paul overtones of sinfulness. It meant man on the merely human level, apart from the indwelling of the Holy Spirit. Thus, Paul meant that the tribulations which marriage causes would be in the human sphere of life.

And I would spare you that: his aim as their spiritual adviser. He was concerned not only with their spiritual welfare, but with their fleshly welfare.

Verse 29: This verse introduces a new thought with reference to marriage and other outward circumstances of life.

I mean: literally, "this I am saying." There is a note of solemnity in the expression. "This" does not refer to what precedes but to what follows. His solemnity of expression was meant to impress upon the Corinthians a feeling of the importance of what would follow. He had counseled no change in their state; now he insisted upon a change of attitude.

The appointed time: There is no word for *appointed* in the Greek, though the word for *time* may have this meaning. *Time* is not *chronos* (temporal time) but *kairos* (fitting time). It was almost a technical term for the time before the end of the world (ICC), and was used in this sense in Romans 13:11. Paul did not always use it in this sense, but this seems to be the sense here. Some commentators have taken the expression to refer to the imminence of death. Though this interpretation makes good sense, it does not fit the context here.

Has grown very short: translates a Greek participial form which means "has been drawn together." Though the verb can be used in the sense of "dejected" or "depressed" with reference to persons, its sense here is "limited." The passive is important. *Time* had not *grown very short;* it had been shortened. Possibly Paul was thinking of an act of God; he may have been thinking of the pressure of persecution as the agent which shortened the time.

From now on: expresses well the meaning of the Greek in this context.

Let those who have wives live as though they had none: the first of five similar admonitions. The exact meaning of Paul's admonitions is not clear. In general, it seems that he was insisting upon a change of attitudes or values in the light of the coming end. For a married man to live as though he did not have a wife would mean that he was to ignore the claims of domestic duties. Whether this meant an absolute renunciation of the responsibilities of marriage or only an admonition against being absorbed with them is uncertain. Perhaps verses 32–35 provide a good commentary on Paul's meaning. If so, he meant that the married man was not to be concerned with pleasing his wife, but to be concerned with pleasing the Lord. At any rate, this admonition would show why Paul felt that marriage was not desirable under such circumstances.

Verse 30: And those who mourn as though they were not mourning: Those who had earthly things to mourn were to dry their tears, realizing that their earthly troubles would soon be over. Instead of mourning, they were to rejoice over the coming glory. This is good advice for all times, though the immediacy of the coming of Christ may not be so apparent.

And those who rejoice as though they were not rejoicing: Those who had earthly ground for rejoicing were to ignore it and rejoice rather in the coming glory. Joys based on earthly circumstances are always transient. It is better to find a heavenly basis.

And those who buy as though they had no goods: It is assumed that those who buy, buy for the purpose of accumulation of wealth in the world. The temptation of the Christian is to think of houses and lands and goods as having real and lasting value. This is true only if life on earth is lasting. In the light of the coming of Christ, Paul insisted that the Corinthians should no longer regard their earthly treasures as of real value. Jesus had much the same to say, but without any implications of the shortness of time. The shortness of time would only emphasize the values which should guide the Christian in all times.

Verse 31: And those who deal with the world as though they had no dealings with it: a poor translation. Literally the clause reads: "and those using the world as not using it to the full." The thought was that men were to use the world to satisfy the necessities of life, but they were not to overuse it. That is, they were not to allow the things which the world had to offer to absorb all their interests. This is good advice for modern as well as ancient days.

For the form of this world is passing away: refers to the transitoriness of the world as we know it. *For* introduces the reason for the immediately preceding admonitions. *The form* is the outer appearance or shape of things, what can be apprehended by the senses. *The world* probably refers to the human society rather than the physical universe. *Is passing away* is a present tense of a verb which means to "pass by." The same verb was used of Jesus' passing by Jericho (Matt. 20:30). Thus, like a moving panorama the shape of human society is passing along. This is always true, but Paul had an immediate sense of a final passing away.

(3) Marriage a hindrance to Christian service (7:32–35)

In this paragraph Paul returned to his main subject of the chapter. To marry or not to marry was the question. Paul defended his central thesis that it was well not to marry by pointing to the impossibility of serving Christ with an undivided mind if one were married.

Verse 32: I want you to be free from anxieties: states his general desire. *Free from anxieties* translates a single Greek negative adjective. The exact form is used only here and in Matthew 28:14. However, verbal forms of the same root meaning are found in Matthew 6:25–34, where Jesus taught that one should "stop worrying" about earthly and material things. Perhaps this passage in the Sermon on the Mount formed the background of Paul's thought. He wanted the Corinthians "unworried" over earthly matters.

The unmarried man is anxious about the affairs of the Lord, how to please the Lord: indicates that Paul did not want them free from all anxieties, but free of the wrong anxieties. He wanted them to be anxious about the affairs of the Lord. Since he considered this possible only for the unmarried man he taught that one should remain unmarried. *The Lord* is Jesus Christ. *The affairs,* literally, "the things," would be all spiritual matters. *How to please the Lord* indicates the direction of the Christian's concern. Paul stated that this was true, but the statement is to be taken as the ideal, not necessarily as fact in all cases. Certainly it should be true.

Verse 33: But the married man is anxious about worldly affairs: the things of the world. His concern is with the things that belong essentially to the human sphere of life, things with no real spiritual significance. *Is anxious* is not to be taken absolutely as if this were the only direction of his concern. It is, however, a statement of general truth. If one is married he must, to some degree, be concerned with the things that pertain to earthly existence.

How to please his wife: indicates the direction of the married man's concern. Instead of being able to give complete devotion to pleasing the Lord, he must give some attention to pleasing his wife.

Verse 34: And his interests are divided: literally, "he has been divided." The perfect tense indicates a present reality based on a past event—in this case, his marriage. The text has many variants in this verse, but the RSV solution seems to be somewhat the best. Thus, this clause goes with the preceding verse and is a description of the state of the married man's mind. Being a Christian, he desires to please the Lord; being a husband, he desires to please his wife. This constituted for Paul a division of interests which was a hindrance to his Christian life.

The unmarried woman: the widow or divorced woman.

Girl: i.e., the virgin. Some variants to the text qualify *girl* with the adjective "unmarried." This seems unnecessary since the word itself implies the fact that the girl is unmarried.

Is anxious about the affairs of the Lord: parallel with the same expression in verse 32.

How to be holy in body and spirit: does not imply that the unmarried woman or virgin is morally superior to the married woman. The clause expresses how the unmarried women seek to please the Lord. They do so by seeking to be *holy,* separated to the Lord, in every phase of life. *Body* does not refer to the physical body but to the human life lived in the world. Thus, even in the affairs that relate to society she is free to be the Lord's. *Spirit* refers to her life in the realm of spiritual matters. Her religious devotion can be without hindrance.

But the married woman is anxious about worldly affairs, how to please her husband: parallel in structure and thought to verse 33. Paul did not add in her case that she had been "divided," but the thought is implied.

Verse 35: I say this for your own benefit: states the motive of Paul in discussing these things. Remember that he had not yet come to the question the church had asked. His discussion had digressed to general, but related, matters. The Greek word for *benefit* is used only here and in 2 Corinthians 10:33, where Paul said that he was not seeking his own "advantage." He was seeking theirs. The expression again emphasizes that Paul was not speaking of right and wrong in this passage.

Not to lay any restraint upon you: statement of purpose from the negative viewpoint. "Lay a restraint" literally means "throw a noose." *Restraint* translates the Greek word for the halter or noose by which animals were caught and guided. Paul's intention was not to fetter their movements, but to provide guidance for them in the exercise of their freedom. This expression denied any attempt to exercise personal authority over the lives of the Corinthians on Paul's part.

But: a strong adversative conjunction meaning "but, on the contrary."

To promote good order: a puzzling phrase. *To promote* translates a Greek preposition which might better be translated "with a view to." The basic meaning of the preposition is "toward." *Good order* translates a single Greek compound adjective composed of two elements, one meaning "well" and the other "shape or form." The meaning would thus be: "with a view to good appearances." However, "good appearances" has a connotation in modern language which is foreign to this context. Perhaps the meaning has to do with that part of the Christian's conduct which is visible to the eyes of men. This should be consistent with the profession of the Christian whether he is married or not. Each one has his problems; he must solve them in the way that is proper to the Christian. There is no suggestion in the phrase that either marriage or the lack of it is essential to Christian devotion.

And to secure your undivided devotion to the Lord: coordinated with the previous phrase and parallel in construction. *To secure* has no Greek equivalent. The preposition in the previous phrase, meaning "with a view to," carries over to this phrase. *Devotion* translates another compound Greek adjective composed of three elements, one meaning "well," another "beside," and the last "seat." Thus the thought of the word is faithful attendance upon a person or thing. The RSV translation, *devotion,* can be accepted in this sense. *Undivided* translates a Greek adverb which means "undistracted." A good commentary on the word is Jesus' comment to Martha: "You are anxious and troubled about many things" (Luke 10:41; cf. vs. 40—the positive verbal form of this same word is used). The meaning is clear. Paul was concerned for fear the Corinthians would be "divided" in their devotion (cf. vs. 34). His discussion in the preceding verses (32–35) had the aim of preventing that attitude. Two suggestions had been given: (1) that they remain unmarried or (2) that they live as if they were not married. His purpose was that they might live consistently before the world and might serve the Lord, undistracted by outside interests. Whether we can agree with his suggestions or not, we can certainly find nothing wrong with his purpose.

(4) Advice to the father of a virgin daughter (7:36–38)

My understanding of these verses is not in agreement with the RSV translation. According to my understanding, the question posed by the church concerned the attitude of the father of a virgin daughter. In those days the daughter did not have power to arrange her own marriage. Social custom dictated that the father should do this. This opinion was the basis of the King James Version, the American Standard Version, and several modern translations. However, an opposite opinion lies behind the RSV translation. It is that the question concerned the attitude of a man toward his virgin partner in a "Joseph marriage." [1] In such marriages men and women lived together as husband and wife, sometimes even sleeping in the same bed, but did not consummate their marriage by sexual intercourse. As suggested above, such attempts were made in later church history; but there is no evidence that they existed in the New Testament period, unless this passage is evidence.

I do not mean to leave the impression that the RSV translation is without any basis. It has two bases. One has to do with the meaning of the Greek word which RSV translates "if his passions are strong" and the KJV translates "if she pass the flower of her age." These seemingly contradictory translations of the same Greek phrase represent possible translations which will be discussed in our comments on verse 36. The other basis has to do with the meaning of the Greek verb which both RSV and KJV translate "let them marry" (vs. 36). However, the context in RSV demands that this phrase be given the meaning, "he should marry her," while the KJV context demands that it be given the meaning, "permit her to get married." I will comment on both of these points below.

Verse 36: This verse is the direct answer of Paul to the church's question.

If any one thinks that he is not behaving properly toward his betrothed: KJV, "but if any man think that he behaveth himself uncomely toward his virgin." *Bethrothed* is based on the Greek word *parthenos,* and should properly be translated "virgin." [2] The RSV translation is based on the suppositions discussed above. The American Standard Version translates it, "virgin daughter." This translation is based on agreement with my position, but it is not a proper translation. The rest of the conditional phrase has the same meaning in both translations. *If,* a particle in the Greek assuming a reality, means that such cases actually existed in Corinth. *Any one* represents the indefinite pronoun and can refer to the father as well as the male partner in a celibate marriage. *Not behaving properly* means to behave in a way that violates the common notions of decency. Since the father was in Paul's mind, the discredit of such behavior was upon him. This consisted of his refusal to arrange a marriage for his daughter. But why was this improper? It could be because he forced her to become an old maid, but it is more likely that the thought is that he subjected her to the danger of seduction (Lenski). If this is correct, the word reflects Paul's thought in verse 2. *Thinks* means to come to the opinion that a thing is true. The same word is used in verse 26 of Paul's views. Of course, in actual practice there would be some basis for this view, and this is given in the next phrase.

If his passions are strong: KJV, "if she pass the flower of her age." *If*

---

[1] Cf. Moffatt, who thinks it was a spiritual bride.

[2] Ford has an unusual suggestion. He thinks the question was one of a Levirate marriage and that "virgin" should be translated "widow." His arguments, however, are not compelling. (J. Massingberd Ford, "Levirate Marriage in St. Paul," *New Testament Studies,* vol. 10, pp. 361–365.) Referred to hereafter as Ford.

assumes a possibility but not a reality. Paul considers this probable, at least in some cases. *His* could just as well be "her." The pronoun is not expressed but is based on the third person of the verb, which can refer to either a male or a female subject. The real problem is the next expression. *Passions are strong* (KJV, "pass the flower of her age") translates a Greek adjective, *uperakmos,* composed of two elements, the first meaning "beyond" and the second "prime" or "highest point." Our English word "acme" is derived from the second element in the word. The adjectival form used here can be either masculine or feminine. Most of the commentators take this word to refer to the virgin, meaning that she is past the bloom of youth (Lightfoot, Lenski, Parry, ICC, Robertson). However, some modern translators take the view that it refers to the man and means that his passions may go beyond his control. James Moffatt argues for the RSV translation on the basis that there would be no need to marry off a woman after she had reached a certain age of maturity. He therefore considers it "obvious" that Paul was dealing with a case of two young people involved in a vow of celibacy while living together. The girl had told the man that this was not fair to her. He was aware of irresistible sexual impulses.[1]

Most recognized Greek lexicons give the primary meaning of the word as "past the bloom of youth." It seems to me that all the objections to my opinion can be met by two considerations. (1) "Past the bloom of age" would refer in the ancient world to sexual maturity, not to spinsterhood by modern standards.[2] Before the girl reached that age, the father would need to have no misgiving. Afterward, he would be faced with the question of the girl's ability to withstand sexual temptation. Thus, the idea of sexual passion is implied, but it is the sexual passion of the unmarried girl who has passed adolescence and is physically ready for marriage. (2) It was the father's business in the ancient world to arrange a marriage for his daughter. Marriage was not the choice of the girl or of her suitor. Thus, if we take the feeling of impropriety as describing the opinion of the father with a marriageable daughter, based upon her sexual maturity and perhaps upon signs of sexual desire on her part, our interpretation makes perfectly good sense.

And if it has to be: literally, "and thus it ought to be." This follows from what has been said. The father feels that he is acting *improperly.* The girl is past her flower of sexual maturity. Now duty enters in. Marriage "ought to be." What then was the problem? It was just the thing that Paul had been discussing. If it is better to remain unmarried, would not the father be contributing to sin if he arranged the marriage?

Let him do as he wishes: let them marry—it is no sin: Paul's answer to the dilemma was that if the father arranged the marriage, he would not sin. He was therefore to do what he wished. The Greek word properly means to "give in marriage." Though this distinction was not always maintained in Paul's day, it seems to have been in his own thought. In verse 28, where it was a question of choice, he used the regular word for "marry." In this verse he changed the form of the word to "give in marriage." The reason

---

[1] Moffatt.
[2] Ford cites a passage in the Misnah which would indicate that this means a girl who has reached the age of puberty.

for the change is that he was making just that distinction. The fathers involved were to give their daughters in marriage, i.e., to arrange for their marriage. The use of this word in this context seems to compel the interpretation given above for the entire paragraph. My comments in verses 37–38 will assume that this is true.

Verse 37: This verse suggests the opposite course of action from that which was permitted. Paul made no secret of his own feelings. His "wish" was that all should remain unmarried.

But whoever is firmly established in his heart: that is, one who had no sense of misbehavior on his part. *Established* has the sense of no vacillation. This would mean that the father had no misgivings about the proper course of action with reference to his daughter. He did not fear that she would suffer seduction by being deprived of marriage.

Being under no necessity: under no external compulsion. External compulsion might come from a previous contract of marriage or in the case of a slave whose master forced him to contract marriage for his daughter. The word which rsv translates by *necessity* can refer to either inner or outer compulsion. It can even refer to distress (cf. 7:26, where it is so translated). The context here calls for the meaning of external pressures. Any other meaning would contradict the previous expression, *established in his heart.*

But having his desire under control: an impossible translation. The Greek is: "but having authority concerning his own desire." This phrase is the antithesis of the former. It is the positive aspect of one who is under no external compulsion. The idea of sexual self-control is found in verse 9, but the Greek word is entirely different.

And has determined this in his heart: the climax of the conditions. They are: (1) that he have no misgivings about his course of action, (2) that he be under no external compulsion but have the authority to act as he wishes, and (3) that he believe that his action is the best. *Determined* comes from a word which means "to judge." It implies a decision based on the exercise of judgment. *Heart,* the seat of man's will, is used here rather than "mind," though the use of thought processes in coming to a decision is not excluded.

To keep her as his betrothed: rather, "to keep his own virgin" (i.e., daughter). This is the decision of the heart to which Paul referred in the previous phrase.

He will do well: reaffirms Paul's belief that the unmarried state was preferred. The next verse shows that *well* is not to be taken as absolute or as a reference to moral right or wrong.

Verse 38: In this verse Paul stated explicitly what we have been saying was true in our comments.

So that he who marries his betrothed does well: wrong translation again. It should be: "So that he who gives his virgin in marriage does well." This was the first time Paul used the expression *well* with reference to marriage.

And he who refrains from marriage will do better: rather, "and the one not giving in marriage will do better." The main point to notice, since the other words have been discussed above, is *better.* This word is the comparative of "well." Paul's whole system of values in this matter of marriage is now clear. He had been speaking of practical values based on expediency rather than of ethical values based on principles of right and wrong. There could be no *well* and *better* in ethical values, especially with reference to the same thing. The true antithesis of *well* in the ethical sense is wrong, not *better*. But when one speaks of what is expedient, one thing may be *well* and the opposite may be *better*.

6. The Christian Widow Was Given Advice (7:39–40)

This section could be regarded as a kind of appendix to the discussion on marriage. Paul had mentioned widows in verse 8 in the context of his advice to remain single if self-control were possible; otherwise to marry. Now he added a section about the remarriage, but reiterated his former opinion that the widow would be happier if she remained unmarried (vss. 39–40*a*). His final assertion that he thought he had the Holy Spirit should be taken as applicable to all that he had said in the chapter (vs. 40*b*).

Verse 39: A wife is bound to her husband as long as he lives: the general principle which rules the thought of marriage in the New Testament. *Bound* is a perfect passive tense of the verb which means "to tie or bind." The thought is that the wife is bound by the ties of marriage, and once bound, she remains so. *So long* translates an adverbial phrase built around the Greek word for "time." Paul used another word for "time" in verses 5 and 29 which meant a special season. The word used here refers only to time in its temporal aspect.

If the husband dies: If assumes the fact to be possible but not actual. Of course, all husbands will die, but not necessarily before their wives. *Dies* is based on the Greek word for sleep. Thus, it should read, "if the husband has fallen asleep." "Sleep" is a euphemistic expression for death. It is used in the Old Testament (Deut. 31:16; 1 Kings 11:21; 2 Chron. 12:16) as well as the New (John 11:11). It was the common Christian word for death, suggesting not only the fact of death but also the hope of resurrection.

She is free to be married to whom she wishes: Since she had the choice, Paul returned to the use of the regular word for "marry." This is in contrast to the word used in verses 36–38 which means "to give in marriage." The widow is free from the ties of her marriage to her husband. "Free" implies the right to remarry.

Only in the Lord: limits her freedom. If she is a Christian widow, she must let spiritual considerations guide her in her choice. Does this mean that she is not to marry an unbeliever? This seems the natural meaning of the expression. Paul used the expression *in the Lord* to mean within the Christian sphere. This is in contrast with his use of the expression "in Christ Jesus," to mean a mystical union with Christ. Opinions vary, however. At the very least, the expression must mean that her remarriage must be within the limits of Christian duty; she must not forget her Christian responsibilities when she remarries. It would be my opinion that Paul meant to restrict the marriage to Christians only. His discussion of the unhappy plight of Christians involved in mixed marriages (vss. 12–16) would indicate that he would frown upon such marriages.

Verse 40: But in my judgment: "according to my opinion." To the modern reader it seems that Paul made too much of his opinion. He had expressed the same sentiment many times in the chapter. Why repeat himself so much? For one thing, he was very sure that this was good advice. For another, he repeated it in each context so that it might not be forgotten. This letter was meant to be read aloud in the church. Ancient Christians did not have the opportunity of turning back a page to see what Paul had said in another connection.

She is happier if she remains as she is: literally, "more blessed she is if she thus remains." The word for "happy" is a difficult one to translate in the New Testament. The same Greek word is used in the Beatitudes (cf. Matt. 5:3–12). It has a higher meaning than mere human happiness. It speaks of a blessedness that comes from God. The context defines it in this chapter. She is happy because she can serve the Lord without the distraction of domestic duties. Thus, as a Christian she is to be congratulated on her state. If Paul wrote the Pastoral Epistles, he seems to have contradicted himself when he said, "I would have younger widows marry" (1 Tim. 5:14). However, he was speaking to another problem there. This tends to show that his advice was to be taken as true only if the conditions existed to make it true.

And I think that I have the Spirit of God: applies to all that he had said. He wanted to assure the Corinthians that he was not speaking from human bias and prejudice. That this danger existed is proved by the number of modern Christians who have accused him of just this vice. *I think* is probably to be taken as meiosis, a figure of speech which emphasizes something by saying less than is meant. Paul believed that his advice had been given under the guidance of the Spirit of God. This does not mean that it was advice for all people in all times. Under other circumstances wise and spiritual men have differed radically from the advice given in this chapter. It does mean that his advice was best under the circumstances then existing. The one point of permanent validity must not be overlooked. The decisions of Christians in all spheres of life should be made in the light of their primary devotion to God in Christ Jesus. If Christians in all ages would make their decisions in view of that which would be most helpful for them in serving the Lord, there would be fewer mistakes to regret.

V. DISCUSSION OF THEIR QUESTION CONCERNING FOOD OFFERED TO IDOLS (8:1—11:1)

This section contains Paul's answer to another question asked by the church at Corinth in their letter. It concerned the eating of meat offered to heathen idols. The question of right and wrong would arise in two situations: (1) in relation to religious festivals held in the pagan temple or associated with the worship of the pagan god; (2) in social meals where such food was served or in buying meat in the marketplace, much of which had been offered to the pagan god and thus, in the opinion of some, contaminated.

Two groups emerge from Paul's discussion—the strong and the weak. The strong seemed to believe that no question should be raised about the matter. They reasoned that pagan gods were really nothing, that offering meat to them in no way changed the nature of the meat. Perhaps they even reasoned that it was all right for them to engage in the religious festivals in the pagan temples. The weak, on the other hand, could not shake off the habits of the past. Meat offered to idols still carried for them the taint of the pagan god and, to them, eating it even in private was a renunciation of faith in the true God.

Paul's discussion of the problem falls into five divisions. First, he laid down the basic principle that love for weaker brethren should restrict one's exercise of freedom (8:1–13). Second, he gave three examples from his own life of the suspension of personal rights for the good of others: He had waived his apostolic rights for the sake of the Corinthians (9:1–18); he had accommodated himself to the customs of others (9:19–23); he continued to subject himself to rigid spiritual discipline (9:24–27). Third, he drew an illustration of the danger of idolatry from the history of Israel (10:1–13). Fourth, he warned the Corinthians against participation in pagan festivals (10:14–22). Fifth, he suggested the use of practical wisdom in making decisions in social circumstances (10:23—11:1).

1. Love Should Control Liberty (8:1–13)

Paul's first principle was that Christian love should be the guiding concern in Christian action. Though the occasion for Paul's discussion no longer exists, the principles which it enunciates apply to a variety of situations in the lives of Christians. Paul's discussion in this chapter falls into three paragraphs: (1) He pointed out the superiority of love to knowledge (8:1–3); (2) He admitted that idols were nothing and that

[127]

Christian liberty existed (8:4–6); (3) He, nevertheless, insisted that brotherly love should guide in the application of Christian liberty (8:7–13).

(1) Love was superior to knowledge (8:1–3)

Much of Paul's discussion in this paragraph anticipated what he would say later in detail. He introduced here the main thrust of his discussion.

Verse 1: Now concerning: marks the discussion as an answer to the church's questions. Whether Paul chose the order in which they were answered, we do not know. Perhaps, if he chose the order, the fact that practical wisdom should be exercised in choices about both marriage and food offered to idols dictated the close connection of the seemingly quite different problems. The suggestion that impurity and idolatry were closely connected loses its validity if we remember that impurity was not the subject in chapter 7.[1]

Food offered to idols: translates a single Greek word of Jewish origin. The word is composed of two elements, the first meaning "idols" and the second "sacrificed." The pagan word for the same thing is found in 10:28. It simply means, "offered in sacrifice." No word for *food* is included in the Greek text, but it is implied. "Meat" would be preferable since the food involved was always meat. Meat of this kind was probably all that was available in Corinth. Unless the animal had been butchered by the Jews, it would have been offered to the idols when it was butchered. This would be true whether the meat was meant for the marketplace or for the temple.

We know that "all of us possess knowledge": probably points to a phrase included in the Corinthian letter.[2] Paul quoted from their letter and then modified or supplemented their statements. Perhaps there is a reference to the apostolic decree in Jerusalem (cf. Acts 15), but the thought there was of abstaining from the "pollutions of idols" (vs. 20), which is a much wider subject than "food offered to idols." On the whole, it is better to assume that Paul was quoting from their letter.

"Knowledge" puffs up: Paul is the only writer in the New Testament to use the word *puffs up.* It is used six times in this letter (here; 4:6, 18–19; 5:2; 13:4) and only once outside this letter (Col. 2:18). Knowledge tends to make one proud, especially if it is inadequate.[3]

But love builds up: shows the superiority of love to knowledge. *Builds up* is a metaphor for Christian growth which was commonly found in Paul's letters. *Love* translates the Greek word which is always used of God's love for men. It contains the thought of unselfish and sacrificial concern for others, rather than the thought of attraction. The best commentary on the meaning of love to Paul is found in 1 Corinthians 13, where it is regarded as the supreme gift of God.

Verse 2: points out the emptiness of imagined knowledge.

If any one imagines: This condition actually existed in Corinth. The form

---

[1] Cf. ICC. The generalization is true, but it is not relevant here.

[2] Moffatt points out that there is a touch of irony in this statement, though Paul agreed in principle with the enlightened Christians. He nevertheless condemned their complacency.

[3] I would agree with Moffatt that the truly learned are usually humble.

of *if* assumes the truth of the statement. *Imagines* points to a fancy or opinion of oneself.

That he knows something: Something is indefinite and tends to make the statement general, though Paul meant it to apply to the present question. *Knows* translates a perfect tense, indicating that the supposition is of enduring knowledge. Greek has two words for "knowledge," one meaning knowledge of facts and the other knowledge of the nature of a thing. "Know" here is the word for knowledge of the nature of a thing. Thus the imagination of knowledge with which Paul dealt is of complete and adequate knowledge, not only of facts but of the nature of something.

He does not yet know: states the emptiness of knowledge without love. *He does not . . . know* translates a single Greek verb in the aorist (past) tense. The meaning is that he did not come to know in the past.

As he ought to know: His knowledge has fallen below the standard of God's demands.[1] *Ought* translates a word which means "it is necessary." Usually in the New Testament it speaks of a necessity connected with the purpose of God. It is tempting to apply this verse generally to human knowledge, and it is applicable in this way. When anyone thinks he knows something completely and fully, this is a sure sign that he has not learned as he should. Full knowledge produces humility and consciousness of ignorance. This, however, was not Paul's intention. He took the general and applied it to the particular—the boasted knowledge of the Corinthians about "food offered to idols." The Corinthians, especially the so-called "strong," imagined that they had complete knowledge of the nature and implications of the question. They knew that idols were nothing. Therefore, the offering of food at their altars did not alter it or taint it in any way. Paul would have agreed with that view. What they did not know was that the eating of such food might become a means of destroying the weaker brother. The nature of the food and the full implications of eating it were not therefore known. They had not learned to know as it is necessary in the purpose of God that Christians should know.

Verse 3: seems to shift the subject, but does not really do so. Verse 2 speaks of a knowledge that one needs to possess as a Christian. This verse points the way to acquiring that knowledge.

But if one loves God: surprising shift of emphasis. We would have expected Paul to have said, "But if one loves his brethren." Love of brethren is obviously that for which he was aiming, but he was aware of the fact that love for brethren comes by way of love for God. *Loves* is in the present tense, pointing to continuous action. Love is not affection for God, but true devotion to God. Some people mistake admiration or affection for the beauty of God for love. Love is much more in the Christian sense of the word, especially when God is the object.

One is known by him: another surprising phrase. We would have expected Paul to say, "one comes to true knowledge." Paul, however, said something far more meaningful. *One* undoubtedly refers to the one who loves God. *Is known* means that he has been accepted into the familiar

---

[1] Allo rightly asserts that the true knowledge of God presupposes love for one's neighbor.

knowledge, has become one of God's people.[1] This is a common use of this verb in both Testaments and is sometimes called the pregnant or dynamic meaning of the term. God knows (perfect tense, indicating permanent reality) us as his own, and this implies the blessings that come from fellowship with him. The application to the full knowledge of the Corinthians is as follows: being known by God enables man to look at things from his viewpoint. Only as he does that does he come into full knowledge of the nature of anything. This is the general statement. The particular application to eating food offered to idols is clear.

(2) Idols were nothing; Christians were free (8:4–6)

In this section Paul acknowledged the truth of the knowledge which the Corinthians claimed to have (vss. 4–5) and added an exalted confession of the true God (vs. 6).

Verse 4: Hence, as to the eating of food offered to idols: indicates a return to the subject. Paul had laid down the principle on which practical decisions must be made—the principle of love. He turned next to a discussion of the validity of their knowledge. *Eating* changes the question somewhat. They had only asked about the food, wanting to know whether or not it had been contaminated. Paul wanted to shift the emphasis to the eating and the implications involved in that. The food in itself, he would have agreed, had not been contaminated; but the eating of it might be dangerous to the weaker brother. This identifies the problem dealt with in this passage and points the way to its application in modern life. The whole discussion centers around something which in itself is not sinful. In such cases, the Christian is certainly free, but his freedom of action must be limited by concern for others.

We know that "an idol has no real existence": probably refers to another statement in the letter from the church. *An idol has no real existence* is literally, "there is no idol in the world." The RSV gives a good meaning but fails to catch the exact overtones of the Greek. An idol was supposed to be a representation of a god. Since there is only one God, an idol does not really exist. This statement repudiates the whole pagan system of gods.

And that "there is no God but one": rather, "none is God but one." This statement is the fundamental premise upon which true religion is built. It has its roots in the Old Testament, being the first statement in the Jewish *Shema* which was recited by every pious Israelite both morning and evening (cf. Deut. 6:4, "Hear, O Israel: The LORD our God is one LORD"). Jesus quoted the Jewish *Shema* as the first and greatest commandment (Mark 12:29–30). Paul is said to have preached the message of one, true, living God in Athens (cf. Acts 17:22–26). We may be sure that it was one of the basic things which he had preached in Corinth. The Corinthians had quoted this saying of Paul's in their letter to him. They did not want him to think that they had forgotten this basic fact of Christianity. From these two premises—the nonexistence of idols and the oneness of God—the logical conclusion was that meat offered to idols had not been

---

[1] Cf. Morris.

contaminated. It followed that such meat, when eaten by Christians with thanksgiving to God, would be as holy as other meat which had not been offered to idols. Paul agreed with this conclusion. But he recognized that it did not settle all the problems connected with eating such meat. There was the problem of the weaker brother, who, though he accepted the premises, could not accept the conclusions.

Verse 5: recognizes that this Christian understanding was contrary to the belief of pagans.

For although there may be so-called gods in heaven or on earth: beliefs that such gods do exist. *So-called* reveals that Paul believed that the worship of pagans was of unreal beings. He would not deny that they believed in their *so-called gods;* he did deny that their gods had real existence.

As indeed there are many "gods" and many "lords": The presence of many so-called deities could not be denied. It is questionable whether this expression is a part of the quotation or a modification of Paul's thought. If the strong in faith had denied the existence of such deities, these words would have been Paul's reminder that they did exist in abundance. If, on the other hand, the strong in faith had merely denied the power of these false gods, this expression could be their contemptuous admission of their existence. The former position is more probable. Paul knew such false deities existed and were worshiped, but he believed that the worship of pagans constituted an offering "to demons and not to God" (1 Cor. 10:20).

Indeed, the existence of "gods" and "lords" could not be denied in the ancient world. The Roman imperial government itself insisted upon the divinity of the emperor, and he was addressed by the title "Lord." It was common in relation to business deals and contracts to burn incense at an altar of the emperor. The Gnostics had peopled the heavens with spiritual beings whom they considered to be more worthy of worship than Christ. The pagan population had idols over the portals of their houses, lining the sides of their streets, and filling the temples. It was commonly said that it was easier to find a god in Athens than it was to find a man. Paul, of course, recognized that these were "gods" and "lords" only in the sense that they were so regarded by those who worshiped them.[1] It is doubtful if any distinction in meaning is to be made between "gods" and "lords" in this connection.

Verse 6: This verse is one of the great confessions of faith in this letter. There is a parallelism, which should not be missed in it, and at the same time a subordination. The parallelism is: *one God—the Father—from whom are all things—for whom we exist; one Lord—Jesus Christ—through whom are all things—through whom we exist.*[2] The subordination of *Jesus Christ* to *God* in function is seen in the contrasting prepositions: *for— from; through—through.* This contrast points to *God* as the ultimate source and reason for both the universe and man, and to *Christ* as the agent of God.

Yet: translates a strong adversative.

For us: the Christians as opposed to the pagans. Their faith was stated above; the Christian faith is stated here.

[1] Cf. Morris.
[2] Cf. Edwards.

One God: the Jewish confession at its highest. This catches up the expression in verse 4.

The Father: the distinctively Christian title for God. The use of Father is based upon the consciousness and practice of Jesus. Of course, Father had been used of God in both the Old Testament and the rabbinical literature, but his fatherhood was of the nation or of the righteous. With Jesus the term came to have a personal and dynamic meaning never before known. God was seen to be the Father of the individual worshiper, concerned about his affairs, answering his prayers, and open to his approach. This conception of God is the unique contribution of Jesus Christ and Christianity to the religious thought of the world. It is interesting to note that God is called Father in the Book of Acts in only three places (1:4, 7; 2:33), all of these occurrences taking place at Pentecost or before. Its use is very common in Paul's writings, usually in such compound titles as "God the Father" or "God, the Father of our Lord Jesus Christ." Sometimes the title "Father" is found alone (cf. Rom. 6:4; 8:15; Gal. 4:6; Eph. 2:18; 3:14; Col. 1:12). Its use is also frequent in the epistles of John and the Book of Revelation. It seems that, contrary to many scholars' opinion, Paul preserved and made common a characteristic of the life of Jesus which the earlier Christians may have nearly forgotten.

From whom are all things: speaks of God as the ultimate source of the universe. *All things,* in the Greek, has the article, which was the common way of designating the totality of all things as a unity.

For whom we exist: the aim of the Christian life. The true goal of every redeemed man and of the redeemed community is the service and worship of God.

One Lord: the Christian title for Jesus Christ. The title, in Paul's thought at least, included the idea of active rulership in the lives of Christians. The correlative of Lord is slaves. He is our Lord; we are his slaves.

Jesus Christ: a proper name in Paul's writings. In the Gospels Christ is usually a title; but it soon came, in Christian usage, to be joined with Jesus as a compound proper name, and Lord became the title.

Through whom are all things: speaks of Christ as the agent of creation, a thought which is found also in other New Testament passages (cf. John 1:1–5; Col. 1:16; Heb. 1:2).

Through whom we exist: that is, through whom we have been redeemed. Not only creation but redemption has its ultimate source in God. Jesus Christ is thought of as carrying out, executing, the wishes of God as his agent. This is not to say that Jesus Christ is an inferior being. The question of the substance of God and the co-equality of Christ had not arisen in New Testament times. Such a question would have been foreign to Hebrew thought. The question of metaphysical equality arose only when Christianity became a Greek religion. The idea is that of subordination in function. Jesus Christ was thought of as the Son, the one who carried out the purposes of the Father. For example, the Christian prayer is commonly addressed to the Father in the name of the Son.

This is not a denial of the doctrine of the Trinity, developed in the fourth century in Greek circumstances. However, it might be better for modern Christians to lay aside doctrinal controversy and recapture the spiritual reality, which is that Christ is our Lord and we are to obey him. All too often Christians, in the name of orthodoxy, have been guilty of maintaining the truth about the being of Christ while refusing him his proper place in their lives. While orthodoxy is necessary to true worship, it must never be allowed to supersede true worship. We must not forget, in our enthusiasm for the confession of Paul, that the primary subject in this chapter is the rightness or wrongness of eating "food offered to idols." The purpose of this confession was to show that such food was neither polluted nor made holy. In itself the food had no spiritual significance.

(3) Brotherly love should guide action (8:7–13)

Having established the basic premise, Paul turned to a discussion of circumstances in which doing that which was not sinful in itself might become sinful. We must remember that Paul's whole discussion involved that which was not sinful in itself. To forget that fact and to try to make all ethical decisions relative would be to misinterpret Paul's thought.

Verse 7: points out the fact that some Christians at Corinth were weak in their faith.

However, not all possess this knowledge: literally, "but not in all the knowledge." *Possess* is a poor translation. The emphasis is not upon having knowledge, but on having inner assurance based on knowledge.[1] All the Corinthians, no doubt, shared in the knowledge. They had been taught the same basic truths of Christianity. Some had it "in them," i.e., emotionally integrated into their attitudes. Others did not. The idea may be illustrated by a modern man's knowledge that walking under a ladder does not bring bad luck. He knows this, but he still avoids walking under a ladder. *This knowledge* is the knowledge discussed in verses 4–6.

But some: recognizes the fact that the weaker Christians constituted a minority.

Through being hitherto accustomed to idols: gives the reason for their weakness. In their past life they had worshiped and revered idols. Their attitudes had become deeply ingrained in their emotional selves. Christianity had not yet stamped out these feelings, though their knowledge was contrary to their emotions.

Eat food as really offered to an idol: literally, "as an idol offering they eat." They felt that they were still partaking in the worship of the idol by eating food which had been offered in the pagan sacrifices. Notice that this feeling was subjective.

And their conscience: rather, "their consciousness." The New Testament does not have a word which equals our word *conscience,* as it is used in theological discussion. In such discussion the compulsion to do what one thinks is right is primary. The New Testament word places the emphasis upon the knowledge of what is right or wrong, the moral consciousness.

Being weak: being overscrupulous. The Greek word *weak* is used in this sense in Romans 14:1–21 and in this letter. In other New Testament

---

[1] Edwards points out that Paul distinguished between *having* knowledge and having it *within.*

passages it usually means "to be sick." Perhaps the word was used by the majority to ridicule the minority. Its use in this way suggests the contempt of those who fancied themselves to be strong. However, Paul recognized the truth of the designation and adopted it, at least for the purpose of discussion. The Corinthians knew whom he meant.

Is defiled: that is, they feel that they are defiled by their action. Again, the subjective element is prominent in the use of the term. This element is brought out by the use of the middle voice in the Greek. It was just this feeling of defilement which made their action sinful.[1] Since they felt that they were insulting God by their action, they were in fact doing so. The same thing would have been true if their act had actually been against the Christian religion. Paul's point was that the feeling of doing wrong made that which was done wrong.

Verse 8: Food will not commend us to God: best taken as a quotation from their letter. The strong had claimed the absolute nonexistence of the idols; they now insisted upon the absolute insignificance of meats. *Commend* is too strong a translation of the Greek, which means "to present." However, it is implied that this presentation would be for the purpose of God's commendation or approval.

We are no worse off if we do not eat, and no better off if we do: continues the quotation of the position of the strong. The expression is hypothetical in quality. It does not state a conclusion of fact but reveals a feeling of the speaker. This form would be perfectly in harmony with the Corinthians' ideas; it would not be in harmony with Paul's advice.

Verse 9: Paul's answer to the assumptions of verse 8 was not that they were wrong, but that they might be dangerous.

Only take care: a warning to be on the alert to the whole situation. *Take care* translates the word for seeing and corresponds to our expression "look out."

Lest . . . somehow: introduces the thing warned against. *Somehow* means "in some manner." Paul was suggesting that the debate about the rightness of eating food offered to idols did not settle the issue, even though the decision might be correct.

This liberty of yours: the right you assert. *Liberty* translates a word which means "authority." Our word "right" would be better. The word suggests that some were insisting upon their right to eat as they pleased.

Become a stumbling-block: a stone against which one stumbles. The idea is that the exercise of one's rights might be a hindrance or obstacle to another.

To the weak: identifies those who may stumble.

Verse 10: This verse is a question. The form demands an affirmative answer.

For if any one sees you: introduces the hypothetical situation.

A man of knowledge: the knowledge of which they boasted, knowledge of the spiritual insignificance of meat offered to idols.

At table in an idol's temple: indicates that some of the strong thought

---

[1] Grosheide points out that such action constituted living in sin, not a momentary lapse into it by the weak Christian.

it permissible to engage in pagan festivals in the temples. This action went beyond the mere eating of such food. In his discussion of this problem (10:14–22), Paul pointed out the danger even to the strong of such action. Here his concern was for the weaker brother.

Might he not be encouraged: ironical expression in the Greek. *Encouraged* translates the Greek word which means "to build up, to edify." It is the same word which Paul used in verse 1, "Love builds up." The man of liberty would educate the weak to defy his scruples without helping him to remove them.

If his conscience is weak: a circumstance which is assumed to be true. *If* does not imply a doubt. The Greek reads: "his conscience being weak," i.e., he being overscrupulous.

To eat food offered to idols: not to join in the pagan festivals, but to violate his own feeling of right and wrong by eating (perhaps in social circumstances) the food.

Verse 11: states the result of the strong Christian's influence over the actions of the overscrupulous Christian.

And so by your knowledge: By translates the Greek preposition *en,* which expresses the idea of sphere. The thought is not that the strong man's possession of knowledge accomplished this, nor that his exercise of liberty accomplished this, but that the weak man's attempt to share the knowledge accomplished it. We could paraphrase by saying: "and so by his attempt to live by your knowledge." In other words, the weak man would be led to suppress his own scruples and judge his own actions in the light of another man's knowledge.

This weak man is destroyed: Ruin, not building up (cf. vs. 10), is the result. *Destroyed* is the present tense, indicating that the weak man by his action is now in the process of being ruined. Though the Greek word is used in the New Testament (cf. John 3:16) for eternal destruction, this is not the thought in this verse. The destruction which Paul had in mind is similar to that which he discussed in his own life (cf. 9:24–27). It is the shipwreck of the Christian life, the slipping away from obedience to God and the insertion of self-gratification. Some have taken *destroyed* to mean eternal destruction, but if that danger had been present, we may be sure that Paul would not have dealt so mildly with the problem. No, the only thing which can lead to man's eternal destruction is his own rebellion against God. A fellow Christian's influence may lead him to be less a Christian than he should be, but it cannot bring about his eternal damnation.

The brother for whom Christ died: contrasts the indifference of the strong for his brother's welfare to the love of Christ for him. The use of the term *brother* reminded the Corinthian of his responsibility for the spiritual welfare of the weak Christian. He was not a stranger; he was a brother. Christian brotherhood should lead to concern for one another's welfare, not to reckless indifference. *For whom* (literally, "on account of whom") gives the reason for Christ's death. It was precisely to rescue him from his ruin. Christian devotion should lead men to emulate the love of Christ and seek the ends which he sought. Thus, the remonstrance of Paul implies that the Corinthians were violating two fundamental principles of Christian life: Christian brotherhood and Christian devotion.

Verse 12: The climax of the strong Christian's sin was seen in the fact that it was a sin against Christ.

Thus, sinning against your brethren: describes one aspect of the strong Christian's behavior. *Sinning* is perhaps to be taken in its classic sense, i.e., "falling short of." The idea would be that the strong Christian "fell short of" his responsibility to his brethren by eating in the temple of idols.[1] He had been so concerned about his own rights, his liberty to do as he pleased in this matter, that he had failed to live up to the standard required in brotherhood. Paul's usual meaning for "sin" is rebellion against God. This sense does not fit the context; so we must find another sense for the word in this verse. The common Greek sense seems to fit best.

And wounding their conscience: the way in which the sin was committed. *Wounding* translates a word which means "to strike a blow." It is a metaphor here. The meaning is that the strong Christian attacked a weak Christian at his weakest point, his scruples.

You sin against Christ: that is, "you fall short of the obligation of full devotion to Christ." *Sin* must again be given the common Greek meaning rather than Paul's usual meaning. The point was that a wrong done to a Christian brother was a wrong done to Christ. Paul had learned this lesson well. On the Damascus road the living Lord had greeted him with the words: "Saul, Saul, why do you persecute me?" (Acts 9:4). Saul's persecution of the Christians was thus defined as persecution of Christ. Jesus himself had taught the same truth when he said: "Truly, I say to you, as you did it not to one of the least of these, you did it not to me" (Matt. 25:45). It is a solemn thought that our treatment of our brethren really reflects our attitude toward Christ. They are his brethren, also.

Edwards takes a slightly different view of this expression. He views sinning against the brother as sin against Christ because (1) it is sin against one whom Christ loved, (2) it is sin against the conscience which Christ liberated, and (3) it is destruction of him for whom Christ died. However, I would think this is more than Paul meant. Edwards' interpretation really rests on his belief that the destruction involved was eternal destruction. This, we have seen, was not the case. It seems that the sense of unity between Christ and his people was the fundamental thought in Paul's mind.

Verse 13: asserts the right course of action in such instances.

Therefore: a very strong expression in the Greek. It should read, "for this very reason," i.e., that such action constitutes a violation of obligations to Christ.

If food is a cause of my brother's falling: should be interpreted in the light of the context. *Falling* would then mean leading the brother to violate his own consciousness of what was right and wrong. The Greek word has a corresponding English word, "scandalize." The King James Version translates the word, "make . . . to offend." The idea is not that the brother criticized the strong Christian for his action, while refusing himself to indulge in it. This interpretation has been given in modern circles. It is rather that the brother admired the strong Christian for his liberty and

---

[1] Barclay succinctly points out that that which may ruin another is not a pleasure but a sin. (William Barclay, *The Letters to the Corinthians* [Philadelphia: The Westminster Press]. Hereafter referred to by the last name of the author, Barclay.)

followed him against his own conscience. *If* is a condition expressing a possibility, not a fact. If such cases actually existed in Corinth, Paul did not know of them.

I will never eat meat: Paul made the statement in the first person but meant to express the Christian ideal which all men should follow.[1] We cannot ignore the fact that this was Paul's own determination. Possibly his discussion of his accommodation to the customs of men (9:19–23) was based on a desire to show that this was actually his practice. On the other hand, we must take the expression in a more general sense, applying to all Christians. *Meat* is substituted here for the more general word, "food," because it was meat which was really in question, not food in general. *Never* is to be taken absolutely. The Greek is "unto the age," and the King James Version, "while the world standeth," catches the meaning well.

Lest I cause my brother to fall: gives the reason for Paul's abstinence from eating meat offered to idols. The expression implies, by omission, that Paul considered the position of the strong Christian correct. He was willing to forego his own liberty, however, for the sake of his brother. *Fall* is to be taken in the same sense as above.

A word needs to be said about the modern application of the principles stated in this chapter. The particular situation is not likely to occur, but the principles have a continuing validity. However, it is possible to be too strict or too lax in applying them. The following conditions must exist for a valid application: (1) a difference of opinion must exist concerning the rightness or wrongness of a particular act; (2) the act must not be sinful in itself, as judged by biblical teachings; (3) a danger must exist that the objector may be led to ignore his own scruples by the action of a stronger Christian. In such cases (it is impossible to be specific since the exact act in question will be different in every age and circumstance), the stronger brother should be willing to abstain from an act which he has every right to consummate for the sake of his brother.

A good illustration of such an act in a particular time and situation would be a woman's use of cosmetics. In the past the use of cosmetics was considered a sign of immorality. This is no longer true. During the period when customs were changing, our principles may often have come into play. A difference of opinion in Christian circles certainly existed. Cosmetics, we may agree, are not in themselves sinful. A danger did exist that women with more freedom of spirit than others might lead some admiring fellow Christian woman to ignore her scruples and indulge in the use of cosmetics before general custom had sanctioned them. As customs change and situations vary, other examples will arise. The principle is that the Christian must not only consult his own consciousness of what is right, but must also consider the effect of his actions on the lives of his brethren.

2. Three Illustrations from Paul's Own Life (9:1–27)

The material in this chapter could be treated as a parenthesis, but its relation to the question of Christian liberty is close enough to consider it a

---

[1] Schlatter points out that Paul's determination included not only meat offered to idols, but all meat.

part of the discussion.[1] The abruptness with which Paul introduced the chapter is puzzling, but Paul often jumped from one thought to another without laying a foundation for the new thought. If he had laid the proper foundation, he might have said, "If you want a concrete illustration of my principles, I will give you three." First, he discussed his own failure to demand his apostolic right to support from the Corinthians (9:1–18). Second, he discussed his habit of adapting himself to the customs and tastes of others so that he might win them to Christ (9:19–23). Third, he discussed his constant self-discipline to avoid being disqualified as an apostle (9:24–27). These three illustrations show that Paul always had been ready to forget his own rights in his concern for others.

A secondary interest in the chapter, seen especially in his choice of topics, was to assert his apostolic position. If he had wished to do so, he might have turned the discussion to a defense of his apostleship. Some commentators have taken the position that the chapter is such a defense. However, the tone he used, as well as the secondary place given to this claim, indicates that his main concern was to show his readiness to subordinate his personal desires to the needs of others.

(1) He had waived his apostolic rights (9:1–18)

The progress of thought in this section is as follows: Paul asserted the reality of his apostleship (vss. 1–2); he insisted that he was entitled to support, for both himself and a wife, if he chose to claim it (vss. 3–7); he pointed to the Old Testament as the basis of such a claim (vss. 8–21a); he explained why he had not insisted upon these rights in Corinth (vss. 12b–18). The divisions of thought are not rigid, however.

Verse 1: a series of rhetorical questions, each one demanding an affirmative answer. The aim of the questions was to show that the Corinthians, if no one else, should recognize his full apostleship.

Am I not free?: connects the discussion to chapter 8. Paul had just declared his determination to abstain from meat in the interest of love for the brethren. The question asserted his freedom, not from sin, but from external law of any kind (cf. 9:19). Love was his reason for waiving his Christian rights.

Am I not an apostle: argues by interrogation that he was. This question introduces the main thought of the section. Not only did Paul have the rights of a Christian, but he also had the special rights of an apostle. He did not think of the right to respect, but of the right to support. The nontechnical meaning of *apostle* is evident in this passage. Not only did Paul list Cephas as an apostle, but also the brothers of the Lord (vs. 5). Further, he included Barnabas under the same designation (vs. 6). In the New Testament *apostle* has the common meaning of one who is sent to carry a message for his principal. The fundamental idea is not that of authority, but of missionary function. In this chapter, our word "missionary" would be more accurate than *apostle* because of our conception of this word.

---

[1] Barrett believes Paul was saying that he did not ask them to do anything that he was not doing.

Have I not seen Jesus our Lord?: vindicated his claim to be an apostle in the same class with the original disciples. When they elected a successor to Judas, the prime qualification was: "One of these men must become with us a witness to his resurrection" (Acts 1:22). Other qualifications were subordinate to this one. Paul qualified as an apostle because he had seen the risen Lord on the Damascus road. He listed himself among those to whom the Lord had appeared (1 Cor. 15:8).

Are not you my workmanship in the Lord?: vindicated his claim to apostleship on the basis of his ministry at Corinth. *Workmanship* is too strong a term; it implies an independence which Paul did not claim. "Work" would be a better translation. The expression is elliptical and should be understood to mean: "It is true, is it not, that your conversion came as a result of my work?" *In the Lord* goes with *you* and means, "your existence as Christians, united to the Lord, living in Him." [1] The reference, of course, was to the founding of the church at Corinth (cf. 3:1–11).

Verse 2: If to others I am not an apostle: implies that others denied the apostleship of Paul.[2] *If* should be translated "though" or "since." Paul was not speaking of the teachers in Corinth, but of others outside the church. Perhaps he had met denial of his apostleship in Ephesus; certainly he had met it in the churches of Galatia.

At least I am to you: good translation.

For you are the seal of my apostleship in the Lord: The order of the English translation obscures the meaning. Literally, "for the seal of my apostleship you are in the Lord." *In the Lord* again modifies *you.* Their conversion, their union with the Lord, constituted the seal. *Seal* is the mark of authenticity. Rulers marked their decrees with their seal, not so much to keep it private as to mark the decree as actually from them. We are familiar with this use of an official seal in our own society.

Verse 3: introduces the paragraph in which Paul discussed the rights of an apostle.

This: refers to the following discussion through verse 18 rather than to the questions asked in verses 1–2. However, some commentators insist that it refers to the preceding claims of apostleship. The matter is not important, but it seems that Paul's apostleship had been challenged on the basis that he was not supported by the churches but must work with his hands for a living. If this is true, my position is correct.

My defense: a legal term for the reply of an accused to the charge against him.[3] Its use here is metaphorical. Paul did not envision a formal court trial, but a private challenge to his apostleship. "Reply" or "answer" would be the sense.

To those who would examine me: a poor translation. *Would* implies a lack of reality. The Greek is in the indicative, and the translation is better if *would* is omitted. *Examine* is another legal term indicating the investigation to determine the facts of the case.[4] The word is always used of the

---

[1] Perry.
[2] Barrett points out that the two epistles give adequate evidence of such doubts.
[3] Cf. Barrett.
[4] Barrett suggests "cross-examine" as a possible translation.

investigation which precedes the decision. This expression tends to confirm the fact that Paul was introducing the discussion to follow in this verse. The investigation would involve the implications of the fact that he was not supported by the churches. The implication of the account in Acts is that Paul was supported on his first missionary journey by the church at Antioch, but that when he began his second journey, the church "commended" him "to the grace of the Lord" (Acts 15:40). From that time onward, he worked at his trade as a tentmaker to support himself and perhaps his party of fellow missionaries.

Verse 4: another rhetorical question.

Do we not have: introduces a question with a form which expects a negative answer. Paul took his place with the investigator and quotes his opinion in the matter. *We* is editorial and means "I."

The right: correct translation in this context of a Greek word which means "authority." It is a metonym for the right or privilege which has been granted one who has authority.

To our food and drink: i.e., at the expense of the church. The question speaks of the fundamental right of all missionaries to be supported by their brethren in the preaching of the gospel. *Food and drink* would include all the physical necessities of life.

Verse 5: another rhetorical question, which surprises us in view of Paul's discussion in chapter 7. However, the question was purely hypothetical and involved the right of Paul. The question of whether he desired this or not is not answered.

Do we not have the right: repeats verse 4 with the same implications.

To be accompanied by a wife: literally, "a sister as a wife to lead about." Some have taken the expression to mean a Christian woman as an attendant, but this interpretation seems to strain for conformity with chapter 7 unnecessarily. Paul was not thinking of the right to marry. No one in that age would have thought to question such a right. The expression expands the idea of the right to food and drink for himself by adding the right for the same support for a wife.

As the other apostles: implies that the other apostles claimed this right.[1]

And the brothers of the Lord: includes them in the apostolic circle. James was recognized as an apostle by Paul (cf. Gal. 1:19). It is likely that the other brothers also were included. They would have been excellent witnesses of the resurrection of Christ.

Cephas: certainly an apostle. We know that he was married and it is possible that he took his wife with him on his journeys.

Verse 6: another rhetorical question but demanding an affirmative answer. The result is the same. The question assumes that it was true that only he and Barnabas did not have a right to support. This represents the opinion of Paul's detractors, not his own.

Barnabas: is assumed to be an apostle. He was one of the members of the Jerusalem congregation and came to prominence by giving the proceeds of a sale of land to feed the poor (Acts 4:36). He had introduced Paul

---

[1] Barrett sees this as justification not only of the right of apostles to have wives, but also of their right to have their wives maintained by the church.

into the company of the Jerusalem disciples after they had rejected him out of fear (Acts 9:26–27). Having been sent by the Jerusalem church to investigate the new church at Antioch (Acts 11:22), he approved of the work and brought Paul from Tarsus to share in it (Acts 11:25–26). He shared with Paul the mission of taking relief funds to the poor at Jerusalem (Acts 11:29–30). Along with Paul, he was designated of the Holy Spirit to be appointed to foreign mission service (Acts 13:2). After their return he desired to give John Mark a second chance; when Paul would not agree, he took Mark with him and sailed to Cyprus (Acts 15:39). Barnabas was thus one of the secondary leaders of the early Christian mission, of which there must have been many. Paul ranked him with the other apostles and demanded that his rights be recognized.

To refrain from working for a living: translates the sense of Paul's question very well. Other apostles might refrain from working and depend on the support of churches. Not so with Paul and Barnabas.

The series of rhetorical questions (vss. 4–6), though in a form which would imply that Paul did not have the same rights as others, are not to be taken in that sense. He merely spoke from the viewpoint of his detractors, leaving it to his readers to recognize that he differed from them. He did have these rights, but he did not exercise them. Succeeding verses tell why.

Verse 7: another series of rhetorical questions, which serve to illustrate the rights of the missionaries to support from their brethren. The argument is that since the soldier, the vine dresser, and the shepherd were paid for their work, the apostle should be.

Who serves as a soldier at his own expense?: The answer is "no one." Originally the word which is translated *expense* meant the rations of the soldier, his food. Later it was expanded to include his pay. *Serves* implies service under another man and for another's cause. Roman soldiers were common in Paul's day, and the illustration would have been easily understood.

Who plants a vineyard without eating any of its fruit?: another common illustration in the Roman Empire.

Who tends a flock without getting some of the milk?: still another common occupation of the day.

Verse 8: shifts the emphasis from human analogies to the support of scriptural teaching.

Do I say this on human authority?: rather, "It is true, is it not, that according to man these things I am speaking?" The assumed answer is affirmative. This expression refers to the analogies in verse 7. They are "according to man," i.e., based on common ways of thinking. *Authority* is too strong a word to use; "analogy" would be better.

Does not the law say the same?: expects an affirmative answer. The law does say the same, as Paul pointed out in the next verses.[1]

Verse 9: For it is written in the law of Moses: an enlarged phrase pointing to the Old Testament Scriptures, particularly to the Torah. Usually Paul introduced scriptural quotations with the phrase, "it is written." Usually he spoke of the law of Moses as simply "the law." Perhaps his

---

[1] *Law* is equivalent to Scripture (Moffatt).

reason for the enlarged statement was that the particular commandment which he quoted seemed too petty for divine regulation. He wanted to be sure that the Corinthians understood that the quotation really came from Scripture.

"You shall not muzzle an ox when it is treading out the grain": comes from Deuteronomy 25:4. The Egyptians threshed grain by having oxen pull a stone or a drag over the grain to separate the grain from the husks. No doubt the Israelites did the same. The ox was to be permitted to eat of the grain; he was not to be muzzled. This was considered fair and humane. The saying, in Deuteronomy, is contained in a series of regulations concerning economic and social justice. It is possible that even there it was metaphorical, referring to human fairness and equity.

Is it for oxen that God is concerned?: indicates that Paul took the saying to mean more than it said. The form of the question in Greek demands a negative answer. Paul did not mean that God was unconcerned for the oxen, but that he was not concerned only for the oxen.

Verse 10: Does he not speak entirely for our sake?: another rhetorical question, which Paul immediately answered in the affirmative. The question is what Paul meant by the term translated *entirely*. The Greek word is *pantōs,* an adverb which can have such various meanings as "by all means, certainly, probably, doubtless, at least, or by any and all means." Paul used the same word in verse 22, where the RSV translates it, "by all means." *Entirely* is too strong. Its use would imply that Paul denied the literal application as being true. Though Paul sometimes allegorized Scripture (cf. Gal. 4:21–31), he never denied the truth of the literal meaning.[1] The point here seems to be that there was a deeper meaning to the regulation than appeared on the surface. It was written surely "for *our* sake." This would be true, even in the literal meaning. It was the inhumanity of the man who would muzzle his oxen and refuse them feed while they worked that God was primarily concerned about. But Paul saw in the regulation more than that. He believed that it had many applications to human life.

It was written for our sake: states Paul's answer to his own question.

Because the plowman should plow in hope: one application of the saying about the oxen. *Should* carries the idea of obligation or duty. It is the duty of the owner of the field to provide for the plowman who cultivates the field.

And the thresher thresh in hope of a share in the crop: another application of the same saying. *In hope* is emphatic in both sayings. *Of a share of the crop* gives a good meaning for the verbal expression in the Greek. The hoping should accompany the working.

Verse 11: comes finally to the point. Paul had built up his case by human analogy and by scriptural statements. In this verse he made the application to the point in question, i.e., the right of the preacher to be paid.

If we have sown spiritual good among you: assumes the fact that they had done so. The *spiritual good* is that good which comes from the Holy

---

[1] Moffatt feels, to the contrary, that the literal meaning had no significance to Paul.

Spirit, though, of course, it ministers to the spiritual needs of man. Its source is the primary emphasis here. *Sown* is reminiscent of 1 Corinthians 3:6, "I planted." *We* is editorial here; Paul meant "I." The reference is to his preaching of the gospel in Corinth and the Corinthians' subsequent conversion and entrance into eternal life.

Is it too much if we reap your material benefits?: argues from the greater to the lesser. The contrast is between the *spiritual good* and the *material benefits. Too much* translates the Greek word for "a great thing." *Material benefits* means bodily things such as food and drink (cf. vs. 4). The question is stated as if the answer were self-evident. It certainly would not be a great thing for Paul to receive his bodily needs from the Corinthians after sharing with them the priceless blessing of the gospel.

Verse 12: returns to the comparison between the rights of Paul and the rights of the other apostles.

If others share this rightful claim upon you: assumes that they do. *Others* is defined by verse 5, i.e., the other apostles and the Lord's brothers and Cephas. They shared *this rightful claim,* i.e., they had been given the privilege of support by the churches.

Do not we still more?: argues from the greater to the lesser. The privilege given these to be supported by the Corinthians was based on a lesser claim. Thus, the granting of it was a greater concession than if they granted the same thing to Paul. He was their spiritual father, the founder of the church.

Nevertheless, we have not made use of this right: begins Paul's discussion of his reason for waiving his rights. *Nevertheless* is a strong adversative, contrasting his rights with his use of them. *We have not made use* means he had never made use of them. We know that this was true at Corinth. We may assume that it was true in other cities as well.

But we endure anything: tells what his practice had been. *Anything* is literally "all things." Specifically, this refers to Paul's working for a living in the midst of the great burden of his missionary labors. Many men have wondered at the possibility of a man's being able to do all that Paul did. *Endure* is a present tense (indicating continuous action) of a verb which originally meant "to cover up, or conceal." Some have interpreted the verb to mean that Paul did not complain about this, that he was silent. He could hardly have said this in the midst of this discussion. Perhaps he was not complaining, but he certainly was not being silent. The derived meaning of enduring is the meaning here.

Rather than put an obstacle in the way of the gospel of Christ: states the primary reason for his enduring all things. Paul had recognized that a claim for support from new converts might become a hindrance to the preaching of the gospel. Thus, he had refused to exercise his claim. *Obstacle* comes from a rare Greek word which means to "cut in." The word is found nowhere else in biblical literature. Perhaps the metaphor arises from breaking bridges to hamper the march of an enemy (ICC). The idea in this context is that of hindering the gospel by cutting in with a claim for personal support.

Verse 13: returns to the question of the right of the apostle to receive support in his ministry.

Do you not know: rather, "you do know, do you not." Both questions in the verse are rhetorical, and both demand an affirmative answer. Paul spoke of things that were known to them.

Those who are employed in the temple service: priests and Levites who ministered in the Temple. The *temple* was the Jewish Temple in Jerusalem, not the pagan temples of which Paul had already spoken. It was probably true that pagan priests also got their living from the temple, but Paul did not appeal to their example.

Get their food from the temple: play on words. The first phrase reads literally, "they the things of the temple working out." The second phrase reads literally, "the things out of the temple eat." Paul was quoting from a word of God to Aaron: "Then the Lord said to Aaron, 'And behold, I have given you whatever is kept of the offerings made to me, all the consecrated things of the people of Israel; I have given them to you as a portion, and to your sons as a perpetual due. This shall be yours of the most holy things, reserved from the fire; every offering of theirs, every cereal offering of theirs and every sin offering of theirs and every guilt offering of theirs, which they render to me, shall be most holy to you and to your sons' " (Num. 18:8–9). Concerning the Levites the regulations were more specific: "The Levitical priests, that is, all the tribe of Levi, shall have no portion or inheritance with Israel; they shall eat the offerings by fire to the Lord, . . . the Lord is their inheritance. . . . And this shall be the priests' due from the people, from those offering a sacrifice, whether it be ox or sheep: they shall give to the priest the shoulder and the two cheeks and the stomach. The first fruits of your grain, of your wine and of your oil, and the first of the fleece of your sheep, you shall give him" (Deut. 18:1–4).

And those who serve at the altar share in the sacrificial offerings: repeats the first question in a more definite form. Only the priests would be involved in serving at the altar, but the basic thought is the same.

Verse 14: draws the conclusion from the illustration and from the instructions of Jesus that preachers should be supported.

In the same way: shows that the instructions of Jesus were in harmony with the regulations of God in the Old Testament.[1]

The Lord commanded: the final proof of the right. *Lord* refers to Jesus Christ. *Commanded* is in the past tense and refers to definite commands of the historical Jesus.

That those who proclaim the gospel should get their living by the gospel: a summary statement.[2] The commands of Jesus to his disciples when he sent them out to preach were: "Take no gold, nor silver, nor copper in your belts, no bag for your journey, nor two tunics, nor sandals, nor a staff; for the laborer deserves his food. And whatever town or village you enter, find out who is worthy in it, and stay with him until you depart" (Matt. 10:9–11). Evidently Paul was familiar with these words of Jesus, probably in an oral tradition. It is true that Jesus modified these instructions when he sent the disciples out into the pagan world, but the principle would remain the same as soon as converts were won. The man who received the spiritual benefit of the gospel ministry should, as a matter of

---

[1] Cf. Morris.

[2] There is no command of Jesus in these exact words (Morris).

duty, share in the material support of the gospel minister. In modern times
our church programs and plants have expanded far beyond that envisioned
by the first disciples. The duty of support is not thereby cancelled but
increased. Our church programs and church plants are designed for the
spiritual good of men. Those who share the spiritual good should share in
the financial support.

Verse 15: gives a further reason why Paul had not used the right to
support.

But I have made no use of any of these rights: repeats the assertion in
verse 12 with some modification. *I* is emphatic here and means "I, for
my part." *Have not made use* is the perfect tense in Greek, indicating a
continuing practice based on a past decision. The idea is the same as verse
12, but more explicit. Paul denied that he had ever exercised any of the
rights which were his.

Nor am I writing this to secure any such provision: denies any overt
motive in his present letter. *Am I writing* is the epistolary aorist in Greek.
Paul took his viewpoint with the readers of the letter and spoke of it as
written in the past tense. It was not his purpose that the support of the
Corinthians should now be turned in his direction.

For I would rather die: a broken expression in the Greek showing great
emotion. Literally it reads: "For good to me rather to die—." The completion of the thought would require some such statement as: "than to
receive support."

Than have any one deprive me of my ground for boasting: a phrase with
several variant readings in Greek manuscripts. The purpose of the variants
seems to have been to smooth out the Greek, which is rough here. Literally:
"My boasting no one shall empty." It is better to take the phrase as an
indicative, expressing Paul's determination that no one should empty his
boasting of meaning, rather than to take it as the completion of the
previous phrase, as the RSV does. Thus the previous phrase would be an
ellipsis with an understood phrase of completion as suggested above. This
phrase is a sentence in itself and expresses Paul's determination, but without the statement that he would rather die than have this happen. His
boasting is explained in verses 16–18.

Verse 16: shows that the ground of Paul's boasting was not in the fact
that he preached the gospel.

For if I preach the gospel: in the form of a hypothetical case. However,
no one in Corinth would doubt that Paul made it his business to preach
the gospel.

That gives me no ground for boasting: There is no word in the original
for *ground.* This comes from the context, but it is justified. Boasting can be
a sinful act, but it can also be a righteous one. The moral quality of
boasting is determined by the reason for it.

For necessity is laid upon me: given the reason why there is no basis for
boasting in the mere preaching of the gospel. *Is laid* is inaccurate. Paul did
not mean that necessity had been laid on him by someone else, but that
it lay upon him.[1] Thus, "lies" would be a better translation. *Necessity*
suggests that Paul had no real choice in this matter. The whole phrase is

---
[1] Morris suggests "presses" as a translation.

somewhat exaggerated. The thought is not that Paul was bound by external pressures which were irresistible. Rather, he was bound by his own devotion to Christ. He had become a slave of Christ by his own free choice. If he wished to maintain that relationship, he must continue to preach the gospel, as he had been commissioned to do on the way to Damascus (Acts 9:6). He was a "chosen instrument . . . to carry my name before the Gentiles and kings and the sons of Israel," said God to Ananias (Acts 9:15). This commission had often been ratified in Paul's own experience, and he found it impossible to reject it—not because he could not, but because he would not. Paul's necessity came from his own devotion to Christ.

Woe to me if I do not preach the gospel!: To Paul, it would be woe to disobey Christ. He was not thinking of punishment but of the emptiness of the Christian heart which has lost its devotion to the Master.

Verse 17: A variety of interpretations have been given to this verse.

For if I do this of my own will: in the manner of a man who chooses his occupation, not by reason of a divine call. The debated expressions in this verse are: *of my own will* and its contrasting statement, *not of my own will.* Some commentators have taken the expressions to refer to the attitude with which the work is done. That is, it may be done cheerfully and willingly; if so, the slave will be rewarded for his work. Or it may be done grudgingly and unwillingly; if so, he is merely working out his duty.

Though this interpretation is tempting, especially as an application to modern Christian service, it seems to miss the point. There was no doubt in Paul's mind about his willingness to preach the gospel, nor is there any suggestion that being a slave, and thus a steward of Christ, is lower than being a free man. The expressions—*of my own will* and *not of my own will*—refer to the reason for undertaking the service. Thus, *will* should be translated by the word "choice." Paul was saying that if he, like some preachers of his day, had undertaken to preach the gospel as a matter of choice, not in response to a divine commission, he would have expected a reward. This thought is enhanced by the natural meaning of the word translated *do.* Literally, it means "practice" and is the natural word for practicing a profession or occupation. Thus, to *do this of my own will* means to practice the gospel ministry as a business, of one's own choice. The main objection to this interpretation is that the Greek words are not ordinarily used in this sense of choice. The lexicons give it as a secondary meaning. However, Paul used it with this meaning in another passage: "for the creation was subjected to futility, not of its own will [i.e., not by choice] but by the will of him who subjected it in hope" (Rom. 8:20). The same Greek word is used in both passages. The meaning adopted in this passage is possible and certainly makes more sense than its alternative.

I have a reward: to be taken in the ordinary sense of pay. Paul would have rebelled against the modern practice of paying preachers a salary as if they were mercenaries selling their services. He would have insisted, I think, that churches should support their ministers. There may not seem to be much difference between giving a minister so much support and paying him the same amount in salary. The money is the same. But the principle is not. "Salary" implies payment for services received. "Support" implies that the church enables the minister to be free from worldly concerns so that he may carry on his ministry. His "reward" should not be earthly, but heavenly. The problem is that the misuse of the word "salary" may lead both the church and the minister to take a worldly view of the ministry.

But if not of my own will: not because I have chosen this, but have been chosen for it.

I am entrusted with a commission: modernizes the language. *Commission* is the word for stewardship. The word was used to describe a slave in the household who had been given a certain task to perform, i.e., a stewardship. *Commission* does not carry the idea fully; but in our free society where slavery is not a common religious figure, it perhaps comes as close to it as possible.

Verse 18: defines the reward which Paul expected in spite of the fact that he was fulfilling a stewardship rather than making preaching a business.

What then is my reward?: a question which assumes that there would be a special reward for Paul. *Reward* is not the same thing as *boasting,* though it seems that both involve the same reality. *Boasting* is the ground of glorying. *Reward* is the pay received for one's ministry.

That in my preaching I may make the gospel free of charge: His pay was to do without pay. *Free of charge* means that the congregation which received the gospel did not support the minister who brought it.

Not making full use of my right in the gospel: result clause. His making the gospel free of charge resulted in his not making full use of his right, i.e., his right to be fed, clothed, etc. Even as slave-steward, Paul had this right. His Master had ordered it. No blame would be attached to his ministry if he availed himself of support. However, his peculiar joy was in making his ministry free. In doing so, Paul followed the example of the Master. Jesus had conducted his ministry so that no hint of profiteering could be found. Paul desired to do the same thing.

(2) He had accommodated himself to the customs of others (9:19–23)

This paragraph is connected with the preceding discussion but goes beyond it. Paul was still dealing with his waiving of rights; now it was his right to be himself. He had also waived this right in the interest of preaching the gospel meaningfully. Two examples are given: his accommodation to the religious customs of those he sought to win (vss. 19–21); his accommodation to the scruples of the men he sought to win (vs. 22*a*). He then stated his reason for this accommodation (vss. 22*b*–23). Paul had been accused of preaching to please men and seek their favor (Gal. 1:10). Perhaps this charge had been leveled at him in Corinth as well. He stoutly denied this charge. His reasoning was that in all things that truly mattered, he was the slave of Christ and could not be the slave of men. He advised others to adopt the same attitude (cf. 1 Cor. 7:23). However, with regard to things that had no spiritual significance, he was willing to make himself the slaves of men for Christ's sake (cf. 2 Cor. 4:5).

Verse 19: states the principle which is the basis of this paragraph.

For though I am free from all men: Paul's claim. No man could dictate to him; no man could define the limits of his ministry. *Free* reflects the thought of verses 1–2 and lays the foundation for his discussion. *From* translates the Greek preposition which means "out of." The meaning is that Paul's freedom came as a deliverance out of bondage to all men. His emancipation had been the work of Christ and was absolute.

I have made myself a slave to all: a paradoxical statement. How could one who was free make himself a slave without surrendering his freedom? The answer lies in the limits of freedom and slavery in the passage. Paul was freed out of his bondage to legalism and the Jewish law. These he had considered to be of spiritual significance before his conversion. His emancipation from sin had proved the insignificance of such things. Therefore he was free. Paul's emancipation was not everyone's emancipation. Others still felt that the law was binding, that food laws should be observed. In his intercourse with such people, Paul had deliberately made himself their slave.

That I might win the more: gives the reason for his action. *Win* translates a commercial term meaning "to get profit or gain." James used it in the literal sense (Jas. 4:13). In this context it is related to "reward." Paul refused payment in money so that he might get payment in men (Edwards). *The more* does not mean the majority, but more than would have been won by other approaches.[1]

Verse 20: begins the enumeration of the classes of society to which he had accommodated his life.

To the Jews: Jews by race, not Jewish Christians.

I became as a Jew: lived according to Jewish customs. Of course, Paul was a Jew and proud of it, but he did not always observe Jewish customs in his missionary work. Perhaps the fundamental characteristic of this kind of life was refusal to eat with Gentiles. Paul and Peter had come to sharp words about this custom (cf. Gal. 2:11-16). Paul ate with the Gentiles and even continued to do so after some of the circumcision party of Christians came to Antioch. Peter ate with them, also, but withdrew when Jewish Christians came. Paul considered this action hypocrisy. Now, however, he insisted that his practice when among Jews was to observe their customs.

How do the circumstances differ? In Antioch, his ministry was primarily to the Gentiles and among Gentiles. He did not wish to attach the gospel to Jewish customs as if one must become a Jew in order to become a Christian. In the case before us, his ministry was to Jews and among Jews. He did not want to attach the gospel to Gentile customs as if one must renounce his birthright in order to become a Christian. In both cases the principle is the same. The gospel must not be made to depend on any outward custom. Further, in his ministry to the Jews, a departure on his part would tend to alienate them from him so that they would not listen to the gospel at all. Therefore, he lived as they did.

In order to win Jews: Paul's purpose in living according to Jewish customs.

To those under the law: another description of the Jews, but could include proselytes and other Gentiles who accepted the requirements of the law. *Under the law* means living in subjection to the law.

I became as one under the law: means that Paul lived up to the demands of the law when he was associated with them. He observed the various regulations concerning washing, eating, etc.

---

[1] Cf. Edwards.

Though not being myself under the law: denies that he should live *under the law* all the time. Christ had freed him from the dominion of the law when he was converted.

That I might win those under the law: parallel with the other purpose clause in verses 19–20.

Verse 21: continues his list of circumstances in which Paul waived his rights.

To those outside the law: literally, "to the lawless." The RSV translation is justified by the context. He meant the Gentiles who did not have, as the Jews did, a written code of behavior.[1] If *outside the law* is to be given its full meaning, it would be a description of Gentiles from the Jewish viewpoint—as outlaws.[2]

I became as one outside the law: lived without observing the various restrictions of the law. *The law* throughout these verses refers to the Mosaic law.

Not being without law toward God: literally, "not being lawless before God." Though Paul did not observe the Mosaic law, he did observe a higher law—the law of his own devotion to God. This parenthetic statement is intended to show that Paul did not regard his emancipation as a license to do as he wished.

But under the law of Christ: literally, "but in the law of Christ." This expression defines the rule by which Paul lived. It was the law of Christ in the sense that he lived under the direct lordship of the living Christ.

That I might win those outside the law: parallel to the previous purpose clauses.

Verse 22: To the weak: the overscrupulous. The word has the same meaning as above (8:7–13). The inclusion of the *weak* here made Paul's example relevant to the whole discussion of eating food offered to idols.

I became weak: observed the scruples of the weak.

That I might win the weak: parallel to previous purpose clauses.

I have become all things to all men: summary of his previous discussion. *All men* includes the classes mentioned above. *Become all things* defines the ways in which Paul accommodated his behavior to the circumstances. These did not include anything sinful, of course. The change to the perfect tense means that this is the permanent result of past action. Paul continued to be all-sided in his various relations. The only limit was the law of Christ.

That I might by all means save some: expresses Paul's purpose in general terms. *By all means* refers to the various methods used in evangelism, including his accommodation to the tastes of others. *Save some* indicates that Paul did not hope or expect to save all. He did not mean to give his example as a sure means to certain success. Rather, he meant that by his accommodation he removed one barrier from his approach to men. The way was thus opened for the hearing of the gospel and the consequent conversion of some.

Verse 23: I do it all for the sake of the gospel: in order that the preaching of the gospel may not be hindered by superficial things. Paul's primary concern was to gain new believers, to win men to surrender to the lordship of Christ. This desire dominated every action and decision.

---

[1] Cf. Barrett.
[2] Cf. Edwards.

That I may share in its blessings: literally "in order that I might be its co-sharer." The meaning seems to be that he did this in order to gain others to share the blessings of the gospel with him.[1] The suggestion that this means, "lest I lose my share in salvation" (ICC), misses Paul's meaning. The context indicates that he was concerned with the salvation of others, but that he had no doubt about his own. Though the RSV translation is possible, it gives the wrong implication. The Greek word is composed of two elements: one meaning "together with," and the other, "partner or sharer." Thus, the interpretation given above is to be preferred. This needs to be remembered as we go on to the next paragraph, which has the same thrust.

(3) He continued to exercise spiritual discipline (9:24–27)

Using the athletic field as his background, Paul told how he continued to exercise discipline in his Christian life to avoid disqualification as a servant of the Lord. He compared the life of the Christian to a race in which all could be winners. But winning required self-discipline in the race of the Christian just as surely as it did in the arena.

Verse 24: Do you not know: introduces a question which demands an affirmative answer. The Corinthians were familiar with the illustration. Since the days of Alexander the Great, athletic games had been popular throughout the Greek world. The most famous of these contests was the Olympic Games, from which our present world meets get their name. Second only in popularity were the Isthmian Games, which were held in Corinth every third year. Paul must have been an avid sports fan, for he often drew illustrations from these contests.

In a race all the runners compete, but only one receives the prize?: There was only one winner in each race, then as now. Though Paul did not say so in so many words, the implication is that every Christian may win the prize in his race.

So run that you may obtain it: run to win. *So* is an adverb describing the manner in which Christians are to run. *Run* is present tense, meaning to keep on running. *Obtain* means to lay hold of the prize, to grasp it as one's right. The point is not the competition, but the self-discipline which is necessary to win. The strong Christians in Corinth were grasping at their rights and exercising their liberty, but they were losing the prize. The application of the illustration must keep the context in mind. *It* refers to the prize, which is not salvation, but the ability to win men to Christ.

Verse 25: compares the prize of the Christian with the prize of the athlete.

Exercises self-control: a technical term for the training program of the athlete. The training program of any athlete requires rigid dieting, constant exercise, and continual practice. The athlete must forego his desire for rich foods and give himself to strict training if he desires to be a winner.

In all things: with reference to all things. The self-control of the athlete

---

[1] Cf. Morris.

knows almost no limit. For the Greek athlete this training period was ten months long.

They do it to receive a perishable wreath: The emphasis lies on *they* in the clause, in contrast to *we* in the following clause. The *perishable wreath* was usually a crown woven of some pine boughs or flowers.[1] It lasted only for a time; thus it was perishable. Even the fame gained at the games was of short duration. The point which Paul made was that if the athlete could endure such rigors for so small a reward, the Christian should certainly be willing to endure discipline for a greater reward.

But we: in strong contrast with *they.*

An imperishable: crown is understood. The Christian's victory wreath is imperishable. We have similar language in other books of the New Testament. James speaks of the crown of life (1:12), as does Revelation (2:10). The expression "crown of righteousness" is found in the Pastorals (2 Tim. 4:8). Peter spoke of "an inheritance which is imperishable, undefiled, and unfading, kept in heaven for you" (1 Pet. 1:4). However, it seems that Paul was not thinking so much of life and salvation and heaven as of effectiveness in service. Paul was not the only ancient writer to use this illustration. Seneca used the same illustration, admonishing men to seek the prizes of "virtue and strength of mind and peace" (ICC).

Verse 26: turns from the impersonal use of the illustration to the personal.

Well, I do not run aimlessly: The Greek is elliptical; that is, a part of the expression is missing. The RSV translation does not do it justice. Paraphrased, the expression reads: "I for my part do run but not as a man who has no goal." *I* is emphatic and made more emphatic by the Greek particle. *Do . . . run* is in the present tense, indicating action. *Not . . . aimlessly* implies that Paul was certain of his goal. One of the cardinal rules for the racer is that he keep his eyes fixed on the goal toward which he runs.

I do not box as one beating the air: changes the metaphor. *I . . . box* is the positive statement. *Not . . . as one beating the air* defines the manner of boxing. The idea is the same as the preceding figure. The boxer who shadow-boxes may look good, but he may not look so good when he has a live opponent. Paul was not on a training program without an aim. He was a preacher of the gospel, seeking to win men to faith in Christ.

Verse 27: But I pommel my body: to be understood metaphorically. *Pommel* translates a word which means literally "to give a black eye by hitting." *Body* is a metonym for "self" with Paul. Our temptation is to take "body" as the mere physical organ. This would be contrary to Paul's thought. Paul did not share the gnostic idea that the physical self was the seat of sin and must be subdued. He thought of his own responsible self as the body. The meaning is that Paul exercised self-discipline. The danger to the Christian is not that his body may get out of hand but that he himself may get out of God's hands. The only answer to our tendency to seek self-gratification is self-discipline.

Subdue it: lead it into slavery. This is a military metaphor of the victor

---

[1] Grosheide points out that the Greek athlete received no money.

leading the vanquished captive as a slave, not to himself but to his master. The verb is in the present tense and means that Paul continuously led himself into slavery to Christ. This does not mean that he found it necessary to be converted over and over again. He did find it necessary in every new situation of life to reexert his faith, to apply anew his devotion to Christ. Surrender to Christ is a once-for-all matter for the Christian, but it must be reaffirmed in relation to every new decision that arises in life. The only way this can be done is through the constant practice of self-discipline.

Lest after preaching to others I myself should be disqualified: continues the metaphor of the games. There was a herald at the games who announced the contests and called out the competitors (ICC). He must explain the rules of the contest, and any runner who failed to observe the rules was disqualified. In modern games this function is divided among announcers, starters, and judges. So much is clear. But how did Paul apply this figure to himself? Certainly he had been a preacher. In verse 24, he had summoned others to the race and laid down the rules for winning. But he was also a runner in the race. His self-discipline had as its aim that he would not be disqualified from the race. Some commentators take this to mean that he feared he would lose his salvation after winning others.[1] This interpretation does not fit the context. He had been talking about the strong Christian's duty to sacrifice his liberty for the good of the weaker Christian (8:7–13) and of his own practice of waiving his apostolic and human rights for the sake of the gospel (9:1–23). The sense of *disqualified* must be sought in the context. Thus, the thought is that he feared that he might lose his effectiveness in service if he did not continue to practice self-control. For a Christian like Paul, this loss would be a tragedy second only to the tragedy of losing his salvation. However, he had no fear of losing his salvation. He did have a fear—which every Christian ought to have—of losing his power to serve others, to bring others to share with him in the blessings of the gospel. We see, then, that Paul's whole discussion in chapter 9 is meant to illustrate his discussion in chapter 8.

3. An Illustration from Israel's History (10:1–13)

This section has a close connection with 9:27. Paul had expressed his fear that he would be disqualified; in Israel's history a whole generation of men were disqualified. They did not go on into the Promised Land to become the agents of God's revelation. However, the connection with the Corinthian situation is even closer. It was contact with idolatry which led to the rejection of the men of Israel. The paragraph is divided into two sections: the failure of Israel in spite of divine favors (10:1–5); the warning of this example for the Corinthians (10:6–13).

(1) The failure of Israel (10:1–5)

In these verses Paul called attention to the fact that God was displeased with most of the men of Israel. He overthrew them in the wilderness in

---

[1] Cf. Moffatt.

spite of the fact that he had delivered them from Egypt. The language in this section is very colorful. Paul used Christian terms to describe the experiences of Israel in the deliverance.

Verse 1: begins the illustration.

I want you to know, brethren: Paul's usual way of introducing a new thought of importance. Literally, it reads: "I do not want you to be ignorant, brethren" (cf. Rom. 1:13; 11:25; 1 Cor. 12:1; 2 Cor. 1:8; 2 Thess. 4:13). The Greek which is translated, *I want you to know,* could have the meaning, "I do not want you to forget." No doubt, the history of Israel was familiar to the Corinthians, and Paul did not want them to forget its implications for the Christian life.

That our fathers were all under the cloud: protected by divine provision. *Our fathers* means the Jewish ancestors of Christians. They could be called that, even though many of the Corinthians were not Jews. Christianity stands in a direct line of descent, on the human side, from Israel. Often scholars speak of the Jewish-Christian tradition. Though Christianity supersedes Judaism, its roots lie in Judaism. *Were all under the cloud* refers to the experience of Israel when pursued by Pharaoh. "And the Lord went before them by day in a pillar of cloud to lead them along the way" (Exod. 13:21). At night the cloud moved behind the Israelites and protected them against surprise attack by the Egyptians (Exod. 14:19–20). The mysterious cloud was the symbol of the Lord's presence.

And all passed through the sea: refers to the passage of the Israelites through the Red Sea. (The story is found in Exod. 14:21–31.) The waters of the sea were rolled back by the Lord; the Israelites passed through as if it were dry land; when the Egyptians tried to follow, the waters returned and destroyed them. "Thus the Lord saved Israel that day from the hand of the Egyptians" (vs. 30). This act of God became the basic touchstone of Israel's religion from that day forward. To recall it reminded them that they were the elect people of God. But their election was to service—to receive a revelation of God and preserve it and thus prepare for the coming of the Messiah. Salvation in Old Testament times was by grace through faith even as it is in Christian times. Each individual Israelite had to find his own personal faith in God to experience personal salvation. Thus, the material in this paragraph has to do with disqualification for service, not with loss of eternal salvation. Many commentators, letting their doctrinal prejudice influence their exegesis in these chapters, fail to consider the context.

Verse 2: interprets the experience of Israel as a type of Christian baptism.

All were baptized: The emphasis is on the *all.* This is to prepare for the contrast with "most of them" in verse 5. All had the same experience. *Baptized* means literally "to be immersed" in something. The textual evidence is about evenly divided between the middle voice (they had themselves baptized) and the passive voice (they were baptized). Since it is more likely that a copyist would change the middle voice to the passive because this was the common voice used in speaking of Christian baptism, the reading of the middle voice should be preferred. The effect of this reading is to emphasize the willingness of the Israelites to accept the baptism. There could be some question concerning Paul's purpose to make this typical of baptism. The Greek word, in itself, speaks only of an immersion. However, it seems best to let the reference to Christian baptism stand.

Into Moses: because of their relation to Moses as leader. The Greek preposition, *eis,* always has this meaning when used with baptism. There are fifteen other uses of these two words together in the New Testament (Matt. 3:11; Luke 3:3; Acts 2:38; 8:16; 19:3–5; Rom. 6:3–4; 1 Cor. 1:13–17; 12:13; Gal. 3:26–27). *Baptized into* seems to have become a technical term in New Testament usage to mean "baptized with reference to" an existing reality. This meaning fits this passage perfectly. The Israelites experienced baptism because they followed Moses, as a result of this fact. Their baptism was a sign of their allegiance to him.

In the cloud: can also be translated "by the cloud." The Greek preposition *en* (in or by) can be used either way, though *in* is the more usual meaning. Thus, because the cloud completely enveloped them, they were said to have been baptized (immersed) in it.

And in the sea: perhaps conceives of the sea as acting in coordination with the cloud to make the immersion complete. It would be more literal to say that the Egyptians were baptized in the sea, since it engulfed them. However, Paul was not always exact in his use of metaphorical language.

Verse 3: continues the list of experiences.

All: emphatic position again.

Ate the same supernatural food: refers to the manna which God sent to feed the Israelites in the wilderness. "When the dew had gone up, there was on the face of the wilderness a fine, flake-like thing, fine as hoarfrost on the ground. When the people of Israel saw it, they said to one another, 'What is it?' For they did not know what it was. And Moses said to them, 'It is the bread which the Lord has given you to eat' " (Exod. 16:14–15). *Supernatural* should be translated "spiritual." It describes, not the kind of bread, but its source.[1] God was its source. Therefore, it was spiritual food.

Verse 4: And all drank the same supernatural drink: water which God provided for them in the desert. This clause reflects the story of God's giving water to Israel from a rock which Moses struck with his rod though he had been commanded only to speak to it (cf. Num. 20:6–11). *The same* does not mean "the same which we Christians drink";[2] it means that all partook of the same water. The reference to the Lord's Supper is forced in this verse.

For they drank from the supernatural Rock which followed them: reflects the Jewish tradition that the Rock which Moses struck followed the Jews in their wanderings and supplied them with water whenever they needed it.[3] This tradition grew out of rabbinic fancy, and Paul used it as a basis for spiritual teaching. It is possible that Paul believed it to be true, but not certain. At any rate, this passage cannot be taken to sanction the truth of the tradition.

And the Rock was Christ: seems to say that it was not the Rock but

---

[1] Cf. Héring.

[2] Edwards.

[3] Ellis speaks of a cumulative legend in rabbinic literature. (E. Earle Ellis, "A note on First Corinthians 10:4," *Journal of Biblical Literature,* March, 1957, pp. 53–56.)

Christ who supplied water for the Israelites. If so, Paul did not believe the legend but corrected it. The tense of the verb is important. Paul did not say "is," which would be required to give the expression a typical meaning. The Rock was not regarded as a type of Christ. He said *was,* which indicates that he thought Christ rather than the Rock was the true source of spiritual drink. There can be no doubt that Paul believed in the preexistence of Christ, his existence before his incarnation. He was present with the Israelites in the wilderness. The point is that just as the Lord provided food in the form of manna, Christ provided water for the Israelites to drink. The emphasis in the four verses is on the fact that all of the Israelites experienced the miraculous presence of God in their wanderings. Thus the defection of the majority was not due to lack of spiritual experience, but to their own rebellion against God's regulations. This had meaning for the situation at Corinth, as will be seen in the exegesis of the following verses. The effort of some commentators (cf. Lenski and Edwards) to interpret these verses as referring to the so-called sacraments of baptism and the Lord's Supper seems to me to be forced. Of course, I must confess to a prejudice against such identification.

Verse 5: the climax of the illustration.

Nevertheless: in spite of their many miraculous experiences.

With most of them: the majority. Only Joshua and Caleb, of the male Israelites who were adult at the time of their deliverance from Egypt, actually entered the Promised Land.

God was not pleased: No reason is given, but the Old Testament shows that it was because they murmured against God. "Of all your number, numbered from twenty years old and upward, who have murmured against me, not one shall come into the land where I swore that I would make you dwell, except Caleb the son of Jephunneh and Joshua the son of Nun. But your little ones, who you said would become a prey, I will bring in, and they shall know the land which you have despised" (Num. 14:29–31). The reason is not given in this context because it was not related to the situation at Corinth. God's displeasure is mentioned because Paul intended to relate it to the situation.

For they were overthrown in the wilderness: the evidence of God's displeasure with them. We must avoid giving this statement emotional overtones. God's displeasure was not emotional but realistic. The Israelites who were overthrown in the wilderness had proved themselves incapable of becoming instruments for God's further gracious activity. By their idolatry, their lack of faith, and their murmuring they had shown themselves incapable of meaningful divine leadership. This explains why they were rejected. They presumed on divine favors and whined for more, when they should have been challenged to greater devotion and stronger faith. This is the thought that Paul desired to present to the Corinthians in their situation.

(2) Warning to the Corinthians to avoid Israel's sins (10:6–13)

Self-discipline as a necessity of the Christian life is the primary subject discussed in this section. The Corinthians were warned that participation in past blessings did not guarantee future righteousness. The warning is couched in general terms, but the implications for the Corinthians' situation are clear.

Verse 6: Now these things are warnings for us: expresses Paul's use of them, not the intention of the events themselves. *These things* is the subject and refers to the things mentioned in verses 1–5. *Are* translates the past tense of a word meaning "to become or to happen." Probably in the context, the translation to be preferred is: "came to pass." *Warnings* translates a Greek word which means "types" or "examples." [1] Taken with *for us,* the meaning is that they happened in the past and had now become, through the Corinthians' knowledge of them, examples of the wrong response of God's grace. In this sense *warnings* may be a justified translation. Paul did not consider the case of Israel as exactly parallel to the situation of the Corinthians. The connecting link is that the Corinthians were following a course of action without realizing its potential danger. Paul thought their attitudes were unsafe and warned against pursuing them by citing the example of Israel.

Not to desire evil as they did: a purpose clause. A literal translation would be: "in order that we should not be desirers of evil, just as those also desired." The RSV translators are to be congratulated for substituting *desire* for the older translation "lust." The Greek word only means to desire strongly without any indication in itself that this is evil. In this context the addition of *evil* (i.e., evil things) defines the desire as sinful. If we seek a particular application in the Corinthian church, it would refer to desiring the pleasures connected with the pagan feasts. However, it is better to take this as a general term which would include any evil thing.

Verse 7: Do not be idolators: worshipers of man-made representations of deity. The command is a prohibition in the form which usually means to stop what you are doing. However, the tense can represent a tendency rather than an accomplished fact. This meaning better fits our knowledge of the situation. Though the Corinthians had not actually become idolaters, they were following a course of action which could well lead them to this sin. Paul's command was that they should stop that course of action. If "evil things" in verse 6 is the general term, idolatry is the first concrete example mentioned. Its position at the head of the list is due not only to the nature of the sin but also to the fact that this sin represented the most pressing danger among the Corinthians.

As some of them were: an understatement. The record shows that all were guilty of worshiping the golden calf (cf. Exod. 32:6).

As it is written, "The people sat down to eat and drink and rose up to dance": quotes Exodus 32:6 from the Greek version of the Old Testament. The quotation describes an idolatrous banquet followed by idolatrous practices. The similarity to the pagan feasts at Corinth must have been striking.

Verse 8: We must not indulge in immorality: more exactly, "let us stop committing fornication." This was already a sin of some of the Corinthians (cf. 5:1—6:20). The relation of idol worship and fornication was often

---

[1] Héring says the Greek word means "imprint." From this literal meaning the sense of "sign" or "pattern" developed.

very close, especially at Corinth. The temple priestesses were little more than harlots. Thus, the second example of evil desire follows the first closely.

As some of them did: The relation between idolatry and fornication is made clear in the case of the Israelites. "The people began to play the harlot with the daughters of Moab. These invited the people to the sacrifices of their gods, and the people ate, and bowed down to their gods" (Num. 25:1–2).

And twenty-three thousand: differs from the Old Testament account, which gives twenty-four thousand (Num. 25:9). Several explanations of this disparity have been attempted: (1) that the number was between twenty-three and twenty-four thousand, and either number is correct; (2) that Paul had a lapse of memory in citing the number and made a natural mistake; (3) that Paul was following a different Jewish tradition. Against (3) is the fact that no other Jewish source has been discovered with the same number as Paul's. Against (1) is the same fact. If Paul had been quoting the Old Testament, he would not have changed the number knowingly. Thus, we must assume that Paul had a lapse of memory and misquoted the Old Testament number. Any attempt to reconcile the two passages rests upon a wrong conception of inspiration. What is inspired in the Bible is the central message of salvation.

Fell: died.

In a single day: shows the enormity of the punishment.

Verse 9: We must not put the Lord to the test: more exactly, "Let us stop trying out the Lord." To do this would be to continue a course of action known to be against the Lord's desire, to see if he would bring vengeance. There is no evidence that the Corinthians were doing this. We must take it as expressing a tendency which Paul could see in their actions but which they could not. There is strong textual evidence for reading "Christ" instead of *Lord,* and much weaker evidence for "God." *Lord* has the strongest manuscript evidence, but to Paul, "Lord" was Jesus Christ.

As some of them did and were destroyed by serpents: The reference is to the story told in Numbers 21:4–6. The particular way in which the Israelites tested the Lord was to bemoan their lack of the rich food they had enjoyed in Egypt. They came to detest the manna which God provided. The anger of the Lord was kindled, and a plague of serpents invaded the camp, destroying the people.

Verse 10: Nor grumble: rather, "stop grumbling." Some of the Corinthians were no doubt guilty of this sin. They perhaps grumbled at the restrictions laid on their liberty by their devotion to Christ. If not that, they at least grumbled because of the scruples of their weaker brethren.

As some of them did: There are two instances of grumbling in the history of Israel in the wilderness: Numbers 14:1–3; Numbers 16:41–50. The instance recorded in Numbers 16 was the one in Paul's mind. The grumbling of the Israelites led, in this instance, to open rebellion against the leadership of Moses and Aaron.

And were destroyed by the Destroyer: the destroying angel, not Satan. No mention is made of the *Destroyer* in the passage in Numbers, but Paul assumed that he was the agent of God's destruction. He was the agent in the slaying of the firstborn in Egypt (Exod. 12:23), in the plague on David (2 Sam. 24:16), and in the destruction of the Assyrians (2 Chron. 32:21)(ICC).

Verse 11: Now these things happened to them as a warning: Warning translates a word which means "typically" or "by way of example." *Happened* is in the imperfect tense in Greek, indicating a series of events. *To them* has the emphasis in this expression. Paul's thought was that the events were typical of sins of God's people. The thought is similar to verse 6.

But they were written down for our instruction: expands the idea of "example." The written record was for the good of future generations, not for those to whom these things had happened. *Instruction* has the idea of positive teaching of the right course of action.

Upon whom the end of the ages has come: expresses Paul's belief that the Christian age was the goal of all past ages. We, the Christians, are those upon whom this age has come. *Has come* is the perfect tense of a Greek verb which means "to come down." *End* is the decisive word in the phrase. It comes from a Greek word which means "complete" as to purpose. The phrase expresses Paul's view of what theologians call salvation history. All the previous ages of history were pointing toward this one. The coming of the Christian age means that the goal has been reached, that the last act in the drama of redemption has begun.[1] The practical conclusion from this thought is that self-discipline is all the more necessary now.

Verse 12: Therefore: introduces Paul's application of what he had just written.

Any one who thinks that he stands: perhaps the one who thought he was immune from the temptations connected with the pagan feasts. The danger of a feeling of security in spiritual matters is that it leads to carelessness.

Let . . . [him] take heed: imperative warning to be on the alert against temptations.

Lest he fall: fall from his secure position and become disqualified in the service of God. The same Greek word refers to death in verse 8. However, Paul was moving from his illustration to his specific warnings to the Corinthians, and the word must be given another sense here.

Verse 13: talks about temptations. Three things are said: (1) temptations will come; (2) our temptations are not different from the temptations of others; and (3) God will provide a way to escape them.[2]

No temptation has overtaken you that is not common to man: Temptation must have its common meaning of inducement to sin. *Common to man* is a good translation. The temptations which they had endured were not unique. The specific situation in Paul's mind was the temptations which came from their pagan friends. The Corinthians had broken with their old religion. They were under temptation not to make that break complete. But this temptation was not uncommon in the first century. Nearly every convert came out of another religion and faced the same temptation.

God is faithful: He can be trusted. Though the temptations were not

---

[1] Cf. Thrall.
[2] Cf. Barclay.

uncommon, they were powerful. Human power alone would inevitably fail to stand up against them. The Corinthians were not asked to resist alone. They had God on their side if they sought to resist. He was faithful; he could be trusted to do his part when they did theirs.

And he will not let you be tempted beyond your strength: one way in which God helps the Christian. Paul limited the temptation to sin. The emphasis was upon the Corinthians in their situation. Paul promised that God would not allow them to be tempted with a temptation beyond their ability to bear as Christians. Notice that Paul did not promise that they would have no temptation. Temptation is one of God's ways of disciplining his children. Not that God desires his children to do evil, but he does desire them to develop their spiritual strength. This can be done only as we meet and overcome temptations.

But with the temptation: as an attendant circumstance. God is not the author of temptation, but he is the author of help.

Will also provide the way of escape: notice the article. It is not *a* way but *the* necessary way of escape. The expression assumes that every temptation has its own way of escape. *The temptation* and *the way of escape* go in pairs. God sees to it that one does not occur without the other being present.

That you may be able to endure it: i.e., without sinning. *That you may be able* meant that the Corinthians would have the power. If sin came, it was not because they did not have the power, but because they did not use it. *To endure it* meant that they could bear up under it without sin. This verse contains a great promise which is applicable to every Christian in every situation. Sin cannot overpower us; we can overpower it. We do this, not with our own strength, but with the strength that God provides.

4. Warning Against Participation in Pagan Festivals (10:14-22)

In this section Paul turned again to the particular problems of the Corinthian congregation. As we noted above, the question of eating foods offered to idols really had two dimensions—social contacts and participation in pagan festivals. This section deals with the second. There is a very close connection with the discussion in verses 1-13. Israel's sins were illustrative of the danger of contact with idols. Here he made this connection specific.

Verse 14: a general admonition.

Therefore: reflects the thought of verses 1-13. Because of the dangers of contact with idols, so well illustrated in the history of Israel, they were to act.

My beloved: an endearing term meant to remind the Corinthians of Paul's love for them. He did not speak as a judge, but as one who had their welfare at heart.

Shun: rather, "keep on fleeing." Flight was the "way of escape" which God had provided for this particular temptation. In some cases it may be better to stand and fight. In this case flight, immediate and continual, was required. This does not mean that they were already contaminated with the worship of idols, but they were in danger of contamination.

The worship of idols: the most sinful sin of all. The first three of the Ten Commandments deal with the problem of idolatry. To bow down before idols is to dishonor God and to show that the true understanding of God has not been achieved. Their attendance at pagan feasts involved an implied worship of idols.

Verse 15: appeals to the natural intelligence of the Corinthians.

I speak: a present tense of the verb.

As to sensible men: men of common sense or natural intelligence. In other passages Paul used the same word with a touch of irony or sarcasm. "For you gladly bear with fools, being wise yourselves!" (2 Cor. 11:19). Here, however, no such implication exists. He simply appealed to them to use their own intelligence to decide whether his argument was sound or not.

Judge for yourselves what I say: The verb is the past tense of the imperative, which means that they were called upon to form a single judgment of his words. *Yourselves* is emphatic in the command. They did not need to depend upon his opinion; they were perfectly capable of forming their own.

Verse 16: Paul stated the basis of his argument that participation in pagan feasts was dangerous, if not sinful. The argument consisted of a comparison of the implications of such practices with the meaning of participation in the Lord's Supper. This and the following verses are difficult of exact interpretation. Interpreters often allow their doctrinal position to influence their exegesis. Paul must not be made to be a supporter of modern ecclesiastical practice. Further, we must remember that Paul's main statement on the meaning of the Lord's Supper comes in 1 Corinthians 11:23–26. In this passage it is mentioned only by way of comparison, and the comparison has perhaps influenced the language. The main debate in church circles is over the way in which participation brings spiritual benefits to the worshiper. Paul did not discuss this factor in this section. He was concerned to show that participation in the Lord's Supper showed that the worshiper was a sharer of these blessings.

The cup of blessing which we bless: wine over which a blessing was pronounced. The third cup of the Jewish Passover was called *the cup of blessing.* It is possible that it was this cup which Jesus used to institute the Lord's Supper. The reference here is to the Christian rite. *Cup* is an expression for the drinking of the wine contained in the cup. *We* may suggest that the blessing was pronounced by the congregation through the agency of the leader, or it may simply mean "we Christians." *Blessing* refers to the prayer of thanksgiving over the cup. The Jews usually began such a prayer with, "Blessed art Thou, O Lord," and followed this beginning with an enumeration of the blessings of God for which thanksgiving was given. *Bless* is in the present tense, pointing to a customary action.

It is interesting that Paul mentioned the cup before the bread. This is the same order which is preserved in the genuine text of Luke (Luke 22:17–19), but it is different from the order suggested in 1 Corinthians 11:23–26. It may very well be that liturgical practices were not crystallized this early in Christian history, and there were differences in the order in which the elements of the Supper were administered. In this context another explanation is possible. The practice which Paul wished to condemn was the eating of food sacrificed to idols. Thus, his mention of bread came last, to bring it into immediate conjunction with the practice to be condemned. If this is so, the mention of the cup is incidental to his argument.

Is it not a participation in the blood of Christ?: a rhetorical question demanding an affirmative answer. Paul argued that one became a partaker by drinking the wine. *Participation* comes from the Greek word *koinōnia,* which means "sharing, partnership, or fellowship." The RSV translates the same word by "fellowship" (1 Cor. 1:9). The Greek has no article and none is needed. It is certainly not "the communion" (KJV), as if there were no other. The meaning is that the drinking of the wine in some way constitutes fellowship with the blood of Christ. No mention is made of the way in which this fellowship occurs. In Christian history much debate has centered, not in the fact of fellowship, but in the way of fellowship. In general four positions have become fairly well defined: (1) Some feel that in the service of the Supper the elements are actually transformed so that the eating and drinking are an actual eating and drinking of the blood and body of Christ. This interpretation is called transubstantiation. (2) Some feel that the elements are not actually transformed, but that there is an actual presence of the body and blood of Christ so that the eating still constitutes an actual eating and drinking of the body and blood of Christ. This interpretation is called consubstantiation. (3) Some feel that we may speak of a real presence of Christ in the elements, but not of an actual presence. (4) Others feel that the elements are purely symbolic of the body and blood of Christ. Either of these views would fit into this verse; none of them are demonstrated to be true on the basis of this passage.[1] Paul dealt more fully with this aspect of the Supper in 11:23-26. Here he was concerned only to remind the Corinthians of a truth with which they were already familiar, i.e., that participation in the Lord's Supper was a fellowship with Christ as well as with each other. *The blood of Christ* should be taken as a metonym for Christ's victory over sin on the cross. Thus the fellowship was a sharing of the spiritual benefits secured by the sacrifice of Christ. The question remains whether the act of drinking created the sharing or merely gave witness to it. I would be inclined, in the light of Paul's later discussion, to think that he meant that it was a witness to a fellowship created by faith.

The bread which we break, is it not a participation in the body of Christ?: parallel in construction and meaning to the preceding question. *Bread* is more exactly the loaf, thus corresponding to the cup. We must beware of reading the modern meaning of "body" into this passage. "Body" in the modern language refers only to the physical self. "Body" in Hebrew thought referred to the totality of earthly life. To share in the body of Christ is to share in the benefits of his incarnation and his perfect human life. I think it is this fact which led the early Christians, if their practice does not represent a genuine reminiscence, to place the loaf before the cup in the service of the Lord's Supper. Our tendency is to make the loaf into another reference to the cross, and thus to rob it of its distinct meaning.

---

[1] Morris insists that Paul said nothing here of "how" this took place.

The insertion of the act of breaking the loaf, when no mention was made of pouring the wine, reflects the ancient custom. Only one cup was used. It was passed around from person to person and each sipped out of it. In many modern churches individual cups are used and the wine is poured into them. In Paul's day this was not done. However, the bread was broken into bite-size bits and distributed to each individual participant.

Verse 17: turns to the fellowship of Christians with one another in the congregation. The details are difficult, but the general sense is clear.[1]

Because there is one bread: gives the basis of his conclusion.

We who are many are one body: refers to the fellowship of the congregation. *Body* was Paul's metaphor for the Christian congregation as an organic unit. This concept will be developed fully in chapter 12. *We* would not necessarily include Paul but would be the same as the *we* in verse 16. The idea is not necessarily that the one loaf makes the many into one body, but that the use of one loaf shows this to be true.

For we all partake of the one bread: repeats the first clause with some modifications. *For* is used instead of *because.* This use would fit into the interpretation that makes the practice conform to the reality. The reality is that the many are one body. The practice that conforms to this is that one loaf is used in the Lord's Supper.

Verse 18: adds another illustration of the fact that participation in religious rites has spiritual significance.

Consider the practice of Israel: a reminder that Paul was appealing to the common sense of the Corinthians to judge the case (cf. vs. 15).

Are not those who eat the sacrifices partners in the altar?: a rhetorical question demanding an affirmative answer; thus, an assertion in the form of a question. *Those who eat the sacrifices* refers to the priests and Levites already mentioned (cf. 9:13). *Partners* translates a Greek word which is cognate with the word used in verse 16 and translated there "participation." The idea of sharing or fellowship is meant. *The altar* is an expression for God. The idea is not that the priests had a fellowship with the physical altar, but they had a fellowship with the God whom the altar visibly represented. I would disagree that the point is that partaking of food is a basis of fellowship (Parry). It is rather to be thought of as a sign of an existing fellowship. This was the meaning of breaking bread in social intercourse. One broke bread with his friends, but not with his enemies. The breaking of bread did not cause the friendship but symbolized it. This fact is the basis of the reproach of Judas. He was "one of the twelve, one who is dipping bread in the same dish with me" (Mark 14:20). Yet, he had already bargained to betray Jesus. His act in breaking bread with Jesus was hypocritical; i.e., it was a false symbol. This meaning must be applied to all physical acts. They do not have spiritual power in themselves; they could not have. They do have symbolic meaning, both in ordinary intercourse and in spiritual rites. Partaking of them symbolizes spiritual realities. The act of partaking may serve to deepen the relationship, but it can never create it.

---

[1] Cf. Morris.

Verse 19: begins the application of the illustrations to the case in question.

What do I imply then?: more exactly "What am I then saying?" This question connects the application to verse 15 and guards Paul's words from what might appear to be an inconsistency.

That food offered to idols is anything, or that an idol is anything?: The answer is "no." This was not the meaning of what Paul was saying. He had already admitted that the opposite was true (cf. 8:4–6). It was the belief that such food was not anything meaningful which led some of the Corinthians to feel that participation in the idol feast meant nothing. Paul did not deny the truth on which they based their action. His purpose was to show that the implications of the action were contrary to the Christian belief. In the mind of the pagan worshiper, the food was something special and the idols were real. Sharing their festivals by the Christians would be tacit recognition of the validity of their belief.

Verse 20: No, I imply that what pagans sacrifice they offer to demons and not to God: rather, "to a no-god." The *not* does not modify the verb, but *God.* The same construction is found in the Greek version of Deuteronomy 32:17. *Demon* is found only here and in 1 Timothy 4:1 in the writings ascribed to Paul. The term "demon" always has the meaning of an evil one in the New Testament, though it had a neutral meaning in Greek thought. The idea is that the sacrifice of the pagans was inspired by evil and was a challenge to belief in God.

I do now want you to be partners with demons: describes the implications of their participation in the religious festivals. *To be,* rather, "to become," either means to "show yourselves to be" or "to act in such a way that you tend to become." Certainly the first would be true. By their participation the Corinthians would show themselves to be, whether falsely or not, partners with demons,[1] in the same way that the participant in the Lord's Supper shows himself to be a partner with Jesus Christ. Not only so, but also Paul seemed to believe that such a practice would tend to make them actually become partners with demons. The action, though it would not create the reality, would tend to lead the participant to a frame of mind where the reality could arise.

Verse 21: You cannot: that is, you cannot with real meaning. Of course, it was not physically impossible to eat of the Lord's Supper and then attend an idol-feast. The idea is that it was impossible to do this with any real meaning. It was morally wrong to try to do it. It would be possible to do this only if one were not aware of the implications of participation.

The cup of the Lord . . . the table of the Lord: reminds us that the Lord is the host when we partake of the Supper. *Table* reflects an Old Testament description of the altar as a "table of the Lord" (cf. Mal. 1:7). Probably on the basis of this passage, coupled with Luke 22:30, the *Lord's table* came to be a name for the Lord's Supper.

The cup of demons . . . the table of demons: the idol-feasts which Paul regarded as feasts in which demons were hosts. Since Paul regarded the

---

[1] The term "demon" is used only here and in 1 Timothy 4:1 by Paul (Edwards).

demons as being under the leadership of Satan, the archenemy of Christ, participation in idol-feasts would be an act of spiritual treason.

Verse 22: Shall we provoke the Lord to jealousy?: rather, "Are we provoking the Lord to jealousy?" The verb is in the present indicative. The saying is reminiscent of Deuteronomy 32:21: "They have stirred me to jealousy with what is no god: they have provoked me with their idols." In the Old Testament, "Lord" referred to Jehovah; here it refers to Christ. To *provoke . . . to jealousy* would be to press the case as far as possible to see if the Lord would be willing to be placed on a level with the demons.

Are we stronger than he?: argues that we are not. The expression is ironical. The Lord can have nothing to do with evil. To suppose that the Christian could do so with impunity would imply that the Christian was stronger than the Lord (Parry). However, the expression could mean that the Corinthians considered themselves strong enough to withstand the judgment of the Lord on their conduct (Edwards). In either case Paul was pointing to the implications of the action of the strong Christians. They were acting as if they would provoke the Lord; they were acting as if they were stronger than he. Paul was indignant. With these questions he concluded what he had to say about the most important aspect of their question. His conclusion, which he felt that their common sense would lead them to share, was that it was utterly impossible for any Christian, strong or weak, to participate in idol-feasts. On this matter there could be no thought of expediency as in the case of eating meat sold in the shops or eating with friends in their homes.

5. Admonition to Use Practical Wisdom in Social Circumstances (10:23— 11:1)

In the preceding paragraph Paul had answered the main question with a resounding negative. In this paragraph he dealt with two subsidiary questions on the basis of expediency. This was possible because there was no moral question involved in eating meat which had been offered to idols. Only the circumstance of the eating had moral meaning. There were two circumstances in which Paul considered the use of wisdom as preeminent: eating meat that had been sold in the market place and eating such meat in the homes of friends. Two considerations were to rule practice in these circumstances: their own interests and the interests of others.

Verse 23: states the two principles on which to base decision.

"All things are lawful": a teaching of Paul which the Corinthians had wrongfully applied to other circumstances (cf. 6:12–20), but which did apply to the present circumstances. Paul believed that Christianity had freed him from the legalistic restrictions of the Jews concerning foods. If these restrictions held good, no Christian could eat meat which had been butchered by pagans lest it be contaminated by the idol offering. But this restriction no longer applied. Such food was not contaminated. *All things* must be taken in this restricted sense. It means all food, not all actions.

But not all things are helpful: The personal good of the Christian must be considered. *Helpful* is to be taken in the sense of spiritual benefit,[1] the growth of the Christian in the likeness of Christ or the winning of the pagan to Christ. A particular action, in this respect, may be harmful, helpful, or neutral. The Christian would do well to seek out those things which are helpful. The things that are neutral are lawful, but this does not mean that one should go out of his way to engage in them.

"All things are lawful": repeated for emphasis and balance of sentence structure.

But not all things build up: insists that the spiritual good of others must be considered. One's actions may have three possible effects on the spiritual life of others. They may tear down; they may build up; they may have no effect. Those which tear down are to be avoided on the basis of love for others. Those which build up should be sought out of love. Those which have no effect may be engaged in without question. It was this principle with which Paul was concerned in this paragraph. He had already dealt with the instance of actions which tended to tear down the brother (cf. 8:7–13). Here he dealt with those which neither built up nor tore down, those which had no spiritual significance either for the individual or his neighbor.

Verse 24: makes the two principles explicit.

Let no one seek his own good: Good is supplied by the translator and is questionable. The Greek has the neuter adjective and constitutes an ellipsis. But the question is: What shall be supplied? Literally, the Greek reads: "Let each one stop seeking the of himself." "The" stands without anything to modify. The RSV choice is followed by most commentators and may be correct. However, it is possible that Paul was thinking of "desire" rather than of "good." The contrast, if this is true, would be twofold: a contrast between what was sought and a contrast between the one for whom it was sought. I would be inclined to think that the double contrast was intended.

But: strong adversative expression.

The good: supplied again by RSV, but is evidently the correct word. Thus, the Christian is to seek the good, the spiritual good of others.

His neighbor: rather "the other." It is noteworthy that Paul did not use "brother" here. His concern had been for the weaker brother in his previous discussion (cf. 8:7–13). However, neighbor fits this context perfectly. The circumstances with which Paul dealt in this paragraph brought the Christian into contact with those outside the church. The Christian was admonished to be concerned about the spiritual influence of his actions on those outside the congregation. The good which he sought was not spiritual growth, but spiritual conversion.

Verse 25: deals with the first circumstance, eating meat which had been offered to idols but which was sold in the market place.

The meat market: probably a correct translation of a rare Greek word, found only here in the New Testament. It comes from a word

---

[1] Grosheide.

which can mean either "enclosure" or "slaughter." It occurs in common Greek for a "provision market." Much of the meat which was sold there, especially that sold to the poor, would come from the sacrifices. An interesting plan of a forum in Pompeii shows the slaughter house, the temple, and the meat market in close proximity (Parry). This would tend to confirm the fact that there was a close connection between the market place and the sacrifice. It would have been difficult for the prospective buyer to determine which meat had been sacrificed and which had not.

Eat . . . without raising any question: the expedient thing to do. *Without raising any question* comes from the same word which we met in 2:14–15. It is a legal term which means "to carry on an investigation." However, its use in this context is not so rigid, and the RSV translation is probably correct. No question was to be asked about the meat.

On the ground of conscience: modifies the whole thought. It is not that they were not to ask conscientious questions. Nor did Paul imply that they were to eat only if their consciousness of right and wrong did not bother them. The thought was that they were not to risk arousing their scruples by asking questions about the meat. This advice would apply particularly to the weaker brother (cf. 8:11). The stronger brother would have no scruples to arouse.

Verse 26: gives the reason why this meat was permissible.

For: introduces a scriptural quotation from Ps. 24:1 which had bearing on the Corinthian situation.

"The earth is the Lord's, and everything in it": the quotation. The thought is that the meat offered to the idols did not cease to belong to the Lord for that reason. It still belonged to him and was his creation. What belonged to him would not pollute anyone. Eating the meat was permissible. Paul took his place alongside the stronger brother in this verse, insisting that the offering of the meat had no spiritual significance. However, his stance was different. He did not tempt the weaker brother to violate his consciousness of right or wrong, but instructed him to avoid the circumstances that would raise the question in his mind.

Verse 27: discusses the other circumstance in which no question was to be raised.

If one of the unbelievers: former acquaintances who did not share their Christian faith. *If* assumes the fact to be true. The word should be translated "when."

Invites you to dinner: There is no word for *dinner* in the Greek, but the RSV translation is justified by the context. Paul clearly had in mind a dinner in the private homes of friends. *You* does not mean the whole church, but any member of the church. *Invites* is the same word which Paul used for God's dynamic call. In the context *invites* is a good translation. Paul assumed that they would not push themselves upon their former friends, but would wait for an express invitation.

And you are disposed to go: rather, "you wish to go." Paul did not encourage them to go, but permitted it if they wished.

Whatever is set before you: the food that is served.

Eat . . . without raising any question on the ground of conscience: same advice as above. Expediency requires that no question be raised. Thus there is no risk that the scruples of the weaker brother will be aroused and create an awkward situation. *Conscience* means the consciousness of what is right or wrong rather than the moral imperative to do the right.

Verse 28: The RSV text makes verses 28–29a parenthetical. This punctuation depends on the meaning assigned to verse 29b. At least, this verse is a modification of the advice given in verse 27.

If: a condition of possibility. The form is different from the *if* in verse 27. There the condition is that of objective reality; here it is that of possibility. Paul did not know this would happen; he thought it might happen. He wanted the Corinthians to be prepared to meet any contingency.

Some one: could be a fellow Christian who was also a guest, or a pagan desiring to see how the Christian would react to the information, or even the host. The pronoun is indefinite, which would seem to eliminate the host.[1]

Says to you, "This has been offered in sacrifice": The term is not, "offered to idols," as one would expect from the previous discussion, but *offered in sacrifice.* The term used would be the natural expression of a pagan who looked upon the offering as to a true god. However, it could be the term used by a weaker brother in deference to the host. Lenski seems quite sure that the one who says the word is a weaker brother, but the context does not support him.

Do not eat it: belongs in this verse rather than the next. The mere mention of the fact that the meat had been sacrificed changed the whole situation. Expediency could no longer be the rule; moral considerations now entered. The present tense would mean, "make a practice of not eating it."

Out of consideration for the man who informed you: gives the first basis for refusal to eat. Again, it is uncertain whether the informant was Christian or pagan. At any rate, his initiative in informing indicated that he thought it wrong for the Christians to eat.

And for conscience' sake: Whose conscience is not said, but it becomes clear in the next verse.

Verse 29: I mean his conscience, not yours: means that the considerations of right and wrong which prompted the fellow guest to divulge the information became a barrier to eating. *His* translates the Greek word meaning "the other's." The same word was used in verse 24; and there we noted that this meant the outsider, not the member of the congregation. If Paul had meant the weaker brother, it seems that he would have said so. Thus, this whole discussion of the meat served in a private dinner had in mind the pagan friend, not the Christian brother. It is often true that the non-Christian has a much stricter opinion of the proper behavior of a Christian than a fellow Christian has. This could well have been true in Corinth. The thought of verses 28–29 seems to have this in mind. If the Christian overrode the feelings of his pagan friend in this matter, he

---

[1] Grosheide thinks the pronoun refers to the weak Christian.

would damage his influence for Christ with that man. To refuse to eat would mean to let one's action be determined by considerations of the "good of his neighbor" (vs. 24).

For why: rather, "to what end or purpose." The expression in Greek is stronger than the interrogative pronoun. RSV has preserved the sense by adding *should* to the particles. The question, if my interpretation is correct, was answered in the foregoing discussion. Paul took his place beside the Christian and asked the question from his viewpoint. If the interpretation of other commentators (Lenski, Edwards, Parry) is correct, the question has no answer. It is rather a cry of rebellion on the part of the strong brother against the restrictions he faces.

My liberty: not, my conscience. The Christian's conscience (i.e., consciousness of what is right or wrong) is his own and cannot be affected by the thoughts and opinions of others. His liberty of action, however, is not free from all restrictions. It must be regulated by the principles of self-concern and concern for others. This fact Paul had made clear.

Determined by another man's scruples: rather, "another man's conscience." *Determined* translates the Greek word meaning "be judged." The idea is not that one's liberty of action is determined by another's conscience, but that it is judged by it. The other man will certainly, on the basis of his own conscience, judge whether a person's actions are right or wrong.

Verse 30: continues in the same vein.

If I partake with thankfulness: assumes that a Christian will. Thankfulness when eating was considered to be a Christian duty. In another context Paul is quoted as saying, "For everything created by God is good, and nothing is to be rejected if it is received with thanksgiving; for then it is consecrated by the word of God and prayer" (1 Tim. 4:4–5). It is probable that this statement was Paul's teaching to new converts everywhere. If so, this conditional clause would only affirm what Paul had taught. The suggestion of the clause is that anything for which one would thank God is done in innocence.

Why am I denounced: more exactly, "Why am I made subject to slander." The same Greek word lies behind the statement: "as some people slanderously charge us with saying" (Rom. 3:8). The use of this word implies that the charges would be false, but would nevertheless be made.

Because of that for which I give thanks?: repeats the thought of the conditional clause. The details of exegesis are somewhat ambiguous in this whole paragraph. Two questions find the commentators in disagreement: (1) Was the "other man" the weaker Christian or the pagan friend? (2) Did Paul think it proper that a Christian should be slandered because of another man's conscience? My own interpretation has led to the conclusion that the "other man" was the pagan friend and that the Christian should regulate his actions by the conscience of others. If he did not, he was properly slandered for his failure to do so. This seems to conform to the principles with which the paragraph began. The fact that a thing is "lawful" is not to be the final word. We must consider whether or not it is "helpful" and whether or not it "builds up" our neighbor. If we fail at these points, we have failed to be Christian and deserve to be criticized.

Verse 31: with the following verses seems to confirm the correctness of my interpretation. There is no change of subjects, as the RSV paragraphing seems to indicate, but a continuation of the same discussion.

So: rather, "therefore." The particle introduces the conclusion based on the preceding discussion. *So* may reach back and include the whole discussion, beginning with 8:1. It is more probable that it reaches back only to 10:23.

Whether you eat or drink, or whatever you do: widens the application to all of the Christian's acts.

Do all to the glory of God: the ruling motive in Christian living. *Do* is in the present tense, meaning "keep on doing." *For the glory of God* means so that it shall truly reflect the glory which God has. The idea is not so much that Christians give thanks, but that their actions shall influence others, particularly the unbelievers, to see what God is really like. "God is glorified when the Christians so act as truly to reveal his character and will for men" (Parry). Thus, the Corinthians would glorify God when they abstained from an action out of a motive of love for others.

Verse 32: defines more clearly what it meant to "do all for the glory of God." It meant that no offense should be given to any of the elements which comprised the population of Corinth—Jews, Greeks, or Christians. To give offense meant to "cause one to stumble into sin." The Christian was to avoid any action which would be the cause of sin in someone else's life.

The first two classes mentioned were the *Jews* and the *Greeks.* Paul thought of the population of Corinth as composed of these two. The *Greeks* were simply those who were not *Jews.*

The church of God: the congregation that belongs to God. This expression reflects the address of the letter: "to the church of God which is at Corinth" (1:2). It was necessary to add the phrase *of God* to avoid misunderstanding. The city council at Corinth was called the *church* (Greek, *ekklēsia)* of Corinth.

By the use of these three terms, Paul made his advice general. He included all the people of Corinth. Some modern commentators take *church of God* to refer to the entire Christian fellowship of the world, but this sense would have been strange to Paul or to any Greek-speaking person. The Greek word which is translated *church* always meant an assembly of people, a congregation. It was only when people who did not speak Greek became Christians that the term could be used in any other sense. Some have suggested that the Greek version of the Old Testament used the term *ekklēsia* to mean the whole of Israel whether assembled or not, but a careful study of the various contexts in which the translation occurs in the Old Testament proves that this is not true. The Greek translators preserved a careful distinction so that this word was never used except to designate an assembly of the people.

Verse 33: enforces teaching by the example.

Just as I try to please all men in everything I do: must be interpreted in the light of Paul's accommodation to the customs of men (cf. 9:19–23). *Everything I do* is not absolute but refers to his practice of waiving his right to be himself in his contact with others. Paul did not compromise on anything of real spiritual significance; he did accommodate himself to the conscience of others on matters that were indifferent in meaning. *Please* is not a happy translation. It seems to imply that Paul habitually curried favor and sought to be well liked. Not so. The word can almost have the meaning, "to be a benefactor to" (ICC). This meaning is nearer to Paul's thought.

Not seeking my own advantage: defines his meaning in the clause above. He sought the advantage of others rather than himself, that is, "of the many."

That they may be saved: defines the advantage which Paul sought for others. This expression emphasizes the fact that Paul was speaking primarily of outsiders in this discussion.

Chapter 11:1: goes with the preceding discussion and contains the exhortation of Paul to the Corinthians in the light of that discussion.

Be imitators of me: the exhortation. Again, the thought must be limited to the context. Paul did not set himself up as a model Christian to be imitated in every respect. This would have been gross egotism. He meant that the Corinthians were to imitate his willingness to waive his rights because of the needs of others.

As I am of Christ: Paul thought of Christ as the supreme example of giving up rights for the good of others. His incarnation and death on the cross is the supreme example of one suffering for the good of others.

VI. INSTRUCTIONS CONCERNING ORDER IN CHURCH SERVICES (11:2–34)

This description could be considered adequate for all the material through chapter 14; but the discussion of spiritual gifts, while related, includes more than what happened in the church services at Corinth. Therefore, I have limited this major division to chapter 11. Two subjects are touched upon: The veiling of women (vss. 2–16) and the service of the Lord's Supper (vss. 17–34).

1. Women Should Be Veiled (11:2–16)

This paragraph begins with a word of commendation—a strange note in this epistle (vs. 2). Some have supposed that it is an insertion into the letter from another epistle of Paul, but there seems to be no solid evidence to support this idea. The reason for the commendation was twofold: (1) Paul was dealing with a matter on which he had not given instruction to the Corinthians, and he did not wish to seem to condemn them for their practice; (2) it lays the foundation for his statement in verse 17: "But in the following instruction I do not commend you." Following the commendation is the statement of a series of subordinations which Paul considered fundamental (vs. 3). Next comes a dogmatic assertion that women should be veiled in the church services and men should not (vss. 4–12). Finally, Paul appealed to the judgment of the Corinthians to justify his stand (vss. 13–16).

The whole discussion of this subject sounds strange to modern ears. The emancipation of womanhood is almost complete in our day, so it seems strange to have special rules for women's apparel in church services. However, we must remember that Paul spoke to women who lived in another social situation, a situation in which women were generally little more than slaves. Paul's instructions were given in the light of that situation. This is not to say that Paul was not himself a child of his times. He was. His instructions were sincere. But we do deny that the instructions in their details have lasting validity in modern society. However, the principles on which the instructions were based do have lasting validity.

The cause of the problem may well have been Christianity itself. The impulse toward freedom which has resulted in the emancipation of women in all societies influenced by Christianity was probably working in Corinth. Though we do not need to assume that there was a strong emancipation movement among the women, it is likely that there was a tendency in this direction. Christ had made all people free, including women. In Christ "there is neither male nor female" (Gal. 3:28). Perhaps the social revolution which is inherent in the Christian gospel was moving too fast in Corinth. If so, the Christian women were leaving themselves open to criticism by acting in ways which were considered unbecoming to a woman of good moral character.

Verse 2: contains Paul's commendation of the church.

I commend you: a strong expression of approval. Paul introduced his new subject without the phrase, "now concerning" (cf. 7:1; 8:1), with which he usually introduced an answer to their questions. It is probable that the church had not raised any question concerning this matter or the Lord's Supper. Their practices in these two matters may have been a part of the report which he had received from "Stephanas and Fortunatus and Achaicus" (16:17). The particular problem was of recent origin. Before entering into a discussion of it, Paul expressed his strong approval of the general practice of the Corinthians in following his instructions. His recommendation was limited to the specific things he mentioned and was not meant to be a blanket approval of their life.

You remember me in everything: refers perhaps to their letter in which they had expressed a desire to follow his instructions.[1] Whether this is so or not, the clause means that *in everything* (i.e., in regard to every question) [2] they thought of him and asked what he would have them do. There is no emphasis on *me* as if Paul were commending them for following him and not following other teachers. This statement is not inconsistent with the rest of the letter. Most of Paul's stern rebukes had to do with matters about which the Corinthians were ignorant. They had written to ask his advice concerning the things which they were debating. Therefore, Paul could say what he did without hypocrisy.

Maintain the traditions even as I have delivered them to you: refers to traditions which were common to the Christian movement. They were not Paul's traditions; he had passed on what he had received from others. "Traditions" was a word often used in Judaism to refer to the rabbinical teachings. Most commentators believe that the Christian traditions included both doctrinal and ethical instructions, but, with Paul at least, the instructions were primary. Paul's use of the word was very limited (cf. Gal. 1:14; Col. 2:8; 2 Thess. 2:15; 3:6). Only here and in the two passages in 2 Thessalonians is the word used to refer to Christian traditions. Second Thessalonians 2:15 refers to doctrinal teachings, while 2 Thessalonians 3:6 refers to ethical instructions. However, the complementary word *delivered* is more frequent in Paul (used in relation to teaching in Rom. 6:17 [in the Greek]; here; 1 Cor. 11:23; 15:3; more often used to refer to the death of Christ). In each of the passages where *delivered* is related to teachings, the teachings are doctrinal in content.[3] Thus, with Paul the doctrinal traditions took precedence. If these were in mind in this passage, as seems likely, Paul's praise was

---

[1] Parry.
[2] Grosheide.
[3] Barrett calls them "the central truths of the Christian faith."

for their doctrinal steadfastness. This interpretation fits perfectly with the fact that the letter never seems to imply that there were any doctrinal deviations in the Corinthian congregation. In summary, Paul's praise was twofold: (1) The Corinthians remembered him when problems arose and sought his advice; (2) They were true to the doctrinal teachings of the gospel. Both of these things could be said truthfully even in the context of this letter.

Verse 3: introduces the series of subordinations which rule the thought of this paragraph.

But I want you to understand: a formula introducing something not previously mentioned. The same formula is found in Colossians 2:1, but the more usual formula with Paul was: "But we would not have you ignorant, brethren" (1 Thess. 4:13; cf. 1 Cor. 10:1; 12:1; 2 Cor. 1:8; Rom. 1:13; 11:25). Paul had not discussed the matter of women remaining veiled while praying or prophesying in his previous contacts with them.

That the head of every man is Christ: The first subordination is that of every man to Christ. *Every man* has the emphatic position in the Greek sentence. The Greek for *man* is not the common word for humanity, but the special word for a male person. *Head* is a metaphor. We do not find it as such in the New Testament except in this passage and in Ephesians and Colossians where Christ is said to be the head of the church. The particular emphasis is that of superiority and rulership.[1] The Christian man has no superior but Christ himself. Paul used this thought to show that a man should not wear a sign of subordination to other men when he prayed.

The head of a woman is her husband: expresses Paul's belief that the man is superior to the woman. He would not have denied that Christ was also the head of the Christian woman; but he believed that, in a lower sense, the woman's husband was superior. The thought of woman's subordination to her husband is perfectly consistent with the idea of equality. The subordination is functional rather than metaphysical. Remember that Paul had written that there was no male or female "in Christ" (Gal. 3:28). He believed in the perfect equality of persons before Christ. However, he believed that in the function of the home and the church the woman should be subordinate to her husband, that she should accept his rule in the same way that he should accept the rule of Christ. This conception of woman's subordination goes back to the creation story itself. "Then the Lord said, 'It is not good that the man should be alone; I will make him a helper fit for him' " (Gen. 2:18).

The head of Christ is God: in the function of redemption, not in personal status. It was God who sent Christ into the world to save men (John 3:16); it was God who worked through Christ to reconcile the world to himself (2 Cor. 5:19). Christ could say: "The words that I say to you I do not speak on my own authority; but the Father who dwells in me

---

[1] Barrett thinks the emphasis is on origin. However, he ignores the fact that Paul was talking about the Christian order, not the human order.

does his works" (John 14:10). At the same time he could say, "He who has seen me has seen the Father" (John 14:9). Why was this clause added here? It had no bearing on the problem. Perhaps the reason was that Paul pointed to Christ as the supreme example of obedience. If Christ could function subordinately to his head, the woman should be willing to do the same.

Verse 4: states the consequences of man's superiority to the woman and his subjection to Christ in the man's religious practices. Many commentators miss the fact that Paul was quite as much concerned with the apparel of the men as with that of the women.

Any man: picks up the *every man* of the previous verse without any connecting particle. Of course, he meant any Christian man.

Who prays or prophesies: shows that the whole question is a matter of religious practices in the church assembly. Prayer could be a private devotion; but since it is linked with prophesying, it refers to public prayer. *Prophesies* is a word often used in these chapters (cf. especially chap. 14). It comes from a Greek word with two elements meaning "to speak" and "before." Probably it meant no more than the act of addressing the congregation.

With his head covered: literally, "having a veil." The injunction for men to be "unveiled" and the women "veiled" in public services was peculiar to Christians. Among the Greeks both men and women were bareheaded. Among the Romans it was customary to cover the head when worshiping. Among the Jews men veiled their faces when praying. It may be that the difference between Jewish and Greek customs caused the confusion in the church at Corinth. As the following verses show, Paul was not concerned with the custom as such, but with the significance of the custom.

Dishonors his head: shames Christ. How? Probably by seeming to acknowledge a superior among men. The veil was a sign of subjection to the authority of another on the human level.[1] This fact seems to lie behind all that Paul said on the subject. Therefore, if the man wore a veil, he dishonored Christ, his head, by having a divided loyalty. Perhaps the background from which Paul derived his ideas was the general custom among the Greeks which dictated that slaves should cover their heads while free men went bareheaded (Lenski). The unveiled head of the man meant that he was accountable only to Christ. The modern mind is understandably confused by this custom because it is so far removed from our own customs.

Verse 5: applies the same thought to the woman.

Any woman: any Christian wife.

Who prays or prophesies: indicates that it was the custom at Corinth for women to take an active part in the public services. He mentioned this fact here without comment, but forbade it (cf. 14:34) later as being a custom peculiar to Corinth. Some have said that Paul had not thought of telling the women to keep silence before he wrote this. This seems unlikely.

With her head unveiled: It was customary in ancient times for women

[1] Edwards.

to remain veiled in any public place. Among the Greeks the only exceptions were the mistresses, women who entertained men but who were not married to them. It is possible that the Christian women were unveiling their heads in the church services to demonstrate their equality with men in Christ. Lenski's suggestion that church services were not under consideration has not convinced others.

Dishonors her head: that is, the man. Some have thought that *head* in verses 4–5 refers to the natural head on which the veil was worn, but it seems that verse 3 should define the *head* in each case in a metaphorical sense. The husband was dishonored by having his wife lay aside her symbol of subjection to him.

It is the same as if her head were shaven: that is, she discards her role as a woman quite as much as if she were shaved. The Greek reads, "it is one and the same thing." There is some question as to the exact significance of the shaven head. Some say it meant either mourning or shamelessness (Parry). Some say it meant disgrace for scandalous behavior or bravado (ICC). Some say it meant that she was either a slave woman or an adulteress (Robertson). The common denominator in all opinions is that the shaven head was a sign of immorality, either imposed upon the woman by society or self-imposed. However, Lenski denies that the suggestion of immorality is involved, pointing out that only the lower class of prostitutes shaved their heads. Most of them attempted to appear as beautiful as possible. Lenski finds the clue to the passage in the belief that women were meant to wear long hair, and that to cut it off was to go against nature and the Creator who stands behind nature. The thought of Paul, nevertheless, seems to demand the idea of moral shamelessness. He had in mind the Christian wives. Any breath of scandal against them would create difficulties in the preaching of the gospel to the pagan population of Corinth. This is perhaps the enduring thought of the passage. If Christian women dress or act in such a way as to shock the sensibilities of society, they will become a hindrance to the preaching of the gospel.

Verse 6: carries this thought further.

For if a woman will not veil herself: The form of the condition assumes that some women were refusing to wear the veil. The problem was real in Corinth. The verb form emphasizes both the fact that this refusal was the act of the woman (middle voice) and that it was a customary thing (present tense).

Then she should cut off her hair: more exactly, "let her be shorn." The verb still has the middle voice, which indicates that it was to be her act. The tense indicates that it was to be a single act. Paul thought that cutting off the hair was equivalent to refusing to wear the veil.

But if it is disgraceful: assumes that it is. Whether this was universally true in the ancient world or not is doubtful. In Corinth it was true.

Let her wear a veil: thus avoiding the implications of shame. The form of the verb is the same as above: the middle voice indicates the woman's own choice; the present tense indicates customary action. The Christian woman was to make a practice of veiling herself to avoid the shame that would otherwise be hers.

Verse 7: appeals to the natural order as vindication of Paul's admonitions.

For a man ought not to cover his head: probably a correct translation. The Greek reads literally, "The man is not under obligation to cover his head." This is probably an understatement for emphasis of the fact that he ought not do so.

Since he is the image and glory of God: reflects the account in Genesis. The immediate implication of the creation of man in the image of God was that he would have dominion over the world. "So God created man in his own image, in the image of God he created him; male and female he created them. And God blessed them, and God said to them, 'Be fruitful and multiply, and fill the earth and subdue it' " (Gen. 1:27–28). This is the thought that lies behind this clause. Man has a supremacy over the created order which constitutes his likeness to God. To wear a veil over his head would deny this supremacy. *Glory* does not appear in the Genesis account, but the thought in this passage seems to be the same. By man's supremacy God's supremacy is made clear to men. Thus, God is glorified and man becomes the glory of God. *Glory of God* usually means the revelation of the glory that is God's rather than the glory itself.

But woman is the glory of man: Paul's interpretation of the fact that woman's creation was secondary. She was made out of Adam in order to be his helper. Therefore, her function in life was to show the supremacy and authority of man. Both *woman* and *man* are without the article in the Greek, which means that Paul was speaking generally. It was not the wife and her husband, but woman and man in their inherent nature that he meant.

Verses 8–9: a parenthetical explanation of the last clause in verse 7. The background of the verses is the creation account in Genesis. Two things are asserted about the woman: she was made *from man* and *for man.* The reverse is specifically said not to be true: *man was not made from woman,* nor *for woman.* The first assertion is supported by the words: "So the Lord God caused a deep sleep to fall upon the man, and while he slept took one of his ribs and closed up its place with flesh; and the rib which the Lord God had taken from the man he made into a woman and brought her to the man" (Gen. 2:21–22). Thus, in the beginning woman was made out of man. The second assertion is supported by the words: "Then the Lord God said, 'It is not good that the man should be alone; I will make him a helper fit for him' " (Gen. 2:18). Thus *woman* was *made for* (Grk. "on account of") *man.* Both the origin of woman and the reason for her being is found in man. Behind this natural explanation of origin lies the purpose of "the Lord God." For Paul, this was the decisive fact. His whole discussion appeals not so much to natural causes as to divine purpose revealed in the natural order.

Verse 10: a very difficult verse. In Paul's mind the thought seemed to flow naturally, but modern commentators are divided about its meaning.

That is why: should be connected with verse 7 and especially the statement, "woman is the glory of man." The expression introduces the reason for Paul's admonition.

A veil: Greek, "an authority." The veil, in Paul's mind, was the symbol of the authority of the man over her. Thus *veil* is a synonym for the "authority" for which it stands.[1] This interpretation is the usual one, but some commentators have differed. They have taken "authority" as referring to the woman's authority over her own natural head. There is justification for this interpretation in the Greek words (i.e., authority upon). This combination of words is found three times in the book of Revelation with the meaning "have control of" (11:6, "over the waters"; 14:18, "over fire"; 20:6, "over such," meaning the saints). In each case the combination of authority plus the preposition (Greek, *epi*) is the same. If this translation is taken, it is possible that the expression means that the woman should maintain control over her head so that it would not expose her to indignity. The woman's veil then became her willing subjection to her husband, her refusal to expose herself to others. However, the ultimate significance of the two interpretations is the same. Willing subjection to her husband's authority was a recognition of that authority, and this is the meaning of the clause. Even so, it would seem that the usual interpretation has the best claim to validity.

Because of the angels: mentioned without explanation as if it were clear to the Corinthians. But it is not clear to modern minds. Some have taken *angels* to be a reference to bishops, presbyters, or the clergy as a whole. This thought proceeds from the fact that the literal meaning of "angel" is "messenger." Some have taken it to refer to the evil angels who, it is supposed, would be tempted to lust by the exposure of the woman's head. Others have taken it to refer to the good angels who, it is supposed, would be tempted to throw off the authority of God over them if the Christian women refused to wear the symbol of the man's authority over them. All of these interpretations are somewhat fanciful, some more so than others. Perhaps the true meaning is the suggestion that Paul was reminding the Corinthians that the heavenly angels watched over them when they prayed and prophesied, and that the Corinthians must be concerned not only with their own pleasure but must also make sure that their actions did not offend the angels.[2]

A modification of this idea is the theory that the angels were thought to be actually present in the public services of the church (Robertson). There seems to be some support for this theory in the Dead Sea scrolls. Whatever the exact meaning, some things seem to be clear. First, *angels* is to be taken in its natural sense and limited to the good angels. Second, Paul thought that the behavior of the women would not only be shocking to the men but also to these angels. Third, concern for the angels seems to be subsidiary to the main thought of the discussion. Fourth, the Corinthians knew what he was talking about. Fifth, the phrase has little or no meaning for modern Christians.

Verse 11: the first verse of a parenthesis. The intent of the two verses (11 and 12) was to avoid an extreme interpretation by the Corinthians of Paul's meaning.

Nevertheless: limits the preceding statement. It would be possible to

---

[1] cf. Edwards.

[2] D. Adolf Schlatter, *Die Korintherbriefe,* Stuttgart: Calwer Vereinsbuchhandlung, 1928. Referred to hereafter as Schlatter.

take Paul's words to mean that man was independent of woman, that there was no place for her in the Christian system of things. Paul did not mean that.

In the Lord: in the Christian sphere. In the natural order woman's place may be insignificant, but not in the Christian order. Only in the Christian sphere are woman's rights respected.

Woman is not independent of man nor man of woman: Independent translates the Greek word which means "without" or "apart from." Perhaps the idea of mutual dependence is the thought.

Verse 12: continues the parenthesis but bases the mutual dependence on a natural background.

For the woman was made from man: in creation.

So man is now born of woman: in the natural order.

And all things are from God: including the natural order. Man is not to be contemptuous of woman because the order of nature and of Christian relations are both the creation of God.

Verse 13: resumes the discussion of the subject of the paragraph.

Judge for yourselves: appeals for a decision which will be binding. The imperative is in the form which demands a once-for-all decision. Paul did not appeal to their common sense, as he did in 10:15, but to their understanding of the natural order and of the Christian system, based on the facts which he had presented. He considered these conclusive. Now he demanded that they decide.

Is it proper: appeals to the Christian sense of propriety. The question is asked without any implications of the right answer. Paul left it to the Corinthians to make their own decision. He had already expressed his opinion. Again, it is noteworthy that Paul did not command, but sought to bring the Corinthians to make their own decisions.

Verse 14: Does not nature itself teach you: rhetorical question asking for an affirmative answer. Paul assumed that it would be self-evident that nature did teach them these things.

That for a man to wear long hair is degrading to him: At this time "civilized men, whether Jews, Greeks, or Romans, wore their hair short" (ICC). Paul appealed to this custom as being an expression of what nature taught.

Verse 15: But if a woman has long hair: assumes that it is probable that she will.

It is her pride?: Again the appeal is to the teaching of nature. *Pride* translates the Greek word for "glory." The woman's long hair reveals her true beauty. The reference is not to the feeling of pride but to the commonly accepted fact that woman's long hair enhanced her beauty.

For her hair is given to her: suggests that God had given her this distinctive sign.

For a covering: more exactly, "instead of a covering." The word for *covering* means something thrown around one. It might be argued that this was covering enough and no other was needed. Paul looked upon this as a sign that the woman should cover herself further in public services. The natural sign of her subjection should be enhanced by the veil which custom required that she wear in public.

Verse 16: best taken as a conclusion to the discussion about the wearing of veils. It is stated in general terms, however, and could have a more general meaning.

If any one is disposed to be contentious: suggests one who fights for the victory, not for the truth. Some people are so fond of dispute that they will contest the clearest conclusions. The Corinthians were fond of this practice in their social life. Perhaps some of the church members brought the habit into their church relations. The Greek construction translated *if* suggests that this was really happening in Corinth.

We recognize no other practice: more exactly, "We do not have such a custom." The RSV translation would seem to limit the expression to the custom of women going unveiled in the church services. The Greek would refer more exactly to the practice of contentiousness. *Recognize* is not a proper translation of the Greek verb "to have." *We* is emphatic in the expression and refers not only to Paul but to all Christians or to all apostles. Probably the implied contrast is between the Greek custom of contention and the Christian custom of peace. Paul would later say: "All things should be done decently and in order" (14:40) and "God is not a God of confusion but of peace" (14:33).

Nor do the churches of God: refers to the various congregations of Christians of which Paul knew. *Of God* distinguishes these congregations, as belonging to God and dedicated to his work, from other *churches* (i.e., assemblies) dedicated to the business of the city or state and belonging to that government.

A footnote from history is perhaps in order. Paul's discussion seems to have had effect in the lives of succeeding generations of Christians. Sculptures in the Catacombs picture men with short hair and women with a close-fitting headdress (Edwards). The church fathers bear witness that such was the universal practice of churches in the postapostolic age, with a few exceptions.

2. The Lord's Supper Should Be Observed Properly (11:17–34)

The second matter of church order with which Paul dealt was the service of the Lord's Supper. Abuses had crept into the service in the church at Corinth, abuses which seem impossible to modern Christians. However, the Christians at Corinth were only a few years old in their spiritual life, and many things, which to a more stable and settled Christian people seem highly improper, did appear among them. It may be that the Supper was served in conjunction with a love feast and that some of the excesses really attached themselves to this service.

The discussion of Paul can be divided into four paragraphs: (1) Their practice was sinful (vss. 17–22). (2) The purpose of the Supper was remembrance of the Lord (vss. 23–26). (3) Each member was responsible for self-examination in this matter (vss. 27–32). (4) The Supper should be an orderly fellowship service (vss. 33–34).

(1) Their practice was sinful (11:17–22)

Paul mentioned three things in this paragraph which made their assemblies sinful. First, there were divisions of opinion among them about the proper procedure (vs. 18). Second, there were factions among them (vs. 19). Third, there were unchristian practices in eating the Lord's Supper or in the love feast which preceded it (vss. 20–22).

Verse 17: states that the assembly of the church was harmful rather than helpful.

But in the following instructions: rather, "but this commanding." The first question is whether "this" refers to what follows or to what precedes. Commentators are divided; all admit that the Greek is ambiguous. Those who believe that it refers to what follows argue that the emphatic position of the demonstrative pronoun "this," together with the adversative particle, indicates a change of subject (Parry). Those who believe that it refers to what precedes argue that the expression *in the first place* (vs. 18) refers to the first of two discussions; they identify the first with the discussion about women wearing veils in public services (Lenski). It seems more likely that we have a change of subject. Verse 16 was an adequate conclusion to the former discussion. The expression *I do not commend you,* if it refers to the custom of women wearing veils while praying and prophesying, would be in contradiction to verse 2. *Following instructions* translates a Greek verb meaning "commanding."

The change of tone in this division from that of chapters 7–10 is striking. In his discussion of marriage and eating food offered to idols, Paul had offered his advice, feeling that he was led by the Holy Spirit, but he had not imposed any commands. In this section he gave commands. This was due, no doubt, to two considerations. First, he was dealing with a practice of the church concerning which he had a direct tradition from the Lord. Second, the abuses were such as to endanger the spiritual life of the church members. Regarding the Lord's Supper there were not two possible ways, one better than the other; there was only one proper way. Paul did not hesitate to speak dogmatically when the occasion called for it, but he was able to discern when dogmatism was called for and when it was not. Modern preachers would do well to follow his example in both ways.

I do not commend you: more exactly, "I am not praising you." Abuses had already crept into the church practice; these called for condemnation rather than praise. Moreover, it seems that no one had remembered Paul's former instructions concerning the Lord's Supper.

Because when you come together: as a church. The assembly of the church is in question throughout this discussion.

It is not for the better but for the worse: Church services were intended to be constructive, to render help in the spiritual development of the Christian. Church services in Corinth were not only failing to be helpful; they were actually harmful. Instead of ministering to spiritual growth, they contributed to spiritual retrogression.

Verse 18: tells one way in which the church services were *for the worse.*

In the first place: has no formal second. It may be that Paul decided to deal only with the most serious aspect of the trouble. More probably he neglected to insert "in the second place" to introduce his change of subject. If he had done so, it would probably have come at the beginning of verse 23.

When you assemble as a church: indicates the strict meaning of the Greek word for *church.* It meant an assembly. Strictly speaking, the church did not exist except when it was assembled. However, the New Testament indicates that the church was thought of as existing even when the members were not assembled.

I hear: present tense, meaning "I keep on hearing again and again." The report seems to have been coming to Paul's ears from several directions.

And I partly believe it: means he was willing to discount some of the talk as exaggerated, but could not discount it all. He wanted to guard himself against being overly credulous and suspicious. The manner in which he proceeded to deal with the reports indicates that he knew that there was an unpleasant amount of them that was true.

That there are divisions among you: differences of opinion. The Greek word is *schismata,* from which we get our English word "schism." However, the Greek word does not seem to have had so strong a meaning in the New Testament. John used the same word (John 7:43; 9:16; 10:19) to describe a difference of opinion among the Jews concerning Jesus, some thinking that he had a demon, others thinking that he was a prophet. Paul used the word three times in this epistle (here; 1:10; 12:25). In each case he seemed to be talking about differences of opinion rather than parties that had split the church. Some commentators have tried to connect the divisions mentioned in 1:12 with this discussion, but there seems no way to make such a connection. Whether this division was along lines of wealth (Parry) or differences of opinion about the proper procedure at the Lord's Supper is not entirely clear.

Verse 19: Paul saw that such *divisions* were necessary in the life of the church.

For: introduces a reason why Paul found it possible to believe some of the reports. This verse should be connected with *I partly believe it,* giving the reason for his belief rather than the reason for the difference of opinion.

There must be: more exactly, "it is necessary that there be." The necessity arose from God's purpose, not from a philosophical acceptance of inevitability. The Greek word *dei* (an impersonal verb meaning, "it is necessary") is used throughout the New Testament to speak of the purpose of God. The cross is the supreme example of how God brings great good out of evil. The same thought is involved here. The evil was necessary in God's purpose to make manifest the good.[1]

Factions: a stronger word than *divisions.* This word comes from the Greek *airesis,* from which we get the English "heresy." The original meaning was that of "seizing," from which came the idea of "making a choice." In rabbinic Judaism it came to mean those who had chosen to depart from the rabbinic tradition. In the New Testament it is found in this sense in Acts, where it describes the Jewish parties of the Sadducees (Acts 5:17) and the Pharisees (Acts 15:5). These parties were not sects in the strictest sense of the word, but rather religious fraternities that existed in the framework of Judaism. Paul did not mean that the church had been split into factions which separated themselves from one another but that there were contending groups. By *factions* he referred to those groups which held doctrinal opinions concerning the Lord's Supper contrary to the

---

[1] Cf. Barrett.

tradition handed down from Jesus. The context indicates that he was speaking of those who had departed from his instructions.

In order that: introduces the clause which explains why factions were necessary. They were not necessary for their own sake, nor for any good that was in them, but for the good which God might accomplish through them.

Those who are genuine: that is, those who pass the test. *Genuine* translates a Greek word which means "approved." The thought is that the Christians who stood up for the truth and followed the tradition were thereby approved. *Genuine* seems too strong. It suggests that others were not really Christians at all. Paul did not seem to imply this.

May be recognized: rather, "manifest." However, the idea of their being recognized seems to be in the context. Paul seemed to think that, through the debates that would arise by reason of the false doctrines, the holders of the true doctrine would be recognized and would win the day in Corinth.

Verse 20: states the consequences of their differences.

When you meet together: assemble as a church.

It is not the Lord's supper that you eat: You cannot by reason of your divisions really eat the Lord's Supper. This seems to be the meaning in spite of the fact that some commentators have taken it to mean either that they had not come together for that purpose, or that when they ate what they called the Lord's Supper it was not really the Lord's Supper. The thought is that their conduct made it impossible for them to have the service. *The Lord's Supper* does not refer to the love feast which sometimes preceded the Supper, but to the church ordinance of that name. However, some feel that it includes both in this context (ICC). It is probable that the abuses detailed in verses 21–22 had to do with the love feast which was connected with the serving of the Supper but which was not a part of it. If this is true, the abuses related to the love feast (not called this until the end of the first century) was one reason why it was impossible for them to have the Lord's Supper in any meaningful way.

Verse 21: This verse with verse 22 describes the abuses which were current in Corinth.

For in eating: the common meal.

Each one goes ahead with his own meal: indicates that it was their custom to do so. The exact picture is impossible to re-create. However, the likelihood is that the free men in the congregation, especially the more affluent, refused to wait for the congregation to gather. Slaves would have had difficulty coming before late at night since they had to fulfill their domestic duties for their earthly masters. The poor, even though free, may not have had anything to contribute to the meal. Thus, those who had brought food went ahead and ate, not waiting for the slaves and not sharing with the poor. The meal was not even a "common" meal.

One is hungry: the poor man or the slave who had no food.

Another is drunk: from excessive drinking of wine. There is a sharp contrast between those who could not even satisfy their hunger and those who, out of their abundance, became drunk. Repulsive as it is to modern Christians, there is no justification for taking *drunk* in any other than its literal meaning. Strange indeed is this if the Corinthians sought to connect the Lord's Supper with this debauchery. No wonder that Paul said they could not eat the Lord's Supper.

Verse 22: What!: an interjection not found in the Greek text, but justified by the context. Paul was horrified at the condition that existed.

Do you not have houses to eat and drink in?: the first of a series of questions in which Paul seemed to search for a reason for their behavior. The thought is: "You do not mean to imply by your action, do you, that you have no houses in which to eat and drink?" There is more than a touch of irony in this question, for he knew that the offenders were just the ones who did have houses. The suggestion is that if they came together only to eat and drink, which is what their actions implied, they would be better off to satisfy their hunger at home.[1] Of course, they were supposed to gather to express and enjoy their mutual love, but their actions made this impossible.

Or do you despise the church of God: Is that what your actions mean? *Despise* means to make a point of slighting or belittling the congregation of Christians. This local congregation is called *the church of God,* to contrast Paul's high regard for it with the implied insult which the offenders were heaping upon it.

And humiliate those who have nothing?: put to shame the have-nots. The have-nots would be the poor, who in regard to food were often worse off than the slaves who ate from their master's table. *Humiliate* is a good translation, for a feeling of shame is included in the word. In all of these questions Paul was speaking ironically. He knew that the offenders did not have this in mind, that they had let their hunger overcome them. But he knew that their actions implied all of this and he wished to make them feel ashamed of themselves.

What shall I say to you?: a rhetorical question. He knew what he wanted to say; but instead of saying it, he asked another question.

Shall I commend you in this?: can be a statement, but is more likely another rhetorical question. The Greek form is probably the deliberative subjunctive which implies the question. However, some translators take this as a statement: "In this I praise you not." The thought is the same in either case. Paul had no intention of praising them for this kind of behavior.

(2) The purpose of the Supper was remembrance of the Lord (11:23-26)

In this section Paul indicated the source of his knowledge of the Lord's Supper (vs. 23), described the institution of the Supper (vss. 24–25), and summarized the meaning of the Supper (vs. 26). This is the oldest written account of the institution of the Supper which we have. The account in Mark's Gospel follows this account very closely; Matthew follows it but with some modification. The account in the Gospel of Luke is different. The probable explanation of these varying accounts was that they were influenced by the practices of the churches in which the accounts took

---

[1] Cf. Barrett.

form. There was a wide divergence of practice and emphasis in the earliest churches. In some the Supper was celebrated in conjunction with a love feast or common meal. It may be, and probably is, true that in some cases the common meal came between the distribution of the two elements of the Supper. In other churches the Supper may have been celebrated in a service dedicated entirely to it, and the two elements were distributed one after the other. This may account for the fact that the true text of Luke places the drinking of the cup before the eating of the bread, while the other accounts reverse the order.

In some churches, if the Gospels are reflections of their practice, the emphasis on the meaning was somewhat different. In all of them three factors were involved: a remembrance of the death of Christ, a reaffirmation of the lordship of Christ, and an anticipation of the messianic banquet in heaven. In our accounts Mark and Matthew place the emphasis on the death of Christ; Paul's writing places it on the lordship of Christ; Luke places it on the coming messianic banquet. It may be that in the same churches different emphases were made at different times. Could it be that modern Christians, by absorption with the death of Christ, have robbed themselves of the other proper emphases?

In modern church practice many issues are in debate with reference to the Lord's Supper. How often is it to be celebrated? What should it be called—a sacrament, a eucharist, a communion, or simply the Lord's Supper? What is the proper qualification for participation in the Supper? Most churches have settled on the fact that only baptized believers are to participate; but since they differ on what is a believer and on what is baptism, their practices vary. What is the meaning of participation in the Supper? Is it an experience of actual and real sharing in the blood of Christ or not? If so, in what way? Finally, church practices differ concerning the relation between the elements and the blood and body of Christ. Some hold that the elements are mystically changed so that they become the actual body and blood of Christ. Others hold that the blood and body of Christ enter into the elements and subsist along with the natural elements. Others hold that there is a real presence of the living Christ in the elements. Others hold that the elements are purely symbolical.

Too often commentators have read their own beliefs into the words of Scripture, and no doubt this commentator will be tempted to do the same. However, we need to remember that many of the questions we ask were not asked in the first century. Each church, though recognizing a spiritual unity with other churches, was independent of them. There were no denominational differences. Answers to many of our questions cannot be found in the New Testament. We must be content to seek to understand their thought and to bring our practice into judgment before it. If our practice is consistent with the spirit of New Testament teachings, we may safely follow it. If not, we should forsake it.

Verse 23: identifies the source of Paul's knowledge.

I received: a word commonly associated with the passing on of tradition.[1] Paul did not say how he received his knowledge, but it is probable

---

[1] Cf. Barrett.

that it was through the tradition handed down by early Christians. Though he affirmed that he did not receive his gospel from human sources (Gal. 1:11–12), he did receive the tradition of church practices. Paul had ample opportunity to find out what the Christian traditions were. Immediately after his conversion, he was in association with the church at Damascus (Acts 9:19). He visited with Peter for fifteen days (Gal. 1:18). We may be sure that they did not talk about the weather. He had many contacts with the Jerusalem church and with men who had been in the Jerusalem chu:ch.

From the Lord: the ultimate source of his knowledge of the Lord's Supper. This is consistent with the opinion that Paul actually received the knowledge through secondary sources. It would be from the Lord just as surely as if the Lord had given it to him by direct revelation. That this knowledge of historical fact came to him by direct revelation is entirely improbable.

What I also delivered to you: Paul became the one who passed on the tradition to the Corinthian church. They had also received it from the Lord, but they had received it through the means of Paul's instructions.

That the Lord Jesus: speaks of Jesus in his historical character. He could be called the *Lord* even then, though his lordship was not recognized until after his resurrection.

On the night when he was betrayed: the night before his passion. All of our accounts of the Lord's Supper agree that it was instituted by Jesus himself on that night.

Took bread: literally, "a loaf." This was one of the thin cakes of bread which was used for the Passover Feast. It was perhaps the thickness and texture of our saltine crackers, but larger. The American loaf would be far different.

Verse 24: And when he had given thanks: The Greek word for "giving thanks" is *eucharisteō*. It is from this word that the Lord's Supper is called a Eucharist in many circles. Certainly the giving of thanks should be an integral part of the celebration.

He broke it: to provide small pieces for each one of the apostles who reclined at the table with him. There is no indication that any spiritual meaning was attached to the breaking of the bread in the genuine texts of the New Testament.

And said: pronounced the words to introduce the meaning of the element.

This is my body: often misunderstood, because we give *body* the modern significance of the physical stuff in which we live. In Jewish thought the body stood for the whole man as an organized being in the world. Thus the bread does not stand for the broken physical body of Christ but for the whole incarnate life of Christ. The whole mystery of the incarnation is included (Parry). All ideas of the substance of Christ being present in the physical elements of the Lord's Supper seem to be ruled out by the language. *This is my body* is not to be taken literally, but as meaning, "this represents my body," much as we may hand a photograph to a friend and say, "This is my grandson." It is not really so, but a pictorial representation of the grandson. So the bread is a pictorial representation of the life of Christ.

Which is [broken]: "Broken" does not appear in the best manuscripts of the Greek New Testament. Its appearance in the variants probably reflects a later date in Christian history when the meaning of body was lost and the bread became another symbol of the cross. Even so, it is inaccurate, since John tells us that the body of Jesus was not broken when the soldiers found him already dead (cf. John 19:32–33). The oft-heard expression, "the broken body," has no New Testament witness to its validity.

For you: becomes a different expression when the preceding expression is omitted. This may account for its insertion. However, the thought is possible and we must deal with the true text, even if it is difficult. The meaning is that the whole incarnate life of Jesus was for the sake of his people.

Do this in remembrance of me: implies that he was thereafter to be absent from them. They were to remember him; and the taking of the Lord's Supper was one way—not the only way, perhaps not even the best way—to accomplish this. "Remember" had a richer meaning to the Hebrews that it has to modern man. It meant to call one into the presence of the one who remembered. The real spiritual power of the celebration of the Lord's Supper is thus seen in the attitude of the celebrant rather than in the material elements that are used. The elements are purely symbolical; the celebration should be dynamically meaningful. Though the Lord is not present in the elements, he should be present in the hearts and minds of the celebrants—they remember him.

Verse 25: describes the second part of the Lord's Supper as Jesus instituted it and as churches should celebrate it.

In the same way also the cup: the wine.

After supper: a descriptive detail that could only have come to Paul from one of the eleven disciples who were present. The most likely source is Peter and the most likely time the period when Paul visited Peter for fifteen days.

This cup is the new covenant in my blood: Both Matthew and Mark change the form of this saying to: "This is my blood of the covenant" (Mark 14:24; Matt. 26:28). Their account is secondary and reflects a development in Christianity which called for uniformity in expression. This is the best evidence that we have that a love feast may have been celebrated between the serving of the two elements. If so, the order would be: breaking of bread and the words, "This is my body," followed by the common meal, followed by the cup with the words, "This cup is the new covenant in my blood." When the common meal was omitted, the desire for parallelism would tend to change the two sayings. Now they would come together: "This is my body" and "This is my blood." This is the probable explanation of the change. If so, Paul's words are more primitive and probably original. The wine does not then represent the blood of Christ, but the *new covenant,* the covenant of forgiveness. Of course, the covenant was established by the *blood,* a metonym for the cross. The importance of distinction is that the original words would leave no room for anyone to think that the wine was changed in substance to the blood of Christ. Also, they indicate the purely symbolical nature of the elements in the Lord's Supper.

Do this . . . in remembrance of me: repeats the same words, with the same meaning, that were used with the bread.

Verse 26: Paul's summary of the point which he wished to emphasize for the Corinthians.

For: marks the transition from the words of Jesus to the words of Paul. The following gives his interpretation of the meaning. *As often:* gives no specified frequency but insists that however often the Supper was celebrated, it should be with this meaning. *Eat this bread and drink the cup:* the loaf and the cup which were used in the Lord's Supper.

You proclaim: shifts the emphasis from the experience of the celebrant (remembering) to the meaning of the service for the church. The service is a way of proclaiming, of preaching the central reality of the gospel. Usually the word proclaim means proclamation by oral words.[1] Here it seems to be proclamation by action. Both the Jews and the Greeks used actions as a means of proclamation; the Jews by their feasts, especially the Passover, and the Greeks by their mystery rites. The Corinthians would have been familiar with this form of proclamation. They had been using the service as a means of selfish indulgence. Their actions had served to proclaim merely human values. Paul rebuked them for failing to proclaim the gospel.

The Lord's death until he comes: involves the three emphases of the Supper. *Death* is the death of Christ on the cross which was considered the foundation of the gospel and the means by which the new covenant was established. *Until he comes* looks to the future hope of the Christians. *Lord* emphasizes the living lordship of Christ. This last emphasis seems to be the one which was primary in Paul's thought. We might say that there was a backward, a forward, and an upward look in the Supper. It was the upward look that Paul was concerned about. Of course all three are involved, no matter where the emphasis lies. Paul's interpretation of the Lord's Supper in this section differs in some material ways from the practice of all modern churches. This is not surprising, since the interpretations given in the Gospel accounts also differ from it. This fact witnesses to the divergence of what we may call the liturgical practices of the early churches. No central authority dictated these practices, and each congregation felt free to follow its own course so long as the essential meaning was preserved. However, in the midst of divergence there was much unity. In all accounts both the loaf and the cup were used, though Luke gives these in reverse order to the rest of the accounts. All the accounts preserve the three emphases of the Supper: Mark and Matthew stress the death, Luke the future expectation, and Paul the present lordship of Christ. Perhaps our modern celebration of the Lord's Supper would be enriched if more variety were practiced in it.

(3) Each member was responsible for self-examination in this matter (11:27-32)

Paul believed that serious consequences followed when Christians celebrated the Lord's Supper in an unworthy manner. These included "pro-

---

[1] Barrett insists that it meant an oral recitation which was connected with the celebration of the Supper.

faning the body and blood of the Lord" (vs. 27); the bringing of judgment upon oneself (vs. 29), which might result in sickness or death (vs. 30) and a chastening from the Lord (vs. 32). The way to avoid these serious results was to practice self-examination to make sure that one did observe the Supper in a worthy manner (vs. 28). Self-judgment would serve to avoid the necessity of judgment by the Lord (vs. 31). The vexed question of "open" or "closed" communion is not settled here, since Paul was writing to an individual church and the admonition was to the members of that church alone. The interpreter can only conjecture what Paul would have said in the modern situation of diverse denominations. It is dangerous to assume that the practices mentioned in this passage are to be followed in detail in modern churches and that these are the only authentic practices. It is equally dangerous to assume that any other practice has biblical authority. Our questions must be solved on the basis of principles. The situation that exists must be such, whether only a local church and its members are involved or a group of Christians of diverse denominations are present, that the Lord's Supper can be truly and meaningfully celebrated.

Verse 27: Whoever: in Paul's situation would include only the members of the Corinthian congregation.

Eats the bread or drinks the cup of the Lord: participates in celebrating the Lord's Supper.

In an unworthy manner: good translation. The thought is not that one must be worthy to do this, but that he must do it in a manner and spirit which are worthy of the character of the ordinance. The context makes clear two things that were involved. First, the Supper must be a meaningful remembrance of the Lord. Second, the Supper must be celebrated in an atmosphere of unity and mutual love. The practice of the Corinthians in making the common meal a matter of selfish indulgence, of creating dissensions in the church, made participation in a worthy manner impossible.[1] They could not remember the Lord.

Will be guilty of profaning the body and blood of the Lord: a poor translation. Literally the expression reads: "shall be answerable for the body and blood of the Lord." The Greek word *enochos,* meaning "liable to" or "liable for," is found rather often in the New Testament (cf. Matt. 5:21, liable to judgment; Matt. 26:66, liable to death; Heb. 2:15, liable to lasting servitude; James 2:10, liable for the whole law). Our word *guilty* is too strong. Perhaps the meaning is that he shall be answerable for *the body and blood of the Lord.* But in what way? The RSV translation is a possible interpretation. It is probably best to think that the offense is against the Lord himself rather than against his body and blood. The thought is that by partaking of the Supper in an unworthy way, one is dishonoring him whom the elements of the Supper represent. Such actions are an insult to the Lord.

Verse 28: suggests the way of avoiding this insult.

Let a man examine himself: literally "put himself to the test." Paul was not thinking of self-examination in the same way that some churches think

---

[1] Cf. Barrett.

of it. The examination was not to see whether there was any sin in the life of the Christian, but to determine whether his mind was sufficiently centered on Jesus Christ so that he could partake of the Supper in a worthy manner. The emphasis is on *examine* which comes from a word meaning "to test or assay." One way in which the word was used was to describe the process of separating the gold from the dross by putting ore in the fire. The resulting product was pure gold. The implication here is that the individual will be able to test himself without the help of anyone else.

And so: in this manner, i.e., after testing himself.

Eat of the bread and drink of the cup: partake of the Lord's Supper.

Verse 29: explains further why one should examine himself before partaking of the Lord's Supper.

For any one who eats and drinks without discerning the body: defines the area in which the examination should take place. To partake meaningfully of the Supper, one must discern the body, i.e., distinguish the reality from the elements. The sin is not the failure to distinguish between the Lord's Supper and a common meal, but the failure to see in the Lord's Supper what is represented by the elements. The bread stands for the body, the life of Jesus. If one eats it without remembering that, he has eaten *without discerning the body.* Paul thought it sinful to engage in a rite of the church without experiencing its spiritual meaning.

Eats and drinks judgment upon himself: makes himself liable to judgment. *Judgment* is a neutral word, not having in itself any indication of innocence or of condemnation. The context indicates that the decision will be adverse. A parallel use of the word is found in Romans 13:2: "Therefore he who resists the authorities resists what God has appointed, and those who resist will incur judgment." The passage abounds with the use of this word and its derivatives. The point which Paul made was that self-judgment was necessary to avoid divine judgment. If one partakes of the Supper in the right manner, after examining himself, he will not be subject to divine judgment. But if he does not partake in the right attitude, he will be liable to judgment. There is no indication that this will lead to damnation; the results of divine judgment will be temporal rather than eternal, corrective rather than punitive.

Verse 30: proves the truth of divine judgment by the fact that some of the Corinthians had suffered.

That is why: literally, "on account of this." This refers immediately to verse 29. The Corinthians had not exercised self-examination and discrimination in their celebration of the Lord's Supper. Now they were experiencing, to some degree, the judgment of God.

Many of you are weak and ill: physically, not spiritually. Some have tried to make this refer to spiritual weakness rather than physical ailments, but the context does not permit it. Paul connected the seemingly prevalent illness of many of the Corinthians with their abuses of the Lord's table. This must be taken as a special interpretation in the spirit of the prophet, not a general statement that such afflictions always follow this particular sin. Nor are we to take this to mean that sickness is always a divine judgment. Paul spoke with certainty.

And some have died: rather, "a sufficient number are falling asleep."

Perhaps the RSV *some* is justified, since that would be a sufficient number to show evidence of God's judgment on the Corinthians. *Died* translates the present tense of the Greek word for "sleep." The past tense of the RSV is misleading. Paul was talking about a thing that was happening at that time in Corinth. Sleep is a common metaphor for death in the New Testament.[1] It was also used among the Jews and heathen. The Christian use had a reference to the belief in resurrection which was not attached to the word among the Jews and heathen.

Verse 31: repeats the thought of verse 29, with the addition that self-judgment prevents divine judgment.

But if we judged ourselves truly: Judged translates the same word used in verse 29 which means "to discern." The whole verse is a contrary-to-fact conditional construction. Paul was asserting that they were not in the habit of judging themselves. There is no word for *truly* in the original, but the thought is justified in this verse.

We should not be judged: conclusion of the contrary-to-fact construction. If the first were true, the second would not be true. But since the first is not true, the second is true. The Corinthians were being judged because of their failure to examine themselves.

Verse 32: continues the thought of divine judgment.

But when we are judged by the Lord: assumes that this was happening in Corinth. The Lord (Jesus Christ) was thought of as the judge who brought sickness and death to the Corinthians.

We are chastened: disciplined with a view to correction rather than punished. *Chastened* comes from the Greek word which signifies a father's disciplining of his child (Eph. 6:4). The idea is that Paul thought of the suffering of the Corinthians as discipline rather than punishment. The purpose was corrective.

So that we may not be condemned along with the world: looks on the world as the men who are in rebellion against God. The world will be condemned at the final judgment. Paul assumed that Christians must be chastened and disciplined so that they would not fall back and become a part of the world and share its destiny.

(4) The Supper should be an orderly fellowship service (11:33–34)

In this section Paul gave instructions for the orderly service which would correct the abuses found in Corinth.

Verse 33: The instructions are introduced by the particle, *so then,* which reminded them of the possibility of judgment. Paul asserted his love and concern for them by calling them *my brethren. When you come together to eat* identifies the instructions as having to do with the celebration of the Supper. On these occasions they were to wait for one another to arrive at the meeting place, even the slaves who would be delayed by domestic duties. This would show their brotherly union, while their past practice had showed their disregard for each other.

Verse 34: continues the instructions. Paul assumed that some would

---

[1] Grosheide.

be hungry and admonished them to eat at home and thus avoid the temptation. This may well have been the beginning of the separation of the common meal from the service of the Lord's Supper. Repeating the thought of verse 31, Paul reminded them that this procedure would prevent their being judged by God. *Condemned* (RSV) is a poor translation.

About the other things: things related to the Lord's Supper. There is no hint as to what the other things were. They may have had to do with regulations concerning the proper distribution of the food and arrangements for the common meals. They may have been other problems.

I will give directions when I come: rather, "whenever I come." Paul spoke with some uncertainty here, though he planned to visit the church in a few months (cf. 16:5). *Directions* means to set things in order. The word has primary reference to external arrangements.[1] It implies authority in its common use, but Paul's authority was only that which the Corinthians were willing to grant him; it was not based on appointment to an authoritative office.

One commentator has summarized what this passage tells us about the celebration of the Lord's Supper in Paul's day (ICC). Negatively, nothing is said about a priest to consecrate the elements or about church officials to serve the elements to the congregation. From this fact we may infer that these practices were not ordained by Christ or the apostles. Positively, the Supper was modeled closely on the action of Christ at the last Passover. The bread and the cup were first blessed and then received. Paul changed the custom by his instructions so as to eliminate the meal from the service and make the Supper into a church ceremony. What had its beginning in Corinth is now the common practice of modern churches, but with some additions.

---

[1] Cf. Edwards, who refers to them as "external, practical arrangements."

VII. INSTRUCTIONS CONCERNING SPIRITUAL GIFTS
(12:1—14:40)

Paul had mentioned, in his instruction to this letter, the spiritual gifts of the Corinthians. He said, "I give thanks to God always . . . that in every way you were enriched in him with all speech and all knowledge . . . so that you are not lacking in any spiritual gift" (1 Cor. 1:4–7). However, the possession of these gifts was not an unmixed blessing in Corinth. It had caused division and jealousy. In this section Paul turned to an extensive discussion of spiritual gifts. The discussion is divided into three major sections: (1) the diversity and purpose of the spiritual gifts (12:1–31); (2) the supreme gift of all—love (13:1–13); (3) the superiority of the gift of prophecy over the gift of tongues (14:1–25). Related to this discussion, but not really a part of it, is the discussion of order in the church services (14:26–40). Two major problems of interpretation are found in this section: the meaning of "tongues" and the meaning of "prophecy." These will be discussed at some length at the beginning of our comments on chapter 14. Since "tongues" enter the picture in chapters 12 and 13, it is necessary to anticipate our longer discussion by saying that the weight of evidence favors the belief that the "tongues" at Corinth were unlearned foreign languages which were used to evangelize the visitors to the port of Corinth.

1. Diversity and Purpose of Spiritual Gifts (12:1–31)

In this chapter Paul reminded the Corinthians that they were one body of Christ, a spiritual organism in which each member had his place and each depended on the other for spiritual usefulness. This is one of the greatest discussions in the New Testament on the nature of the Christian congregation. First, Paul reminded the Corinthians of the need for spiritual understanding, recalling the contrast between their former pagan life and their new Spirit-led life (12:1–3). Second, he pointed out that the Holy Spirit was the source of all gifts and that these were distributed according to his will (12:4–11). Third, he told them that the church was a spiritual organism (12:12–13). Fourth, he reminded them that the gifts were functions of the one body and should be used for mutual edification (12:14–26). Finally, he insisted that mutual service, not uniformity of gifts, should be the Christian's aim (12:27–31). The problem seems to have been that the Corinthians who had the more spectacular gifts were parading them before the church and claiming a spiritual superiority to other members.

Many attempts have been made to identify this group with either the "Christ party" or the "Cephas party" in Corinth, but such attempts have been unconvincing. It is probable that the gifts did not follow so-called party lines at all. Therefore, any attempt to press the matter of a polemic against one party or the other in this section is unwarranted. Paul seems to have said all he wanted to say about the dissensions in Corinth in the first four chapters. He was against all dissension and never indicated his preference for one "party" or the other.

(1) Need for spiritual understanding (12:1–3)

Paul's first concern was to remind the Corinthians for the need of spiritual understanding. He expressed his hope that they should not be ignorant with reference to spiritual gifts (vs. 1). He reminded them of their subjection to "dumb idols" prior to their conversion (vs. 2). Then he insisted that any spiritual action without the aid of the Holy Spirit was impossible (vs. 3).

Verse 1: introduces the subject of spiritual gifts.

Now concerning: like similar phrases in 7:1 and 8:1, introduces a subject about which the church had written him. Unlike the problems discussed in chapter 11, the church was aware of the danger of their current practice of spiritual gifts.

Spiritual gifts: The Greek can be either masculine or neuter and may refer either to spiritual gifts or to the spiritually endowed. The same word is used, however, in 14:1 in a form which can only be neuter, and we should interpret this expression as neuter. Of course, Paul discussed the people who had the gifts, but his main concern was with the gifts. It may be that the church had written concerning only one gift—speaking in tongues. If so, Paul widened the discussion to include the use of all gifts. The gifts were spiritual because they were bestowed by the Holy Spirit. In some cases they were miraculous, in some temporary, in some connected with human talents. In every case they were endowments of the Holy Spirit, given for the purpose of proclaiming the gospel.

Brethren: softened the thought of their ignorance by reminding them of the brotherly affection which Paul had for them.

I do not want you to be uninformed: a formula similar to 10:1 which Paul often used to introduce important subjects (cf. Rom. 1:13; 11:25; 2 Cor. 1:8; 1 Thess. 4:13). *Uninformed* translates a Greek word meaning "ignorant." Paul did not want the Corinthians to be ignorant of a matter which was of such importance to them.

Verse 2: reminded them of their subjection to "dumb idols" before their conversion. This thought was introduced as a contrast to their leadership by the Holy Spirit (vs. 3). The syntax of the Greek sentence is not clear, but perhaps the RSV solution is correct.

You know: reminded them of their former life.

When you were heathen: before your conversion. *Heathen* is too strong; the Greek is "Gentiles." This word had no overtones of cultural deprivation as our word "heathen" does. The reference was purely religious. Being Gentiles, they did not know the true God. The contrast between being a Gentile and being a Christian is unusual.

You were led astray to dumb idols: implies a bondage to a power outside themselves. The power was not identified, but Paul would have thought of it as the power of Satan. *Were led* suggests only that their going was not premeditated. Paul did not mean that they did not give their consent to being led. *Astray* comes from the context and is not in the Greek. *Were led* translates a Greek expression which emphasizes the thought of continuous and habitual action. *Idols* are images, not realities. Paul had already expressed his feeling about idols (cf. 10:19–20). They were nothing in themselves, but they represented subjection to demons. *Dumb* (i.e., speechless) was a common Jewish term of contempt for idols (cf. Ps. 115:5; Hab. 2:18), but is used only here in the New Testament.

However you may have been moved: attempts to translate an obscure phrase in the Greek. Two thoughts are present in the expression: that of repeated action and that of external forces. They were repeatedly led. They were led by something external to themselves. This force may have been local customs or the commands of priests and kings, but it is probable that Paul had Satan in mind. While Paul never sought to minimize personal responsibility, he often insisted that conversion constituted a change of masters. One of the continuing illusions of sinful men is that they are free. On closer examination, their freedom is seen to be only an illusion. Sin is bondage, bondage to the power of evil in the world. Christianity is bondage, also, but bondage to God in Christ. Man's choice is the choice between a master who brings death and destruction and a master who brings life and fulfillment.

Verse 3: Paul believed that conversion brought one under the leadership and power of God.

Therefore I want you to understand: rather, "I want to make known to you." The expression introduces the thought that life in Christianity was completely different from life in paganism or sin.

No one speaking by the Spirit of God ever says "Jesus is cursed!": The work of the Spirit is effectual,[1] making it impossible for anyone to curse Jesus. It is possible that the phrase "Jesus be cursed!" was hurled at the Christians by Corinthian Jews. This is more likely than that it was used by the Gentiles. It is even improbable that Paul himself had used it in the days when he persecuted the church. If so, he spoke from experience, saying that such speech was not inspired by the Holy Spirit. *By the Spirit of God* could be translated "in the Spirit of God"; perhaps that would be more accurate. However, the active influence of the Spirit of God on the speaker was in Paul's mind.

No one can say: emphasizes ability. Paul meant that one did not have the ability to speak thus by himself.

"Jesus is Lord": the Christian confession. From its beginning Christianity consisted of a confession of allegiance to the person of Jesus. He was called "Lord" with the full meaning of the title. In Greek life "Lord"

---

[1] Edwards.

was comparable to our "Mister." It was used as a term of respect to address anyone. But its most common use was in the recognition of complete power, as in the case of a master of slaves or the ruler of the Empire. In Jewish life it had this common meaning, but it was further enriched as the title most often used in the Old Testament for God. The Christian meaning of the confession was the recognition of the complete authority of Jesus over their lives. No one was thought to be a Christian unless he had surrendered himself to the lordship of Christ.

Except by the Holy Spirit: The Christian confession was possible only under the guidance and influence of God's Spirit. His work was absolutely necessary to conversion and to continued Christian living.[1] Of course, Paul did not mean that the words could not be repeated by men acting under their own power. He meant that the full meaning of the words could not be expressed by such a man. Thus Paul gave a test of the Spirit's presence. It was not the exercise of strange and spectacular phenomena, but the simple confession of the lordship of Jesus. Paul's test was essentially the same as that given later by John: "Beloved, do not believe every spirit, but test the spirits to see whether they are of God; for many false prophets have gone out into the world. By this you know the Spirit of God: every spirit which confesses that Jesus Christ has come in the flesh is of God" (1 John 4:1–2).

(2) The Holy Spirit, the source of all gifts (12:4–11)

The essential characteristic of the spiritual gifts was diversity in unity: the diversity was evident in their action, usage, and effects; unity was evident in their origin. The origin of the gifts is the main concern of verses 4–7, 11; the diversity of the gifts is the main concern of verses 8–10. Verses 4–6 contain the clearest example of the trinitarian formula in the reverse order—Spirit, Lord, God. Though it is probable that Paul did not raise the questions which led to the formulation of the doctrine of the Trinity, it is clear that the doctrine is based on data which he furnished.

Verse 4: Varieties: good translation of a noun which can mean either "distinctions" or "distributions." The noun is used only here in the New Testament, but the verbal form of the same word is found in verse 11, where it is translated "apportions." By using this word, Paul wished to emphasize the fact that the congregation was not furnished with a uniform equipment for service.

Gifts: comes from the word which is usually translated "grace." A transliteration of the Greek word is common, *charismata*. The word is used chiefly in Paul's writings (cf. Rom. 12:6) but is also found in Peter (1 Pet. 4:10). The emphasis is upon the fact that the gifts were a divine favor, bestowed upon unworthy subjects. There could be no reason for pride in the possession of a gift of grace.

But the same Spirit: emphasizes the unity in the diversity.[2] The Spirit was the origin of the gifts. In verse 1, they are called *pneumatika,* i.e.,

---

[1] Cf. Edwards.
[2] Cf. Edwards.

things of the Spirit. The reference there, as here, was to the origin of the gifts.

Verse 5: Service: usefulness. This translates a Greek word from which the English word "deacon" comes. The idea was that the gifts had various uses in the ministry of the church. The word implied that all the gifts were given for service, not for self-glorification or private edification.

But the same Lord: that is, Jesus Christ. *Lord* is his official and Christian title. He is mentioned in connection with the service or use of the gifts because he is the head of the church. Unity is preserved, not by identity of function, but by the Lord of all spiritual functions.

Verse 6: There are varieties of working: effects of their use. The gifts, when used in service, accomplish various results. *Working* is the word from which we get our English word "energy." The primary meaning is that of effectual operation. In the church some of the gifts might be used for evangelism, others for the edification of the church members, others for the administration of the affairs of the church. Each had its own peculiar use and its own peculiar result.

But it is the same God: the Father.

Who inspires them all in every one: rather, "who produces all things in all people." *Inspires* is a weak translation of the word, similar to *working* above, which means, "to produce." The thought of Paul was not that God inspired men to do their best, but that he used men's lives as instruments of his own working. *Them all,* literally, "all things," has reference to the use of the gifts. *In every one* meant anyone in which any function is present and any result produced. The expression strikes a note that is common in the New Testament. We do not work for God; God works through us. Only as we yield ourselves to God, so that he can work through us, are spiritual results attainable.

Verse 7: To each: implies that the spiritual gifts were universal. No Christian was so lowly that he did not have a spiritual gift.[1]

Is given: emphasizes the sovereignty of the Holy Spirit in the giving of the gift. The present tense means that these gifts were repeatedly given by the Holy Spirit when they were given at all. The gifts were not mere human attainments, though they might make use of natural endowments. They were gifts.

The manifestation of the Spirit: The construction is somewhat obscure. It can mean "the manifestation that the man has the Spirit." Or it can mean "the Spirit manifests himself." The second meaning is the more likely. *Manifestation* is a rare word, found only here and in 2 Corinthians 4:2.

For the common good: indicates the purpose of the spiritual gifts. Any thought of conceit or selfishness was excluded. The possession and use of the gifts were for the spiritual benefit (i.e., the *good*) of the whole congregation.

Verses 8–10: lists the gifts of the Spirit which were present in Corinth. That this list does not exhaust all the possible gifts is evident from the

---

[1] Cf. Barrett.

companion lists (Rom. 12:6–8; 1 Pet. 4:10–11). The Romans passage
has "prophecy" in common with this list and "teaching" in common with
the other list in this chapter (vss. 27–28). Romans adds, "service, ex-
horting, contributing, giving aid, and doing acts of mercy." The passage in
Peter has only "rendering service and speaking," neither agreeing with
the Corinthian list, but "rendering service" agreeing with the Roman
passage.

Many attempts have been made to classify the gifts listed in this passage.
Most are based on the repetition of the word for "another of a different
kind" (Greek, *heteros*) at the beginning of verse 9 and before "various kinds
of tongues" in verse 10. The division would be: intellectual powers (utterance of wisdom and utterance of knowledge); powers involving faith (faith,
gifts of healing, working of miracles, prophecy, ability to distinguish between spirits); gifts involving tongues (various kinds of tongues and
interpretation of tongues).[1] Edwards finds five divisions: intellectual powers
(utterance of wisdom and utterance of knowledge); miraculous powers
(faith, gifts of healing, working of miracles); teaching power (prophecy);
critical power (ability to distinguish between spirits); ecstatic powers
(various kinds of tongues and interpretation of tongues).[2] While some of
the divisions are apparent, others are strained. It is doubtful that Paul had
any particular division of powers in mind. His list seems to follow an order
of gifts which were current in Corinth as they came to his mind. Nor
should we try to make the list one of descending values. Paul made his
sense of values plain in chapters 13–14. Love heads the list. Prophecy is
superior to tongues. Beyond that it is impossible to go with certainty.

To one is given through the Spirit: a constant refrain in these verses,
to remind the Corinthians that each manifestation of the Spirit had its
origin in the Holy Spirit.

Utterance: literally, "a work," the power of expressing oneself so as to
communicate to others. Perhaps *utterance* is a good translation, though
"communication" would be better.

Wisdom . . . knowledge: clearly related but to be distinguished. The
difference between the two words is not always clear. Paul combined them
in Colossians 2:3. Usually *wisdom* has a practical meaning for Paul, the
ability to make the right choices. In this epistle, however, it is synonymous
with revealed truth. Thus, the gift of speaking wisdom would be the higher
gift of making known revealed truths through the Spirit of God. *Knowledge*
would be more common knowledge such as all Christians might have.
Perhaps the knowledge involved here would be the historical facts upon
which Christianity rests. If so, speaking knowledge would be the same as
teaching.

Verse 9: Faith: a strange word to be found in a list of special charismatic
gifts, since all Christians must have faith to be Christians at all. Seemingly,
some of the Corinthians were especially gifted with faith, and this was
called a spiritual gift. Some commentators have taken *faith* to be the power

---

[1] Cf. Lenski.
[2] Cf. Edwards.

to work miracles; others have taken it as the foundation of all great spiritual achievements. The context (13:2) would favor the idea that this is wonder-working faith.[1]

To another gifts of healing: gifts which result in *healings.* It may be that these gifts were distributed in such a way that some could heal certain diseases and others different diseases. It is not stated that anyone had power to heal all diseases. The healings may have been accompanied by medical practice, but this seems unlikely.

Verse 10: To another the working of miracles: covers other wonderful works which were not healings. Such *miracles* as casting out demons, stilling the storm, or bringing blindness to Elymas may have been included.

To another prophecy: an especially high ability to proclaim and make known the truths of God. See the beginning of chapter 14 for an extended study of this word and its meaning in the New Testament.

The ability to distinguish between spirits: the power to distinguish in various cases (note the plural) whether the extraordinary powers were from God. This was a companion gift to that of prophecy. John warned his readers to test the spirits because many false prophets were around (1 John 4:1–2). It is implied that there were no objective tests which could be used, so some Christians must be given the gift of intuitive judgment. In modern days preachers are judged in the light of their fidelity to the Bible. Early Christians had no objective test of this kind. Those who claimed to be prophets, who said they had a revelation from God, must be judged.

Various kinds of tongues: the ability to speak different foreign languages (see comments on 14:1 for an extended study of this phenomenon). The gift was given to certain Christians to enable them to proclaim the gospel to the visitors to the docks of Corinth from many lands. Used in its proper place and for its proper function, this was a useful gift in a city like Corinth. The problem at Corinth was that men brought this gift into the church services for display purposes. There was no use for it there.

The interpretation of tongues: the power to translate foreign languages. This gift was a companion to the gift of speaking in these languages. Prob-ably even the speaker of a foreign language did not understand what he said; he was under the power of the Spirit. If he spoke in a church service, his language must be translated or it would have no meaning. This problem is the subject of chapter 14.

Verse 11: reemphasizes the source of all the gifts.

All these: the various gifts mentioned in verses 8–10. *All* is very em-phatic.

Are inspired by one and the same Spirit: the working of the Holy Spirit. *Inspired* is a poor translation; the Greek word is the same one used in verse 6. It means "to produce" rather than to inspire another to produce. The idea is that the Holy Spirit wrought these things; they were manifes-tations of his presence and power. The individual who practiced them became an instrument of the Holy Spirit. Thus, he could not claim any

---

[1] Cf. ICC, which argues that it cannot refer to initial faith.

credit for them or their results. *One and the same* emphasizes the identity of the power which worked in each manifestation.

Who apportions to each one individually as he wills: The free, sovereign choice of the Spirit determined the recipient of each gift and the scope of its practice.[1] This thought again erased any ground for conceit on the part of the gifted ones.

(3) The church, a spiritual organism (12:12–13)

Taking up the thought of verse 7, "for the common good," Paul turned to the nature of the congregation. He emphasized that it was one body in spite of its various members (vs. 12). He then brought the practice of Christian baptism into relation with this truth (vs. 13*a*) and asserted that all members of the congregation experienced the operation of the Holy Spirit (vs. 13*b*). The doctrine of the church and the doctrine of baptism were both important elements in Paul's discussion. His thought in these two verses can be summarized thus: (1) The unbeliever becomes a Christian by the activity and work of the Holy Spirit. (2) Each convert is spiritually united with the congregation by the Holy Spirit. (3) Baptism follows as a sign of this unity of the body of Christ. (4) In that body, the Christian congregation, all earthly distinctions are superseded by the new spiritual oneness of the members. (5) This unity creates an instrument for Christ to use to minister to the community as a whole; the church becomes a body of Christ.

Verse 12: The body is one: refers to the human body, which is the basis of Paul's metaphorical discussion throughout this chapter. *One* means that the body is a unity.

And has many members: such as the eyes, legs, hands, sexual organs, and feet. This is common knowledge and universally true with reference to the human body.

And all the members of the body, though many, are one body: a repetition for emphasis. The members do not lose their identity by being a part of the body; rather, they find it. Separated from the body, they have no being. Connected with it, they are able to function.

Just as . . . so: presents the comparison. On the one side is the human body; on the other side, Christ. The point of comparison is unity in spite of diversity.

Christ: We would expect "church" instead of Christ, for it is obvious that Paul was talking about the church in this chapter. In some way Christ is identified with the church. One way of solving the problem of language is to suppose that there is an ellipsis which must be filled out to read, "the body of" Christ.[2] Another way is to suppose that we have a metonym in which *Christ* means the church. Lenski suggests that Paul was speaking of Christ as the head of the church, thus identifying the two but not dis-

---

[1] Cf. Schlatter, who points out that it is not the desire of the recipient that determines the gift.

[2] Moffatt points out that the use of "body" in a corporate sense was original with Paul.

solving the person of Christ. The first suggestion is the simplest and fits the context perfectly. Therefore, we assume that it is the "church of" Christ which is meant.

Two questions immediately arise. Was the church which Paul had in mind the local congregation of Christians at Corinth? The answer seems plain if we approach the material without a preconceived conclusion. Verse 27 reads, "Now you are the body of Christ and individually members of it." "You" in this verse is governed by the addressee of the letter, which is "the church of God which is at Corinth" (1 Cor. 1:2). Thus it is clear that the body of Christ which was in Paul's mind was the congregation at Corinth. But how can this local congregation be called the body of Christ? The answer is in the meaning of the figure of speech. Two possible meanings are: (1) "body" means something which is indivisible and of which there can be only one; (2) "body" is the means of active life in the world. If the first meaning is accepted, we must force the thought of the so-called "universal" church into every passage where Paul spoke of the church as the body of Christ (fifteen in all). This does great violence to some of the passages (as here) and misses Paul's thought in the others. If the second meaning of the figure is true, it fits all the passages where Paul used the expression. The meaning, then, is that each church is a body of Christ, a means by which Christ continues to live and operate in the community where that church exists. With this meaning of the figure, it is quite right to think of many bodies of Christ, many reincarnations, many media through which Christ lives and operates in the world. This is the meaning which will be adopted in this commentary. The thought predominant in Paul's mind was that the congregation was a spiritual organism, that its members with their various gifts formed a unity in which Christ lived and through which Christ ministered (cf. vs. 5).

Verse 13: explains how the unity of the congregation comes about.

For by one Spirit: rather, "in one Spirit." The Greek preposition *en* can be translated "by." This is not its common meaning and does not fit the context. However, there are problems of interpretation. Does *Spirit* refer to the Holy Spirit or to the spirit of man? This question is easy to answer. The context makes it clear that the Holy Spirit was in Paul's mind. Is the baptism water baptism or Spirit baptism? Though the expression can mean Spirit baptism, it is better to take it to refer to the regular practice of Christian baptism. What, then, does "in one Spirit" mean? Edwards solves the problem by supposing the "Lord is the Spirit" (cf. 2 Cor. 3:17) who dwells in the church and makes it one. Lenski solves it by supposing that "in the Spirit" is a mystical expression similar to "in Christ" and means "in union with one Spirit." Perhaps this solution is the best, though it is not entirely satisfactory. If so, the expression means that the convert, prior to his baptism, has come into union with the *one Spirit,* i.e., the Holy Spirit.

We . . . all: all the members of the congregation. Paul included himself because he was not speaking of a particular act of baptism but of the universal Christian practice of baptism. What is said in this verse about baptism would apply in Jerusalem or Rome quite as well as in Corinth. There seems to have been no instance in New Testament times of Christians who refused to accept baptism. Though we must insist that baptism was never thought of as a part of the saving act, it was always thought of as the first Christian act of the new convert. In most cases, if not all, it followed the conversion immediately.

Were . . . baptized: to be taken to mean the physical immersion of the new convert in water in the name of Christ. *Baptized* literally means "immersed." There is no evidence of any departure from this basic meaning of the word in the New Testament.

Into one body: a doubtful translation. The Greek preposition *eis* means "into" when it refers to physical movement. When it is used with *baptized,* it always has the meaning "with reference to." Thus people were baptized "with reference to repentance" (Matt. 3:11), "with reference to forgiveness of sins" (Acts 2:38), "with reference to the name of Jesus" (Acts 8:16), "with reference to the death of Christ" (Rom. 6:3). This is the meaning here. Christians were baptized "with reference" to the *one body.*[1] This would imply that they were already a part of the one body before they were baptized. How? Perhaps the best commentary is the statement: "The Lord added to their number day by day those who were being saved" (Acts 2:47). The idea is that it was the Lord who created the union of the new convert with the congregation which existed in his community. Baptism followed as a sign, for one thing, of this union. If our interpretation is correct, it has bearing on the modern practice of Christian baptism. First, it would indicate that Christian baptism must follow conversion. Second, it would indicate that Christian baptism is not entrance into the church, but a sign of the unity which already exists. Third, it would indicate that the older church members accept the new convert along with responsibility for his spiritual nurture.

Jews or Greeks, slaves or free: the classes of people in the church at Corinth. Some were Jews; some were Greeks. The racial barriers broke down. Some were slaves; some were free. The social barriers were superseded. Of course, these four classes of people were in almost every church in New Testament times.

And all were made to drink of one Spirit: a metaphor of debated meaning. We may exclude the thought that this referred to the Eucharist. *And* introduces an explanatory statement of the preceding rather than a new subject. *All . . . one* points to a universal Christian experience. *Made to drink* finds its explanation in the words of Jesus: "On the last day of the feast, the great day, Jesus stood up and proclaimed, 'If any one thirst, let him come to me and drink. He who believes in me, as the scripture has said, "Out of his heart shall flow rivers of living water." ' Now this he said about the Spirit, which those who believed in him were to receive" (John 7:37–39). Thus the expression is meant to explain Paul's phrase, *by one Spirit* or, rather, "in one Spirit." Each convert was *made to drink* of that *one Spirit* in his conversion. The testimony of the New Testament is that each Christian received the Holy Spirit at the time of his conversion.

---

[1] Grosheide points out that baptism does not incorporate one into the body. This is the work of the Holy Spirit.

(4) All gifts functions of the one body (12:14–26)

Almost belaboring the point, Paul wrote a long and sometimes involved treatment of the human body as an analogy of the church. The discussion in vss. 14–23 is concerned with the basis of the analogy—the human body as a physical organism. The thought blends into the mutual care of the members of the spiritual body in verses 24–26.

Without stating his application in so many words, Paul suggested several points of comparison between the physical body and the congregation: (1) Each is an organism composed of many parts. (2) Each body is complete only when the various parts perform their diverse functions. (3) In a body each member is dependent on every other member. (4) Discord destroys the reality of a body in each case.

Verse 14: states the basic premise which is the foundation of the analogy.

The body: the physical organism—the human body.

Does not consist of one member: a truism.

But of many: such as the hands, feet, eyes, sexual organs, and legs.[1] The verse reflects verse 12, and the comparison between the human body and the congregation is implied throughout.

Verse 15: begins a statement that each member is a part of the body, even though it does not function as other members function. The thought, which may have been current in Corinth, that only those members who had particular gifts were in reality a part of the body may be in the background. If so, it would be a direct negation of an idea which we find in some quarters today, that a particular manifestation of the Holy Spirit is the only real manifestation. Some hold that professed Christians who do not speak in tongues, for instance, have not received the Holy Spirit at all.

If the foot should say: a personification. The foot is invested with the power of speech for the sake of the figure. *If . . . should say* is a form of the conditional clause which presumes a possibility but not a probability. Of course a foot could not say this, but a member of the congregation could say something like this.

"Because I am not a hand, I do not belong to the body": a statement which is obviously absurd.

That would not make it any less a part of the body: states the obvious. Saying so or thinking so does not make it so.

Verse 16: repeats verse 15 with other illustrations. This time it is the ear which feels that it is no longer a part of the body because it is not an eye. Other portions of the verse are exactly parallel with verse 15.

Verse 17: consists of two rhetorical questions meant to show that the very existence of the body depends on a variety of members which function differently.

If the whole body were an eye: a grotesque assumption. If it were so, man could do nothing but see.[2]

Where would be the hearing?: The obvious answer is that it would be lacking.

If the whole body were an ear, where would be the sense of smell?:

---

[1] Morris points out that diversity is the very essence of the body.

[2] Cf. Edwards.

parallel with the preceding question. Paul could have continued through the whole category of human parts, but these were sufficient to make his point.

Verse 18: states Paul's belief that the organism of the human body has its origin in the creative act of God.

But as it is: as we actually find it to be so.

God arranged: presupposes the Christian doctrine of creation. Nothing is said about the intermediate means by which God accomplished his creation. The positive assertion is that God is the ultimate source of the arrangement we find. *Arranged* translates a Greek word which means "set" or "placed." "Placed" would be a better translation. The word implies a plan which was executed. Since each member functions according to the plan of God, there is no place in the body for selfishness or conceit. If the analogy is assumed, this would mean that no member of the congregation has reason for selfishness or conceit with reference to spiritual gifts. Even granting that one gift is inferior to another, it was not the fellow church member but God who ordained it to be so.

The organs in the body: in their functions.

As he chose: repeats with reference to the bodily organs a thought already expressed with reference to spiritual gifts (cf. vs. 11).

Verse 19: a rhetorical question which has the same meaning as verse 17.

If all were a single organ: which they are not.

Where would the body be?: There would be none. The very idea of a body implies the many members. If all tried to be the same, no body would exist. The implications of this thought are made explicit in the following verses.

Verse 20: speaks of the body as we actually experience it in our living. It is not composed of a single part, but has many parts. This does not mean that it is not a unity; it is, in spite of that, one body.

Verse 21: Though the body is a unity with many parts, each part is dependent on each other part for the perfect functioning of the body. Thus, for example, the eye has a need for the hand. It therefore cannot say to the hand that it has no need for it. What the eye sees, the hand must execute. If the eye sees food to eat, the hand must bring the food to the mouth before it can be eaten. The same principle applies to the relation between the head and the feet.

There are many parts, yet one body: Since each part performs its own function in unity with each other part, a body exists.

Verse 21: begins a statement of the mutual interdependence of the various parts of the body.

The eye cannot say to the hand: in the unity of the body.

"I have no need of you": In the human body, what is seen by the eye is executed by the hand. The eye may see food to eat; the hand must bring the food to the mouth.

Nor again the head to the feet: continues the thought.

"I have no need of you": Both the head and the feet must perform their functions for the body to exist.

Verse 22: On the contrary: denies the absurd assumptions previously made. The following is a description of human action current in the first century, but it reflects a more or less universal practice among normal people.

The parts of the body which seem to be weaker: The emphasis is on the words *seem to be.* Perhaps no particular member of the body is in mind, but the occasional weakness of certain members through disease. One need only have a broken arm or leg, defects of sight or hearing, to learn how indispensable each member of the body is. When disease or defects weaken one part of the body, we must try to compensate for its function in some other way. Thus they are indispensable. Insurance policies for accidents commonly have a sliding scale of payments for various disabilities. Thus the loss of an eye or of both eyes is compensated for by more money than the loss of a hand. However, most of us have no parts of the body with which we would willingly part.

Verse 23: And those parts of the body which we think less honorable: the sexual organs, which in most societies are considered less honorable.

We invest: comes from a word which is usually used to designate putting on clothing. Literally, it means "to place around" as a garment (Matt. 27:28). There is no need to seek a mystic explanation. We may take the word to mean that we clothe such members so as to hide them from common view.

With the greater honor: must mean with "greater beauty," if we take the former word to refer to clothing.

And: introduces an explanation in other terms of the previous statement.

Our unpresentable parts: equals the part which we think less honorable, i.e., the sexual organs.

Are treated with greater modesty: a poor translation but probably a good interpretation. Literally, it reads "have more abundant comeliness." The expression is understandable if we take it to mean the investing with clothes of those parts of the body. The use of clothes is almost universally for the purpose of adornment as well as for the purpose of modesty.

Verse 24: Which our more presentable parts do not require: literally, "the more beautiful parts have no need." Probably some such part of the body as the eye was in Paul's mind. It has no need for adornment because it is already beautiful.

But God has so adjusted the body: begins the shift of thought to the spiritual body, but the natural body is still present, also. *But* marks a strong contrast with the imagined discontent of the members in the previous section. *God* is the actor both in the natural and in the spiritual body. *Adjusted* literally means "blended together." The past tense refers to the past creative act of God in which this was accomplished.

Giving the greater honor to the inferior part: The sexual organs which men think dishonorable and uncomely have the function of procreation. Thus greater honor is given to those members of the body which men tend to think of as inferior. While the natural body seems to be primarily in mind, the thought is easily transferred to the spiritual body.

Verse 25: That there may be no discord in the body: states the purpose of the divine blending of the parts. Here it seems that the spiritual body begins to take the primary place. *Discord* translates the same Greek word, *schism,* which Paul used to describe the dissensions in the Corinthian congregation (cf. 1:10). It more aptly describes the discord of various members of the congregation than an imagined tug of war between the various organs of the body.

But that the members may have the same care for one another: But is strongly adversative. The opposite of *discord* is common *care. The same* emphasizes that the care of one member for another should be equal to that which he has for himself. While this applies to the various physical members of the human body, it is more descriptive of the Christian fellowship. God's purpose is that each member of the congregation should be concerned about every other member.

Verse 26: If one member suffers: a medical term. It is assumed that he will suffer.

All suffer together: an indicative statement, not an imperative. Paul did not say, as if it were a Christian duty, that all members should suffer together. His thought was that the fellowship of the congregation was so close that this result would be inevitable. Of course this is true of the physical body, as everyone who has hit his thumb with a hammer knows. It is also true of the true Christian fellowship.

If one member is honored: assumes that this may be so.

All rejoice together: an indicative. The members do rejoice together because they are one body. A very human illustration is found in family life. The father is as proud of the achievement of his son as if it were his own achievement, sometimes even more so. The fellowship of the congregation should be of this nature. In these last few verses it is difficult to say whether Paul was still speaking of the members of the body in a personified way or whether he was speaking of the spiritual body. Probably he consciously continued his discussion of the human body, but let his subconscious application to the spiritual body affect his language. In this verse *suffer,* since it is a medical term, seems more appropriate to the physical self, but *honored* and *rejoice* seem more appropriate to the congregation of Christians.

(5) Mutual service, not uniformity, the Christian's aim (12:27–31)

In this paragraph Paul made the application of his analogy explicit (vs. 27) and followed it with a discussion of the various gifted ones whom God had set in the church (vs. 28). He followed this with a series of rhetorical questions which showed that variety rather than uniformity was the order of the day (vss. 29–30). Finally, he urged the Christians to seek the gifts and introduced his discussion of love (vs. 31).

Verse 27: contains the application of the analogy to the congregation of Christians.[1] As noted above, Paul had begun to shift to this subject in verse 24. However, in verse 27, the human body is left behind and the spiritual body of Christians becomes the sole concern.

---

[1] Edwards suggests that we supply: "Therefore, there ought to be no schism in the church."

You: is emphatic in the sentence. The extent of the pronoun is defined by the address of the letter. *You* means the congregation of Christians at Corinth who are called the "church of God" (1:2).

Are the body: no article in the Greek. The thought of a Greek noun without the article is difficult to express in English. We usually substitute an article, either "a" or "the." This is inadequate and sometimes mis-leading. The absence of the article in Greek emphasizes the quality of a thing. In our context a paraphrase would be: "You constitute that which has the nature of being body to Christ." The emphasis is upon the quality of the church's existence. The church is the means by which Christ lives in the world. Many commentators, most of them in fact, take another direction. They believe that the body of Christ is composed of all Christians everywhere. Thus the Corinthian church could not be called the body. Nor could it be called, they argue, a body, since there is only one.[1] This opinion rests upon the assumption that the expression *the body of Christ* refers to the universal church. As we have seen, this is not the case. In Paul's mind each individual congregation was the body of Christ. The Corinthian church was one such body; the Roman church was another. There is no strain on this if we take "body" to be a figure of speech pointing to the instrument through which Christ lives.

And individually members of it: each one being an organic part of the whole. The idea of individuals being members of the congregation is unique to Christianity in the first century. In modern days the term has lost its original meaning and is used in all sorts of connections. We need to rediscover and recover the meaning of membership in the Christian con-gregation. The Greek phrase which is translated *individually* has given rise to debate, but the rsv translation is correct. The phrase is literally "out of parts." In 13:9, the same phrase means "partially" in contrast to "perfectly." This has led some commentators to take the words in this meaning in this verse and say that Paul meant that Christians were only imperfectly members of the body of Christ. This interpretation is certainly incorrect. *Individually* is a good translation in this context.

Verse 28: an enumeration of various functions in the Christian order. The list is closely akin to the one in Ephesians 4:11. While the list in verses 8–10 is entirely a list of the gifts given, this list begins with people who exercise gifts. Even so, the two lists in this chapter do not conform to each other.

And God has appointed: the functions are still regarded as the gifts of God. *Appointed* means "set in their proper place" in the ministry of the church.

In the church: the Christian congregation. The question may arise: How can we say that apostles were set in each congregation? It is unlikely that even in this early age each church had the advantage of an apostolic ministry. However, the church at Corinth had had such a ministry. Either Paul had this one congregation in mind or else he thought of each church as based on the fundamental function of all the apostles. In another passage Paul spoke of the church as "built upon the foundation of the apostles and

---

[1] Cf. Lenski, Parry, ICC.

prophets, Christ Jesus himself being the cornerstone" (Eph. 2:20). Since the apostles gave the primary testimony to Christ and the prophets interpreted the meaning of that event for life, each church was built upon their testimony and witness.

First apostles: men who were eyewitnesses of the ministry of Jesus. The primary qualification of an apostle is expressed in the words of Peter when the Jerusalem church elected a successor to Judas: "So one of the men who have accompanied us during all the time that the Lord Jesus went in and out among us, beginning from the baptism of John until the day when he was taken up from us—one of these men must become with us a witness to his resurrection" (Acts 1:21–22). Paul, though he was not such a witness, became an apostle. His primary qualification was that he had seen "Jesus our Lord" (1 Cor. 9:1). It seems then that this function was to give eyewitness testimony to the resurrection of Jesus Christ. The function of the apostles was not to exercise authority, but to give testimony.

Second prophets: men who received a divine revelation of the will of God for his people (see extended study at 14:1). These men seem to have been gifted with the power to discern the will of God for his people in particular situations.

Third teachers: men who instructed others in Christianity. The body of material which they taught was that which came from the testimony of the apostles and the revelations communicated by the prophets.

Then workers of miracles: The Greek changes from the concrete to the abstract. The RSV may be correct in continuing the parallelism, but it would be better to follow the Greek. Thus the correct translation would be "miraculous acts." The thought is not so much that certain men were miracle workers, but that various members at various times were given the gift of performing miraculous acts. The remainder of the list is of the same nature.

Then healers: rather, "healings." Gifts of healing were probably a special class of miraculous acts. Notice that Paul placed these spectacular acts on an inferior plane to apostles, prophets, and teachers.

Helpers: rather, "helps." The Greek word was in common use to express the assistance given to government officials by inferiors. This word marks a passage from the miraculous powers to the practical administration of the church.[1] Though not much is said about such matters in the New Testament, it must be assumed that early churches had need of such gifts, just as modern churches do. Again the reference is not to specific men who retained this gift, but to the exercise of the gift at various times.

Administrators: rather, "administrations." Administration is a function of government. This exact term is found only here, but other words are used in the New Testament to indicate those who superintended the church (cf. "leaders," Heb. 13:7, 17; "bishops" or "overseers," Phil. 1:1; 1 Tim. 3:2). Any orderly society needs such a function. The gift of administration would be the ability to function with spiritual meaning in such a role.

---

[1] Barclay thinks this refers to those who succored the poor, the orphans, the widows, and the strangers.

Speakers in various kinds of tongues: This expression fits well with our interpretation that *tongues* means "foreign languages" in this whole discussion (see extended study at 14:1).

Verses 29–30: a series of rhetorical questions to enforce the fact that no one person has all of these gifts. The emphasis is upon the variety of gifts and functions within the church fellowship. Each question is phrased to demand a negative answer. Thus, "all are not . . . are they?" The list of gifts conforms broadly to that given in verse 28. However, *interpretation* (i.e., translation) is added at the end to conform to the *tongues. Helpers* and *administrators* are omitted from the previous list. Comparing the three lists in this chapter, we find the following results:

12:8–10	12:28	12:29–30
	1. Apostles	1. Apostles
	2. Prophets	2. Prophets
	3. Teachers	3. Teachers
4. Word of wisdom		
5. Word of knowledge		
6. Faith		
	7. Miracles	7. Miracles
8. Gifts of healing	8. Gifts of healing	8. Gifts of healing
7. Miracles		
2. Prophecy		
9. Discernment of spirits		
	10. Helps	
	11. Administrations	
12. Kinds of tongues	12. Kinds of tongues	12. Speaking in tongues
13. Interpretation of tongues		13. Interpretation

The only gifts found in all three lists are prophecy, miracles, healings, and tongues. This rather strange fact probably reflects the situation in Corinth. The question was, "Which kind of gift was more important, the edificatory or the spectacular?" Paul answered this question in chapter 14. In each of our lists, he was concerned to include the most representative examples of these two kinds of gifts.

Verse 31: The first part of the verse belongs with the previous discussion and prepares the way for chapter 14; the second part serves as an introduction to chapter 13.

Earnestly desire: a general injunction to the congregation. The imperative is in the present tense, meaning "to continue to seek." The Greek word translated *desire* is generally used in a bad sense in the New Testament; Paul's writings alone use it in a good sense. In a bad sense the basic word means "jealousy, envy." In a good sense, it means "zeal, desire." Instead of coveting the more spectacular gifts, the Corinthians were urged to turn their desire in a different direction.

The higher gifts: rather, "the greater gifts." How was this greatness to be ascertained? Paul made it clear in chapter 14 that a gift which edified the whole congregation was the greater gift. However, in this chapter he had not made this clear except in a general way (cf. vs. 7).

And: a correct translation. The following is in accordance with Paul's injunction to seek the greater gifts.

I will show you: refers to chapter 13.

A still more excellent way: i.e., a way to something greater than even the greatest gifts, perhaps. The wording is obscure and the interpretations are diverse. It is possible to take this entire clause in different ways. First, it is possible to take it as continuing the thought of the injunction or in contrast with the injunction. Second, it is possible to take the *more excellent way* as meaning that love is the supreme gift, or that it is the way to the achievement of the greater gifts, or that it is neither of these but a greater thing in itself. On the whole it is better to follow the suggestions of our interpretation. Thus the clause is taken as a continuation of the previous clause with the following thought: "keep on desiring the greater gifts and I will now show you something that is even greater than that." However, the connection between love and the spiritual gifts is close. Love is the motive that makes the spiritual gifts meaningful in the life of the individual and the congregation.

2. Love—the Supreme Gift (13:1–13)

To call love a gift in the same sense of the other gifts is perhaps a mistake. What we mean is that love comes from God. Paul named it first in a list of fruits of the Holy Spirit (Gal. 5:22–23). John said, "Love is of God, and he who loves is born of God and knows God. He who does not love does not know God; for God is love" (1 John 4:7–8). There is no doubt that Paul thought that love was the supreme virtue of the Christian life. This beautiful chapter points out that love gives meaning to all the other spiritual gifts (13:1–3). It is the most Christian of all gifts (13:4–7). It is one of the enduring gifts, the greatest of all (13:8–13). Lenski suggests that chapter 13 is what Paul had to say about Paul, that love was the motivating power of all his mighty works and great sacrifices. This may be, but we do not believe that the chapter was consciously written with this in mind. The pattern, if there was one in Paul's mind, was Christ himself.[1] In the beautiful description of the characteristics of love (vss. 4–7), the name of Christ could be substituted for love without doing violence to the facts of his life.

(1) Love gives meaning to all other gifts (13:1–3)

Four gifts are mentioned in this list as characteristic of the rest. The order may reveal the values placed on these gifts by the Corinthians, but of that we cannot be sure. Certainly they do not reflect the order of values in the mind of Paul. In each case the gift is said to be meaningless without love.

Verse 1: If I speak in the tongues of men and of angels: the gift most

---

[1] Parry has well said that this chapter shows a loving and loyal intimacy with the character of Jesus as portrayed in the Gospels.

prized by the Corinthians. *Tongues of men* mean foreign languages which men speak. The expression . . . *of angels* has given rise to speculation. The Jewish rabbis thought this tongue was Hebrew; others have thought it to be a kind of speech which surpassed the speech of men, as the speech of men surpasses the babbling of babies. No one knows for sure what is meant. Perhaps Paul meant it to be a hyperbole. Some of the Corinthians were boasting of speaking in diverse tongues. Paul said that even if that were true, that even if one should speak in the *tongues . . . of angels,* this in itself was not enough. In the Greek order *and of angels* seems to be added as an afterthought.

But have not love: unselfish concern for others. *Love (agapē)* in this passage is one of the three Greek words used for various kinds of love. The other two are *eros,* from which we get our word "erotic"; and *philos,* which forms a prefix to many English words such as "Philadelphia"—the love of men. *Eros* describes a love of selfishness, either a search for gods or the passion of a man for a woman. *Philos* describes a reciprocal love, love which responds to that which is attractive to others. It might be directed toward members of the same sex or those of the other sex. *Agapē* describes a colder, less emotional type of love—the love of concern and devotion such as a mother might have for her child. Seemingly passion was never thought to be a part of this type of love. This fact made it appropriate to describe the love which God has for men and the love which men should have for God. Its use to describe the concern of Christians for each other is derived from this usage. Such love is a divine kind of love in which the one who loves stands willing to give himself without reserve for the good of the object of love. In the New Testament Christians are commanded to love not only God and their fellow Christians but their enemies also. This is the love which Paul saw as the foundation of all Christian life, giving meaning to all else when it was present.

I am a noisy gong or a clanging cymbal: i.e., no better than the pagan priests who proclaimed nonsense in the name of religion. The noise of gongs and cymbals was not uncommon in Corinth. Many pagan rites, especially those of the Dionysian cult, were accompanied by such displays (Moffatt). The Corinthians would have known what Paul meant. If they spoke the message of God, even in foreign languages or the language of angels, but did not speak it with love, they would class themselves with pagans who sought only to enslave the people.

Verse 2: And if I have prophetic powers: the gift of prophecy, the ability to speak by direct revelation from God (see extended study at 14:1).

And understand all mysteries and all knowledge: describes the result of having prophetic gifts. *Mysteries* means the secrets of divine providence (Rom. 11:25). *Knowledge* means the knowledge of God and his ways (cf. 1:5). Such understanding would be a valued gift, but without love it becomes meaningless in the Christian community.

And if I have all faith: i.e., to perform miracles. This is clearly the meaning of this context.

So as to remove mountains: the result of faith.

But have not love: a recurring refrain in this section.

I am nothing: a stronger indictment than in verse 1. There the thought is that one's exercise of gifts has no meaning in the Christian community. Here the thought is that the exercise of such gifts leaves one a nonentity, not even a Christian. The verdict of Jesus on such people was, "I never knew you; depart from me, you evildoers" (Matt. 7:23).

Verse 3: If I give away all I have: rather, "if I give away for food all my possessions." *Give away* translates a Greek word which means "give food in small portions." [1] It was often used of feeding the young. Here it is obviously used for feeding the poor. The Jews made a virtue of almsgiving, and the Christians seem to have followed in their steps. It was said of the Jerusalem church, "There was not a needy person among them, for as many as were possessors of lands or houses sold them, and brought the proceeds of what was sold and laid it at the apostles' feet; and distribution was made to each as any had need" (Acts 4:34–35). The Gentile churches were, at the time Paul wrote, involved in gathering a collection for the poor saints (cf. chap. 16). There was virtue in such giving, but not without love.

And if I deliver my body to be burned: presents a textual problem. The better texts have, instead of *to be burned,* "in order that I might glory." In the Greek there is only a difference of the letter in the two words. At first glance the better-attested reading seems to violate the context. Therefore, most translators and many commentators argue for the secondary reading *to be burned.* However, this reading is almost as difficult because there is no record of this kind of martyrdom in the time of Paul. The best rule to follow is to accept the better-attested reading, which in this case is also the more difficult reading. How can we reconcile the idea of self-glory to the context? It would seem self-evident that any act motivated by self-glory would gain nothing. Perhaps the key to understanding the passage is to read "in order that I might glory" with both clauses—the surrender of possessions and the surrender of life. In this case the latter would be only an extreme case of the former. At a later period in Christian history, it is said that some Christians sold themselves into slavery and used the proceeds to feed the poor (ICC). It may be that such an extreme sacrifice was known in Paul's day. If so, the reference would not be to martyrdom but to voluntary servitude.

But have not love: If the solution above is correct, this would be a true antithesis of self-glory. Thus the thought would be: "if I do these things for self-glory instead of love."

I gain nothing: no spiritual reward. Such gifts, even when given for self-glory, bring benefits to those who receive them. They bring no benefit to those who give them. Notice the different results in these three verses: in verse 1, the result is that the loveless speaker produces nothing of value for others; in verse 2, the loveless prophet and miracle worker are of no value themselves; in verse 3, the loveless giver gains nothing of value for himself.

(2) Love is the most Christian of all gifts (13:4–7)

This is a beautiful poem of praise to love. It enumerates love's charac-

---

[1] Cf. Barrett.

teristics, sometimes in negative terms, sometimes in positive. Fourteen qualities of love are mentioned, in pairs.

Verse 4: Patient: rather, "longsuffering." The Greek word is a compound of two elements, one meaning "long" and the other "wrath." The quality is the opposite of being "short-tempered." One who loves is slow to wrath against the one he loves.

Kind: related to usefulness. Kindness is not so much a sweet disposition as it is the practice of useful, beneficial, friendly acts. Love seeks the good of its object. Edwards is wrong in finding the opposite meaning to be "sharpness, severity."

Not jealous: of the earthly goods or position of another. Love rejoices in the benefits that the loved one has, even if he must do without. Paul thought of jealousy as the source of strife and characteristic of men who did not know God (cf. 1 Cor. 3:3).

Not . . . boastful: does not play the braggart. Ostentation is the keynote of the word. Boasting creates envy in others; it has no place in the life of love.

Verse 5: It is not arrogant: rather, "does not puff itself up." Paul had used the word often to describe factious Christians (cf. 4:6, 18–19; 5:2; 8:1). Colossians 2:18 is the only instance of the word outside this letter. Paul would remind those Corinthians who boasted of their knowledge and their freedom and ignored the good of their brethren that they were not living a life of love.

Not . . . rude: does not practice self-assertion. Perhaps Paul had in mind those who insisted on speaking in tongues even though it did not profit the congregation, or of the rich who ate their meals ahead of the poor. In the New Testament the word is used only here and in 7:36, where it is translated "behaving properly." There the thought of propriety is the desire or needs of others. The same meaning should be used here.

Love does not insist on its own way: its own interests. The thought of love is always for the interests of others.

Is not irritable: translates a Greek word from which we get our English word "paroxysm." However, the Greek word means "does not yield to provocation." Love is not embittered by slights, whether real or imagined. The idea of great anger being restrained by love was in Paul's mind.

Is not . . . resentful: rather, "does not reckon up the evil." Love does not store up resentment or bear malice against those who do wrong. "Reckon up" is a bookkeeping word for keeping accounts with the idea of squaring them at a later date.

Verse 6: It does not rejoice at wrong: the evil committed by others. Love always takes the right side in a moral conflict.

But rejoices in the right: rather, "rejoices with the truth"—i.e., when truth prevails. "Truth" is contrasted with "wrong," meaning a way of life that is true and right.

Verse 7: Love bears all things: The interpretation is debated. The Greek word which is translated *bears* originally meant to "cover over." From this came two figurative uses: (1) to excuse the faults of others, and (2) to bear without resentment the injuries inflicted by others. Paul used the same verb in 9:12 with reference to his refusal to claim his rights but to "endure anything" to avoid putting an obstacle in the way of the gospel. Either of the two figurative meanings could fit this context, but in view of the passage quoted (9:12), the second meaning should be given. Thus love endures afflictions without resentment.

Believes all things: has no reserves in, or lack of, faith. This does not mean that love is gullible, but that it strives to ascribe the best motives to others in their actions. Love puts the best possible construction on the acts of others.

Hopes all things: even when it is difficult to believe. It still hopes even when hopes are repeatedly disappointed.

Endures all things: remains true in the most adverse circumstances. *Endures* translates the verbal form of the word which is usually translated "patience." It is formed by two elements, one meaning "under," and the other "remains." The idea is that love remains under the load in all circumstances. Not patient endurance, but active steadfastness is the primary idea.

(3) Love is one of the enduring gifts (13:8–13)

In contrast to *prophecy, tongues,* and *knowledge,* love has enduring validity, even beyond this life. It shares this ability to endure with *faith* and *hope,* but it is greater than these. The spiritual gifts mentioned are for this world only; the qualities of love are imperishable.

Verse 8: strikes the note which runs throughout this paragraph.

Love never ends: never disappears. *Ends* translates the Greek word for "falls," but the RSV catches Paul's meaning.

As for prophecies: the more valuable gift for the benefit of the congregation. Prophecy was the gift of receiving and communicating divine revelations.

They will pass away: be abolished. The idea is that the need for prophecy will no longer exist in the future world when the fellowship of all Christians with God will be perfect and direct.

As for tongues: languages by which men communicate with one another. The gift in Corinth was the gift of speaking in an unlearned foreign language. Perhaps this is the forefront of Paul's thought, but *tongues* can be more general, meaning language itself.

They will cease: stop. The need for various languages will no longer exist; perhaps the need for any language will cease. Of course, if *tongues* is taken to mean ecstatic speech, there will be no need for this in the world to come. All that Paul meant by this statement may go beyond the ability of the human mind to understand. Notice that the other two gifts will be superseded by something better; this gift is said to cease absolutely.

As for knowledge: the knowledge of the ways of God, based on revelation and instruction. This knowledge always ends in a mystery in this life.

It will pass away: be abolished as imperfect to make place for full knowledge.

Verse 9: For our knowledge is imperfect: rather, "we know partially." The thought is not that our knowledge itself is imperfect as if it were wrong or had a flaw in it. The point is that our knowing is only partial.

Paul would have said that the knowledge which the Christian had, if it were indeed a spiritual gift, was true knowledge.

Our prophecy is imperfect: same construction as above. "We prophesy in part." The revelations from God were true, but they were never complete.

Verse 10: But when the perfect comes: rather, "the complete." *Perfect,* though often used to translate the same Greek word that we find in this verse, is an inadequate translation. The Greek word means "mature" when applied to natural man, "complete" when applied to things.

The imperfect will pass away: rather, "The incomplete will be abolished or superseded." There will be no need for the partial knowledge or prophecy, when the full knowledge of God becomes universal.

Verse 11: To illustrate his thought, Paul took the example of human growth, a contrast between the child and the man. The illustration was suggested by the word "mature" in the previous verse.

When I was a child: an infant. The word for *child* was applied to the very young.

I spoke like a child: imperfect tense, meaning, "I made a habit of speaking."

I thought like a child: same construction. *Thought* does not refer primarily to intellectual exercise, but to one's interests. Paul meant to say that the normal strivings of childhood characterized his childhood.

I reasoned like a child: still the imperfect tense. *Reasoned* brings in the intellectual exercise. It is doubtful that Paul meant to draw subtle comparisons with the spiritual gifts in Corinth. He simply chose three characteristics of human life in which the immaturity of the child is universally apparent.

When I became a man: perfect tense, stressing a point when this happened. The continuing reality is also present in the Greek verb. Paul had become a man in the past, and he still remained one.

I gave up childish ways: Gave up translates a form of the same verb used above for the passing away of prophecy and knowledge. The perfect tense means, "I abolished once and for all" the ways of the child.

Verse 12: carries the illustration to its application in spiritual matters. The contrast is between the *now* of this life and the *then* of the life to come.[1]

Now: in this life as a Christian on earth.

We see in a mirror dimly: Paul included all Christians by the change from *I* to *we.* It is characteristic of Christian life in this world that our sight is dim. The ancient mirrors were much inferior to our modern ones. They consisted of some kind of polished metal which gave an imperfect reflection. Thus the illustration was valid in Paul's day. *Dimly* really means "in a riddle." The emphasis is on the obscurity of the revelation.

But then: in the life to come after the resurrection.

Face to face: reflects the Old Testament story of Moses (Num. 12:8), where the contrast was between the direct revelation of God to Moses and the indirect revelation through dreams and visions to others. Paul longed to see God in that direct way and believed that he would.

Now I know in part: changes the pronoun to the singular. Perhaps the

---

[1] Allo suggests 1 John 3:2 as a parallel verse to this.

reason is that Paul's knowledge would be recognized by the Corinthians as superior to their own. Yet even his knowledge was partial.

Then I shall understand fully, even as I have been fully understood: seems to contradict verse 8. However, Paul changed the Greek word to indicate a different kind of knowledge. In verse 8 and in the previous clause, he used the simple word for knowledge; here he used a compound word which means perfect knowledge or experiential knowledge. Though the difference between these words was becoming blurred in the first century, their use in this context should be given the full classical meaning.

Verse 13: the climactic statement of this paragraph.

So: a good translation of the Greek particle. The particle is "now," but it has a logical rather than a temporal sense.[1]

Faith, hope, love abide, these three: a surprising list. We would have expected only *love* in this context, but Paul added *faith* and *hope.* In what sense do faith and hope continue in the next world? The answer may be found in the nature of faith and hope and an understanding of the heavenly life. *Faith* is not, as some believe, merely intellectual belief; it is surrender to God. In this world faith functions also to make real what cannot be seen (Heb. 11:1). In the coming world this function of faith will be superseded by seeing God face to face, but faith as surrender to the rulership of God will abide. Hope likewise will continue. Paul seemed to indicate that heaven will not be a place of stagnation; we will not in one giant step reach the limits of our development. Entrance into heaven will open the way for progress and growth such as man never dreams of in this world.

But the greatest of these is love: In what way does love surpass faith and hope? Paul did not say, but we can guess. Perhaps the best answer is that love is the most Godlike characteristic of the Christian. Love is the central quality in God's character. To love is to be most like him. Love is supreme, not only because it is more useful, but because it is more divine than any other quality of life.

3. The Superiority of Prophecy over Tongues (14:1-25)

In this section Paul dealt with the chief problem in the church at Corinth in relation to spiritual gifts. His discussion in the previous chapters was general; his discussion here is specific. He was adamant concerning the superiority of prophecy over tongues, giving four reasons for his stand: (1) Prophecy edifies the whole congregation and ministers to its spiritual good (vss. 1-5). (2) Tongues, when used in the church services, do not help others; such use is essentially selfish (vss. 6-12). (3) Prophecy enables the outsider to understand what is going on in the church services (vss. 13-19). (4) Therefore, prophecy is serviceable in evangelism (vss. 20-25). We must remember that Paul was talking about the public services of the congregation. If our interpretation of tongues is correct, tongues did have their use on the docks of Corinth. However, before we can understand this chapter, we must attempt to find out what is meant by *tongues* and *prophecy.*

---

[1] Cf. Morris.

Digression: The meaning of "tongues" in Corinth

Concerning the phenomenon of speaking in tongues which existed in Corinth, some things can be said with certainty:

1. It was a genuine gift of the Holy Spirit (12:10–11).

2. Paul considered it the lowest of the gifts which the Holy Spirit had given (it is listed eighth in both lists of the gifts, only interpretation of tongues being lower: 12:10, 28).

3. Not all Christians who had the Holy Spirit were endowed with this particular gift (cf. 12:30).

4. The gift was useless for the edification of fellow church members (14:9).

5. The trouble in Corinth arose from the desire of those who possessed the gift of tongues to parade their gift and perhaps to insist that it was the greatest of gifts.

6. The phenomenon was limited to Corinth. There is no evidence of its existence in other churches. Paul did not mention it as a gift of the Spirit in his other lists of such gifts (cf. Rom. 12:6–8). It may be, but it is not certain, that the same phenomenon occurred at Pentecost (cf. Acts 2:1–11). But there, as in the other passages in Acts where speaking in tongues is mentioned (cf. Acts 10:46; 19:6), the gift seems to have been temporary. None of the apocryphal writings mention it, and the ancient writers of Christianity viewed it as a strange thing.

Concerning the nature of the phenomenon, there is wide difference of opinion. Neither the New Testament nor early evidence outside the New Testament permits one to form a precise opinion of the nature of speaking in tongues. Later and current practices of "speaking in tongues" cannot be identified with the New Testament phenomena with certainty. At least three differences seem to exist. (1) Modern practitioners usually think of the gift as an indispensable sign of the possession of the Holy Spirit or at least as superior to other spiritual gifts, which was not true in the New Testament.[1] (2) Modern practitioners usually speak in tongues only in the church services or in private, whereas Paul thought the signs were a "sign . . . for unbelievers" (cf. 1 Cor. 14:22). (3) Modern practitioners seem to be unable to control the phenomenon, while Paul seemed to imply that it could be controlled (1 Cor. 14:27–28).

There is background material for four possible interpretations of this phenomenon:

1. It could have been speaking an unlearned human language.

2. It could have been speaking a nonhuman language, such as the language of angels or of a god (cf. 1 Cor. 13:1).

3. It could have been an exalted and enigmatic form of speaking which had to be interpreted for the common man.

4. It could have been ecstatic speech consisting of cadences of vocalization which did not really constitute a language at all.[2]

---

[1] Beare points out that it was not regarded by any New Testament writer as a "normal or invariable accompaniment of the Christian faith." (F. W. Beare, "Speaking in Tongues," *Journal of Biblical Literature,* Sept., 1964, p. 246.)

[2] This is an adaptation of Currie's list (cf. Stuart D. Currie, "Speaking in Tongues," *Interpretation,* July, 1965, p. 294).

The commentators are almost evenly divided between the first and fourth alternatives. ICC and Edwards believe it consisted of ecstatic speech; Robertson and Lenski believe it consisted of an unlearned foreign language. No one, it seems, can justifiably be dogmatic about his opinion, though many are. Since the choice seems to be between ecstatic speech and speaking a foreign language, let us examine the evidence of the New Testament which would favor one or the other of these.

There are some factors which would tend to support the idea that the tongues were ecstatic speech:

(1) "For one who speaks in a tongue speaks not to men but to God; for no one understands him, but he utters mysteries in the Spirit" (1 Cor. 14:2).

(2) "For if I pray in a tongue, my spirit prays but my mind is unfruitful" (1 Cor. 14:14).

(3) "Tongues of . . . angels" might imply this type of speech (1 Cor. 13:1).

There are some factors which would tend to support the idea that the tongues were foreign languages:

(1) This was a common use for the word "tongues" in the New and Old Testaments (cf. Rev. 5:9; 7:9; 10:11; 11:9; 13:7; 14:6; 17:15).

(2) If the speech were the same as that at Pentecost, the Acts account (2:1–11) strongly supports the idea that the speech there was in foreign languages, though many scholars find ways to explain it otherwise.

(3) The complex of Greek words which is translated "interpret" or "interpretation" (1 Cor. 12:10, 30; 14:5, 13, 26–28) is used, with one exception, in the New Testament with the meaning of translating a foreign language (cf. Acts 9:36; John 1:38–42; 9:7; Heb. 7:2). The one exception where the meaning is the more common Greek meaning of explaining something is Luke 24:27.

(4) The analogy between the Old Testament passage and the tongues in Corinth (1 Cor. 14:21) would support the idea of a foreign language, for the Old Testament passage clearly has this meaning (cf. Isa. 28:11–12).

(5) The statement that the tongues were a sign for "unbelievers" (1 Cor. 14:22) would be in favor of a foreign language which the unbeliever could understand.

(6) The strong supposition that all spiritual gifts were for the purpose of gospel proclamation would favor the idea of foreign languages as the meaning of the phenomenon at Corinth.

In view of these considerations, it would seem that the weight of the evidence is in favor of giving the "tongues" at Corinth the meaning of speaking unlearned foreign languages. The only real objection to this is found in 1 Corinthians 14:2 and 14 and possibly 23. If, however, we suppose that the speaker did not himself understand the language, but spoke it in the grip of the Holy Spirit, these passages could be so interpreted. It is difficult to see how the factors which support the meaning of a foreign language can be reconciled to the interpretation that the "tongues" were a form of ecstatic speech. Thus, without being dogmatic, the following interpretation will assume that the "tongues" in Corinth were foreign languages.

Digression: The meaning of "prophecy" in Corinthians

The New Testament use of the complex of words—prophet, prophecy, and prophesy—is concentrated in these chapters of 1 Corinthians. This is true if we exclude the references to the prophets of the Old Testament. Our purpose is to seek an answer to the question: What was a Christian prophet in Paul's thought? Was this a synonym for a preacher of the gospel, a proclaimer? Was prophecy a peculiar gift which occurred only in the first century in connection with the founding of Christianity and then vanished? The answer to the problem is not easy.

The prophet of the Old Testament was primarily a "forth-teller," not a "foreteller." It is true that they sometimes foretold the future, but their main characteristic was to speak out for God to the people about their present situation. The distinguishing mark of the prophet's message was "Thus saith the Lord." The prophet was primarily a spokesman for God.

The prophet disappeared from the scene of Israel's life after Malachi, and prophecy lay dormant for a considerable period of time. There was a lively hope that the coming of the Messiah would be accompanied by the return of the prophet. The first intimation of prophecy in the New Testament surrounds the birth of Jesus. Zachariah (Luke 1:67) is said to prophesy; Anna is called a prophetess (Luke 2:36). In the song of Zachariah, we find the words, "And you, child, will be called the prophet of the Most High" (Luke 1:76). When John the Baptist began his ministry, he was held to be a prophet by the people (Mark 11:32; Matt. 14:5). Jesus said concerning him, "Why then did you go out? To see a prophet? Yes, I tell you, and more than a prophet" (Matt. 11:9; Luke 7:26). Seemingly the thing which made John the Baptist recognizable as a prophet was that he spoke an authoritative message from God.

Jesus himself was often identified as a prophet; the two disciples on the road to Emmaus, for example, said, ". . . Jesus of Nazareth, who was a prophet mighty in deed and word before God and all the people" (Luke 24:19). The people commonly thought he was a prophet (Matt. 16:14). The woman at the well in Samaria called him a prophet (John 4:19). Seemingly his power to perform miracles, his authoritative teaching, and, perhaps, his ability to read the thoughts of men lay behind this designation.

In the Book of Acts, we have a few passages which speak of Christian prophets. Peter identified the phenomenon of Pentecost with the prophecy in Joel which said among other things, "Your sons and your daughters shall prophesy" (Acts 2:17). Agabus is spoken of as a prophet who foretold the famine in Jerusalem (Acts 11:27-28) and the imprisonment of Paul (Acts 21:10-11). The church at Antioch had five men who were called "prophets and teachers" (Acts 13:1). Judas and Silas, who accompanied Paul and Barnabas back to Antioch with the apostolic letter, were called prophets (Acts 15:32). The disciples at Ephesus "spoke with tongues and prophesied" when Paul laid his hands on them, and they received the Holy Spirit (Acts 19:6). The four daughters of Philip the evangelist "prophesied" (Acts 21:8-9).

Omitting the Corinthian correspondence, the rest of the New Testament has very little to say about prophets. Paul commanded the Thessalonians, "Do not despise prophesying" (1 Thess. 5:20). Timothy's separation to the ministry and his gifts were recognized and accompanied by prophetic utterances (1 Tim. 1:18; 4:14). The church is said to have been "built upon the foundation of the apostles and prophets" (Eph. 2:20). In the gifts of the ascended Christ, prophets are mentioned along with apostles and before evangelists, pastors, and teachers (Eph. 4:11). The Book of Revelation is called a prophecy (Rev. 1:3; 22:7, 10, 18–19). Two prophets are among the mystic figures of Revelation (11:6, 10). Prophets are also mentioned in Revelation 10:7; 18:20, 24. The lone passage which may give some light on the meaning of prophecy is, "The testimony of Jesus is the spirit of prophecy" (Rev. 19:10).

In this section of 1 Corinthians the whole complex of words is used with remarkable frequency. The noun "prophecy" is used five times (12:10; 13:2, 8; 14:6, 22). The noun "prophet" is found five times (12:28–29; 14:29, 32, 37). The verb "prophesy" occurs eleven times (11:4–5; 13:9; 14:1, 3, 4, 5, 24, 31, 39). In most instances mention is made of the gift without any contextual clue as to its nature. It was certainly thought to be a gift of the Spirit (14:1); it ranked second to the apostles in the gifts given to the church (12:28); not all the church members could prophesy (12:29); prophecy along with knowledge would cease (13:8); prophecy edified the church (14:4); prophecy led to the conviction and conversion of the outsider (14:24–25); prophecy was a gift earnestly to be desired (14:39). One passage is helpful: "And if I have prophetic powers, and understand all mysteries and all knowledge" (13:2).

What then is the answer to our question? It would seem that the prophet of the New Testament was one who received his message directly from God and spoke to the people concerning the meaning of Christ and the gospel. He differed from the modern preacher in the source of his message. The modern preacher interprets the Bible and speaks to men for God on that basis. The ancient prophet, though he may have used the Old Testament to some extent, spoke with direct authority. He differed from the apostle in the content of his message. The apostle gave testimony to Jesus based on his own eyewitness observation of his life. The prophet gave testimony to God's will and explained the meaning of the lordship of Christ. Of course, the apostles could also be prophets and probably were. The need for this gift would vanish when the canon of the New Testament was completed. Thus there is no modern equivalent of the New Testament prophet. The distinguishing mark of the prophet was that he (or she) received a revelation from God and communicated it to the people. It was possible for false prophets to arise; thus the attendant gift, "the ability to distinguish between spirits" (1 Cor. 12:10), was essential to the life of the church.

(1) Prophecy edifies the church (14:1–5)

The central thrust of this paragraph is the edification of the church. Paul thought that prophecy accomplished this (vss. 3–5). He felt that speaking in tongues did not accomplish it (vss. 2, 4). This seems to have been his basis for the preference of prophecy over speaking in tongues.

Verse 1: connects this discussion with chapter 13.

Make love your aim: rather, "keep on pursuing love." The metaphor is that of the chase. Love is to be the aim of the Christian search. *Love* has the article, which means that the *love* is identified as that about which Paul had been writing. The search for love is to continue along with other interests of the Christian life, but it is always to have the supreme place. Though love is a fruit of the Spirit, the Christian is to exert continuous and eager effort to achieve it.

And earnestly desire the spiritual gifts: indicates that Paul did not place love in the same category with the other spiritual gifts which he discussed. Though these gifts are distributed by the Holy Spirit as he alone wills (cf. 12:11), it is proper for the Christian to desire them.

Especially that you may prophesy: reveals Paul's evaluation of prophecy in comparison with tongues. The special desire of the Christian should be to be able to receive a communication from God and share it with his fellow Christians.

Verse 2: states that the use of tongues in the church services is essentially selfish.

For one who speaks in a tongue: a foreign language which he has not learned, and speaks it in the service of the church.

Speaks not to men: since they cannot understand what he says.[1] This does not necessarily mean that no one understood him, but that none of those present understood him. If we assume that the statement is absolute, we would have to believe that ecstatic utterance was the nature of the tongues in Corinth.

But to God; for no one understands him: Paul did not deny that God understood; he only denied that men could.

But he utters mysteries in the Spirit: implies that the man himself was not aware of what he spoke. *Spirit* refers to the man's spirit, not the Holy Spirit. The contrast is with the man who speaks with the mind (vs. 19). Seemingly, those who had this gift had words placed upon their lips by the Holy Spirit without any intelligent reflection on their own part. *Utters mysteries* looks on his speech from the standpoint of the congregation. Since they did not understand him, he was speaking mysteries.

Verse 3: On the other hand: in contrast to the speaker in tongues.

He who prophesies: communicates God's revelation.

Speaks to men: because they can understand him.

For their upbuilding: growth in spiritual status. The Greek makes this a direct object of *speaks.* "He speaks upbuilding." The idea is that of result. His speaking resulted in the spiritual improvement of all the congregation.

Encouragement: rather, "admonition." The verb of this noun is quite frequent in these letters.

Consolation: encouragement to continue faithful in Christian living.[2] The three words are coordinate and represent necessary help in Christian living. Prophecy gave this help by making known the will of God and thus building up character, quickening will power, and encouraging men to remain faithful.

Verse 4: In contrast to the beneficial powers of prophecy, tongues only serve for self-edification.

---

[1] Cf. Lenski.
[2] Cf. Edwards.

Edifies himself: builds up his own Christian character.

Edifies the church: rather, "a church." There is no article in the Greek.

Verse 5: Paul expressed his wish that all should be able to have some spiritual gift, but desired that they should have the higher gift of prophecy.

Now I want you all to speak in tongues: Paul had no wish to depreciate tongues; he recognized them as a genuine gift of the Spirit which had some value. His desire for his converts was that each of them would have some spiritual gift.

But even more to prophesy: exalts the gift of prophecy without depreciating the gift of *tongues.*

He who prophesies is greater than he who speaks in tongues: not in character, but in usefulness.

Unless: introduces the exception to the general statement.

Some one interprets: translates the language into the language of the people.

So that the church may be edified: defines the area in which prophecy is normally superior to tongues. Paul's concern was that spiritual gifts would serve to benefit others. In church services tongues must be translated if the content of the message was to be helpful to the congregation.

(2) Tongues do not edify others (14:6–12)

Having introduced this thought in the previous paragraph, Paul discussed it at some length. He illustrated his thought by reference to musical instruments and to foreign languages.

Verse 6: expands the thought of verse 5 as preparation for the following statements.

Brethren: reminds them of his brotherly concern for them.

If I come to you speaking in tongues: a possibility, since Paul claimed to "speak in tongues more than you all" (vs. 18).

How shall I benefit you: a rhetorical question assuming that he would not bring them any spiritual profit.

Unless: introduces the exception.

I bring you some revelation or knowledge or prophecy or teaching: obscures the Greek. The four examples are in pairs that correspond. *Revelation* was communicated through *prophecy. Knowledge* was communicated through *teaching. Teaching* is a noun, but the active sense seems to be called for here. Paul did not include the necessity of translation of the tongues even if they expressed intelligible content, but translation is assumed.

Verse 7: The first illustration of the necessity of intelligible speech concerns musical instruments.

If even lifeless instruments: stresses the inanimacy of the instruments (Greek, "voices"). Lifeless though they are, and therefore without control of their sounds, they must give distinctions if they are to mean anything.

Such as the flute or the harp: rather, "pipe and harp." These are given as representative of all wind and stringed instruments. They were the most common instruments used in banquets, funerals, and religious ceremonies (ICC).

Give distinct notes: probably so as to play a tune. *Distinct* comes from a

Greek word which means "to make a difference." *Notes* comes from a word which may mean either vocal or instrumental sounds, usually but not always musical in nature (cf. Rom. 10:18).

How will any one know what is played?: rhetorical question with an obvious answer.

Verse 8: The second illustration is the trumpet used in battle. The trumpet was used to play out various commands in ancient days as in modern days.

And if the bugle gives an indistinct sound: when it plays "to arms."

Who will get ready for battle?: correct translation. The obvious conclusion is stated in the form of a rhetorical question.

Verse 9: The illustrations are given their application to speaking in tongues.

So with yourselves: when you speak.

If you in a tongue utter speech that is not intelligible: Aside from the context, this could be interpreted to mean clear enunciation of tones in any kind of speech. In the context it must refer to the gift of tongues (i.e., foreign languages). This kind of speech would not be *intelligible* (Greek, "easily understood") when spoken in the congregation.

How will any one know what is said?: an obvious conclusion in the form of a rhetorical question.

For you will be speaking into the air: i.e., "You will be like a man speaking to the winds." *You will be speaking* is a form of Greek construction that signifies continuous action. The thought is that one who speaks thus will never have a message of meaning for the congregation.

Verse 10: may be taken as another illustration or as a direct discussion of the uselessness of the gift of tongues. If our interpretation is correct, verses 10–11 are a direct discussion of the uselessness of speaking in a foreign language unless the hearer knows the meaning of the language.

There are doubtless many different languages in the world: poor translation. Literally, it reads, "There are, it may be, so many kinds of voices in the world." "Voices" mean sounds made by any means. The same word was used in verse 7 for the sound of musical instruments. It is tempting to accept the RSV translation because it supports our interpretation, but this is not true to the Greek text. *Different languages* should therefore be "so many kinds of voices or sounds." "It may be" does not express doubt of the fact but doubt of the number of such sounds.

And none is without meaning: rather, "and voiceless." None of these sounds is without some meaning to someone or something. The entire gamut of sounds, human and subhuman, come into play. Even the sounds made by cats, for example, have meaning to other cats.

Verse 11: comes to the point of foreign languages. All kinds of languages were spoken in commercial Corinth. Difference of language was a frequent barrier to understanding.

But if I do not know the meaning of the language: probably a correct translation. *Meaning* is literally "power." Probably the idea is that of "significance" and hence *meaning*. *Language* is literally "the voice." The context in this verse justifies the use of the word *language*.

Foreigner: in both clauses, is "barbarian." However, the word meant "someone who spoke a foreign language." The hearer was like a foreigner to the one speaking, and the reverse was also true.

Verse 12: So with yourselves: Act on this same principle. Always speak in the language of the hearer rather than in a foreign language.

Since you are eager for manifestations of the Spirit: gifts coming from the Holy Spirit.

Strive to excel in building up the church: Seek the kind of spiritual gifts which can be used for this purpose.

(3) Prophecy enables the outsider to understand (14:13–19)

Though prophecy is not mentioned in this section, it is the implied subject of it. While the edification of the congregation was the main concern of the last paragraph, the outsider also enters into this one.

Verse 13: Therefore: a connective word, showing a continuation of thought.

He who speaks in a tongue: a foreign language.

Should pray for the power to interpret: literally, "Let him pray in order that he may interpret." Three interpretations have been suggested for this clause: (1) Let him pray for the power to interpret (note: RSV translation). (2) Let him refrain from praying in a tongue unless he can interpret. (3) Let him pray in a tongue with the purpose of interpreting afterward what he says in his prayer. Either interpretation is possible grammatically. Probably the RSV translation is correct. He who makes a habit of speaking in tongues should pray for the attendant gift of interpretation (i.e., translation). These two gifts could be exercised by the same person, it seems. No mention is made of praying in a tongue in this verse.

Verse 14: For if I pray in a tongue: assumes that this would be an unusual thing. Even those who have learned foreign languages find it difficult to pray in them.

My spirit prays: assumes that the one who prays thus did not understand what he was saying. His spiritual self was exalted because of its communion with God; therefore his prayer was not wholly useless. This would indicate that such praying, if it were done, should be done in private, not in public. However, Paul seemed to think it should not be done at all.

My mind is unfruitful: My intelligence does not come into play, and the praise that I offer to God bears no fruit in the congregation. *Unfruitful* refers to the effect on the congregation, not to the result in the individual's life.

Verse 15: What am I to do?: rather, "What are the consequences of this fact?" The question is rhetorical. Paul sought to focus the minds of the Corinthians on his conclusion.

I will pray with the spirit and I will pray with the mind also: The same prayer experience is in mind. The one who prays in the language of the congregation prays with the spirit just as truly as the one who prays in a tongue, having communion with God. But he also, at the same time, prays intelligibly, and so his mind becomes fruitful to the congregation.

I will sing with the spirit and I will sing with the mind also: parallel with the previous statement. *Sing* indicates that the public services of the church were in the mind of Paul. Singing was thought by Paul to be a means of instructing other Christians (cf. Eph. 5:19). The word which is translated *sing* originally meant "to play the harp" and then came to mean "to sing to the accompaniment of the harp." The last is the more frequent meaning in the Greek Old Testament and probably is the meaning in the New Testament.

Verse 16: Otherwise: i.e., if you pray or sing in a tongue.

If you bless with the spirit: Bless means to "speak well of." No doubt, in ancient times as in modern, praise of God was an element of both praying and singing. Thus the word bless includes both of the former exercises. *With the spirit* means only with the spiritual self, but not with the mind, i.e., intelligibly.

One in the position of an outsider: The Greek word which is translated *outsider* had two meanings: (1) a private person, as contrasted with a public official; and (2) an unpracticed or ignorant man, as contrasted with the learned.[1] There is considerable doubt concerning the exact status of this outsider or private person. Some have taken it to mean the lay person as opposed to the church officials, but this seems highly unlikely. There is no evidence of such a distinction in the first century. In Corinth the gifts of the Spirit seem not to have been restricted to any particular class of people. Some have taken it to mean the ungifted Christian, but again Paul did not intimate that any Christian was ungifted. The gifts seem to have been bestowed on various people at various times. It is better to take the word to mean the outsider, i.e., one who had not been converted but who attended the public services, perhaps with the expressed purpose of learning about the Christian gospel. Verse 23 seems to indicate that there was the possibility of a church meeting without these outsiders. Also, the same verse puts them on a different plane from unbelievers. Most evangelical churches have people of this kind today, people who are interested in Christianity but who have not yet surrendered to the lordship of Christ. They are not, strictly speaking, unbelievers nor are they believers.

Whether *one in the position of* refers to a seating arrangement or one who has this nature is uncertain. It seems likely that Paul used the expression as another way of saying who was an outsider.

Say the "Amen" to your thanksgiving: indicates that he could not. The custom may have prevailed in the church of saying *"Amen"* (i.e., true). The Christian part of the congregation could do this, even if the praise were in a tongue. The outsider could not. *"Amen"* approves and appropriates the word of another.

When he does not know what you are saying: Since the praise was in a tongue, it was not intelligible.

Verse 17: For you may give thanks well enough: points again to the limited usefulness of the tongues.

But the other man is not edified: The *other man* is still the *outsider.* The

---

[1] Cf. Edwards.

Greek adjective (*heteros*) means "another of a different kind" and would support the thought that the outsider was not a Christian. *Edified* means "built up." The non-Christian hearer needed to understand so that he could be brought nearer to true faith.

Verse 18: I thank God that I speak in tongues more than you all: a claim of superiority in this matter. Paul could have learned his languages, but it is probable that he also possessed this gift. If our interpretation of *tongues* is right, Paul was not saying that these tongues should be used in private rather than public (the usual interpretation). In both verses (14 and 16) where mention is made of praying in a tongue, the expression indicates doubt that this would ever be done. Tongues were used as a method of proclaiming the gospel to those who could not otherwise understand. They were properly used when addressed to such an audience. The whole thought is of speech in the church services where the congregation spoke a common tongue, such as Greek. In this context foreign languages would be out of place.

Verse 19: Nevertheless: in spite of the depth of the gift.

In church: i.e., in the church services. This use of the word *church* is peculiar to this chapter.

I would rather speak five words with my mind: i.e., intelligibly.

Than ten thousand words in a tongue: i.e., and not be understood. The contrast between *five words* and *ten thousand words* is extreme. Paul made it extreme on purpose so that his estimate of the value of tongues and the worth of prophecy could be made clear.

(4) Prophecy is serviceable in evangelism (14:20–25)

This paragraph deals specifically with the value of prophecy in the church services. Paul made his appeal to the mature wisdom and the experience of the Corinthians.

Verse 20: appealed to the Corinthians to exercise their minds.

Brethren: constantly repeated in this discussion, in which so much must be taken as a rebuke of some of their practices. Paul wanted them to realize that he held them to be Christian brethren even though he must condemn their practices.

Do not be children in your thinking: an appeal to exercise mature wisdom in understanding their problems. *Children* translates a Greek word which is better taken to mean "youth." Greek words to indicate ages overlapped even as English words do; but whereas we have four (baby, child, youth, adult), the Greeks only used three. The word for baby (here and 13:11) covered the ages from infancy to ten. *Children* would cover the school years (about six to fourteen). After this the Greek youth was considered a man. The negative admonition means that they were to be grown men in their ways of thinking. The figurative use of these designations was common in Paul's day.

Be babes in evil: The fundamental idea in the use of *babes* is that one should not have any experience with evil. In respect to evil, it is better to be ignorant than learned.

But in thinking be mature: positive statement of the first clause.

Verse 21: appeals to an Old Testament Scripture to show the folly of speaking in foreign languages.

In the law it is written: refers to Isaiah 28:11–12. *The law* is a general word which may be used for the entire Old Testament.[1]

"By men of strange tongues and by the lips of foreigners will I speak to this people, and even then they will not listen to me, says the Lord": The connection of thought between the Old Testament and this passage is not entirely clear. The Israelites had refused to heed the plain message of God's prophets. God threatened to send the Assyrians, whose speech would be strange and alien to the Jews, to speak to them in judgment. The only connection with our passage is the ineffectiveness of tongues (i.e., foreign languages) as vehicles of God's grace and mercy.

Verse 22: The only positive statement of the function of tongues in Corinth.

Thus: indicates that Paul saw some connection between this verse and the thought of the Old Testament passage.

Tongues: foreign languages.

Are a sign: rather, are meant for a sign, when spoken to those who understand them. The Greek makes it clear that Paul did not say that they were actually a sign. In the way that they were being used in Corinth, they were not. The phrase expresses God's intention in imparting the gift. This is a difficult statement and commentators debate its meaning. In what sense were tongues a sign, an external symbol of spiritual reality? Some have suggested that they were a sign of God's judgment (ICC), whether the unbeliever understood them in this way or not (Edwards). Some, referring to verse 23, have said they were only a sign of madness (Parry). It seems best to suppose that God gave these gifts to men to speak his gospel to unbelievers as they encountered them. Thus a Greek-speaking Christian could communicate the gospel to one who spoke Coptic. In such cases they would constitute a sign that God loved the unbeliever. The Christian took them as a sign of God's presence through his Spirit, but this was not their intended use.

Not for believers but for unbelievers: The fact that the tongues were intelligible speech in a foreign language finds its strongest support here. Verse 23 states the reaction of an unbeliever who found the church people speaking in foreign languages which he did not understand. This would be the universal reaction of the unbeliever, either to ecstatic speech or some unknown language. If God meant them to be a sign for unbelievers, it must mean that they conveyed a message to the unbelievers. How could this be? Simply by those who had the gift of speaking in Latin making a practice of speaking to those who understood Latin because it was their native tongue. This seems to have been the way it was at Pentecost. The unbelievers exclaimed: "Are not all these who are speaking Galileans? And how is it that we hear, each of us in his own native language?" (Acts 2:7–8). The account in Acts is abbreviated, but it is likely that one had the gift to speak

---

[1] Cf. ICC.

in the language of the Medes and did so. The Medes were attracted by hearing their own language and gathered to hear what was said. Thus it seems that a number of speakers were simultaneously speaking various languages to different groups. The same sort of thing could have happened on the docks of Corinth, and probably did. The traveler would hear the gospel in his own language and the gift of tongues would fulfill its intended function.

While prophecy is not for unbelievers but for believers: expresses God's purpose for prophecy (i.e., the communication of direct revelations). The unbelievers would not be impressed with such statements; the believers would be. "For a sign" may or may not be understood in this second clause.

Verse 23: Though tongues, when spoken to men who understand them, were valuable, they were a hindrance to the gospel when spoken in the wrong place and at the wrong time. The desire of the Corinthians to display their gifts in the church services served only to make the service seem bedlam to the outsider.

If, therefore, the whole church assembles: makes it clear that Paul had been speaking of church services rather than private use of gifts.

And all speak in tongues: supposes that no other kind of utterance takes place. All who spoke in tongues would display their gifts of speaking unlearned foreign languages. Whether all spoke at once or only one at a time is not clear. Verse 27 seems to indicate that this would be a mass speaking, i.e., all speaking at once.

And outsiders: those convinced of the truth of Christianity but not yet converts.

Or unbelievers: people who had no Christian belief whatever.

Will they not say that you are mad: The implied answer is, "yes." Such a display of bedlam could lead only to this conclusion on the part of those who were unable to recognize the presence of the Holy Spirit. The Corinthians were indeed possessed, but by the Spirit of God rather than the spirit of frenzy.

Verse 24: Though prophecy was meant primarily for believers, it, when used in the public assembly, could have spiritual results even with unbelievers.

But if all prophesy: one at a time. Verse 29 seems to indicate that there was no problem with more than one prophet speaking at a time.

And an unbeliever or outsider enters: assumes that this may happen, but not likely.

He is convicted by all: i.e., of his sins. The thought is that he would hear the communication of divine truth and come under conviction of his own sin. *All* means the inspired speakers, not the congregation.[1]

He is called to account by all: i.e., examined by all. The Greek word is the word for investigation or examination to determine guilt. This verse reflects Hebrews 4:12: "For the word of God is living and active, sharper than any two-edged sword, piercing to the division of soul and spirit, of joints and marrow, and discerning the thoughts and intentions of the heart."

---

[1] Cf. ICC.

Every Christian knows how the Word of God seeks out his inner self and reveals himself as he really is. This is the thought in this verse. The proclaimed word of God has this power.

Verse 25: The secrets of his heart are disclosed: to himself. The court of his conscience saw his life as God saw it. This expression shows how the conviction and self-examination spoken of in verse 23 were effected.

And so, falling on his face, he will worship God: His self-condemnation would lead to self-surrender. The Greek word translated *worship* is used only here by Paul. His usual word for "worship" is much more dynamic. This word means to "bow down before" or "kiss the feet of." The emphasis is on the external sign of submission. However, the context shows that Paul meant to use it to describe a dynamic action on the part of the unbeliever or outsider.

And declare that God is really among you: a reversal of the opinion he had when he heard them speak in tongues. Then he thought they were mad; now he recognized that God was in their midst. This emphasized the superiority of prophecy over tongues. *Declare* is a present participle showing that his declaration was an act contemporaneous with his falling on his face and worshiping God.

4. Order in the Church Services (14:26–40)

Having established the superiority of prophecy over tongues Paul turned to instructions about the orderly procedure in church services (vss. 26–33*a*). This led him to a further instruction concerning the action of women in church services—they were to keep silence (vss. 33*b*–36). Finally, Paul demanded recognition that his instructions were from the Lord (vss. 37–40).

(1) Conforming to God's character should be the aim of church services (vss. 26–33a)

Starting from the assumption that God is not a God of confusion (vs. 33*a*), Paul instructed the Corinthians about their conduct in church services. All things were to be done for edification (vs. 26). Tongues were permitted only if one spoke at a time and they were interpreted (vss. 27–28). Only two or three prophets were to speak in one service (vs. 29). If someone else received a revelation, the speaker was to yield the floor (vss. 30–32).

Verse 26: This verse teaches that each gift has its place in the services of the church, but they are to be used only for edification of the church and not for self-display. The verse is introduced by a rhetorical question, *what then,* which Paul answered in the following verses.[1] The subject of the discussion is the church services in Corinth *(when you come together).*

The idea is that various members of the congregation would come prepared to edify the whole congregation in some way. Those who are so

---

[1] Barrett calls these verses "final instructions."

prepared are not to be denied opportunity to participate in the service, but certain restrictions are placed upon such participation (vs. 27).

One member might have a message in the form of a *hymn* (Greek, "Psalm"), probably the chanting of one of the psalms of the Old Testament, but perhaps a Christian psalm.[1] Another would have a teaching based on the Christian tradition (i.e., a *lesson*). A prophet might be present who had received a *revelation* from God which he wanted to share. One who spoke in a foreign language (i.e., a *tongue*) might be present with a message for the congregation. If so, an *interpretation* of the message was required.

The rule in all things was that it should be done for edification (i.e., the spiritual good of the congregation). The desire of each gifted member is assumed. The permission to participate had to be judged in the light of the good which he had to offer to others.

Verse 27: begins the special instructions for those who spoke in foreign languages.

If any speak in a tongue: probably a correct translation. The Greek particle is "whether." The expression reads, "whether anyone speaks in a tongue." However, there is no second part to the construction. We would expect, "or sing a psalm," but the second member is lacking. *If* is the best way of smoothing out the rough grammar.

Let there be only two or at most three: instead of all (cf. vs. 23). The exercise of the gift was to be limited.

And each in turn: in contrast to all at once.

And let one interpret: translate as the other speaks.

Verse 28: But if there is no one to interpret: in the absence of a translator.

Let each of them keep silence in church: They were not to speak in the public services at all.

And speak to himself and to God: To himself is emphatic. It means that he was to speak in the privacy of his own home, not that he was to speak under his breath. *To God* is an afterthought, showing that God would understand him.

Verse 29: begins the special instructions for the prophets. These follow the general lines of, but are less explicit than, the instructions about tongues.

Let two or three prophets speak: limits the number to speak in one public service. No more than this number could be heard with profit at one meeting.

And let the others weigh what is said: refers to the other prophets who were silent. They were to *weigh* (i.e., discern) whether what was said was inspired or not. "Ability to distinguish between spirits" was a companion gift of prophecy (12:10). Verse 37 seems to indicate that the ability to recognize genuine revelations from the Lord was also given to prophets.

Verse 30: If a revelation is made to another sitting by: i.e., another prophet. The first was allowed to continue speaking until another was

---

[1] Barrett thinks it was a spontaneous composition.

moved to speak. *Sitting by* implies that the audience was seated in the Jewish synagogue and perhaps that the speaker stood. The other prophet would, no doubt, give some sign that he had received a revelation.

Let the first be silent: The speaker was to close his remarks and yield the floor to the other prophet. The prophets, like some modern preachers, would be tempted to continue speaking even after they had delivered their message from God. These instructions indicate how free and unstructured the public services were. The people waited on a revelation from God; the Spirit was in control of the service. Seemingly, no particular person was the leader; all members held themselves in readiness to receive from God and communicate to their fellow church members.

Verse 31: For you can all prophesy one by one: literally, "You have the power, one by one, all to prophesy." The prophets had power over their speech; they were not carried along by the Holy Spirit, it seems. Thus in successive services of the congregation, all would have the opportunity to speak. But they, like the speakers in tongues, must speak one by one.

So that all may learn: Whether *all* means all the prophets or all the congregation is uncertain. Perhaps it was possible that all the congregation could be prophets at one time or another. In either case the object of the prophesying was that all might learn the total will of God, not just that part revealed by one prophet.

And all be encouraged: the second purpose of prophecy. *Encouraged* comes from the word, much used in these epistles, which implies the strengthening of the heart to remain faithful to God. In ancient churches, as in modern, knowledge was not the only need of Christians. Knowledge must be put into practice to have Christian meaning. Learning is essential that practice may be right; practice is essential that knowledge may be effective. The two go hand in hand in the mature Christian life.

Verse 32: And the spirits of prophets are subject to prophets: a contrast with the sibyls and pythonesses of the pagan religions. These pagan priests could not control their speech; they continued until the impulse died. Not so with the inspired prophets of God. *Spirits of prophets* refers to the human spirits of the people who prophesied. *Are subject to* is a present tense, pointing to an established principle. This principle justifies the instruction in verse 30. The prophet could control his spirit and thus could be silent when another received a revelation.

Verse 33a: states the principle which underlies this section of material. The church services should reflect the character of God. Since *God is not a God of confusion,* the services of the church should not be characterized by turbulence and disorder. Since God is a *God of peace,* the church services should not reflect conflicts between those who wanted to speak. This orderliness and sanity of approach was in marked contrast to the pagan religions which were characterized by frenzy and confusion. Paul did not want the Corinthians to become known as another religious sect among many, but as the representatives of the one true God. The same principle, that church services should reflect the character of God, is valid today. Most of our churches are no longer guilty of confusion and disorder, but they often are guilty of stiffness, formality, and insipidity. This type of service is no more representative of God than was the type of services which Paul sought to correct in Corinth.

(2) Women should keep silence in the church services (14:33b–36)

This paragraph seems strange in the light of Paul's discussion in 11:2–15. There he seems to have thought that it was proper for a woman to pray or prophesy. Here he admonished them to keep silent. The seeming contradiction may be solved by supposing that he was speaking here against a common cause of disorder in the services of the church. But what was the disorder? No certain answer can be given. We may assume that women who were recipients of special edificatory gifts would be allowed to speak along with the men. It seems, then, that some women, in order to declare their equality, were speaking without that special gift. This would cause confusion in the services and perhaps draw reproach upon the church from outsiders. The application to modern-day churches is likewise in question. Perhaps the best we can do is to have recourse to the general principle—women should not try to usurp that which is not rightfully theirs. We must remember that two factors entered into Paul's thinking and the thinking of the ancient churches. One was the common social standing of women as inferior to their husbands and subject to them. Paul, as a child of his day, seems to have approved this. The other was the flagrant use of women's bodies in the worship of pagan gods. It would have been fatal to the gospel if the Christian congregation seemed to flaunt the women before the public. Paul's answer was for the women to be silent. Some have supposed that Paul had not thought of this when he wrote his instructions in 11:2–15, but this seems highly improbable.

Verse 33b: belongs to this discussion rather than the previous one. The statement that God is a God of peace is complete in itself.

As in all the churches of the saints: congregations composed of saints (i.e., people who belonged to God). Paul appealed to the universal practice of Christian congregations. Though each church was free and independent, Paul felt that common practice should prevail in all congregations.

Verse 34: The women should keep silence in the churches: not speak in the public services.

For they are not permitted to speak: reinforces the previous clause.

But: strongly adversative.

Should be subordinate: rather, "subject." "Their own husbands" is implied in the statement.

As even the law says: appeals to the statements of the Old Testament. Perhaps the creation story is the particular passage in mind, but the whole of the Old Testament reinforces the thought.

Verse 35: If there is anything they desire to know, let them ask their husbands at home: forbids even the asking of questions. No provision was made for the widow or for the wife whose husband was either not a Christian or did not know the answer. Paul dealt only in general principles.

For it is shameful for a woman to speak in church: Shameful is a strong word used of women who had shaved heads (cf. 11:6). Its use here would seem to indicate that Paul had in mind the violation of social customs.

Verse 36: addresses the whole congregation. The tone is ironical. The Corinthians were acting as if they alone were the standards of proper Christianity.

What!: that is, "Do you mean to say by your actions concerning spiritual gifts that this is true?"

Did the word of God originate with you: obviously false. Paul himself had brought the gospel to them. They were the recipients, rather than the originators, of the gospel.

Or: if that is not true.

Are you the only ones it has reached?: in its fullness. The Corinthians seemed to be saying by their attitudes that they alone knew the full meaning of the gospel. Their attitudes were an implied insult to all the other Christian congregations of the first century.

(3) Paul's instructions were a command of the Lord (14:37–40)

This is the closing paragraph of the entire discussion of spiritual gifts, but the subject is still governed by the thought of the superiority of prophecy over tongues and order in the church services.

Verse 37: a demand for recognition of the divine origin of Paul's instructions.

If any one thinks that he is a prophet: as many of the Corinthians did.

Or spiritual: possessed of a spiritual gift, perhaps of tongues.

He should acknowledge: rather, "know by experience." The word does not mean that he should publicly acknowledge this to be true, though that may be implied. It means that he himself should continually (present tense) recognize from his own experience in receiving spiritual gifts. Paul was himself speaking as a prophet, and this should be apparent to other prophets and spiritually gifted people.

That what I am writing to you is a command of the Lord: because it was a revelation from him. *Lord* equals Jesus Christ, the head of the congregation, the only one who had the right to order its life. *Lord* is emphatic in the sentence structure. Paul claimed that his words constituted a command which had its origin in the Lord.

Verse 38: If any one does not recognize this: literally, "if anyone is ignorant." The context would justify the RSV translation.

He is not recognized: The same word is used as above. A textual problem is present. Some texts have, "He is ignorant"; others, "Let him be ignored." The difference is between the indicative and the imperative. The idea seems to be that one who was unable to recognize the gifts of Paul was either not recognized by God as gifted or should not be so recognized by the congregation. In the light of the context and the textual evidence, it would seem that the second reading is to be preferred. Thus, Paul's command was that the congregation should not recognize the claims of the pretender. His ignorance of Paul's source of authority was evidence of his own lack of spiritual gifts.

Verse 39: a repetition of the thought of verse 1.

So: in the light of Paul's discussion.

My brethren: a sign of Paul's affection for them.

Earnestly desire to prophesy: Seek the highest gift, the most useful one.

And do not forbid speaking in tongues: Let those who have this inferior gift use it, provided, of course, that it is interpreted.

Verse 40: But all things should be done decently and in order: Should be done is a present imperative, meaning, "Let them continue to be carried out." *Decently* is the opposite of egotistic disorder. The word expresses the idea of beauty and harmony which ought to prevail in the church assemblies. *In order* refers to the instruction that only one was to speak at a time. The Greek word is a military metaphor, meaning each in his own place and performing his own function.

In these three chapters (12–14) Paul dealt with the danger of spiritual anarchy which would prevail if each gifted member believed his gift the most important and insisted on exercising it without consideration for others.

VIII. TEACHINGS ABOUT THE RESURRECTION OF THE DEAD (15:1–58)

The problem dealt with in this chapter is not the problem of a future life, but the problem of the resurrection of the body. It seems that "some" of the Corinthians were denying that there was a resurrection of the dead (vs. 12). The idea of resurrection, though deeply imbedded in Judaism and accepted without question in Christian circles, was essentially repugnant to the Greeks. Plato had taught that the human body was a prison from which men escaped at the time of death. A resurrection to them would be only a second descent into hell.

Paul dealt with the problem with great restraint. There is no sign of the extreme fire which we find in the letter to the Galatians. The reason is that the error (he left no doubt that he considered it an error) did not strike at the heart of the Christian gospel. One who believed it could still believe in salvation by grace through faith alone. Those who held to the idea of a spiritual future life were not condemned as heretics but reasoned with as men of faith.

Paul dealt with the problem though the church had not asked for his opinion. There is no suggestion that they had raised the question at all. On the contrary, he raised it. Perhaps his source of information was the same visitors who had furnished him with information about the dissensions in Corinth.

There are two major divisions in his discussion. First, he presented the proofs of the certainty of the resurrection (15:1–34). Second, he discussed the nature of the resurrection body (15:35–57). He closed his discussion with an appeal for steadfastness (vs. 58).

1. The Certainty of the Resurrection (15:1–34)

Paul gave four arguments for the resurrection of the body: (1) The historical argument that the resurrection of Christ is an essential part of the gospel message (vss. 1–11). (2) An experiential argument showing that the resurrection of Jesus, the resurrection of the believer, and the reality of the gospel are all bound together (vss. 12–20). (The argument is that if any one of these great truths is false, then all are.) (3) A theological argument consisting of the fact that the future triumph of God is possible only if the resurrection takes place (vss. 21–28). (4) The argument from Christian devotion, showing that such devotion with its dangers

[234]

and trials has no meaning if there is no resurrection from the dead (vss. 29–34).[1]

(1) Resurrection an essential part of the gospel (15:1–11)

In this section Paul reminded the Christians of the terms in which he had preached the gospel to them at the beginning (vss. 1–2), used a Christian confession which was familiar to the Corinthians to describe the content of the gospel (vss. 3–5), gave further historical proof of the appearances of Jesus (vss. 6–8), and discussed his own case as a witness to the resurrection (vss. 9–11).

Verse 1: Now I would remind you: probably a correct translation. The Greek verb literally means, "I make known to you." Since they already knew what he was to say, his statement was by way of a reminder.

Brethren: a reminder of his brotherly concern for them.

In what terms I preached to you the gospel: appealed to his original preaching of the gospel in Corinth. The Greek contains a play on words. It is "the gospel which I gospelized you." *Gospel* literally means "good news." Paul had come announcing the good news of God's redemptive work in Jesus Christ.

Which you received: points to the fact that they did really receive his gospel. The word *received* was the regular word in Jewish life for the reception of a tradition handed down from past teachers. It implies that Paul acted as one who passed on the Christian tradition—the gospel. The Corinthians were reminded that they accepted the gospel in its entirety, which would include the teaching of the resurrection of Christ.

In which you stand: perfect tense. The expression means that they took their stand in the gospel and still stood in it. The permanent state of the Corinthians was involved. The immediate implication is that when they denied the resurrection, they denied the very thing in which they stood.

Verse 2: By which you are saved: present tense. Salvation was looked upon as a process still going on within the permanent state. *Saved* is a word that has three dimensions in the New Testament. First, it is used to describe the initial conversion of the sinner to Christ. In this sense Paul would have said, "You were saved." Example of this usage: "For in this hope we were saved" (Rom. 8:24). Second, the word is used to describe the progressive growth in grace of the Christian in this life. This verse is an example of that use of the word (cf. also Phil. 2:12–13). Third, the word is used to denote the final entrance of the believer into heaven—the consummation of his salvation (cf. Rom. 5:9–10). Paul wanted to remind the Corinthians that their present progress in Christlikeness had its basis in the gospel which he had preached to them in the beginning.

If you hold it fast: does not express doubt, but insists on the necessity of holding fast to the gospel. *If* in the Greek could perhaps better be translated "since." In Paul's thought there is a balance between assurance and presumption. The man who wrote the words found in Romans 5:9–10

---

[1] Cf. Edwards.

could not doubt that his salvation was secure, that nothing would ultimately bring about his damnation. On the other hand, he recognized the obligation of the Christian to remain a Christian, to be true to his confession of faith. In modern circles debate over the security of the believer has led to extreme statements that color our thinking on this subject. Some have looked on salvation as a sort of quicksilver which we must always be in fear of losing. Others have looked on it as a security which one may presume on, and have implied that one will forever remain a Christian if he once was one, no matter how he lives. Neither of these extremes fits the thought of the New Testament. Salvation is a dynamic experience which will change a man's whole life, but it is always assumed that a changed life is essential to final salvation. Our assurance rests upon the dynamic nature of the experience, rather than on some mechanical premise.

Unless you believed in vain: i.e., "unless you became believers without any real basis." The thought goes with the previous clause. If they had a good basis for their belief, they would hold fast to the gospel. Paul's appeal was to the experience of the Corinthians. Notice the continuity: they learned the gospel; they took their stand in it; they were being saved on the basis of it; they were holding to it. If all of this was not true, they had believed in vain. *In vain* refers not to their own experience but to the objective reality on which it was based. "Without a solid basis" would be a good paraphrase of the word.

Verses 3–5: contain an ancient Christian confession which Paul had adopted as the terms in which he would preach the gospel.[1] There are several factors in these verses which show that this was not an original formulation of Paul's. "I delivered . . . what I also received" (vs. 3) is the regular formula for passing on a tradition. The parallelism of the formula is apparent. It has four members: "That Christ died . . . that he was buried, that he was raised . . . that he appeared." This may have been the original form of the confession. To the first member of the four had been added "for our sins" and "in accordance with the scriptures." To the third member had been added "on the third day" and "in accordance with the scriptures." To the last member, "to Cephas, then to the twelve." The use of the Aramaic "Cephas" instead of the Greek "Peter" marks the confession as originating in the Palestinian community before the spread of the gospel to the Greek world. It is impossible to mark the end of the confession and the beginning of Paul's additions. Verse 8 certainly marks an addition to Paul. It seems likely that verse 6 begins a listing of appearances which Paul knew of from other sources.

This understanding of these verses has led scholars to reassess the originality of Paul. Not only here, but in several other passages in Paul's letters, there is evidence of use of older Christian formulas by Paul. It would seem that Paul was at one with the general Christian witness to Christ. Some have denied this on the basis of his claim to independence in Galatians 1 and 2. However, in that instance he was denying the human

[1] Conzelmann thinks the formula was originally written in Greek but that it is very ancient. (Hans Conzelmann, "On the Analysis of the Confessional Formula in I Corinthians 15:3–5," trans. by Mathias Rissi, *Interpretation*, Jan., 1966, pp. 15–25.)

origin of his gospel. Here he was recognizing that his preaching of the gospel was in the common terms of all Christians. Paul was an original thinker, but he was original within the framework of the Christian witness.

For I delivered to you: the regular expression for passing on a tradition.

As of first importance: probably a correct interpretation of the Greek word *first.* The meaning could be "in the first place" or "first of all." It seems that Paul meant it to refer to the basic truth of the gospel rather than to the first thing that he preached. Thus, *of first importance* should be accepted.

What I also received: correlative with *I delivered to you.* The expression marks Paul as a link in the chain of Christian tradition.

That Christ died: the historical fact of his death on the cross.

For our sins: the Christian confession of the meaning of that death. We must always remember that the heart of Christianity is a confession of faith rather than a historical fact. Of course, the historical fact is essential, in this case, to the confession of faith; but it, in itself, is not a confession of faith. It is historically true that Christ died. This fact is open to historical investigation and proof or disproof (it has been proved to be true). The confession of faith is not subject to historical investigation at all. Historical research can neither prove nor disprove that he died for our sins. The use of the plural *sins* is a further mark of the un-Pauline character of this formula. Paul usually used the word in the singular. "Sin" to him was not a number of acts contrary to the law of God, but an attitude of rebellion in the heart of man against God.

In accordance with the scriptures: is no problem with reference to this first member of the formula. The Old Testament could be used to show that the death of Christ was vicarious (cf. esp. Isa. 53). It is a problem with regard to the resurrection. The expression could mean according to the Christian Scriptures, i.e., writings. There is little doubt that the passion stories were already in written form when Paul wrote this letter. However, the scholars are against this interpretation, though it is appealing.

Verse 4: That he was buried: a necessary part of the formula because his burial was proof of the reality of his death. It seems that early in the course of Christian preaching, men had said that Jesus had not really died at all. The story in John of the piercing of his side is designed to set at rest such stories (cf. John 19:34–35).

That he was raised: from the dead bodily. The Gospel according to Luke is very careful to show that his resurrection was a resurrection of the body, not just a living beyond the grave (cf. Luke 24:36–42).

On the third day: after his death.

In accordance with the scriptures: If this refers to the Old Testament Scriptures, it must refer only to the fact that he was raised from the dead, not that it occurred on the third day. In his speech at Pisidian Antioch, Paul quoted three Old Testament Scriptures to prove the resurrection (Acts 13:33–35—cf. Ps. 2:7; Isa. 55:3; Ps. 16:10). Peter, at Pentecost, quoted also from Ps. 16:8–11 to show that "it was not possible for him to be held by" death (Acts 2:24–28). If this expression refers to the Christian passion stories, it could also include "the third day." It is tempting to take the *scriptures* here to mean the Christian writings (the same Greek word would be involved) rather than the Old Testament.

Verse 5: And that he appeared: Though the Greek is the passive of "to see," *he appeared* is the better translation. The Gospels show that Jesus was not perceived merely by the physical eye; he had to appear (cf. esp. Luke 24:13–35). The resurrection appearances were more in the nature of revelations than of discoveries.

To Cephas: The Aramaic means "the rock" just as the Greek "Peter" does. This fact marks this word as a part of the formula. Peter is mentioned because he seems to have been the first apostle to see Jesus alive (cf. Luke 24:34). The appearance to the women at the tomb is not mentioned in this list.

Then to the twelve: an official designation of the body of apostles.[1]

Verse 6: probably begins a listing of appearances from another source. This is the first written list, being older than any of the Gospels which contain accounts of the appearances (Matthew, Luke, and John). It is not always possible to parallel this list with the Gospel accounts.

Then he appeared to more than five hundred brethren at one time: possibly the appearance recorded in Matthew 28:19–20, but this is not likely. This seems to have no parallel in the Gospel accounts. However, the appearance stories were chosen by each Gospel writer according to his own purpose. There was no need to attempt a complete list. The central fact of the resurrection was attested even if only one appearance was made.

Most of whom are still alive: mentioned to show the possibility of checking the truth of the story.

Though some have fallen asleep: i.e., died.

Verse 7: Then he appeared to James: his half-brother. This appearance is mentioned only here in the New Testament. Paul had had contact with James (cf. Gal. 1:18) and perhaps had learned of this appearance from him.

Then to all the apostles: includes more than the Twelve. "Apostle" was not reserved for the original twelve in Paul's time. The aim of Paul was to enumerate a wide range of appearances so that no doubt could remain of the reality of the resurrection of Jesus.

Verse 8: Last of all . . . he appeared also to me: refers to the experience on the Damascus road at the time of Paul's conversion (cf. Acts 9:4–5). Paul believed that Christ's appearance to him was of the same nature as the appearances to the others. He looked upon the fact that he had seen the risen Lord as his primary qualification for being an apostle (cf. 1 Cor. 9:1).

As to one untimely born: an abortion.[2] The Greek word is a technical term for the abortion of a child. This is a difficult statement. It is clear that Paul meant to demean himself, to call attention to the fact that he was different from the other apostles. Three suggestions have been given as interpretations of this term (Edwards): (1) that Paul meant that he no

---

[1] Lenski points out that this was a standard term even though the defection of Judas had left only eleven.

[2] Morris suggests "miscarriage."

more deserved to be called an apostle than an abortion deserved to be called a man; (2) that Paul meant that his conversion was sudden and violent; (3) that Paul meant that he saw the Lord even before his birth as a Christian. The context would favor the first interpretation. Whether he meant exactly that or not, he did mean that he was the least worthy of all the apostles for the honor which God had given him.

Verse 9: should be taken as Paul's own interpretation of what he meant by calling himself an abortion.

For I am the least of the apostles: inferior to all the others.

Unfit to be called an apostle: unworthy of the honor God had given him in making him an apostle.

Because I persecuted the church of God: a fact that Paul often mentioned to show two things: his own unworthiness and the greatness of the grace of God. Paul was the chief persecutor of the church at Jerusalem (Acts 8:1–3) and was on his way to Damascus to carry out his persecutions there when he was converted. One of the great miracles of early Christianity was the transformation of the chief persecutor into the chief preacher.

Verse 10: Though inferior to the other apostles in merit, Paul was not inferior to them in labors and success in the ministry.

By the grace of God: the unmerited favor of God. This expression is a constant refrain in the writings of Paul. He ascribed his salvation, his equipment for the ministry, and his success in the preaching of the gospel to the work of God.

I am what I am: The Corinthians knew what he was. He did not press his claims; he was concerned only to establish the validity of his witness to the resurrection.

And his grace toward me was not in vain: not empty of fruit. In verse 2, Paul had used a word for *vain* which means "empty of reality"; here another word is used which means "empty of result."

On the contrary: strong adversative.

I worked harder than any of them: rather, "I labored more abundantly than all of them." There is no doubt that the word for *worked* (Greek, labored) emphasizes exertion. The question is: Does the Greek word meaning "more abundantly" mean *harder* or "with greater result"? The next clause would seem to indicate that he was thinking about the results of his labor rather than the hardness of it. The hardness with which one works is due to his own devotion; the results are due to the grace of God. Paul was quick to say, *though it was not I, but the grace of God which is with me.*

Verse 11: asserts the uniformity of the preaching of the apostles.

Whether then it was I or they: who labored more abundantly. The comparative results of apostolic labors might be in question. Paul did not wish to make a point of his superiority in this regard.

So we preach: present tense. The apostles kept on preaching this gospel. Their gospel had not changed.

And so you believed: past tense. The play on tenses is intended. *You believed* reiterates the thought of verses 1–2. The Corinthians had come to have faith on the basis of the gospel which asserted the resurrection of Christ from the dead; and without that assertion there would be no gospel, no good news. He wanted the Corinthians to know that their Christian faith was involved in the discussion of the resurrection of the dead.

(2) The resurrection of Christ as insuring the resurrection of believers (15:12–20)

In this paragraph Paul linked the resurrection of Christ, the resurrection of believers, and the reality of the Christian faith. If one was true, he reasoned, all were true. If one was false, all were false. The paragraph could be called, "the results of denying the resurrection of the dead."

Verse 12: If: rather, "since." Paul assumed the truth of his statement.

Christ is preached: present tense, pointing to continuous proclamation. This statement reflects the apostolic preaching which was mentioned in verse 11. *Christ* is the subject of the proclamation, not his resurrection. Christian preaching never centers on an event, but on a person.

As raised from the dead: the form in which Christ was preached. *Raised* points to the past event of his resurrection. Christ was not preached as a dead Savior but as a living one. *The dead* does not have the article in Greek. This means that there is an abstract quality to the expression. Literally, it would mean, "from among dead people." Actually, the thought seems to approximate our word "death." The thought was not that Christ came out from among dead people, but that he was victorious over death itself.

How can some of you say: in the light of this fact. *Some* shows that more than one Corinthian held this error, but not a majority. *Some of you* shows that it was members of the congregation who were saying this. Perhaps Paul knew their identity; certainly the Corinthians did. However, there is no way of identifying these with one of the parties to the dissensions in Corinth.

That there is no resurrection of the dead: their statement denied that there was any such thing as resurrection from death. Probably what was meant was that the after-life would be entirely spiritual in quality. It is not likely that *some* reflected the doctrine of the Jewish Sadducees, who denied any after-life at all. These people reflected the thinking of Greek philosophy which thought of the body as a prison and death as an escape. To them a resurrection (which implies a bodily resurrection) would be a reentrance into prison. It is also possible that they held to Gnostic views concerning matter, i.e., that matter was evil. At any rate, their error consisted of denying the possibility of any resurrection of the dead.

Verse 13: begins Paul's argument for the resurrection of the dead based on the resurrection of Christ.

But: a continuative particle, not adversative.

If there is no resurrection of the dead: begins a contrary-to-fact sentence. *If* it is assumed true, though it is not true.

Then Christ has not been raised: the necessary conclusion if the truth of the premise is accepted. Christ was a man; he died as other men die. If men cannot rise from death, neither could he.[1] Paul's argument assumed

---

[1] Dahl points out that the denial is one of utmost seriousness since it denies the basis of the gospel. (M. D. Dahl, *The Resurrection of the Body: A Study of 1 Corinthians 15* [Naperville, Ill.: Alec R. Allenson, Inc., 1962], p. 75.)

the real incarnation of Christ, that he became fully man. It assumed also that his resurrection was bodily, that he lives now in a real human body and always will.

Verse 14: If Christ has not been raised: begins another contrary-to-fact sentence. *If* introduces a premise which, if accepted as true, would negate what follows.

Then our preaching is in vain: i.e., empty of content. If Christ did not really rise from death, the proclamation of the gospel was not based on objective fact. The gospel would cease to be a proclamation, a *preaching,* a message with real content. It would become a philosophy, a speculative message. This was the very thing that Paul argued against in chapters 1–3. The gospel is not a speculative message calling for intellectual acceptance; it is a proclamation of God's act in Christ, calling for surrender.

And your faith is in vain: since it was based on the message (cf. vss. 1–2). *Vain* still has the meaning of being void of content, rather than useless so far as result is concerned. Of course, it is true that faith without content would be useless in effecting salvation no matter what else it might effect. This assumes that faith is more than intellectual belief, that it is surrender to the lordship of the living Christ. The argument is that if our surrender is to a Christ who did not rise from death, there is really no one to whom to surrender. Thus it is vain.

Verse 15: continues the thought of verse 14. There is no period in the Greek text.

We are even found: rather, "and we are also found." *We* means the apostles and witnesses to the resurrection. *Found* begins a legal analogy as if God were on trial before men.

To be misrepresenting God: rather, "false witnesses against God." The language is an analogy of the courtroom. The apostles are pictured as "false witnesses" against God, who is on trial. They have perjured themselves in preaching the resurrection of Christ, if indeed it is true that he has not risen. This assumes that God raised him. When the resurrection is spoken of, the passive tense is usually used. Christ did not arise; he was raised.

Because we testified of God that he raised Christ: the substance of their testimony "against" God.

Whom he did raise if it is true that the dead are not raised: completes the circle begun in verse 13. The resurrection of the dead, the resurrection of Christ, the preaching of the apostles, the faith of the Corinthians, the testimony of the witnesses to the resurrection form a whole.

Verse 16: begins an emphasis upon the faith of the Corinthians and other Christians.

For if the dead are not raised, then Christ has not been raised: repeats the substance of verse 13. The form is slightly different.

Verse 17: If Christ has not been raised: begins another contrary-to-fact sentence. Since the premise is false, the conclusions will also be false.

Your faith is futile: another word for "vain" in the Greek. The RSV translation catches the meaning of emptiness of result. Faith in Christ would be aimless, without result or purpose, if he were not the living Christ.

And you are still in your sins: defines the futility of faith if Christ were not alive. The Christian gospel supposed that Christ had died for their sins, that his death effected for them an open way to God. The ancient

Christian hymn quoted by Paul in another passage (Phil. 2:6–11) makes the exaltation of Christ depend upon the victorious quality of his death. To suppose that he was not alive would mean a denial of the quality of his death.

Verse 18: Then . . . also: continues the thought of verse 17. If they were still in their sins, if that were the situation indeed, then the following must also be true.

Those . . . who have fallen asleep: This was a common Christian euphemism for dying.

In Christ: in union with Christ, substituted for "faith" because union with Christ was the result of faith. If the faith were proved empty of results, then the results commonly associated with faith would not be true.

Have perished: forever. "Perish" means the loss of all hope and consequent death in sin. To Paul this would be the climactic result of doubt concerning the resurrection. Such Christians as Stephen, whose martyr death had prepared him for the revelation of Christ, were proved to be men of false hopes.

Verse 19: pursues the thought of hope and sums up the sad condition of Christians if there is no resurrection.

If for this life only we have hoped in Christ: a rather difficult clause. The emphasis lies on *in this life* and *only,* but they are. not connected as if the hope were only in this life. Perhaps the translation should read "If all that can be said about us Christians is that we have hoped in Christ in this life." *Only* is thus taken with the entire clause rather than with one element in it. More than this must be said of Christians if Christianity is to be meaningful. The clause itself is conditional, introducing a contrary-to-fact conclusion. The thought is that Christianity is not meaningful unless the hope that Christians have is based on reality.

We are of all men most to be pitied: because the difference between our hope and the reality is so great. Paul did not mean to say that Christian life on earth was inferior to life without Christ. He would have denied this vehemently. What he meant to say was that one who has high hopes, only to see them dashed to the ground, is an object of human pity. Since the Christian hope is so magnificent, to have it turn out to be nothing would be the most pitiable thing in human experience. Thus Christians are the most to be pitied.

Verse 20: usually taken with the next paragraph, but it seems to form a fitting climax to Paul's argument in verses 12–19. We take it then as the climactic confession of Paul's assurance that his message was true, that his faith was not in vain, that Christ is alive.

But in fact: introduces Paul's statement of triumph. He had been arguing by reducing the error in Corinth to its absurd conclusions. Now he spoke with no doubt.

Christ has been raised from the dead: Any other thought is not true. The resurrection of Christ becomes the basic fact upon which the gospel rests, and the gospel is true.

The first fruits of those who have fallen asleep: leads to the next section, but is not out of place in this one. *First fruits* implies the unity of Christ and *those who have fallen asleep.* The symbolism reflects the law of the Old

Testament. During the Passover the first sheaf of grain was brought to the priest to be consecrated (Lev. 23:10–11). The fact that some fruit had been yielded by the plants meant that the harvest was coming. Thus the resurrection of Christ was the first harvest over death. It predicts and guarantees the full harvest at the final resurrection.

(3) The resurrection essential to the fulfillment of God's purpose for the world (15:21–28)

The mention of Christ as the firstfruits of the Christian resurrection (vs. 20) led Paul to expand this idea. Paul introduced for the first time his analogy between Adam and Christ, the head of the natural human race and the head of the spiritual order (vss. 21–22). He then stated the order in which the resurrection takes place—Christ first, believers next (vs. 23). No mention is made of the resurrection of unbelievers. Then he pointed out that the completed resurrection will constitute the end of Christ's mediatorial ministry, and the kingdom will be delivered up to God (vss. 24–28).

Verse 21: introduces the necessity of a new head of humanity.

For: introduces the necessary implication of the firstfruits.

As by a man came death: refers to the Genesis account of the cursing of Adam. Death was the penalty of sin. Paul thought that the universality of death proved the universality of sin (Rom. 5:12). Adam brought sin into the stream of human life. With sin he brought death. This does not deny that each man is guilty of his own sin and worthy of death in his own right. It speaks only of the mediatorship of the one man through whom human death was inaugurated.

By a man has come also the resurrection of the dead: completes the analogy. Christ, to be the mediator of life, had to become a man. The incarnation is as essential to the gospel as the resurrection. The whole argument assumes the full humanity of Jesus and the acceptance of its implications. The point is that Jesus had to become a part of the stream of human life in order to introduce into it a new dynamic, a dynamic that leads to life rather than to death. The argument is condensed in this passage, but is worked out more fully by Paul in other passages (cf. Rom. 5:12–21).

Verse 22: carries the analogy further and makes it concrete.

For as in Adam all die: a fact of human experience. *All* includes all men. *In Adam* means because of their relation to him, a relation which is necessary and unavoidable. *Die* does not mean the mere biological experience of dying, but the suffering of the curse of sin. The modern way of speaking of death as bodily and spiritual stems from the Greek way of thinking. Paul never adopted that meaning. Death to him was the death of the whole man. Death was the wages of sin (Rom. 6:23). He did not mean that Adam's sin brought death to all, but that it inaugurated sin and death into human life. Each man, in his own turn, sins and so suffers death.

So also in Christ shall all be made alive: completes the specific analogy. *All* cannot mean all men, but must mean all believers. There is no hint of universalism in Paul's writings, and modern attempts to make him say that all men will ultimately be saved is based on a misconception. *In Christ* means "in union with Christ." This relationship is formed through faith.

As was Paul's custom when discussing this analogy, he omitted the mediating factors—sin in one case and faith in the other. *Shall be made alive* points to the future and final resurrection. To paraphrase the verse, we might say: "As it is in Adam that all who die die, so it is in Christ that all who are made alive are made alive" (ICC).

Verse 23: states the order in which the resurrection must take place.

But each in his own order: a military term for the ordering of the troops so that the advance guard came first and then the body of troops. The thought is of temporal order. Two movements are included in the verse, and only two. If we assume that the Corinthian error was teaching a spiritual resurrection which took place at the death of the Christian, we may see the reasoning of Paul. The resurrection was to take place in two movements—Christ and then believers as a whole. The resurrection of unbelievers is not mentioned here, or elsewhere in Paul's writings.

Christ the first fruits: the first movement in the resurrection from death. Paul did not think of two resurrections, but one. This one was to take place in two movements. Christ as the firstfruits was to come first. The analogy of the harvest still governs the language. There will be one harvest, the harvesting of the firstfruits and then the full harvest.

Then at his coming: The Christian hope is that Christ will appear or come again at the end of the present age (cf. Acts 1:11). The word adopted to express this hope was a Greek word (*parousia*) which literally means "presence." This was a word often used for the visit of a dignitary such as a king or the emperor in the Greek world. However, the origin of the term is probably Jewish rather than Greek. The event which Paul had in mind is commonly called the second coming of Christ (a term found only in Heb. 9:28). The writers of the New Testament were careful to avoid the intimation that is current in modern days. Christ was not considered to be away; he was present with them in their congregations and in their personal lives. They did not think of him as one who sat on a throne in the sky and who therefore must "come back." Nevertheless, they believed that the end of the world would be heralded by a visible appearance of Christ when "every eye will see him" (Rev. 1:7). Human language is strained in trying to express both ideas at once. *Then* means "at that time." The time is indefinite. No doubt, Paul hoped that he would live to see it, but he never said so in so many words.

Those who belong to Christ: the believers. The point is that they will all be raised at the same time, not one by one. The problem of the state of those who have died is not dealt with in the New Testament, and we would be wise to follow that example.

Verse 24: begins the discussion of the central thought in this paragraph— the full resurrection will effect the accomplishment of God's purpose for the world. All that is involved in the Christian gospel moves toward this end. The resurrection is necessary to its attainment. Therefore, to deny the resurrection is to deny that the purpose of God will be fulfilled.

Then comes the end: Then means after what has preceded, but necessarily immediately afterward. However, it would seem that in this context it means immediately after. *The end* would mean the close of this present age if it is taken with temporal meaning. However, the Greek word (*telos*) would be better translated "the goal." This translation fits the context better as well as being a more accurate translation of the Greek. The implication is that God has a goal toward which he is working in history. The decisive event in history was the Christ event, but the climactic event in which that event finds its consummation is the perfect rule of God.

When: correlative with *then.* The Greek is indefinite—"whenever."

He delivers the kingdom to God the Father: The subject of the sentence is Christ i.e., *he.* The picture that is involved is that Christ now exercises the sovereignty of God over men spiritually; he is the one who rules. This is the meaning of the expression, "He sat down at the right hand of the Majesty on high" (Heb. 1:3). Christ rules over the world as the vicegerent of God, but this is not the permanent state of affairs. He will deliver, hand over, the *kingdom,* i.e., the exercise of rulership, to God at that time. *Delivers* is a present tense, but due to the nature of the act describes only one single act. "Kingdom" in the New Testament means "rule" rather than "realm." God is identified as *the Father,* that is, of Jesus Christ.

After destroying every rule and every authority and power: Each of the words is qualitative, i.e., *"every* kind of *rule,"* etc. Each is considered to be evil in that it opposes the perfect rule of God in the hearts of men. The present work of Christ, beginning with his victorious death, is the destruction of all opposing powers. "Destroy" translates a word which means "to bring to nothing." The same Greek word was used in the expression, "When the perfect comes, the imperfect will pass away" (13:10). The victory of Christ over these hostile powers will be absolute and complete—they will be made to pass away. *Rule* (Greek, *archē*) is in the singular and has an abstract sense. The word literally means "beginning" and is frequently found in the New Testament in that sense. Only Paul and Luke use it to mean "rule" (Paul, nine times and Luke, two). "Authority" is often used in Paul's writings in conjunction with "rule." *Power* is unusual in this connection. The thought is that every kind of rule, authority, or power, whether human or superhuman, must be abolished before Christ can hand over the reins of government to God. It is doubtful that we can find the Gnostic hierarchy of angels in this verse, though they would not be excluded. Nor do we need to seek for identification of the various powers in Paul's mind; the abstract nouns forbid this.

Verse 25: For he must reign: Must translates an impersonal verb meaning "it is necessary." The usual implication of this verb in the New Testament is that it is necessary in the will of God. God's purpose includes the active rule of Christ.[1] *Reign* comes from the same stem as *kingdom* and shows that *kingdom* has the active sense of rulership.

Until he has put all enemies under his feet: a classic symbol for complete subjugation. The source of the expression is perhaps the statement: "The Lord says to my lord: 'Sit at my right hand, till I make your enemies your footstool'" (Ps. 110:1). Paul, however, changed the symbolism. Now it is the one who sits at the right hand of God who puts his enemies under his feet.

Verse 26: The last enemy to be destroyed is death: explains why the full

---

[1] Grosheide points out that Christ's reign is a part of his duty as Savior.

resurrection must precede the final consummation. Death reigns as long as men die. Only the resurrection will abolish death.[1] When this enemy is brought to nothing, the kingdom can be handed over to God. *To be destroyed* is inaccurate. The Greek is in the present tense and the sentence reads: "Last enemy he is destroying—the death." The process of destruction has already begun with the resurrection of Christ. "The death" is the penalty of sin, not the mere biological experience which moderns call death.

Verse 27: "For God has put all things in subjection under his feet": quotes Ps. 110:1 partially. The quotation, in Paul's mind, meant that God had granted Jesus authority over all things, but Jesus must himself subject his enemies. *God* is properly understood as the subject, though the Greek has only "he."

But when it says, "All things are put in subjection under him": the words of the Psalm.

It is plain that he is excepted who put all things under him: that is, God is not himself in subjection to the Son. The Son still works under the sovereignty and for the sovereignty of God. This statement reflects the series of subordinations in the redemptive work which governed Paul's thoughts.

Verse 28: describes the goal toward which God has been working through the Son.

When all things are subjected to him: when the victory of Christ is complete (cf. vs. 25).

Then the Son himself: The incarnate Son who in his lordship has achieved authority over all things.

Will also be subjected to him who put all things under him: i.e., to God, the Father.

That God may be everything to every one: the final object or goal. The ultimate object of the subjection of Christ, after having won the victory over all enemies, will restore the original order, the supremacy of God over everyone.

(4) Hope for the resurrection giving meaning to Christian devotion (15:29–34)

Having shown that the resurrection of the dead is implied in the resurrection of Jesus, that Christian faith and preaching have validity only if the doctrine is true, and that it is an essential part of God's redemptive purpose, Paul turned to Christian practice. The main thrust of this paragraph is that denial of the resurrection makes sacrifice meaningless. He began with one of the most difficult verses in Scripture (vs. 29) and continued with the assertion that he died every day (vss. 30–31). Next he said that his sacrifice was meaningless if there was no resurrection (vs. 32). Finally, he attacked the error as being the result of association with evil companions and due to ignorance of God (vss. 33–34). The result is that it is impossible for Christians to deny the resurrection.

---

[1] The absence of the Greek article places emphasis on the character of death as an enemy (Morris).

Verse 29: is a most difficult verse to interpret. What did Paul mean by baptism for the dead? This we must try to discover.

Otherwise: if all that has been said is not true, if Christ was not raised, if believers will not be raised, if God will not triumph.

What do people mean: rather, "What are they doing?" However, the RSV translation is probably a good interpretation.

By being baptized on behalf of the dead: a poor translation. Literally, the expression reads, "those who are being baptized for the dead." *On behalf of* is a possible translation,[1] but it excludes other possible translations. "For" is neutral and allows us to seek an interpretation. Over three hundred interpretations have been given of this difficult saying. The number warns us that dogmatic certainty is impossible.[2] Some have removed the difficulty by making *baptized* refer to something other than Christian baptism. Some examples are: [3] (1) washing the bodies of the dead in preparation for burial, (2) washing self to remove the defilement of touching dead bodies, (3) undergoing affliction and martyrdom.[4] Others have removed the difficulty by a strained meaning of the phrase: "for the dead." Some examples are: (1) being baptized over the tombs of the martyrs, (2) being baptized on the point of death, (3) being baptized to fill up the ranks of dying Christians, and (4) accepting baptism because they have seen the heroic behavior of those who have died for their faith.[5]

Both of these attempts to relieve the verse of difficulty must be rejected. *Baptized* refers to Christian baptism.[6] *For the dead* points to one object of baptism. Two interpretations, it would seem, are possible. One is to suppose that Paul was referring to a practice of vicarious baptism; the other is to suppose that he was speaking of the convert's hope of the resurrection, expressed in his baptism. In the first case the RSV translation is the correct interpretation. In the other case the expression would read, "by being baptized with reference to the resurrection from the dead." Either interpretation is possible since the Greek preposition (*huper*) can either mean, "in behalf of" or "with reference to." Our feeling is that the second alternative is correct; thus the expression means that Christian converts were being baptized with reference to their own future resurrection, that this was one meaning of baptism.[7] Our argument for this opinion must be in

[1] Many modern interpreters take the verse to refer to vicarious baptism which was practiced at Corinth, but believe that Paul did not approve of the practice. IB calls it a "superstitious practice" but believes it lies behind the words. Parry calls any other interpretation an "evasion." Morris agrees that this practice must have been behind the verse.

[2] ICC says it will remain "doubtful." Schlatter says there is no clear meaning.

[3] The following summary is based on the discussion by Edwards.

[4] Schlatter suggests it was suffering death as a witness to Christ. He points to Jesus' calling his death a baptism as background.

[5] EGT believes that Paul was referring to a normal Christian experience which was true not only in Corinth but in other places as well: that "the death of a Christian leads to the conversion of survivors, who . . . in the hope of reunion, turn to Christ." Lenski substantially agrees with this interpretation.

[6] Barrett insists that *baptized,* without further explanation, should be taken in the sense of Christian baptism, Paul's normal meaning for the word.

[7] I am indebted to Lockhart for this interpretation and for some of the arguments used to substantiate it. (Clinton Lockhart, *Principles of Interpretation* [Fort Worth, Texas: S. H. Taylor, Printer, © 1901], pp. 157–159.)

two parts—factors that favor this interpretation and reasons why vicarious baptism could not be the correct interpretation.

First, let us notice the factors that favor our interpretation. They are: (1) This fits the context. (2) This is in harmony with the total New Testament teaching on baptism. (3) This is the best way to treat the Greek text. Number (1) is apparent. Paul had been speaking of the resurrection of the dead. In the paragraph itself he repeated, "If the dead are not raised" (vs. 32). To say that new converts who joined the ranks of Christians publicly through baptism and made themselves subject to the persecutions inherent in their faith would be acting foolishly unless the resurrection was true fits into Paul's thought. Number (2) is likewise apparent. Baptism was the public act by which a new convert identified himself as a Christian. It had a number of meanings. It pictured the spiritual death and resurrection of the believer. It symbolized the death and resurrection of Jesus. One passage seems to make the hope of the resurrection a meaning of baptism. "You were buried with him in baptism, in which you were also raised with him through faith in the working of God, who raised him from the dead" (Col. 2:12). Number (3) is not so apparent. It is necessary to suppose an ellipsis. In the statement, "those baptized with reference to the dead," it is necessary to insert "the resurrection of." The result is: "those who are baptized with reference to the resurrection of the dead." However, such ellipses often occur in the writing of Paul and such an insertion, we believe, is justified.

The following are arguments against taking this to mean vicarious baptism: (1) Paul did not condemn the practice but spoke of it as if it were normal. (2) There is no evidence that such a practice existed among professing Christians at this time. (3) Such a practice is contrary to the teaching of the New Testament on salvation. Number (1) has been circumvented by saying that Paul did not condemn it or approve it, because he only wanted to use it as an example. Few commentators, if any, outside the circle of that Christian sect which practices vicarious baptism think that Paul approved the practice. But is it reasonable to suppose that Paul would have mentioned a practice so contrary to the doctrine of salvation through faith without condemning it? To the contrary, this whole letter is devoted to correcting problems which the Corinthians had. It seems highly improbable to suppose that Paul would not have condemned the practice of vicarious baptism if it had existed. Number (2) is an argument from silence, but it is a resounding silence. Number (3) should be apparent. The New Testament teaches that salvation is by grace through faith alone. Baptism is not essential to salvation, even for the living; it comes after salvation, not before it. It is a result of salvation, not a cause of it. Thus no possible good could come to dead men by having someone baptized in their behalf.

In the light of these arguments it would seem that our opinion is best supported. Paul meant that Christians were being baptized with a view to the resurrection of the dead.

If the dead are not raised at all: a constant refrain in this chapter.

Why are people baptized on their behalf?: rather, with a view to their own resurrection. The same interpretation and arguments must stand here as above.

Verse 30: continues the same thought as verse 29, but with a personal reference.

Why: if there is no resurrection, no hope of the future. Hope is not the only motive, but it is an essential motive, of sacrifice.

I: rather, "we." The change of the pronoun to *I* in the RSV is unaccountable. The Greek has "we also." "We" refers to the apostles as a group. "Also" shows that their peril was of the same nature as those who were baptized for the dead and supports the interpretation given above, i.e., that such baptism brought those who were baptized into peril.

Am . . . in peril every hour?: rather, "are in danger every hour." The expression describes well what we know of Paul's career and probably what was true of the other apostles as well. Paul was in danger almost from the moment of his conversion. He had to be let down over the wall in a basket to escape the plotting of the Jews in Damascus (cf. Acts 9:23–25). He was sent to Tarsus by the Jerusalem disciples because the Hellenists were seeking to kill him (Acts 9:28–30). He was never out of danger and often involved in positive suffering (cf. 2 Cor. 4:7–12). *Every hour* is not hyperbolical in his case. Such subjection to danger must come from a conviction that the work being done is worth the risk. This is easily understood if the preaching of the gospel brings men to eternal salvation and rescues them from eternal damnation. It is difficult to understand on any other grounds.

Verse 31: From dangers he had in common with the other apostles, Paul turned to his own personal dangers.

I protest: translates a Greek affirmative particle that introduces an oath. Though no oath is present in the verse, at least not in the sense of calling God to witness the truth of the assertion, the expression is very solemn.

By my pride in you which I have in Christ Jesus our Lord: the basis of his affirmation. Rather than saying, "I swear by God," he said, "I swear by my pride in you." To swear by something means that one is willing to forfeit that if his word is not true. Paul was proud of the work he had done in Corinth and made this a ground of *pride,* i.e., glorying. However, he saved himself from the charge of egotism by immediately giving credit to his Lord. He had that pride because of his union with Christ Jesus, and it was that union that made his work successful in Corinth. As always for Paul, Christ Jesus was acknowledged as Lord.

I die every day: has the emphatic position in the Greek sentence. The expression is the substance of his oath. The expression meant that he was in peril of dying every day (cf. 2 Cor. 4:11). This expression is often lifted out of its context and made to mean that Paul died to himself every day so that he could live for God. This does not fit the context. It means rather that Paul, in his own mind, forfeited his life every day when he went out to preach the gospel. He counted himself as marked for death.

Verse 32: presses the point of his self-sacrifice further.

What do I gain: What is the profit to me personally? Paul did not confess here, as some have charged, that his motives were selfish. His point was that there was no point in living as he did if his fundamental view of life was wrong.

Humanly speaking: The meaning of this expression depends on the context. In the Greek sentence it is placed first for emphasis. It indicates that he was speaking hypothetically and from a merely human point of view. Here the expression should be taken with the question: *What do I gain?* When judged from the human point of view, by human standards, is it worth the risk? It has always been true that the unbeliever has regarded Christian devotion as a form of madness. The reason is that they judge it from the human point of view. From this point of view it is madness. The Christian seems to gain little from his devotion. He gets sick, suffers ills, and dies. What has his devotion to Christ gained him? Nothing, unless you view it from the Christian rather than the human viewpoint. When eternity is brought into the picture, the devotion of the Christian is seen to be well worth the risk and the loss he has taken. This is not the only dimension of the answer, but it is one dimension.

If . . . I fought with beasts at Ephesus: probably a figurative expression describing his conflicts in Ephesus with human opponents.[1] It is unlikely that he would have omitted mention of this in his list of his perils in 2 Corinthians 11:23–29 if it had been a literal conflict. The meaning is: "Why, right here at Ephesus, I have faced death in the same manner as those who fight with beasts in the arena." Acts tells us of the riot instigated by Demetrius, the silversmith, in which Gaius and Aristarchus were dragged to the theater and Paul was restrained with difficulty from going in among the crowd (Acts 19:23–30). No doubt there were other perils concerning which we know nothing, unless some of the experiences Paul mentioned in 2 Corinthians 11:23–29 took place in Ephesus. No doubt the Corinthians had heard of his trials in Ephesus, and this expression would have been understood by them.

If the dead are not raised: quotes the foolish error of some of the Corinthians for the sixth time in this chapter.

"Let us eat and drink, for tomorrow we die": a quotation from Isaiah 22:13 without regard to the context there. The words are meant to express the rule of life which dominates those who have no hope for the future. They represent the natural reaction of men who have lost the hope that lifts their lives to new levels. Paul meant to say that if death ends all, life has little to offer except the creaturely comforts of eating and drinking. The words, or at least the substance of them, are universally found among men who have no Christian hope. To Christians they seem to be blasphemy. We have found a deeper dimension to earthly life; but that dimension, though it is present, always looks also to the future.

Verse 33: Do not be deceived: i.e., led astray. The present tense in the Greek carries the meaning, "Stop doing what you are doing." The implication is that the Corinthians were being *deceived,* i.e., led away from Christian truth, by the preaching of the error in Corinth. At least, they were tending in that direction, and Paul wished to stop them.

"Bad company ruins good morals": a quotation from the Greek poet

---

[1] Morris, with some reluctance, agrees that this is metaphorical.

Menander, but it may have been a current proverb. *Bad company* means "evil associations." *Ruins* means "to corrupt." *Good morals* is rather, "good habits." The application to the Corinthians' situation is clear. If they continued to associate with those who were evil, their own Christian ways of thinking would be destroyed. Paul implied that the denial of the resurrection had already undermined the moral tone of the Corinthians.

Verse 34: brings the argument to a conclusion with an imperative.

Come to your right mind: literally, "sober up in the right way." The RSV translation is a good interpretation. Paul had appealed throughout to the mind of the Corinthians; he had used logic to destroy the error. Now he commanded the Corinthians to start thinking as they should.

And sin no more: rather, "stop your sinning." The literal meaning of the Greek word *sin* is to miss the mark. In this context that meaning should be given to the word. Thus, "stop missing the mark" is equivalent to "stop being deceived."

For some have no knowledge of God: Some suggests that Paul knew whom he was talking about. Whether this *some* is equivalent to the *some* who denied the resurrection is uncertain (cf. vs. 12). Probably not. Rather, it seems that Paul referred to professed Christians, perhaps members of the Corinthian congregation, who remained ignorant, i.e., had no real knowledge, of God. Denial of the resurrection shows an ignorance of God.

I say this to your shame: i.e., to move you to be ashamed. The Corinthians prided themselves on their intellect; Paul wanted them to see that they were gullible if they allowed themselves to be swayed by men who did not really know God at all.

2. The Nature of the Resurrection Body (15:35–57)

Paul turned his attention to a question which has bothered Christians through the ages—the kind of body with which we will be raised. He dealt with this problem because it seems to have been a talking point with those who denied the resurrection. They saw the problem as insoluble. Such an attitude Paul considered to be foolishness (vss. 35–36). Illustrating his point from nature, Paul taught that the resurrection life will have continuity with the present body but will be different in kind (vss. 36–41). He turned then to stress, in a number of contrasts, the difference between the two lives (vss. 42–50). Finally, in a song of victory, Paul pointed out that the resurrection will herald the final and complete victory of the believer over sin (vss. 51–57).

(1) Having continuity with, but different from, the present body (15:35–41)

First, the question is raised as some would raise it (vs. 35). Paul then proceeded to show the foolishness of the man who would doubt the reality of the resurrection because he could not understand the nature of the resurrection body (vss. 36–41).

Verse 35: introduces the problem and difficulty of the doctrine of the resurrection.

But: adversative particle, marking the question as Paul's own statement of it.

Some one: may be a Christian who was genuinely puzzled rather than a proponent of the error itself.[1]

Will ask: assumes the probability that this question would be raised.

How: that is, in what manner.

Are the dead raised: when they are raised, or if they are raised.

With what kind of body do they come?: the same question in a different form. Edwards thinks we have two questions, the first of which Paul answers in verse 36, the other in the following verses. It seems better to take the questions as only one, the second being explanatory of the first.

Verse 36: removes the assumption that a man has only one mode of existence, that which we now experience.

You foolish man!: rather, "senseless one!" A severe rebuke which assumes that the objector prided himself on his intelligence. This is often the case with objectors. They think they see a flaw in Christian doctrine and pounce on it, priding themselves on their acuteness in seeing it. Often just the opposite is true. Objections often stem from the inability to understand rather than from intelligence.

What you sow does not come to life unless it dies: introduces the analogy of the seed which continues through verse 38. Paul's appeal was to the observed processes of natural life. The seed does not sprout until the old form of its existence dies. Jesus used the same illustration to show the necessity of his own death (cf. John 12:24). The expression is not meant to be scientifically correct, but only true to human observation.

Verse 37: And what you sow is not the body which is to be: when the plant comes forth from the ground. Of course, eventually the plant will reproduce the same kind of body that was sown, but this was not in Paul's mind.

But a bare kernel: when it is sown. The grain at that time has no resemblance to the plant that is to come.

Perhaps of wheat or of some other grain: a good translation. Wheat was the chief food crop of the ancient world, but other types of grain were also grown.

Verse 38: But God gives it a body as he has chosen: expresses Paul's faith in the sovereignty of God, even in the processes of nature. According to the New Testament, what we call natural law is only God ruling the earth in an orderly manner.

To each kind of seed its own body: the body which belongs to it. The parallel with the new life of the believer after resurrection is intended. Men, as well as natural seeds, are capable of more than one kind of existence. *Body* throughout this discussion means more than the material substance; it speaks of a kind of existence.

Verse 39: turns to an analogy from different kinds of flesh. Again, the thought is of different kinds of existence.

For not all flesh is alike: states the basic premise.

But there is one kind for men, another for animals, another for birds, and

---

[1] Dahl (p. 80) suggests that anyone who asks this question is an "idiot."

another for fish: The difference is not in kinds of matter but in the modes of life, going from the higher to the lower.

Verse 40: illustrates the point of the paragraph from the different kinds of existence in heaven and on earth.

There are celestial bodies: perhaps angels. Paul did not use *bodies* in the sense that we use the word, as masses of material. He always used it to designate a kind of organic life. It may be that the ancients thought of the sun, moon, and stars as such organisms and that Paul shared this idea. If so, in the light of verse 41, the *celestial bodies* would be these bodies. However, it is more likely that he thought of modes of existence that were fitted for life in heaven, and the only such beings of which he was aware were angels.

There are terrestrial bodies: such as mentioned in verse 39. *Bodies* equals modes of existence on the earth.

But the glory of the celestial is one: introduces the idea of glory in the modes of existence. The fundamental meaning of *glory* is manifestation, whether of being or character. The Shekinah glory manifested the presence of God in the Jewish temple. The point is that the heavenly, or celestial, being has a peculiar mode of manifesting itself according to the sphere in which it acts.

The glory of the terrestrial is another: of a different kind. Terrestrial, or earthly, organisms have a different way of manifesting themselves than the heavenly. There is no hint in the passage of one being superior to the other; they are merely different. The illustration prepares the way for the thought that the resurrected Christian, though belonging to the celestial sphere, will of necessity have a mode of life and a means of manifestation different from that which now prevails.

Verse 41: The mention of *glory* in the previous verse suggests the various manifestations of what we would call the "heavenly bodies," i.e., the sun, moon, and stars.

There is one glory of the sun: The sun manifests itself in one way.

Another glory of the moon: Another means, "another of the same kind." The moon was considered by the ancients to be an independent body without relationship to the sun.

Another glory of the stars: the same construction as above. *Stars* is plural rather than singular to prepare the way for the next statement.

For star differs from star in glory: reflects the observation from the earth. Some stars are bright, others dim. Their way of manifestation, their glory, though of the same kind, is different from each other.

Paul's thought throughout this paragraph had to do with the varieties of existence and manifestation. His purpose was to show that the difficulty which some had with the doctrine of the resurrection was not a difficulty at all. If God is able to provide so many ways of existence that we know of, can he not provide still another which is a mystery to us? One who stumbles at this difficulty is indeed senseless.

(2) A spiritual, imperishable body (15:42–49)

In this paragraph the difference between the present mode of existence and the resurrection life is stressed. After introducing the subject (vs. 42a), Paul made a series of contrasts between the present life and the future life—perishable-imperishable; dishonor-glory; weakness-power; physical-spiritual (vss. 42b–44a). The rest of the paragraph is given to the development of the idea of physical and spiritual modes of existence. Paul brought into play the Adam-Christ comparison. He asserted that Adam, as the progenitor of the race, left the stamp of his existence on all his descendants, but Christ, who is the head of the new spiritual race of believers, likewise leaves the stamp of his existence on all Christians (vss. 44b–49).

Verse 42: begins with a direct application of the former analogies to the resurrection of the dead and starts the series of contrasts between this life and the resurrection life.

So is it with the resurrection of the dead: refers back to the series of analogies in previous verses—analogies of seed, flesh, modes of existence, and glories of the heavenly bodies. In the previous verses the comparison was indirect; here it is direct. The thought of the continuity of the future life with this one is left behind, and the difference is stressed.

What is sown: rather, "There is a sowing." The verb is impersonal, and it is best to preserve this in translation. The analogy of the seed was in Paul's mind (cf. vss. 36–38).

Is perishable: rather, "in corruption." The thought does not seem to be that the corpse which is put in the grave is corruptible, but that the whole life of man from the cradle to the grave is lived out in the sphere of corruption. In this sphere a sowing takes place. This sowing—death and burial—closes life in the sphere of corruption. "Corruption" has moral overtones as well as physical.

What is raised: rather, "There is a raising." The construction is parallel with that above.

Is imperishable: rather, "in incorruption." The whole of heavenly life, beyond the resurrection, is in mind. At the beginning of that life there is a resurrection. The whole new life is lived in the sphere of incorruption. Peter spoke of the future life as "an inheritance which is imperishable, undefiled, and unfading, kept in heaven for you" (1 Pet. 1:4). This means not only that we will not die but also that no sin will be involved in that new, heavenly life. It is fair to point out that some commentators disagree with this interpretation, taking the reference to be to the corruptibility of the corpse that is buried in the grave (cf. Lenski). This is subject to two objections. One is that we are reading back into Paul our own conceptions of the human life as body and soul. The other is that some of the antitheses in this list do not fit with that conception. We believe that we must be consistent.

Verse 43: continues the series of antitheses.

It is sown: rather, "There is a sowing."

In dishonor: i.e., in the sphere of a life that is characterized by dishonor. *Dishonor* covers all the mean, sinful, unworthy circumstances of human life. Man by his sin becomes less than human and fails to manifest his true self. The Christian partially escapes the dishonor of human life, but not wholly.

It is raised in glory: rather, "There is a resurrection in the sphere of glory." The thought is that man in his resurrection life will have *glory,* a manifestation of his true manhood. The biblical witness is that God created man without flaw, that he made himself a sinner by rebelling against God, that redemption begins the process of restoring man to his true stature, and that the resurrection will consummate redemption. This does not mean that man will be like Adam in the resurrection life, but that he will be all that Adam could have been if he had not sinned.

Verse 44: It is sown in weakness: rather, "There is a sowing in the sphere of weakness." *Weakness* describes well the state of man's life on earth, but it does not describe the corpse in the grave. The corpse is not weak; it is dead. This is one of the couplets which shows that Paul was not speaking of the burial of the corpse. Man in his whole life is weak, even those who are relatively strong. He is subject to disease, disappointment, failure, heartache, and finally, death. He is unable to achieve his desires or fulfill his dreams. In some ways he is the weakest of all God's creatures. The Christian, by his union with Christ, overcomes some of the limitations that plague his fellowman, but not all of them. The resurrection life is not a return to the former life of weakness, but a resurrection to a higher kind of life.

It is raised in power: rather, "There is a resurrection in the sphere of power." The resurrection life will be a life of power, power received from God, of course, but power nevertheless. The Christian, in his new life, will never need to know the sting of defeat, the bitterness of disappointment, the shame of sin, or the futility of efforts. He will live in the sphere of power.

Verse 44: It is sown a physical body: a correct translation. The construction in the Greek changes at this point. This phrase comes nearest to suggesting burial, but it is not meant to do so. *Body* means the living organism, not the dead corpse. When the body (in our use of the word) is laid in the grave, it is no longer (in Paul's use of the word) a body at all. Thus, there is a sowing of life, but it is a life which is designed for living in this world. *Physical* gives a wrong impression because our meaning for the term is different from Paul's. In English, "physical" means "that which is composed of or has to do with matter." The English word is opposed to "mental, moral, or spiritual." Not so with the Greek word *(psychikon).* This word is a form of the same word which is translated "soul" or "life" in the New Testament. Thus, the *physical body* is the living self in the thought of Paul. The same adjective is used to describe the natural man, untouched by the Spirit of God, unable to understand the gifts of the Spirit (1 Cor. 2:14). It is also used to describe Adam as a "living being," a man from the earth (cf. vss. 45–47). The thought, then, is that the Christian, so long as he lives on earth, is plagued by being a natural man. Though his union with Christ enables him to overcome the natural self in many ways, he is never able to escape himself. It is this living self which is sown and dies and rises a new kind of self in the resurrection.

It is raised a spiritual body: i.e., a new kind of self that is perfectly adapted to life under the leadership of the Holy Spirit. *Spiritual* is not meant to describe the composition of the body (in our sense) of the resurrection self. It describes the kind of life which that self lives. *Body,* of course, equals self in Paul's vocabulary.

The question which troubled the Corinthians and which troubles many modern people was not answered by Paul. He preferred to leave it a mystery. Perhaps we would do better to do the same. The only clue which we have of the "heavenly dwelling," "a building from God, a house not made with hands" which is in contrast to our "earthly tent" (cf. 2 Cor. 5:1–3; notice how Paul avoided the use of "body" to describe either) is the resurrection appearances of Jesus. He could appear or disappear at will; he could walk through locked doors without opening them; he could, at the same time, eat fish and bread. Again, borrowing the words of Paul, he was not a "naked" self but a "clothed" self (cf. 2 Cor. 5:4). It is certain that we shall have the same kind of "clothing" which he had and still has, but the exact nature of it is unknown to us. The main point of this statement is that the resurrection will not be a mere resuscitation, a being brought back to the same kind of life; it will be a resurrection of the whole self to a new and glorious kind of existence. Is it any wonder that Paul longed for that life?

If there is a physical body: a natural mode of existence in the world.

There is also a spiritual body: a supernatural form of life. *There is* is the assertion of Paul's faith in the resurrection. "This sentence . . . gives the key to the whole of Paul's thought on this subject. He conceives of individual life as necessarily implying an organism for its own self-expression and development, and for entering into relation with others. The kind of organism depends on the kind of life" (Parry).

Verses 45–49: These verses are an expansion of the thought of the physical body and the spiritual body. Paul reasoned that, since the natural self was an expression of the life derived from Adam, the new spiritual self will be a full expression of the life received from Christ. Some modern theologians make the Adam-Christ analogy a key to the theology of Paul, but this seems to exaggerate the importance of a type of reasoning which Paul used only occasionally, here and in Romans 5:12–14. It seems unlikely that an analogy used so seldom would have had a dominating influence on the theology of Paul. In both passages where it is used, Adam was only the background out of which Paul set forth the achievements of Christ for mankind.

Thus it is written: introduces a quotation from the Old Testament.

"The first man Adam became a living being": quotes Genesis 2:7, but inserts *first* and *Adam* in the quotation. *Living* comes from the same word group *(phychē)* as the word which the RSV translates "physical" in the previous verses. The *first . . . Adam* marks the beginning and sets the pattern for man's natural life. All men become like him in that they too are living beings. .

The last Adam: Jesus Christ. He is called the *last Adam* to show that his work of redemption was a new beginning for human life.[1] His ministry marked the beginning of the Christian gospel which opened the way for

---

[1] Thrall suggests that Christ is like Adam because "what happens to him potentially affects the whole human race."

all men to become like him. The limits of the analogy must be set at this point. Nothing more is meant than that Christ, like Adam, was the beginning of a new kind of life and a pattern of that life.

Became a life-giving spirit: marks the contrast between Adam and Christ. Adam received a natural life from God; Christ imparted an infinitely higher kind of life to men. One was the recipient of creation; the other is the Creator. *Life-giving* always implies divine action. In John 5:21, it is said: "The Father raises the dead and gives them life, so also the Son gives life to whom he will." The giving of life is a prerogative of God; the natural way in which Paul ascribed this act to Jesus Christ shows that he believed in the deity of Christ. Paul stopped short of saying that Christians would be like Christ in this respect. They will indeed bear his image (vs. 49), but they will not have the power to give life. *Became* marks a point in Paul's past in which this became true. Commentators have argued about the point of time involved. Some have said it was the resurrection; others, that it was the bestowal of the Holy Spirit at his baptism; others, that it was the incarnation. This last interpretation seems to be correct, though it is impossible to draw a distinct line between the incarnation, the Spirit-filled life, the victorious death, and the resurrection of Jesus. In the New Testament these are considered to be parts of one redemptive movement of God in Christ Jesus.

Verse 46: But it is not the spiritual which is first but the physical, and then the spiritual: marks the order in man's experience in which he may become the image of the first Adam and the last. Man becomes like the first Adam at birth, like the last Adam when converted (partially), but fully when he experiences resurrection.

Verse 47: The first man was from the earth, a man of dust: describes the creation account in Genesis 2:1–7. God formed man of the dust of the earth and then breathed into his nostrils the breath of life, and he became a "living soul" (i.e., a living being).

The second man is from heaven: expresses the faith of the Christian that Christ was sent from God. "The Lord" appears after *the second man* in some Greek manuscripts, but its omission is more strongly attested by manuscript evidence. Also, it is an obvious explanatory insertion. Some commentators take the phrase *from heaven* to refer to the Second Advent, but this violates the context and is not demanded by the words.

Verse 48: As was the man of dust, so are those who are of the dust: Men bear the likeness of Adam in two respects. They are living beings; they are subject to corruption and decay. The expression in verses 42–43— *perishable, dishonor, weakness*—explain the meaning of Paul. *Those . . . of dust* include the whole of the human race.

As is the man of heaven: Question: Does this refer to the present state of Christ in heaven, or is it synonymous with "from heaven"? Commentators differ. There is no verb in the Greek. *Of heaven* is a Greek adjective in this expression, meaning "heavenly one." The decision is difficult because it carries over into verse 49. If verse 49 is hortatory, as some important textual variants make it, this would have to refer to Christ in Paul's past. If it is indicative, as our translation makes it, it would refer to the present state of Christ in heaven. On the whole—and more will be

1 CORINTHIANS 15:48 [258

said about it—we should adopt the RSV translation and let this expression refer to the present, heavenly state of Christ.

So are those who are of heaven: rather, "the heavenly ones." The same adjective is repeated to describe those who belong to Christ. They are not "from heaven" as he was, but they are "heavenly ones" as he is. This being so, the expression does not refer to Christians on earth who are spiritual in their desires and strivings, but to Christians in heaven who have experienced the transformation brought about at death. They share the heavenly life with him, the freedom and purity of his glorified humanity.

Verse 49: Just as we have borne the image of the man of dust: in our earthly life. This is true of all men, including Christians. This expression is synonymous with the previous statement: "As was the man of dust, so are those who are of dust." *Of dust* is a modernization of the Greek "clayey." However, it is not misleading.

We shall also bear the image of the man of heaven: rather, "the heavenly man." *Image* supposes a prototype from which it is drawn. It is more than mere "likeness," in which one man resembles another man or one egg resembles another egg. Christ is envisioned as the prototype of the Christian, and it would not be too much to suppose that in the resurrection life this will include his mode of existence. *We shall . . . bear* is a disputed reading. If adopted, the expression refers to the resurrection life of the Christian in heaven. If the alternative reading, "Let us bear," is adopted, the whole expression would be an exhortation to progressive growth into the likeness of Christ during our earthly life. Either reading would be in accord with Paul's teaching, but the thought of exhortation breaks into the continuity of his thought in this passage. Thus, in spite of every strong manuscript support for the subjunctive reading, we will assume that the indicative is correct.

This still leaves us with a problem—the extreme distinction which Paul drew between the earthly life of the Christian and the future life. This is explained when we remember that Paul was speaking to the question in debate. In other passages he made man's fellowship with God a foretaste of the heavenly life itself (cf. Eph. 1:13–14). However, in this context he was anxious to show why the resurrection was an essential part of the gospel message. Even though we assume that the present Christian life is a foretaste of the future, the future must indeed be far more wonderful. This is the emphasis of this chapter.

(3) The resurrection completing the victory over sin (15:50–57)

Having answered the objection to the resurrection based on the kind of body, Paul turned to the transformation of the living (vss. 50–53). The main thrust is that something akin to the "sowings" mentioned above must take place for those who survive until the time of Christ's return. Finally, he pointed out that when the dead are risen and the living changed, the consummation of God's rule in human life will have been achieved (vss. 54–57).

Verse 50: belongs to this new section rather than to the last, contrary to the paragraphing of the RSV. The thought is that even the living Christians cannot experience the full meaning of the new life in their present state. The natural man can never be escaped on this earth.

I tell you this: introduces the new thought. The same Greek phrase occurs at the beginning of 7:29 and nowhere else in the New Testament.

Flesh and blood: human nature under present conditions. The same combination is found in Matthew 16:17 and Galatians 1:16. It is found in inverted form in Ephesians 6:12 and Hebrews 2:14. That the two words refer to a single thing is shown by the fact that the verb is singular rather than plural. The expression denotes man as a frail creature, different in kind from God. The phrase is equal to *the physical body,* the natural life in verse 44. However, the material part of man is predominant since it is most obviously subject to decay and corruption.

Cannot inherit: come into possession of, or enter in. *Cannot* is absolute, meaning "not able to." The thought is that by reason of his corruptibility man cannot, in his present mode of existence, experience the full meaning of redemption.

The kingdom of God: the future reign of God after Christ has handed over the kingdom (cf. vs. 24). "Kingdom," as it is used in the New Testament, has two dimensions. Most often it refers to the present spiritual rule of God in the hearts of men, but the futuristic dimension of the word is never lost. This present rule moves toward a future consummation. The future consummation was in Paul's mind here.

Nor does the perishable: that which is subject to corruption.

Inherit the imperishable: that which is not subject to corruption. These statements seem to leave out the living Christian; they seem to say that he must die in order to inherit the kingdom. However, there is another way, which Paul explained in the next verses.

Verses 51–52: explain how the Christian who is still alive at the consummation can inherit the kingdom also.

Lo! I tell you a mystery: graphic way of introducing a new thought. *Mystery* has the common meaning of "secret." It was a secret of God's purpose which Paul now divulged to the Corinthians.[1]

We shall not all sleep: i.e., die. *Sleep* is a common euphemism for death. *We* seems to imply that Paul expected to be among the number who would not die. The pronoun included only the Christians. The fate of unbelievers was not dealt with by Paul.

But we shall all be changed: in the mode of our existence. Paul did not say, "transformed," as if only the form of life were changed. He meant that the change in the living Christians would be the same change effected by dying and being raised to new life.

Verse 52: In a moment, in the twinkling of an eye: expresses the idea of instantaneousness. The change will not be a process.

At the last trumpet: which heralds the final appearance of Christ (cf. 1 Thess. 4:16; Matt. 24:31; Rev. 8:2). We do not need to suppose that the trumpet calls the dead forth from the grave; God does that. The trumpet sounds in order to call the attention of the living to the coming Christ.

For the trumpet will sound: when the time comes.

---

[1] Dahl (p. 83) says Paul had received his knowledge by revelation.

And the dead will be raised imperishable: at the same time.

And we shall be changed: at the same time. The three expressions form a majestic description of the event.

Verse 53: returns to the thought of verse 50.

For this perishable nature: our present mode of life.

Must: in God's purpose. The impersonal verb, "it is necessary," here translated *must,* has reference to the redemptive purpose of God. That purpose cannot be fulfilled until the last enemy, death, is overcome (vs. 26).

Put on the imperishable: be clothed with the new mode of life.

And this mortal nature must put on immortality: obviously synonymous with the previous expression. *Mortal* means that which is subject to death, *immortality* that which is not. In Greek thought, mortality was identified with the life of men, immortality with the life of the gods. In later thought among the Greeks, immortality was thought to be a property of the soul of man which dwelt within the mortal body. Modern thought has taken this up, and it is characteristic of Christian language today. However, we need to remember that the immortality of the soul is a Greek teaching, not a biblical doctrine. The thought in New Testament teaching is not that man is inherently immortal, but that he is mortal. Immortality is received at the resurrection when man enters the new heavenly life. It is not inherent in the nature of man (as the Greeks thought) but is a miraculous gift of God. The Greek word is used only in this passage and in 2 Timothy 6:16, where it is said concerning Christ that he "alone has immortality." Of course, when the word is used by Christians, it no longer has the Greek implications. In common speech it means only that men shall continue to exist beyond death. This thought, we believe, is true. However, it is improper to say that man is now immortal, or that any part of him is. He is mortal, i.e., subject to death; but the Christian man will receive immortality at the time of the resurrection.

Verses 54–57: constitute a song of victory that rose to Paul's lips as he contemplated the glory of what he had said.

Verse 54: When the perishable puts on the imperishable, and the mortal puts on immortality: repeats the thought of verse 53.

Then: at that time and not until that time.

Shall come to pass: be brought to its ultimate fulfillment.

The saying that is written: in the Old Testament.

"Death is swallowed up in victory": quotes Isaiah 25:8: "He will swallow up death for ever." Paul translated directly from the Hebrew, which meant that death would be annihilated. The saying, even in its Old Testament setting, is strongly eschatological and looks forward to the ultimate deliverance of Israel. Paul appropriated it, justifiably, to speak of the ultimate deliverance of all Christians.

Verse 55: "O death, where is thy victory? O death, where is thy sting?": a quotation, but not exact, from Hosea 13:14: "O Death, where are your plagues?/O Sheol, where is your destruction?" Paul's wording has been influenced by the Greek translation of the Old Testament and the demands of the present context. The questions have the tone of one who jeers at conquered enemies.

Verse 56: The sting of death is sin: Paul's own interpretation. Death is personified as if it had a weapon, sin. Personification of abstract ideas was common with Paul (cf. Rom. 7:7–25). The thought is that sin brings death; death is its wages (cf. Rom. 6:23). The victory over sin which comes in the resurrection will spell the defeat of death.

The power of sin is the law: repeats the thought which Paul developed at length in Romans 7:7–25. In that passage sin is personified and pictured as using the commandments of the law, which are in themselves good, to bring about the destruction of man. But "Christ is the end of the law" for the believer (Rom. 10:4). His redemption frees us from its power to destroy. The resurrection will be the time of complete victory.

Verse 57: a song in Paul's own words, repeating the substance of the Old Testament passages in Christian language.

But thanks be to God: the ultimate source of victory.

Who gives us the victory: present tense. Full victory is yet to come, but the victory is already being given. Conversion and the overcoming of temptation are parts of that final victory.

Through our Lord Jesus Christ: Jesus Christ is the agent through whom God gives the victory, and he is the Christian's Lord.

3. The Present Implications of the Hope of the Resurrection (15:58)

This final verse of the chapter contains Paul's exhortation to the Corinthians in the light of their hope.

Therefore: in the light of this hope. The word refers primarily to the song of victory, but includes all that leads up to it.

My beloved brethren: a full and affectionate appeal which Paul used only here and in Philippians 4:1. Seemingly, his final burst of song aroused a flood of affection for the Corinthians, who would share his victory.

Be steadfast, immovable: two words of the same meaning, both figures of speech. *Be* is really "become" in the Greek and may suggest that they had not always been so, but now must become so. The thought is primarily that of doctrinal stability. The Corinthians needed to strive to be so securely tied to the gospel that no false teaching would move them from their moorings.

Always abounding in the work of the Lord: turns to their practice. Perhaps there is a suggestion that they should cease their speculation and turn to the work that they had to do.

Knowing that in the Lord your labor is not in vain: i.e., empty of results. The assurance of success in the ministry depends, now as then, on being in the sphere of Christ's lordship. *In the Lord* means "in the Christian sphere," as it does in 7:39.

IX. CONCLUSION OF THE LETTER (16:1–24)

Paul concluded the letter to the Corinthians with a series of personal notes (vss. 5–18), preceded by instructions about the collection for the poor in Jerusalem (vss. 1–2) and his plans for the administration of the joint gift (vss. 3–4), and followed by various greetings (vss. 19–20), and the final malediction and benediction (vss. 21–24).

1. Instructions Concerning the Collection for the Poor (16:1–4)

It was the custom for Jews of the dispersion to send gifts to their poorer brethren in Judea (Edwards). This custom was transferred to the practice of Christian brotherhood. Paul and Barnabas had brought the gifts from Antioch (Acts 11:30). Paul concluded his record of the Jerusalem Council with the words: "only they would have us remember the poor, which very thing I was eager to do" (Gal. 2:10). Thus, caring for the poor was considered a Christian duty, and caring for the poor in Jerusalem was one of the side issues in Paul's missionary journeys. The poverty of the Jerusalem Christians stemmed from two causes: the poverty of the land in general and the large number of widows who resided there (cf. Acts 6:1).

(1) Systematic collection (16:1–2)

The first part of the instructions concerned the gathering of the contribution from the Corinthian congregation.

Verse 1: Now concerning: introduces the discussion abruptly with a phrase which indicates a previous question from the church.[1] They had probably included a question about this matter in their letter to him.

The contribution: regular word for the collection of money. The same Greek word is found in papyrus documents which speak of a collection of money from members for club purposes (Parry).

For the saints: i.e., the people of God. Nothing is said as to their identity, but verse 3 makes it clear that they were the Jerusalem Christians.

As I directed the churches of Galatia: mentioned because they knew of his arguments. The project had probably begun as Paul visited these churches on his way to Ephesus. He had sent word to the Corinthians

---

[1] Barrett suggests that the Corinthians had heard of the offering and had asked what part they should take in it.

about the matter. If this is not the case, he wanted the Corinthians to know that the instructions were common to all the churches. *Directed,* in the Greek, suggests detailed arrangements.

So you also are to do: suggests a note of confidence that they would do it.

Verse 2: describes the arrangements.

On the first day of every week: Sunday. This is the first suggestion that Christians used this day as their time of meeting. It was natural that they should do so in commemoration of the resurrection of Christ. The Jewish sabbath commemorated the completed creation; the Christian day of worship and work commemorated the completed redemption. However, it is wrong to think of Sunday as the Christian sabbath, since the nature of the day changed when the nature of the religion changed.

Each of you: means that each member of the congregation was to share in the collection.

Is to put something aside: probably meant that each member was to do this himself, not that it was to be brought to a common fund. It was to be done on the day dedicated to Christ as a real act of worship.

And store it up: present participle in the Greek, thus, "continuing to treasure it." The sum was to be increased each week.

As he may prosper: or be prospered. The form of the Greek word is uncertain. It may be passive or active, present or perfect, indicative or subjunctive. The word has two components, one meaning "well," the other, "journey." The idea was originally of a prosperous journey, but prosperity in general came to be the dominant use. Proportionate giving is certainly enjoined, but the exact proportion is not mentioned. It is possible, even probable, that the Jewish custom of tithing had carried over into Christian practice.

So that contributions need not be made when I come: Since each one, if he followed this arrangement, would have his portion stored up and ready, there would be no need for further collections.

(2) Paul's plans for its administration (16:3–4)

The plan for delivering the gift was simple; yet it provided for security against the accusation of misappropriation.

Verse 3: And when I arrive: Paul expected to come soon to Corinth (vs. 5).

I will send those whom you accredit by letter to carry your gift to Jerusalem: The church would choose the messengers and give Paul a written statement of that fact.

Verse 4: If it seems advisable: rather, "important." Paul did not imagine it would, but it might. *Advisable* comes from the Greek word meaning "worthy." In this connection it would mean "worthwhile" or "important."

That I should go also, they will accompany me: Paul still refused to become wholly responsible for delivering the gift.

2. Paul's Personal Plans (16:5–9)

Verse 5: I will visit you after passing through Macedonia: suggests for the first time that he was about to depart from Ephesus. The proposed itinerary would naturally cover a period of several months, since the distance was considerable and he wished to confirm the Macedonian churches in their faith.

For I intend to pass through Macedonia: states his purpose not to come directly to Corinth.

Verse 6: Paul had the intention of spending some time at Corinth, perhaps even spending the winter there. This would suggest that the letter was written in the early spring, and that he thought he had time before the winter months to pass through Macedonia and arrive at Corinth. He hoped that the Corinthians would speed him on his way when he left, which was a nice way of saying that he hoped they would pay his expenses to his next destination, wherever that might be.

Verse 7: Paul explained why he did not come first to Corinth. He did not want to make them a mere visit in passing, but wished to spend considerable time with them. Of course, his plans were always subject to the will of God; so he added, *if the Lord permits.*

Verse 8: Paul stated his intention to remain in Ephesus until Pentecost, which comes fifty days after the Jewish Passover Feast and our Easter, about the middle of June. This verse confirms a spring date for the writing of the letter.

Verse 9: states the reason why he lingered at Ephesus.

For a wide door for effective work has opened to me: a metaphor for a new opportunity. Many suggestions have been given for the meaning of this expression, but the most natural one is to assume that something had happened which promised new success in the preaching of the gospel.

And: We would expect "but."

There are many adversaries: Paul saw the presence of the many adversaries as a challenge to remain longer. Among his adversaries were the men who threatened his life, including probably both Jews and pagans.

3. Instructions Concerning Timothy (16:10–11)

Seemingly Paul had already sent Timothy to Corinth on some mission. We have a record of this mission in Acts: "Now after these events Paul resolved in the Spirit to pass through Macedonia and Achaia and go to Jerusalem, saying, 'After I have been there, I must also see Rome.' And having sent into Macedonia two of his helpers, Timothy and Erastus, he himself stayed in Asia for a while" (Acts 19:21–22). Since Paul wrote the Roman letter from Corinth and sent greetings from "Erastus, the city treasurer" (Rom. 16:23), it is probable that he was Timothy's companion.

Verse 10: When Timothy comes: supposes that he had not yet arrived. *When* is really the Greek for "if." Paul did not doubt that he would come, but he did not know whether Timothy would arrive ahead of his letter.

See that you put him at ease among you: literally, "See to it that he is without fear among you." The RSV translation probably catches the meaning of the rather strange word, "without fear." Why Timothy would be "in fear" at Corinth is a mystery. Perhaps the suggestion that Timothy was naturally a timid man might account for the word, though this suggestion is based on language which does not support the idea very strongly. Perhaps his youthfulness was in the mind of Paul.

For he is doing the work of the Lord, as I am: gives the reason why the Corinthians should put Timothy at ease. If they hindered his work, they would hinder the work of the Lord in which he was engaged.

Verse 11: Let no one despise him: treat him as if he were of no account. The tendency to do this might arise from their disappointment that Paul himself had not come.

Speed him on his way in peace: with the blessing of the church.

For I am expecting him with the brethren: states why the church should speed him on the way with peace. Seemingly, Paul planned to wait for Timothy's return before he set forth on his own journey.

4. Information about the Plans of Apollos (16:12)

Perhaps the Corinthians had asked that Apollos visit them.

As for our brother Apollos: intimates that Apollos was with Paul at this time.

I strongly urged him to visit you with the other brethren: shows that Paul had no sense of jealousy for the gifted speaker who had also labored in Corinth.

But it was not at all his will to come now: God is not a part of the text, but is supplied by the translators. The *will* was that of Apollos, but it is probably true that it was subject to God's will. The insertion may be justified, but Apollos should not have been left out. *Not at all* means that Apollos met all of Paul's appeals with stronger reasons.

He will come when he has opportunity: Apollos may have felt that his presence at Corinth, in view of the dissension with which his name was associated, would be awkward at this time. *Opportunity* means "seasonable time."

5. Admonition to Watchfulness (16:13–14)

These short verses repeat common Christian admonitions.

Verse 13: Be watchful: present tense, meaning, "Be continually on guard."

Stand firm in your faith: against those who would deceive them.

Be courageous: have moral courage to stand up for what is right, even though it is unpopular.

Be strong: in the strength of the Spirit.

Verse 14: Let all that you do be done in love: the climax of Christian duty. Dissension, not love, was the characteristic of their common life. Paul wanted the trend reversed. For the meaning of love, see comments on chapter 13.

6. Instructions Concerning Various Leaders (16:15–18)

These instructions concern some of the Corinthians themselves: Stephanas, Fortunatus and Achaicus.

Verse 15: Now, brethren, you know that the household of Stephanas were the first converts in Achaia: The Greek sentence is rough grammatically, but the RSV translation probably catches the meaning. The reason for this special commendation is not clear, unless it is to suggest to the church that they should follow his example.

They have devoted themselves to the service of the saints: indicates that their service was voluntary. Paul had not appointed them; they had appointed themselves. *Service* is usually used for service to God, but the *service of the saints* was a way of serving God.

Verse 15: I urge you: not a command but an appeal.

To be subject to such men: follow their leadership.

And to every fellow worker and laborer: to everyone who lends a helping hand in the work of Christ. Perhaps Paul was thinking of leadership assumed by those who fancied themselves to be wise; he wanted to remind the Corinthians that leadership should be granted to those who were useful.

Verse 17: I rejoice at the coming of Stephanas and Fortunatus and Achaicus: three members of the Corinthian congregation who had visited Paul. Perhaps they were the source of much of his information.

Because they have made up for your absence: literally, "for your lack they have filled up." It is not certain that Paul intended "your lack" to mean his own deprivation of their company. This is possible and would express his affection for them and his joy in having some of them with him when he could not have all. On the other hand, he could have meant that, since the whole congregation could not come and lay their problems before him, these three had performed that function quite well. If this last is true—and it is perhaps more probable—these three had been official delegates from Corinth, bearing their letter to Paul and supplementing it with other information.

Verse 18: For they refreshed my spirit as well as yours: Their coming had showed Paul how anxious the church was to have his advice and thus refreshed him. He was sure that their return would accomplish the same for the Corinthians.

Give recognition to such men: Their service to the church, at some personal sacrifice, no doubt, should be rewarded by adequate recognition.

7. Various Greetings (16:19–20)

These two verses contain various greetings from Christians who were with Paul in Ephesus.

Verse 19: The churches of Asia: indicates that more than one church had been founded in Asia. Paul's work at Ephesus had extended to other cities.

Aquila and Prisca: had been tentmakers in Corinth and with whom Paul had dwelt while there.

Together with the church in their house: reflects a custom in those days of Christians meeting in house-congregations. Possibly these congregations were a part of the larger congregation in the city. Since there was no central meeting place, the Christians would, no doubt, meet in smaller groups most of the time.

Verse 20: All the brethren: inclusive of those not before mentioned.

Greet one another with a holy kiss: Peter called it "the kiss of love" (1 Pet. 5:14). The kiss was the usual way of greeting friends and loved ones. The thought is not so much that they should kiss each other, but that one of them should kiss the rest in the name of Paul to express his affection for them.

8. Final Malediction and Benediction (16:21–24)

Verse 21: Paul's usual formal way of closing a letter. He dictated the body of it to someone else and then added a subscript in his own hand. This verse is the beginning of that subscript and is quite formal: *I, Paul, write this greeting with my own hand.*

Verse 22: The first part of the verse is a malediction, the second part a Christian prayer for the coming of Christ. The malediction is quite unusual in Paul's letters, the only parallel being Galatians 1:8–9.

If any one has no love for the Lord: probably refers to those who did not know God, but sought to be leaders in the church anyway. *Love* is not the higher word for Christian love, but the lower word which merely means "affection." [1] The thought is that a man's life must find its center in the Lord or it is not a Christian life.

Let him be accursed: set aside for the Lord to curse, and treated as an unbeliever. This reveals that the person or persons which Paul had in mind were professing members of the congregation at Corinth. Such a malediction would be unnecessary for pagans in general since they were already regarded as under the curse of God.

Our Lord, come!: a Christian prayer for the return of Christ.[2] The King James Version transliterated these two words and joined them together: "Anathema Maranatha." "Anathema" is the transliteration of the word which is properly translated, "Let him be accursed." This was a curious combination in the older translation but probably reflects a misunderstanding of the meaning of the second word. "Maranatha" has a vocal similarity to the word (Shammatha) which expresses the highest form of Jewish excommunication. However, it is really two words: *Maran atha.* Both are Aramaic terms. The first means, "Our Lord." the second means, "Come." The RSV translation is thus correct. It is to be doubted that the words were added to the curse as a kind of prayer for the Lord to come and execute it. Even less fitting in this context is the idea that these words were spoken at the beginning of the Lord's Supper.

Verse 23: a common formula of blessing which Paul often used: *The grace of the Lord Jesus be with you.* The only departure from his customary benediction is the omission of "Christ." However, this omission is probably accidental rather than purposeful.

Verse 24: furnishes a final tender touch to the farewell greetings. Paul asked that his love should be their constant companion in their union with Christ Jesus.

---

[1] Barrett suggests that it means "the adoration and religious consecration of the believer to God."

[2] C. F. D. Moule argues, but not convincingly, that this was a prayer for the immediate, unseen presence of the Lord ("A Reconsideration of the Context of Maranatha," *New Testament Studies,* Vol. 8, pp. 307–310).

2 Corinthians

INTRODUCTION

2 Corinthians

The authorship of 2 Corinthians is not in doubt. The unity is. In some ways 2 Corinthians is the most Pauline of all of Paul's epistles. Furthermore, the elusive (from the standpoint of the modern reader) references to movements, people, and events is just what one would expect from an authentic letter. No forger would write of these matters so artlessly. Therefore, we do not need to spend time arguing the case for Pauline authorship; it may be assumed.

THE UNITY OF THE EPISTLE

Modern scholars are not nearly so skeptical concerning the unity of the epistle as older scholars were. However, the question of unity cannot be dismissed without discussion. This is true in spite of the fact that there is no ancient manuscript of the letter which does not contain it as it is in our modern translations—as one letter. There is no *external* reason for doubting the unity of the epistle, but there are *internal* reasons for doubt.

The epistle naturally divides itself into three distinct parts. Part one (1:1—7:16) contains Paul's explanation of his failure to visit the Corinthians as he had promised. Even here an extended discussion of the Christian ministry (2:14—6:10) seems to interrupt the explanation. Furthermore, a smaller section (6:14—7:1) seems to contain an abrupt change of subject, not conforming to the immediate context. Part two (8:1—9:15) contains a discussion of the collection for the poor. Again, the two chapters seem to be unrelated. Part three (10:1—13:14) contains what seemed to be an attack on his enemies which is in complete contrast to the report of Titus that all was well at Corinth (cf. 7:5–16).

The seeming internal inconsistencies of the letter have led many scholars to suppose that the epistle is a collection of fragments of several epistles of Paul to the church at Corinth. We know that Paul had written an epistle to the Corinthians before he wrote our 1 Corinthians (cf. 1 Cor. 5:9). Some have supposed that 2 Corinthians 6:14—7:1 is a fragment of that epistle. We know that he wrote a painful epistle after he wrote 1 Corinthians and before he wrote 2 Corinthians (cf. 2 Cor. 2:3–4). Many have supposed that this "painful letter" is actually chapters 10–13 of this letter. However, in view of the fact that the letter has always existed as a unity (so far as we have known the letter), we must seek to explain these apparent inconsistencies and contrasts without resorting to a theory of division. If these can be explained, we may suppose that the letter as we have it is in the same form in which it was originally composed by Paul.

Let us deal with the easiest problem first—the relationship between chapters 8 and 9. 2 Corinthians 9:1–2a reads: "Now it is superfluous for me to write to you about the offering for the saints, for I know your readiness." Yet, if the letter was written as it stands, Paul had just finished writing a full chapter encouraging them to be liberal in their giving (cf. 8:1–24). This apparent inconsistency is really an evidence of Paul's pastoral skill. Christians may sometimes feel driven to do something and rebel against it for that very reason. A wise pastor persuades. One way he does this is by leading his congregation to feel that he has confidence in their *readiness* to do the will of God. Seen in this light, there is no real inconsistency between the admonitions of chapter 8 and the expression of confidence which begins chapter 9. As a matter of fact, the rest of chapter 9 is further encouragement to liberality and is quite consistent with the tone of chapter 8. The unity of the situation presupposed in these two chapters forbids any separation.

The problem of the small paragraph admonishing the Corinthians not to be "mismated with unbelievers" (6:14—7:1) is more acute. There is no doubt that there is an abrupt break of thought in the context. First, there is a plea for the Corinthians to open their hearts to Paul (6:11–13). The same thought is continued in 7:2–4. An admonition against fellowship with unbelievers seems definitely out of place. However, the solution offered by some that this is a fragment of the letter mentioned in 1 Corinthians 5:9–13 is worse than no solution at all. The Corinthians had understood Paul to mean (in the letter mentioned in 1 Cor. 5:9) that they should not associate with "the immoral of this world." Paul denied that this was the meaning of the letter to which he referred, saying, "I wrote to you not to associate with any one who bears the name of brother if he is guilty of immorality" (1 Cor. 5:11). This paragraph (2 Cor. 6:14—7:1) manifestly deals with fellowship with unbelievers. It could not, by any stretch of the imagination, be interpreted to mean that one should not associate with immoral Christians.

What then is the solution? It is probably found in the fact that Paul was dictating this letter and some thought caused him to digress for a moment to an unrelated problem. Speakers often do this. The evidence of the correctness of this solution is that when Paul resumed his thought, he repeated the substance of the last words of the sentence spoken just before he broke off—"widen your hearts also" (6:13); "open your hearts to us" (7:2). There is a real break in Paul's thought at this point, but it is the kind of break which is natural when a letter is dictated rather than written. There is no reason, therefore, to assume that this paragraph is a fragment of another, lost letter to the Corinthians.

The problems connected with chapters 10–13 are the most acute. The contrast in tone between the two sections of the letter is apparent. 2 Corinthians 7:6–7 reads: "But God, who comforts the downcast, com-

forted us by the coming of Titus, and not only by his coming but also
by the comfort with which he was comforted in you, as he told us of
your longing, your mourning, your zeal for me, so that I rejoiced still
more." 2 Corinthians 13:2 reads: "I warned those who sinned before
and all the others, and I warn them now while absent, as I did when
present on my second visit, that if I come again I will not spare them."
At first glance it seems impossible that these two passages could be
written by the same man to the same people on the same occasion. Many
scholars, including Alfred Plummer,[1] find it impossible to believe that they
were.[2] Plummer gives the most extended and cogent arguments for
believing that the four chapters in question were a major portion of the
"painful letter" and were written before the rest of this epistle. His
arguments may be summarized as follows: (1) The tone of the letter
changes abruptly at 10:1. (2) Logical inconsistencies exist between language in chapters 1–7 and chapters 10–13 (cf. 7:11 and 11:3 for instance). (3) There are passages in chapters 1–9 which seem to refer to
things mentioned in chapters 10–13 (cf. 10:6 and 2:9 for instance).
(4) The statement of Paul that he hoped to preach the gospel "in lands
beyond you" (10:16) is inconsistent if written from Macedonia.

Cogent as Plummer's arguments are, they are not convincing.[3] Similar
inconsistencies can be found in 1 Corinthians, the unity of which has
never been doubted. For instance Paul's statement, "I commend you
because you remember me in everything and maintain the traditions
even as I have delivered them to you" (1 Cor. 11:2) is difficult to
reconcile with the rest of the letter in which Paul found so much to
criticize in the behavior of the Corinthians (see commentary on the
passage).

It is possible to explain all the arguments against the unity of 2
Corinthians by supposing that there was a recalcitrant minority in Corinth
which had not been reconciled to Paul. Against this minority Paul found
it necessary to write as he did. Our commentary on these chapters will
make this clear. Thus it may be concluded that this letter never existed
in any form other than that in which it is found in our versions today.

PAUL AND THE CORINTHIANS

The exact sequence of visits, emissaries, and epistles to the Corinthians
is difficult to reconstruct. The main outline of Paul's relations with the
Corinthian congregation is clear, but some of the details are doubtful.

---

[1] Alfred Plummer, *A Critical and Exegetical Commentary on the Second Epistle
of St. Paul to the Corinthians,* Edinburgh: T. & T. Clark, © 1915. Hereafter referred
to by the last name of the author, Plummer.

[2] Bornkamm agrees substantially with Plummer and adds evidence from the
early church fathers, primarily from their silence about the letter. (G. Bornkamm,
"The History of the Origin of the so-called Second Letter to the Corinthians," *New
Testament Studies,* Vol. 8, pp. 258–264.)

[3] The integrity of the epistle is defended by W. H. Bates ("The Integrity of 2
Corinthians," *New Testament Studies,* Vol. 12, pp. 56–69) and by P. E. Hughes
(*Paul's Second Epistle to the Corinthians* [Grand Rapids, Mich.: Wm. B. Eerdman's
Publishing Co., 1962]; hereafter referred to as Hughes).

The following sequence seems to do justice to the references in the two letters.

1. Paul visited Corinth and founded the church there during his second missionary journey (cf. Acts 18:1–18; 1 Cor. 3:10).

2. He wrote them a letter warning them not to associate with immoral Christians (1 Cor. 5:9–13).

3. He received communications from the Corinthians during his stay at Ephesus: by oral report from Chloe's people (1 Cor. 1:11) and by letter from the church raising various questions (1 Cor. 7:1).

4. He wrote a letter to the Corinthians answering their questions and seeking to deal with the problems of the church as he knew them—our 1 Corinthians (2 Cor. 4:14; 9:15; 14:37).

5. Meanwhile, he had sent Timothy as an emissary to the congregation (1 Cor. 4:17), but was not sure whether Timothy would arrive before his letter (1 Cor. 16:10). However, since Timothy is not mentioned in 2 Corinthians, it is possible that he never arrived at Corinth. If he did, his visit did not influence the relations of Paul with the church.

6. At this stage the sequence of events becomes uncertain. Paul mentioned a letter which he wrote "out of much affliction and anguish of heart and with many tears" (2 Cor. 2:4). He mentioned a report he had received from Titus (2 Cor. 7:6). He spoke of his reluctance to make another painful visit to them (2 Cor. 2:1) and spoke of his forthcoming visit to them as his third visit (2 Cor. 12:14; 13:1). The most probable sequence of events is as follows: (1) Paul learned, possibly by the return of Timothy, that his letter (our 1 Corinthians) had not settled the problems in Corinth and that a faction of the church had turned against him. (2) He made a hurried visit to them which was painful in the extreme and which failed to solve the problems. (3) Returning to Ephesus, he wrote the "painful" letter and sent it with Titus to attempt a solution to the various problems in Corinth and to express his love (2 Cor. 2:4). (Note: it is very improbable that this reference is to the epistle which we know as 1 Corinthians.) Then he went to Troas to await his report. (4) Worried over the outcome, he left Troas and made his way to Macedonia, expecting to go on immediately to Corinth. (5) At Macedonia he met Titus with good news from the church; he determined to stay on at Macedonia for the time being and wrote 2 Corinthians (2 Cor. 13:10).

If this is the true sequence of events, this epistle was written to explain his delay in coming to Corinth as he had promised to do, and to prepare them for his third visit.

THE OPPONENTS OF PAUL IN CORINTH

Our commentary on the various passages involved will make the situation in Corinth clear, but it seems profitable to pause at the beginning for a brief look at the opponents of Paul at Corinth. In writing 1 Corinthians, Paul intimated that there were teachers at Corinth who were puffed up and did not recognize his authority (cf. 1 Cor. 3:18–23). By the time 2 Corinthians was written, these teachers or others had become the avowed enemies of Paul and sought to destroy his influence among the Corinthians. Paul called them the ministers of Satan (11:14–15), insisted that they were mere peddlers of the word of God (2:17), and indicted them as "false apostles, deceitful workmen, disguising themselves as apostles of Christ" (11:13). Seemingly they preached a different gospel than Paul did, for he remonstrated with the Corinthians by saying, "For if some one comes and preaches another Jesus than the one we preached, or if you receive a different spirit from the one you received, or if you accept a different gospel from the one you accepted, you submit to it readily enough" (11:4).

Paul's opponents in Corinth seem to have made various accusations against him, most of which we must infer from statements that Paul made about himself. They accused him of not knowing his own mind (1:17–18), of lording it over his converts (10:8), of writing like a lion while being weak when present with them (10:10), and of being a braggart (3:1).

Who were these opponents? The best guess is that they were Judaizers like those who had caused so much trouble in the churches of Galatia. These teachers insisted on keeping the law of Moses to an extent which threatened the existence of the gospel itself. They insisted that Gentile converts be circumcised and obey the various regulations of the law which Paul thought to have been superseded by the gospel of Jesus Christ. No doubt their attack on Paul at Corinth was due to the firmness with which the Corinthians held to the gospel. Not being able to persuade the Corinthians, they attacked the preacher of the true gospel in an effort to undermine his influence. Even after the main body of Christians had been reconciled to Paul, they remained adamant in their opposition. This explains the tone of the last four chapters of this epistle.

PLACE AND DATE

From internal evidence it can be ascertained that the letter was written from Macedonia (2:13; 7:5; 8:1; 9:2–4). Since Philippi was one of the chief cities and we know Paul had a special love for that church, we may assume that it was written from there. Some ancient manuscripts which have subscriptions agree with this assumption.

The date must probably be placed within a year of the writing of 1 Corinthians. Since the exact year of that letter is uncertain, we cannot be more definite about this letter. We would be inclined to accept the date of A.D. 56 for 1 Corinthians, and either late in the same year or early in the following year appears to be the most probable date for 2 Corinthians.

OUTLINE

2 Corinthians

I. INTRODUCTION (1:1–11)

   1. Salutation and Greetings (1:1–2)
   2. Paul's Hymn of Thanksgiving (1:3–7)
   3. Paul's Deadly Peril and Deliverance (1:8–11)

II. PAUL'S EXPLANATION OF HIS CHANGE OF PLANS (1:12—7:16)

   1. Reason for Paul's Change of Plans (1:12—2:13)
      (1) He insisted that he always acted sincerely (1:12–14)
      (2) He insisted that his plans were always subject to the will of God (1:15–22)
      (3) He wished to spare them another painful visit (1:23—2:4)
      (4) He had admonished them to forgive the sinful brother for their own sake (2:5–11)
      (5) His great concern for them had forced him to leave Troas before he had meant to (2:12–13)
   2. Paul's Relation with the Corinthians a Discharge of His God-given Commission (2:14—6:10)
      (1) Paul's sufficiency, as well as his commission, came from God (2:14—3:6)
      (2) Paul's ministry was superior to that of Moses in the same way that the new covenant is superior to the old (3:7–18)
      (3) Paul had been saved from despair by the surpassing grace of God (4:1–18)
      (4) Paul's ministry was characterized by hope, faith, and love (5:1–21)
      (5) Paul made a plea not to accept the grace of God in vain (6:1–10)
   3. Paul's Various Pleas and Warnings (6:11—7:4)
      (1) A plea to open their hearts to him (6:11–13)
      (2) A warning not to be mismated with unbelievers (6:14—7:1)
      (3) A continuation of the plea to open their hearts (7:2–4)
   4. Paul's Rejoicing at the Report of Titus (7:5–16)

III. ENCOURAGEMENTS TO LIBERALITY IN THEIR GIFTS FOR THE POOR (8:1—9:15)

1. Encouragement by the Example of the Macedonians (8:1–7)
2. Encouragement by the Example of Christ (8:8–15)
3. Encouragement by Sharing His Plans for the Offering (8:16–24)
4. Encouragement by His Boast of Them (9:1–5)
5. Encouragement by Giving Reasons for Liberality (9:6–15)
    (1) Their own enrichment depended on their liberality (9:6–11)
    (2) Their liberality would glorify God (9:12–15)

IV. A PLEA TO THE CHURCH IN THE LIGHT OF THE OPPOSITION OF SOME (10:1—13:10)

1. An Entreaty to Hold Fast to the Gospel Paul Had Preached (10:1–18)
    (1) The reason for the entreaty—Paul did not wish to be severe with all (10:1–6)
    (2) The basis of the entreaty—Paul's ministry had been for the purpose of building up the church (10:7–12)
    (3) The purpose of the entreaty—Paul hoped that his field of labor would be greatly increased (10:13–18)
2. An Entreaty to Avoid Being Led Astray by False Apostles (11:1—12:13)
    (1) The reason for the entreaty—Paul feared they would be led astray (11:1–6)
    (2) The basis of the entreaty—Paul's credentials of apostleship were superior to those of false apostles (11:7—12:10)
    (3) The necessity of the entreaty—the church failed to accept his apostleship (12:11–13)
3. An Entreaty to Be Prepared for his Third Visit (12:14—13:10)
    (1) The basis of his entreaty—his dealings with them had always been in love (12:14–18)
    (2) The reason for the entreaty—he intended to deal harshly with the unrepentant (12:19—13:4)
    (3) The purpose of the entreaty—Paul hoped they would repent and escape the necessity of harsh severity (13:5–10)

V. CONCLUSION (13:11–14)

1. Final Appeal (13:11)
2. Salutations (13:12–13)
3. Benediction (13:14)

COMMENTARY

2 Corinthians

I. INTRODUCTION (1:1–11)

The introduction to this epistle is longer than in most of Paul's letters. Not only does it include his usual salutations and greetings (1:1–2), but it also contains a hymn of thanksgiving (1:3–7) and an account of a recent peril which Paul had experienced and his deliverance by the hand of God (1:8–11).

1. Salutation and Greetings (1:1–2)

The salutation and greetings are very similar to the beginning of 1 Corinthians.

Verse 1: Paul: identifies the author of the epistle. There is no reason to doubt the authenticity of this letter. Of all the epistles in the New Testament which are ascribed to Paul, these two letters to the Corinthians are least debated in regard to authorship.

An apostle: a commissioned messenger. *Apostle* is used in the New Testament to refer to a number of disciples other than the original twelve. Since the apostle was a commissioned messenger, he had the responsibility to speak for his principal, and his words were to be accepted as authoritative pronouncements of that principal. Paul began the following letters with an emphasis upon his apostleship: 1 and 2 Corinthians, Galatians, Ephesians, Colossians, and 1 and 2 Timothy. Though apostleship is mentioned at the beginning of Romans and Titus, it is appended as a secondary matter. It would seem that Paul insisted upon his apostleship only in those cases where he had to deal with internal problems in the churches and where his right to speak might be challenged.

Of Christ Jesus: identifies Paul's principal. He spoke for Christ and his words were to be accepted as from Christ.

By the will of God: stresses the source of Paul's appointment. Since Paul did not meet the normal requirements for an apostle (cf. Acts 1:21–22), he had to point to an act of God's will as the source of his right to call himself an apostle. He gave a fuller explanation of the meaning of this term in Galatians 1:1–12. Here he mentioned it as if it were well known to his readers. His appointment *by the will of God* is mentioned also in Galatians, Ephesians, Colossians, and 2 Timothy, as well as in both letters to the Corinthians.

And Timothy: associated with Paul in the greetings but not in the authorship of the letter. Timothy has the same relation to Paul in his addresses to the Philippians, Colossians, 1 and 2 Thessalonians, and Philemon.

Our brother: the title which belonged to Timothy. The use of the title accomplished two things: it identified Timothy with the Corinthians as a Christian, and it denied the apostleship of Timothy.

To the church of God which is at Corinth: This expression identifies the primary readers of the epistle as the congregation of Christians (i.e., the church) which belonged to God and which was located in the city of Corinth. Paul was anxious that the congregation remember that it belonged to God, that he was its founder and ruler. They were not free to make whatever decisions they thought best; they were required to submit their decisions to his will. *Church* refers to the local congregation of Christians. For a discussion of the city of Corinth, see the introduction to 1 Corinthians.

With all the saints who are in the whole of Achaia: the secondary readers of the epistle.[1] They were not associated with the Corinthians in the trouble that Paul had had with that congregation, but the material in the letter would be of benefit to them, as it is to modern Christians. They were called *saints*, the generic term for the people of God—i.e., the Christians. The term *saints* is generally used only in the plural and thus means approximately the same thing as our modern term "the universal church." *Achaia* was the Roman province of which Corinth was the capital. There were other churches in the province, but the letter was not sent to the churches as such. This mention of other Christians probably indicates a custom which arose early, that of churches sharing with others the religious writings which they possessed. Later in Christian history, the various epistles and writings were copied and circulated in blocks of material and finally in the New Testament as we have it today.

Verse 2: Grace to you: looks back from the gift to the giver. This was the usual Greek salutation, but Paul Christianized it. *Grace* means the unmerited favor of God.

Peace: was the Jewish salutation, but it was also Christianized. Paul took the common greetings of the day and gave them new meaning in the Christian vocabulary. *Peace* means wholeness of life, being far more meaningful than mere serenity of spirit.

From God our Father and the Lord Jesus Christ: links the Father and Son as coequal givers of grace and peace. The single preposition, *from,* indicates that Paul thought of Jesus Christ as equal to God. *Father* is the distinctive Christian name for God. *Lord* is the Christian title for Jesus Christ. In modern language *Lord* tends to become a lifeless term. In New Testament times it was a dynamic term, representing the position, dignity, and authority which Christ had won in the hearts of believers.[2] Of course, Paul was not a speculative theologian. His conception of God the father

---

[1] R. C. H. Lenski, *The Interpretation of St. Paul's First and Second Epistle to the Corinthians* (Columbus, Ohio: Wartburg Press, 1946). Referred to by the last name of the author, Lenski.

[2] Strachan gives a very good discussion of the word. (R. H. Strachan, *The Second Epistle of Paul to the Corinthians* [New York and London: Harper and Brothers Publishers, n.d.]. Hereafter referred to by the last name of the author, Strachan.)

and of Jesus Christ arose from a real experience of redemption through Jesus Christ.

2. Paul's Hymn of Thanksgiving (1:3–7)

This is not a hymn in the formal sense of the word, but it is in the sense that it contains praise for God. It probably is related to Paul's deliverance from the deadly peril (vss. 8–11), but it seems better to treat it separately.

Verse 3: Paul's pronouncement of a blessing on God.

Blessed be: introduces an ejaculation of praise. *Be* is not in the Greek, *blessed* standing alone. *Blessed* comes from a compound Greek word, one element meaning "to speak" and the other, "well." Thus it means "to speak well of." The word occurs eight times in the New Testament and is always used of God. Another form of the same Greek word is used when speaking of the blessedness which men receive.

The God and Father of our Lord Jesus Christ: an abbreviated statement of Paul's theology. His thought of God did not begin with nature or with speculation. It began with Jesus Christ. The God whom Paul recognized and worshiped was the God who revealed himself in Jesus Christ and who was acknowledged by him to be his Father. Of course, Paul recognized God as the creator of the world, but his worship was defined by his religious experience. God is also the Father of Christians, but his fatherhood of Christians is derived from their relation to Christ. It is not based upon creation but upon redemption.

The Father of mercies: the Father who shows mercy. *Mercies* is in the idiomatic plural, but can probably be rendered by our singular "mercy" or "compassion." The expression reflects the thought of Ps. 103:13, "As a father pities his children, so the Lord pities those who fear him." God is the fountainhead from which all mercies flow, but it was the particular mercy of God by which Paul came to know Christ that he had in mind.

And God of all comfort: the source of every kind of comfort. *Comfort,* either in the verb or the noun form, is used ten times in this paragraph. It is a favorite word of Paul, being used seventy-four times in his epistles, twenty-nine times in this epistle. The Greek word is a compound word composed of two elements, one meaning "to call" and the other, "alongside of." Thus, to be comforted in the New Testament sense is to experience the enabling presence of God. The English word "comfort" has the same meaning in its original connotation, being made up of two elements, *co* (together with) and *fort* (strength). In modern speech "comfort" has come to mean ease and does not adequately translate the Greek word. The meaning of the Greek word is akin to the strongest meaning of the English "encouragement"—i.e., "to give courage, hope, or confidence to; embolden, hearten." Perhaps "encouragement" would be a better translation. Comfort is a special attribute of God. Jesus called himself a comforter and promised to ask the Father to send another comforter like him when he departed—i.e., the Holy Spirit (John 14:16). No doubt, Paul's recent experience, in which he had despaired of his life and had been delivered by God, led him to a new realization that God was the God of every kind of encouragement.

Verse 4: an expansion of the thought that God is the God of all comfort. God's encouragement not only heartens the oppressed Christian; it also qualifies the recipient to be a dispenser of comfort.

Who comforts: present tense. The thought is of the continuous act of God. He comforts his children, not once or twice, but perpetually, without a break.

Us: includes all Christians. The word does not need to be limited to Paul and Timothy, but extends to all men who, like them, suffer affliction in the service of God.

In all our affliction: God's comfort is not limited to particular types of affliction but is active on all occasions. *Affliction* comes from a word which refers to the pressing of grapes to extract the juice. Paul defined some of his afflictions in this letter as being: "weaknesses, insults, hardships, persecutions, and calamities" (12:10). In comparison to others, he said that he had "far greater labors, far more imprisonments, with countless beatings, and often near death" (11:23). *In* means "upon the occasion of."

So that we may be able to comfort those who are in any affliction: comfort is not to stop with the recipient. Having received comfort in his own afflictions, he is able to encourage others (Christians) on the occasion of their sufferings.

With the comfort with which we ourselves are comforted by God: The encouragement to be dispensed comes from God. The Christian is not a psychologist pointing to human solutions of man's problems, but a witness pointing to divine solutions.

Verse 5: The translation of this verse is questionable, but may be correct. The only other place in the New Testament where the afflictions of Christians are called "Christ's sufferings" is 1 Peter 4:13. In other passages the expression always refers to the cross of Christ and his own suffering.

For as we share abundantly: literally, "just as [they] overflow with reference to us." Whether RSV is correct or not depends on the meaning given to the next expression.

Christ's sufferings: This expression has been given several interpretations by commentators. (1) It means the sufferings which the Christian endures because of his identification with Christ (cf. 1 Pet. 4:13). (2) It means the sufferings which the glorified Christ suffers when Christians suffer. (3) It means the sufferings of the Messiah on the cross, and they abound to us in the sense that we share in the benefits of the cross. In favor of (3) is the fact that the Greek word for *sufferings* (pathēmata) is used, with only a few exceptions, in the New Testament for the death of Christ on the cross. In favor of (1) is the context in which Paul had been speaking of his own afflictions (using another Greek word). The context must be the deciding factor in this instance. Thus *Christ's sufferings* are the sufferings of Christians, but only those which come to them as a result of their identification with Christ. Paul believed that Christian discipleship implied the willingness, even the necessity, of a partnership in the sufferings of Christ. Jesus himself had prophesied that this would be true: "Remember the word that I said to you, 'A servant is not greater than his master.' If they persecuted me, they will persecute you" (John 15:20).

So: introduces the second part of the comparison.

Through Christ: as the center of the Christian's life. Apart from him, suffering leads to despair. Through his agency sufferings lead to encouragement.[1]

We share abundantly in comfort too: literally, "our encouragement overflows also." The thought is that the Christian's sufferings are matched, and more, by the comfort which overflows to him through Christ.

Verse 6: relates the sufferings and comfort of Paul to the spiritual welfare of the Corinthians.

If we are afflicted: a form of condition which assumes the truth of the statement. Paul was afflicted, constantly so.

It is for your comfort and salvation: His afflictions were suffered in the course of bringing them the gospel. Paul did not mean that his afflictions were redemptive in quality. They came to him in the course of his ministry. The ministry, in turn, was aimed at bringing the Corinthians the gospel from which they received comfort and salvation.

And if we are comforted: as we are. *We* is editorial, meaning "I."

It is for your comfort: God encouraged Paul so that he might in turn encourage the Corinthians. The encouragement which the teacher received overflowed to them.

Which you experience: rather, "the being made to work." The Greek participle is probably passive. The comfort of the Corinthians did not work of itself; it must be made to work by the one who bestowed it—God. Some commentators take the participle as middle (the form is the same in Greek). If this is true, the thought is that the comfort makes itself felt. However, it would seem that the passive fits the context better. Paul had already said that God is the source of all comfort.

When you patiently endure: rather, "in the sphere of endurance." "Endurance" means steadfastness without cowardly shrinking. Lenski points out that the Corinthians were assumed to be in the realm of endurance already, and the comfort was made to work for the purpose of increasing it. This seems to be the thought. When the Corinthians suffered and endured, they would be encouraged further to continue their steadfastness.

The same sufferings that we suffer: not identical with Christ's sufferings but are the same kind. Had the Corinthians already suffered persecution? If so, there is no hint of it in these letters, unless 1 Corinthians 10:13 indicates that they had been ridiculed for their refusal to join in pagan festivals. The probability is that Paul was speaking in anticipation of future persecution, or that he meant the sufferings of anxiety and concern connected with preaching the gospel. Not all suffering is physical. Much of it is mental and spiritual. Modern Christians, though they seldom suffer physically for their faith, must, if they are true, suffer from anxiety and concern in the gospel enterprise.

Verse 7: an expression of Paul's confidence in the church.

Our hope for you is unshaken: a strange statement in the light of what

---

[1] Héring regards and interprets this to mean that Christ is the intermediary of comfort. (Jean Héring, *La Seconde Épitre de Saint Paul Aux Corinthiens* [Paris: Delachaus et Niestlé, 1958]. Referred to as Héring.)

follows in this letter, especially chapters 10–13. However, if we assume that the church as a whole stood reconciled to Paul and true to Christ, with only a minority still rebellious, the expression is consistent with the letter as a whole. *Unshaken* comes from a word which means "stable, sure." The verbal form means "to plant the feet down." *Hope* expresses the idea of confident expectation.

For we know: gives the reason for the *hope.*

That as you share in our sufferings: rather, "to the degree that you are partners in our sufferings." Paul believed that they would be "partners" with him in his sufferings.

You will also share in our comfort: not that he would comfort them, but God would.

3. Paul's Deadly Peril and Deliverance (1:8–11)

This section continues the thanksgiving motif and explains why Paul blessed God for mercies extended to him. The exact nature of the peril is obscure. Perhaps the Corinthians already knew what it was, and Paul wrote only to express the intensity of his suffering and thus encourage them to steadfastness in their lighter afflictions, relatively speaking.

Verse 8: For we do not want you to be ignorant, brethren: a formula used six times by Paul, always with *brethren* (1 Cor. 10:1; 12:1; Rom. 1:13; 11:25; 1 Thess. 4:13). The expression always introduces something to which Paul wished to call special attention.[1]

Of the affliction we experienced in Asia: an obscure reference (to the modern reader) to a recent experience of Paul. *Affliction* is the word for "pressure" and may mean physical suffering or mental anguish. *Asia* is a general term which could mean Ephesus or Troas. Hughes points out several things that can be known about the affliction in mind. The positive conclusions are: (1) Paul wrote to tell them how great his affliction was, not what it was. (2) Since it is not mentioned in 1 Corinthians, it must have occurred after the writing of that letter. (3) Since it happened in Asia, it happened before his coming to Macedonia. (4) Only divine intervention enabled the apostle to survive it. (5) It belonged to "Christ's sufferings" (cf. vs. 5). The earliest suggestion as to what the affliction was took the reference to fighting with wild beasts (1 Cor. 15:32) literally and made that the affliction referred to here. However, this is unlikely. Several other suggestions have been made: (1) It was a rebellion against Paul in Asia similar to, and sparked by, the rebellion in Corinth (Plummer). (2) It was a second and more nearly successful attempt on Paul's life by his enemies in Ephesus (the first being that recorded in Acts 19:23 ff.). (3) It was not a particular affliction, but a series of persecutions. (4) It was a physical illness, perhaps associated with the "thorn in the flesh" (cf. 2 Cor. 12:7). Since there is a lack of evidence in the letter itself, the nature of the affliction remains a question. We must leave it there.

For we were so utterly, unbearably crushed that we despaired of life

---

[1] Plummer points out that this is Paul's common way of introducing important matters.

itself: literally, "that we were weighed down beyond measure, beyond our power to bear, so that we were without a way of escape, even with our lives." The total expression speaks of the depth of Paul's suffering and affliction. No comment could improve on his own words.

Verse 9: Why, we felt that we had received the sentence of death: literally, "We ourselves, in ourselves, had received the sentence of death." The RSV translation gives the sense of the expression, but does not capture its depth of feeling. The expression is meant to strengthen the sense of despair expressed in verse 8. *Sentence of death* is a technical, judicial term, i.e., "the death sentence."

But that was to make us rely not on ourselves but on God: Paul saw in his affliction a lesson to be learned. Paul had been brought to the point where no human power could deliver him. He could no longer trust in himself; he had to rely on God. This is the second beneficial result that Paul mentioned with respect to Christian sufferings. One was that he might have the ability to comfort others because he had received comfort (vs. 4). The Greek has the particle which introduces a purpose clause here. We do not need to water that down. One purpose, in the mind of God, in letting Paul suffer was that he might learn not to trust in himself. Modern Christians need to learn this same lesson. Suffering is not necessary to learn it, but sometimes it is the only way.

Who raises the dead: The present tense points to a timeless characteristic of God. He alone has the power of life and death. Paul's rescue seemed to him to be tantamount to a resurrection from the dead.

Verse 10: a résumé of Paul's experience and his hope.

He delivered us: past tense, pointing to the experience referred to in verse 8.

From so deadly a peril: rather, "from so great a death." Paul had considered himself as good as dead. He did not say that God delivered him from *peril,* but from *death* itself. The death is described as "so great." "Death" is in the plural in some texts and this may be the true reading. If so, the plural is probably idiomatic, pointing to the quality of the thing and enforcing "so great."

And he will deliver us: seems superfluous in the light of the next clause. Some manuscripts have changed this to the present tense to make a parallelism, but the future is probably the correct reading. The thought is that God would continue to deliver Paul from any danger in his present circumstances.

On him we have set our hope that he will deliver us again: includes all possible future circumstances. *Again* translates a word which means "yet." *We have set our hope* translates a perfect tense in the Greek. It means that Paul had set his hope in the past, and his hope was still set there.

Verse 11: This is one verse where Paul spoke of the power of intercessory prayer. He believed that the ability of God to deliver was contingent in some degree upon the prayers of his Christian brethren.

You also must help us by prayer: rather, "provided, or while, you help us by prayer." The construction continues the sentence from verse 10. The present participle may be translated either "provided" or "while."

Paul felt himself to be as secure as the prayers of the Corinthians were certain. *Help* translates a Greek word of three elements: "with," "in behalf of," and "work." Perhaps our English word "cooperate" is a better translation. But with whom or what were the Corinthians to cooperate? Several answers are possible: "with Paul in his prayers" or "with one another" or "with the particular situation" or "with God." We need not try to define the expression too closely. The thought is that the prayers of the Corinthians would contribute in some way to the effectiveness of God in delivering. We must avoid the idea that God's act is only partly his. On the other hand, we must not shrink from the idea that the effectiveness of God's action in human lives depends upon constancy in prayer.

So that many will give thanks on our behalf for the blessing granted us in answer to many prayers: an attempt to translate a difficult clause. There is no doubt that the clause is a purpose clause. *So that* is a good translation. *Many* translates a phrase which literally means "out of many faces." "Face" is used often in the New Testament. It may mean "face," "appearance," or "person." It occurs twelve times in 2 Corinthians and obviously means "face" in eight of them (Robertson). Perhaps the best solution is to let it mean "faces" here and suppose that Paul was thinking of the "faces" of men upturned in prayer (Robertson). This would be equivalent to many "persons," but the Greek is more impressive. In spite of the difficulties of translation, the meaning is clear. Paul felt that his deliverance, helped by the prayers of the Corinthians, would become an object of thanksgiving on the part of many others who prayed.

II. PAUL'S EXPLANATION OF HIS CHANGE
OF PLANS (1:12—7:16)

The immediate concern of this section is Paul's failure to visit Corinth as he had promised. His failure to come had given his opponents opportunity to accuse him of fickleness. Paul answered that charge in 1:12—2:13. His answer encompassed not only his failure to visit them but an admonition to forgive the offender (2:5–11). However, he did not satisfy himself by merely answering the charges brought against him. He included an extended discussion of his ministry to show that his relationships with the Corinthians were a discharge of that ministry (2:14—6:10). His discussion of his ministry is followed by various pleas and warnings (6:11—7:4), and by an expression of his rejoicing over the report of Titus that all was well at Corinth (7:5–16). The whole section is marked by evidences of Paul's strong feeling which makes it impossible to develop a concise and coherent outline. Nevertheless there is progress in his thought, and we have attempted to mark that progress.

1. Reason for Paul's Change of Plans (1:12—2:13)

In answer to some slurs which had been made about Paul's stability and trustworthiness, he insisted that his dealings with the Corinthians had always been marked by openness and sincerity (1:12–14). Regarding his failure to carry out his promise to visit them, he insisted that his plans were always subject to the will of God and that this explained his delay in coming (1:15–22). Furthermore, he insisted that he did not wish to make another painful visit to them, and thus had delayed his coming until he could receive a report of their reconciliation (1:23—2:4). He also included, because it was related to the same accusation, an admonition to forgive the brother who had caused so much pain (2:5–11). Finally he pointed out that it was his concern over the Corinthian situation that had led him to depart from Troas while there was still a great opportunity for service there (2:12–13).

(1) He insisted that he always acted sincerely (1:12–14)

Behind this paragraph and shaping it are some accusations leveled against Paul by his Corinthian opponents. He had been accused of using underhanded and cunning methods; he replied that his behavior had been single-minded and candid (vs. 12). He had been accused of writing obscure letters with hidden meanings; he replied that his letters always had been such as could be understood and made public (vs. 13). The paragraph closes with an expressed hope that all of them would come to understand him, as some had already done.

Verse 12: an answer to the charge that Paul's methods had been underhanded and cunning.

For: marks these verses as transitional, being closely connected with the thanksgiving and hope expressed in the previous paragraphs (vss. 3–11) and preparing the way for the justification of his recent actions.

Our boast is this: a confession that he did engage in boasting. *Boast* translates a Greek word which refers to the act of glorying, while *proud* (in vs. 14) translates a word built on the same Greek stem which means "the ground of glorying." The English translations fail to preserve the play on words which is apparent in the Greek. This word group is almost peculiar to Paul's writings, found elsewhere in the New Testament only in James (three times) and Hebrews (one time). Moreover, the frequency of its use in this particular letter is striking. The noun "boasting" occurs six times in this epistle as compared with four times in the rest of Paul's epistles. The noun, *boast* (i.e., ground of boasting), occurs three times in this epistle but only seven times in the rest of Paul's epistles. The verb "to boast" occurs twenty times in this epistle and only fifteen times in the rest of Paul's epistles. The word group is used twenty-nine times in this epistle and twenty-six times in the rest of Paul's epistles. The words may have either a good sense or a bad one. Paul's opponents boasted; their boasting was marked by insincerity and pride. Paul boasted, but his boasting was marked by sincerity because what he boasted of was attributed to the grace of God.

The testimony of our conscience: appositional with *boast.* Paul was saying that his glorying found its basis in the testimony which his own consciousness bore to his behavior. *Conscience* is more aptly translated "consciousness." The thought is that there was no nagging memory of insincerity in behavior to mar the boasting of Paul. He had searched his memory and was unaware of any lapse into the use of underhanded and worldly methods of work.

That we have behaved in the world: This expression includes the entirety of Paul's missionary efforts. Not only in Corinth, but elsewhere, he had renounced the tools of the world in preaching the gospel (cf. 1 Cor. 2:1–5).

And still more toward you: does not imply that Paul had been less sincere in his behavior in other places, but that they had had more opportunity to observe his behavior than elsewhere. His contacts with the Corinthian church had been more intimate and more numerous than with any other church.

With holiness: probably an incorrect reading. "Simplicity" is, on the whole, better attested as the correct reading. There is only a small difference in spelling between the two words in the Greek. *Holiness* is *agiotēti;* "simplicity" is *aplotēti.* The probability is that the scribal error was due to a slip of the eyes. "Holiness," as a noun, is used in only one other passage in the New Testament and then as an attribute of God (cf. Heb. 12:10). It is very unlikely that Paul would have used this noun to describe his own behavior. The meaning is that his behavior had been marked by singleness of mind, by simplicity. "Simplicity" means openness or singleness of purpose. It is a distinctive Pauline word used with reference to giving (Rom. 12:8; 2 Cor. 8:2; 9:11, 13), with reference to devotion to Christ (2 Cor. 11:3), and with reference to a slave's service to his master (Eph. 6:5; Col. 3:22).

Godly: is a noun in the Greek and should go with both words. Thus his behavior had been marked by simplicity and sincerity which came from God. These were God-given qualities of life rather than human achievements. This explains why Paul did not hesitate to boast in them. They reflected God's action; so his boasting was true Christian glorying rather than human pride.

Sincerity: synonymous with "simplicity." The word means "transparency" or "ingenuousness" and hence *sincerity* (Plummer). The word is a compound word in Greek, composed of two elements, one meaning "sun" and the other, "judgment." Hence it means that which is subject to the light of the sun or tested by the light of the sun. Paul was not afraid to subject his behavior to the test of sunlight.

Not by earthly wisdom: rather, "not in earthly wisdom." "In" indicates the sphere in which Paul's behavior moved. *Earthly* is actually "fleshly." Paul used "fleshly" five times; it is found only two times in the rest of the New Testament. His meaning for the term was "that which is merely human." Paul regarded men who did not know God as "fleshly" in their entire life. *Wisdom* means practical wisdom. The phrase means that Paul's behavior was not dictated by cunning and underhanded methods which might win for him an advantage over others. Such methods would be the exercise of earthly wisdom.

But by the grace of God: stresses the idea that is contained in *godly.* Paul's behavior found its source in the grace of God and thus was characterized by simplicity and sincerity.

Verse 13: turns to his letters. He had been accused of sly behavior. Verse 12 is his answer to that accusation. He had been accused of writing with hidden meanings. This verse is the answer to that accusation.

We write: a present tense, which could mean either "what I am now writing" or "what I habitually write." The second is probably the meaning in this verse. This is the fourth letter that we know of which Paul had written to the Corinthians. Perhaps it is this which justifies his statement in verse 12, "and still more toward you." The Corinthians had a larger exposure to his written word than any other church.

Nothing but what you can read and understand: contains a play on words in Greek which is impossible to reproduce in English. The word for *read* (anaginōskete) really means to read aloud to the congregation. *Understand* (epiginōskete) translates another form of the same Greek word. The background of the expression assumes that some of the Corinthians, like some modern commentators, were looking for hidden meanings in Paul's letters which were not there.[1] He intended for them to understand what he wrote, so that what he wrote could be read aloud in the congregation and taken in its plain meaning.

---

[1] Tasker believes it is clear that Paul had been accused of being insincere in his letters. (R. V. G. Tasker, *The Second Epistle of Paul to the Corinthians* [Grand Rapids, Mich.: Wm. B. Eerdmans Publishing Company, 1958]. Hereafter referred to by the last name of the author, Tasker.)

I hope you will understand fully: probably an incorrect translation. Literally the clause reads: "I hope that unto the end you will understand." "Unto the end" could have the meaning of completeness or fullness, but that does not seem to fit the context. He had just said that his letters could be understood. Why add a hope that they would be understood? The thought is temporal. He hoped that they would continue to understand "to the end," either of their own lives or of the world, what they now understood.

Verse 14: continues the sentence begun in verse 13, but changes the thought from an understanding of the writing of Paul to an acknowledgment of him as a person.

As: a comparative article. He hoped that their understanding of his letters would be to the same degree that they now understood him.

You have understood: rather, "you understood us." The omission of the pronoun "us" by the RSV is wrong. *Understood* can mean "acknowledged," but that is probably not the meaning in this verse.

In part: can be "part of you" or "part of me." Probably the meaning is that some of them, the church *in part,* had come to understand Paul. He hoped that all would come to the same understanding. The report of Titus (cf. 7:5–16) lies behind the expression.

That: can be understood in three ways. It can mean "because" and give the reason for their past recognition. It can mean "that" and continue the thought of "read and understand" in verse 13, with the intervening words being regarded as parenthetical. It can mean "that" and continue the thought of "understood in part" in this verse. The last option is the best. Thus the verse should read: "as you, some of you, have understood that you are the ground of my boasting and I of yours in the day of the Lord Jesus." If this is the correct connection, the RSV translation will need to be corrected in the rest of the verse.

You can be proud of us: rather, "We are the ground of your boasting." By this expression Paul meant that his ministry was the ground upon which their glorying in the grace of God stood.

As we can be of you: rather, "as you are the ground of my boasting." This expression reflects the same thought that lies behind the expression: "You yourselves are our letter of recommendation" (3:2). Paul had been accused of pride in himself and of looking down on the Corinthians. He reversed that in this expression. They were his pride and his joy.

On the day of the Lord Jesus: the end of the world. Paul probably still looked for this to come soon. *On* translates the Greek preposition, *in.* *On* gives the impression that the glorying of Paul in the Corinthians and theirs in him would take place only at the time of the end of the world. This gives a false impression. The Greek preposition *en* can have the meaning "with reference to." This may be what Paul meant. His glorying and theirs was a present reality, but it was related, not to earthly and temporal realities, but to eternal realities (Lenski).

(2) He insisted that his plans were always subject to the will of God (1:15–22)

Paul had been accused of fickleness in his dealings with the Corinthians, of saying "Yes and No" (vs. 18) at the same time. He met this accusation in this paragraph by pointing out that his plans were always subject to change because he was under orders. He did not plan as worldly men planned (vs. 17), but as a steward with a commission from God (vs. 21).

Verse 15: looks back to the assurance which he had expressed in verses 13–14.

Because I was sure of this: literally, "in this persuasion." He was sure of the mutual trust and respect which existed between him and the Corinthians. The Greek noun for "persuasion" is used in the New Testament only by Paul. He used it six times, four in this espistle (here; 3:4; 8:22; 10:2).

I wanted: rather, "I was intending." The verb is in the imperfect tense in the Greek, meaning a continuous action in past time. The word expresses something stronger than a wish; it speaks of plans already laid.

To come to you first: that is, before going on to Macedonia (cf. vs. 16).

So that we might have a double pleasure: Instead of *pleasure,* the better texts read "grace or favor." [1] Paul referred to the double visit which he had proposed to make, first mentioned in verse 16. To call such a visit a "grace" implies that his visits to them would be attended by the manifestation of God's presence. There may be a subtle reference to the lack of grace which accompanied his painful visit.

Verse 16: gives the details of his plans. He wanted to visit them on the way to Macedonia, which marks the plans as different from the ones he had detailed in 1 Corinthians 16:5, where he had said: "I will visit you after passing through Macedonia." If this visit had been promised, which is uncertain, it must have been promised in his painful letter. There is no mention of a promise, but the context implies that the Corinthians knew of his plans. After visiting Macedonia, he had planned to return from there and be sent on his way to Judea by the church at Corinth. This verse helps in some ways to clarify the various visits and letters of Paul to Corinth, but the obscurity still remains. We must guess at the exact sequence of events.

Verse 17: expresses surprise that the Corinthians could have so misunderstood him that they thought his change of plans was a change of attitude toward them.

Was I vacillating when I wanted to do this: rhetorical question expecting a negative answer. It means, "I was not, was I?" This is argument by interrogation. The implication is that his opponents accused him of making promises without thinking. *Vacillating* comes from a Greek word which implies shallowness of character that leads one to make promises without thinking whether he can carry them through or not. It does not indicate so much a change of mind as a lack of mind. Perhaps the English word "frivolous" comes nearer to the Greek here. Paul was accused of being giddy and without sober sensibleness. This he denied.

Do I make plans like a worldly man: changes from the past to the pres-

---

[1] Denney agrees that this is the correct text. (James Denney, *The Second Epistle to the Corinthians* [New York: Eaton & Mains, n.d.]. Referred to hereafter by the last name of the author, Denney.)

ent tense, from the particular to the habitual. The implied negative answer still stands. *A worldly man* is "according to the flesh" in this verse. The *worldly man* is the one not ruled by the Spirit of God. Surely the Corinthians would recognize that Paul was not such a man. His plans were not "according to the flesh" but "according to the leadership of the Holy Spirit."

Ready to say Yes and No at once: describes the way the worldly man makes his plans. This kind of man says "yes" from one side of his mouth and "no" from the other. The point is that one is never able to depend on what he says.

Verse 18: Instead of explaining at once why he had changed his plans (he did so in 1:23—2:4), Paul stopped to affirm the truth of his message and character.

As surely as God is faithful: may be a correct translation. If so, it is a call to God to be a witness to the truth of what Paul was to say. This would make the verse an oath.[1] But both Lenski and Plummer object to this. The expression does not have the formal form of an oath in the Greek. It is a simple indicative, "God is faithful." *Faithful* is often used as a special attribute of God. It means that God can be relied upon, that one can take him at his word.

Our word to you has not been Yes and No: the verb is a present tense in the Greek. It should be, "Our word to you is not now Yes and No." *Yes and No* means a wavering between the two. The point of joining the two expressions, if our interpretation is correct, is that Paul's word—the gospel—takes its nature from God. Since God is faithful, the message from God is not a message full of misleading statements. It can be depended upon just as surely as God can be depended upon.

Verse 19: defines the word of Paul.

For the Son of God, Jesus Christ: full title which is solemnly impressive. There was no doubt in the mind of Paul about the deity of Christ.

Whom we preached among you: Jesus Christ is the content of the gospel message. The gospel is not a message about Christ, but a proclamation of him. *We preached* is in the past tense and refers to the original mission of Paul to Corinth. *Among* is a correct translation of the Greek preposition ordinarily translated "in."

Silvanus and Timothy and I: the members of Paul's missionary team when he first came to Corinth.

Was not Yes and No; but in him it is always Yes: God's promises are faithfully kept in him. The Corinthians' own experience had taught them that the promises of life and salvation were always faithfully kept in him.

Verse 20: continues the thought of the truth of the gospel.

It should be noticed that Paul expressed, in this verse, a unique Christian claim that is still debated by unbelievers, as it was debated by unbelievers in the New Testament times. The claim that God's promises had been fulfilled in a single person and in history is one of the scandals of Christianity, perhaps *the* scandal. The Christian gospel is not a system of

---

[1] Allo calls it a "sort of oath" (Le P. E. B. Allo, *Saint Paul Second Épître aux Corinthians* [Paris: Libraire Lecoffre, 1956]. Referred to as Allo.)

ideas, teaching a new way of life; but the witness to a person, demanding submission to him as the Lord of life. True, Christian submission leads to the authentic human life, but it does so by bringing the man to submission to the Giver of life.

For all the promises of God: emphasis is on *all.* All the promises, however many there may be and whatever their nature, are included in the expression. This expression describes the Old Testament in its essential character as promise.

Find their Yes in him: that is, in his person and work. *Yes* means their fulfillment. Christ gave the affirmative answer to all that God had promised in the Old Testament. Paul believed that the history of salvation came to its culmination in the redemptive meaning of the Christ event. This conviction is basic in the New Testament writings and is expressed by the feeling that the Christian era is the "last days" (cf. Heb. 1:1-4).

That is why we utter the Amen through him: refers to the "Amen" uttered in the public services of the church (cf. 1 Cor. 14:16). It seems to have been the custom in the churches for the congregation to respond with "Amen" when the speaker gave thanksgiving or uttered a message from God. Amen comes from the Hebrew word which means "truth." [1] Thus, to say "Amen" was to affirm the truth of what the speaker said and to claim his words for oneself. The Corinthians had, no doubt, often uttered "Amen" to the preaching of Paul and his companions. The article *the* marks "Amen" as the customary Christian "Amen." *Through him* means that the "Amen" to what God had done came through the completed work of Christ. The Book of Revelation has a striking passage in which "Amen" is ascribed to Christ as a title: "The words of the Amen, the faithful and true witness, the beginning of God's creation" (Rev. 3:14).

To the glory of God: rather, "to God for glory through us." *To . . . God* belongs to *Amen.* It was to God that the "Amen" was said in the congregation. The message came through the speaker, but the affirmation from the congregation was that God is true. *Glory* is the recognition of the true character of God as he has manifested himself, primarily in Jesus Christ.

Verse 21: Paul had been discussing (vss. 18-20) the faithfulness of God as it applied to the gospel. Now he turned to discuss it as it applied to the experience of the Corinthians and his own ministry.

It is God who establishes us with you: Establishes translates a present participle in the Greek and points to the continuous action of God. *With you* means "in company with you." The Corinthians shared in the same grace of God which Paul and his companions had. Paul wanted to penetrate behind the squabbles of the church to the spiritual realities that made it a church. The Corinthians needed to have their attention called to the unique character of their religion and to realize that both they and Paul shared a common spiritual foundation of life.

In Christ: rather, "with reference to Christ." God was continually giving them stability in their relation to Christ.

And has commissioned us: turns to a unique experience of Paul and

---

[1] Tasker stresses the fact that "Amen" has an affinity with the Hebrew verb which means "to confirm."

his fellow preachers. "With you" is dropped. *Commissioned* translates a Greek word which means "anointed." *Christ* is the noun form of the verb used. The background of the expression was the Old Testament custom of anointing one to an office. The hope of the Messiah's coming was the hope of the unique Anointed One. Paul regarded his own "anointing" to the office of apostle as related to the anointing of Jesus to the office of Messiah. This expression arrives at the heart of the paragraph. Paul's primary defense against the charge of fickleness was that he did not make his own decisions. God made them.

Verse 22: continues the thought of verse 21. The statements still refer to the commission of Paul and his fellow teachers.

He has put his seal upon us: marked as genuine. The sealing of documents was widespread in New Testament times, as it is in modern times.[1] The seal gave validity to documents, guaranteed the genuineness of articles, and proved that a container contained the specified amount (ICC). Whatever was sealed could be accepted without question if the one who sealed it was honest. God had sealed Paul and his fellow teachers, thus guaranteeing the integrity of their message and their ministry.

And given us his Spirit in our hearts as a guarantee: Guarantee translates a Greek word which was in common use in commercial transactions. The guarantee was really a down payment, usually a considerable portion of the purchase price itself, which promised that the full price would be paid. If one failed to pay the full price, he lost the down payment. Paul is the only New Testament writer who used this word with a spiritual meaning (here; 5:5; Eph. 1:14). The idea involved is that the Holy Spirit is God's down payment on the final redemption of his children. This down payment is a payment in kind, a foretaste of heaven itself. Thus the Holy Spirit is the first installment of eternal life.

The mention of *God, Christ,* and the *Holy Spirit* in this paragraph is noteworthy. Paul was not thinking of a speculative doctrine of the Trinity, but his statements later became a foundation of that doctrine. He spoke with reference to the redemptive work or function of each member of the Triune God. God is the source of all blessings, the one confirming his teacher. Christ is the fulfillment in history of God's promises and the Lord of the Christian. The Holy Spirit is the seal of the Christian, the down payment on heaven. The Spirit dwells in the heart of the believer and makes God real to him through his union with Christ.[2]

(3) He wished to spare them another painful visit (1:23—2:4)

This paragraph is Paul's direct answer to the accusation of fickleness. He began the paragraph with an oath (vs. 23a), calling God to witness that he refrained from coming to Corinth in order to spare them (vs. 23b). Next he denied that he had any desire to act as their lords (vs. 24). Then he stated his determination not to make another painful visit to them

---

[1] Plummer points out that the papyri show "sealing" to have had extended use in the East.

[2] Hughes says that verses 21–22 have trinitarian implications.

(2:1–2), followed by a reference to the painful letter that he had written (2:3–4).

Verse 23: I: is very emphatic. Paul disassociated himself from his fellow-workers and began to speak of his own integrity.

Call God to witness: words that fit into a formal oath such as one might take on the witness stand in court. The Corinthians had already judged him without a full knowledge of his motives and heart. God knew Paul, as he knows all men, completely and perfectly. All the secrets of man's heart are open to him. Thus he alone can give a true witness.

Against: figure of speech. Paul pictured himself as being on trial in the courtroom with witnesses testifying against him.

Me: literally, "my soul." However, the translation is justified. Paul used "soul" for the whole person, following the Hebrew and Christian way of speaking rather than the Greek.

It was to spare you: His motive had been one of love and concern for them. The Greek word group translated "spare" is found only eleven times in the New Testament, eight in Paul's writing, and four of these are in 2 Corinthians. It means to spare someone something. His delay in coming had not been due to levity or fickleness, but to a desire to give them time to repent. Of course, if they had not repented, he would have come (cf. 13:10).

That I refrained from coming to Corinth: rather, "no longer I came to Corinth." The idea is not that he refrained from coming but that he did not come "again." This expression implies that there had been a second, painful visit to the Corinthians which had only served to deepen the separation of Paul from the Corinthians rather than to heal the breach.

Verse 24: Paul hastened to correct a possible wrong impression. Power to spare might imply authority over them. Possibly also, he had been accused of acting as lord over their faith.

Not that: an elliptical statement standing for, "I do not say this with the thought that." Such ellipses are common in the New Testament, as they are in modern speech, and are easily understood. *We:* includes his colleagues once again.

Lord it over: exercise authority which belongs only to Christ. Such was not Paul's intention.

Your faith: dedication to Christ. Faith is a primary virtue of the Christian life as well as the way to salvation. It must be the free, voluntary attitude of the individual; it cannot be subject to any authority except that of Christ. Paul knew this and wanted the Christians of Corinth to know that he was not trying to violate their necessary devotion to Christ.

We work with you: as your fellow-workers. A direct contrast to the thought that he wanted to lord it over them in any way.

For your joy: the object of their mutual striving. This is a surprising word in the context. It may imply that what the Corinthians lacked was not faith but joy in their faith (Phil. 1:25). Of course, such happiness is a fruit of the Holy Spirit (cf. Gal. 5:22), but faithful preachers can help Christians to attain that joy. However, it is implied as well that the Christian himself must strive to receive this gift.

For you stand firm in your faith: rather, "for in faith you have taken your stand." *In your faith* means in the sphere of your devotion to Christ, your surrender to him. "You have taken your stand" is a perfect tense, pointing both to the original act of faith and to the continuous exercise of faith.

Verse 1 of chapter 2: continues Paul's answer to the charges against him.

For: presents a textual problem with little meaning. Some manuscripts have "but." The evidence is about evenly divided, but *for* is probably the correct reading. Paul was still explaining that their mutual concern was for the joy of the Corinthians.

I: changes back to the singular. Paul's decision was his own and did not include his fellow-workers.

Made up my mind: literally, "judged this within myself." The RSV is correct. If he was to cooperate with them to further their joy, he had to decide against another visit that would bring pain.

Not to make you another painful visit: rather, "not again in pain to come to you." The implication is that one painful visit had already been made; he was not going to make another. However, it is possible to interpret the Greek to mean that since his first visit was a happy one, he did not want his second one to be painful. "In pain" means in the sphere of sorrow; whether his or theirs is uncertain, probably theirs in the light of verse 2. "Sorrow" is probably a better translation of the Greek word than "pain." If "pain" is retained, it must be understood in the sense of mental anguish and turmoil, rather than in a physical sense.

Verse 2: gives one reason why Paul refused to make another painful visit. It would bring him sorrow as well as them.

If: assumes that he would do this if he came.

I cause you pain: I is emphatic in the sentence.

Who is there to make me glad but the one I have pained: rhetorical question. The implication is that he could not be made glad by those whom he had pained. Their sorrow would be his, just as their joy had been his. *Who* is singular in the Greek and looks upon the congregation as a unity.

Verse 3: turns to the discussion of his painful letter.

I wrote: a past tense which is most naturally taken to refer to a former letter. However, it can be, and sometimes is, interpreted to be an epistolary aorist in which the writer puts himself in the position of the readers and speaks of what he is doing as having been done in the past. The best example of this type of past tense is 1 John 2:12–14. In that passage verses 12–13 use the present tense in Greek, verse 14 uses the past (Greek, aorist) tense three times, but the translation is present in each case. However, the present instance is best taken as a true past tense. Paul was referring to a letter which he had written them. Some have suggested that this was our 1 Corinthians, but the context does not really fit that letter.

As I did: rather, "this very thing." The translation is justified but loses something of the color of the Greek. The meaning is that Paul had decided to deal with their problems by a letter rather than make them a painful visit. If this is true, we may be sure that there was a letter written between 1 and 2 Corinthians.

So that when I came I might not be pained: rather, "in order that I might not by coming have sorrow." The RSV gives the wrong impression. Paul did not write the letter to prepare for a coming joyful visit, but to avoid making any visit at all. He knew that a visit while the breach between him and the Corinthians was wide could only result in sorrow for him as well as for them.

By those who should have made me rejoice: a gentle reminder to the Corinthians that they should always bring joy to him who founded the church. They were his spiritual children. They should have made him happy by their adherence to his preaching and example.

For I felt sure of all of you: expresses a confidence which Paul had had and contains a subtle invitation for them to make it true. He refused to believe that the Corinthians would want it any other way. Even though they had been rebellious, he still had confidence in their sympathy and love for him.

That my joy would be the joy of you all: the confidence which he had. He believed that the Corinthians would want nothing else than to have him happy.

Verse 4: explains how and why Paul wrote the letter.

For: introduces the explanation.

I wrote you out of much affliction: mental anguish caused by the breach with the Corinthians. *Out of* indicates the source from which the letter flowed. *Affliction* (i.e., pressure) can apply either to physical or mental anguish caused by outside factors. Paul had looked upon the troubles in Corinth which necessitated the letter as being much affliction. *Much* stresses the depth of feeling and anxiety out of which Paul wrote.

Anguish of heart: a synonym for *affliction.* Lenski suggests that *affliction* describes the sorrow which Paul had received from the Corinthians instead of the joy which he should have had, while *anguish* describes the worry which he had concerning the effects of the letter in Corinth. *Anguish* comes from a Greek word which means "to hold together." This phrase expresses the contraction of the heart in the grip of great emotion.

With many tears: rather, "through a flood of tears." The change of preposition is significant. He wrote "out of" affliction and "through" many tears. "Through" has the meaning of attendant circumstances, and so the RSV *with* is perhaps justified. The expressions, taken together, are meant to describe a situation so painful to Paul that he could hardly bear it.

We have already discussed the identity of this letter in the introduction, but it may be well to summarize what we said there. Many commentators take the reference to be to 2 Corinthians 10–13. Indeed, the composition of that portion of this letter fits the description of the letter here, providing it is assumed that chapters 10–13 are addressed to the church as a whole. However, in the light of the fact that there is no manuscript evidence of the independent existence of that portion of this letter, and in view of the fact that the four chapters are an appeal to the church in the light of the opposition of some, we have decided in favor of the unity of this epistle.

Other interpreters have taken these verses to be a reference to 1 Corinthians and have denied the writing of another letter between the two. While this is possible, the tone of 1 Corinthians does not conform to the description of the circumstances contained in these two verses. True, some portions of 1 Corinthians could fit this description—especially the discussion of the case of incest (cf. 1 Cor. 5:1–8). The letter as a whole, however, could not. Thus, it seems likely that the reference here is to a lost letter of Paul to Corinth which no longer exists.

Not to cause you pain: This was not the purpose of the painful letter. Some of the Corinthians may have supposed that Paul was unfair in his criticism. He denied that this was true.

But to let you know the abundant love that I have for you: the real purpose of the letter. The order of the Greek clause is worthy of notice. It is: "but the love to let you know which I have abundantly for you." It was the custom of Greek structure to place the word which was to be emphasized first and the word which received the secondary emphasis last. Thus the two expressions which receive the emphasis are: *love* and *for you*. He wanted them to know that the letter was meant to express his loving concern, and that that concern was especially for them. He could have spared himself the tears; he could have come at once to deal with them harshly. He did neither. He wrote the letter and gave them time to repent because he loved them.

(4) He had admonished them to forgive the sinful brother for their own sake (2:5–11)

This paragraph has proved puzzling to modern commentators. Who was the offender? From the paragraph itself we can gather some information. It seems that the Corinthians felt that the offense was primarily against Paul (vs. 5), but he insisted that it was primarily against the congregation. The majority of the congregation had joined in censoring the offender in some way, whether by excommunication or not is uncertain (vs. 6). The Corinthians seemed to think that their punishment was inadequate, but Paul insisted that it was sufficient (vs. 6). Paul asked them to forgive him and reaffirm their love for him (vss. 7–8). He had written them about the offender to test their obedience (vs. 9). He now wrote that he was willing to join them in forgiving the offender and insisted that this was for their sake "to keep Satan from gaining the advantage over us" (vss. 10–11).

Many commentators have supposed that the offender in question was the incestuous person mentioned in 1 Corinthians 5:1–8.[1] If so, Paul's first letter had led to his excommunication from the congregation, which in turn had led to his repentance. Now Paul asked that the congregation receive him back into their fellowship. In favor of this interpretation is the fact that Paul could have heard of this sequence of events and dealt with it in the painful letter. Against it is the fact that the Corinthians felt that the offender's offense was primarily against Paul. This would not have been true with regard to the incestuous man.

On the whole it is better to suppose that the offender was the ringleader of the opposition against Paul.[2] If so, Paul had to deal with the problem,

[1] Hughes supports this position.
[2] Plummer takes this position.

but he could not do so alone. The congregation must deal with him as well. This, it seems, the majority had done in some way—probably by excommunicating him from the congregation (vs. 6). Titus' visit to them had brought to light the fact that the man had repented and wished to become an obedient member of the congregation. In response to this report, Paul now asked the congregation to forgive him and restore him to its fellowship (vss. 6–7). Perhaps the reason he had to do this was that the congregation, feeling that such action would be a sign of disloyalty to Paul, had refused to forgive the man while Titus was there, in spite of Titus' suggestion that they should forgive him (vs. 5).

The sequence, if this is true, would be as follows: (1) After 1 Corinthians had been received, some of the Corinthians under the leadership of a ringleader had rebelled against Paul. (2) His painful visit to them had uncovered this state of affairs but had failed to resolve it. (3) He had written them a painful letter, demanding that they excommunicate the ringleader and that the church should reaffirm their obedience to his gospel. (4) He had sent Titus to them to discover the status of the situation in Corinth. (5) Titus had found that the congregation had indeed reaffirmed its loyalty to Paul and had excommunicated the ringleader of the opposition. (6) Titus had also discovered that the ringleader was contrite and wished to be reinstated in the fellowship of the congregation. (7) The church had refused to reinstate him, feeling that to do so would be a sign of disloyalty to Paul. (8) Paul now wrote that they should forgive him because his punishment by the majority had been enough and because a refusal to forgive would subject the Corinthians to further temptation from Satan. We will base our commentary on the verses on the supposition that this is the true interpretation.

Verse 5: But if any one has caused pain: assumes that he had indeed done so. The *if* clause is in the form which assumes the truth of the statement. There is no doubt that Paul was dealing with a real case of grievous offense in Corinth. *Any one* is an indefinite pronoun, understandably so, since the Corinthians would know full well of whom he spoke.

He has caused it not to me: Paul refused to take the affront as a personal matter. The ringleader had indeed refused to accept Paul's authority, but his affront was not to Paul alone. *Not to me* should probably be taken to mean "not to me alone."

But in some measure—not to put it too severely—to you all: The whole congregation had suffered by reason of the man's rebellion. *In some measure* translates a Greek expression which means "in part." Some had not been distressed by the scandalous treatment of Paul; they had joined the ringleader in his rebellion. This expression indicates that there was still a minority of the Corinthians who had not been reconciled to Paul. This is important to remember as a justification for the harsh tone in 2 Corinthians 10:1—13:10.

Verse 6: speaks of the punishment by the majority, probably by excommunication, but this is not certain.

For such a one: the kind of person who would do this.

This punishment: perhaps refers to excommunication, but this is not certain.

By the majority: indicates a democratic procedure in the affairs of the church at Corinth. Some had not joined in the action of the majority.

Enough: has the position of emphasis in the Greek. But in what sense was the punishment sufficient? Adequate to the offense? Or adequate to lead to repentance? Probably the latter. If our reconstruction of the sequence of events is correct, the rebel had come to repentance and wished to be forgiven. The obligation of the Christian community in such a case is to forgive a sinning brother. Seemingly the Corinthians had refused this forgiveness on the basis of their loyalty to Paul.

Verse 7: confirms the belief that the offender had repented. The duty of the church now became clear. Paul's concern was that the brother should be reclaimed.

So you should rather: literally, "so that on the contrary rather." This expression implies a contrast between the duty of the church and some other action. *So* gives the natural consequence from the fact that the penalty had been sufficient to lead to repentance. Perhaps the contrast is between their former expulsion of the offender and the contemplated restoration. More probably, the contrast is between the continued desire of some to add to the punishment and Paul's desire for his restoration.

To forgive: remove the offense as a barrier to future fellowship. Forgiveness does not mean that the offense is forgotten or belittled. It is rather to act in grace, like that of God's, and use the ruptured fellowship as a steppingstone to a more loving fellowship in the future.

To . . . comfort: encourage to renewed efforts to live the true Christian life. *Comfort* has the same meaning here that it does in the rest of the epistle—"to encourage, hearten, strengthen." Since the man had seen the error of his way and wished to remedy his actions, it was the duty of the church to encourage him in that direction. It is always the duty of Christians to encourage the penitent. It is sadly true that Christians are often slow to forgive rather than slow to anger.

Or he may be overwhelmed by excessive sorrow: literally, and more colorfully, "lest in some way by the more abundant grief such a one should be swallowed up." The Greek word which the RSV translates *overwhelmed* means "to drink down, swallow up, devour." It is found in the expression: "Your adversary the devil prowls around like a roaring lion, seeking someone to devour" (1 Pet. 5:8). Paul meant to imply that the church, if it did not forgive, would be doing the devil's work for him. The offender would be discouraged by his excessive sorrow, sorrow beyond what he should have, and give up his desire to live a Christian life.

Verse 8: Paul's appeal to the Corinthians to act as Christians.

So: rather, "wherefore." The idea is that Paul's appeal followed naturally from the situation as he had expressed it in verse 7.

I beg you: rather, "I encourage." This is the same Greek word which was translated "comfort" in verse 7, speaking of the action of the church toward the offending brother. Paul fulfilled his duty by comforting, i.e., encouraging the church to do its duty. It is noteworthy that Paul never invoked any kind of authority when dealing with church actions. The church was independent. It could follow his advice or not, as it chose. However, when speaking of gospel truths, Paul often spoke as one who had authority.

To reaffirm your love for him: Reaffirm translates a legal term which means "to make valid" or "ratify." The same word is used of a legally valid or ratified will (cf. Gal. 3:15). *Your* is inserted by the translators; the Greek has only *love*. *Love* stands out more boldly and absolutely if *your* is omitted. It is the Christian love and concern for the welfare of the man that is meant.

Verse 9: gives the reason why Paul was writing the present admonition to the church.

For this is why I wrote: rather, "am writing." *Wrote* is probably an epistolary past tense. When they read the letter which he was now writing, his writing would be in the past. *I wrote* therefore refers to this present letter.[1] Otherwise, we would have to assume that he had written them in his previous letter—perhaps the sorrowful letter—to forgive this brother. However, this does not seem to fit into the sequence of Paul's relationships with the church at Corinth.

That I might test you: rather, "know the proof of you." *Test* translates a Greek word which means "proof." It was the word used to describe the test of the genuineness of precious metals.

Whether you are obedient in everything: Their forgiveness of the brother would be evidence that they were ready to give complete obedience. The form of the Greek expression does not imply doubt on the part of Paul, but confidence. But to whom or what was their obedience to be rendered? To Paul or to the gospel? Either makes good sense in this context. However, Paul did not usually use "obey" with himself as the object. His practice, when using the word, was to speak of obedience to Christ or to the gospel. We must conclude, in the light of this fact and in the light of his words in verse 8, that the obedience was obedience to the gospel or to Christ.

Verse 10: is a promise on the part of Paul to share their forgiveness of the offending brother, and a statement that his willingness to forgive was based on a desire for their benefit.

Any one whom you forgive, I also forgive: limited to this present case, not a general statement. It was a promise to share their forgiveness. *Forgive* is the present tense in Greek, but the context demands that it be given a future meaning. Paul anticipated that they would forgive when they received this present letter.

What I have forgiven: introduces another reason for his writing the letter. It was not only to test their obedience (vs. 9) but also to benefit them. *I have forgiven* speaks of a forgiveness which was already a fact in the case of Paul. No doubt he meant that when Titus had returned and informed him of the penitence of the offender, he had as a matter of fact forgiven him.

If I have forgiven anything: parenthetical statement, expressing doubt that he really had anything to forgive. There is no doubt that he had forgiven. The doubt is whether he had been offended.

---

[1] Bernard, on the contrary, takes it to refer to 1 Corinthians (J. H. Bernard, *The Second Epistle to the Corinthians,* Vol. III of *The Expositor's Greek Testament,* edited by W. Robertson Nicoll [Grand Rapids, Mich.: Wm. B. Eerdmans Publishing Company, reprint edition]. Referred to in this work as EGT).

Has been for your sake: your benefit.

In the presence of Christ: literally, "in face of Christ." *Presence* is probably the correct translation. The idea is that Paul's action in forgiving the offender was consciously carried out with the feeling that the eyes of Christ were upon him.[1] Not only the benefit of the church, but the pleasing of Christ, accounted for his forgiving spirit.

Verse 11: explains further what is meant by "for your sake" (vs. 10).

To keep Satan from gaining the advantage over us: The spirit of unforgiveness opens the way for Satan to defraud the Christian. *Gaining the advantage over* translates a single Greek word which means "to take advantage of, to overreach." The thought is that Satan, by unchristian attitudes on the part of the Corinthians, would gain the upper hand over them in their Christian lives. *Us* includes both Paul and the Corinthians. The thought is not that the offender would be thrown back into the hands of Satan (Plummer), but that the church would be. This verse tells us that a church or an individual Christian may be overcome by evil simply by failing to do right. We often think that evil has power over us only when we actually do something that is wrong. Not so. Righteousness is a positive way of life, not a negative one. Failure to do right is in itself the most common sin of Christians.

For we are not ignorant: i.e., we are fully aware of. The statement is an understatement for emphasis. *We* is probably editorial. Its use does not imply that the Corinthians shared the knowledge of Paul at this point.

Of his designs: i.e., his evil plans and purposes. There can be no doubt that Paul believed in the existence of a personal devil who sought to bring about the ruin of God's people as well as to prevent the salvation of the lost.

There are four designations for the evil one in this epistle: "Satan" (here; 11:14; 12:7); "the serpent" (11:3); "Belial" (6:15); and "the god of this world" (4:4). In other epistles he is called: "the tempter" (1 Thess. 3:5); "the devil" (Eph. 4:27); "the evil one" (Eph. 6:16); and "the prince of the power of the air" (Eph. 2:2).

(5) His great concern for them had forced him to leave Troas before he had meant to (2:12–13)

Paul completed the first part of his discussion of his change of plans by showing that his concern for them was so great that it took precedence over his desire to stay at Troas. The purpose of the paragraph is to show how wrong it was for them to think that his failure to visit them was due to fickleness or lack of love for them.

Verse 12: tells about his coming to Troas and the great opportunity which he had there.

When I came to Troas: refers to the beginning of the journey from Ephesus to Macedonia to Corinth.

---

[1] IB says Paul felt obligated to act in the spirit of Christ with nothing done from caprice or pride. (Floyd V. Fisson, *Interpreter's Bible,* Vol. 10, Edited by George A. Buttrick, © 1953.) Referred to as IB.

To preach the gospel of Christ: may be a correct translation, but the Greek is more general, meaning that he came with reference to the gospel. It may be that Paul had only meant to stop at Troas for a few days and strengthen the church that existed there.

A door was opened for me: rather, "stood open." *A door* means an opportunity to evangelize.

In the Lord: Paul's way of speaking of the general sphere of Christian work. *In the Lord* does not have the personal and dynamic dimension of such expressions as "in Christ" or "in Christ Jesus."

Verse 13: Though the door of opportunity stood open, Paul could not take advantage of it because of his concern for Corinth.

But my mind could not rest: a tame translation of the Greek expression, which means, "I did not have any relief in my spirit." The picture is of a man in the turmoil of anxiety.

Because I did not find my brother Titus there: his emissary to the church at Corinth. Probably plans had been made for Titus to meet Paul at Troas and report the outcome of his mission.

So I took leave of them and went on to Macedonia: where this letter was written after Titus had come and reported the good news from Corinth.

The natural connection would have been for Paul to go on to the report of Titus (7:5–16), but he digressed from the immediate situation to discuss his ministry.

2. Paul's Relation with the Corinthians a Discharge of His God-given Commission (2:14—6:10)

This section has often been called a great digression on the Christian ministry, but this misses the point.[1] True, the statements of Paul seem, at times, to be far removed from the situation to which he addressed himself. Just as true, they often seem quite pertinent. How can this be explained? The answer seems to be that Paul was claiming authority for his gospel. His concern for the Corinthians was in harmony with his commission as an apostle of Jesus Christ. His attempts to point this out led at times to an enlargement of the theme of the ministry to the proportions of an essay. However, it is impossible to understand this section without realizing that it was meant to answer the objections of his opponents. They believed that he was presumptuous when he spoke to them with apostolic authority.

The progress of thought is not even; an exact outline is impossible. However, there seem to be five things, in general, which he wished to say and did say: (1) He pointed out that his sufficiency, as well as his commission, came from God (2:14—3:6). (2) He pointed out that his ministry was superior to that of Moses to the same extent and in the same way that the new covenant was superior to the old (3:7–18). (3) He told the Corinthians that he had been saved from despair by the surpassing grace of God (4:1–18). (4) He claimed that his ministry was characterized by the three supreme Christian virtues—hope, faith, and love (5:1–21).

---

[1] IB calls it a "great parenthesis."

(5) The final paragraph is an appeal to the Corinthians not to accept the grace of God in vain (6:1–10).

(1) Paul's sufficiency, as well as his commission, came from God (2:14—3:6)

Three subsidiary thoughts may be found in this section of material. (1) The ministry of Paul was such that men's decisions concerning his gospel had ultimate significance (2:14–17). (2) The experience of the Corinthians was Paul's letter of commendation (3:1–3). (3) Paul's sufficiency for this kind of ministry came from God (3:4–6).

Verse 14: An outburst of thanksgiving to God for his wonderful grace is in marked contrast to the report of his dejection when he left Troas. The change of spirit marks the beginning of a new thought.

Thanks be to God: The order of the Greek words is different from Paul's usual order. It is literally: "To God be the thanks." The same order is found in 1 Corinthians 15:57. Here, as well as there, we have an outburst of gratitude of noble magnitude. No doubt this outburst was caused by the contrast between his dejection as he left Troas, which he well remembered, and the report of the triumph of the gospel which he had received from Titus.

In Christ: personal and dynamic union with Christ. It is through union with him that the apostles were led in triumphal procession.

Who . . . leads us in triumph: has as its background the triumphal procession of a victorious Roman general. The greatest honor that a Roman general could receive was such a procession. It was granted only under certain circumstances. The general must have commanded an army which had been completely victorious, with at least five thousand of the enemy fallen. The procession had the following order: first the state officials and the senate, then the spoils of war taken from the conquered land, then pictures of the conquered land and its citadels and ships, then the white bull destined for sacrifice, then the captives in chains (enemy princes, generals, and leaders) destined to be executed or imprisoned, then the lictors and musicians, then the priests, then the general himself (clothed in a purple tunic, carrying an ivory scepter with a Roman eagle at the top), riding in a chariot drawn by four horses, then the family of the general, and finally the army which he had commanded in the field.[1] It is uncertain just what part Paul conceived himself playing in God's triumphal procession, whether that of one of the captives or that of a soldier in the victorious army, shouting the praise of the general. Possibly, in view of the fact that he considered himself to be a slave of Christ, he thought of himself as a captive, not meant, however, for execution but for enslavement.[2]

Always: indicates the continuous nature of God's triumphal procession.

Us: probably refers to the apostles as a whole, but it should be true of any Christian.

---

[1] William Barclay, *The Letters to the Corinthians* (Philadelphia: The Westminster Press, 1954). Hereafter referred to as Barclay.

[2] Denney says Paul was not the soldier who won the battle but the captive who was led in the procession.

And through us: through our ministry of preaching the gospel. They were the agents through whom God worked and accomplished his victories.

Spreads the fragrance: continues the picture of the triumphal procession. It was customary for sweet odors to be released from the burning of spices in the streets.

The knowledge of him: which the gospel gives. This knowledge is considered to be the fragrance of heaven which men smell when they receive the gospel.

Everywhere: the thought of victory in Corinth led to the thought of the universal victory of the gospel. Paul believed that the gospel was universal, that it met the needs of all men. He spoke hyperbolically here, perhaps meaning everywhere he went.

Verse 15: In figurative language Paul pointed to the decisive significance of his ministry among those who heard him.

We: perhaps all the apostles, but the primary emphasis is on Paul's own ministry.

Are an aroma: a different word from *fragrance* in verse 14. This is the word which is used in the Old Testament (Greek version) for the sweet smell that the burnt offerings gave off. Paul thought of his ministry as a sacrifice to God.

Of Christ: the source of the aroma. *Of Christ* has the place of emphasis in the Greek sentence. It was Christ whom the apostles preached, and such preaching was pleasing to God.

To God: God is pictured as the one who smells the aroma and is pleased by it.

Among those who are being saved: one by one. The present tense is distributive in sense. The believers of the gospel are meant.

And among those who are perishing: one by one. The repetition of the preposition is significant. Paul believed that the human race was divided into two divisions—believers and unbelievers.

Verse 16: explains the way in which the gospel ministry is decisive for the two classes of people and asks a question concerning human sufficiency for such things.

To one: the unbelievers.

A fragrance from death to death: from one evil condition to another. This should not be pressed as a literal saying. The meaning is that of progress, movement from bad to worse. The unbelievers were already lost when the gospel came to them; its preaching only confirmed and deepened their condition. This is a solemn thought. When the gospel is preached, men respond to it, either with faith in Christ or by being driven deeper into doom. There are Jewish sayings which indicate that the words of the law are medicine to the wise and poison to fools (Plummer).

To the other: believers.

A fragrance from life to life: Again the idea of progress from one state to another is meant. The acceptance of the gospel and surrender to Christ leads to life. Continued hearing of the gospel by the believer leads to a deeper experience of that same life in Christ.

Who is sufficient for these things?: i.e., who is equal to such a responsi-bility? The answer expected is "No one." The question is an expression of great humility on the part of Paul as he thought of the consequences of his own preaching. At the same time it is an indication of how wrong the Corinthians were to think of him as flippant and giddy in the discharge of his ministry. He was aware that his ministry, by the grace of God, had ultimate significance to his hearers. One can never afford to be flippant when performing a heart operation that is a question of life or death for the patient. Nor can he be flippant when facing the dread responsibility of preaching the gospel which is a matter of eternal life or death. Paul's answer to his own question would be that no one was sufficient for these things.

Verse 17: Paul stated the seriousness with which he took his commis-sion of preaching, in contrast to the flippancy with which his opponents approached the task of preaching.

We are not . . . peddlers: Peddlers had an evil connotation in the business practices of the day. They often adulterated their product.[1] This practice forms the background of Isaiah 1:22: "Your silver has become dross, your wine mixed with water." Paul's claim was that his gospel was the pure gospel, without adulteration. Probably he had been accused of just this because he had not insisted that his converts be circumcised and keep the Mosaic law. His opponents were men who, like the heretics in Galatia, insisted that the Gentile convert must become a Jew if he was to be saved.

Like so many: Paul's countercharge against his opponents. They, not he, were the hucksters who contaminated the word of God with human teachings and demands. Such an admixture of foreign elements in the gospel had the effect of changing the gospel, from the good news of what God had done in Christ leading to salvation by grace alone, into a system of religion, merely human in origin, which called for human achievement. Thus meaningful issues were at stake, and Paul did not shrink from the necessity of condemning those who would change the gospel.

God's word: a frequent expression in the New Testament for the gospel. The same expression occurs nearly forty times in the New Testament, being especially common in Acts and Paul (Plummer). Instead of *God's word* one should read, "the word of God," i.e., the word that has its source in God.

But: strong adversative introducing contrast between the true preacher and the peddler of God's word.

As men of sincerity: The RSV translation obscures the connection of words in the Greek sentence. A literal translation of this clause would read: "But as out of sincerity, yes, as out of God before God in Christ we continue to speak." This expression is: "We speak . . . out of sincerity." *Sincerity* indicates that motive of heart which can stand the light of the sun (cf. 1:12, where the same Greek word is used and discussed). Sincerity was the internal source of all of Paul's speaking.

As commissioned by God: rather, "yea, out of God." Speaking "out of God" was synonymous with speaking "out of sincerity," in Paul's mind.

---

[1] Strachan applies this to wine-sellers.

There is no word for *commissioned* in the Greek. The purpose of the clause was not so much to describe the men, but the preaching as coming from sincere purposes and inspired by the faithful God (cf. 1:18), who could not lie (cf. Titus 1:2).

We speak: present tense meaning, "We continue to speak as a habit of life."

In Christ: as united with him, representing him to the world. This is the last of several characteristics of the true minister, both negative and positive, which are mentioned in this verse. Negatively, he must not be one who is concerned only for himself and is willing, therefore, to water down the gospel in order to avoid offending his hearers or to make their Christian life easier. Positively, he must speak from an open and sincere heart without guile, be inspired of God, speak as one on whom God's eyes rest, and be a reincarnation of Christ. Such a man would be sufficient for the task of the gospel ministry.

Verse 1 of Chapter 3: continues the thought introduced in the previous verses, but introduces a new subject as well—letters of recommendation. The custom of writing letters of recommendation was common in ancient times, as it is in modern times. There are two instances of such letters in the New Testament. When Apollos went to Corinth the first time, "the brethren encouraged him, and wrote to the disciples to receive him" (Acts 18:27). This was an instance of one group of disciples (those in Ephesus) sending a letter of recommendation to another group of disciples (those in Corinth) in order to introduce and certify a preacher. Romans 16:1–2 is a more formal note of this kind, inserted into the longer writing: "I commend to you our sister Phoebe, a deaconess of the church at Cenchreae, that you receive her in the Lord as befits the saints, and help her in whatever she may require from you, for she has been a helper of many and of myself as well." It is this custom which lies behind verses 1–3.

Verse 1: raises the question of Paul's need of such letters.

Are we beginning to commend ourselves again: indicates that such accusations had been made against him in Corinth. His statements in the previous verse (2:17) might well be taken by hostile minds as an attempt at self-commendation. The question is rhetorical.

Or do we need . . . letters of recommendation: another rhetorical question expecting a negative answer.

As some do: an ironical reference to his opponents, the hucksters of the gospel. The anonymous *some* gives point to the irony.

To you, or from you: suggests that Paul's opponents had gained entrance and hearing in Corinth on the strength of letters of recommendation. They would ask for such letters from the Corinthians when they departed. Perhaps some of them had already left Corinth and received such letters. There is no evidence of the identity of those who had given the letters of recommendation. Perhaps some of the prominent Christians in Jerusalem had done so.

Verse 2: Paul insisted that he did not need such letters of recommendation.

You yourselves are our letter of recommendation: rather, "our epistle, you are." *Letter* is in the place of emphasis in the Greek. *You* is emphatic and the addition of *yourselves* in the RSV is justified. No other testimonial was needed by Paul.

Written on your hearts: based on an inferior text. *Your* should be "our." The textual evidence is so strong for "our" that the retention of *your* by the RSV translators is inexplicable. Yet the true reading creates a problem. The metaphor becomes more mixed and difficult. How could that which was written on Paul's heart be read by all men? Perhaps the two thoughts need to be separated. "Written on our hearts" expresses the grateful remembrance of Paul. The Christian life of the Corinthians was impressed on his heart in an unforgettable way.[1]

To be known and read by all men: should be connected with the first part of the verse; thus, "You are our letter of recommendation . . . to be known and read by all men." Their Christian life, in such marked contrast to their former pagan life, was apparent to all who knew them. Thus, it was their life which was known and read by all men. The expression may be an indirect blow at his opponents whose testimonial letters were read by only a limited audience. Note the change of tenses. *Written* is a perfect participle; *known* and *read* are present participles. The testimonial had been written long ago on the heart of Paul; it was continually known and read.

Verse 3: continues the metaphor and the sentence from verse 2.

And you show: another present participle, parallel with *known* and *read*. The idea is that they were continually showing that they were Paul's epistle of recommendation.

That you are a letter from Christ: an obscure phrase. Does it mean that they were a letter from Christ, or a letter about him, or a letter belonging to him? Either interpretation is possible. Perhaps the RSV choice is correct, and Paul was saying that Christ was the author of his credentials. Thus he would disclaim all credit for the writing, asserting that the composition of the letter was by Christ.

Delivered: rather, "ministered." This means that Paul and his fellow-workers were the ministers through whom the letter came into existence. We need not press the metaphor and ask whether Paul thought of his ministry as that of the secretary who wrote the letter or of the postman who delivered it.

Written: returns to the perfect participle. Thus the letter had been written in the past and still stood as it was penned.

Not with ink: an ancient writing liquid made by mixing soot, gum, and water. It could be easily blotted out. The transitoriness of the writing is the main thought of the figure.

But with the Spirit of the living God: stresses the permanence of the writing. The illumination of the Spirit of God is contrasted with the fading ink. God is often described both in the New Testament and in the Old as "living."

Not on tablets of stone: a reference to the giving of the Law to Moses.

---

[1] Baird suggests an alternative, that is, that the letter is written by Christ on the hearts of all Christians. Christians in general, not Paul alone, are bearers of the letter (William Baird, "Letters of Recommendation: A Study of 2 Cor. 3:1–3," *Journal of Biblical Literature,* June, 1961, pp. 166–172).

True, those tablets were written by the finger of God, but they were essentially external things without power to touch the hearts of men.

But on tablets of human hearts: a reasonable translation of a difficult phrase in the Greek. The expression would be better if *tablets* were omitted, but the textual evidence does not permit this. Perhaps Paul unthinkingly repeated *tablets* under the influence of the previous phrase. The thought is clear. The writing of the Holy Spirit is on hearts, not on tablets of stone. The Corinthians could not disregard such a testimonial. Not only was it written on Paul's heart, but also, undoubtedly, on theirs. In other words, their memory of the operation of the Holy Spirit in their lives when they responded to his gospel should be all the commendation that he needed.

Verses 4–6: return to the thought of the sufficiency of the minister. Paul asserted that it was a gift from God. What Paul had said in the previous verses might have led some to think that he was overly confident. In these verses he was anxious to point out that his sufficiency was not an innate quality, but that it came from the qualifications which God had given him.

Such is the confidence: the confidence expressed in verses 1–3 that he needed no other credentials than those which the Corinthians in their Christian life furnished him. That fact alone sufficed to prove his apostleship and the genuineness of his gospel.

That we have through Christ: not through any power of his own. Christ was the channel through which Paul's confidence was mediated.

Toward God: rather, "face to face with God." The Greek preposition means "face to face" when used with a person. God is not spoken of as the object of his confidence. The proper preposition for expressing the object of confidence is "in" or "with reference to" or "on." God is spoken of as the one who judges the validity of one's credentials and is contrasted here with the opponents who doubted Paul's credentials.

Verse 5: Not that we are sufficient of ourselves to claim anything as coming from us: reminds us of the question, "Who is sufficient for these things?" (2:16). *Sufficient* comes from a Greek word which means "qualified." The statement has in mind the particular work of Paul in Corinth.

Our sufficiency is from God: states the source of his qualification for his work. There is a fanciful interpretation of the Old Testament name for God, *El Shaddai,* which gives it the meaning: "The Sufficient One." It is possible, but not likely, that Paul had this in mind and was saying, "Our sufficiency is from The Sufficient One."

Verse 6: Who has qualified us: same Greek word which was translated "sufficient" above. *Qualified* is in the past tense, pointing to the time when Paul was called to be an apostle.

To be ministers: general word for ministry or service from which we get our English word "deacon" by transliteration. It did not designate any official class of the clergy, but all Christians.

Of a new covenant: introduces for the first time the contrast between the Christian gospel and the old covenant which God had made with Israel. Jeremiah 31:31 contains the promise of that new covenant which would be characterized by forgiveness of sins and direct knowledge of God.

Covenant is really a mistranslation of the Greek word which means "will or testament." The word for *covenant* or "contract" is found in the Greek Old Testament, but never in the New. That word is not suitable for describing a covenant between God and man since it suggests a contract between equals. The biblical writers appropriated the term "testament" to describe the arrangement which God made with men for their salvation. The word is to be taken in a figurative sense, however. The idea is that God has graciously promised redemption and salvation; he has made a covenant with man, but the idea is that of gift rather than contract. *New* in this expression is the word which means new in quality and always suggests the superiority of that which is new over that which is not.

Not in a written code but in the Spirit: rather, "not of letter but of Spirit." The idea of *code* is not contained in the expression and is misleading. The expression modifies the new covenant and suggests the way in which it is superior to the old. The old was characterized by a multitude of legalistic requirements that men must keep if they were to live; the new guides men to a knowledge of God and enables them to do what is right. The contrast is between the gospel with its promise of life and the whole Jewish law with its threat of death.

For the written code kills, but the Spirit gives life: continues the contrast. It is the nature of law to kill. This does not refer to the threat of death on those who disobeyed the law, but to the way of law which leads men along a path of religious endeavor that can only end in death. Law sets up standards of behavior which are unattainable. On the other hand, the Holy Spirit gives life by bringing forgiveness from sin and the power to live as God wants one to live.

(2) Paul's ministry was superior to that of Moses in the same way that the new covenant is superior to the old (3:7–18)

Paul did not deny the glory of Moses' ministry. But as the car headlights which appear bright in the dark fade to nothing in the bright sunlight, so the glory of the law fades to nothing in the presence of the gospel. In this paragraph Paul took up two words mentioned in verse 6—"minister" and "new covenant"—and discussed them with reference to the old covenant of which Moses was the minister. The ministry of the old covenant came with a glory which made it impossible for the Israelites to look on Moses' face (vs. 7). Paul reasoned that the coming of the new covenant must be attended by greater glory (vss. 8–11). The results of the two ministries are also different. The ministry of the law leads to blindness; the ministry of the new covenant leads to transformation of life (vss. 12–18). The main object of the paragraph is to show the superiority of the Christian ministry. Perhaps this is Paul's answer to those who would accuse him of boasting. He did not boast so much in himself as in his gospel.

Verse 7: introduces the glory which attended the ministry of the old covenant.

Now if: introduces the conditional clause which assumes that the following statement is true.

The dispensation: rather, "the ministry." This is still the word, used in verse 6, for ministry in general. Perhaps the whole sweep of Jewish history is involved in the word, but the primary emphasis is on the giving of the law to Moses on Mount Sinai. This event was one of the highlights of Jewish history, pointed to by all Jews as the foundation of their religion. The Judaizers in Corinth had, no doubt, made much of the glorious manifestations of God on that occasion.

Of death: characterizes the law by the effects which it produced in those who followed it as a way of religious life—death. This expression takes up the statement in verse 6: "The written code kills." Paul well knew the results of the legalistic way of life. He had said in another letter: "For sin, finding opportunity in the commandment, deceived me and by it killed me" (Rom. 7:11). In his first letter to the Corinthians he had written: "The sting of death is sin, and the power of sin is the law" (1 Cor. 15:56). Whereas the Judaizers had been promising a superior life through the law, Paul insisted that the law brought death.

Carved in letters on stone: rather, "in letters, engraved on stones." Two characteristics of the law are involved, not one. First, the law was in letters which might never be read and understood. Second, it was carved on stone, not on the hearts of men as the gospel is. Two contrasts with the gospel are involved here. The gospel is a person, not letters. The gospel is written on the hearts of men. The historical reference is to the giving of the law. "And Moses turned, and went down from the mountain with the two tables of the testimony in his hands, tables that were written on both sides; on the one side and on the other were they written. And the tables were the work of God, and the writing was the writing of God, graven upon the tables" (Exod. 32:15–16). The Ten Commandments are used for the law as a whole.

Came with such splendor: rather, "came in glory." They came into existence accompanied by a manifestation of the glory of God. *Such* is not a part of the Greek text, but its presence is justified by the comparative particle used to introduce the next clause.

That the Israelites could not look at Moses' face because of its brightness: The Old Testament passage has: "And when Aaron and all the people of Israel saw Moses, behold, the skin of his face shone, and they were afraid to come near him" (Exod. 34:30). In Jewish tradition this verse had been enlarged to mean that the splendor was so bright that the people could not look at Moses' face. Plummer cites a Jewish tradition that the light which shone on his face was the light which inaugurated creation.

Fading as it was: present tense indicating that it was fading even as the people looked upon it. The verb which is translated *fading* means "to make of no effect." The same Greek word is used in 1 Corinthians 2:6, where it is said that the rulers of this world were passing away.

Verse 8: begins the reasoning of Paul that the inauguration of the gospel and its ministry should be attended by a greater splendor.

Why should not: rather, "how shall not rather." The combination of particles is impressive, but the sense is that of the RSV translation.

The dispensation: rather, "the ministry." Same word as above. The reference is not to an abstract idea, but to the concrete inauguration of the gospel and its ministry through the preaching of the apostles.

Of the Spirit: characterizes the gospel ministry from the standpoint of its results. Those to whom the gospel is ministered receive the *Spirit,* and "the Spirit gives life" (vs. 6).

Be attended with greater splendor: completes the argument of Paul. He was saying that the gospel was attended in its inauguration by a glory, i.e., a manifestation of God, which was superior to that of the coming of the law. The events on the day of Pentecost form the background of the statement.

Verse 9: contains an argument from the lesser to the greater. Paul had already said that the old covenant was accompanied by the manifestation of God's glory (i.e., *splendor*). He now repeated this with emphasis, changing only the "of death" (vs. 7) to *of condemnation.* The old ministry was a ministry of death because it led to condemnation.

The conclusion is that the new ministry (i.e., *dispensation*) must far exceed it in splendor. This means that the manifestation of God's glory in the new covenant far surpasses that which accompanied the giving of the law. The reason follows from the results of the new covenant, it is a covenant of righteousness which is the opposite of condemnation. Righteousness is one of the great theological words of Paul. It means "the act of God's grace by which the sinner is forgiven and received into the fellowship of God." It is called "righteousness" because the experience of salvation is the basis and the germ of righteousness in the life of the Christian.

Verse 10: states that the law, which once had great glory, now had none. It had been surpassed. The verse is introduced by a phrase *indeed, in this case* (rather, "in this respect") which modifies the whole statement. There was a sense in which the law no longer had any glory at all.

What once had splendor: refers to the glory with which the law was inaugurated.

Has come to have no splendor at all: has faded as the moonlight fades when the sun rises.

Because of the splendor that surpasses it: the inauguration of the gospel ministry.

Verse 11: For if: as is true.

What faded away came with splendor: as it did.[1]

What is permanent: i.e., continues to abide as the way in which God deals with men. The law was temporary; the gospel has come to stay. This is the third contrast between the law and the gospel found in this paragraph. The first is found in verses 7–8: The law is a ministry of death; the gospel is a ministry of the Spirit. The second is found in verse 9: The law is a ministry of condemnation; the gospel is a ministry of righteousness. Now the third speaks of the law as temporary and of the gospel as permanent.

Must have much more splendor: because it is the consummation and climax of God's gracious provisions for man's salvation.

Verses 12–18: continues the argument for the superiority of the

---

[1] Wendland says that the law and the death it brought are in the past. (Heinz-Dietrich Wendland, *Die Briefe an die Korinther* [Göttingen: Vandenhoeck & Ruprecht, 1954]. Referred to by the last name of the author, Wendland.)

ministry of Paul to that of Moses. The contrast is between the results of the ministry of the law and of the ministry of the gospel in those who receive the ministry.

Since we have such a hope: Hope is used in the sense of a confident expectation. The object of the hope is that the gospel will prove permanent, that God has indeed reached the climax of his redemptive dealings with men, that the Christian era is indeed the "last days."

We are very bold: rather, "We continue using much openness." *We are* translates a Greek verb which means "to make use of, or to act." It is in the present tense, indicating continuous action. *Bold* translates a word which means "openness." It implies that there is a public exhibition of frankness in either action or speech. It is the opposite not only of timidity but of reserve. The contrast is between Paul's habit of speech and Moses' withdrawal after he had completed the giving of the law. *Very* means "much, or full." The idea is that Paul's speech was fully open and above-board, without hidden meanings.

Verse 13: Not like Moses: introduces the contrast between his ministry and the ministry of Moses.

Who put a veil over his face: refers to the story in Exodus 34:33–35: "When Moses had finished speaking with them, he put a veil on his face; but whenever Moses went in before the Lord to speak with him, he took the veil off, until he came out; and when he came out, and told the people of Israel what he was commanded, the people of Israel saw the face of Moses, that the skin of Moses' face shone; and Moses would put the veil upon his face again, until he went in to speak with him." The brightness was, in each case, caused by his conversing with God. It would fade away when he was out of the divine presence. This, at least, was the conclusion of Paul, though it is not stated as the reason in the Exodus account. However, there is nothing inconsistent with the Exodus account in what Paul said.

So that the Israelites might not see the end of the fading splendor: states what Paul assumed was the reason for the veil.[1] The main point to Paul was that the fading glory represented the temporary nature of the law. Of course, this was Paul's own interpretation, and he was not intimating that the Old Testament story was told for that purpose.

Verse 14: turns to the effects produced on the Israelites by this display of glory.

But: strong adversative. Instead of what might have been expected, the contrary took place.

Their minds were hardened: probably refers to the fact that the Israelites of Moses' day had their minds, i.e., their thoughts, hardened. The past tense could be timeless and include both the ancient and contemporary Jews, but it is better to take it as a true past tense. *Hardened* is passive, but the agent is not named. Probably Paul thought of God as the agent who hardened their minds in judgment.

For to this day: turns to the contemporary Jews of Paul's day. They were the true spiritual descendents of their fathers.

---

[1] Barclay points out that the Old Testament does not say this.

When they read the old covenant: in their synagogues. The reading of the Old Testament was a regular part of the Jewish worship, as indicated in Luke 4:17–21. The old covenant includes all the books of the Old Testament.

That same veil remains unlifted: not the same one which Moses wore, but one with the same effect. *Veil* is used in a figurative sense for that which prevents the clear sight of what one is looking at. The metaphors are mixed here. The idea is that the Israelites did not see the glory of God in the reading of the law. Their eyes were veiled.

Because only through Christ is it taken away: probably parallel with the previous clause. The veil remains because it can only be taken away when one comes into union with Christ. The Jews had rejected him and were still blind.

Verse 15: expands and stresses the statement in verse 14: "That same veil remains unlifted."

Yes: a correct translation of the Greek particle which usually means "but." In this case, as is often true, the particle has the function of stressing a fact and is thus properly translated, "indeed" or *yes.* Here it functions to continue the thought with renewed emphasis.

To this day: makes it clear that Paul's mind was absorbed with contemporary conditions.

Whenever Moses is read: Moses is used as a metonym for the whole Old Testament, especially the law. *Whenever* is indefinite. *Read* means "read aloud." Paul had in mind the periodic meetings of the Jews in their synagogues for the reading of the law and the prophets, the recitation of the Shema, and the singing of psalms.

A veil: not the same veil as in verse 14, but that which has the quality of a veil. The absence of the article in Greek stresses the quality of the thing. Previously the veil had been something external which hid the truth from the Jews: here the veil was an internal condition that prevented its being lifted.

Lies: present tense of a permanent state of being.

Over their minds: rather, "upon their hearts," hiding the dawn of the new day in Christ. Whether there was an intentional change from, "their minds were hardened" (vs. 14) to, "upon their hearts" is debatable. It would seem that Paul deliberately changed the wording to stress the fact that the veil was internal and affected the center of existence among the Jews. Certainly the hindrance to the gospel was not merely intellectual. The hindrance lay in the whole way of life of the Jewish people.

Verse 16: stresses the power of the gospel to remove the veil from the heart of the Jew who believes. Paul knew this to be true because he had experienced the lifting of the veil. He had been a persecutor of Christians, convinced that Christ was an impostor and the gospel a lie. He became the foremost preacher of the gospel, convinced that Christ was the true Messiah and that the gospel was true.

But: adversative in meaning, marking a contrast between the thoughts of verses 15 and 16.

When: rather, "whenever." The expression is indefinite and is almost the same Greek construction as that translated "whenever" in the previous verse. At the time that this happens, no matter when it happens, the veil is removed.

A man turns to the Lord: probably a Jewish man is meant, since the Jewish man is the subject of discussion in this context. Perhaps there is an implied accusation against Paul's opponents, who seemed still to have the veil over their hearts. Otherwise, why would they try to proselyte Gentile converts to Judaism? This is a quotation from the Old Testament, but Paul appropriated the Lord to mean Jesus Christ, the Lord of all Christians.

The veil: i.e., the veil that lay over their hearts (cf. vs. 15).

Is removed: at once. The context justifies the thought that the veil is removed at once and for all time at the moment of the Jew's conversion.

Verse 17: is one of the most difficult theological verses in Paul's epistles. It seems to identify the Holy Spirit with Jesus Christ.

The Lord: that is, Jesus Christ, to whom the new convert turns when he repents.

Is the Spirit: has the article in Greek, which stresses identity. If *Spirit* were not used with the article, the translation could be, "The Lord is spirit." But this is impossible with the present construction. The problem is alleviated somewhat by the next phrase, "the Lord's Spirit," in which the usual distinction is maintained. However, this clause has been the cause of much theological debate, sometimes used to prove the deity of the Holy Spirit and sometimes used to prove the identity of the Spirit and Christ. This debate misses the point; it tries to force language which describes experience into a theological and metaphysical mold. It tries to use the words of Paul to answer questions which did not arise for centuries after his death. This is unfair in the extreme. We must remember that Paul was not writing theology; he was explaining his experience. In the experience of the Christian, it is impossible to distinguish the power of the risen Christ from the power of the Holy Spirit. In experience they are one and the same. We may try to make such distinctions when we are speaking theologically, but we do not try to do so otherwise. Why should Paul be forced to do so? It is clear that Paul did not confuse the persons of the Trinity, but it is equally true that he did not separate one from the other and conclude with three Gods. Theological discussion through the ages has had to try to walk the tight rope between these two unchristian alternatives.

In our present verse we must not lose sight of the main thrust of Paul's language because of a theological detour caused by our use of language. He was trying to say that when one turned to the Lord, the veil of prejudice was removed by the Holy Spirit. Thus, coming to the Lord meant to experience the power of the Holy Spirit. In this context it is easy to say that the Lord and the Holy Spirit are one in their action in the human heart, and this is what Paul meant to say by the expression, *The Lord is the Spirit.*

And where the Spirit of the Lord is: rather, "the Lord's Spirit." In this expression the distinction of persons is properly made. The Holy Spirit is the Lord's in the sense that he was sent by Christ to minister salvation in the hearts of those who believed in him.

There is freedom: spiritual freedom of all kinds, but especially freedom from the bondage of the law and sin. A good commentary on this statement is Paul's own words: "For the law of the Spirit of life in Christ Jesus has set me free from the law of sin and death" (Rom. 8:2). Service under the law was the service of unwilling bondage to the letter of the law; service under the Spirit is willing servitude to Christ, which is itself the true liberty of men.

Verse 18: a continuation of the metaphor of the veiled and the unveiled face, with a somewhat confusing shift of emphasis.

We all: all Christians, those who have found liberty in Christ. Two contrasts with the Jews are implied: one is, we who are Christians, in contrast with the enslaved Jews; the other is the contrast between *all* and "one," i.e., Moses.

With unveiled face: the third contrast in the verse. Moses veiled his face after speaking to the Jews so that they could not see the fading reflection of God's glory which lighted it. Christians have no need to veil their faces for the reflection of God's glory in their lives is permanent, not fading.

Beholding: rather, "reflecting." RSV has "reflecting" as a marginal translation in some editions; it should be given the preference. The Greek word means "to reflect," as a mirror reflects the image of the one before it.[1] Furthermore, the context in which Moses is said to have reflected, by his shining face, the glory of God makes this the preferred interpretation. Still more to the point, the idea of contemplation of the Lord is not a New Testament teaching. Christians are not transformed into God's image by contemplation but by shining forth with the glory of God themselves.

The glory of the Lord: the true manifestation of Christ as he has shown himself to be. This is what is reflected by the Christian when he lives a Christlike life, especially when he lives a life of love. Jesus said: "By this all men will know that you are my disciples, if you have love for one another" (John 13:35).

Are being changed: rather, "transformed." The present tense marks this as a continuous process going on in the lives of the Christians. "Transformed" does not refer to outer change, but to inner transformation.

Into his likeness: rather, "into the same image." Christ himself was the "image of the invisible God" (Col. 1:15). His life showed men what God is really like. The Christian is being transformed into the same kind of image, i.e., a true image of God.

From one degree of glory to another: probably a good translation of the meaning of the Greek, which reads, "from glory into glory." The idea of gradual progress toward the ideal is involved in the expression.

For this comes from the Lord: the transformation. The origin and source of the true manifestation of God in the lives of Christians is the Lord, i.e., Jesus Christ.

Who is the Spirit: a confusing phrase with three possible meanings, since the article is not used with either *Lord* or *Spirit*. The three possible translations are: (1) "by the spirit of the Lord"; (2) "from the spirit which is the Lord" (RSV); or (3) "from a sovereign spirit." Parallels can be found in Paul's writing for either of the three. The first two are parallel with the two expressions in verse 17. The sovereignty of the Holy Spirit is

---

[1] Allo prefers this translation though recognizing the possibility of the other.

affirmed in 1 Corinthians. The idea is that a spiritual effect must have a spiritual cause. Further, a spiritual change of such magnitude must have an adequate cause. The simplest way to solve the problem is to take *Lord* as the primary word—the change is effected by him. The Spirit is sent by the Lord (cf. John 16:7). The translation would then read: "from the Lord of the Spirit," i.e., the Lord who sends the Spirit.

(3) Paul had been saved from despair by the surpassing grace of God (4:1–18)

The key words in the chapter are: "We do not lose heart" (vss. 1, 16). First, Paul stated that the ministry of the gospel could not fail (vss. 1–6). Next, he noted the fact that this was true in spite of the fact that "this treasure" was contained in "earthen vessels" (vss. 7–12). Next, he asserted his faith in him "who raised the Lord Jesus and will raise us also" (vss. 13–15). Finally, he insisted that he did not lose heart, because the afflictions of the ministry were preparation for the coming glory (vss. 16–18).

Verses 1–6: are a statement of Paul's confidence that the ministry which God had given him could not fail. The thought can be divided into three subsections: Verses 1–2 are a reiteration of Paul's refusal to use worldly methods to preach the gospel. Verses 3–4 are a statement of the reason why the gospel was veiled in the case of some people. Verses 5–6 state the content and glory of the gospel.

Therefore: literally, "on this account," connecting this section very closely with what went before. The particular thought that is caught up and carried on is the thought of the *veil* on the hearts of the Jews. This thought is expanded to include all unbelievers.

Being engaged: translates the Greek word which means, "having." The RSV translation is perhaps a good one.

In this service: rather, "in this ministry." The same general word for *service* is used which was used in chapter 3. It is the gospel ministry which Paul had in mind.

By the mercy of God: literally, "just as we were mercied."

Having this ministry by the mercy of God: refers to Paul's ministry to the unmerited goodness of God. *Ministry* translates the same Greek word which was used in chapter 3 (8–9); it refers to the gospel ministry. *Having* means to be engaged in the ministry. Paul often attributed his conversion and call to the ministry to the mercy of God, which is, no doubt, what he meant here (cf. 1 Cor. 7:25; 1 Tim. 1:13, 16). Emphasis on this was needed in this letter since he had been accused of egotism and self-assertion by his opponents. Much of Paul's language in these verses, as throughout the epistle, was influenced by the opposition in Corinth. Sometimes he seemed to be answering charges. Sometimes he seemed to be making countercharges by stating things that he did not do. In some cases both motives might be present.

We: primarily Paul, but also includes Timothy and other fellow-workers.

Do not lose heart: present tense, meaning, "We never lose heart." The Greek word which is thus translated means "to lose heart or despair."

It indicates a timidity that shrinks from speaking out, a faintheartedness that takes refuge in silence and inactivity. Such faintheartedness is the opposite of the openness claimed in 3:12, "We are very bold." Some think that the word has the meaning of bravery, but this would apply only in the case of soldiers in battle. With regard to the ministry, our translation is to be preferred. One who is fainthearted, who gives up easily in the face of difficulties, is worthless in the gospel ministry.

Verse 2: describes the decision of Paul and his coworkers to renounce worldly methods of preaching the gospel.

We have renounced: points to a past decision which has continuing validity (cf. 1 Cor. 2:1–5). There is no need to ask when the decision was reached. Certainly it would not have been at his conversion but in relation to his mission. Perhaps it was first made when Greek audiences would be attracted by the use of persuasion. Some have believed that Paul tried worldly methods in Athens and found that they did not work, then decided to avoid them in Corinth. This is highly improbable. Of course, when speaking to the Jews, such methods were meaningless. The Jews asked only for scriptural proof of the correctness of a man's doctrine. With the Greeks the situation was different. They did not believe the Scriptures; they wanted to be persuaded by the display of reason. Paul refused this, knowing that such a display of wisdom would imply that the gospel was a system of philosophy. Such an implication was foreign to the nature of the gospel, which is good news of God's action in Christ. Good news needs to be proclaimed, not proved by processes of logic. Thus the nature of the gospel dictated and still dictates the correct methods of its proclamation.

Disgraceful, underhanded ways: literally, "the hidden things of shame." However, the translation is justified, since he was not talking about Gentile vices in general but about methods of proclaiming the gospel. This is, perhaps, a subtle assertion that his opponents—the Judaizers—used such methods.

We refuse to practice cunning: first of three result clauses. His renunciation of underhanded methods led to these results—two negative and one positive. *Cunning,* or "craftiness" (the more literal meaning), is the unscrupulous use of any means to gain one's point. The same Greek word is used to express the accusation made against Paul by some: "I was crafty, you say" (12:16).

Or to tamper with God's word: the second and parallel result clause. *Tampering* comes from a Greek word, used only here in the New Testament, but common in the papyri, where it was used for adulterating gold or wine (Robertson). This expression should be related to the statement: "We are not, like so many, peddlers of God's word" (2:17). This was just what the Judaizing opponents were doing. They were watering down the gospel so that it became insipid and tasteless. By suggesting that Christians voluntarily come under the law, they were denying the primary obligation of the Christian to obey God in all things.

This is always the way of legalistic living. Men who preach a system of rules think they are making Christianity more vital, when, as a matter of fact, they are draining it of its vitality. Rules may define behavior, but they also tend to limit it and create self-righteousness. The lack of rules may be dangerous, but it leaves man with the obligation to unlimited obedience to God. Perhaps the best solution is to look upon definite guidance as guidelines within the larger obligation. It is true that the weak Christian needs guidelines to help him determine, in the beginning, how he should live a Christian life. But the guidelines should never take on the nature of rules or law.

But by open statement of the truth: the third result clause in the positive sense. Since Paul had renounced underhanded methods, he used the method of *open statement* (i.e., manifestation) *of the truth*.[1] The truth, in the New Testament, always refers to the gospel, not to truth in general. The inscription of the saying of Jesus: "The truth will make you free" (John 8:32) on public school buildings is entirely out of place. Often the teaching of the gospel truth is prohibited by law in such schools, and the implication is that truth in general creates liberty. This simply is not true.

We would commend ourselves: present tense meaning, "We keep on commending ourselves." This expression looks back to 3:1–3. Paul needed no other recommendation than his open statement of the gospel truth.

To every man's conscience: a poor translation. The Greek should be translated to read: "to every kind of consciousness of men." The appeal was to every kind of human judgment that men used; not to logic alone, but to every faculty that could be brought into play to recognize the truth. By implication Paul denied any appeal to passion or prejudice, neither of which was a way of recognizing truth.

In the sight of God: the climax of the sentence. Not only did Paul appeal to men to judge him and his message; he lived and ministered in the sight of God. He claimed, by implication, a consciousness of God's approval of his ministry.

Verse 3: begins Paul's statement of why the gospel truth did not win universal acceptance.

And even if: admits that it is true. In spite of the open statement of the truth, the gospel did not win everyone to its side. Some remained blinded to its truth.

Our gospel: the good news which Paul preached.

Is veiled: perfect participle meaning "remains veiled." The expression is intensive.

It is veiled only to those who are perishing: in the case of unbelievers. The gospel had not reached their hearts; therefore they were perishing.

Verse 4: explains why unbelievers refuse the gospel.

The god of this world: that is, Satan. *World* translates the Greek word which means "age." This age, in the New Testament, is the present evil age (Gal. 1:4) which stands in contrast with the coming age (Eph. 1:21) in which God alone shall reign supremely (1 Cor. 15:28). Paradoxically, both ages are present in this present time. The thought is not so much of time, but of spheres of action. The separation is invisible and partial now; in the future it will be absolute.

By calling Satan a god, Paul did not mean to suggest an absolute dualism in which two eternal, coexisting deities, one evil and one good, battled

---

[1] EGT says this means the "plain statement of the gospel in public preaching."

for supremacy over human life. This was a Persian idea. The dualism of
Paul and John, like that of the Qumran communities, was moral. God
alone is God. Satan, however, has usurped the place which God should have
in some lives. In this sense he can be spoken of as their god, just as we
often speak of money as the god of some people. It is a god in the sense
that it has the supreme place in their lives. However, Paul obviously
thought of Satan as a personal being who exercises influence in the lives
of men. He shared the common New Testament conception that Satan is
the adversary of Christian men.

Has blinded the minds of the unbelievers: probably means that their
unbelief (i.e., their rebellion against God) opened the way for Satan to
exercise his leadership over them. Unbelief is both the cause and the result
of Satan's power. The *perishing* (vs. 3) and the *unbelievers* (here) are
coextensive. They are the same people regarded from a different viewpoint. *Perishing* describes their doom; *unbelieving,* their condition. *Minds*
means "thoughts." To speak of minds being blinded is a common form of
inconsistency for emphasis.

To keep them from seeing the light: states the purpose of Satan in
blinding the minds of unbelievers. The English expression, "to see the light,"
is a common metaphor for understanding something. The Greek verb can
be either transitive or intransitive. If transitive, it means "to see." If
intransitive, it means "to dawn." Probably the RSV translation is correct.
The sequence of words in this verse is stately and impressive: *see—
light—glory—likeness.*

The gospel of the glory of Christ: the message which contains and
proclaims the glory, i.e., the manifestation, of Christ. *Christ* [1] has the
article here and perhaps should be taken as a title and translated "the
Messiah."

Who is the likeness of God: the climax of the sentence. When one,
through the gospel, sees the glory of Christ, he sees the reality of God, for
Christ is the likeness (literally, "image") of God. This expression reminds us of the Christian hymn which Paul quoted: "He is the image of
the invisible God" (Col. 1:15). The glory of Christ consists of the fact
that when one sees him, he sees God. This was a basic tenet of early
Christianity and, indeed, of Christianity in all ages. It proclaims the belief
that knowledge of God gained from other sources is at best partial and
incomplete, and at worst misleading and erroneous. To know God in
truth is to know him as the "Father of our Lord Jesus Christ" (Eph. 1:3).
Neither philosophy nor nature nor introspection nor mysticism can lead
to a true and complete knowledge of God. Only by seeing the glory of
Christ through faith can we see God as he really is.

Verse 5: gives the content of the gospel.

For what we preach: continually (the verb is in the present tense).
We includes all of the apostles and Paul's fellow-workers. To *preach* is
to proclaim the authoritative message which one receives from his ruler.

Not ourselves . . . as Lord: a negative assertion. *Lord* is to be taken

---

[1] EGT suggests "the glorious revelation of Christ."

with both words. His opponents had obviously accused Paul of usurping the authority which did not rightly belong to him and of trying to become their master.

But Jesus Christ as Lord: the true content of the gospel message. It is a message of Jesus Christ. It is a message which proclaims the lordship of Christ.

With ourselves as your servants: defines the proper relation between Paul and the Corinthians. *Servants* translates the Greek word for "slave." Usually Paul thought of himself as the slave of Jesus Christ, but here he was willing to take the place of "slave" to the Corinthians. The word indicates his willingness to subjugate all personal desires and advantages for the good of the Corinthians. Their need was his command.

For Jesus' sake: explains why he was willing to be the slave of the Corinthians. It was to enable him to accomplish the will and purpose of Jesus, his true Lord, through his ministry to them.

Verse 6: states the basis on which the gospel message was preached.

For: a causal conjunction connecting this verse with the previous one.

God: has the place of emphasis in the sentence. The Greek has: "the God the one who said."

"Let light shine out of darkness": an inexact quotation of the Old Testament (cf. Gen. 1:3; Isa. 9:2). In this context the background is probably the passage in Isaiah, which reads: "The people who walked in darkness have seen a great light; those who dwelt in a land of deep darkness, on them has light shined." This passage—Isa. 9:1–7—is messianic. The background here is the redemptive purpose of God rather than creation.

Who has shone in our hearts: past tense. This expression is a satement of Paul's belief that his understanding of the centrality of Christ was a divine illumination, as indeed it must be in every heart. The reference is primarily, but not exclusively, autobiographical.[1] *In our hearts* marks the illumination as internal and spiritual.

To give the light of the knowledge of the glory of God: a stately series of expressions, parallel to that in verse 4. The whole expression is reminiscent of Paul's commission: "I have appeared to you for this purpose, to appoint you to serve and bear witness to the things in which you have seen me and to those in which I will appear to you . . . to open their eyes, that they may turn from darkness to light and from the power of Satan to God" (Acts 26:16–18). Thus Paul was saying that God had shone in his heart to illumine others. The illumination is the light that comes from a knowledge of God as he has revealed himself, i.e., his glory.

In the face of Christ: metaphor for, "in the person of Christ." It was in that person that the perfect illumination of the glory of God was given. He was the true mediator of the knowledge of God. The reflection of God's glory in his servants is a perfect illumination mediated through Jesus Christ, whereas the reflection in Moses' face was imperfect.

Verses 7–12: speak of the earthen vessels which contain the divine

---

[1] Hughes says the past tense points back to the time of Paul's conversion.

treasure. The contrast between the suffering and frail ministers of the gospel and the gospel itself is great. The paragraph continues the thought that Paul did not despair.

But: mild continuative particle. No break in thought is evident.

We have: present tense emphasizing continuity. The emphasis is upon the divine possession with which the minister has been entrusted.

This treasure: the gospel which brings the "light of the knowledge of the glory of God in the face of Christ" (vs. 6).

In earthen vessels: not a reference to the physical body but to the frail persons who possess the gospel. *Earthen* emphasizes the relative worthlessness of the vessel when compared to the treasure it holds. The meaning of the metaphor demands that *vessels* be taken in the sense of jars rather than other articles to which the word might be applied (furniture in a house, Luke 17:31; a sheet, Acts 10:11). The reference should be taken to the whole personality of the ministers.

To show that the transcendent power: i.e., the power that created the gospel and gave it entrance into the lives of men. This is transcendent because it goes beyond any power that men have. Men may persuade, but the gospel transforms. Men may pass on tradition, but the gospel reveals God.

Belongs to God: rather, "is from God." He is the origin of the power.

And not to us: the instruments through which God's power works.

Verses 8–10: contain four illustrations in which the frailty of the vessels might have proved fatal to the gospel but did not. All of them are taken from Paul's own experience.

We are afflicted in every way: rather, "in every way pressed." This was the first and least serious of the ills that Paul had suffered. Perhaps the idea of mental turmoil and anguish fits the context here. Many preachers feel that they live in pressure cookers. Some commentators take this to be a general word of which the next three expressions are explanatory, but this is not likely.

But not crushed: rather, "not hemmed in"; i.e., not without a way of escape from the pressure.

Perplexed, but not driven to despair: poor translation. The Greek contains a play on words which the English does not preserve. The translation, "being at a loss but not having lost out," would be effective. The word translated despair is an intensified form of the same word which is translated *perplexed.* These words are reminiscent of the language in 1:8: "We were so utterly, unbearably crushed that we despaired of life itself."

Verse 9: Persecuted, but not forsaken: pursued by men but not forsaken of God. *Persecuted* comes from the Greek word which means "to pursue." As the hunter pursues his prey, so the enemies of Paul pursued him with the hope of destroying him. The thought is that the onslaughts of his enemies would have destroyed Paul except for the sustaining power of God.

Struck down, but not destroyed: or, to modernize, "knocked down but not knocked out" (Barclay). It is probable that the last two illustrations, and perhaps all four, reflect the combat in the arena. They all reflect the pathway of thorns over which Paul walked to carry out his commission from God. There was enough to cause despair, but he never despaired.

Verse 10: a fifth contrast which sums up the meaning of the others in extreme language which might be changed to conform with the other four expressions and read, "always dying, yet never dead."

Always: perpetually without cessation.

Carrying in the body: experiencing in my life as an apostle. *Body* is to be taken to mean the whole life of Paul as he existed in this world. This is the usual meaning of the term for Paul, and there is no need to change its meaning here.

The death of Jesus: death that was threatened to him because of his fidelity to Jesus. The missionary of the first century faced the constant threat of death. Enemies were seeking his life as they sought the life of Jesus.

So that: introduces the purpose of his living under the threat of death.

The life of Jesus: the life which Jesus gives. These phrases express Paul's thought of a mystic union with Christ Jesus in which he himself had died and now lived Christ's life for him (cf. Gal. 2:20).

May also be manifested: made clear and open to the gaze of all men.

In our bodies: i.e., in our lives on earth.

Verse 11: repeats for emphasis the thought of verse 10.

For while we live: rather, "for always we the living." The thought is of the disciples of Christ and especially those who proclaim his gospel. While they are "the living," they are the living prey of their enemies and his.

We are always being given up to death: subject to the sentence of death. *Given up* (i.e., delivered over) is the verb used for the deliverance of Christ to death.[1] Those who follow him in his glory must follow him also in his cross.

For Jesus' sake: on account of our relation to him.

So that the life of Jesus may be manifested: repeats the statement in verse 10.

In our mortal flesh: another expression for the human life in its frailty and is synonymous with "body." The flesh, the self, is subject to death; therefore it is called mortal. Thus the paradox of the paragraph is restated. It is just in the self which is subject to death that the life of Jesus finds its true manifestation.

Verse 12: marks the contrast between the missionaries and the converts.

So: as a result of all this.

Death is at work in us: already beginning and carrying on its work: *Death* is personified and pictured as carrying on a program of destruction in the lives of the apostles.

But life in you: eternal life that is the gift of God to all believers. Paul did not mean that the Corinthians did not share his concern for the preaching of the gospel. When they did and to the extent that they did, the

[1] Tasker points out that the missionaries could never be sure that they would be alive tomorrow.

processes of death would work in them as it did in him. His thought of them was purely in the role of converts. In that role the life of Jesus which was manifested in his mortal flesh worked in them.

Verses 13–15: state the reason why Paul continued to speak without discouragement in spite of his trials. The reason was his faith in the one who raised Jesus from the dead (vss. 13–14) and for the sake of the Corinthians (vs. 15).

Since we have the same spirit of faith: an expression which has given rise to much speculation. There is no doubt that Paul turned to a new, but related, thought. *Since* is mildly adversative. The continuity of thought is: "Even though death works in us and life in you, we will not be silent but continue to speak." Two problems of interpretation arise: Does *faith* refer to personal faith or to doctrinal beliefs? And does *the same* refer to the Corinthians' faith or to the faith of the ancient psalmist whom he quoted? *Spirit* refers to the Holy Spirit as the giver of faith, not to the internal disposition of Paul and his fellow-workers. First, it would seem that *faith* is the personal faith of the ministers in the power of God, rather than a doctrinal belief. Verse 14 speaks of his knowing that he would be raised from the dead. Thus it would seem that *faith* is equivalent to knowing or to confident expectation. The thought is that though he recognized that death was now working in him, he realized as well that death would not have the final say. This was his faith.

Concerning the meaning of the expression *the same,* there is a wide divergence of opinion. Strachan believes that Paul meant the same as that which the Corinthians had, so that the expression turned from the contrast between Paul and the Corinthians to the likeness that existed.[1] While this makes good sense, it does not seem to be the best interpretation. It is better to take it as referring to the faith of the psalmist[2] and that kind of faith which characterized the prophets of old. Thus the RSV translation of the next phrase, *as he had who wrote,* is to be accepted as the true interpretation.

"I believed, and so I spoke": These are the exact words which are found in Ps. 116:10 in the Septuagint. It is probable that Paul had the whole Psalm in mind, though he quoted only a few words from it. If so, the Psalm fitted the occasion perfectly. Verses 10–11 of the Psalm read: "I kept my faith, even when I said, 'I am greatly afflicted'; I said in my consternation, 'Men are all a vain hope.'" Paul did not mean that his faith was regulated by the psalmist, but that it was like that of the psalmist, the faith which was bestowed by the same Spirit who inspired the psalmist.

We too believe: present tense of continuous action.

And so we speak: present tense of continuous action.[3] The continued speaking arose from and expressed the permanent faith.

---

[1] R. H. Strachan, *The Second Epistle of Paul to the Corinthians* (New York and London: Harper and Brothers Publishers, 1935). Hereafter referred to by the name of the author.

[2] Cf. Tasker.

[3] Denney remarks that "faith naturally speaks."

Verse 14: Knowing: more aptly expresses the idea of hope than of faith. Yet, there is only a fine line of distinction between the two words in the New Testament. Paul's knowledge was the same as his faith in this instance.

That he who raised the Lord Jesus: i.e., God. This is the usual way of speaking of the resurrection of Jesus. He did not rise; he was raised.

Will raise us also: expresses the confidence of Paul that he also would be raised from the dead. This hope is discussed further in the next chapter.

With Jesus: to share his glory. This does not mean that Jesus will be raised up again when we are raised, but that our resurrection is dependent on his life. His resurrection was the first fruits of the resurrection which promised and guaranteed the final harvest (cf. 1 Cor. 15:20).

And bring us: rather, "present us." The verb used is the common word for the presentation of a sacrifice. Peter wrote that Christ died for us that he might present us to God (1 Pet. 3:18). In another epistle Paul wrote: "And you, who once were estranged and hostile in mind, doing evil deeds, he has now reconciled in his body of flesh by his death, in order to present you holy and blameless and irreproachable before him" (Col. 1:21–22). This presentation of the Christian before God will be the final consummation of our salvation. We may have confidence in it to the extent that we have confidence that we are saved.

With you: expression of Paul's confidence in the salvation of the Corinthians. His hope was the common Christian hope.

Into his presence: not in the Greek, but justified by the metaphor in the light of the rest of the New Testament.

Verse 15: turns to another reason for Paul's continued faithfulness in speaking the word of God. By doing this, he benefited the Corinthians and added to the host of those who in the final day would glorify God.

For it is all for your sake: All is placed in the position of emphasis and is literally, "all things." All that Paul suffered, all that he did, is included. *For your sake* means for their salvation and growth in Christian graces. The particular idea is explained in the next phrase.

So that as grace extends to more and more people: through the ministry of the Corinthians. This expression shows what Paul meant by *for your sakes.* He did not contemplate the Corinthians as a reservoir, receiving and keeping the grace of God, but as a river, receiving and spreading it.

May increase thanksgiving: rather, "abound." The translation of the whole phrase is difficult. The RSV is perhaps as good as can be done with the Greek. However, the thought seems to be clear. Paul believed that his ministry to the Corinthians would lead to their ministry to others. This would be an abounding of the grace of God. In turn the increased number of converts would lead to the abounding of thanksgiving, the expression of gratitude.

To the glory of God: All this would lead to giving glory and recognition to God. Thus, the reasons for his continued speaking rested ultimately in God. First, he had faith in the operation of God. Second, he had a desire for the glory of God.

Verses 16–18: are transitional from the statement of certainty concerning the resurrection (vss. 13–15) to the discussion of the future life (5:1–5). However, the subject is still that of God's surpassing grace which prevented despair on the part of the apostle. The contrast in these verses is between the light afflictions of the ministry when compared to the eternal quality of unseen things.

So: rather, "wherefore." The expression looks back to the statements of the previous verses and makes them the foundation of the statements in these verses.

We do not lose heart: repeats the assertion of verse 1.

Though: weak translation of the Greek particles. Literally they read, "but, even if." "But" is strongly adversative to the preceding statement, meaning, "We are far from losing heart." "If" assumes the truth of the following statement. "Even" is emphatic. "Even if" this is true, fainthearted-ness is not the result.

Our outer nature: literally, "our outer man." "Man" was often used by Paul as equivalent for "self," as it is here. In this verse we have the con-trast between the *outer* and the *inner self;* in verse 18 the contrast is between the *seen* and the *not seen.* Thus, the outer self is man in contact with the realities that are seen. It is wrong to take the outer self to mean only the material parts of man. Paul meant his whole self as a person living in the world and dealing with it.

Is wasting away: rather, "is in the process of being destroyed." The thought is not of internal factors which are decaying, but of external forces that bring about the destruction of the earthly self. In Paul's case these were the persecutions, the afflictions which meant that his days as a minister of Christ on earth were numbered. He felt himself to be in the process of being destroyed.

Our inner nature: i.e., our inner self, the self that has to do with unseen realities.

Is being renewed: the present tense points to the continuous process of renewal which Paul experienced. By comparing this word with "being destroyed" in the previous verse, we see something of the meaning of both words. Through ceaseless hard work, anxieties, ill health, and per-secutions Paul felt a constant drain upon his powers to deal with the problems of the ministry, a drain that heralded the final moment of death when the outer man would be no more. At the same time he felt a re-surgence of inner power through the continued presence of the Holy Spirit that was a foretaste of the eternal fountain of youth which he expected to find after death. It is difficult to explain the thought of this verse. Only ex-perience in the ministry can lead one to understand it.

Every day: rather, "day by day." As the strength was needed, it came.[1] Each day showed some progress in spiritual stature.

Verse 17: is a comparison between the affliction of the present and the glory of the future.

For this slight momentary affliction: an expression that is possible only

---

[1] Cf. Denney.

in the light of the coming glory. This verse reminds us of the statement of Paul in another passage: "I consider that the sufferings of this present time are not worth comparing with the glory that is to be revealed to us" (Rom. 8:18). However, the thought is not so much a comparison between affliction and glory, but rather a statement that God sometimes uses affliction for man's spiritual good.

Is preparing for us an eternal weight of glory beyond all comparison: rather, "is constantly working out for [or in] us more and more beyond measure an eternal weight of glory." The thought is that God was using the evil to work out in Paul and for Paul his spiritual good. This thought is one of the great statements of faith in the New Testament. God is never overcome by evil, nor are his people. Contrariwise, God uses the evil to work out the good; evil unwillingly becomes the servant of God. The supreme example of this, of course, is the cross. It was the supreme evil of the ages; yet, through it God worked out the redemption of all men. Paul applied this faith to his own afflictions. They were evil. How evil they appeared to him is told in verses 8–10. Yet, as he saw what God was doing through them, they appeared light. "The weight of glory more and more beyond measure" is a stately sequence of words to express Paul's unmeasurable hope.

Verse 18: Because we look not: i.e., do not direct our gaze. It is a participial construction in the Greek and may be interpreted as having conditional force. The point is that the working of God depends on the attitude of the men in whom he works. It is not enough that men suffer evil; this, in itself, does not work glory. It does so only if the concern of the Christian is for the things that really matter. If his concern is for the material and earthly realities, his evil can only be evil; it can never be good.

To the things that are seen: the values and standards of the world. This goes far beyond material things. It includes all the ambitions and desires of men who live in this world untouched by the Spirit of God.

But to the things that are unseen: the values and standards of God. These things are at present, to us, unseen. Yet they are real in the heart and mind of the Christian. The New Testament has many passages related to this one. The admonition of Jesus not to lay up for ourselves treasures on earth but to lay up treasures in heaven (Matt. 6:19–20) is one. The Beatitude which pronounces: "Blessed are those who hunger and thirst for righteousness" (Matt. 5:6) is another. As a matter of fact, this thought —that the Christian's concern should be with spiritual realities—forms a part of the fabric of the New Testament message.

For the things that are seen are transient: This is their nature. Even if one attains wealth and position and power on earth, all these end with death. Often they end before death.

But the things that are unseen are eternal: This is their nature. *Eternal* includes the idea of lasting beyond death, but it involves more than that. It involves the notion of a quality of being which is like that of the Eternal One—God. Though the thought of Paul was concentrated on the future world, the world beyond death, we must not forget that these unseen realities are present realities as well. The writer to the Hebrews tells us that they are so through our faith which makes them real (Heb. 11:1).

(4) Paul's ministry was characterized by hope, faith, and love (5:1–21)

This is one of the most important chapters in 2 Corinthians when judged from the standpoint of its modern significance. In the context of the epistle itself, it does not, however, outrank other chapters.

It is impossible in these chapters to mark out an exact break in the sequence of thought. Paul seems to have started speaking about his ministry as it related to the situation he faced and, without consciously organizing his thought, continued on to this climax. It is probable that the words, "the things that are unseen are eternal" (4:18), led Paul to expand on the subject of the Christian's hope (5:1–5). This discussion, in turn, led him to discuss the present situation of the Christian who is "away from the Lord" (vss. 6–10). This life is one of faith: "we walk by faith, not by sight" (vs. 7). The minister seeks to please the Lord, knowing full well that he must "appear before the judgment seat of Christ" (vs. 10). The mention of the judgment seat led Paul to develop the theme of the compelling love for Christ which motivated his entire ministry (vss. 11–15). Finally comes the climax of the chapter in which Paul asserted, in the light of all that he had said, that nothing was to be judged from the "human point of view" (vs. 16)—a point of view that is concerned with "things that are seen"—not even Christ (vs. 16), nor union with Christ (vs. 17), nor the ministry of reconciliation (vss. 18–21). This final section is climactic for the whole discussion of the ministry. If man views his life with reference to the transitory values of earth, his response to sufferings and difficulties is far different from what it would be if he viewed life from the standpoint of eternal realities. As a matter of fact, the only paragraph which has a distinct subject is the first (vss. 1–5). The heading for the chapter is an attempt to be broad enough to cover the entire chapter and at the same time to emphasize the central motifs.

Verses 1–5: a discussion of Paul's hope for the life after death. The primary problem from the modern theological viewpoint is whether Paul thought that the resurrection took place immediately after death or not. The relation of the material to the immediate context of Paul's ministry is that this material gives a further reason why Paul was not dismayed by the realization that his sufferings would ultimately result in his death. Death was not, to Paul, the end but a new beginning, especially if it were followed immediately by the resurrection.

For: a continuative particle, relating this paragraph to the previous one but marking a new departure of thought as well. It may introduce the reason why Paul continued to be concerned about unseen, rather than seen, things.

We know: is related to "knowing" in verse 14. In both verses the knowledge goes far beyond that which is possible through the exercise of human logic. Paul knew from his experience that Christ had been raised from the dead, that he himself had often been rescued from imminent death. His knowledge of his own resurrection and of the future spiritual body came to him by revelation. He was taught this by the Holy Spirit. Here he spoke as a prophet who had received knowledge from God of spiritual realities, not as an apostle giving witness to the action of God in Christ Jesus. Yet there is no doubt in his knowledge—it is confident knowledge. We must not confuse this knowledge with belief in immortality, which was a Greek thought and has characterized many non-Christian religions. Paul's doctrine of the resurrection was far different from belief in immortality. It was confidence in the future resurrection, in his coming glorification with Christ.

That: introduces the noun clause which is the direct object of *we know.* The object clause extends only through verse 1. Verses 2–5 speak from the experience of the apostle and his hopes in the light of his certain knowledge which is expressed in this verse.

If: does not express doubt of the fact, but uncertainty as to the time that the change from one state of existence to another would take place. The uncertainty as to time involved two things: the time of his death and the relation of the resurrection to his death, i.e., whether it took place immediately following death or at the coming of Christ if he died before Christ came.

The earthly tent we live in is destroyed: an expression of the possibility of death before the end of the world. Paul had expressed his certainty that the earthly tent would not be destroyed but transformed for living Christians when Christ returned (1 Cor. 15:51–52). In this verse he faced the possibility that he would not be among the living who would be "changed" but among the dead who would be "raised imperishable" at the sounding of the last trumpet. Some commentators on this verse have remarked that Paul had faced some new danger which shook his confidence in living until the end of time. Indeed, he had faced such a danger. He had faced the prospect of dying and had even given up hope that he would continue to live (2 Cor. 1:8–11). But this does not mean that he had changed.[1] There is no evidence that he ever had anything more than a hope that he would survive until Christ returned. Perhaps this hope (using "hope" in the modern sense as a wish) had dimmed in the interval between the writing of 1 and 2 Corinthians. Probably it did.

The earthly tent: is Paul's equivalent to our modern use of "body." Since "body" always meant more to Paul than the physical organs, he could not use the term to express this conception. *Earthly* does not refer to the material out of which the physical is composed, but to the sphere in which it operates. *Earthly* stands in opposition to "eternal in the heavens." *Tent* is used in contrast to *building,* to stress the transitory nature of the physical. The Greek actually mixes metaphors and reads: "the house of our earthly tent."

Is destroyed: translated by some, to conform with the context, "is taken down." Perhaps this is the best translation because the Greek word is the very word which was used for striking down a tent in preparation for

---

[1] Hughes remarks that the theory of a radical change in Paul's eschatological outlook is "more specious than substantial."

moving on (Robertson). Thus Paul's idea of death, for the Christian, was simply the idea of striking one's tent in preparation for removal to a new sphere of life.

We have: a present tense. We already have the new building though we have not yet possessed it. Coupled with *building,* the suggestion is that the building is in the process of being built.

A building: a deliberate contrast to tent. *Tent* describes that which is temporal and transitory; *building,* that which is permanent. The word which is translated *building* is actually the Greek word for a building in the process of being built (Plummer). This agrees with the above suggestion.

From God: the builder of the new building. This does not deny that the earthly tent also proceeds from God, but is added here to stress the thought of the transcendence of that new building.

A house not made with hands: and therefore spiritual in quality. *Not made with hands* translates a single Greek word which is also used in Colossians 2:11 to refer to circumcision and in Mark 14:58 to describe the new temple which Jesus promised to build. The thought, in each case, is a contrast between that which is physical and that which is spiritual.

Eternal: describes a quality of indestructibility. If it is eternal, it has a quality which is not subject to decay. The idea of indefinite duration seems to be derived from the quality of what is called eternal, rather than being the primary thought involved in the word.

In the heavens: the environment in which life will be lived. Modern skeptics have sometimes tried to discredit the Bible on the basis of its cosmology, insisting that heaven is not a place above the earth. The expression reflects the ancient cosmology, it is true, and that cosmology has been discredited by the discoveries of modern science. However, the thought that is expressed is not thereby negated. Heaven was regarded as the abode of God, and the thought is one that transcends the limitations of earth.

Verse 2: turns to the present condition of the embattled apostle.

Here: rather, "in this," i.e., in this earthly tent in which we now live.

Indeed: a possible translation of the Greek particle, but "also" is the probable meaning. Not only is there knowing but also a groaning in this present state of existence.

We groan: describes the inner suffering because of undesirable circumstances. *Groan* implies a complaint.

And long: rather, "longing." The word is a present participle indicating continuous action. The connection with *groan* is either temporal (while longing) or causative (because we long). Perhaps the best choice is to look on it as a causative participle. Thus the particular thing that causes the circumstances of life to be undesirable is that we have not yet reached the consummation of salvation. The verb which is translated *long* is a common one with Paul, but the connection is unusual. Everywhere else that Paul used the verb (cf. Rom. 1:11; Phil. 1:8; 2:26; 1 Thess. 3:6; 2 Tim. 1:4), he used it to express his intense desire to see absent friends. However, we do not doubt that Paul was serious in saying that he longed for his heavenly dwelling.[1] A similar statement is found in another passage: "For to me to live is Christ, and to die is gain. If it is to be life in the flesh, that means fruitful labor for me. Yet which I shall choose I cannot tell. I am hard pressed between the two. My desire is to depart and be with Christ, for that is far better" (Phil. 1:21–23).

To put on: a graphic description. The words are those which are used in putting on clothes. Paul looked upon death and resurrection as going to sleep and awaking to dress oneself for the new day.

Our heavenly dwelling: synonymous with "a house . . . eternal in the heavens" (vs. 1).

Verse 3: Paul departed in this verse from the figure of a building and changed the metaphor to that of a robe. His shift of metaphors came from the use of "put on" in the previous verse.

So that: literally, "if so be." However, the RSV translation catches the meaning.

By putting it on: rather, "having put it on." The expression is an aorist participle in the Greek, pointing to a time prior to that indicated by the words *we may not be.*

We may not be found naked: doubtless refers to a state of existence in which the person has no body (in the modern sense of the term) at all. The same figure of speech is found in the writings of Plato, who spoke of "the soul naked of the body" (Hughes). However, there is a great difference between the thought of Plato and the thought of Paul. Plato believed that the body was a dungeon or prison; Paul thought that it was an essential part of the human personality.

The question arises from this verse: Did Paul believe in an intermediate state between death and the final resurrection, or did he believe that the resurrection took place immediately after the Christian's death? From 1 Corinthians 15:20–28, it would seem that Paul believed that the resurrection would take place at the coming of Christ and the ushering in of the eternal order. But what of those who died before the coming of Christ? Would they exist naked while waiting for the final advent? A certain answer is not to be found in Paul's writings. If there is an intermediate state between death and the resurrection, it is not that for which he longed, but the completed resurrection.[2] It would seem that Paul was here expressing a common human and Christian revulsion at the possibility of a disembodied existence, but this is far from certain. Perhaps, in this matter as in many other matters, we must be content with our ignorance and leave the future in the hands of God, as indeed it must be. There is no reason to think that Paul ever speculated on this subject at all (Strachan).

Verse 4: continues the expression of Paul's longing.

For while we are still in this tent: during our earthly life.

---

[1] Robertson suggests that Paul had a "heavenly homesickness." (A. T. Robertson, *The Glory of the Ministry* [New York: Fleming H. Revell Company, 1911]. Hereafter referred to by the title, *The Glory of the Ministry.*)

[2] Ellis also argues cogently that the subject here is not the intermediate state but the contrast between this age and the age-to-come (E. Earle Ellis, "II Corinthians V. 1–10 in Pauline Eschatology," *New Testament Studies*, Vol. 6 [Apr., 1960], pp. 211–224.).

We sigh with anxiety: not parallel with the thought of verse 3, "We groan, and long." The thought here is of deep anxiety caused by a fear of something in the future.

Not that we would be unclothed, but that we would be further clothed: expresses the reason for the anxiety. It was a very human dread of dying. Though Paul looked upon death as the gateway to a new and more glorious life, he did not think of the process of dying, of being unclothed, as merely passing from one room to another. This fact may seem to be inconsistent with some of his statements made in the immediate context, but it seems to express the true interpretation of the words. Paul, like all Christians, had not reached a point of perfect consistency in his emotions. His belief was sure; his confidence unshaken. Yet, he shrank from the experience of dying. What he wanted was not to be unclothed but to be clothed. (There is no Greek equivalent for *further* in the context, and the word is not needed to express Paul's thought.) The prospect of death is not a pleasant one for any human being, and it is false interpretation to try to make the Christian face death without qualms or fears.

Verse 5: expresses Paul's confidence and faith in spite of his fears.

He who has prepared us for this very thing: The idea is that the life of the Christian is at present a process preparing him for the resurrection life. The idea of some, that death and resurrection will be a complete break with life on earth, is false. We may not be able to take anything with us into the future life, but we must take ourselves. This verse echoes the thought: "For this slight momentary affliction is preparing for us an eternal weight of glory" (4:17).

Is God: accomplishes two things. It denies that the resurrection or preparation for it is in any way a human achievement; it comes from God. It also expresses the confident faith of the apostle. If God is the one who does it, there can be no doubt that it shall be done.

Who has given us the Spirit as a guarantee: rather, "as a down payment." This explains how God has prepared us and is preparing us for the future inheritance. The Spirit gives us a foretaste of the heavenly life and creates thereby a desire for the full redemption. The Spirit guarantees the future resurrection and thereby inspires hope and confidence.

Verses 6–8: Paul asserted his continuing good courage while he was still alive, although he preferred to be with the Lord.

Verse 6: So: rather, "therefore." The new thought is consistent with the previous verses and explanatory of them. Perhaps the particular point of reference is the gift of the Holy Spirit as a down payment.

We are always of good courage: There is no thought of a craven shrinking from death or from the experiences of life. *Always* means that Paul had this courage in any event, life or death. *Good courage* translates a rare form of the Greek verb which was a favorite word with the Stoics. The meaning of the word varies according to the context. Sometimes it has the meaning of daring, but that would be foreign to this passage. The idea of quiet confidence is perhaps at the center of the use of the word in this context. The opposite idea would be included in the expression "lose heart" (cf. 4:1, 16).

We know: is a participle coordinate with the participle which is translated, "we are of good courage." The connection is: "being of good courage and knowing," etc.

That while we are at home in the body: still living in this world. *At home* translates a Greek word meaning "one among his own people." *In the body* means "in this earthly mode of existence." Thus, "while we still live in the world in our present mode of existence" expresses the sense of the expression.

We are away from the Lord: rather, "we are abroad from the Lord." Paul did not mean that the Lord was absent from him in his earthly existence. He had just said that the Lord's presence was mediated to him through the Holy Spirit. Yet, in spite of Christ's constant presence (Matt. 28:20) and our union with him (Gal. 2:20), there is a sense in which the Christian is away from, separated from, the Lord as long as he lives in this world. The Lord's presence is not direct and unmediated with us, but is indirect.

Verse 7: explains what is meant by being "away from the Lord."

For: introduces an explanatory note.

We walk: a common metaphor in the New Testament for living one's life.

By faith, not by sight: In this life men walk in the sphere of faith and apprehend the unseen world through the means of faith (cf. Heb. 11:1). No matter how strong faith may be, no matter how real the unseen world is to us, it is not the same as walking by sight, seeing the things which we know to exist and having direct and unmediated fellowship with the Lord. This expression reminds us of a common tension in New Testament interpretation. The desire to emphasize the ultimacy of the Christian experience sometimes leads us to make assertions which leave the impression that there is nothing better to come. Not so. Christian life at its best is far inferior to that which is to be. On the other hand, some are guilty of emphasizing the world to come with such stress that the glory and transcendence of the Christian life is lost sight of. The New Testament writers were conscious of this tension and never made the mistake of belittling either the present glory of the Christian or his coming glory.

Verse 8: We are of good courage: present tense of the verb which was used at the beginning of verse 6. This is a reiteration of Paul's confident assurance in the face of all circumstances.

And we would rather: literally, "we are well pleased rather." Probably the rsv translation suggests the correct interpretation. Though quietly confident of God's continued presence with him, Paul would, if he had his own preference, be well pleased if he had already made the transition to the next world. *Rather* suggests a comparison between the two modes of existence.

Be away from the body: absent from this present mode of existence. *Body,* here as elsewhere in Paul, includes the whole person as living in this world.

And at home with the Lord: same word as in verse 6. There he talked of being at home in the body. Here he spoke of being with the Lord as being at home. *With* expresses the idea of face-to-face fellowship, a direct and unmediated entrance into the presence of the Lord, i.e., Jesus

Christ. This verse implies that such a fellowship occurs immediately following death and does not await the resurrection.

Verse 9: So: rather, "wherefore." The particle in the Greek is a strong continuative particle. The immediate reference is to his desire to be with the Lord. This desire created another—a desire to please the Lord.

Whether we are at home or away: whatever may be the case when Christ comes. *At home* probably refers back to verse 6 and means "at home in the body." *Away* would then mean "away from the body and present with the Lord." [1] Whether this is the exact reference or not, it would seem that these are the two factors involved in the expression.

We make it our aim: translates an old and common Greek verb which literally means, "we love honor." Thus it means to act from a love of honor, or to have the ambition, in the good sense, to do something. The same verb is used in 1 Thessalonians 4:11, where Paul exhorted the Christians "to aspire to live quietly." It was also used by Paul in discussing his future plans with the Romans to preach the gospel where it had never been preached: "thus making it my ambition to preach the gospel" (Rom. 15:20). These are the only three passages in the New Testament where the word is used.

To please him: i.e., the Lord. The ambition of Paul was to live in such a way that he would be well pleasing to the Lord when he came regardless of how the Lord found him, either in the body or already absent from it. This expresses Paul's ambition, an ambition which he exhorted the Christian slaves at Colossae to share: "Whatever your task, work heartily, as serving the Lord and not men, knowing that from the Lord you will receive the inheritance as your reward; you are serving the Lord Christ" (Col. 3:23–24). The pleasure of the Lord was the consuming passion of Paul, the motive of all his actions, as indeed it should be of the actions of all Christians.

Verse 10: continues the thought of verse 9. It reveals that Paul was thinking of the judgment day as the time in which his life would be revealed to be either well pleasing or displeasing to the Lord.

For: a continuative particle giving the reason why Paul made pleasing the Lord the ambition of his life.

We must all appear: literally, "It is necessary for us to be made manifest, the all of us." *All* means all Christians without exception. *Appear* means more than just standing before the judgment seat; it means that our whole life with its actions, motives, and desires will be made manifest. This is "necessary" in the purpose of God. To whom we shall be made manifest is not stated here. It may be that Paul merely used the word to express the idea of appearing before God in judgment. However, this is not likely. Some have said that we will be made manifest to the whole world of men and angels so that they may know what we really are (Lenski). This is possible, but we find it difficult to accept. The better probability is that Paul thought of our being made manifest to ourselves so that we can see what kind of persons we really are. It

---

[1] Allo believes they mean "at home" (i.e., with the Lord) or "away" (i.e., from the Lord).

certainly would not mean that we are made manifest to the Lord, for he already knows "the secrets of man's heart."

The judgment seat: translates a common Greek word from which we get the English expression "the bench." Every Greek city had its "bench" where the affairs of men were judged by the ruling authority. Paul adopted the word and used it to express the belief that all Christians would come under the judging authority of God. This does not mean that there is any doubt about the salvation of the Christian. It implies rather that our lives as Christians will be brought into account before God. Plummer points out that the word which is translated *seat* (Greek, bēma) was a platform on which the seat of the presiding officer was placed, either in a court of justice or in a military camp.

Of Christ: the judge. Sometimes in the New Testament God is spoken of as the judge, sometimes Christ is. Perhaps the idea in Paul's mind was the judgment as the final act in which Christ subdued his enemies and disciplined his followers before he turned the kingdom over to God (1 Cor. 15:20–28).

So that each one: each Christian. The judgment of the unsaved was not in Paul's mind in this verse, but the judgment of Christians. The unsaved will be judged on the basis of their relationship to Christ and condemned because they refused him. The Christian will be judged on the basis of his works.

May receive good or evil: suggests that there is a difference between Christians at the judgment seat of Christ. This implies that there are degrees of bliss in heaven itself, not that one will be consigned to a lower part of heaven than another, but that one will be more able to enjoy the heavenly life than another. *Evil* does not mean punishment, but a lesser degree of bliss.

According to what he has done in the body: i.e., during his earthly life as a Christian. *What he has done* will include not only the outward works which he has accomplished, but the inner motives of the heart from which his works proceeded. This expression teaches that there is a definite continuity between the life of the Christian on earth and his future life in heaven. Those who have been faithful, who have sought to please God with all their hearts, will be rewarded more generously than those who have merely received salvation and have done nothing in the service of God thereafter.

Verses 11–15: state, as their central thought, that Paul's ministry was motivated by his love for Christ. It seems, however, that some had attacked his sincerity of motive and had persuaded the Corinthians to doubt it. Perhaps he had been accused, as he had in Galatia (cf. Gal. 1:10), of seeking to win the favor of men for his own selfish ends. To this accusation he answered that he was indeed busy trying to persuade men to believe in his sincerity, but this was not for selfish ends but for their sake.

Verse 11: Therefore: connects this passage with the thought of final judgment, expressed in verse 10.

Knowing: being conscious of this as a continuous reality of life.

The fear of the Lord: not the dread of the ungodly, but the fear of sons who love and revere their father, knowing that punishment awaits any failure to do right and reward awaits those who do right.[1] The notion that this should be connected with "we persuade men" so as to make it mean, "we persuade men to fear the Lord," misses the connection entirely. Paul meant that the fear of the Lord was one of the strong motivating factors of his own ministry.

Though this thought is not so common to the New Testament as it is to the Old, it should not be forgotten and lost in Christian piety. In the Old Testament fear of the Lord, or of God, is one of the fundamental bases of piety. "Fear God, and keep his commandments; for this is the whole duty of man" (Eccles. 12:13). "Behold, the fear of the Lord, that is wisdom" (Job 28:28). "The fear of the Lord is the beginning of knowledge" (Prov. 1:7). These are only a few of the Scriptures that could be cited. The same expression is found in the New Testament. "Be subject to one another out of reverence [Greek, fear] for Christ" (Eph. 5:21). We see that Paul was motivated by this fear and taught that his converts should also be motivated by it. Modern Christians who seem to think that they can sin with impunity need to remember that our heavenly Father is a God of judgment as well as a God of love.

We persuade men: not a conative present (i.e., "we are trying to persuade men") as Robertson thinks,[2] but a durative present (i.e., "we are busy persuading men") as Lenski says. Several questions of interpretation arise: Does this refer to charges made against Paul? Does this mean that he was busy persuading men to believe in his sincerity? Or does it mean that he was trying to persuade men to accept Christ? Much as we might like to believe the latter, the context forbids it. The meaning of the word which is translated *persuade* is "to win the favor of" or "to conciliate." This meaning becomes clear when we look at two New Testament passages where the same word is used. "If this comes to the governor's ears, we will satisfy [Greek, persuade] him and keep you out of trouble" (Matt. 28:14). "Now Herod was angry with the people of Tyre and Sidon; and they came to him in a body, and having persuaded [i.e., won the favor of] Blastus, the king's chamberlain, they asked for peace" (Act 12:20). Thus, we must believe that the meaning is that Paul was busy persuading men of the sincerity of his motives, to win their favor. But since he did this in order to prepare the way for the preaching of the gospel, no selfish motive was involved.

But what we are is known to God: Is known translates *paphanrerōnetha,* a perfect tense which literally means "we are manifest." The same word was used in verse 10 for the appearance before the judgment seat of Christ. The connection is antithetical to the previous expression, "We persuade men." This antithesis deserves to be preserved: "God knows

---

[1] Hodges remarks that "fear of the Lord" often stands for true religion in the Scripture. (Charles Hodge, *An Exposition of the Second Epistle to the Corinthians* [New York: George H. Doran Company, 1859]. Hereafter referred to by the last name of the author, Hodge.)

[2] A. T. Robertson, *Word Pictures in the New Testament,* Vol. IV. *The Epistles of Paul* (New York: Harper and Brothers Publishers, 1931). Referred to as Robertson.

all about us through and through and always has, but we have to persuade
men to believe in our sincerity." The thought is that Paul was long ago
made manifest to God. The perfect tense reaches into the past and extends to the present.

And I hope it is known also to your conscience: expresses Paul's hope
that his sincerity did not need to be defended before the Corinthians. The
same Greek word, "made manifest," is used and in the same tense—the
perfect. He hoped that to them, as to God, his motives had always been
transparent and still were. *Your conscience* is in the plural in the Greek.
He did not appeal to the church as a whole but to the conscience of each
member. *Conscience* means "consciousness." In this context it almost
has the meaning which we express by the term "subconsciousness."
Though they may have been led to doubt his sincerity, he hoped that this
was only superficial and temporary, and that they really knew better
"down deep in their hearts" (as we would say).

Verse 12: In answer to a possible misinterpretation of his words as
self-commending, Paul said his real reason in calling attention to his
own sincerity was to enable his friends, the Corinthians, to defend him
against the slurs of his enemies.

We are not commending ourselves to you again: the same words were
used as a rhetorical question in 3:1.[1] The two verses are related. 2
Corinthians 3:1 was an answer to a possible misunderstanding of his
words in 2:17 which might have been taken as a boastful self-assertion.
The statement here answers a possible misinterpretation of verse 11. Of
course, if the hope that he expressed in verse 11 was well founded, he
would have no need to commend himself to them. At least he asserted
that that was not what he did.

But: strong adversative, introducing the real reason for his language.

Giving you cause: providing you with an opportunity. The Greek word
which is translated *cause* is peculiar to Paul in the New Testament (cf.
Rom. 7:8, 11; 2 Cor. 5:12; 11:12; Gal. 5:13; 1 Tim. 5:14). The common meaning of the word in the common speech of the day was to
indicate the starting point or base of operations for an expedition. From
this the word took on the meaning of the resources necessary to carry
out the expedition, sometimes even meaning the capital necessary for a
commercial undertaking. In the New Testament the meaning seems to
be "occasion, opportunity, or pretext." Paul said that sin found opportunity in the commandments to bring about his spiritual death (Rom. 7:11).
The thought in 2 Corinthians 11:12 seems to be "pretext" rather than
"claim," as the RSV translates it. Paul warned the Galatians against letting
their freedom in Christ become an "opportunity" for the lower nature
to exert itself in their Christian lives (Gal. 5:13). He suggested that
widows marry and raise children so as to "give the enemy no occasion
to revile us" (1 Tim. 5:14). The meaning here seems to vary between
"occasion" and "opportunity." His thought was that when the opponents
seized on his words to bring their accusations, this would give the

---

[1] EGT, contrary to my outline, thinks Paul was returning to his theme after a
long digression.

Corinthians the opportunity to defend him on the basis of their knowledge of his integrity.

To be proud of us: rather, "to boast of us." The thought is not of an internal feeling of pride but of active "boasting" to the opponents of Paul.

So that you may be able to answer those: probably a good translation of an elliptical expression in Greek. Literally, the expression reads, "in order that you may have ————— against those." Something needs to be supplied to complete the sense of the clause, and RSV has supplied *answer.* This may be a good decision, or it might be better to assume the repetition of the word from the previous clause, "opportunity." This clause reinforces our understanding of the previous one.

Who pride themselves on a man's position and not on his heart: describes the opponents who were guilty of superficiality. This expression shows that his opponents were not Corinthians but persons who had come to Corinth armed with letters of recommendation from those who, according to their claim, had high position. Perhaps James, the brother of the Lord, had sent along such letters. This is entirely possible without his having been a party to the disruption of the church. In Jerusalem their Judaizing principles would have had no need to come to the surface. All the members of that church were already Jews. Thus, they may have been good and faithful members of the church in Jerusalem and have deserved letters of recommendation. However, when they came to Corinth and met Gentile converts for the first time, their own basic superficiality would have come to the surface. They boasted in their position as Jews, as descendants of Abraham, perhaps of their friendship with James. Paul looked on that as boasting in a man's position rather than his heart. The letters of recommendation seem to have impressed the Corinthians and led them to doubt the integrity of Paul, who had said nothing to them of the need for circumcision and obedience to the Mosaic law. He wrote now to call them back to confidence in him and to furnish an opportunity for them to silence the voices of their tormentors.

Verse 13: For: introduces an example in which his opponents might cry out one thing and his friends another.

If we are beside ourselves: i.e., crazy. Paul had faced the charge of madness in his lifetime. No doubt, his Jewish friends thought he had gone mad when he turned from Judaism to Christ. Festus, on hearing Paul preach the resurrection of the dead, cried out, "Paul, you are mad; your great learning is turning you mad" (Acts 26:24).[1] Some interpreters have taken the Greek word to refer to the ecstasy of speaking in tongues or receiving visions from God, but there is no evidence that this is an accepted meaning for the word. But what made his opponents think that Paul was crazy? It could have been that he was afflicted with epilepsy, though this doubtful. It could have been because of his claim of superiority in speaking in tongues (1 Cor. 14:18) or because he claimed to have had surpassing visions of God (2 Cor. 12:2). It could have been because he preached the gospel with such fervency that men thought he was mad, i.e., a fanatic. More probably, the charge is related to the con-

---

[1] EGT suggests that Paul's enemies in Corinth pointed to his visions as proof of his madness.

text and refers to the charge of self-commendation. His opponents may well have said that his thirst for recognition was a mania, that he was mad for it.

It is for God: i.e., to judge the truth of the accusations. The usual interpretation is to suppose that Paul meant that he was mad, if he was, for the sake of his devotion to God. It would seem, in the light of the context, that he meant to say that *God* was the only one who could judge his integrity, i.e., whether or not he was driven by a frenzied desire for recognition. If our interpretation of the previous phrase is correct, this would have to be the meaning of this phrase.

If we are in our right mind: i.e., sane. This expression was meant to be the opposite of the charge that he was mad. The same kind of meaning must be given to the phrase. Thus, this would mean that Paul's seeming self-commendation was not a sign of madness but of sobriety. His reason for it had a basis in his mission and his desire to carry on his ministry.

It is for you: to judge. This is exactly parallel in structure to the previous statement. If God alone could judge whether or not he was mad, at least the Corinthians, from their knowledge of him, could judge that he was sane.

Verse 14: is one of the great statements of Paul on the motivation of the ministry. The disinterestedness of Paul is nowhere better seen than in this passage.

For: possibly refers back to verses 10–11 and gives another basis for Paul's ministry. He was not driven by fear of God alone, nor by the prospect of judgment. There was also something in the present which constituted a driving force in his life.

The love of Christ: can be either Paul's love for Christ or Christ's love for Paul. Probably the latter is the primary reference, though Christ's love for him would certainly bring from him a response of love for Christ. The love which Christ had for him never ceased to be a marvel to Paul. One of the noble statements of Paul's wonder at the love of God is found in the words: "I have been crucified with Christ; it is no longer I who live, but Christ who lives in me; and the life I now live in the flesh I live by faith in the Son of God, *who loved me and gave himself for me*" (Gal. 2:20; italics mine).

Controls us: a neutral translation of a word with a variety of meanings in the New Testament. The question is: Did Paul mean that the love of Christ was a driving force that held him to his task (Lenski, *et al.*) or did he mean that it was a restraining force that kept him from being insincere (Plummer)? The basic meaning of the word is "restrain, take hold of, or grip." Paul's only other use of the word (Phil. 1:23) describes the tension between two desires, the desire to depart and be with the Lord and the desire to remain alive and be of service to the Philippians. In the rest of the New Testament, the word is used in three passages to describe the "grip" of a fever or disease on someone (cf. Matt. 4:24; Luke 4:38; Acts 28:8). In other passages it describes the physical pressure of a crowd or army (Luke 8:45; 19:43; Acts 7:57), and the physical restraint of captors who held Jesus captive (Luke 22:63).

Two passages might have bearing on the meaning of the word in this passage. Jesus said: "I have a baptism to be baptized with; and how I am constrained until it is accomplished" (Luke 12:50), probably meaning that he was driven forward to the hour of his cross. Another passage reads: "And when Silas and Timothy came down from Macedonia, Paul was being constrained by the word, bearing witness to the Jews that Jesus was the Messiah" (Acts 18:5; my translation). The meaning of this passage is probably that Paul was under a compulsion from the word to testify as he did. If this is true, it would reinforce the common meaning given to the word in this passage, i.e., that the love of Christ impelled him to continue his ministry of preaching. Movement within the grip of something is possible if that grip is urging one toward something (Strachan). Thus, we must reject the interpretation that would make this verse mean that Paul was "restrained" by the love of Christ from acting insincerely (Plummer). This interpretation makes the verse conform to the context in verses 11–13, but would limit the meaning too much.

Because we are convinced: possibly refers to the period of reflection which preceded his missionary activity and followed his conversion (cf. Gal. 1:17–18). The expression is in the past tense and indicates a judgment reached by reflection on the implications of the cross.

That one has died for all: The reference is to the death of Jesus on the cross. In this passage Paul did not insist upon the substitutionary nature of the death of Christ, though he believed in it (cf. Gal. 3:12–13). He used the preposition which is translated *for* meaning "in behalf of" or "for the benefit of." This preposition does not exclude substitution. *All* would be all men, but the effect of the death was real only in the lives of Christians.

Therefore all have died: All has the article and should be translated "the all," i.e., the all for whom he died. True, this has not taken place in the experience of the unsaved; but when Christ died as the representative of the race, all did really die, at least potentially. Paul refused to think of the benefits of the cross as limited in any way in their potential efficacy. *Died* is in the past tense and points to the death of all as taking place in the death of Christ.

Verse 15: takes up, repeats, and expands the thought of the last part of verse 14.

And he died for all: reaffirms the fact of the vicarious nature of the death of Christ.[1] The same expression is used as in verse 14 except that *he* is substituted for *one.*

That: in order that, expressing the purpose of the death of Christ for all.

Those who live: literally, "the living ones." The thought here is of the Christians who have experienced in their own lives the benefits of the cross.

Might live no longer for themselves: motivated by selfish concerns.

But for him who for their sake died and was raised: be motivated by a desire for his glory and honor. This expression defines more fully what

---

[1] Allo remarks that Paul's doctrine of salvation appears in these verses with all its force and plenitude.

Paul meant by being constrained "by the love of Christ." Living for the
one who died means that one should live his whole life with Christ as
its motivating center. Two things are worthy of notice in passing. One
is that Paul spoke of the death of Christ three times in this passage. The
cross was the center of Paul's theology. He never tired of pointing to it as
the event in which salvation was procured by the sacrifice of Christ. The
other is that he added, quite unnecessarily, *was raised*. This he did in
many passages. His Christ was not a dead Christ but a living one, and
he never forgot that fact. He preached Christ as the living Lord in the
character of one who had died to secure the salvation of all men.

Verses 16-21: the climax of Paul's discussion of his ministry. He
asserted that he judged nothing from the "human point of view" (vs. 16),
not Christ (vs. 16), nor union with Christ (vs. 17), nor the ministry
of reconciliation (vss. 18-21). His point was that the gospel had created
a new dimension of life which could never be pressed into the mold of
earthly ambitions and strivings.

From now on: probably does not mean from the moment of writing.
Now has the article and should be translated, "the now." By this term·
Paul meant to encompass his whole Christian life. It was "the now" of
his Christian life, as his life as an unsaved rabbi was "the then." He looked
upon his conversion as a new beginning in his life, and all that came after
it was included in "the now" time.

Therefore: connects this verse with verses 14-15. In view of the fact
of Christ's death and the resultant obligation of all Christians to live
for him, what he was about to say was true.

We: very emphatic in the structure of the Greek sentence. Thus it
means, "No matter what others may do or how they may look at life,
it is otherwise with us." *We* is probably editorial and means "I." Paul
could not have spoken about so personal a thing for others; he could
only speak for himself.

Regard no one: Greek, "we know." The sense is probably that of
appreciation of value.[1] He was saying that he judged the value of no one
by the old terms of reference. The differences between "Greek and Jew,
circumcised and uncircumcised, barbarian, Scythian, slave, free man"
(Col. 3:11) were all obliterated by the new set of standards.

From a human point of view: Greek, "according to flesh." The RSV
translation mistakenly assumes that "according to the flesh" describes
the subjective view of the one who sees. The point, however, is that it
is objective and means that Paul now refused to judge men by external
distinctions, by what he was in "the flesh."

Even though: a correct translation of the Greek particle, "if." The
form of the statement assumes the truth of what is said.

We once regarded: rather, "we knew." The word has the same meaning

---

[1] Martyn (wrongly, I think) makes this a key verse in Paul's conflict with his
enemies (he thinks they were Gnostics) and believes the point of conflict was
epistemology (J. Louis Martyn, "Epistemology at the Turn of the Ages: 2 Corinthians 5:16," *Christian History and Interpretation: Studies Presented to John Knox.*
Edited by W. R. Farmer, C. F. D. Moule, and R. R. Niebuhr. Cambridge at the
University Press, 1967).

as above. It means, "we valued or appreciated." *Once* is not in the Greek, but is justified by the meaning. Paul referred back to his standard of values before he was converted.

Christ from a human point of view: rather, "Christ according to the flesh." The sense seems to be that Paul, prior to his conversion, had judged the claims made for Jesus to be the Christ from the standpoint of the external, especially the Jewish hopes of the Messiah, and had found him wanting. He therefore had regarded him as an impostor and had persecuted his followers in an attempt to obliterate the new and heretical sect of Jews who followed him. After his conversion he no longer judged Christ by those standards of value, but by standards of value "according to the Spirit" which proved him to be the true Messiah indeed.

This makes perfectly good sense, but it is necessary to notice and refute some false ideas that have arisen from the interpretation of this expression. Some have taken this to mean that Paul was not interested in the earthly Jesus, that he did not know of his marvelous works and transcendent teachings, and that, if he did, he cared nothing about them. This idea has led some to a sort of anti-Jesus Christology which is contrary to the teachings of Paul. It is true that Paul did not often quote the teachings of Jesus, but he sometimes did (cf. 1 Cor. 7:12). There are doubtless many reflections of the teachings of Jesus in Paul's writings which are not readily identifiable. Paul mentioned a two-week visit with Peter (Gal. 1:18), and we may be certain that Peter passed on to him much of the Christian tradition concerning the teachings and works of Jesus. Paul was no supporter of a Christology which separated itself from the earthly Jesus.

There have been many other suggestions made of this phrase in Paul's writing, but we need not delay to notice them all and answer them. It may be that the exact meaning of the phrase is not clear to all—the multitude of opinions would confirm this. However, the context seems to support the interpretation given above. To view Christ "according to the flesh" would be to make external matters the final judge in deciding the validity of his claims. If this were done, he must be rejected. He had no high position; he possessed no wealth; he ruled no armies; he did not meet the expectations of the Jews. There was nothing externally to recommend him either to the Jews or to the Romans. But when judged by the standards of the Spirit, he eminently qualified to receive the supreme devotion of men. His works proclaimed him to be from God; his teachings transcended anything men had ever heard; his death was the death of an innocent one for the guilty; he arose from the grave; he changed the lives of his followers. What else is needed to show that Jesus of Nazareth was truly the Messiah?

We regard him thus no longer: reiterates the point made in the first part of the verse. Paul's conversion had led to a radical change of opinion about Christ. It may be that a charge against Paul lies behind this verse, but we cannot know that for a certainty. If he had been charged with such a view of Christ, he denied it completely.

Verse 17: Therefore: introduces a consequence from what has been said, but the exact reference is uncertain—either verses 14–15 (in which

case this verse is parallel to vs. 16) or verse 16. I would choose the
last option. Paul's refusal to judge men on the basis of external conditions
applied also to men who were in Christ.

If any one: indefinite pronoun marking the possibility of the new life
in Christ as unlimited.

Is in Christ: has a spiritual and dynamic union with him. This is one
of Paul's most used phrases, the depth of which is often lost to the
modern interpreter. Paul, here as everywhere in his epistles, was building
on his own personal experience. Faith-union meant nothing short of being
overpowered by Christ. The whole man—thought, feeling, and will—was
unconditionally surrendered to Christ. It is difficult to express the depth
of the expression *in Christ* to the modern mind. We are so accustomed
to thinking of our religion in terms of church membership and external
factors that we have often lost sight of the real proportions of an experience with Christ. The only true commentary on this expression is an
experience like that which Paul had—an experience in which we have
given our lives over to Christ for his use, for him to live in. When it becomes true of us that we are actually a modern incarnation of Christ in
our world, then we will know what Paul meant by the phrase *in Christ.*
It is the kind of union which a husband has with his wife when perfect
love prevails—the two become one flesh. It is like the union between a
building and its foundation, in which the separation of the one from the
other would be its destruction. It is like the union which the parts of the
physical body have with the head, so that they are perfectly subservient
to the authority of the head. It is like the union which branches have with
the vine, receiving their life from it and expressing in their fruit the
reality of the vine.

He is a new creation: Greek, "new creation" or "new creature." There
is no verb in the Greek phrase, and both words are without the article.
The stark simplicity of the expression in the Greek is obscured when it
is translated into English. The word for *new* is *kainē,* meaning "new in
kind, of a different order." The other Greek word for *new (neos* which is
commonly used as a prefix in English words) means new in time without
any implication of a new quality of being. This is an important distinction. Paul thought of the life which the Christian had in Christ as completely different from the life which he had had before his conversion.
When judged from external realities, this is not always evident. The
unbeliever gets sick; so does the Christian. The unbeliever has difficulties
in life; so does the Christian. The unbeliever eventually dies; so does the
Christian. But when judged from the internal realities, there is as much
difference between the life of the unbeliever and the believer as between
day and night, between black and white, between solid and liquid. They
belong to an entirely different order of things.

The word which is translated *creation* may also be translated "creature."
There is no way of knowing which meaning Paul had in mind when he
wrote the word. In either case, the point is that this new life of the
Christian comes by way of a creative act of God. It does not come from
works, or by progress in righteousness, or by any human act or achievement. God is the source of that new life. The same power which brought

the world into existence with a word is used in changing the nature of man from that of a rebel to that of a child.

The old has passed away, behold, the new has come: explains the meaning of the creative act of God. This means the *old* and *new* things, as is indicated by the use of the neuter plural in both adjectives. The things that characterized the old life have passed away, have been made a part of the past. The things which characterize the new life have come into being, have been created. Practically speaking, this does not mean that the Christian no longer has some of the habits and sins of life which he developed before he was a Christian; it means rather that he has been changed at the center of his being; his attitudes, hopes, and aspirations have become new. There still remains the task of bringing life into conformity with the new principle. In this sense there is progress within the Christian life. But this does not mean that there is progress toward the Christian life. Man is made a Christian instantaneously, not from within himself but from without, by the power of God acting in his life.

Verse 18: continues the discussion of the new life and forms a bridge to the thought of the ministry of reconciliation.

All this is from God: by his creation. The expression expands the idea expressed in *new creation.* To say that it is *all . . . from God* is to deny that it is in any way based on human action or merit.

Who through Christ: the means of God's action in the lives of men. It is through faith in Christ that God acts in the life of the individual.

Reconciled us to himself: describes the creation as an act of reconciliation. The meaning of this term has often been debated by Christian theologians. Some have asserted that it means little more than a discovery on man's part that God is friendly, followed by a change of attitude, entirely on man's part, toward the friendly God. This sort of interpretation violates the meaning of the word and of the experience.

Three things need to be noticed and discussed. First, the word is active in voice. Second, the word means a mutual change of attitude. Third, the New Testament confirms that there is a mutual change of attitude in the experience itself. The thought which is emphasized by the first statement (the word is active) is that God invades the estranged human heart to accomplish his purpose. God's reconciling love is not the idea of a passive love that indicates only that God has a subjective disposition to forgive man if he will turn to God. No. God takes the initiative; he is the aggressor; he seeks to bring the estranged sinner to salvation. This is one of the deep and abiding teachings of the New Testament, one which must never be ignored if we hope to understand God and his ways.

Also, the word has the meaning of a mutual change of heart on the part of two estranged parties and a consequent fellowship which is established by this change.[1] Many have denied that this is true with regard to the use of the word by Paul. They have argued that God does not change; therefore there could be no change of attitude on his part. The teachings of the New Testament show that this is not the case, that the word does

---

[1] Denney remarks that there is "something in God as well as something in man which has to be dealt with before there can be peace."

describe a change of God as well as a change in man. This is most clearly seen by a comparison of Paul's use of the term in two passages: "As regards the gospel they are enemies of God, for your sake; but as regards his election they are beloved for the sake of their forefathers" (Rom. 11:28). This verse shows that, for Paul, being "beloved" was the opposite of being "enemies." Since "beloved" must describe God's attitude toward Israel, "they are enemies" must also describe God's attitude. If we turn to another passage, our thought will become clear. "For if while we were enemies we were reconciled to God" (Rom. 5:10). Here being "enemies" is the opposite of being "reconciled." We have seen above that being enemies describes the attitude of God toward sinners rather than their attitude toward him.[1] It follows that "reconciled" must also describe the change of attitude that God has toward the sinner. Thus, when Paul wrote, *God has reconciled us,* he meant that God had changed his attitude toward men so that they were no longer regarded as enemies but as children. Such a change must inevitably lead to a change of men's own attitude toward God, so the mutual change must be involved in the word itself in the New Testament as it is in the common Greek usage.

And gave us the ministry of reconciliation: transfers the thought from salvation to ministry. *Ministry* is again the common word for service. The idea is that the Christian, having himself been reconciled, now has the task of proclaiming the good news, the gospel, of God's reconciliation to men. In the New Testament this ministry was considered to be the common task of all Christians, not just that of a selected few. All were not prophets; all were not apostles; all could not speak in tongues; but all were ministers. This concept of ministry is one which desperately needs to be recaptured in our modern churches. In too many instances our churches are sharply divided between the laity and the ministry, and no obligation is felt by the laity to minister the word of God. This was not the New Testament pattern, and it should not be ours. Each member is to be a missionary; each Christian is to be a minister. This is the New Testament pattern; this should be the pattern of modern church life. There may be different methods of ministry, but the object is the same. It is to proclaim the fact of God's reconciliation and lead men to open their hearts to God so that he may reconcile them to himself.

Verse 19: explains further what is meant by the ministry of reconciliation.

That is: continues the thought of verse 18. The Greek participle is "as," but the RSV translation has caught the idea of continuity which was involved in the verse.

God was . . . reconciling: a combination of verb and participle which stresses the durative nature of an action. Paul had in mind the whole ministry of Christ. It was a ministry in which God was continually acting. The purpose of his action was reconciling. Lenski, however, interprets the Greek structure differently, taking *was* with *in Christ* and making it a statement of the fact that God was united with Christ in all that Christ

---

[1] I am indebted to Conner for this argument (W. T. Conner, *The Faith of the New Testament* [Nashville, Tenn.: Broadman Press, 1940]. Hereafter referred to as Conner).

did. However, this seems to strain the Greek and is not necessary to express the idea.

In Christ: the way in which God was acting, parallel to *through Christ* (vs. 18). The point is that there was no separation between the Father and the Son in the accomplishment of redemption. Some older theologians had the notion, based on either the feudal system of society or on an extreme penal view of the atonement, that God was a reluctant bystander while Christ accomplished man's redemption. Some even went so far as to picture an imaginary conference in heaven in which the Son begged the Father not to judge mankind but to allow him to save them, to which the Father reluctantly gave his consent. Others have taken the view that God regarded Christ on the cross as a sinner and visited the divine wrath on him instead of on guilty sinners. Such language attempts to explain by logical processes what cannot be explained, and it tends to slander God. God was the initiator of redemption; he sent his Son to accomplish that redemption; he filled his Son with the Holy Spirit; his Son suffered redemptively, not penally. We may be sure that there was never a time in the life of Jesus when God was more pleased with him than in the moment of his death on the cross. Attempts to understand the meaning of the cross must always end in a mystery. But where theology fails, experience succeeds. There is no problem in experiencing the benefits of the cross.

The world: stands for all mankind and defines the limits of the redemption achieved on the cross as universal. He died for all men; therefore all men may be saved.

Not counting their trespasses against them: explains in negative terms what is meant by the expression, "God was in Christ reconciling the world to himself." God brought about their redemption by *not counting their trespasses against them.* This expression reminds us of one of the statements of John: "For God sent the Son into the world, not to condemn the world, but that the world might be saved through him" (John 3:17). The expression is the equivalent of the word "forgiveness." Instead of holding the evils that man had done against him and thus condemning him to eternal perdition, God forgave their trespasses and received them into his fellowship.

Entrusting to us: as a treasure is entrusted to the steward who will administer it. The Greek means literally, "he has put [in our hands]."

The message of reconciliation: defines the ministry of reconciliation as the proclamation of a message. The idea is not that we participate in the actual work of reconciliation as the co-workers of God. But we proclaim what God has done and seek to lead men to respond to the gospel in such a way that God can do his work of reconciliation.

Verse 20: So: rather, "therefore," because we have been entrusted with the word of God.

We are ambassadors for Christ: rather, "on behalf of Christ, we are acting as ambassadors." "On behalf of Christ" is placed at the beginning of the sentence for emphasis, and the translation should preserve this distinction. The word for *ambassadors* is a verb derived from the Greek word which means "old." Since kings usually entrusted great responsibility only to old and experienced men, the word came to have that meaning. The translation is correct. Ambassadors represented, in ancient as in modern times, their government or their king. They spoke with the same authority as the head of state. To scorn them was to scorn the government which sent them. To send them away was to break relations with the government that sent them. Paul chose the word to indicate the closest possible relationship between the messenger of reconciliation and his Lord, Christ, who sent him. To be an ambassador was a great privilege, but it was also a great responsibility. The ambassador could never let his own thoughts, words, or feelings hinder the full and exact expression of the words, thoughts, and feelings of his principal. He must also receive his orders directly from his principal; he could not *ad lib*. The thought contained in the word, when applied to the Christian's ministry, is clear. It is the task of the Christian minister to speak for Christ, to express exactly what Christ would have expressed, to subjugate all personal feelings to the task which he has received as a trust. *For Christ,* i.e., "for the benefit of Christ," may have the meaning "instead of Christ." The Greek preposition can have this meaning, and the use of "instead" rather than "for" is more apt to describe the place of the ambassador.

God making his appeal through us: our speaking is as though God were speaking and making a direct appeal to the sinner to repent. This is one of the ways in which God takes the initiative in reconciling men to himself.

We beseech: one of the regular words for prayer in the New Testament. It expresses a depth of feeling and fervency that should always characterize the minister as he seeks to bring men to salvation. The word is not admonish, warn, or command, but "beg."

You: if retained, probably marks this as an unconscious quotation from Paul's appeal to unbelievers. It is not likely that he would direct such an appeal to the Corinthians, who had been spoken of as reconciled. Actually, *you* is not expressed in the Greek, and the resultant translation without its use is more impressive: "We make it our habit to beseech on behalf of Christ."

On behalf of Christ: i.e., speaking as an ambassador for Christ.

Be reconciled to God: a passive verb which means "allow yourselves to be reconciled." This would be Paul's common plea to unbelievers. The passive voice stresses the fact that unbelievers do not accomplish their own salvation but merely receive it.

Verse 21: This is one of Paul's great statements concerning the benefits of the cross.

For our sake: indicates that the cross was meant to secure benefits for the Christian. This expression repeats the substance of what Paul had said in verses 14–15, i.e., "he died for all."

Who knew no sin: is placed first in the Greek sentence for emphasis. Christ did not become acquainted with sin from his personal experience. This expresses Paul's concept of the sinlessness of Jesus and conforms to the statement: "For we have not a high priest who is unable to sympathize with our weaknesses, but one who in every respect has been tempted as we are, yet without sin" (Heb. 4:15). The sinlessness of Jesus in his own life is a common teaching of the New Testament writers. The passion stories in the gospel are constructed to emphasize the fact that he did not die for crimes that he had committed, but "for our sins."

He made him to be sin: cannot be taken literally. It must be taken`to mean "made him to suffer the consequences of sin." *Made* is not to be taken as if God exerted force on Christ. His redemptive sufferings were his own choice. If the expression is taken literally, it would mean that Christ and sin became the same thing. This, of course, cannot be true. The history of Christian theology is filled with interpretations of this verse, each proponent of a theory of atonement taking it to support his theory. We must remember that Paul had no theory of the atonement. He had experienced its benefits. But he did not seek to explain *how* the death of Christ could accomplish these benefits; he only knew that it did. There was no doubt that the cross was the cause and salvation was the effect. There is no sin in trying to understand the *how* of this, but one makes a mistake when he lets his attempts to theorize the *how* hide from him the glorious fact that it is true. Perhaps the best approach to this verse is through the Christian teaching of the humanity of Christ. As one with the race, he became subject to all the ills of the race, including the dread consequences of sin. These he bore vicariously for all men, and as a result all men may share in the benefits of the cross. The unity of the race explains why some men suffer for the evils of other men; it does not explain how anyone can be thought to be guilty of the evils of another man.

So that: introduces the statement of the purpose or effect of the cross.

In him: through our union with him, a faith-union. This clearly teaches that the benefits of the cross come only to believers. There is no tinge of universalism in the teachings of Paul.

We: has the position of emphasis in the Greek sentence. *We* means all Christians.

Might become the righteousness of God: parallel in structure and meaning with the previous clause, "He made him to be sin." The literal meaning cannot be taken. It would result in the ridiculous statement that Christians are the righteousness of God. What is meant is that Christians receive the consequences, the benefits, of the righteousness of God. *Righteousness of God* would mean the righteous act of God in Christ. Thus the whole verse, in perfect parallelism, might be paraphrased to read: "He who knew no sin in his own experience was made to suffer the consequences of our sin for our sakes, so that we who had sinned could secure the benefits of the righteous act of God in him."

(5) Paul made a plea not to accept the grace of God in vain (6:1–10)

This section has two prominent ideas. First, there is a plea to the Corinthians which continues the thought of the statement in verse 20: "We beseech you on behalf of Christ, be reconciled to God" (vss. 1–2). The remainder of the material continues the self-vindication of Paul which has been prominent in so much of this division (vss. 3–10). Yet there is only one sentence.

Verse 1: contains the plea of Paul.

Working together with him: The Greek has only *working together with.*

Whom Paul "worked together with" is not stated. The RSV would imply that Paul meant that he was cooperating with God in his ministry. There are three other possible choices: (1) with Christ; (2) with the Corinthians; and (3) with his fellow-workers. There are good reasons for believing that he meant that he worked together with God. This is the most natural meaning from the context, where he had spoken of "God making his appeal through us." Against each of the other suggestions, strong objections can be raised. Against (1) is the fact that there is no preparation for this in the context. Against (2) is the fact that this whole section deals with the ministers and not the hearers. Against (3) is the fact that the Greek participle is already in the plural and probably includes his fellow-preachers. Since Paul was God's ambassador, it was not irreverent for him to think of himself as working with him, i.e., in association with God. There was no thought of equality in the mind of Paul. He did not think of his ministry as a cooperative effort between equals.

We entreat: rather, "encourage." The Greek word is not the one used in 5:21 which was translated there "beseech." It is the familiar word which Paul had already used so often in this epistle and which we have decided to translate "encourage." The Greek word *(parakaleō)* means literally to "call alongside of" and has a variety of meanings ranging from "exhortation" to "entreaty." It seems that the context here would be in favor of the weaker translation, "encourage you."

You: is expressed and placed in the emphatic position here. There is no thought of a general entreaty to the unsaved world. The encouragement is directed toward the Corinthian church.

Not to accept: literally, "not to receive." The infinitive is in the past tense in Greek but may refer to a present action. However, it seems best, in the light of the context, to take it as a true past tense. Therefore, Paul would be referring to their conversion in past time. The expression should be translated, "not to have received."

The grace of God: is the saving grace of God by which they became Christians.

In vain: i.e., to no purpose or profit. Many interpretations have been given of this appeal. Some make it to be an appeal not to lose their salvation by turning away from God. Others relate it to James 1:22 and make it an appeal not to have made a superficial profession which would not produce good works. Others relate it to 2 Corinthians 5:10 and make it an appeal to produce fruits that would stand in the judgment. Perhaps the best interpretation relates it to the present context, the Judaizing teachers. If the Corinthians were misled by those who would preach "another Jesus . . . a different gospel" (cf. 11:4), they would have to turn their backs on the gospel Paul had preached and on the Jesus they had accepted. To do this would mean that their acceptance of the grace of God had been in vain. It had counted for nothing. Thus the appeal was primarily an appeal to stand true to the gospel as they knew it and not to be led astray by false teachers. The tone of the passage does not indicate that the danger was very great, but it was nevertheless a continuing danger.

Verse 2: a quotation from the Greek version of Isaiah 49:8. In its Old Testament setting the passage speaks of the ministry of the Suffering

Servant of God, the call of which is universal, extending to the Gentiles. Paul appropriated the language to point out that the salvation which he had preached in Christ was the true salvation.

Now: in both cases is the eschatological *now,* the now of the Christian age in contrast to the "then" of Old Testament times. *Now, i.e.,* this Christian age, *is the acceptable time . . . the day of salvation.* The point is that the wonderful time which the prophet foresaw was the time which the Corinthians had experienced.

Verse 3: begins the vindication of Paul's own ministry. This vindication is related to the appeal which he had just made. The appeal was an appeal to stand firm in the faith of Christianity. This is valid if Christianity is valid. For the Corinthians the validity of their faith was connected to some degree with the validity of Paul's ministry.

We put no obstacle in any one's way: resumes the thought of verse 1 after the parenthesis (vs. 2). *No obstacle* has the emphasis in the clause. The word for *obstacle* comes from the Greek verb meaning "to strike against, stumble." Hence, the meaning is that Paul put up no stumbling block, no reason for sin. The negative in the Greek is in the form which looks at the matter from the subjective point of view. Thus the assertion is that he put nothing which could be regarded as cause of sin in the way of anyone. This is the form of negative regularly used with the participle in Greek, but the subjective meaning still holds. The whole expression is related to the statement, "Only take care lest this liberty of yours somehow become a stumbling-block to the weak" (1 Cor. 8:9).

The concern of every Christian, as well as of every preacher, ought to be to live in such a way, with such love for others, that his life does not become the occasion for another's sin. This does not mean that one can lay the responsibility for his sin on someone else. Each is responsible to God for his own sin, but it is possible that one's actions may become the occasion for another's sin. This we should all seek to avoid.

So that no fault may be found with our ministry: a weak translation of a rare Greek verb which means "vilified" or "blamed." The literal translation would be: "so that shall not be vilified the ministry." *Our* is a justifiable translation of the Greek article, which often has a possessive sense. The same Greek verb is found in the statement: "We intend that no one should blame us about this liberal gift which we are administering" (8:20). The thought in that verse is that no one should accuse him of maladministration of the gift of the churches, of taking some of their money for his own personal use. "Vilify" would be a good translation there as it is here. Paul's aim was to conduct his ministry in such a way that, if someone failed to find the true way of life, he could not place the blame on the ministry.[1] If blame was to come to him, it must be wrongfully placed. This should be the aim of every minister of the gospel (as we noted above, this should include all Christians). We should seek to conduct our ministry with such thoughtfulness, love, and devotion to the needs of people that no one could blame the ministry for the lapses of those to whom we minister.

---

[1] Tasker remarks that Paul could make his appeal with confidence because his conscience was clear.

Verse 4: continues the thought of the previous verses. The Greek has a series of present participles which the RSV, in its translation, obscures. The whole paragraph (vss. 1–10) is a single sentence in the Greek, held together by the following participles: "working together with him" (vs. 1); "not giving anyone an occasion for stumbling" (vs. 3); but "commending ourselves" (vs. 4). The remainder of this paragraph contains a series of phrases which are in apposition with "in every way."

But: is strongly adversative, meaning "on the contrary." The contrast is between the possible accusation against the ministry (vs. 3) and the ways in which Paul commended his ministry.

As servants of God we commend ourselves: literally, "commending ourselves as servants of God [should do]." He remembered the accusations of self-commendation which had been leveled against him and admitted that he was commending himself, but in the ways that servants of God should commend themselves—by their lives.

In every way: has the position of emphasis in the Greek structure. The rest of the paragraph is a commentary on what this meant for Paul. The listing of the ways is impressive, falling into three parts. The first part introduces each way with the preposition "in" (Greek, *en).* Using the RSV translation of the main words but repeating the preposition with each one, the first list, running through verse 7*a,* reads as follows:

1. in great endurance,
2. in afflictions,
3. in hardships,
4. in calamities,
5. in beatings,
6. in imprisonments,
7. in tumults,
8. in labors,
9. in watching,
10. in hunger,
11. in purity,
12. in knowledge,
13. in forbearance,
14. in kindness,
15. in the Holy Spirit,
16. in genuine love,
17. in truthful speech, and
18. in the power of God.

The second list (vss. 7*b*–8) uses the preposition "through" (Greek, *dia)* to introduce each word. It reads as follows:

1. through weapons of righteousness for the right hand and the left,
2. through honor and dishonor, and
3. through ill-repute and good repute.

The third list is composed of seven contrasts, each introduced by the conjunction "as" (Greek, *ōs)* (vss. 8*b*–10). It reads as follows:

1. as impostors, and yet true,
2. as unknown, and yet well known,
3. as dying, and behold we live,

4. as punished, and yet not killed,
5. as sorrowful, yet always rejoicing,
6. as poor, yet making many rich,
7. as having nothing, and yet possessing everything.

It remains now to examine the RSV translation in each case and discuss the meaning of the various items in the lists.

Through great endurance: a good translation except for the preposition. It should be "in" rather than *through. Endurance,* a word which in older translations was often rendered by "patience," comes from a Greek word with two elements: one meaning "under," and the other "remain." The idea is that of steadfastness in the face of opposition. Jesus gave great stress to this quality of life in his teachings (cf. Luke 8:15; 21:19). The word is found in Paul's writings sixteen times. As a quality of the ministry, it stands first, and rightly so, in this list. Some of the items in this list are so personally Paul's that the modern minister cannot hope to have these opportunities to commend his ministry. This quality of endurance, however, is of universal validity.

In afflictions: pressures of life. The word can be used to indicate external sufferings, but it is best used to describe the internal pressures of a minister who is greatly concerned about his ministry.

Hardships: often coupled with "afflictions" (cf. 1 Thess. 3:7; Job 15: 24; Ps. 119:143; Zeph. 1:15). Its meaning is similar to that of the word which is translated "afflictions," coming from the Greek verb which means "to compel" or "force," with reference to either internal or external compulsion.

Calamities: a word derived from another word which means "narrow," as when one is in a tight place. Possibly the meaning is that of being hemmed in by a feeling of anxieties. *Calamities* seems too strong as a translation. "Distresses" might be better.

Verse 5: Beatings: rather, "stripes." Probably "stripes" is derived from *beatings* so that the translation is justified. We get our English word "plagues" by transliterating this Greek word.

Imprisonments: a good translation. The plural suggests that Paul had been in prison more often than the account in Acts indicates. At the time when he wrote this letter, we know of only one imprisonment, that suffered in Philippi (cf. Acts 16:23).

Tumults: good translation. From the account in Acts we know of several popular uprisings against Paul (cf. Acts 13:50; 14:5, 19; 17:5; 18:12) prior to this letter, one of them having taken place in Corinth (Acts 18:12).

Labors: good translation. The strongest possible meaning of "labor" must be understood. The word indicates toil to the point of exhaustion, work that is severe and tiring.

Watching: literally, "sleeplessness." The same word is used in the expression "through many a sleepless night" (11:27). Paul had no doubt had many such nights, caused by his concern for his converts and perhaps spent in prayer.

Hunger: good translation. The same word may be translated "fastings," but it is probable that it refers to involuntary hunger rather than voluntary abstinence from food. There is no indication that "fasting" carried over into Christian practice from Jewish piety, where it was considered of great value.

Verse 6: Purity: i.e., moral purity and earnestness. Its use in 11:3 (if genuine) is the only other passage in which the word is found in either biblical or classical Greek.

Knowledge: good translation of a common Greek word which was often used by Paul.

Forbearance: good translation. The word is composed of two elements in the Greek: "long" and "tempered." The quality is the opposite of being "short-tempered." Endurance is the courage to endure adversity and opposition. *Forbearance* is the quality of enduring evil deeds without being provoked to anger.

Kindness: good translation. The word describes not only the attitude of graciousness toward others, but also an attitude that results in beneficial works.

The Holy Spirit: a natural but debated translation. Plummer finds it incredible that the Holy Spirit should be mentioned in a list of human virtues, and suggests that the phrase should be translated "a spirit of holiness." However, "power of God" (vs. 7) is also mentioned in this list; so we need not assume that the list is a list of human virtues. It is a list of the ways in which Paul commended his ministry to his hearers. He had said, concerning his preaching, that he had deliberately spoken in simple terms so that his preaching was "in demonstration of the Spirit and power" (1 Cor. 2:4). Here it would seem that his meaning was that his ministry was commended by a manifestation of the Holy Spirit. We retain the translation. Perhaps (as Lenski suggests) *the Holy Spirit* is placed just here in preparation for the next three items in the list, all of which depend on the Holy Spirit.

Genuine love: good translation. *Genuine* comes from a word which could be literally translated, "unhypocritical." This is the first word in the list which has a qualifying adjective. *Love* is itself a concern for the object of love (cf. 1 Cor. 13). Paul wanted to add that his concern for the Corinthians was a real concern, not feigned.

Verse 7: Truthful speech: a doubtful translation. The phrase has two words which, translated literally, read: "word of truth." "Word" can mean speech, but the expression "of truth" can have several meanings; "the word which is the truth" or "the word which belongs to the truth" or "the word which declares the truth." The expression could refer to the general virtue of truthfulness (Lenski thinks this is a trivial interpretation; Plummer regards it as preferred). However, it seems that the expression means "the proclamation of the gospel truth." "Truth" is without the article and therefore refers to that which has the quality of "truth." Nevertheless, it would seem consistent with the purpose of the list (i.e., to list ways in which Paul commended his ministry) to regard the "truth" as the gospel.

The power of God: good translation. The reference is no doubt related to the preaching of the gospel which the Corinthians had experienced as the power of God (cf. 1 Cor. 1:18). The ministry of Paul was accompanied by power, power which came from God.

With the weapons of righteousness for the right hand and for the left: begins the second division of the list and is a good translation. *Weapons* is a military metaphor of which Paul was fond. *For the right hand and for the left* probably carries out the metaphor. The Roman soldier carried his sword in his right hand and his shield in the left. The sword was the offensive weapon; the shield the defensive. Two fanciful interpretations have been given to this expression: (1) It means that one is equipped to meet attack from any quarter. (2) It means that Paul fought on in all kinds of times, adversity and prosperity (the right hand was considered to be the sign of good fortune; the left, of ill). *Of righteousness* describes the weapons as used in the cause of righteousness (cf. Rom. 6:13, where the Christian is admonished to yield his members as weapons of righteousness to God).

Verse 8: In honor and dishonor: rather, "in glory and dishonor." "Glory" must be given its usual meaning. The meaning of "glory" is the recognition of worth or value.[1] In this sense Paul received "glory" from his converts. The modern term "popularity" might well give the meaning of the word here. Dishonor was Paul's in a plentiful sense. It came from his opponents at Corinth, and this is probably the primary reference here.

In ill repute and good repute: rather, "through evil report and good report." The phrase does not repeat the previous one but goes on to the notion of "report." "Glory" and "dishonor" have found words. No doubt the reference here is to the things which had been said about him in Corinth, behind his back.

We are treated as impostors, and yet are true: poor translation. There is no Greek equivalent for *we are treated*. The list continues, but with a change from the prepositions to a conjunction. *Impostors* is used to translate a Greek word which means "deceivers." One of the reports which circulated in Corinth was that Paul was a "deceiver" who misled his converts. *True* is a good translation and expresses Paul's denial of the charge that he was a "deceiver."

Verse 9: As unknown, and yet well known: good translation.[2] *Unknown* expresses another accusation against Paul, i.e., that he was not known to the leaders of Christianity. If this were true, he would be an apostle without credentials, an impostor who had no knowledge of God. *Unknown* would thus have the meaning of a nonentity. *Well known* is Paul's answer. It probably is not an exact opposite of *unknown*, but means that he was well known to God. It may mean, also, that he was well known to the Corinthians and wherever believers were to be found.

As dying, and behold we live: good translation. Paul turned from what his enemies were saying against him to look at his ministry from his own viewpoint. The best commentary on this expression is found in a previous section (4:16–18). Though he was facing death every day and might be

---

[1] Wendland rightly sees a change of style at this point. Following is a list of contrasts.

[2] Plummer says the two words are present participles in the Greek and speak of what is habitual and constant.

thought of as in the process of dying, yet the life of Christ became increasingly his.

As punished, and yet not killed: poor translation. The word which is translated *punished* means "chastised." It is the word used to describe the chastisement which a father gives to his son. Paul was thus thinking of himself as one who needed to be chastised by his Father—God. He had often received chastisement, and his opponents may have regarded that as a sign of God's wrath when, as a matter of fact, it was a sign of God's love. (Cf. Heb. 12:7, "God is treating you as sons; for what son is there whom his father does not discipline?") *Not killed* is added to show that the chastisement of God was discipline rather than a visitation of wrath. Perhaps the statement: "The Lord has chastened me sorely, but he has not given me over to death" (Ps. 118:18) lies behind Paul's thought here.

Verse 10: As sorrowful, yet always rejoicing: the translation does not mark a change in the Greek structure, which is important but difficult to capture in an English translation. The two words, *sorrowful* and *rejoicing,* are not placed in strong contrast, but as elements of the same life. He was saying that he was always sorrowful and rejoicing at the same time. This is a paradox of the Christian life and the ministry of Christ. Of sorrows he knows many—friends fail, converts falter, the work of Christ goes slowly. But in the midst of his sorrows, there is always rejoicing. Perhaps the best commentary on this expression is the Book of Philippians, which was written from prison but which rings with the sound of joy throughout. In the closing verses of that epistle, Paul reached the climax of rejoicing as he admonished his friends: "Rejoice in the Lord always; again I will say, Rejoice" (Phil. 4:4).

As poor, yet making many rich: The same structure as above is carried over to this expression. Paul knew himself to be poor with regard to earthly treasures, but he knew that his poverty was contributing to the enrichment of many. This is not a reference to the collection for the poor, but to the spiritual enrichment that came from the ministry of Paul.

As having nothing, and yet possessing everything: returns to the structure which implies a true contrast. He had nothing, not even himself, since he was a bondslave of Jesus Christ. It would seem to Paul that nothing was the state of his earthly possessions. Yet, he possessed all things. This expression reflects a previous statement of Paul: "For all things are yours, whether Paul or Apollos or Cephas or the world or life or death or the present or the future, all are yours; and you are Christ's; and Christ is God's" (1 Cor. 3:21–23). As it was with his converts, so it was with Paul. He possessed everything.

3. Paul's Various Pleas and Warnings (6:11—7:4)

This heading has been given to a block of material which contains heterogeneous elements. First, Paul made a plea to the Corinthians to open their hearts to him (6:11–13). Second, he gave a warning against "being mismated with unbelievers" which seems to break the continuity of thought and which some have thought to be a part of the letter written before 1 Corinthians and mentioned in it (6:14—7:2). Finally, Paul resumed his plea to the Corinthians to open their hearts to him (7:2–4). This material is not a unity. 6:14—7:2 is parenthetical, if not an insertion. This problem will be discussed in connection with that section.

(1) A plea to open their hearts to him (6:11–13)

The plea is connected with the foregoing paragraph. Paul had just poured out his heart to the Corinthians and reminded them of this fact (vs. 11). Then he pointed out that any restraint that might be felt in Corinth did not come from him but from them (vs. 12). Then follows his plea, as of a father to his children, that they open their hearts to him (vs. 13).

Verse 11: reminded the Corinthians that Paul had spoken without reserve in the previous paragraph.

Our mouth is open to you: Open is the perfect tense and means, "It stands open." The expression refers to what he had just said and constitutes a picturesque statement that there had been no reserve on his part in speaking to them. Perhaps, as is often the case, Paul was a bit surprised at the extent to which he had opened his heart to them.

Corinthians: an address which is included to express his personal concern and affection for them. It was a very rare thing for Paul to address his converts in this manner. He did so in two other of his letters (cf. Gal. 3:1; Phil. 4–5), but nowhere else except here. The tone of this passage is exceedingly tender.

Our heart is wide: Paul reached out to enfold the Corinthians in the embrace of love. Just as he had felt no restraint in speaking to them, he now assured them that he felt no reservations in his affection for them. When he looked into his heart, their misdeeds, their faltering in their loyalty to him, even their suspicions of his sincerity were all forgotten.[1]

Verse 12: states that the only reason for restraint in their relations lay with them.

You are not restricted by us: states the fact that he held no feeling of animosity toward them. *Restricted* translates a word which means "to narrow down, to crowd." It is in the passive voice, which means that they were not "crowded in" by anything in his attitude toward them. These words are a perfect example of the attitude and words which must be used for the final healing of the breach between alienated friends. The offender in such a case often feels, though he has changed his mind, that the one offended will not be ready to forgive and forget. Paul had received the report of Titus that the Corinthians had indeed changed their attitude toward him; now he wanted to reassure them that the way was open for a renewal of the old fellowship of mutual trust and affection.

But you are restricted in your own affections: Perhaps the Corinthians had expressed a fear that Paul would not receive them back into his love.

---

[1] Barclay says he spoke "with the accents of purest love."

He reminded them now that the only thing which crowded them in was their own affections. *In your own affections* translates the Greek expression for deep affection, "in your own viscera." The KJV always translated the word, "bowels," but this is a misleading interpretation. The word encompasses the higher organs of the body such as the lungs, liver, and heart. The word was used interchangeably with "heart" as the seat of emotions. The point of the expression was that nothing stood between Paul and them except their own wrong "feelings" toward him. There was no justification for these feelings.

Verse 13: Paul's plea for a like response from the Corinthians.

In return: literally, "but as the same requital." The expression called for them to give him an exact equivalent for what he gave them: to meet his open heart with an open heart.

I speak as to children: parenthetical statement of his affection for them. "My" should be understood. Paul was not writing to them as if they were merely children, young in the faith and thus unable to respond with adult feelings. He was writing to them as his children. He meant that he was their spiritual father and they were his spiritual children. To refuse to open their hearts to him would be unnatural in such a relation. Both Paul and John were accustomed to calling those whom they had won to the faith their children (cf. 1 Cor. 4:14, 17; Gal. 4:19; 1 John 2:1, 28; 4:4; 5:21).

Widen your hearts also: repeats the same word which he had used (vs. 11) to describe the wideness of his own affection for them. As he had reached out and embraced them in his affections, he asked that they reach out and embrace him in theirs. The change of tense is instructive. When speaking of his heart as *wide,* Paul used the perfect tense, which indicated that his heart had always been wide and still was. In his plea to them, he used the past tense of the imperative. This form of the Greek verb indicates that their hearts were not yet opened, but that he pleaded earnestly with them to open their hearts.

(2) A warning not to be mismated with unbelievers (6:14—7:1)

This section consists of: the plea (vs. 14*a*), various rhetorical questions designed to show that there could be no real fellowship between Christians and unbelievers (vss. 14*b*–16*a*), a medley of Old Testament Scriptures to enforce the plea which Paul made (vss. 16*b*–18), and a final repetition of the plea in the light of the promises which God gave (7:1). In itself this paragraph is a self-contained whole, but the relation to the context in this letter is nonexistent. That is, there is nothing in the immediate context which would prepare one to expect this paragraph.

Scholars have tried to solve this lack of relation to the context by two hypotheses. One hypothesis is that the material is an insertion in the letter of a fragment from a previous letter which Paul had written to the Corinthians. The other is that it is an insertion of inauthentic material, material written by another person. Against both of these hypotheses is the fact that no ancient manuscript exists in which this paragraph is not found in its present position in the letter. There is no external evidence to support the notion that the material is an insertion of any kind. Furthermore, neither of the hypotheses has very strong internal evidence.

The case for the hypothesis that this is non-Pauline material rests entirely upon the fact that there are six Greek words in the paragraph which are not found anywhere else in the New Testament. Using the RSV translation of these words, they are: *mismated* and *partnership* (vs. 14), *accord* and *Belial* (vs. 15), *agreement* (vs. 16). One must admit that this comprises an impressive list of such words in so small a compass. However, this is not unusual; "there are more than three dozen such words in each of the three Epistles, Ephesians, Colossians, and Philippians" (Plummer). Therefore, we may reject this theory with confidence and insist that this paragraph was written by Paul.

The case for the hypothesis that this is a fragment of a former letter from Paul to the Corinthians, a letter mentioned in 1 Corinthians (cf. 5:9) is more widely held. But it is our opinion that the support for this theory is quite as slim as that for the other. In describing this previous letter Paul said: "I wrote to you in my letter not to associate with immoral men; not at all meaning the immoral men of this world . . . since then you would need to go out of the world" (1 Cor. 5:9–10). Obviously Paul had meant one thing by his letter and the Corinthians had taken him to mean another thing. He meant that they were not to associate with sinful Christians; they thought he meant that they were not to associate with sinful unbelievers. When we look at our present paragraph, no such misunderstanding could be imagined. This paragraph deals with unbelievers rather than Christians—there can be no doubt of that. Further, the words describing fellowship are much stronger in this paragraph than in 1 Corinthians 5:9–13, as my exegesis will show. My point is that this paragraph does not conform to Paul's description of his former letter. It could not be a part of that letter.

Both theories were manufactured to explain the lack of continuity in this letter. This needs explanation, but we need look no further than the way in which the letter was written. It was dictated by Paul to a secretary who wrote down what he said. It probably was dictated at various intervals, since the writing of so long a letter in laborious longhand would have consumed more than one day of labor. Under such conditions it was entirely possible for the mind of the one dictating to wander and for him to insert a paragraph which had no obvious relation to the context. The repetition of the substance of the last words of 6:13 at the beginning of 7:2 sounds very much like a speaker returning to the previous subject after a digression. Thus we will accept the paragraph as a part of this letter and confess that there is no clue to explain the reason for the digression.

Verse 14: Do not be: literally, "stop becoming." The Greek words consist of a present tense with a subjective negative, which was the regular construction for prohibiting continuance in a course of action. Notice that Paul did not say, "stop being," but, "stop becoming." The idea is that the Corinthians were on a course of action which tended in this direction, and Paul wanted them to reverse that course.

Mismated: good translation, but the figure of speech is lost in the translation. The Greek word is composed of two elements: "other" and "yoked." The picture behind the word is of the team of oxen, yoked together to pull the plow or wagon. The "other" in the word is the form which means "another of a different kind." [1] Perhaps the picture behind the word in Paul's mind was the Old Testament prohibition: "You shall not plough with an ox and an ass together" (Deut. 22:10). The idea indicated by the word *mismated* is not mere association, but union of the two lives in a common purpose.

With unbelievers: i.e., men who reject Christ and the gospel. Paul's thought was that believers and unbelievers were two different species. The unbeliever belonged to one class of mankind; the believer to another. They could not be true yokefellows; they could not be a team. Association would be inescapable as long as the believers were in the world, but any tendency toward yoking up together must be stopped. There is no indication of the exact nature of the "yoking" which Paul had in mind. It could have been the "yoke" of marriage or of business partnership. Paul deliberately left it indefinite so that it might apply to all such relationships.

For: because. The word gives the reason for the admonition.

What partnership have righteousness and iniquity: the first of five rhetorical questions which constitute an argument by interrogation. The implied answer to *what?* is "none." Paul meant that there was no ground for partnership between these two diverse elements. *Partnership* translates another of the distinctive words of these verses and is a good translation. *Righteousness* equals "salvation" in Paul's vocabulary. *Iniquity* is a poor translation. The word should be translated, "lawlessness." It is the word which describes the unbeliever as in open rebellion against the rule of God in his life. The thought is that there is no basis of partnership between those who have received salvation and those who reject the rule of God.

Or: introduces the second rhetorical question which forms a pair with the first.

Fellowship: another Greek word with a similar meaning to the previous word *partnership.* The Greek word for *fellowship* is much stronger than the English word. It is formed from the word which means "common," and thus means that the *fellowship* is one in which the two have things in common. It is a sharing of life rather than a moment of pleasure in another's company. Thus it is a synonym for *partnership.* This word is quite common in Paul's vocabulary.

Light . . . darkness: common metaphors in the New Testament for righteousness and sin. John said, "God is light and in him there is no darkness at all" (1 John 1:5). Paul said in the Ephesian letter: "Once you were darkness, but now you are light in the Lord; walk as children of light. . . . Take no part in the unfruitful works of darkness" (Eph. 5: 8–11). This question repeats in different words the thought of the first question.

Verse 15: continues the rhetorical questions with two which are couched in concrete terms.

---

[1] Lenski suggests "heterogeneously yoked."

Accord: translates a Greek word which is transliterated by our English word "symphony." It is composed of two elements, "with" and "voice," and means to speak with the same or harmonious voice.

Christ: Lord of Christians, the head of the heavenly society.

Belial: a word with indefinite meaning. The Greek spelling is "Beliar," which means "worthless." In the Old Testament *Belial* has the meaning of "worthlessness, ruin, desperate wickedness." Later it came to be a name for Satan (Plummer). This last is the probable meaning here. The antithesis is between the Prince of Peace and the prince of this world. The assumption of Paul was that there could be no accord between the two.

Or: Introduces the fourth rhetorical question and indicates that it forms a pair with the third.

Has . . . in common: i.e., what part or portion does the one have in the other.

A believer . . . an unbeliever: concrete statement of the antithesis which is implied in all the questions.

Verse 16: begins with the final and fifth question and continues with Paul's application of the term "temple of God."

Agreement: a correct translation of a Greek word which was common in the Greek world but is found only here in the New Testament. Its literal meaning is "to approve by putting the votes together."

The temple of God: rather, "the inner sanctuary of God." The word for *temple* is that for the "inner sanctuary," the holy of holies. It was here that the Jews believed that God dwelt.

With idols: the objects of pagan worship. The contrast is the absolute incongruity of having an idol, an image of a false god, in the inner sanctuary in which not even an image of God could be placed. Nothing more clearly marked the difference between Jewish and pagan religion than the absence of any image of man or god in the Temple at Jerusalem and the multitude of images found in pagan temples. Christianity adopted the Jewish idea of God, but transformed the notion of a temple, as the next sentence indicates.

For: gives the reason for the admonition in verse 14, or, rather, introduces the sentence that makes clear the reason implied in all the questions.

We: very emphatic in the Greek. There is good support for a variant reading, "you." However, in this passage *we* should probably read in preference to "you," which is the true reading of 1 Corinthians 3:16.

Are the temple: i.e., the inner sanctuary, the dwelling place of God. Some readings have "temples," to make the reference to the individual Christian rather than to the church. However, the meaning would be the same, since the idea is that God dwells no longer in temples made with hands (Acts 7:48) but in the hearts of those who love and adore him. This is one of the important teachings of Paul which has been lost in modern Christianity. We are inclined to transfer to our church buildings a concept which is akin to the Jewish religion rather than an expression of the Christian. To call a church building a temple, or a part of it a sanctuary or any furniture therein an altar is to deny the very meaning of the

Christian religion. Yet this is commonly done in our day. The only sanctuary that exists in Christianity is the human heart. The only altar is the cross of Jesus Christ. We would do well to guard our language lest we fall into the error of thinking that God does "dwell in buildings made by human hands."

The living God: God is described as living, to emphasize the incongruity of thinking that his presence can be limited to any kind of building.

As God said: introduces a series of Old Testament quotations which looked forward to the new order and confirmed Paul's thought that God now dwells in human hearts.

Verse 16b: is a paraphrase and quotation of Lev. 26:11–12 with a mixture of other passages (cf. Exod. 25:8; Isa. 52:11; Ezek. 37:27; Jer. 31:1). It is likely that Paul was quoting a medley of Old Testament passages which had already been formed into a Christian formula.

I will live in them and move among them: describes the personal nature of the new relation with God which is found in Christianity.

And I will be their God, and they shall be my people: expresses the identity of Christians with God. Each pronoun should be qualified in thought by "only." Thus, *I* and only *I,* and *they* and only *they.*

Verse 17: continues the quotations but is primarily derived from Isa. 52:11.

Therefore: because of this new relation.

Come out from them, and be separate from them: a call to complete spiritual separation from the world by those who follow Christ.

Says the Lord: reiterates that this is a message from God. *Lord,* since it is in an Old Testament quotation, should be given the meaning of God.

And touch nothing: rather, "stop clinging to." The middle voice of this verb means "clinging to," while the active voice means "touch." The negative marks it as a command to "stop" doing what was already being done.

Nothing unclean: either things or persons.

Then I will welcome you: i.e., receive you with favor.

Verse 18: comes from Hosea 1:10 and Isaiah 43:6.

And I will be: may mean, "I will become."

A father to you: rather, "for a father to you." The promise was that God would take the place of a father. The Old Testament never rose to the heights of the New in conceiving of the relation between God and his people as the relation of father and son. The RSV has missed the point by omitting the Greek preposition "for."

And you shall be: probably, "You shall become."

My sons and daughters: rather, "for sons and daughters." The Greek preposition "for" is again missed by the RSV.

Says the Lord Almighty: emphasizes the right of God's rulership. *Almighty* does not stress the power of God to do anything, but the right of God to have all subjection by men.

Chapter 7:1: Since we have these promises: indicates Paul's conception of the Old Testament as a whole as well as of the particular passages cited.

Beloved: reemphasizes his devotion to the Corinthians.

Let us cleanse ourselves from every defilement: from everything that would interfere with our relationship to God. If God is to dwell in our hearts, we must cleanse them.

Of body and spirit: the two areas in which defilement may take place. It may be in the *body,* i.e., in the normal relations of our earthly life, such as marriage, business, or society as a whole. It may be in the *spirit,* i.e., in our distinctively religious life.

And make . . . perfect: i.e., bring to its proper goal.

Holiness: our holiness, i.e., our relation to God. The ethical meaning of the word is secondary and derived; the primary meaning is that of relationship. The thought is that, having come into this relationship with God, a relationship in which God dwells in our hearts, we are now obligated to push on to the goal of actual right living which is involved in the new relationship.

In the fear of God: with realization that God, as the Father, chastises his sons when they sin. This fear is a missing element in much of modern piety, but it needs to be recaptured. A child cannot with impunity disobey his father, nor can a Christian with impunity ignore the demands of God.

(3) A continuation of the plea to open their hearts (7:2–4)

Having digressed to warn the Corinthians against undue fellowship with unbelievers, Paul turned back to his plea for open hearts. First, he made his plea (vs. 2a); next, he denied that he had wronged anyone (vs. 2b); next, he reiterated that his purpose in writing was not to condemn but to open the way to full fellowship (vs. 3); finally, he expressed his great confidence in them (vs. 4).

Verse 2: Open your hearts to us: resumes the thought of 6:13 with similar words. The indication is that Paul, when he returned to his plea to them, repeated the substance of his last words and then went on from there. If this is true, it supports our contention that 6:14—7:1 stands in the letter in the place where Paul wrote it originally. *Open your hearts* translates a single Greek word which means "to leave a space, to make a space for" (Robertson). However, the translation is justified because the thought is, "Make room for us" in your hearts. This expression prepares the way for a series of rapid negatives in which Paul attempted to destroy any reasons which they might have for not opening their hearts to him.

We have wronged no one: No one comes first in the Greek sentence for emphasis. He meant it absolutely. *Wronged* means "to treat unjustly or unfairly." The verb is in the past tense, which in the Greek means that he could not remember a single time when he had been unfair in his treatment of the Corinthians. Evidently he had been accused of this. True, he had sometimes had to say harsh things, but his severity was always deserved and was not unfair.

We have corrupted no one: The exact reference is uncertain. In what sense could Paul have been accused of corrupting, "ruining," someone? The reference may be to morals or money, but it is much more likely that this was an answer to an accusation that he had corrupted their doctrine. The Judaizers would have accused him of preaching a corrupt doctrine because he did not insist on the circumcision of his converts. Also, his teaching of Christian freedom may have left him open to the charge of encouraging immorality.

We have taken advantage of no one: No one, as in the two previous clauses, is in the emphatic position in Greek structure. Perhaps the reference here is to a charge that Paul took money from others and acted dishonestly. His care in detailing the arrangements for the transportation of the offering for the saints may have been caused by such a charge. If such a charge was made, we have no certain knowledge of it and must leave it as a hypothesis.

Verse 3: denies that Paul's purpose was to condemn the Corinthians.

I do not say this to condemn you: He was not interested in recriminations, though he may have been justified in them. He did not seek to find fault with, to condemn, the Corinthians for their suspicions of him and their faltering in their devotion to Christ. All that was past and Paul was willing for it to stay in the past. He had defended himself, of course, from the accusations of his enemies. This was natural. But he did not want the Corinthians to misunderstand. There was no barrier on his part to a renewed fellowship.

For I said before: probably refers to the statement, "Our heart is wide" (6:11). The words used are not the same, but the thought of this verse, though more emphatic, is the same.

That you are in our hearts: the substance of what he had said before. This goes further than the statement, "Our heart is wide" (6:11), but it is substantially the same. To say, "Our heart is wide," is to say that we are ready to receive you into our hearts. This statement goes further. It asserts that they were already in his heart.

To die together and to live together: emphasizes the depth of affection which Paul had for the Corinthians. The meaning of the words as they stand means that Paul was ready to share either death or life with them. However, the statement is not limited to Paul, but includes his fellow-workers, as the plurals indicate.

Verse 4: a statement of Paul's confidence in the Corinthians.

I have great confidence in you: This expression reflects the report of Titus which had informed Paul of their obedience and affection. He felt that the troubles were over and the future would justify his confidence in them.

I have great pride in you: literally, "much to me the boasting in your behalf." The RSV translation is good. Paul implied that he had boasted of the Corinthians to his fellow-workers (8:24), and now he told them plainly that he was proud of them.

I am filled with comfort: reflects the encouragement of Paul's heart at the report of Titus. Surely, the days of turmoil had been days of doubts and fears. Now the clouds were removed, and Paul could look forward to renewed fruitfulness in his relations with the Corinthians. The sun was shining; he was encouraged.

With all our affliction, I am overjoyed: literally and more colorfully, "I am overflowing with joy amid all our afflictions." This is a Christian paradox—joy amid afflictions; yet it is often true. It was with Paul and his fellow-workers. In the midst of their troubles, the situation in Corinth caused Paul (note the singular pronoun) to bubble up with joy.

4. Paul's Rejoicing at the Report of Titus (7:5–16)

Paul took up in this paragraph where he had left off (2:13) the story of his movements and emotions prior to the writing of the letter. First, he told of his longing for the arrival of Titus and of his relief at the good news which he had brought (vss. 5–7). Next, he spoke of the painful letter which he had written and rejoiced that it had accomplished the desired end, even though it had caused pain to the Corinthians (vss. 8–12). Finally, he spoke of his encouragement at the report of Titus, which had not disappointed his confidence and boasting in the Corinthians (vss. 13–16).

Verse 5: tells of the afflictions which Paul suffered in Macedonia as he waited for news from Corinth.

For even when we came into Macedonia: picks up the story where he had left it off (2:13): "So I took leave of them and went on to Macedonia." This indicates that the long discussion of his ministry (2:14—6:10) was a digression, but not unrelated to the problems of Corinth.

Our bodies had no rest: rather, "Our flesh had no relief." The meaning of this phrase is difficult for us to comprehend because we use terms like "flesh" with a technical meaning. In 2:13, Paul had described his unrest in Troas before departing for Macedonia in the words: "There was no relief for my spirit" (2:13; my translation).[1] In this relation the "flesh" and "spirit" are approximately synonymous. "Flesh" should not be taken in Paul's usual sense as "the sphere of sin," but in a related sense as "the sphere of suffering." In this sense "flesh" would encompass the whole of man: his mind, his emotions, his nerves. The phrase was meant to express the continued unrest of Paul as he awaited word from Corinth.

We were afflicted at every turn: rather, "in every way being under pressure." The Greek adjective "every" does not mean *at every turn* but "in every way." *Afflicted* translates the word which we have met so often in this epistle which means "to press in." It may refer to either physical or mental sufferings.

Fighting without and fear within: explains what Paul meant by saying that he was under pressure in every way. We are ignorant, from other sources, of fighting which he had without. The expression does not necessarily imply physical fighting but may refer to clashes which he had which were non-physical. Whether this was with believers who opposed his plans or with unbelievers is not known. *Fear within* probably expresses the anxiety that Paul had concerning the situation in Corinth. It had remained unrelieved even in Macedonia until the arrival of Titus with his report.

Verse 6: speaks of the comfort that Paul received when Titus came.

But God, who comforts the downcast, comforted us: reminds us of the

---

[1] Thrall sees the two expressions as synonymous.

beautiful passage which opened this letter (cf. 1:3–4). Even though the
comfort, i.e., "encouragement," came by means of the report of Titus,
Paul attributed it to God. God comforts (note the present tense).[1] This
is his habitual practice. *The downcast,* literally, "the lowly," describes
the recipients of God's habitual encouragement, but is meant also to
describe the state of mind which Paul had before the news came.

By the coming of Titus: It was the arrival of Titus with the long-hoped-
for news from Corinth which God used as the instrument for the encouragement of Paul. *Coming* translates the Greek word which was used
for the visit of a high official and is also the common word in the New
Testament to describe the coming of Christ. It implies not only his arrival,
but his staying. Thus, Paul meant not only the coming but the company
of Titus.

Verse 7: adds other factors to the coming of Titus as means by which
God encouraged Paul.

And not only by his coming: indicates that more is to be added.

But also by the comfort with which he was comforted in you: In you
should be translated, "with regard to you." Titus came with a spirit of
optimism concerning the affairs in Corinth. He had been encouraged by
what he saw and heard while there, and his optimism was contagious.
Thus, Paul was further encouraged, not only by the report, but by the
spirit of Titus.

As he told us: rather, "reported to us." The Greek is a present participle,
indicating that the optimism of Titus accompanied his report. Strictly
translated, the expression says: "but also by the comfort with which he
was comforted with regard to you while he was reporting to us."

Your longing: first of three things which Titus reported with respect
to the Corinthians. The thrice-repeated *your* lends a special emphasis.
Longing is a compound Greek verb composed of a preposition which
indicates direction and the simple verb which means "longing" or "yearning." Thus the thought expressed was of their "yearning toward" Paul.
This expression speaks of the Corinthians' deep desire for reconciliation
with Paul and his fellow-workers.

Your mourning: literally, "lamentation." The Greek word is found only
here in the New Testament and indicates not only a sense of mourning but
the outward expression of that mourning by "lamentation." Their "lamentation" was raised, no doubt, because of the troubles they had caused.

Your zeal for me: indicates a desire on their part to carry out his wishes
and to repudiate his opponents. These three terms tell much concerning
the new situation in Corinth. The Corinthians had completely repudiated
their past disloyalty and suspicions. They wanted nothing more than to
be reconciled to Paul.

So that I rejoiced still more: Paul's own joy was enlarged by the encouragement which Titus had received from them.

Verse 8: begins the discussion of the painful letter which he had written and expresses his lack of regret for it.

---

[1] IB says that the repetition of the word "comfort" (vss. 6–7 and vs. 13) shows
what a joy and relief the news from Corinth was.

For even if I made you sorry with my letter: assumes the truth of the statement. He had indeed made them sorry. This had not been his purpose in writing, but it had been the result. His purpose had been to cause them to repent.

I do not regret it: because it did lead to repentance (cf. vss. 9–10).

Though I did regret it: a parenthetical statement of his regret for having written the letter while the issue was still in doubt. This is a very human expression and shows that the apostle was made of the same stuff that composes common men. Those who picture the apostles of the New Testament as spiritual giants who never had a doubt or fear would be surprised by this expression. And well they might be. The truth is, the apostles were not spiritual giants, but common men. They had their weaknesses, doubts, and fears as we all do. The marvel is that God's grace was sufficient to take such men and use them so mightily. This thought should encourage us to believe that God can use our lives for his glory.

For I see that that letter grieved you: statement of the fact which Paul learned from the report of Titus.

Though only for a while: literally, "if even for an hour." The RSV translation catches the meaning. Their grief was only temporary, and this letter would completely extinguish it.

Verse 9: As it is: as the situation now stands.

I rejoice: reiterates Paul's joy.

Not because you were grieved: It was not his letter which had caused him joy, but their way of receiving it. Even so, it was not their grief but their repentance that produced the joy.

But because you were grieved into repenting: But is strongly adversative. *Into* expresses the idea of result. They were grieved but their grief resulted in repentance. Repenting comes from a Greek word which literally means "change of mind." But to the Greeks, "mind" was not a mere intellectual faculty, but described the whole bent and purpose of life. Thus, Paul's use of the word here probably has that meaning. Paul seldom used the word at all, since it was subject to misunderstanding by the Greeks. Jesus' use of it was controlled by the Jewish word which meant "change of heart." Perhaps, in this context, the word comes nearer the Greek meaning. The Corinthians had changed their "mind"; they had repudiated their past suspicions and were ready now for reconciliation.

For you felt a godly grief: literally, "you were grieved according to God," i.e., in God's way. God's way is opposed by the way of men and the devil.

So that you suffered no loss through us: a purpose clause which looks upon the situation from God's point of view. It was according to his purpose that the Corinthians would suffer no loss as a result of the letter of Paul. If he had not written, they would have suffered loss. Paul looked upon the letter and its results as being dictated by the will of God.

Verse 10: contrasts two kinds of grief by the results which they produce. The statements in this verse do not refer to the case in point; they are rather suggested by the language in verse 9. It is possible that this verse contains a common Christian saying or axiom with which Paul was familiar. The reason for suggesting this is that Paul seldom related "repentance" and "salvation." The only possible exception is Rom. 2:4, where Paul was addressing himself to the Jewish objector and was perhaps influenced by the Jewish meaning of the word. The only other passage where Paul used the word "repentance" was 2 Timothy 2:25, where the reference is to those professed Christians who opposed the true teachings of salvation. It is noteworthy, also, that John never used the word at all. Thus, the two great apostles to the Gentiles did not demand repentance as the way of salvation, but faith. On the other hand, Jesus often used the word, and it is fairly frequent in the Book of Acts.

The reason is to be found in the diverse cultures. Among the Jews "faith" was identified with a mere intellectual belief in some truth. "Faith" would have been a poor word to use in demanding a complete surrender of life to the Lord Jesus Christ. Among the Greeks "faith" was a much more dynamic word, being used for the fidelity of man to his ruling powers. Thus, among them "faith" was the proper word to use in making the demand for surrender to Jesus Christ.

The opposite was true with regard to "repentance." Among the Jews the word was related to the Hebrew word which means a change of heart. It was an excellent term to use to present the demands of the gospel. The meaning of a radical reorientation of life with Christ as its center would have been made plain to them. But among the Greeks the word had a narrower meaning. It referred to a change of mind or purpose with regard to a specific thing. It was not of significance in preaching the gospel; it did not express the demands of the gospel sufficiently.

In modern language the word has more of a Greek flavor, but even that is watered down. The primary meaning in modern language is "regret." It means to feel sorry for what one has done, to be contrite. Even in its religious meaning, it usually has the meaning of reformation of way. Thus, neither in Paul's context nor in the modern context is "repentance" a good word in which to express the demands of the gospel for the surrender of one's life to Jesus Christ.

It is for this reason that we think that verse 10 is an insertion into this passage of a common Christian saying or axiom suggested by the language of verse 9, rather than being an expansion of the thought in verse 9 with reference to the Corinthian situation.

For: is continuative rather than causal. It introduces a Christian saying which was suggested to Paul's mind by the words of verse 9. A paraphrase would read: "for as it is often said."

Godly grief: grief that is "according to" God. This is exactly the phrase, in the Greek, which Paul had used of their grief (vs. 9). It is probable that this phrase is the cause of his insertion of this saying.

Produces: literally, "works." The rsv translation is good. Paul was expressing a cause-effect relation between one thing and the other.

Repentance: has a different meaning than in verse 9. There the idea was a change of mind or purpose with regard to their treatment of Paul. Here it means the complete reorientation of life with Christ as its center. It is gospel repentance that is meant. See our discussion in the introduction of this verse.

That leads to salvation: probably a good translation of the Greek phrase, "unto salvation." The thought is that true repentance opens the way for God to give salvation to the sinner.

And brings no regret: should be connected with *repentance.* Salvation would not, of course, be regretted.

But worldly grief: literally, "the grief of the world." It is the grief which characterizes the world of sinful men which was in Paul's mind. This kind of grief is the kind that we find in the biblical stories of Esau, Cain, and Judas, all of whom regretted their actions. It is the grief of the thief, not because he stole but because he was caught doing it. It is the grief of the drunkard whose physical health is destroyed by drink, a grief not because he drank but because of the illness that resulted.

Produces: a stronger word than that which was translated *produces* in the previous clause. This word translates a compound Greek word which means "to work out to its completion." The contrast is important. Repentance "works" salvation, but it does not "work it out to completion." It only opens the way for God to "work out to completion" a man's salvation. Thus repentance is only an intermediate cause of salvation. Here the thought is that worldly grief is the effectual cause of working out death.

Death: in the sense of the curse of sin, death as complete and eternal for the whole man because he has rejected God. Worldly grief works this out in the sense that it becomes the substitute for repentance. Man regrets the effects of his sins, but is not led to change the center of his life from rebellion to subjection to God.

Verse 11: Paul returned to the effect of godly grief on the Corinthians and saw in this an illustration of the truth of the Christian axiom which he had just quoted.

For see: an exclamation, usually translated, "for behold."

What: translates a Greek word which means "how much" or "how great." He held up each of the effects produced in the Corinthians by their godly grief and exclaimed, "Behold, how great each one is."

Earnestness: i.e., diligence. The word comes from a Greek word which means "to hasten." They were diligent to mend the breach which they had caused.

This godly grief has produced in you: This is very emphatic, meaning "this very same." *Produced* is the compound form of the verb and means "worked out to its completion." The use of this compound form of the verb marks this verse as being different from verse 10.

What eagerness to clear yourselves: comes from the Greek word which is transliterated into English as "apology." The meaning is that of defense against attack or accusation. They were anxious to vindicate themselves and to show that they had not abetted the offender or condoned his offense (Plummer).

What indignation: at the shame brought on the church.

What alarm: i.e., "fear." Perhaps fear of God's judgment was meant, though fear of the consequences to their church might be meant. Certainly, Paul did not mean fear of himself.

What longing: yearning for Paul's favor and return to them.

What zeal: same word as in verse 7. There it is modified by the words, "for me." Probably the same meaning is meant here.

What punishment: meted out to the offender. Their willingness to punish him showed the completeness of their change of mind toward Paul. Perhaps this effect is placed last because Paul no longer considered it of primary importance.

At every point you have proved yourselves guiltless in the matter: rather, "In everything you recommended yourself to be pure in this matter." Paul acquitted them of all responsibility by these words. Their reception of Titus and the reform instituted by Paul's letter had shown them to be without blame.

Verse 12: So although I wrote to you: indicates that the painful letter which he had written still weighed on his mind. He could have closed his remarks with verse 11, but he further explains his reasons for writing and to reiterate his joy at the results.

It was not on account of the one who did the wrong, nor on account of the one who suffered the wrong: reveals Paul's Hebrew way of thinking. The negatives are not to be taken absolutely, for it was partly on account of these that he had written the letter. Our way of speaking would have said, "not primarily." The *one who did the wrong,* i.e., the offender, probably refers to the ringleader of the opposition. *The one who suffered the wrong* is probably to be taken as Paul himself.[1] He spoke with reserve about the matter because it was painful. The Corinthians would have understood.

But: strongly adversative, introducing the primary reason why he wrote.

Your zeal for us: your concern for our position and leadership.

Might be revealed to you: implies that the zeal had always existed, but that the Corinthians needed to be reminded of how great it was.

In the sight of God: placed last for emphasis. Plummer suggests that this should be connected with, "I wrote to you." If this is true, it would express Paul's feeling of responsibility to God for his actions. This, however, is not likely. It should be connected with the manifestation of the Corinthians' zeal for Paul. This was to be *in the sight of God,* i.e., an expression of their feeling of responsibility to act as God would have them act.

Verse 13: Therefore: rather, "for this season," i.e., because his purpose in writing the letter had been accomplished.

We are comforted: rather, "We have been encouraged." The tense of the verb is perfect, reaching back to the time of Titus' report and forward to the time of the writing of this epistle. As the RSV paragraphing indicates, this expression should be considered a part of verse 12. Just as a teacher is encouraged by the progress of his pupils, so Paul had been encouraged, and still was, with the progress of the Corinthians.

And besides our own comfort: i.e., over and above the personal encouragement that he had felt in the report.

We rejoiced still more at the joy of Titus: Double joy had come to Paul

---

[1] Hodge states that Paul's primary purpose was not to have the offender punished, nor to secure justice.

because of the joy Titus felt at their response to his visit. *Still more* is an attempt to express a very strong Greek expression which might be translated, "overflowed rather."

Because his mind has been set at rest: rather, "has received refreshment." The form of the Greek verb here speaks of temporary refreshment and relief from worries and burdens. *Mind* literally means "spirit." Paul was careful to speak of Titus in this chapter because he was to return to complete arrangements for the collection for the poor.

By you all: that is, "at the hands of all of you."

Verse 14: For if I have expressed to him some pride in you: indicates that Paul had boasted of them to Titus.

I was not put to shame: He did not have to retract any good thing that he had said about them. It is probable that Titus had undertaken the mission with some misgivings, but encouraged by the boasts of Paul. Paul had assured him that there was a basic integrity in the Corinthian church that would bring about the cessation of hostility. Now Paul could say, "I told him so."

Just as everything we said to you was true: reflects his preaching to the church. This had proved true.

So our boasting before Titus has proved true: by their response to his mission.

Verse 15: And his heart goes out all the more to you: More compares the present eagerness of Titus to return to Corinth with his previous misgivings.

As he remembers the obedience of you all: If obedience were to Titus, it indicates that he had brought definite commands to them with which they had complied. If it is to the gospel, as is probable, he had seen that they conformed to the demands of the gospel.

And the fear and trembling with which you received him: Fear and trembling is a strong expression defining a nervous anxiety to do one's duty (Plummer). No other New Testament writer used this expression except Paul. He used it four times (here; 1 Cor. 2:3; Eph. 6:5; Phil. 2:12).

Verse 16: reiterates Paul's confidence in the Corinthians.

I rejoice: present tense, indicating a continuing rejoicing on Paul's part.

Because: introduces the reason for his rejoicing.

I have perfect confidence: literally, "I am of good courage." *Confidence* in their continued obedience to the gospel may be the meaning of the word here and, perhaps, confidence in their response to his appeal to give liberally to the collection for the poor.

In you: with respect to you.

III. ENCOURAGEMENTS TO LIBERALITY
IN THEIR GIFTS FOR THE POOR (8:1—9:15)

The material in these two chapters can be divided into five sections, each giving encouragement to liberality. The encouragement sprang from the example of the Macedonians (8:1–7), from the example of Christ (8:8–15), from sharing his plans for the offering (8:16–24), by referring to his boasts of them (9:1–5), and by giving reasons why liberality rather than stinginess should be displayed (9:6–15).

In these chapters we see history in the making. It seems that the church at Jerusalem had more than its share of poor and destitute Christians. This could have arisen from two causes. In the first place, the economy of Jerusalem and its surroundings was the poorest in the Roman Empire, at least in those portions in which Jews resided. At the same time Jerusalem was considered the Holy Land, the one place where a devout Jew could live most truly as a Jew. This tended to make it a city with much poverty and no middle class. When Christianity began its course, its converts were from these poor people and possibly from the poorest of the poor. Not only so, but many pilgrims were in Jerusalem on the Day of Pentecost, and many of them stayed there. Naturally, the ones who stayed were the poor and widows. They had nothing calling them back to their former residences, and so they remained in Jerusalem. One of the earliest problems of the church in Jerusalem was the equitable feeding of the widows (Acts 6:1).

Early in the history of the spread of Christianity, the Christians at Antioch sent relief to the church at Jerusalem by the hands of Barnabas and Saul (Acts 11:29). When the Jerusalem council was held and the hands of Paul and Barnabas were freed to preach the gospel wherever the Lord led them, the leaders of the Jerusalem church asked Paul and Barnabas to remember the poor (Gal. 2:10). Paul added to his account of that council by saying, "which very thing I was eager to do" (Gal. 2:10).

It seems that when Paul began his third missionary journey, he determined to make a real effort to raise a considerable fund from the Gentile churches in Asia Minor and Greece. Our first knowledge of this enterprise is 1 Corinthians 16:1–4, but it was spoken of as if it were a matter with which the Corinthians were well acquainted. Romans was written from Corinth, probably a few months after the writing of this epistle. In it Paul said: "At present, however, I am going to Jerusalem with aid for the saints. For Macedonia and Achaia have been pleased to make some contribution for the poor among the saints at Jerusalem" (Rom. 15:25–26). We know that the offering was not restricted to Macedonia and Achaia. When Paul left Corinth, after writing Romans and visiting with them, there accompanied him a considerable number of men. Acts does not say that they were taking the collection, but it would seem that this was the reason for their going. The committee (if we may call it that) consisted of: "Sopater of Beroea, the son of Pyrrhus; of the Thessalonians, Aristarchus and Secundus; and Gaius of Derbe, and Timothy; and the Asians, Tychicus and Trophimus" (Acts 20:4).

In these chapters Paul encouraged gifts of money for the collection. Since Corinth was one of the wealthier cities and contained some men of substance in its membership, Paul was greatly concerned that they would respond liberally to the appeal. This explains the reasons for this section of the epistle.

1. Encouragement by the Example of the Macedonians (8:1–7)

Paul's first approach was to point to the unprecedented liberality of the Macedonian Christians—those in the churches at Philippi, Thessalonica, and Beroea. Their response was such that Paul called it "the grace of God" (vs. 1). In spite of their great poverty, their eagerness to give led them to give beyond their means (vss. 2–4). But their giving of money was also accompanied by a renewed spiritual devotion to God and to Paul (vs. 5). This had led Paul to send Titus back to Corinth to complete the work of the collection (vs. 6). Finally, he made an earnest plea that they should abound in "this gracious work" also (vs. 7).

Verse 1: introduces the subject of the liberality of the Macedonians. There is an untranslated Greek particle at the beginning of the verse which might be translated "now." It marks the change to a new subject, but not a complete change. The force of the particle may be something like this: "Now let us not become so absorbed in our renewal of fellowship that we will forget the sufferings of others."

We want you to know: calls attention to what he was about to communicate and suggests that he was bringing news to them that they did not know about.

Brethren: an expression of his affection and feeling of kinship for them in Christ.

About the grace of God: Paul regarded the response of the Macedonians as being instigated by the grace of God, not by purely human motives. Furthermore, he regarded God's leadership in giving as an evidence of a favor which he showed to unworthy people. The grace of God was still operating in Macedonia, producing a Christian response to the needs of the church in Jerusalem.

Which has been shown in the churches of Macedonia: a poor translation. The Greek reads: "which was given in the churches of Macedonia." Probably, "given in" meant "given to." Of course, this grace was manifested openly in their response, but Paul looked on the matter from the standpoint of the Macedonians who had received the grace. By *Macedonia* Paul referred to the ancient kingdom of that name rather than to the

Roman province. The ancient kingdom included Philippi, Thessalonica, and Beroea; the Roman province included Thessaly and Epirus. Plummer records the fact that the Romans had been very hard on the Macedonians, expropriating their richest sources of income—the gold and silver mines—and taxing the right to smelt the minerals. They had also reserved to themselves the trade in salt, timber, and shipbuilding. All of this had reduced the territory to deep poverty. Added to the burdens of the Christians were the various persecutions which they had experienced. Yet it seems that they, of all Paul's churches, were most generous in their support of him. At least this was true of the church at Philippi (cf. Phil. 4:10–19).

Verse 2: begins Paul's account of the generosity of the Macedonians.

For: rather, "that." This particle introduces the objective clause that goes with, "We want you to know." The sentence structure is clear if we make a few changes in the translation: "We want you to know, brethren, with reference to the grace of God given to the churches in Macedonia, that . . ."

In a severe test of affliction: that is, in a severe test brought about by affliction. *Affliction* is the same word which Paul had often used in this epistle, coming from the verb which described the crushing of grapes to extract their juice. It can refer to either mental or physical pressures. The exact nature of these afflictions in Macedonia is not recounted unless they had to do with the affliction of poverty. It is possible that a clue to the afflictions may be found in Paul's letter, written some years prior to this, to them: "For you, brethren, became imitators of the churches of God in Christ Jesus which are in Judea; for you suffered the same things from your own countrymen as they did from the Jews, who killed both the Lord Jesus and the prophets, and drove us out, and displease God and oppose all men" (1 Thess. 2:14–15). However, this letter does not mention a continuation of persecution, so it is not safe to say with certainty that this was what Paul meant here. Whatever the afflictions were, they had been a *test* of the devotion and faith of the Macedonians, a test that Paul described as *severe* (Greek, "much").[1] They were probably severe in the sense that they were prolonged as well as involving intense sufferings.

Their abundance of joy: a strange expression to be found coupled with affliction, but we have noticed on several occasions that joy in the midst of sufferings is one of the marks of true Christians. Paul spoke of the evangelization of the Thessalonians: "Our gospel came to you not only in word, but also in power and in the Holy Spirit with full conviction. . . . And you became imitators of us and of the Lord, for you received the word in much affliction, with joy inspired by the Holy Spirit" (1 Thess. 1:5–6). Seemingly, the Macedonians were Christians who never forgot how amazing God's grace was.

And their extreme poverty: And joins this expression with their joy as the source of their liberality. *Extreme* translates a Greek word which means "the according to depth." Their poverty was deep-down poverty.

---

[1] Plummer says the Greek word usually means "proof," but "test" is correct here.

Poverty has the ordinary meaning that it does today, referring to financial deprivation. They had no money for themselves; yet they had money to give to others.

Have overflowed: as a flooded river overflows. This is a striking metaphor to describe the liberality of the Macedonians.

In a wealth of liberality on their part: There is a play on words. *Wealth* and *poverty* begin with the same letter in the Greek words. *Wealth* is the word from which we get our English word "plutocrat." It describes wealth as abundant. However, the wealth of the Macedonians was not an earthly wealth, not sudden riches visited upon them by God in response to their needs. It was a richness of the spirit that produced liberality.

Liberality is probably a good translation of the Greek word which means "single-mindness" or "simplicity." [1] Paul, the only writer to use the word in the New Testament, employed it in the ordinary sense in 11:3; but in these two chapters and Romans 12:8, the meaning of *liberality* holds. It seems to mean the "simplicity" of purpose and generosity which places the needs of others above one's own. We are reminded of the saying of Jesus as he watched the multitude bring their gifts to the Temple when a widow came with her small coins, all that she had: "Truly I tell you, this poor widow has put in more than all of them; for they all contributed out of their abundance, but she out of her poverty put in all the living that she had" (Luke 21:3–4). God does not measure the greatness of one's gifts by the amount given, but by the spirit in which it is given; not by the amount given, but by the amount retained.

Verses 3–5: one sentence in the Greek text, in which four additional statements are made concerning the giving of the Macedonians. Paul had already, in verses 1–2, said three things: (1) Their giving was in a time of great affliction. (2) Their giving was in spite of great poverty. (3) Their giving was with great joy. He added in these verses: (4) Their giving went beyond their means to give. (5) Their giving was voluntary. (6) Their giving was a privilege for which they begged Paul. (7) Their giving included placing themselves at the disposal of Paul. The RSV has preserved the sentence as a unity, but has inserted a few words to make smooth reading.

Verse 3: states that the giving of the Macedonians was beyond their means and voluntary.

For: rather, "because." The particle connects this sentence with the statement, "have overflowed in a wealth of liberality on their past." "Because" introduces Paul's description of that "overflowing" giving.

They gave: inserted by the RSV to make smooth reading. It is a justified insertion from the context. The word is borrowed from verse 5.

According to their means: correct translation of a Greek phrase which says, "according to power." The thought is that they gave to the limit of their ability to give.

As I can testify: from personal knowledge. *Testify* has its regular meaning, indicating the giving of testimony by one who has personal knowledge. *Testify* is the same word which is used in the New Testament for the

---

[1] Allo translates it "generosity."

giving of one's Christian testimony. In later Christian history the giving of testimony often led to death, and so the word has come over into the English language as "martyr." "Martyr" is simply a transliteration of the Greek word used here.

And beyond their means: adds a note of emphasis to the liberality of the Macedonians. They had given beyond what could be expected of people so poor. Their giving was a sort of contradiction of their poverty.

Of their own free will: translates a single Greek word composed of two elements: one meaning "self" and the other, "choice." It meant that their giving was voluntary, on their own initiative. It excludes the thought that Paul had asked them to give at all. Perhaps he had mentioned the collection without any thought that they would give and without asking them for money; yet they initiated a movement to allow them to participate in the offering.

Verse 4: explanatory of the meaning of the expression, "of their own free will."

Begging us earnestly: literally, "with much entreaty begging us." The expression is a striking way to describe the initiative that the Macedonians took in their giving. *Begging* is one of the regular words for "praying" in the New Testament.

For the favor: The Macedonians considered giving to others a favor, not from Paul, but from God. The word which is translated *favor* is the regular word for "grace." Perhaps they had heard and believed the saying ascribed to Jesus, "It is more blessed to give than to receive."

Of taking part: literally, "and the partnership." The Greek word for "fellowship" is used with its meaning of sharing or being partners with someone in something.

In the relief: rather, "the ministry" or "the service." This is the same word which Paul used so often to describe his ministry. Its use here suggests that this kind of giving is a part of the Christian ministry.

Of the saints: i.e., the people of God. The location of the saints for whom the ministry was to be accomplished is not mentioned in this context, but there is no doubt that they were the poor saints in the church at Jerusalem.

Verse 5: recounts the "extra" in the giving of the Macedonians.

And this, not as we expected: a phrase meaning "far beyond our expectations." What follows shows what Paul meant.

But: This is a strong adversative meaning "on the contrary."

First they gave themselves: The emphasis is on *themselves.* Instead of just giving money, even though their gifts far exceeded their ability, they gave themselves as well. *First* probably means "of first importance." It could mean "before they gave their money" or "before I asked," but neither of these meanings is as satisfactory as the one suggested.

To the Lord: shows the primary direction of their devotion as it expressed what should be the first devotion of every Christian.[1] To give oneself to the Lord is to make all one's powers and resources available for his use.

---

[1] Plummer comments that the "crowning point of their generosity was their complete self-surrender."

And to us: Their devotion to the Lord led them to make themselves available to Paul and his fellow-workers. It is probable that Paul used them in the spread of the gospel, the work of the ministry. This expression states what should be the attitude of all Christians. Their devotion to Christ should lead to their submission to the leadership of God's leaders. The New Testament pattern was that the pastor should be the captain of the troops, the leader of God's soldiers. It was not his task to minister, but to equip the saints for ministering (cf. Eph. 4:11–13). All too often, in our modern churches, the pastor is looked upon as a servant of the congregation, as one who ministers to their needs. This is contrary to the New Testament pattern of church life. The members of the congregation should be ministers themselves rather than being persons requiring ministry. They should be led by the pastor to qualify themselves for a dynamic ministry to people in the name of the Lord.

By the will of God: Their actions, both in giving themselves to the Lord and in giving themselves to Paul, were governed by the will of God. *Will* translates a Greek word which means "wish" or "desire." It is not the word used to express the purpose of God, but his desire. Every Christian should be anxious to please God, to give him what he desires from them. This passage suggests three things which would please God: sacrificial giving, full devotion, and constant participation in the ministry of the church.

Verse 6: turns to Paul's plans with regard to Titus and his mission to the church at Corinth.

Accordingly: supplied by the RSV translators to avoid continuing the sentence as the Greek does. The thought is that "as a result" of the example of the Macedonians, Paul was led to make the plans for Corinth which he now divulged.

We have urged: rather, "encouraged." The same Greek word is used that we have met so often in this epistle.

Titus: the bearer of good news from Corinth, therefore a logical choice to return there to carry on the work of the collection.

That as he had already made a beginning: Possibly the work of collecting the money for the poor saints at Jerusalem had sadly lagged during the days of turmoil prior to this letter. Titus, we may assume, had made a beginning in urging them to make their gifts before he returned with the good news of the reconciliation of the church.

He should also complete: bring to final fruition. *Complete* translates a word which means "work out to its completion." Paul planned, within a few months, to take the offering to Jerusalem, and he did not want the rich gifts which he expected from Corinth to be lacking.

Among you: that is, the Corinthian congregation.

This gracious work: rather, "this grace." However, the RSV translation is probably justified. Titus would have had nothing to do with completing the grace of God. It was the collection for the saints that he was to complete. "Grace" in this sense may be a gracious work, or it may mean a virtue of the Christian life. However, since the development of Christian virtues was the work of God, it may be that Paul had in mind the unmerited favor of God in bestowing upon the Corinthians the spirit of liberality such as had been evident in Macedonia.

Relative to this verse, it may be remarked that the pastor who urges his people to give is opening the way for a bestowal of grace upon them. Some pastors hesitate to urge the stewardship of money lest the people think that they are not concerned with spiritual things. Some Christians criticize pastors who seek their money and say that he is not concerned with spiritual things. But there is nothing more spiritual than the giving of our money for the cause of Christ. As a matter of fact, it is doubtful that a Christian can be truly spiritual unless he is a good steward of the money which God has put into his hands. As long as our hearts are ruled by selfishness (this alone explains why some do not give as they should), it is doubtful that we can pray, sing, or witness with any real meaning. Full devotion to God means that our pocketbooks must be devoted to him as well—yes, and our bank accounts.

Verse 7: introduces another incentive to giving on the part of the Corinthians—what God had given them.

Now as you excel in everything: reminded the Corinthians of God's grace bestowed upon the church. In our 1 Corinthians, Paul had said: "I give thanks to God always for you because of the grace of God which was given you in Christ Jesus, that in every way you were enriched in him with all speech and all knowledge . . . so that you are not lacking in any spiritual gift" (1 Cor. 1:4–7). Much of 1 Corinthians had been occupied with helping the Corinthians to understand the nature and use of the spiritual gifts of which they boasted (cf. chaps. 12–14).

Faith: the first of the spiritual gifts which Paul mentioned in this verse. It could mean faith in Jesus Christ which brings salvation, or it could be the faith that performs miracles. Since, however, this list seems to include only those gifts which were common to all the Corinthians, it would be better to take faith as the act which begins the Christian life.

Utterance: probably a correct translation, though Lenski takes it in the sense of "doctrine." The Greek is "word." Often in these two epistles Paul used "word" for speech. It should be given that meaning in this context.

Knowledge: is knowledge of God through the gospel. The Corinthians set a great value on "wisdom," but Paul insisted that what they needed was knowledge.

In all earnestness: The Greek word combines the ideas of eagerness, earnestness, and carefulness (Plummer). By its use Paul meant the dedication of the Corinthians to the Christian cause.

In your love for us: translates a phrase of doubtful meaning. Literally, the phrase reads: "the out of us in you love." A textual variant of considerable value reads: "the out of you in us love." Probably, "the love that comes from us and dwells in you" (Plummer) is the correct meaning.

See that you excel in this gracious work also: probably catches the meaning of the purpose clause. Paul believed that the signal grace of God on them called for a response from them, the response of giving in the same way that the Macedonians had given. *Excel* translates the Greek word which means "overflow." Two words dominate this paragraph.

"Overflow" as a noun is found twice in verse 2; as a verb, it is found in verse 2 and twice in verse 7. "Grace" is found in verses 1, 4, 6–7. The idea of "overflowing" in the "grace" that comes from God was central both in the actual practice of the Macedonians and in the hoped-for response of the Corinthians.

2. Encouragement by the Example of Christ (8:8–15)

Though the example of Christ is mentioned and discussed in only one verse (vs. 9), it seems to dominate this paragraph. Paul mentioned that his suggestion (vs. 7) was not a command but an appeal to their love (vs. 8). The mention of love led naturally to the voluntary impoverishment of Christ in order to secure the riches of all Christians (vs. 9). The following verses (10–12) continue to play on the theme of voluntariness in giving. Paul reminded them of their readiness to give and suggested that they now complete what they had begun (vss. 10–11). He reminded them that God accepts a man's gifts according to what he has so long as the readiness to give is there (vs. 12). Finally, he pointed out that the sharing of their prosperity with those who were impoverished (another theme of the example of Christ) is meant only to secure equality (vss. 13–15).

Verse 8: states that Paul was not commanding something from the Corinthians, but appealing to their love. This verse was probably inserted to avoid a misunderstanding of verse 7.

I say this: present tense. Thus it reads, "I am speaking." The reference is to verses 1–7.

Not as a command: a Pauline phrase. The words, with the negative, are used only here and in 1 Corinthians 7:6. Without the negative the phrase is found in three passages (Rom. 16:26; 1 Tim. 1:1; Titus 1:3), always followed by the words "of God." Paul never assumed the place of a dictator in the lives of the churches. When he spoke "by way of command," it was always the command of God and not of himself. He wanted the Corinthians to know that he did not assume that he could command them in this respect. They were free to do as they pleased in regard to the giving of money.

But: strong adversative. Having told them what he was not doing, he told them what he was trying to do.

To prove: rather, "as proving." The thought is that his suggestions to them were an attempt to *prove,* i.e., to demonstrate, something. This word is a distinctively Pauline word, being used seventeen times. In common Greek it simply meant to test something. Paul always used it with the implied hope of a favorable result.

By the earnestness of others: the Macedonians. Their earnestness or eagerness in this matter could be used as the standard of comparison. If the Corinthians measured up to that standard, they would stand the test and fulfill the hopes of Paul.

That your love also is genuine: probably a true translation. Plummer suggests that it was to prove "whatever was genuine in your love also." But this seems to press the figure of speech too far. It is true that the word for *prove* was commonly used of the process of placing precious ores in a crucible, burning out the dross, and having the genuine metals (gold or silver) left. However, in this context the figure should not be forced to suggest that Paul was hoping to burn out the dross of their selfishness and have only genuine love left. *Genuine* is an old adjective formed by the contraction of the word "to be born," and implies that what is genuine is legitimately born, hence not spurious (Robertson).

Verse 9: The minds of the Corinthians were directed to the sacrifice of Christ as the true example of what genuine loves does.[1]

For: introduces the reason why Paul did not have to speak by command. He knew that if love was genuine, their response would be freely given and generous.

You know: appeals to a fact of which they were well aware. They knew this from the preaching of the gospel itself.

The grace of our Lord Jesus Christ: Grace is generally used with God in the New Testament, but in this case the word has the same meaning as in the previous verse. It would be rendered, "the gracious work." The full title, *our Lord Jesus Christ,* is impressive, though it was seldom used by Paul.

That: introduces the definition of the gracious work of Christ.

Though he was rich: in his preexistent glory. This expression proves that Paul shared the common Christian belief in the preexistence of Christ. He quoted a Christian hymn (Phil. 2:6–11) which indicated that this belief was common to early Christians rather than a late development in the case of only a few. Many modern theologians, in spite of the evidence, attempt to make belief in the preexistence of Christ a late development in Christian history, seemingly with the implication that the doctrine is false. However, the evidence is quite clear that by the mid-fifties of the first century, Christians did commonly accept the truth of the preexistence of Jesus. Paul did also.

This belief is a natural and necessary deduction from the conception of the exalted Jesus. If the man who died on Calvary arose and became the exalted Christ of the Christian movement, it would inevitably follow that he must be more than man, though he was man. The only answer to the exaltation of the Crucified One was the answer of his preexistence and its attendant belief in his true deity. Paul had already spoken of Christ as the agent of creation: "There is . . . one Lord, Jesus Christ, through whom are all things and through whom we exist" (1 Cor. 8:6). To speak of his riches here is to imply the same truth that was expressed in the Christian hymn which said: "though he was in the form of God, did not count equality with God a thing to be grasped" (Phil. 2:6). The expression is a concessive clause, assuming the truth of the fact stated.

Yet . . . he became poor: speaks primarily of the incarnation, but implies the cross as well. The parallel statement in the Christian hymn is: "but emptied himself, taking the form of a servant, being born in the

---

[1] I believe this is the thrust of the passage, although Craddock has argued cogently that the purpose of introducing the Christological formula at this point was to set the offering in the larger context of Christian life (Fred B. Craddock, "The Poverty of Christ: An Investigation of II Corinthians 8:9," *Interpretation,* Apr., 1968, pp. 158–170).

likeness of men. And being found in human form he humbled himself and became obedient unto death, even death on a cross" (Phil. 2:7–8). In early Christian thought the incarnation was never regarded as an isolated fact, but as a prelude to the cross. The absence of any mention of the cross may mark this verse as an early Christian formulation which Paul adopted and stated because it met his purposes in this context.

For your sake: made the sufferings of Christ personal to the Corinthians.[1] There are two diverse ways of looking at the sacrifice of Christ. One is to view it in its universal significance; the other is to view it in its personal significance. When seen in the light of its universal meaning, one may say, "One has died for all" (2 Cor. 5:14). When seen in its personal significance, one may say, "Who loved me and gave himself for me" (Gal. 2:20). Paul never forgot either dimension of the sacrifice of Christ. Here he wanted to remind the Corinthians that it was for their sake, i.e., "on your account," that Christ had made his sacrifice.

So that: introduces the results in the lives of the Corinthians of Christ's sacrifice.

By his poverty: his assuming the place of poverty.

You might become rich: enjoy the riches of the grace of God in salvation. The choice of the two words, *poverty* and *rich,* was dictated by the circumstances. Paul was speaking to those who were relatively rich in material goods; he hoped to lead them to generous giving to alleviate the poverty of the Jerusalem saints. What better example could be found of one who sacrificed his riches that those who were poverty stricken could be rich than Christ?

Verse 10: begins the application of the example to the collection for the poor, starting with the idea of voluntary sacrifice.

And in this matter: the collection for the poor.

I give my advice: synonymous with: "I say this not as a command." *Advice* translates a word which means "opinion." Paul had used the word before and said that his opinion was worth considering (1 Cor. 7:40).

It is best for you: wrongly connected in the RSV translation. The Greek reads literally: "for this to you is profitable." The expression is a complete clause in itself and follows in the Greek with the rest of the sentence, thus: "who are such that not only to do but also to desire you before began, a year ago." Therefore, the connection of the expression before us is uncertain. It could mean that their liberal giving was morally profitable to them. It could mean that giving an opinion instead of making a command was best for them. It is probable that the latter connection is the one meant. Thus the expression would mean: "To give advice rather than commands is expedient for you." The implication is that they did not need to have commands.

To complete: is not a part of the Greek text, but is borrowed from verse 11.

The words "who are such" are omitted by the RSV but are necessary to complete the meaning of the sentence and to express Paul's thoughts.

What a year ago you began not only to do but to desire: rather, in the

---

[1] Hughes comments that the significance of Christ's self-impoverishment "is grasped only in a manner that is intensely *personal.*"

Greek, "not only to do but to desire you before began, a year ago." It is necessary that the comments follow the Greek meaning rather than the RSV translation in this instance. "Before began" probably refers to the fact that the Corinthians were the first in the field in their doing and desiring to alleviate the condition of the poor. "Before" does not refer to a time element, but is comparative in significance. It does not necessarily refer to "before" the Macedonians, but probably means, "before anyone else." "To do" and "to desire" is a strange order of words. We would expect, "to desire and to do." The background implied is that the Corinthians actually began to give and expressed a desire to continue their giving. *A year ago* marks the time when they began their doing and desiring. The expression literally means "from last year." There is no need to argue whether Paul used the Roman or Jewish calendar. 1 Corinthians was written some months prior to 2 Corinthians, and the year had changed in the meantime. Whether it was literally a full year or not may be doubtful (cf. discussion of date in the introduction).

Verse 11: completes the sentence begun in verse 10. The RSV translation has added to verse 10 the first part of verse 11.

"But now complete the doing also": This phrase in the Greek is not represented by any portion of the RSV translation in verse 11. Paul had boasted of the Corinthians as being first in the field in their doing and desiring, but this did not mean that their doing was completed. The present admonition is to complete, i.e., bring to its culmination, the doing which had been begun the previous year.

So that your readiness in desiring it: refers to the voluntary way in which they had expressed a desire to have a worthy part in the collection for the saints.

May be matched by your completing it: It would have been a sad thing if the church that was first in the field of giving should now, at the end, prove unable to complete their project.

Out of what you have: an expression that has little point in this form. If they gave, it must of necessity be out of what they had. The expression should be given the meaning of proportion: Their giving was to be proportionate to their having. Paul had enunciated this principle of giving in the first epistle (1 Cor. 16:2). Paul did not suggest that the Corinthians match the sacrifice of the Macedonians, but that they give in proportion to their own ability to give.

Verse 12: enunciates the principle that God judges man's giving according to his ability to give.

For if the readiness is there: assumes that it is. *If* could be translated, "since." *The readiness* translates an old Greek word with two elements: one meaning "before"; the other, "temper." The literal meaning is "forwardness, eagerness." *Is there* translates the Greek word meaning "lies before." Paul assumed that the eagerness to do lay before, i.e., in the presence of, the Corinthian congregation.

It is acceptable: that is, in the eyes of God. Paul did not mean to set himself up as a judge of what was an acceptable gift on the part of any man. He was stating principles by which a man might know whether what he gave was acceptable to God.

According . . . not according: Both express the idea of proportionate giving.

Verse 13: states the purpose in Paul's mind as he wrote these things.

I do not mean that others should be eased: by not having to give according to their ability. There may have been those in Corinth who accused the apostle of trying to get them to carry the whole burden of the collection. If not, Paul anticipated such a complaint in these words. He did not want to relieve others of the necessity of giving.

And you burdened: literally, "pressed." He did not want the Corinthians to think that he was trying to lay an intolerable burden on them.

Verse 14: The first part, as punctuated by the RSV, belongs to verse 13; the second part, to what follows.

But: a strong adversative introducing the alternative to the preceding, i.e., the positive statement of Paul's purpose.

As a matter of equality: rather, "out of equality." The thought is that the principle of proportionate giving made the burden equal on those who participated in it. The ones who had little to give could give some, and in the sight of God their readiness made their gift acceptable. Those who had much to give, gave much; but it was not the amount of their giving which pleased God, but the readiness to give.

Your abundance: indicates that the Corinthians were relatively prosperous when compared to the Macedonians and, especially, to the saints in Jerusalem.

At the present time: in the present circumstances.

Should supply their want: their needs. *Their* translates the Greek demonstrative pronoun "of others." Some have supposed that these "others" were the Macedonians, but the likelihood is that the pronoun refers to the saints of Jerusalem.

So that their abundance may supply your want: probably refers to a future and possible time when the tides of fortune, political or commercial, changed.[1] In that time the ones who had received the bounty of the Corinthians could come to their rescue. In both cases material help is involved. Against this suggestion is the idea that Paul was speaking of a double equality—both material and spiritual (Lenski). According to this opinion, he had in mind that the Jerusalem church would share their spiritual riches with the Corinthians. This seems unlikely as an interpretation of Paul's thought. He never conceived of the Jerusalem church as richer than his Gentile churches. He was thinking of equalizing material conditions according to the shifts of fortune.

That there may be equality: carries the thought to its completion. By urging the Corinthians to share in the relief of the needs of the Jerusalem saints, he was setting a pattern of relief which might well return to bless the Corinthians in the future. In this way equality would always exist.

Verse 15: is an Old Testament quotation which illustrates equality of a sort, not necessarily of the same sort of which Paul had been speaking. In the case under consideration, equality would result from voluntary sharing. In the Old Testament quotation the equality was involuntary. The

---

[1] Lenski comments that Christian giving is not *"a one-sided matter."*

quotation is from Exodus 16:18. The context is that of the gathering of the manna in the wilderness. Each Israelite was commanded to gather only so much as he could eat. Some were greedy and gathered more. Some, through indifference, gathered less than the prescribed amount—"an omer" (Exod. 16:16). However, when they came to measure the manna, each man's gathering weighed exactly the same. There was an equality, but it was an equality enforced upon them from without. The resemblance between the two cases was verbal only, but Paul sometimes quoted Old Testament Scripture where the verbal resemblance existed but where there was no material resemblance between the two situations. He did so here. The word which he was illustrating was equality.

3. Encouragement by Sharing His Plans for the Offering (8:16–24)

The central thought in this paragraph is expressed in the words: "We intend that no one should blame us about this liberal gift which we are administering" (vs. 20). To avoid any breath of scandal about the handling of the money, Paul had made various arrangements. Titus, not only because Paul wanted him to come but also because he himself desired it, would come to Corinth and help to complete the offering (vss. 16–17). With him the brother who was well known to the churches for preaching the gospel would come (vs. 18). He was qualified in this matter, not only by his fame as a preacher, but by appointment by the churches (vs. 19). Verse 21 completes his statement of purpose. Another brother would likewise accompany Titus and *the brother,* one whom Paul could personally recommend (vs. 22). Verses 23–24 further recommend the brothers who would come to them. Finally there was an appeal for the Corinthians to demonstrate their love and the validity of his boasting (vs. 24).

Verse 16: is a thanksgiving to God for the love which Titus had for the Corinthians.

But: a mild continuative particle.

Thanks be to God: Paul's regular formula of thanksgiving.

Who puts: present tense of verb meaning "gives." God was continually giving this gift to Titus.

The same earnest care for you: Earnest care translates the same word which we have found often in this context, which means "eagerness, earnestness, carefulness." Titus was zealous for the welfare of the Corinthians. *Same* probably means the same kind of concern which Paul himself had for them.

Into the heart of Titus: His care was not external show, but a matter of the heart.

Verse 17: tells of the gladness with which Titus welcomed the appeal of Paul to go to Corinth. The point is that Titus was not a reluctant minister.

For: rather, "because." The particle introduces the basis on which Paul had decided that the words of verse 16 were true.

He . . . accepted: rather, "welcomed." The Greek word means more than a passive acceptance: it has the sense of eager acceptance. Thus, it could be translated, "welcomed." The past tense points to the time of Paul's appeal as the time when he welcomed it.

Our appeal: our encouragement to go to you.

But being himself very earnest: comparative form of the adjective which was translated "earnest care" in the previous verse. It means, "more earnest than ordinarily" or "more than I expected."

He is going to you of his own accord: His own accord translates the same Greek adjective which was translated "their own free will" in verse 3. The picture drawn by the words of this verse is of a minister who was asked to do something which he already wanted to do. The Corinthians should accept the ministry of such a man with gladness.

Verse 18: introduces the other brother whom Paul would send with Titus.

With him: as his associate in the ministry.

We are sending: past tense in the Greek, but is to be taken as an epistolary past tense. The sending would be past when he arrived with the letter. The RSV changes the tense to view the sending from the standpoint of Paul.

The brother: Some commentators have taken this in the literal sense as meaning the brother of Titus, and have supposed that the person involved was Luke. Thus they have built a hypothesis that Luke and Titus were blood brothers. This may be true, but evidence does not sustain the hypothesis. Many other names have been conjectured—Barnabas, Silas, Mark, Erastus, Trophimus, Aristarchus, Secundas, and Sopater of Beroea (Plummer). All that is certain is what is said in this passage, and this is insufficient to be of any real value. As Romans 16 suggests, there must have been many faithful preachers of the gospel whose names have been lost to us. Plummer insists that the best guess is Luke; he suggests that Luke had been left at Philippi when Paul left there, and he had remained for six years in the city. If so, he may have become a favorite of the church and be the person involved. But this can be only guesswork.

Who is famous among all the churches: states the widespread fame of the brother being sent. He was no nonentity, but a very much respected minister of the gospel. The extended introduction of this brother might indicate that the Corinthians did not know him personally.

For his preaching of the gospel: rather, "in the gospel." This does not necessarily refer to preaching; it could refer to writing. However, if it refers to the gospel in written form, it could not refer to "the gospel according to Luke," which had not yet been written. Perhaps the RSV suggestion is better. In this case he would have been a well-known and popular preacher.

Verse 19: continues the recommendation of the brother.

Not only that: refers back to verse 18. His preaching was one recommendation, but there was another to come.

But: literally, "but also." The expression is strongly adversative.

He has been appointed: rather, "elected." *Appointed* comes from a Greek word which means "to stretch out the hands" (Robertson). The idea was that he had been elected by a public vote. This word suggests that the democratic process of government prevailed in the churches of the first century.

By the churches: The plural indicates that he was elected by all the churches of Macedonia—Philippi, Thessalonica, and Beroea.[1]

To travel with us: to be our assistant. The word means "to be our companion in travel," but suggests a subordinate position. He was not a colleague like Barnabas.

In this gracious work: the work of gathering and delivering the collection for the saints. It was a "grace" in the sense that it was inspired of God. *In* is probably the true reading, though there is strong support for "with." The meaning would not be materially changed in either case.

Which we are carrying on: literally, "which is being ministered by us." Paul did not think of himself as continuing this ministry, but acting as a servant of the Lord who was its originator.

For the glory of the Lord: to manifest the true character of the Lord as one who was concerned about the needs, material or spiritual, of his people.

And to show our good will: literally, "our readiness." Paul wanted to make it clear that he was doing this voluntarily, that it expressed his own love as well as that of the Lord.

Verse 20: the key verse in this paragraph.

We intend: literally, "arranging this." The idea of taking precautions against a possible accusation is involved in the verse. The verb is the present tense and middle voice. This indicates Paul's own continuing arrangements to avoid any breath of scandal.

That no one should blame us: indicates the purpose of Paul's arrangements.

About this liberal gift: literally, "with reference to this bounty." *Liberal gift* translates a Greek word which originally meant "fullness and firmness," with reference to speech or the human body. From this meaning it came to indicate any kind of abundance. The suggestion is that Paul expected the collection to be large and abundant. For this reason he must secure himself against any suspicion with regard to it.

Which we are administering: rather, "which is being ministered by us." The same word is used that we found in verse 19. The idea of ministry under the leadership of the Lord is involved. It included not only the *administering,* i.e., the delivery of the gift, but also the collection of it.

Verse 21: continues the thought of verse 20.

For: a continuative particle introducing an explanatory statement.

We aim at: literally, "we take thought of." The idea of intention is included in the verb. This word and the following words—*honorable, before the Lord, and men*—come from Proverbs 3:4 in the Greek version of the Old Testament. The Hebrew has: "so you will find favor and good repute in the sight of God and man."

What is honorable: literally, "the good."

Not only in the Lord's sight: as he sees it. The Lord would view the

---

[1] IB says he was an official representative.

motives and intents of the heart. Paul had no doubt that his ministry of the bounty would be approved by the Lord; he knew his heart was free of ulterior motives.

But also in the sight of men: who would view the matter from the viewpoint of its exterior arrangements. This phrase is the true object of the verb. It was for men that these arrangements were being made.

Verse 22: introduces another companion of Titus.

And with them: as their associate in this matter.

We are sending: rather, "we have sent." The past tense views the sending from the viewpoint of the Corinthians when they received the letter.

Our brother: fellow-Christian. This does not refer to Paul's blood brother any more than "the brother" meant Titus' blood brother. There is no need to try to guess the identity of this emissary. He wants to be their associate.

Whom we have often tested and found earnest in many matters: suggests that the emissary was a long-time companion of Paul. *Tested* does not mean that Paul had deliberately put the man to the test, but that circumstances had proved him to be true.

But who is now more earnest: more eager to engage in this ministry. The comparative refers to the previous clause which stated that Paul had found him *earnest in many matters.*

Because of his great confidence in you: suggests that this brother may have been in contact with the Corinthians. He may or may not have been in Corinth.

Verse 23: returns to Titus and places him on a higher plane, with reference to Paul, than the other envoys.

As for Titus: changes the subject back to Titus. No verb is found in the Greek. The thought is, "if anyone asks about Titus."

My partner: a partaker of my whole ministry. Paul could have said nothing more meaningful about Titus than this.

And fellow worker in your service: In your service belongs only to this expression. That he had been a fellow worker in their case would have been well known to the Corinthians. He seems to have had a large part in effecting their reconciliation to Paul.

And as for our brethren: the other two associates of Titus in this particular ministry.

They are messengers of the churches: Messengers translates the Greek word "apostles," but it probably has this meaning in this context. The word literally means "messenger" or "sent one." The idea is that they had sufficient recommendation from the fact that they had been elected as official delegates of the churches with reference to the collection.

The glory of Christ: men through whom the true nature of Christ was manifested. "One person is another person's glory when he exhibits the glorious work of that person" (Lenski).

Verse 24: is an admonition to the Corinthians.

So: rather, "therefore."

Give proof: obscures the play on words which exists in the Greek. The two words are built on the same stem, one a noun and the other a verb.

"Demonstrate the demonstration" would catch the meaning of the phrase. Plummer suggests, "exhibit the exhibition."

Before the churches: to these men as representatives of the churches. Paul conceived of the churches being present in the person of their delegates.

Of your love: your Christian concern for the needs of others.

And of our boasting about you to these men: refers to Paul's boast that the Corinthians would do their part in the offering. He did not want to make this his only plea to them, but he did not want them to be ignorant of his confidence.

4. Encouragement by His Boast of Them (9:1–5)

Paul professed to feel that there was no necessity to write to Corinth about the offering (vs. 1) and stated that he had boasted in Macedonia of the readiness of the Corinthians (vs. 2). The purpose of his sending the brethren was to make sure that his boast of them would not prove in vain (vs. 3), lest he be humiliated when he found the Corinthians unready for the offering (vs. 4). This fear of humiliation, he said, was the reason that he sent the brethren to prepare them for the offering (vs. 5). In all of this Paul revealed his skill as a pastor, using solid principles of psychology. By assuring the Corinthians of his confidence in them, he would make them ashamed not to live up to his expectations. Some commentators have thought that chapter 9 and chapter 8 belong to different letters, but this reveals a misunderstanding of Paul's methods. It is more likely that the chapter division is misplaced. This paragraph connects very closely with what immediately precedes.

Verse 1: a statement of his feeling that he need not write them at all about the offering.

Now: a particle of continuation.

It is superfluous for me to write to you: a polite statement with which skillful speakers and writers often introduce additional statements. It is equivalent to our: "I need not say." Yet, after saying this, we often proceed to discourse at some length on what we "need not say."

About the offering: rather, "concerning the service." The same word which we met often in chapter 8 to describe the ministry of relief is used here. There is no doubt, however, that this "service" involved an offering.

For the saints: rather, "unto the saints." The ministry of relief was directed toward the *saints,* i.e., the people of God.[1]

Verse 2: introduces the reason for his feeling that he need not write them about this matter.

For I know your readiness: reflects the statement in 8:10–11. They had professed their readiness to complete the offering, and Paul knew about that.

Of which I boast about you: present tense meaning, "I keep on boasting." Though the Corinthians had lagged in their gathering of the offering, Paul still boasted of their *readiness,* i.e., their forwardness.

---

[1] Hodge says that the term refers to all believers.

To the people of Macedonia: the members of the congregations at Philippi, Thessalonica, and Berea.

Saying that Achaia has been ready since last year: the words of his boast. *Achaia* was the province of which Corinth was the main center of Christian work. Paul used the term here meaning primarily Corinth. *Has been ready* is a perfect tense in the Greek of the verb meaning "to be prepared." It meant that they had been prepared and were still prepared for the offering. *Since last year* is the same expression used in 8:10 and points to the definite time when the Corinthians had begun to gather the offering.

And your zeal has stirred up most of them: indicates that Paul had used the readiness of the Corinthians to stir up the Macedonians. *Stirred up* translates a verb which is used only here and in Colossians 3:21 in the New Testament. The fundamental meaning is "to provoke." It may have either a good or bad sense. The good sense prevails here; the bad, in Colossians 3:21. *Most of them* means the majority and intimates that there were still those in Macedonia who had not been "provoked" to emulation of Corinth.

Verse 3: explains why Paul sent his envoys to Corinth.

But I am sending: past tense in the Greek, looking at the sending from the standpoint of the Corinthians when they received the letter.

The brethren: the three brethren mentioned in 8:16–24.[1] Titus is the only one whose name we know.

So that our boasting about you may not prove vain in this case: Paul feared they might be neglectful in organizing the collection. He did not question their readiness but their performance. His purpose in sending the brethren was to organize the offering and see that performance matched the readiness. *Vain* translates the Greek word which means "empty of results."

So that you may be ready: i.e., prepared with the money already gathered.

As I said you would be: repeats the boast that Paul had made concerning the Corinthians.

Verse 4: continues the explanation begun in verse 3.

Lest if some Macedonians come with me and find that you are not ready: an expression that indicates that Paul did not think that the Corinthians would be found wanting. The probability of some Macedonians coming with him was strong. It is possible that the brethren who accompanied Titus were not Macedonians, but it is more likely that at least one of them was. However, Paul was anticipating his own visit to them.

We be humiliated—to say nothing of you: Paul put his own shame before that of the Corinthians; but, of course, they would be put to shame also. Perhaps he had done more boasting about them than they had done about themselves, and his shame would therefore be the greater. Perhaps he was acting the part of a wise pastor and appealing to them to spare him rather than appealing to a selfish motive.

---

[1] Héring does not believe this connection is necessary.

For being so confident: rather, "in this confidence." The word which is translated "confidence" has two elements: one meaning "under" and the other, "stand." Thus, it meant literally a foundation or standing ground, and came to mean the basis of hope and then hope or confidence. The same word is used in Hebrews 11:1 in speaking of faith as "the conviction of things not seen."

Verse 5: continues Paul's explanation of the sending of the emissaries to arrange for the collection. He wrote in the past tense (the epistolary past). He had felt it necessary in the light of the circumstances in Corinth to send an advance guard to Corinth. His envoy therefore would precede him in going to the city. They would make arrangements for the gift to be gathered together according to the promise of the Corinthians. *Gift* translates a word which originally meant "good words" and then came to mean "good deeds." Here it refers to the benefit which the Corinthians would bestow on others. In the light of this context, *gift* is a justified translation.

So that it may be ready not as an exaction but as a willing gift: rather, "as a matter of bounty and not of covetousness." *Willing gift* is the same word as above. *Exaction* translates the word which is usually translated "covetousness." The meaning is that the Corinthians should not give grudgingly.

5. Encouragement by Giving Reasons for Liberality (9:6–15)

This paragraph is closely related to the preceding ones. It adds further motives for giving liberally to the collection for the poor saints in Jerusalem. The first additional motive seems to be an appeal to selfish interests. It is a suggestion that giving is not a sacrifice but a sowing of seed which will be reaped by the giver (9:6–11). However, since the harvest to be reaped is spiritual in nature, it is not correct to think of this as an appeal to selfishness. The second additional motive is that giving will lead to the glorification of God (9:12–15).

(1) Their own enrichment depended on their liberality (9:6–11)

Verse 6 introduces the figure of speech which dominates the paragraph—the figure of sowing and reaping. Within limits, the more one sows, the more he reaps. This is followed by an appeal to give cheerfully (vs. 7). Verse 8 is a statement of the ability of God to provide an abundant spiritual harvest for those who give. Verse 9 is a quotation from the Old Testament which Paul thought to be relevant to the matter of giving. Verse 10 contains the promise of God's abundant harvest in their lives. Verse 11 constitutes a bridge between this thought and the thought of the next paragraph: the first part saying, "You will be enriched," and the second part, "This will produce thanksgiving to God."

Verse 6: introduces the figure of speech.
The point is this: a good translation of the Greek demonstrative pronoun. Paul wished to call attention to his words as being a summary of

what he had already said regarding giving. The Greek particle is merely transitional and does not need to be translated.

He who sows sparingly: The present tense points to a habit of life and describes the farmer who constantly sows fewer seed than the ground can sustain.[1] Of course, the figure is overdrawn because it pronounces a principle that is clear to every farmer. No farmer would think of being niggardly in the amount of seed sown. The figure is purposely overdrawn in order to make the spiritual point clear.

Will also reap sparingly: rather, "sparingly will reap." The future tense refers to what may naturally be expected to happen.

And he who sows bountifully: probably a correct translation. *Bountifully* translates a Greek prepositional phrase which literally means "upon blessings." "Upon" may mean either "on principles of," "on condition of," or "for the purpose of." "Blessings" is a plural form of the same word which was used twice in verse 5, where the RSV translated it "gift." Lenski insists that the meaning of "blessings" be retained. He would translate literally: "He who keeps sowing on the basis of blessings, on the basis of blessings shall he also reap." If this is accepted, it would seem that the thought has already shifted from the figure of speech to the giving of money. However, the expression can be rendered "bountifully" or "generously," and this is probably the better choice. If so, the figure is continued with a perfect parallel between the sparing sower and the bountiful sower. Again, we must recognize that Paul overstated the case from the standpoint of farming. There is a limit to the amount of harvest that a piece of ground can produce. There is the possibility of oversowing and thus lessening the harvest. However, the figure was constructed in view of the spiritual application he wished to make.[2]

Will also reap bountifully: The RSV translation obscures the chiasmus, which is continued in the second part of the verse.

Verse 7: is an application of the figure to the matter of giving.

Each one: places the decision of giving on the shoulder of each Christian in Corinth.

Must do as he has made up his mind: literally, "as he has determined in his heart." The Corinthians were urged to make their giving a matter of deliberate choice. This expression introduces the thought that God is concerned not only with what we do but also with the motive that lies back of our deeds. Though the need was great in Jerusalem, Paul wanted each Christian to make his giving a matter of generosity of heart.

Not reluctantly or under compulsion: two ways of stating the same thought. *Reluctantly* indicates an unwillingness to give that is overcome by some kind of compulsion from without.[3] The statement is related in thought to the command of God to Moses concerning the gifts made for the building of the Tabernacle: "Speak to the people of Israel, that they take for me an offering; from every man whose heart makes him willing you shall receive the offering for me" (Exod. 25:2). The same thought

---

[1] Héring comments that an agricultural sentence is given a fiscal-moral application.
[2] Strachan comments that "the fruits of true giving are as really guaranteed by God as the fruits of the earth."
[3] Tasker says that such attitudes rob giving of "its loveliness and its joy."

is contained in the instructions concerning giving to the poor: "You shall give to him freely, and your heart shall not be grudging when you give to him" (Deut. 15:10). The implication is that gifts which come from a reluctant heart and are begrudged are really no gifts at all in the sight of God.

For God loves a cheerful giver: rather, to preserve the emphasis, "a cheerful giver God loves." *A cheerful giver* is placed first in the Greek in order to put emphasis on it. *Cheerful* translates the Greek word from which our English word "hilarious" is derived. Some translators translate, "hilarious." The word indicates that giving is to be lighthearted, happy, joyous, even gay. One is to feel that giving is a happy privilege which God has granted rather than an onerous duty. When the opportunity to give comes and we are able, it is to be welcomed and rejoiced in as much as any other spiritual blessing that comes from God. This kind of spirit should characterize the Christian giver in every age. The phrase is a partial quotation from Proverbs 22:9: "He who has a bountiful eye will be blessed." However, Paul changed the wording to substitute *loves* for "blessed," and to bring together the two words which are separated in the Greek translation of the verse in Proverbs—*cheerful* and *giver.*

God loves: is a difficult statement. It seems to say that God loves a cheerful giver but does not love the begrudging giver. This is not exactly true. When love is thought of as the attitude of concern which God has for men, it must be as great or greater for the begrudging as for the cheerful giver. What Paul had in mind was not the attitude of love but the manifestation of love in real blessings. It is true, today as in the first century, that the cheerful giver is loved or "blessed" by God in many ways in which the begrudging giver cannot share. Some of these blessings are immaterial; some are material; all are spiritual: (1) There is the consciousness of doing what is pleasing in the sight of God. The cheerful giver stands cleared in the judgment of his own consciousness; the begrudging giver stands condemned. (2) There is the blessing of growth in Christlikeness.The cheerful giver becomes more like Christ by his joyful spirit in giving; the begrudging giver less like him. Begrudging giving nurtures the spirit of covetousness; cheerful giving drives it out. (3) There is the blessing of oneness with the congregation. The cheerful giver becomes at one with the churches of Christ in their effort to win the world to Christ and to manifest the spirit of love for all men; the begrudging giver, though he participates materially, can never be spiritually at one with God's people. (4) God bestows material as well as immaterial blessings upon the cheerful giver. This does not mean that the cheerful giver can expect a dollar-for-dollar return of his gifts; it does mean that his spirit of joy in giving opens the way for God to give him prosperity in order that he may continue his giving. Of course it needs to be said that the cheerful giver is not motivated in any sense by a hope of reward. He gives only because he loves God and takes delight in doing his will. In giving he seeks no blessings, but he receives many.

Verse 8: states that both the farmer's crop and the Christian's blessing depend on the power of God.

That God is able: an indisputable statement.

To provide you with every blessing in abundance: literally, "every kind of grace to overflow toward you." This expression continues the thought of verse 7. Making his grace overflow in the direction of the Christian is God's way of loving the cheerful giver. Plummer takes this to mean that God is able to inspire generosity in the heart of the Christian, but this does not seem to be the meaning.

So that you may always have enough of everything: includes, if it does not mean, material gifts. The Corinthians were not to think that they would impoverish themselves by their giving. God would see to it that this did not happen. *Enough* translates a Greek word which means "self-sufficiency." It indicates a state in which one is not dependent on external circumstances.

And may provide in abundance for every good work: rather, "in order that you may abound in every good work." The phrase expresses the purpose of God's grace in the life of the Christian. It is not that he may simply have enough, but that he may be able to participate in every good work.[1] This verse is filled with the Greek adjective "all." It is used, in one form or another, five times in the verse. The RSV translation obscures this play on words by translating it variously: *every . . . always . . . everything . . . every.*

Verse 9: quotes Psalm 112:9, which reads: "He has distributed freely, he has given to the poor; his righteousness endures forever." The Psalm is a song dedicated to the blessings of "the man who fears the Lord" (Ps. 112:1). The reference was probably suggested to the mind of Paul by the equation of the cheerful giver with "the man who fears the Lord."

As it is written: Paul's regular formula for introducing an Old Testament quotation.

He scatters abroad: corresponds to the sowing of seed, not sparingly.

He gives to the poor: indicates purpose in his giving. He is not a man who scatters his wealth without thought; he sees that it goes to help the needy. The word for *poor* is used only here in the New Testament. It is the Greek word from which we get our English word "penury." The general sense is of one who works for his living. Paul had used another word for poor in previous verses, one which means "abject poverty."

His righteousness endures forever: may be either the righteousness of the man who gives to the poor or the righteousness of God. The subject is not stated. However, the subject is still probably the man who fears God. *Righteousness* would mean his righteous acts, i.e., his almsgiving. Plummer lists five possible meanings for this statement: (1) The almsgiving of the God-fearer will continue all during his life, since God continues to supply him with the ability to give. (2) His prosperity will continue as long as he lives as a reward of his righteous acts. (3) His good deeds will always be remembered by men. (4) God will always remember his good deeds and reward them in both this world and the next. (5) The results of his good deeds will continue, influencing succeeding generations of men. In the light of the context, it would seem that (4) is the meaning which Paul had in mind when he quoted the verse.

Verse 10: states that what God does in the realm of nature, he will

---

[1] Tasker suggests that God will provide the generous spirit with resources for its expression.

do in a richer way in the realm of spiritual life. The thought that generosity is not ruinous is continued.

He who supplies seed to the sower: The present tense indicates the habitual action of God. *Supplies* is emphatic in meaning. The word signifies a bountiful supply. Interestingly enough, the English word which is derived from this word is "chorus." The original application of the word was to the leader of a singing group who supplied the needs of the group. From this came the meaning of "supply" in a general sense. Paul's theology of nature is revealed in this verse. He looked upon the processes of nature as being the action of God.

And bread for food: through the harvest from the seed. There is no thought of miraculous feeding, but a further recognition of God as sovereign over the natural order.

Will supply and multiply your resources: rather, "your sowing." Paul carried the figure over into the realm of Christian giving. He looked upon giving as a sowing of seed which, through the grace of God, would bring a bountiful harvest.

And increase the harvest of your righteousness: from the Greek translation of Hosea 10:12. The Old Testament passage does not mean the same thing that Paul had in mind. The Hebrew of the verse means: "Sow for yourselves righteousness, reap the fruit of steadfast love." The idea that Paul had in mind is parallel to the previous clause: God will *increase* (i.e., cause to grow) the *harvest* of (rather, which is) *your righteousness.* *Righteousness* is in apposition with *harvest.* The result of their liberality would be progress in righteousness on their part. Thus, Paul revealed that he was not thinking of material rewards for giving, but of immaterial ones.

Verse 11: continues the thought of God's reward.

You will be enriched in every way: probably a good translation of the Greek passive participle. *Every way* indicates that the enrichment would take place in every area of life.

For great generosity: probably a correct translation. The Greek means literally, "with reference to all single-mindedness." The word which RSV translates *generosity* originally came from the action of spreading cloth flat so that nothing was left hidden in the folds. Lenski insists that the word should be given that meaning in this verse so that the translation would be, "unto all single-mindedness." However, the word can have the meaning of "liberality," and in this context it should be given that meaning. The idea was that generosity, through the grace of God, would breed generosity (cf. 8:2).

Which through us: through the ministry of the gift in Jerusalem, through Paul and his fellow-workers.

Will produce: i.e., "will work out to completion." The Greek verb has the meaning of completing a thing in its entirety.

Thanksgiving to God: on the part of the Jerusalem saints who would receive the results of their generous giving.

(2) Their liberality would glorify God (9:12-15)

This paragraph attaches itself to the last words of verse 11 and explains more fully the results of the offering. Paul stated that it would not only accomplish its goal of relieving need on the part of God's people (vs. 12a) but would also have spiritual results (vs. 12b). Thus the gift would accomplish a dual purpose. It would help those who needed help and would also glorify God (vs. 13). Further, their generosity would lead the Jerusalem saints to long for and pray for the Corinthians (vs. 14). The final verse is an exclamation of thanksgiving on the part of Paul (vs. 15).

Verse 12: For: rather, "because." The particle introduces Paul's explanation of what he meant by speaking of "thanksgiving to God."

The rendering: rather, "the ministry." This is the same word which Paul had often used in the context of the offering. It was considered to be a religious ministry.

Of this service: translates a Greek word which means "public service." In the Greek Old Testament this word was used almost exclusively for the priestly service in the Temple, the offering of sacrifices. It is the word from which we get our English word "liturgy." The thought of Paul was dominated by the thought of the gift being a sacrificial service to God.

Not only supplies the wants of the saints: meets their needs. *Supplies* translates a compound Greek word which means, "to fill up by adding to." The gifts of the Corinthians would be added to those of other churches, and this would meet what was lacking.

But also: strong adversative.

Overflows: the figure of a flooding river.

In many thanksgivings: by those who receive the gifts.

To God: placed at the end with special force. The thought is that the gifts of the Corinthians would be traced to God, their true source.

Verse 13: should be connected in thought to verse 11. Verse 12 is parenthetical.

Under the test of this service: The call for liberality was regarded by Paul as a test of the devotion of the Corinthians which he felt confident they would pass with flying colors.

You will glorify God: manifest his true being. Their giving would show that God was a God of love and concern, that he cared about the needs of his people even at the lowest level of existence. Thus their giving would glorify him. This is probably the meaning, but the Greek construction is obscure. It could mean, "they will glorify God." If so, *glorify* would be equivalent to "thanksgiving."

By your obedience: rather, "upon the occasion of your submission."

In acknowledging the gospel of Christ: rather, not *acknowledging* but "of your confession." The construction is somewhat confused, but the thought seems clear. It would seem that Paul felt that their giving of the money would be a form of confessing the gospel of Christ and show that they were obedient to him who was their Lord. By doing this, they would manifest the true nature of God.

And by: No word for *by* is in the Greek. Probably the connection should go back to the thanksgiving of many (vs. 12). Thus the thanksgiving would be "for" their generosity.

The generosity: same word as above, literally, "simplicity," but *generosity* gives the sense in this context.

Of your contribution: rather, "your partnership." Of course, the "partnership" of the Corinthians in the needs of the saints in Jerusalem took the form of a contribution, but the word means more than this. It looks upon the Corinthians as being sharers in the lives of the saints. The contributions were signs of a deeper reality of the Christian life—that of sharing life with others.

For . . . for: rather, "with reference to," or "in relation to." The change of English preposition is necessary if we take the fuller meaning of the previous word.

Them and . . . all others: indicates that the partnership of Christian life should be universal rather than limited to one group, and that it should be continuous rather than limited to a situation of need. There is no indication that the Corinthians would send money for relief to other congregations. But there is an indication that they would consider themselves partners with all Christians.

Verse 14: suggests the kind of partnership that would be returned.

While they long for you and pray for you: rather, "while they themselves also, with supplications on your behalf, long for you." *Pray for you* is subordinate in the construction. The emphasis falls on *long for you.* The idea was that the manifestation of partnership in life by the Corinthians would lead to a like manifestation on the part of the Jerusalem saints. While the Corinthians showed their partnership by giving money, the saints of Jerusalem would show theirs by intercessory prayer.

Because of the surpassing grace of God in you: the basis of the longing and praying of others for the Corinthians.

Verse 15: an exclamation of thanksgiving on the part of Paul.

Thanks be to God: reveals the inspiration of the thoughts of this paragraph to the heart of the apostle. He saw the reality of a united Christendom for which he had long labored. The Jewish Christians had been suspicious of the Gentile Christians. Through this offering he hoped that their suspicions would be allayed. Such a manifestation of God's grace in the hearts of the Gentile Christians would show that their confession of Christ was no superficial matter, but a genuine turning to the Lord.

For his inexpressible gift: one which cannot be expressed in speech. If Paul could not express it, we would be foolish to try.

IV. A PLEA TO THE CHURCH IN THE LIGHT
OF THE OPPOSITION OF SOME (10:1—13:10)

Modern writers have fallen prey to the same misapprehension which Paul feared that his readers would have. "Have you been thinking all along that we have been defending ourselves before you?" (12:19). He insisted that this was not the true purpose of his writing, but that he meant the section to be for their "upbuilding" (12:19). Yet most commentators have entitled their discussion of the section with words which indicate that they do not take Paul's own interpretation of his purpose seriously. One calls it, "St. Paul's Vindication of his Apostolic Ministry: The Great Invective" (Plummer). Another has, "Paul Affirms his Apostolic Authority" (Hughes).[1]

However, if we take Paul's own statement of purpose seriously, we must find the progression of thought in his appeal, not in his defense. Progression, do we say? It is difficult to discern; yet it exists. It would seem to me that we find first an entreaty to hold fast to the gospel as Paul had preached it to the Corinthians (10:1–18). This is followed by an entreaty to avoid being led astray by false prophets (11:1—12:13). Finally, there is an entreaty to the church to be prepared for his third visit to them (12:14—13:10). The climax of his statements is found in these words: "I write this while I am away from you, in order that when I come I may not have to be severe in my use of the authority which the Lord has given me for building up and not for tearing down" (13:10).

But if this is the true case, how can we account for the invective in these chapters? For invective there is. Many, finding it impossible to reconcile this with the first seven chapters of the book, have assumed that this is a portion of a former letter. We have discussed this idea in the introduction and have decided that the evidence for a division of the letter is not strong enough to overcome the force of the manuscript evidence. The letter has always appeared in the oldest manuscripts as one letter. There must be an explanation, however. It lies in the fact that a rebellious minority of the church were still trying to lead the Corinthians away from the true gospel. In doing this, they had made accusations against Paul which he had to answer. Six of the accusations which were made against Paul can be discerned: (1) His enemies accused him of writing severe letters, but of being a coward when present with the

---

[1] Munck also thinks apostleship is the subject under discussion (cf. *Paul and the Salvation of Mankind*, pp. 168–195).

church (they had mistaken the forbearance of Paul for cowardice) (10:1, 9–10). (2) They insisted that Paul's spirit was of the world, that he acted in a worldly fashion (10:2*b*; 11:11; 12:16). (3) They accused him of boasting and self-commendation (10:8). (4) They insisted that he knew himself to be an inferior apostle (11:5; 12:11; 13:3). (5) His enemies ridiculed Paul's ministry by saying that he was unskilled in the art of speaking and repulsive in his bodily appearance (11:6; 10:10). (6) They pointed to his refusal to receive support from the church and insisted that this showed that he felt himself to be inferior (12:13–14, 16).

Who were these opponents of Paul? We know only what we read in these chapters, but this reveals much. They preached "another Jesus . . . a different spirit . . . a different gospel" than that which Paul preached (11:3–4). They seemed to delight in argument (10:5). Paul accused them of practicing self-commendation (10:12), of boasting in other men's labors (10:15), of being "false apostles, deceitful workmen, disguising themselves as the apostles of Christ" (11:13). To Paul they were the servants of Satan (11:15), preying upon the Corinthians and seeking to take advantage of them (11:20). It would seem that they also reveled in their "visions and revelations of the Lord" (12:1*b*). All of this could be descriptive of any kind of false teacher in any age. One passage seems to identify these false teachers as Judaizers: "Are they Hebrews? So am I. Are they Israelites? So am I. Are they descendants of Abraham? So am I" (11:22). These opponents were men who boasted in their relation to Abraham, to the law, and to the traditions of Israel.

When we combine this knowledge with other passages, a good picture is drawn of that group of Christians (seemingly rather large in Jerusalem) who insisted that all converts from paganism must be circumcised and become practicing Jews as well as having faith in Christ. The Jerusalem council (Acts 15:1–35) had settled this question officially, but some had refused to accept the decision of the churches. They became active propagandists of their system of error.[1] It seems that they had come to Corinth after Paul's departure and had insinuated themselves into the confidence of the Corinthians by various claims. Paul, therefore, found it necessary to make one last appeal to the church to avoid their enticements before he was ready to come in peace to the church.

1. An Entreaty to Hold Fast to the Gospel Paul Had Preached (10:1–18)

The material in this chapter can be divided as follows: the reason for Paul's entreaty (vss. 1–6); the basis of his entreaty (vss. 7–12); and the purpose of his entreaty (vss. 13–18). The reason for his entreaty is most fully stated in verse 2. The basis of his entreaty was an appeal to his former ministry, which had been constructive rather than destructive (vs. 8). The purpose of his entreaty was that he hoped to be freed from the care of the Corinthians and extend his field of labors (vss. 15–16).

---

[1] This is the usual opinion but there are those who think the perennial enemies of Paul were Gnostics (cf. Martyn, *op. cit.*) and Munck thinks they had no theological axes to grind at all.

(1) The reason for the entreaty—Paul did not wish to be severe with all (10:1–6)

Paul began by introducing himself ironically in terms which had been used by his accusers (vs. 1) and pledged that he might not have to act with severity toward the whole church when he came (vs. 2). He identified his warfare as a spiritual rather than a worldly one (vs. 3), no doubt reflecting yet another accusation against him. However, he stated his readiness to use spiritual weapons to destroy strongholds, arguments, and every obstacle to spiritual progress, even being ready to punish the rebellious minority when the church as a whole returned to obedience to God (vss. 4–6).

Verse 1: Paul's ironical introduction of himself.

I, Paul, myself: may be an indication that Paul took the pen from his amanuensis (secretary) and wrote the rest of the letter in his own hand.[1] He often did this near the close of a letter (cf. Gal. 6:11–18). However, the formula itself does not demand this interpretation, and it would be unusual for him to have written so much as a conclusion to the epistle. The words could be merely an emphatic way of calling attention to himself and his appeal to them, following the extended discussion of what he hoped Titus and others would accomplish among them with reference to the collection for the saints.

Entreat you: translates the same Greek word so often used in this epistle, a word with meanings that range from "entreat" to "exhort." We have usually taken a middle course and interpreted the meaning as "encourage." However, in the light of the material in this section, *entreat* is justified. Obviously, he spoke with great feeling. The verb is in the present tense, which means that Paul was continuing to entreat them. *I beg* (vs. 2) is a synonym in this context.

By the meekness and gentleness of Christ: the basis of his entreaty. The example of Christ gives point and meaning to the entreaty. *Meekness* is the characteristic of a godly man toward God. It means that one is subject to the will and desire of God rather than insistent on his own way. *Gentleness* combines graciousness with forbearance. In Greek ethics it denotes "the 'equitable' man who does not press for the last farthing of his rights." Paul mentioned these two qualities of Christ to indicate the attitude in which he made his plea. He did not demand his rights nor exert his apostolic authority. Rather, he pleaded in the spirit of Christ for the restoration of love and harmony.[2]

I who am humble when face to face with you, but bold to you when I am away: reflects the charge made against Paul by his enemies. They mistook his forbearance for cowardice. *Humble* is used in a bad sense, which is unusual in the New Testament. "Socrates and Aristotle used it for

---

[1] This is the opinion of Gordon J. Bahr, "The Subscriptions in the Pauline Letters," *Journal of Biblical Literature*, Mar., 1968, pp. 27–41.

[2] Ragner Leivestad thinks Paul used the saying to show that humility in an apostle was not something to be derided, but this seems improbable ("The Meekness and Gentleness of Christ," *New Testament Studies*, Vol. 13, pp. 156–164).

littleness of soul" (Robertson). *Bold* means "to have good courage." In essence the two words could be equivalent to our words "cowardly" and "brave."

Verse 2: picks up the *entreat* of verse 1 and continues the sentence. It reveals the real purpose of Paul in writing these chapters.

I beg: synonymous with *entreat* and shows that the translation in verse 1 is correct. Plummer, however, thinks that the two words are not the same. He insists on translating thus: "I exhort, nay I beseech you." This is a possible translation but the suggested meaning seems better.

When I am present: indicates that Paul contemplated a third visit, a fact which dominates these chapters.

I may not have to show boldness: proves that he was not a coward, as his enemies had charged.

With such confidence as I count on showing: equivalent to saying that his mind was made up to act with courage and openness against his enemies. He expected the necessity of so acting.

Against some: important distinction between *some* and the majority of the church (cf. 2:6). Even in the first chapters of the letter, Paul showed a consciousness that the reconciliation of the church was not complete. Some were the enemies of Paul and the gospel against whom he now warned the church as a whole.

Who suspect us: literally, "who count us." *Suspect* is a good interpretation in this context.

Of acting in a worldly fashion: literally, "of walking according to the flesh." "Flesh" is equivalent in Paul's vocabulary to the whole man aside from any godly influence. Therefore the charge brought the motivation of Paul into question. His enemies accused him of acting from unspiritual motives.[1] There is probably no reference to immorality but a contention that he did not deserve to be respected as a man of God.

Verse 3: For though we live in the world: a concessive clause. *In the world* comes from the Greek "in the flesh." The meaning is about the same. Paul was conceding the fact that he lived (i.e., walked) in a common human way.

We are not carrying on a worldly war: rather, "We do not fight according to the flesh." Though he walked in the flesh, he did not follow "fleshly" ways in his warfare. This verse denies the allegations of his enemies that he "walked according to the flesh" (vs. 2). There is a play on prepositions in this verse. *In* is contrasted with "according to." The thought is the same as that expressed in the words of Jesus: "They are not of the world, even as I am not of the world" (John 17:16). The Christian must live his life "in the world," but he should guard himself against becoming a part of the world—dominated by its standards and principles.

Verse 4: begins a statement of Paul's warfare and his weapons of warfare.

For the weapons: the methods by which we fight. The figure is clear. The weapons of ancient warfare were much different from those of modern

---

[1] IB comments that this means to act without consistency, principle, or Christian character.

warfare, but the same principles hold. The soldier does not fight bare-handed, but with weapons.

Of our warfare: carries on the figure with the thought that the Christian ministry is a warfare i.e., it is carried on in the face of opposition.

Are not worldly: rather, "not fleshly." The meaning is that Paul refused to use the weapons his enemies used. They used appeal to pride and position. These were the weapons which men ordinarily used in trying to carry the day, and were thus "fleshly" weapons.

But: a strong adversative.

Have divine power: a poor translation. The Greek has "powerful to" or "for" God. The antithesis is between "fleshly" weapons and "powerful" weapons. This is an unusual antithesis. Ordinarily Paul would have used "spiritual." He seems, however, to have been thinking of the effects of his weapons, and so he called them "powerful." "God" is in the dative case in Greek and cannot be used, as the RSV does, adjectively. The thought seems to be that the weapons were used in the service of God, for God's advantage, hence, "for God."

To destroy strongholds: the fortresses which hinder the progress of the gospel. This is a continuation of the military figure of speech.

Verse 5: begins the application of the figure to the situation in Corinth.

We destroy arguments: plausible fallacies by which the Judaizers were leading or attempting to lead the Corinthians astray. Paul did not seek to destroy men, but the arguments which men used in opposition to God.

And every proud obstacle: rather, "every high thing that is lifting itself up." The figure is of the high walls of a fortress lifting itself against the attacking forces. *Obstacle* interprets the meaning rather than translating the Greek.

To the knowledge of God: rather, "in opposition to the knowledge of God." Paul looked upon the arguments of his opponents as fortress walls that stood against the knowledge of God. They were thus hindrances to the gospel and needed to be destroyed.

And take every thought captive: continues the military metaphor. Having destroyed the fortress, the army takes captive the survivors. Paul hoped to "imprison" the thoughts of men.

To obey Christ: expresses the purpose of the imprisonment. He did not want to capture the thoughts of men and hold them captive. He wanted to bring them into the service of Christ.

Verse 6: Being ready: indicates that Paul was holding himself in readiness, prepared to act if necessary.

To punish: a legal term which means "to do justice." Some have carried over the military metaphor and translated this, "to court-martial." There is no doubt that Paul was threatening some drastic action against his enemies.

Every disobedience: by the minority.

When your obedience is complete: speaks of Paul's hope that the church as a whole would set right the things that were not in order before he came. *When* is indefinite, meaning "whenever" or "as soon as." *Obedience* and *disobedience* are different forms of the word, which means in its root form "to listen." *Obedience* is "to listen and heed." *Disobedience* in this

context means "failure to listen," or "to listen amiss." The disobedience
indicated by the Greek word is less deliberate than the English word indicates.

(2) The basis of the entreaty—Paul's ministry had been for the purpose of building up the church (10:7–12)

The connection of this paragraph with the preceding is that Paul was
insisting that he had a right to ask the Corinthians to hold fast to the
gospel he had preached. The integrity of his past ministry should have
created confidence in the validity of his gospel. The paragraph begins
with a reminder that they looked only at what was before them (vs. 7a).
This is followed by a bit of boasting on Paul's part as he compared his
ministry with that of his detractors (vss. 7b–12). The implication is that
they should consider the situation from a wider and deeper viewpoint.

Verse 7: Look: may be imperative or indicative. If indicative, it may
be either a statement or a question. The form of the word would be the
same in either case, but it seems better to take the word as an indicative.
It would then read, "You are making a practice of looking" (Plummer and
Hughes). Paul reminded them that they were taking a superficial view of
things.

At what is before your eyes: comes first in the Greek sentence for
emphasis. The expression means that they saw only the superficial realities,
not the true realities of their situation. It implies an appeal to take a more
careful look.

If: indicates that the condition is a true condition.

Any one: points to Paul's detractors but does not necessarily single
out one. The pronoun is indefinite.

Is confident: rather, "is confident in himself." It was in his own mind
that the opponent had such confidence. The verb is in the perfect tense,
implying that the confidence still existed.

That he is Christ's: i.e., that he belongs to Christ.

Let him remind himself: rather, "this let him reckon again in himself."
The implication is that he should take another look at his confidence and
see if it was valid for him to assume that he alone belonged to Christ.

That as he is Christ's, so are we: a denial that his opponent had any
exclusive claim to Christ. Paul also belonged to Christ.

Verse 8: For even if I boast a little too much of our authority: implies
that it may be true that he boasted a little too much. His opponents had
undoubtedly accused him of this. *A little too much* is a good translation
of the Greek phrase, which literally means "somewhat more abundantly."
Our should probably be taken as an editorial plural. A mixture of the
singular and plural persists through this chapter; then the singular becomes
dominant in the remaining chapters of the letter. Paul conceived himself
as having authority in the sense that he was an authorized messenger of
Jesus Christ.

Which the Lord gave: the source of his authority. This expression robs
the paragraph of any hint of egotism on the part of Paul.

For building you up: The results of Paul's ministry had been constructive. This word is usually translated, "edification."

And not for destroying you: translates the same word which is used
in verse 5 in the expression: "We destroy arguments." This may intimate
that his opponents had accused him of being destructive or that he held
their ministry to be destructive. It could be a statement of plain fact, but
some intimation beyond the fact is more likely.

I shall not be put to shame: connected with the first part of the verse.
"If I indeed boast too much, I shall not be put to shame." [1] The verb is a
simple future tense and speaks of the confidence of Paul. His thought was
that no one would be able to disprove his boasts, since they were based
on solid reality.

Verse 9: is a purpose clause in the Greek which should be closely
united with verse 8. The RSV translation destroys the connection.

I would not: should be introduced by a particle of purpose and read,
"in order that I would not." The connection is as follows: "I shall not be
put to shame by being exposed as a pretentious boaster who only seeks
to scare people."

Seems to be frightening you with letters: anticipates the charge made
against Paul by his opponents, which he quoted in the next verse. They
were saying that he was a pretender who dared only to write strong letters
but was afraid to press his authority when face to face with them.

Verse 10: quotes the charge of Paul's opponents.

For they say: rather, "one says." The exact reading in the Greek text
is debated. Some take the word as a plural (as RSV), others as a singular.
The singular seems to be better attested. The reference then is to the
statement of one person, perhaps the leader of the opposition.

"His letters are weighty and strong": a true estimate, as the Corinthians
well knew. Paul himself said of his letter: "For even if I made you sorry
with my letter, I do not regret it . . . for I see that that letter grieved you,
though only for a while" (7:8). His letter had indeed been powerful in
its effects. Thus it could be called *strong. Weighty* probably means "impressive." The word can mean "burdensome" or "grievous."

"But his bodily presence is weak": probably also a true estimate concerning Paul's personal appearance. It would seem that he did not make
a good impression at first appearance, as did Barnabas (cf. Acts 14:12).
He had some defect in his eyes (Gal. 4:14) which may or may not have
been his thorn in the flesh (12:7). A second-century writing described
him as "small, short, bow-legged, with eye-brows knit together, and an
acquiline nose" (Robertson). A fourth-century forgery is even less flat-
tering, describing Paul as "a bald-headed, hook-nosed Galilean" (Robertson). Thus, the quotation so far was a true estimate of Paul.

"And his speech of no account": not so. It is true that he spoke simply,
but his speech had been attended in Corinth by the demonstration of the
power of God (cf. 1 Cor. 2:1–5). The sneering reference is probably to a
second visit of Paul in which he tried to heal the breach at Corinth by
kindness and love. His love had been mistaken for cowardice. He had

---

[1] Hughes remarks that Paul's glorying was never "hollow or self-centered."

failed. Yet it would be untrue to say that his failure on that occasion meant
that he did not have a powerful way of speaking. This verse shows how
any enemy may take a half-truth and turn it into a whole lie.

Verse 11: contains Paul's answer to the ridicule in verse 10.

Let such people: rather, "let such a one." The singular is quite clear in
this instance. Paul was still speaking of one who was "such a one" that
he would resort to ridicule to accomplish his ends.

Understand: rather, "take into account." The same word is used here
as in verse 7. He was asking that the opponent take into account what
came next.

That what we say by letter when absent: literally, "that what we are in
word through a letter while absent." The RSV obscures the thought by its
translation. Paul was speaking of what he was, not what he said. Of
course, what he was, was revealed by what he said in his letter. Possibly
this present letter is meant. Paul wanted them to take into account the
fact that his were no idle threats.

We do: rather, "we are." Again, the accent is on character, not on acts.

When present: looks forward to his proposed third visit. He would be
the same man when he came that he was when he wrote.

Verse 12: is placed in the next paragraph in the Greek text, but we need
not quibble at that. It obviously builds a bridge to the next thought, but
it can be connected with this paragraph.

Not that we venture: or "dare."

To class or compare ourselves: translates two cognate Greek words,
built on the stem which means "to judge." Perhaps the play on words in
the original could be preserved by translation, "to pair or compare."
Paul did not wish the Corinthians to judge him by comparison with others,
nor did he dare do so himself.[1]

With some of those who commend themselves: If Paul had called for a
comparison on this basis, the war would have been one of idle boasting.

But when they measure themselves by one another: forming a mutual
admiration society. The expression indicates that they set themselves up
as the standard of perfection and found their own conformity to it pleasing.

And compare themselves with one another: repeats the substance of the
previous clause.

They are without understanding: i.e., of the true standard of judgment,
which is Christ. The practice of the opponents of Paul is not unknown in
modern days. Some people seek self-satisfaction by comparing their lives
with one another, never realizing that the true measuring stick of the
Christian life and ministry is Christ.

**(3) The purpose of the entreaty—Paul hoped that his field of labor
would be greatly increased (10:13-18)**

Paul was a man who had a mission. He wrote to the Romans that
he aimed "to preach the gospel, not where Christ had already been named,
lest I build on another man's foundation" (Rom. 15:20). His hope was

---

[1] Hughes suggests that Paul was speaking ironically.

that the Corinthian church could be stabilized so that he could feel justified in going on to other fields (vs. 15). He insisted that he would not boast beyond the limits God had set (vs. 13), but reminded them that he was the first to come to Corinth with the gospel (vs. 14). He then shared his dream of preaching the gospel in lands beyond Corinth (vs. 16). The last two verses return to the theme of boasting, repeating the insistence that one should boast in the Lord (vs. 17) and realize that the Lord accepts only those whom he himself commends (vs. 18).

Verse 13: But we: very emphatic in the Greek. Paul drew a sharp contrast between his own boasting and that of his opponents. Some texts omit these words and the last words of verse 12: "They are without understanding." However, the manuscripts which omit all of these words belong to the Western group of manuscripts, while all other groups retain the words. Therefore it seems likely that the RSV represents the true text.

Will not boast beyond limit: possibly, "beyond our measure." The expression means "unlimitedly." However, in the context the "measure" of Paul's boasting is set forth. In the light of this, the meaning is that Paul refused to go beyond the measure or limit which God had set for him. He refused, in other words, to accept the standards of other men as the basis of judging himself.

But: strongly adversative, introducing the limits which Paul set on his own boasting.

Will keep to the limits God has apportioned us: shortened translation of the Greek, which reads: "according to the measure of the length which God apportioned to us as a measure." The shortened form makes better English and preserves the meaning of the Greek. However, there is a question concerning the Greek word *kanon,* translated "length." It is the word from which our word "canon" is derived. It was used to define the "rod which measured," but it was also used for the "territory which had been measured." Some commentators have translated it "province" in this verse. However, it seems that Paul was using the figure of measuring off the limits beyond which he could not go in boasting. God had provided the measuring rod.

To reach even to you: expresses the purpose of God in calling Paul. It was God's intention that Paul should reach the Corinthians with the gospel. That he had done so was indisputable.

Verse 14: This is a puzzling verse. The connection is in doubt. The punctuation is in doubt. Remember that the original manuscripts of the New Testament had no punctuation. Punctuation has been the work of various editors. A literal translation of the Greek reads: "For not as not reaching to you do we overstretch ourselves, for as far as even you we came in the gospel of Christ." The question is: should another comma be inserted to make the verse read: "For not, as not reaching to you, do we overstretch ourselves," etc? The RSV has chosen this punctuation and reversed the order of the clauses. This is probably the correct solution. The other question is the connection of the verse. Does it complete verse 13, or does it introduce the thought of verses 15-16? The correct solution, since verse 15 begins with a participle in the Greek, is to connect this verse with the following ones.

For we are not overextending ourselves: in our boasting.

As though we did not reach you: implies that if he had not reached them with the gospel, as God intended, his boasting would have been, like that of his opponents, beyond the measure which God had appointed.

We were the first to come all the way to you: literally, "for even as far as you we came." *First to come* is a justified translation, since the word for "came" has the classic meaning of "coming first" or "preceding."

With the gospel of Christ: in the preaching of the gospel, which was Paul's appointed mission. Hughes suggests that the figure behind Paul's language in these verses is that of the Isthmian Games for which Corinth was famed throughout the Roman world. In these contests, as in modern racing events, runners were required to keep to the lane which had been marked off for them. Paul's lane had led him to Corinth. His opponents were not even in the race; they had no lane marked out for them.

Verse 15: We do not boast beyond limit: closely related to the preceding verse. Perhaps it should be translated, "thus not boasting beyond our limit." *Our limit* would be, if we accept the figure of the Games, the lane which God had marked out for Paul.

In other men's labors: implies that his opponents were boasting on the basis of what others had done rather than on the basis of what they had done. Paul did not wish to invade someone else's appointed course.

But our hope is that as your faith increases: At the time of this writing, Corinth was the western limit of Paul's missionary activity. From his letter to the Romans, written from Corinth only a few months after this letter, we know that he dreamed of going to Spain with the gospel (cf. Rom. 15:24). He could not do so until the trouble in Corinth was solved. This verse was an appeal for them to set their house in order.

Our field among you may be greatly enlarged: a poor translation. The Greek reads: "among you to be magnified according to our length [or province] unto further abundance." Paul hoped that the complete solution of their problems would result in his "magnification" among the Corinthians, but according to his own province of labor. In other words, he seems to have meant that he hoped the Corinthians would return to his gospel and hold him in the esteem he deserved. If they did so, it would result in a "further abundance" which is explained in verse 16.

Verse 16: explains the dream of Paul.

So that we may preach the gospel in lands beyond you: explains the meaning of "further abundance" in verse 15. He hoped to extend his ministry into Rome and Spain. That he was able to go to Rome, we know. Whether he ever went to Spain is uncertain.

Without boasting of work already done in another's field: probably catches the meaning of the Greek. *Boasting of work already done* translates a Greek expression which literally reads: "to boast in respect of things ready to hand." *Another's field* translates words which literally mean "in the province of another." The thought seems to be the same as we have noted in the letter to Romans. He did not wish to preach the gospel in places where others had laid the foundation; he looked upon his ministry as a pioneering ministry. If he did, there certainly would be no ground of boasting in what others had done, though his opponents seem to have fallen into this error. Indeed, there would be no ground for boasting in great results done in his own province, since the results came from the power of God.

Verse 17: reminds us of the first three chapters of 1 Corinthians.

Who boasts: whoever he may be.

"Let him . . . boast of the Lord": since it is the Lord who accomplishes the results. The same words are found in 1 Corinthians 1:31 and are an adaptation of Jeremiah 9:24.

Verse 18: sums up what Paul would say about his opponents in Corinth by stating a basic principle of Christian life.

For it is not the man who commends himself: the one who advertises his own virtues and accomplishments.

That is accepted: rather, "that is approved." The word was commonly used of metals that had been tested and found to be pure.

But: strong adversative.

The man whom the Lord commends: will be accepted. There is no doubt that Paul was drawing a contrast between himself and his opponents. They praised themselves. He, in his ministry there, had shown himself to be commended by the Lord. The church itself was his letter of commendation. Surely there could be no question which leadership they would follow if they took a deeper view of their situation.

2. An Entreaty to Avoid Being Led Astray by False Apostles (11:1—12:13)

This section is the heart of the last four chapters. In it the fear of the apostle that the Corinthians would be led astray "from a sincere and pure devotion to Christ" (vs. 3) gives the reason for his entreaty and justifies a little foolish boasting (11:1–6). In it Paul met the charges of his opponents head on and returned insult for insult as he pointed out that his credentials of apostleship were superior to those of the false apostles (11:7—12:10). In it the apostle chided the Corinthians for not coming to his defense against these "superlative apostles" (12:11–13). Lenski calls this section a magnificent example of Paul's ironical polemics.

(1) The reason for the entreaty—Paul feared they would be led astray (11:1–6)

Paul began by asking their forgiveness for his foolish boasting (vs. 1) but justified it on the basis of his "divine jealousy" for those whom he had devoted to Christ (vs. 2). He expressed his fear that they would be led astray, as Eve had been deceived by the serpent (vs. 3). Nor did he think that his fears were unfounded. They had proved ready enough to submit to those who preached another Jesus, a different spirit, a different gospel (vs. 4). He ended the paragraph with an introduction to the next as he insisted that his credentials were in no way inferior to those of the superlative apostles (vss. 5–6).

Verse 1: introduces the whole section and labels it *a little foolishness.* He knew that if he won the battle on the grounds of boasting, he would not really win at all. However, he felt that his boasting was justified by the circumstances. The Corinthians had to be challenged to compare what they knew of Paul with the false claims of the false apostles. There seemed no other way for him to proceed than to meet them on their own ground.

I wish you would bear with me: a request for their indulgence. *I wish* translates a word which is almost an expletive in the Greek. It should be translated "would that." It is equivalent to one crying, "Oh!" in expressing a desire for something that is almost too good to become true.

In a little foolishness: What he was about to say concerning himself was foolishness.[1] He had just said that self-commendation did not make a man accepted. Only the commendation of the Lord was important (10:18).

Do bear with me!: could be either indicative or imperative. Probably the imperative is to be preferred. The expression becomes a form of prayer or request addressed to the Corinthians.

Verse 2: justifies his request.

I feel a divine jealousy for you: literally, "I am jealous over you with a jealousy of God." Whether "God" should be translated as an adjective and rendered *divine* is questionable. The implication is that the honor of God was at stake. Paul's jealousy for God's honor led him to be jealous of the Corinthians.

For I betrothed you to Christ: words based on the function of the bridegroom's friend, who arranged the betrothal and watched over the bride's conduct in the interval before the marriage.[2] The "marriage supper of the Lamb" when all Christians of all ages will be united with Christ is a feature of the final days (Rev. 19:9). Paul's thought was not that the church was the bride of Christ, but that it was betrothed to him to become his bride. This figure of speech is based upon the Old Testament idea that the nation was the wife of God (Isa. 54:5-6; Jer. 3:1).

To present you as a pure bride to her one husband: There is no Greek equivalent for *you.* Paul's aim was to present *a pure bride* to Christ but this would include more than the church at Corinth. Notice that these verses make it clear that this section was addressed to the church and not to the rebellious minority.

Verse 3: Using the temptation of Eve as a background, Paul expressed his fear for the Corinthians.

But: a mild continuative particle which could better be translated "now."

I am afraid: present tense expressing a continuous fear.

That: a poor translation. The Greek reads, "lest somehow." The expression is indefinite, expressing a fear of something that is possible, but not expected. Paul did not trust the Corinthians fully, nor did he distrust them completely. He looked on the state of affairs as being fluid, with the possibility of turning in one direction or another.

As the serpent deceived Eve by his cunning: reflects the temptation story in Genesis 3. *Eve* is mentioned only twice in the New Testament, here and 1 Timothy 2:13. In both passages she is pictured as one who was deceived

---

[1] Denney suggests that Paul was forced to play a role he despised.
[2] EGT. However, Lenski thinks the figure is that of the bride's father.

entirely. The *serpent* becomes in religious language a synonym for Satan. *Cunning* comes from a Greek word which indicates a willingness to adopt any means in order to gain one's ends. Paul had implied that this same word aptly described the ways of his opponents (4:2). The word could be translated "subtlety" or "craftiness." It connects this verse with the statement in the original story: "Now the serpent was more subtle than any other wild creature" (Gen. 3:1).

Your thoughts: the same word which Paul had used in an evil sense in 2:11. Here the word has its modern meaning. To corrupt one's thoughts would be to fill them with evil ambitions. No doubt, the story of Eve's deception was still in Paul's mind. She had eaten the forbidden fruit under the impression that it would bring a blessing to her.

Will be led astray: rather, "corrupted." This fear involved the Christian community, not the individual members. Some of them had already been corrupted.

From a sincere and pure devotion to Christ: rather, "from your single-mindedness and purity in reference to Christ." The sense of the expression seems quite clear. "Single-mindedness" translates the same Greek word which Paul used to speak of "liberality" (cf. 8:2). However, the common meaning of the word is to be preferred here. "Purity" is a cognate word with "holy" and means "separation to the use or service of God." [1]

Verse 4: The instability of the church was the basis of Paul's fears in regard to them.

For if: a weak translation of the Greek, which reads, "for if indeed." The form of *if* indicates that Paul assumed the truth of what he was saying. He was not basing his fears on a mere possibility, but upon the past performance of the Corinthians.

Some one comes and preaches: rather, "the one coming preaches." No doubt, Paul had in mind an intruder into the Corinthian fellowship, either an individual or a group. Thus he stressed the fact of coming in order to remind the Corinthians that it was not one of their number who was causing the trouble. *Preaches* is in the present tense, indicating continuous action. The intruder made a habit of preaching.

Another Jesus: Jesus in a similar way in which Paul had preached him but with nuances that changed the gospel. There is a play on *another* in this verse. The Greek had two words which could be translated in this way. One, the one used here, meant another of the same kind. The other, used in the next two expressions, meant another of a different kind. The RSV has preserved this distinction by translating, "a different spirit" . . . "a different gospel." How could the intruder preach another Jesus without preaching a "different" Jesus? In this case it was not difficult. The Judaizers believed that Jesus was the Messiah, as Paul did. But they preached that he came to make Judaism perfect rather than that he came to supersede the law and the institutions of Judaism. Thus, adherence to Jesus in their eyes meant for one to come into Judaism. Primarily, the difference was not in the Jesus preached but in the messianic role with which they invested

---

[1] Denney suggests that the figure of the virgin still ruled Paul's words.

him. In modern days we have much the same thing but in a different form. Some men preach Jesus as man's example only, or with other nuances of meaning which actually destroy the substance of the gospel. We must be sure that we preach the same Jesus, Jesus in the same character and role which the New Testament gives him.

Than the one we preached: when we came as evangelists. The past tense refers to Paul's first visit when he preached Jesus and they received him as their Lord.

A different spirit: different in kind. It is sometimes difficult to know whether by *spirit* Paul meant the Holy Spirit or an attitude of the human mind and heart. In this instance it would seem that he was speaking of the attitude. Thus a *different spirit,* i.e., another of a different kind, would mean a spirit of legalism as opposed to a spirit of surrender to the lordship of Christ.

A different gospel: The message of the Judaizers was indeed a different gospel. It demanded that Christians submit to the rite of circumcision and take upon themselves the responsibility of keeping the Jewish law. Paul described this gospel by saying: "Not that there is another gospel, but there are some who trouble you and want to pervert the gospel of Christ" (Gal. 1:7).

You submit to it readily enough: an ironical statement. If they could bear with the interloper, surely they could bear with Paul in his boasting. The same Greek word is translated *submit* in this verse that was translated "bear" in verse 1. This expression again indicates that this whole section is addressed to the church as a whole, not to a minority group.

Verse 5: I think: rather, "I reckon." Paul had counted up the account and came to believe that what he said about himself was true.

That I am not in the least inferior: rather, "I fall short in nothing."

These superlative apostles: a sarcastic description of the Judaizing teachers, who fancied themselves to be superlative. Some have thought that Paul was referring to the most prominent apostles of the Twelve—Peter, James, and John. They are called the "pillar" apostles (Gal. 2:9). However, this interpretation is based upon the supposition that there was a marked cleavage between Paul and Peter in the first century, a supposition that has been surrendered by nearly all New Testament scholars of repute. There is no indication in the context that Paul was comparing himself with these apostles, and it is highly improbable that he would have done so. Rather, we are to suppose that Paul was speaking ironically of the interlopers in Corinth who claimed for themselves this high position. With reference to them, he did not find himself falling short in anything.

Verse 6: Even if: as is true. Paul admitted it.

I am unskilled in speaking: Unskilled comes from the Greek word from which we get our English word "idiot." However, the implications of the word were far different from the English transliteration. It comes from the root meaning of "one's own"; hence it came to be applied to one who minded his own private business and did not engage in public affairs. In relation to skills, it came to mean one who had no professional training, thus being the equivalent of our "layman." In the text the expression *unskilled in speaking* means that Paul was not a trained orator. Paul was glad to admit that he did not use the devices of oratory to gain his point. In this respect he might indeed be inferior to others, but it was an inferiority which he regarded as superior equipment for the preaching of the gospel.

I am not in knowledge: He knew what he was talking about when he spoke in his untrained way, and this was the important thing. *Knowledge* is no doubt the knowledge of God, the truth of the gospel. With respect to this, Paul said of himself in another context: "I did not receive it from man, nor was I taught it, but it came through a revelation of Jesus Christ" (Gal. 1:12). His thought was that in spite of his defects in speaking, the Corinthians should recognize his superiority in knowledge.

In every way: probably a correct translation of a phrase which could mean "in all things." With respect to preaching, it would have the meaning of "in every particular."

We have made this plain: i.e., manifested the knowledge which God had given him.

To you: rather, "with regard to you" or "to you-ward." We may paraphrase the thought of Paul: "My fellow-workers and I have manifested the knowledge of God in every way publicly with the intention of bringing this knowledge to you."

In all things: possibly, "among all men." In both phrases in this verse, the form of the Greek makes the meaning obscure. Literally read, the Greek says: "In all [things or ways or men] I have made it manifest in all [things or men or particulars] in regard to you." Possibly the best solution of this phrase is that Paul was speaking of the public manner in which he preached. There had been no secrecy about his preaching. Thus it was "among all men."

(2) The basis of the entreaty—Paul's credentials of apostleship were superior to those of false apostles (11:7—12:10)

In this rather long section Paul met the false apostles head to head. First he noted the charge that his refusal to take support from the Corinthians was a sign that he did not love them and denied this insinuation (11:7–11). Next, he asserted his purpose to undermine the claim of the false apostles, whom he characterized as "servants of Satan" (11:12–15). Paul admitted, next, that he had been too weak to make slaves of them as others did (11:16–21a). Next, admitting that he was playing the fool, he listed his credentials of apostleship (11:21b–29). Next, he insisted that if he must boast, he would boast in his weakness (11:30–33). Then he recounted his experience of prayer in which he tried to rid himself of his "thorn in the flesh" and the victory that came when he became willing to rely in the grace of God (12:1–10). Finally he reminded them of his ministry in their midst and apologized for not demanding their support (12:11–13).

Verses 7–11: deal with the charge made against Paul that his refusal to accept support from the Corinthians was a sign of lack of love for them.

Did I commit a sin: a rhetorical question with overtones of irony.

In abasing myself: refers to his humbling himself by making tents to support himself. To the professional orator this would be self-abasement. Paul did not mean to imply that working with one's hands was abasing. He was meeting his detractors on their own ground.

So that you might be exalted: lifted up to the position of sons of God. There is a fine play on ideas in this verse. Paul spoke of his own labors as an abasement. He spoke of the results of his labors as an exaltation of the Corinthians.

Because: introduces the explanations of his self-abasement.

I preached God's gospel without cost to you: Note the irony. "Was it a sin to give you God's gift for nothing?" "Is that what you mean to say?" In this verse Paul demonstrated his God-given ability to put things in the right words so as to rip off the false implications which others had put on his actions.

Verse 8: returns to the account of what actually happened.

I robbed other churches: Paul's own statement, not that of his opponents. *Robbed* is to be taken figuratively rather than literally. It means to strip a fallen foe of his armor.

By accepting support from them: indicates what he meant by saying he had robbed them. They paid his wages; this is the meaning of the phrase *accepting support.*

In order to serve you: the reason for his accepting wages from other churches. The Corinthians had not only Paul to thank for their hearing the gospel, but other churches as well.

Verse 9: continues the account of his support.

And when I was with you and was in want: startles one. The expression reveals the precariousness of the apostle's position as he preached the gospel. He was never ahead; he was always behind.

I did not burden any one: Burden comes from a Greek word which means "to become numb." Paul did not benumb the Corinthians with a demand for support.

For my needs were supplied: filled up my shortage.

By the brethren who came from Macedonia: probably means Philippi. Paul mentioned in his letter to the Philippians that they had "entered into partnership with me in giving" (Phil. 4:14). No doubt, they had sent to supply his needs in Corinth.

So I refrained and will refrain from burdening you in any way: Burdening comes from another Greek word which means "to place a weight on." In the first place, a demand for support would have denumbed them; now it would have been only an added weight. Paul insisted that he would continue his practice with regard to them. He would ask no support.

Verse 10: Paul reminded them of his boast concerning which he had written them before. "What then is my reward? Just this: that in my preaching I may make the gospel free of charge, not making full use of my right in the gospel" (1 Cor. 9:18).

As the truth of Christ is in me: rather, "The truth of Christ is in me indeed." There is no suggestion of an oath in the original as in the RSV translation. Paul had previously claimed to have the mind of Christ

(1 Cor. 2:16). In another letter he claimed that the spirit of Christ abode in him (Rom. 8:9). This truth or sincerity that comes from Christ and is like his prevented Paul from deceit and selfishness.

This boast: that he made the gospel free.

Of mine: rather, "with regard to me" or "so far as I am concerned." The thought is that if the Corinthians sent support, it would have to be on their own initiative, for he did not plan to ask for it.

Shall not be silenced in the regions of Achaia: and therefore not in Corinth. *Silenced* translates a word which means to "fence in, to stop, to block." The metaphor is uncertain. It could come from a dam that stops the river or a barricade that blocks a road. Perhaps the barricading of a road is more pertinent to the thought of stopping one's mouth.

Verse 11: And why: a rhetorical question which Paul answered in the next words.

Because I do not love you: reflects the charges of the interlopers. They had insinuated that this refusal to take money from them indicated that he did not care sufficiently for them. Such gifts would, of course, be voluntary, as they were among the true philosophers of the Greeks. Later in Christian history, many preachers were peripatetic preachers; that is, they walked around from place to place and received their support from the people to whom they preached. While Paul did not deny, but rather insisted on, the right of preachers to be supported, he seems to have refused to take money from the Corinthians.

God knows I do: It was not lack of love for them that led Paul to follow his practice. Whatever the explanation of it may be (and it still remains somewhat of a mystery), this was not it. The Greek has only, *God knows,* but the added words *I do,* are probably justified. God knew all about Paul, the reason why he refused pay and his attitude of heart toward the Corinthians. The expression is almost an oath.

Verses 12–15: a head-to-head meeting between the embattled apostle and his opponents. Paul frankly admitted that he was out to undermine their claims, to show them up in their true colors to the Corinthians.

And what I do I will continue to do: i.e., continue to refuse remuneration for his services from the Corinthians.

In order to undermine the claim of those who would like to claim: rather, "in order to cut off the occasion of those who wish an occasion." His opponents pretended that his refusal to take money showed that he was not an apostle at all, while their willingness to take it showed them to be true apostles. However, they recognized that this was a thin line of attack. The Corinthians might well see that their taking money was a sign of selfish grasping. They wanted Paul to do what they did. He refused and meant to retain his vantage point.

That in their boasted mission they work on the same terms as we do: a weak translation. The Greek literally reads: "in order that in what they boast, they may be found just as also we are." The meaning of the expression is obscure because we are ignorant of the exact state of affairs in Corinth at the time. The RSV gives the wrong impression. It suggests that the opponents wished to be thought of as working on the same terms as Paul. The Greek indicates the opposite. They wished to be thought superior. It was Paul who wished to show that they were, in some way, "just as we also." Many proposals have been made in an effort to clarify the meaning of the verse, none of them wholly convincing. Lenski and Hughes agree substantially with the RSV translation, believing that the opponents wished to be accepted on a level with Paul. However, the syntax of the sentence is against that and we must try to follow the syntax.

The exact thinking of Paul is difficult to ascertain. Certainly he did not wish to place his opponents on a level with him in general or even in the matter of accepting support. They already accepted support, and he intended to continue refusing to do so. Also, he thought of himself as an apostle of Christ and of them as servants of Satan. What then was his thought? A guess might be that he wished to have the Corinthians judge his opponents on the same terms in which he himself was willing to be judged—on the basis of their work in the gospel. Still, we must confess that there is no real answer to the problem of the meaning of this verse.

Verse 13: a diatribe against his opponents.

For such men: men who have such a character and do such things.

False apostles: The idea of "false prophets" is quite common in the Old Testament. They were men who claimed to have a revelation from God but in fact toadied to men, especially to rulers, in an effort to gain position for themselves. Perhaps this is a good commentary on Paul's meaning of *false apostles.*

Deceitful workmen: There was no denying that they worked, but their devotion to Christ was a sham (Plummer). They had accomplished a great deal of mischief in Corinth, but they were deceitful because they led the Corinthians to believe that they were representatives of Christ. This expression is a commentary on Paul's meaning for *false apostles.*

Disguising themselves as apostles of Christ: masquerading as such. *Disguising* comes from a word which means "to change the outer form of." It suggests that these men met the external standards of true apostles, but inwardly were far from being so. *Disguising* is a good translation. It catches the meaning of the Greek.

Verse 14: And no wonder: This is not a surprising thing.

For even Satan disguises himself as an angel of light: Disguises, in the present tense in Greek, indicates that this is the habitual action of Satan. There is no need to suppose that Paul was quoting a Jewish legend in this verse, though some such legends exist. If there was any historical basis for his statement, it could be found either in the temptation of Eve in the garden or in the temptations of Jesus in the wilderness. The point that Paul wished to make was that Satan's envoys would not hesitate to use the same guile which Satan himself habitually uses. The modern idea that Satan has horns, carries a pitchfork, and has a long tail is misleading. He always comes to men with the suggestion that what he wants them to do is a wonderful boon. He appears as an angel bringing light to men. It is not surprising that many of the great heretics in Christianity have assumed that they had discovered new light which superseded the revelation of God in Christ Jesus.

Verse 15: So: in the light of this fact.

It is not strange: rather, "not a great thing."

If his servants: those who minister to his desire as Christians minister to the will of God.

Also disguise themselves as servants of righteousness: seeking to make men think they serve God and promote righteousness.

Their end will correspond to their deeds: rather, "works." *Deeds* is not as strong as "works." *Deeds* indicates only what men do; "works" includes the results of their actions. Thus it was the "works" of the false apostles which would determine their end. What that end was to be is not specified. It was left in the hands of God with the full assurance that it would be just and right.

Verses 16–21: a paragraph filled with sarcasm, as Paul boasted as a "fool" would boast. He confessed at the end that he had been too weak to enslave the Corinthians to himself.

I repeat: possibly refers to verse 1. Paul had asked their forbearance as he acted foolishly. In both passages he was anxious that the Corinthians should realize that he thought self-praise a foolish thing. However, there seems to be a difference in the two verses. In verse 1, he seems to have expected that they would grant his request; here he seems to have doubted that they would.

Let no one think me foolish: in spite of the fact that he was going to act the fool. Behind his apparent folly was a wisdom which they were invited to perceive.

But even if you do: think me a fool. This indicates a doubt on Paul's part that they would be able to perceive the wisdom of his actions.

Accept me as a fool: Give me a hearing. All that Paul asked was that they listen to what he had to say and consider the implications of it.

So that I too may boast a little: He had not started the stupid rivalry of boasting; his opponents had (Plummer). *I too* is emphatic. He meant: "You listened to them; now listen to me. It is my turn to boast." *A little* may indicate that the intruders called their boasting a little; it may mean that Paul meant to restrict his boasting.

Verses 17–18: are parenthetical. Paul wanted to be sure that the Corinthians knew that he was not speaking with the authority of the Lord, that he was only, for a while, meeting his opponents on their own ground.

What I am saying I say not with the Lord's authority: rather, "What I say I do not say according to the Lord." He intended to boast, to present his credentials in terms that worldly eyes could recognize, but this was not "according to the Lord." Whether this meant, as the RSV translation suggests, that he was not speaking by a command of the Lord is doubtful. Probably it meant that he was deliberately departing from the norm or standard that the Lord had set up for his apostles. It could mean, "according to the example of the Lord."

But as a fool: rather, "as in foolishness." The Greek word is used only four times in the New Testament, three of them in 2 Corinthians. A cognate word is used in the New Testament eleven times, five in 2 Corinthians. Paul was speaking sarcastically, with the implication that his opponents made a habit of indulging in foolishness.

In this boastful confidence: rather, "in this undertaking of boasting." This refers to the boasting which Paul intended to do.

Verse 18: Since many boast: refers to his opponents, who made a habit of boasting.

Of worldly things: a poor translation. The Greek reads: "according to the flesh," i.e., according to the norm which the world sets. There is a deliberate antithesis between "according to the Lord" in verse 17 and "according to the flesh" here.

I too will boast: indicates his intention, not only to boast, but also to boast on the same level as his opponents. He planned to meet and vanquish them on their own ground.

Verse 19: resumes the thought which was left off at the end of verse 16.

For: continuative particle.

Gladly: is emphatic in the Greek construction, being placed first in the sentence.

You . . . bear with fools, being wise yourselves: ironical expression. There is a play on words which the English translation obscures. *Fools* and *wise* translate two Greek words built on the same stem. The play on words would be preserved if we substituted "unwise" for *fools.* However, the translation of the words is a problem in itself. *Wise* is too strong a translation. The word which is translated *wise* means "prudent, thoughtful," etc. If we sought an English equivalent for the word in this context, perhaps the word "smart" in a bad sense would be fitting. Paul was speaking ironically of the Corinthians' opinion of themselves as prudent men who acted on the basis of intelligence.

Verse 20: sarcastic reminder that the Corinthians, in bearing with his opponents, had borne with far more than folly.

For you bear it: describes their gullibility in putting up with the pretensions of the interlopers. The thought is: "Surely you can stand a little foolishness from me since you have borne tyranny, extortion, craftiness, arrogance, violence, and insult from my enemies" (Plummer). What follows is Paul's description of how the Judaizing teachers treated the Corinthians. Of course, his description was not in harmony with the understanding of either the Corinthians or the Judaizers. But he wanted them to see the situation as he saw it and to judge their behavior on the basis of truth.

If a man: assumes the truth of the statement. *A man* translates an indefinite pronoun. The Corinthians would be able to identify the man.

Makes slaves of you: reduces you to abject slavery. This word is found only here and in Galatians 2:4, where it also refers to the efforts of Judaizers to destroy the Christian freedom of Paul and his converts. The form of the Greek word is active, indicating that Paul did not think that his enemies were seeking to enslave the Corinthians to themselves (a middle voice would indicate that). Probably what he had in mind was that the teachers were seeking to enslave the Corinthians to the Mosaic law. The kind of legalistic bondage to which Judaism led was described by Paul in these words: "Formerly, when you did not know God, you were in bondage to beings that by nature are no gods; but now that you have come back to God, or rather to be known by God, how can you turn back again to the weak and beggarly elemental spirits, whose slaves you want to be once more?" (Gal. 4:8–9). Thus, in Paul's theology legalism was as much a bondage to the elemental spirits of the world as paganism.

Preys upon you: literally, "devours you." His thought was that the opponents did this by claiming support from the Corinthians for themselves.

Takes advantage of you: literally "takes you," as a bird is caught in a snare or fish with bait (Plummer).

Puts on airs: literally, "lifts himself up." The RSV translation catches the meaning well.

Strikes you in the face: probably a metaphor meaning "insults you grossly." The literal meaning could be true, as was the case with Christ (Mark 14:65) and with Paul (Acts 23:2); but it is unlikely that physical violence had been done to the Corinthians at this time. However, the Judaizers had treated the Corinthians with contempt.

Verse 21: an ironical confession of Paul's own dishonor. This was meant to be a real rebuke of the Corinthians, who accepted those who treated them so and criticized one who had treated them with great consideration.

To my shame: literally, "dishonor." Judged by the standards of the "flesh," Paul had fallen short of honor on the field of combat. He had won no trophies for himself.

We were too weak for that: similar in meaning to the slang expression, "I could not stomach that."

Verses 21b–29: turn in dead earnest to the "little boasting" that Paul had indicated he would engage in (vs. 16). Lenski calls this paragraph "the first grand gush of foolish boasting." Perhaps that is overstating the case, but it is indicative of the tenor of the material. It seems as if the river of Paul's thoughts on this matter had been dammed up, and now burst forth in a flood. Yet the language is under control. First, there is a general statement that he could match boast with counterboast (vs. 21b). Next, he listed the things which marked one as a true Israelite and claimed that he could match that boast (vs. 22). He then turned to the specific area of Christian service and claimed to be a better servant of Christ than his opponents, protesting again that he was talking like a madman (vs. 23). There follows a list of twenty items from his apostolic experience, many of which we find only in this passage, on which he based his claim of superiority as a servant of Christ (vss. 24–28). Finally he asserted his sympathy with those who were weak or offended (vs. 29).

Verse 21b: a general challenge.

But whatever any one dares to boast of: One is the indefinite pronoun in the Greek and refers to a leader of the opposition who would be well known to the Corinthians. There is no Greek for *to boast of*. The phrase is left indefinite and should read "whatever one dares." *Dares,* though a good translation, should perhaps be given the meaning, "shows real courage." The RSV insertion of *to boast of* is perhaps justified by the context, however.

I am speaking as a fool: a protest against comparing himself with others who commended themselves. He did not fear comparison but recognized that nothing could be settled by a battle of words. Even though Paul intended to launch into a vigorous statement of his own claims, he knew that such boasting was being a fool. Paul was anxious that the

Corinthians should not think his unusual behavior on this occasion was to be emulated. Rather, it was a folly to be shunned by them, even as it was a folly of which he was ashamed, though he thought it necessary.

I also dare to boast of that: literally, "I also dare." *I also* is emphatic.

Verse 22: a series of rapid questions directed to the same point—Paul could claim to be a true Jew on an equality with his opponents. Though the three questions seem to be synonymous, they are not really so. There is a descending scale of values to which one could point in asserting his right to be recognized as a true Jew, though Plummer regards it as an ascending scale.

Are they Hebrews? So am I: Hebrews were the most orthodox among the Jews.[1] They preserved the customs of the nation; they spoke Aramaic, the official language of the nation; they usually lived in Palestine. In another passage Paul described himself as "a Hebrew born of the Hebrews" (Phil. 3:5). Broadly speaking, the Jews of the first century were divided into Hebrews and "Hellenists." "Hellenists" were Jews who had adopted Greek customs and speech and who usually lived outside of Palestine, though residence itself was not the sole criterion. Paul himself had lived in Tarsus but considered himself a Hebrew. Possibly his opponents, having come from Jerusalem, the heart of the Holy Land, had accused Paul of being a traitor to the traditions of the race—a common accusation against "Hellenists." Paul replied that he was as good a Hebrew as they. Notice that he did not claim to be a better one than they, though in another passage he had said, "I advanced in Judaism beyond many of my own age and among my people, so extremely zealous was I for the traditions of my fathers" (Gal. 1:14). Either Paul did not wish to press his claims, or the opponents were his equal in this area.

Are they Israelites? So am I: Israelites described the Jews who preserved in their lives the idea of the sacredness of the nation. The term is derived from "Israel," the new name given to Jacob by the angel which had wrestled with him (Gen. 32:28).

Are they descendants of Abraham? So am I: speaks of the blood lines of the true Jew. Though Gentiles were admitted to membership in the nation, there was always a feeling that the native-born Jew had a superiority to the proselyte. Honesty demands that we note that other commentators (EGT, Plummer) hold this to be the highest dignity of which Paul boasted. However, it seems to me that it is the lowest of the three. One could be a descendant of Abraham without holding to the sacredness of the nation as an Israelite, and one could be an Israelite without maintaining the customs and language of the Jews as a Hebrew. Thus it seems that Paul meant this to be a descending list of words. Of course, the main point of the verse is to show that Paul matched his opponents at every point in their claims to be good Jews. As a matter of fact, Paul was intensely proud of his heritage, even though he came to recognize as a Christian that such a heritage had no real spiritual significance.

Verse 23: turns to the area of life where real spiritual significance lies —one's service to Christ.

---

[1] Paul's opponents probably boasted of their descent (Tasker).

Are they servants of Christ: rhetorical question meaning, "Is that what they claim?" *Servants* translates the Greek word meaning "ministers." Paul had used this word often in his discussion of the collection for the saints as being a "ministry." His thought was that such a person performed a religious ministry. Paul had just accused the interlopers of being Satan's servants. They could not be Christ's servants. This shows that Paul did not recognize their claim.

I am a better one: rather, "I more." It is possible that Paul allowed for the sake of argument that the "superlative apostles" were Christ's servants. If so, the RSV translation is correct. But this is improbable. It is more likely that he meant, "I have a greater claim to this recognition than they." We must remember that Paul never made such an odious comparison between himself and the other apostles. But with reference to the interlopers who were no real ministers of Christ, he did not hesitate to advance his superior claim to recognition.

I am talking like a madman: a parenthetical statement stronger than the previous, "I am speaking as a fool." Probably the intensification is due to the fact that he considered boasting in the area of service to Christ a greater madness than boasting about courage.

With far greater labors: begins a general listing of the basis of Paul's claim for recognition. The use of *greater* is surprising if one feels that he was comparing himself to the Judaizers. However, it could mean "greater than most Christians." The comparative is dropped after the next phrase and we must suppose that the idea of comparison is secondary even in these first two phrases. It is possible that the adverb could merely mean "very abundant." *Labors* comes from the word which stresses the exhaustion of the worker, rather than the results of his work. There can be no doubt that Paul stands preeminent among Christians of all ages in this respect. No man in history has been more unflagging in missionary toil and zeal. A mere reading of his journeys in the Book of Acts makes one marvel that a human being could survive such arduous labors.

Far more imprisonments: We know of only one imprisonment prior to the writing of 2 Corinthians—the imprisonment at Philippi (cf. Acts 16: 24). However, it is possible that he had been in prison at Ephesus, and there may have been others which are unrecorded in any way.

With countless beatings: rather, "in stripes very exceeding." The RSV translation is totally misleading. He would not have said his "stripes" were countless. He counted them in verses 24–25. He did consider them very great. Lenski feels that the comparative idea still persists and that the word means "very greatly beyond them." However, this does not seem to be the sense here. "Stripes" is a general word which could be used of the results of either the lashings by the Jews or the beatings by the Romans.

Often near death: probably a good translation of the Greek, which literally reads, "in deaths many." The meaning would be that on a number of occasions and in a variety of ways he faced death. Verses 25b–26 give a commentary on this expression.

Verse 24: tells of the sufferings he had endured at the hands of his own countrymen.

Of the Jews: placed first in the Greek sentence for emphasis.

Five times: We do not know of any time from any other source, but this is no reason to doubt Paul's accuracy.

I have received . . . the forty lashes less one: the official Jewish way of punishing an offender of the law. This kind of punishment is mentioned first in Deuteronomy 25:1–3: "If there is a dispute between men, and they come into court, and the judges decide between them, acquitting the innocent and condemning the guilty, then if the guilty man deserves to be beaten, the judge shall cause him to lie down and be beaten in his presence with a number of stripes in proportion to his offense. Forty stripes may be given him, but not more; lest, if one should go on to beat him with more stripes than these, your brother be degraded in your sight." Jesus had warned the disciples that they might suffer such floggings: "Beware of men; for they will deliver you up to councils, and flog you in their synagogues" (Matt. 10:17). Paul confessed to the risen Christ that he, as a Jewish persecutor, had "in every synagogue . . . imprisoned and beat those who believed in thee" (Acts 22:19).

Forty lashes less one describes the Jewish custom. It was forbidden to give any man more than forty lashes. Thus, the one administering the flogging always stopped one short, lest he miscount and be guilty of breaking the law himself. There is considerable difference of opinion about the exact way in which the floggings were administered, whether thirteen blows with a whip that had three lashes or thirty-nine with a whip which had a single lash. Josephus, the Jewish historian, speaks of this punishment, but it is debatable whether he intimated that it often ended in death. Plummer thinks not, feeling that the Jewish authorities would not have risked so extreme a result. At any rate, the punishment was severe, and Paul could easily remember each occasion on which he had suffered it.

Verse 25: turns to beatings at the hands of Roman officials and follows with other experiences.

Three times I have been beaten with rods: This was a Roman punishment. Of the three times we know of one, that inflicted at Philippi illegally (Acts 16:22–23, 37). It was illegal to beat a Roman citizen in this way, but some Roman officials were brutal and did not obey the law. The verb indicates that the punishment was inflicted by Roman courts.

Once I was stoned: at Lystra on the first missionary journey. We have a full account of this stoning (cf. Acts 14:19). His tormentors left him for dead, but he revived and continued his work. He had barely escaped stoning at Iconium, prior to this (Acts 14:5–6). This was the Jewish way of execution, but it was illegal during Roman times. However, it occurred.

Three times I have been shipwrecked: We know of one such occasion, but it occurred after the writing of 2 Corinthians. Such a danger was probably not uncommon in Paul's day when so much travel was by sea, often in small boats.

A night and a day I have been adrift at sea: The Greek in this expression is a very rare word, being a compound which means a complete day and night. Probably this was in conjunction with one of his shipwrecks. *I have been* is a Greek perfect tense, whereas the other verbs in the series are simple past tenses. The change of tense indicates that the experience was still vivid in the mind of Paul. The Greek word (poieō) which is translated *I have been* literally means "I have done." However, it was commonly used to express the idea of spending time at something. Literally, this expression would be: "I have done a night and a day in the deep." *At sea* translates a word which originally meant "the bottom of the sea." However, common usage had changed it to mean "at sea." There is no justification for the idea that Paul had a Jonah-like experience and spent a day and a night under water.

Verse 26: continues the account of Paul's perilous life as a missionary in the first century.

On frequent journeys: literally, "by journeyings often." The construction is changed to indicate that this and the following experiences came to him as a result of his preaching mission. Concerning these journeyings we have an excellent account in the Book of Acts.

In danger from rivers: the first of eight dangers listed.

Danger from robbers: a frequent danger of travelers in the first century.

Danger from my own people: the Jews.

Danger from Gentiles: those who were not Jews. Notice the pairing of the dangers.

Danger in the city: where he spent most of his time in proclaiming the gospel. The Corinthians could well remember the dangers that he faced while among them.

Danger in the wilderness: probably includes all rural areas outside the city.

Danger at sea: from which his shipwrecks came.

Danger from false brethren: the most insidious peril of all. The other dangers threatened his life or property; this one imperiled, and sometimes, ruined his work (Plummer). In both Galatians and this letter, these false brethren were the Judaizers, Jewish Christians who wished to impose the Mosaic law on the Gentile converts.

Verse 27: turns from danger to hardships encountered in his life as a missionary. Remember that his purpose in recounting all of this was to give the basis of his claim to be a servant of Christ.

In toil and hardship: rather, "by labor and travail." *Toil* translates the same Greek word which was translated "labors" in verse 23. The emphasis is upon the weariness caused by the work. *Hardship* translates a word which indicates struggle in the course of work. Either obstacles or enemies may explain why the work was accompanied by hardship, i.e., "travail." Probably the reference is to his having to work with his hands to support himself.

Through many a sleepless night: literally, "in watchings often." This probably does not refer to insomnia, but to the necessity of working late in the night while others slept.

In hunger and thirst: may correspond to his shipwrecks. It is not likely that he would have been deprived of water otherwise.

Often without food: literally, "in fastings often." The question is: Does this refer to involuntary hunger or to religious fasting? Commentators differ,[1] but it' seems better to take it as involuntary hunger which may

---

[1] Hodge takes it to mean voluntary fasting. IB takes it to mean the necessary privations while traveling.

have arisen in the midst of journeys. Perhaps Hughes' suggestion that Paul neglected to eat because of his absorption in the work of the ministry has merit.

In cold and exposure: literally, "in cold and nakedness." Plummer suggests that this occurred when he was cast into prison, drenched by rain, or stripped by robbers. All of these experiences in the pursuit of the ministry were in marked contrast to the comfortable life of his opponents in Corinth. It has been suggested that Paul never counted his converts, but his sufferings. These, rather than success, proved the reality of his devotion to the ministry.

Verse 28: Apart from other things: a doubtful translation. Literally, the expression reads: "besides those things that are without." Probably he was thinking of the list of sufferings which he had just enumerated as coming from "without." They were not essential to the conduct of the ministry, but arose incidentally as he conducted his work. Next listed are those things which came from the ministry itself, being essentially connected with it.

There is the daily pressure upon me of my anxiety for all the churches: a correct translation. *Pressure upon me* translates a phrase, the meaning of which depends on the form of the pronoun. If the pronoun were genitive, it would mean "my daily observation" or "my daily attentiveness." However, since the pronoun is locative, the RSV translation is accepted as correct. He looked upon his concern for the churches as a sort of pressure that set upon him each day. Anxiety was caused by just the sort of thing that was happening in Corinth. It is not the pressure of work that became a burden to him, but the pressure of concern as he asked himself whether his converts would be able to stand firm in the gospel.

Verse 29: two examples of the anxiety that Paul felt with reference to all the churches (vs. 28).

Who is weak, and I am not weak: rhetorical question meaning that Paul shared in the weakness of every Christian. Examples of this true sympathy for the weaker brethren are to be found in Paul's writings. "To the weak I became weak, that I might win the weak" (1 Cor. 9:22). He admonished the strong Christians to act in such a way that they would not offend the more scrupulous members of the church, saying that they sinned against Christ himself if they did so (1 Cor. 8:11–12). He forbade those who felt free to eat meat to sit in judgment on those who were vegetarians (Rom. 14:1–2). Of course, other kinds of weakness might be involved in Paul's thought, but his regular designation for those who were overscrupulous was that they were weak. In this, Paul probably acted in marked contrast to the Judaizers, who were impatient with those who did not conform to their own ideas of the Christian life. Lenski takes this to refer to an humble spirit in Paul, a spirit that saw nothing but weakness in himself; but the Greek construction would have been different if this were the thought.

Who is made to fall, and I am not indignant: another rhetorical question. *Made to fall* translates the Greek word from which we get our English word "scandalized." Its meaning in Greek is stronger than the English equivalent. It means to cause one to stumble so as to fall into sin. Jesus pronounced a definite curse on one who "causes one of these little ones who believe in me to sin" saying that "it would be better for him to have a great millstone fastened round his neck and to be dropped in the depth of the sea" (Matt. 18:6). The thought is of one of Paul's brethren being seduced to sin by someone. Perhaps there is a hidden reference to Paul's estimate of the ministry of the Judaizers. *I am not indignant* translates a Greek phrase which literally means "I do not burn." Whether this should be given the meaning of indignation is questionable. It may mean that his heart was "ablaze with pain" (Plummer). "When a brother stumbles, Paul is set on fire with grief" (Robertson). *I* is emphatic in this instance, stressing Paul's personal involvement in the troubles, and especially the sins, of the Christians. One can readily see that a pastor with so great a heart that he suffered grief when a church member sinned would be filled with anxiety.[1]

Verses 30–33: Paul turned from his credentials of apostleship which might be stated in a positive sense and gave his attention to his credentials which were based on God's sustaining power in weakness. In this section the example of his escape from Damascus is cited. Certainly no one could boast of his courage when he had to flee the city at night through a hole in the wall.

Verse 30: a general statement of the fact that he intended to boast in the things that showed his weakness. The future tense of the verb is to be taken as an indication of his whole direction of boasting, but marks as well a change of direction. He meant that if he were forced to go through the parody of boasting, he would find the grounds of it in the very experiences that led some men to despise him. However, Paul found in these experiences a greater ground of boasting because they had developed him in his likeness to Christ. At the same time they marked him as distinctly different from his opponents.

Verse 31: Paul asserted in the most solemn way that he was not lying. Neither by playing with words nor by false innuendo was he misleading his readers.

God . . . knows that I do not lie: reminds us of verse 11, where he asserted, "God knows." No doubt the necessity of the solemn assurance came from the accusations of his opponents, who said that he meant "no" when he said, "yes." The present tense of *lie* makes this statement broader than this context. It included what he was now saying but it also pointed to his habit of life.

Father of the Lord Jesus: reveals the basic premise of Paul's theology. He did not begin his thought of God with creation or history, but with the Lord Jesus. Jesus had addressed God in the most familiar terms as Father and had taught his disciples that God was their Father as well. Perhaps this thought of the fatherhood of God is the most distinctive contribution of Christian thought to the world of religion. It has been corrupted to make God the Father of all men, but this is not the thought of the New Testament. Fatherhood is a spiritual relationship with the individual believer; it is not a statement of the creative act of God in making all men.

---

[1] Tasker sees these two attitudes as expressions of true love.

Who is blessed forever: indicates the reverence of Paul. *Blessed* comes from a compound Greek word which has two elements: one meaning "well" and the other, "speak." Thus it means to speak well of someone. God is to be spoken well of by all men throughout all ages and into eternity. His work of redemption should be the central song of every Christian heart and the central theme of every Christian sermon.

The Lord Jesus: the correct reading, though some manuscripts have added "Christ." This compound unites the earthly Jesus with the living Lord of the Christian.

Verses 32–33: an account of Paul's escape from Damascus as one of the first instances in which he found it necessary to boast in his weakness.

At Damascus: Many find a strange abruptness in Paul's shift from the exalted language of the previous verse to the prosaic description of his escape from Damascus. Some feel that there is an awkward interpolation including these two verses and the first clause of 12:1. However, the verses make perfectly good sense when connected with thought of weakness to which Paul turned his attention in this section.

Damascus is at present the capital city of modern Syria, a city well watered by springs and rivers, forming an oasis in the desert. It had a long and colorful history even in the times of Paul. We remember that Paul was on his way to Damascus to persecute the Christians there when he had his vision of the risen Christ and became a Christian. Stricken with blindness, he went into the city and was baptized by Ananias. It is possible that he withdrew into the desert for a period of meditation and study (Gal. 1:17–18) and returned to Damascus to preach. It is said: "Saul increased all the more in strength, and confounded the Jews who lived in Damascus by proving that Jesus was the Christ" (Acts 9:22). It was his success in this respect that led to a plot by the Jews to kill Paul (Acts 9:23). When this plot became known, "his disciples took him by night and let him down over the wall, lowering him in a basket" (Acts 9:25).

The governor . . . guarded the city of Damascus in order to seize me: not mentioned in the Acts account. The governor was acting under the instigation of the Jews. It was not unusual for the Jewish leaders to call upon the authorities to act in their behalf and carry out their schemes (note the arrest and crucifixion of Jesus).

Under King Aretas: raises historical questions, the answers to which are difficult. This would have been Aretas IV, who was the ruler of the Nabatean kingdom from 9 B.C. to A.D. 40. The kingdom, under his reign, extended from the Euphrates to the Red Sea. He attacked and defeated Herod Antipas and debated with him over the boundaries of his kingdom. It may very well be that he exercised rulership over Damascus during the period in question since there are no Roman coins for the years A.D. 34–62 among the coins of Damascus. Plummer suggests three possible explanations for the rulership of Aretas over Damascus at that time: (1) Caligula, the Roman Emperor, because he disliked Antipas, may have given Damascus to his enemy. Plummer thinks this the most probable explanation. (2) It may be that Caligula gave Damascus to Aretas to secure his friendship. (3) Plummer considers it impossible to believe that Aretas ruled over Damascus by conquest.

Verse 33: But I was let down in a basket through a window in the wall: differs in details from the account in Acts, but agrees in substance. There is still a "little door" in the walls of the ancient city of Damascus which is the traditional window through which Paul was let down. The basket is mentioned in Acts 9:25, but window is not.

Chapter 12, verses 1–10: Paul continued his boasting in the area of weaknesses in his life, pointing out that "when I am weak, then I am strong" (vs. 10). However, he depreciated the value of boasting again (vs. 1). He then told of a mystical experience in which he had received visions and revelations (vss. 1*b*–6). But the main thrust of the paragraph in this context is the so-called thorn in the flesh (vs. 7). Paul recounted how he had prayed for it to leave him, but the Lord gave him a greater gift—grace to prevail in spite of his weakness (vss. 7–10).

Verse 1: presents a variety of textual problems, but the text on which the RSV translation is based seems to be the best attested.

I must boast: reiterates that the boasting is forced upon him by his opponents. Textual variants read: "but to boast" and "if it is necessary to boast." Both are rejected.

There is nothing to be gained by it: rather, "It is indeed not expedient." Paul would hardly have said, "There is nothing to be gained by it," and then gone ahead with the boasting. Rather, he meant that such action was not the best way of promoting the cause of the gospel. He did not expect to confer spiritual blessings on the Corinthians by his boasting, but he felt it necessary in the light of the Corinthian situation to boast.

But I will go on to visions and revelations of the Lord: i.e., sent from the Lord. *Of the Lord* is to be taken as subjective genitive rather than objective. It was not experiences in which he saw the Lord, but experiences that came from the Lord. *Visions and revelations* are plural and imply a number of such mystical experiences from which Paul singled out a particular one in the following verses. The two words overlap each other but do not necessarily mean the same thing. Revelation could occur without a vision; a vision could come without a revelation. Strachan points out that stories of translations to heaven were common to later Christianity and were not unknown among Jewish writers. He believes that Paul's Jewish-Christian opponents also laid stress on ecstatic experiences as authenticating their teaching. This may or may not be true. It is just as possible that Paul had recounted some of his experiences and had been called a deluded enthusiast (Plummer).

At any rate, Paul did not lay great stress on his ecstatic experiences, and we would have known nothing about them if the circumstances had not demanded that he tell them, or if others had not told them. We know of two. The first was his conversion experience on the road to Damascus (Acts 9:3–6). The other was his call to Macedonia (Acts 16:9–10). In the first he saw the risen Lord, and it was revealed to him that Jesus was the Messiah. In the second he saw a man calling for him to come over into Macedonia, and concluded that "God had called us to preach the gospel to them" (Acts 16:10). Of course, the main thing about such experiences is that they come from the Lord. One can have counterfeit experiences of this nature which are deluding. It is true, also, that revela-

tion through visions were far more common and far more likely in the
first century than in the twentieth. We have the New Testament for our
guidance.

It is important to remember that Paul was still glorying in his weaknesses. His mention of various visions and revelations was a necessary
prelude to his recognition of the weakness that prevailed in his life as a
"thorn in the flesh."

Verses 2–5: an account of one of his mystical experiences. The language shows that Paul had thought and meditated on it, showing as it does
a rhythmical structure and suggesting more than it states.

I know: present tense. He did not say that he had known such a man,
but that he still knew him.

A man in Christ: hence, a Christian man. There is no doubt that Paul
was speaking of one of his most exalted experiences; yet he spoke of himself in the third person. Perhaps the reason is that he was speaking of a
rapture which he had when he was outside of himself, so to speak. The
ecstasy of the experience was outside the realm of his practical experiences
and not to be related in the same way.

Fourteen years ago: which would place the vision around A.D. 43. However, there is no way of identifying this vision with any experience recorded in the Book of Acts. His conversion vision was a coming of the
Lord to him rather than his being raised to heaven (cf. Acts 22:17). The
conjecture that the vision was related to his being stoned at Lystra (cf.
Acts 14:19) can be nothing more than conjecture. It may be that it
occurred during the silent years, before Paul came to Antioch and began
the mission work which is recorded in Acts.

Who . . . was caught up to the third heaven: the abode of God. In Jewish cosmology the first heaven was the abode of the birds, the second the
place of the stars, and the third the abode of God and his angels. *To* is
to be given the meaning of "as far as." [1] *Was caught* is a passive verb
which stresses the fact that the one who had this experience exercised no
initiative in himself. He was "snatched up" by God himself.

Perhaps we should notice for a moment the habit of the Bible of
speaking of the abode of God as a place in space. This kind of speech is
evidence of man's inability to think without the use of time and space
dimensions. God, of course, is not confined to a place in space, either on
earth or in the heavens above. Paul was speaking from the viewpoint of
ancient cosmology in which he was steeped. He had no knowledge of the
immensity of space or of the difficulty that modern man has with the concept of heaven being above us. On the other hand, even in modern days
it is difficult to improve on biblical language. We need to express two
ideas when we speak of God—the otherness of God and the closeness of
God. To say that heaven is God's abode and earth his footstool is a colorful way of saying that God is other than man. When we read such language in the Bible, we are not forced to accept ancient cosmology in order
to understand its meaning. The Bible was not written to give a view of
the cosmos, but to help men come to know God in reality.

---

[1] Denney comments that this expresses the idea of vast spaces.

Whether in the body or out of the body I do not know: does not indicate a doubt as to the fact of the vision but ignorance concerning its mode. Paul was not sure whether his mode of existence had been changed for the time of the vision or not. This was not important. He did know that he was there. This was important. This would indicate that Paul was alone at the time of the vision; otherwise his companions could have told him whether he had been absent in body or not.

God knows: since he knows all things.

Verse 3: repeats verse 2 with only slight alterations.

And I know: repeats the verb in verse 2.

That this man: rather, "such a man." Paul was speaking of himself in both instances.

Was caught up into Paradise: probably a synonym for *the third heaven.* Jesus used this word in his words from the cross to the dying thief: "Truly, I say to you, today you will be with me in Paradise" (Luke 23:43). The only other passage in the New Testament where the word is found, aside from this passage, is Rev. 2:7: "To him who conquers I will grant to eat of the tree of life, which is in the paradise of God." Many commentators have supposed that Paul was speaking of two separate visions or of one vision in two stages, basing their conclusion on the use of *Paradise* in this passage instead of *the third heaven.* Yet, the evidence does not seem to support a marked difference between the two terms.[1] Jesus, after promising the thief that he would be with him in Paradise, commended his own spirit to the Father (Luke 23:46), which would indicate that he thought of Paradise as God's dwelling place. The Book of Revelation identifies heaven as the place where the tree of life is to be found (Rev. 22:2). Therefore it seems that no distinction was made between the two. Paul was simply repeating his description of the vision which he had already given in verse 2.

Out of the body: Out is based on a different Greek word here than in verse 2, but the meaning is the same. In verse 2, "out of" is a proper translation. Here "apart from" would be a better translation.

Verse 4: And he heard things that cannot be told: obscures the word play in the original. Literally, it reads: "He heard unutterable utterances." Paul said nothing about what he saw in Paradise; he chose only to mention the "utterances" heard there. The adjective "unutterable" is found only here in biblical Greek, but was sometimes used in Greek mystery religions of secrets which could be told only to the initiated. However, though some commentators have thought that Paul borrowed the word from this source, it is likely that it was borrowed from the classical Greek. There it simply meant things that could not be expressed in human words, or things too sacred or too horrible to mention (Plummer). The following clause shows that the meaning here is "things too sacred to mention."

Which man may not utter: rather, "which things it is not lawful for a man to speak." This may indicate that they could not be spoken; but if they could, it would be "unlawful" to do so. However, the meaning seems to be that they could be told but that it was "unlawful" to tell

---

[1] Denny thinks it is a second stage of the same rapture.

them. Much conjecture has centered in the content of this revelation, quite without reason. The only thing that can be said with certainty is that Paul received nothing which God meant for him to communicate with others. His mention of the vision is restrained and almost reluctant. Only the force of the circumstances at Corinth led him to mention it at all.

Verse 5: On behalf of this man I will boast: This translates a Greek word which means "such a man." The kind of man who could receive such visions and revelations was the kind of man about whom one could properly boast. Of course, Paul had received the vision, but he wanted to make it clear that he felt that it was based on no merit or capacity in himself. The man who received the vision was under the complete domination and influence of the Holy Spirit, a state which Paul could not claim for himself in everyday circumstances of life.

But on my own behalf I will not boast: as if there were two Pauls, as indeed there were. If we understand the words in the sense that Paul meant them, there is no reason why we could not accept this as true. He meant that in his everyday existence he was not the kind of person who walked around in Paradise. He claimed no special category for himself when compared to other Christians. When he walked around in Paradise, he had not been himself, but had been snatched up out of himself to a unique and extraordinary degree of fellowship with God. He had been entirely passive throughout the experience. Though he had found himself stronger because of it, he had not found himself to be materially changed by it.

Except of my weaknesses: returns to the major theme introduced in 11:30. Notice that he did not say he would boast of himself as the kind of man who was victorious in spite of weaknesses. This would have been egotism. Rather, he boasted of his weaknesses themselves as evidence that he was in himself nothing at all. There is no hint here of the abnormal self-abnegation which is found in other men, but there is clear evidence of the fact that Paul considered himself a nonentity except as he received the grace of God.

Verse 6: parenthetical remark in which Paul claimed that he might right-fully boast if he so desired.

Though if: a form of conditional particle which indicates that this, though possible, is not probable.

I wish: future tense. Combined with the conditional particle, this might be translated, "if I ever wish."

To boast: same word which is used often in this passage. The word is used thirty-seven times in the New Testament, thirty-five of them by Paul. He used the word twenty times in 2 Corinthians, seventeen in these last four chapters. Paul considered it a Christian thing to boast in the Lord, an unchristian thing to boast of anything else.

I shall not be a fool, for I shall be speaking the truth: indicates that there were experiences in his life of which he might boast, but it was unlikely that he would. There is probably a sarcastic intimation that his opponents were fools in their boasting. There is no intimation of contradiction with 11:1, 16, where Paul had labeled all boasting as foolish. Here he was speaking only of possibilities, not of realities.

But I refrain from it: shows that Paul had no intention of entering a boasting contest. The Corinthians were to remember, when they read the letter, that Paul could have boasted truthfully of other things than his weaknesses had he chosen to do so.

So that no one may think more of me than he sees in me or hears from me: indicates Paul's purpose in refraining from boasting. He wished to be judged, not by what he could tell about the exceptional experiences of life, but by what their own contact with him had led them to see and hear.

Verse 7: In pursuit of his intention to boast only in his weaknesses, Paul turned in this verse to his thorn in the flesh.

And to keep me from being too elated: rather, "in order that I may not be lifting myself up unduly." The Greek verb in this expression means literally "to lift up beyond." Since the standard is not noted "beyond" which Paul should not lift himself up, "unduly" catches the meaning. The verb is in the middle voice, which means that Paul was thinking of "lifting himself" up. It is in the present tense, which indicates a continuous action. The word is found only here and 2 Thessalonians 2:4, where it speaks of "the man of lawlessness" as one "who exalts himself against every so-called god or object of worship, so that he takes his seat in the temple of God, proclaiming himself to be God." The word speaks of a self-exaltation which goes beyond any limit of self-opinion which a Christian ought to have. The same expression is repeated at the end of the verse, the repetition giving strong emphasis to the idea. Paul considered that he was in real danger of exalting himself beyond the limits of Christian propriety.

This, of course, is a danger in the lives of all Christians and especially in the life of a preacher. God gives to the preacher many experiences of helpfulness to others, of communication with God, which lay possible foundations for self-exaltation. We are prone to forget that such experiences are not due to our own merit or worth, but to the grace of God. All too often we, unlike Paul, begin to think that there is some special merit or capacity in us that explains our extraordinary privileges. We must avoid this idea at all costs.

By the abundance of revelations: the basis on which Paul might have been egotistical if God had not provided a counteracting reality. Some editors have arranged the verse differently and connected this statement (it comes first in the Greek) with the preceding verse. One has made it another basis of Paul's boasting, suggesting the reading, "I will not boast, except of my weaknesses and the abundance of my revelations." However, such a connection would, it seems, contradict the tenor of the passage. It is better to take it, as the RSV has, as the beginning of a new thought. *Revelations* is plural as in verse 1, but this does not mean that verses 3–4 are descriptions of two different revelations. As we noted above, Paul had had the privilege of several revelations, out of which he had chosen one to mention in this context.

Was given me: by God. Since Paul had come to recognize the thorn as a deterrent to spiritual pride, he considered it as a gift of God. He called the thorn "a messenger of Satan." However, Paul was often conscious of the fact that Satan unwittingly and unwillingly became the servant of God, carrying out God's designs in the life of the Christian, even as he had in the case of Job. Thus there is no contradiction of thought in looking at the same thing as given by God and at the same time as coming from Satan.

A thorn . . . in the flesh: a phrase which has raised many questions, both of translation and interpretation, none of which can be answered with absolute certainty. *In the flesh* should perhaps be translated, "for the flesh." The answer lies in the case of the Greek word, which could be either dative or locative. However, it was more common to use the preposition *(en)* when the locative case was meant, and this is missing in this instance. The thought, then, is that the thorn was meant "for the flesh," i.e., for the earthly life of Paul.

Thorn comes from a Greek word which can be translated "stake." In classical Greek the common meaning was "a stake" which was used either for building a palisade or for impaling someone. However, the regular meaning of the word in the common Greek of the first century was "a thorn." So this translation should be retained. What was this thorn "for" the flesh? There are a number of conjectures by various scholars, and only conjecture is possible. Four are worthy of note: (1) It was some bodily ailment.[1] (2) It was opposition which he encountered.[2] (3) It was carnal temptations. (4) It was spiritual trials which he faced in his ministry. The latter two, it seems, can be eliminated as valid conjectures, and the choice must lie between the first two.

In favor of the second conjecture, that it was a personal enemy, is the context in which so much has been said about his opponents and especially about one who seemed to be the ringleader. That Paul was sometimes beset by personal enemies is shown by his reference to Alexander the coppersmith: "Alexander the coppersmith did me great harm; the Lord will requite him for his deeds" (2 Tim. 4:14). It is also possible to trace the use of this Greek word in this way. "If you do not drive out the inhabitants of the land from before you, then those of them whom you let remain shall be as pricks [the Greek Old Testament uses the same Greek word as Paul] in your eyes" (Num. 33:55). "And for the house of Israel there shall be no more a brier to prick or a thorn to hurt them among all their neighbors who has treated them with contempt" (the Greek Old Testament translates the Hebrew word behind "brier" by the same Greek word which Paul used) (Ezek. 28:24). Thus, both the context and the background make room for the conjecture that Paul's thorn was a personal enemy. However, this conjecture seems to be wrong on two counts. (1) Paul's thorn was something granted to him of God to keep him from self-exaltation, and seems to have been peculiar to him.

---

[1] The usual interpretation is that the "thorn" was a physical handicap of some kind (IB). Goodspeed translates it a "bitter physical affliction." Phillips translates it "a physical handicap." Neil Gregor Smith agrees that it was a physical malady or handicap ("The Thorn That Stayed: An Exposition of II Corinthians 12:7–9," *Interpretation,* Oct. 1959, pp. 409–416).

[2] Terrence Y. Mullins seeks to prove by the context and by Jewish usage that this was a reference to a personal enemy ("Paul's Thorn in the Flesh," *Journal of Biblical Literature,* Dec., 1957, pp. 299–303).

This does not fit the thought of a personal enemy. (2) Paul prayed that God would take away his thorn, and he would hardly have prayed in this way regarding a personal enemy. The reference in 2 Timothy 4:14 shows how he reacted to one personal enemy—by leaving his judgment in the hands of the Lord.

The most probable solution is to believe that Paul's thorn was a physical malady of some kind, so acute, so painful, and such a hindrance to his work of the ministry that he could regard it as the work of the devil.[1] That Paul was afflicted by some recurring malady which hindered his ministry is shown by his reference to his first visit to the Galatian churches: "You know it was because of a bodily ailment that I preached the gospel to you at first; and though my condition was a trial to you, you did not scorn or despise me, but received me as an angel of God, as Christ Jesus. What has become of the satisfaction you felt? For I bear you witness that, if possible, you would have plucked out your eyes and given them to me" (Gal. 4:13-15). From this reference we may suppose that Paul was subject to some kind of bodily ailment, and that it affected his eyes in such a way that he was repulsive to those who saw him. A type of malarial fever fits this description, but some have conjectured that his malady was epilepsy, ophthalmia, or hysteria. On the whole, though the evidence does not warrant dogmatism, it would seem that a type of malarial fever was the thorn in Paul's flesh.

A messenger of Satan: seems to be, but is not, contradictory to Paul's conviction that his thorn was a gift from God. Perhaps this expression shows Paul's first thought of the thorn, while the belief that it was a gift of God shows his mature conception of it. However, ancient people often thought that physical ailments were caused by Satan, and Paul may have been reflecting this belief. At any rate, though it comes from Satan, it was used of God for Paul's spiritual maturity; this shows how the power of God can overcome and thwart the designs of Satan.

To harass me: literally, "to fisticuff me" (Lenski). Paul used a word which came from the Greek word for "fist." Speaking metaphorically, he thought of his thorn as having personality and continually or periodically slapping him in the face. *Harass* is a good interpretation of the meaning of the metaphor.

To keep me from being too elated: repeats the first clause of the sentence, thus laying stress upon God's purpose in giving the thorn.

Verse 8: recites the unsuccessful prayers of Paul for the removal of the thorn.

Three times: probably refers to three different occasions of prayer rather than a thrice-repeated prayer on one occasion.

I besought the Lord: in prayer. *The Lord* probably means Christ, though prayer addressed to Christ is unusual in the New Testament.

About this: the thorn.

That it should leave me: the substance of his prayer. There is no doubt of what Paul wanted. He wanted to be rid of the dread affliction. Probably,

---

[1] Smith, *op. cit.*, rightly says Paul did not attribute this to God.

however, his motives were pure. He did not ask so much that he might be relieved of suffering as that he might be rid of a hindrance to his ministry.

Verse 9: records God's answer to Paul, though he refused to grant the petition.

But: rather, "and." Paul did not look upon the answer of God as contrary to his prayer. We might well find here the reason why God does not grant some of our requests. He wanted to give Paul something better than he asked; so he refused to give him what he asked.

He said to me: perfect tense, "He has said." The implication is that the answer stood true at the time Paul wrote 2 Corinthians.

"My grace is sufficient for you": direct quotation of what the Lord said. *Sufficient for you* is placed first in the Greek clause for emphasis. The implication is that the grace, the unmerited favor of God, was greater than the thorn. God's grace would enable Paul to overcome the hindrance of the thorn and carry out his ministry in spite of it. Difficult as it is to see when one suffers, this is a greater blessing than having difficulties removed. To live with the constant knowledge of one's own weakness but with the consciousness of God's sustaining grace is a far more glorious life than to live with no hindrances at all.

"For my power is made perfect in weakness": continues the direct quotation of what the Lord had said. *Made perfect* translates the Greek word which means "brought to completion." There is no indication that God's power is ever imperfect. The thought is that his power, working through human weakness, accomplishes its purpose. Perhaps the idea is that the results are thus shown to be the result of divine power rather than human achievement. When human strength is great, it is easy to overlook divine power and to think that the results are due to man's work.

I will all the more gladly boast of my weaknesses: should begin a new verse, since the words are now Paul's. The translation is not good. It should read, "most gladly therefore will I rather glory in my weaknesses." The thought is that Paul would do this rather than pray for the removal of the weaknesses.

That the power of Christ may rest upon me: rather, "that may tabernacle on me the power of Christ." The order of the Greek words is important, though a literal translation is awkward. *Rest upon me* is a bold metaphor in the Greek. The word means "to tabernacle" or "to pitch a tent." The idea is of temporary rather than permanent residence.

Verse 10: continues the thought of Paul's willingness to be weak so that the strength of Christ might operate through him.

For the sake of Christ: the basis of his contentment with a life that was less than satisfactory when judged by human standards.

I am content: weak translation of the Greek verb meaning "well pleased." Paul was not stating a passive attitude but a positive one. Having seen the reason for the Lord's refusal to free him of his thorn, he was "well pleased" with his life as it was.

Weaknesses: the first of five words describing Paul's life. If the thorn in the flesh was a physical malady, as seems most likely, this word would include it. Perhaps this general term includes the others which come as a result of it.

Insults: weak translation. "The word implies wanton injury, insolent maltreatment, and therefore it is occasionally used of apparently wanton damage done by storms, as in Acts" (Plummer). This word refers to mistreatment of Paul by his enemies, inquiries which he refused to meet with the spirit of retaliation.

Hardships: such as he had enumerated in 11:26–28.

Persecutions: derived from the word which means "to pursue." The persecuted man was pursued by his enemies, who sought his downfall. Paul, instead of meeting persecutions with wrath as a strong man might, endured them as a weak man.

Calamities: rather, "distresses." The word indicates one who is in a tight place and can do nothing but suffer. *Calamities* is too strong a translation of the Greek word.

For when I am weak, then I am strong: reverses the whole worldly standard of judgment. Paul meant that when he recognized his own weakness, he relied upon the strength of the Lord and thus was indeed strong. His weakness opened the way for the power of Christ to become operative.

(3) The necessity of the entreaty—the church had failed to accept his apostleship (12:11–13)

Paul recognized that his boasting in the previous verses had been foolishness (vs. 11*a*), but he insisted that he had been forced to it by the failure of the Corinthians (vs. 11*b*). He reiterated that he was in no way inferior to the superlative apostles, even though he was nothing (vs. 11*c*); and he rebuked the church for their blindness to the true signs of apostleship which they had seen in his ministry (vs. 12). Finally he apologized for having favored the Corinthians above other churches (vs. 13).

Verse 11: I have been a fool: almost an exclamation of annoyance as Paul realized that he had engaged in what he knew was foolish. He admitted his folly but threw the responsibility for it on the Corinthians.

You: emphatic use of the pronoun in the Greek.

Forced me to it: insists that the Corinthians should at least share the responsibility for his folly.

For I: emphatic use of pronoun in the Greek. *I,* in contrast to my enemies.

Ought to have been commended: rather than suffering the indignity of having his converts listen to sneers and insinuations from others.

By you: emphatic use of pronoun in the Greek. *You,* of all people, should have been my defenders. Paul felt that he had a right to commendation from them, that it was a debt they owed him.

For I am not at all inferior to these superlative apostles: states the reason why they could have commended him with a good conscience. Paul called his opponents *superlative apostles* in a note of sarcasm. This was what they thought they were.

Even though I am nothing: ironical conclusion to the verse. Paul meant that he need not brag to state that he was not inferior to such people. Even a nobody could say that, and Paul was a nobody apart from Christ.

Verse 12: gives the reason why the Corinthians should have rushed to Paul's defense. They had evidence of his divine commission.

The signs of a true apostle were performed among you: changes the verb to the passive. Paul did not say, "I performed them." He said that they were performed, thus giving the credit for them to the operation of the power of God through him. The signs are further explained in the following words of the sentence.

Signs and wonders and mighty works: three words to describe the same thing—a miracle. It is a *sign* because it points to the power of God and is a means to something else rather than an end in itself. It is a *wonder* because it produces awe in the one who beholds it. It is a *mighty work* because it can be accomplished only by divine power. It is doubtful that Paul had three different kinds of miracles in mind by the use of the three words (as Plummer suggests). This verse points out the true function of miracles in the redemptive work of God—to authenticate the messenger and induce people to listen to him. Even in the life of Jesus, miracles were never used for the sake of the miracle, but to show people that Jesus was the messenger of God. So it was with the apostles. There is no longer a need for the messengers of God to be authenticated in this way. Preachers are judged by their conformity to the gospel. But, in the beginning of the Christian movement there was a real need for signs. Paul had been thus authenticated by the power of God, but his opponents had not been.

Verse 13: returns to the thought of Paul's refusal to accept support from the Corinthians or, at least, his refusal to demand it. This seems to have been a pressing question in the minds of the Corinthians. Evidently the opponents of Paul had harped upon this fact until the Corinthians had begun to see it as an insult rather than a concession to them.

For in what were you less favored than the rest of the churches: implies that they thought they had been neglected in some way.

Except that I myself did not burden you: by demanding financial support. This was the only way in which Paul was willing to concede that he had mistreated the Corinthians.

Forgive me this wrong: sly irony. Paul was willing to admit that he had not taken support from them. If they thought this an injury instead of a manifestation of his love, he asked their forgiveness.

3. An Entreaty to Be Prepared for His Third Visit (12:14—13:10)

The material in this section revolves around Paul's forthcoming third visit, which he mentioned three times (12:14; 13:1,10). Paul's main concern is expressed in the words: "I write this while I am away from you, in order that when I come I may not have to be severe in my use of the authority which the Lord has given me for building up and not for tearing down" (13:10). First, he pointed out that his dealings with the Corinthians had always been motivated by his love and concern for them (12:14–18). Next, he reiterated his intention of dealing with harshness and severity with the recalcitrant minority when he arrived (12:19—

2 CORINTHIANS 12:14—13:10

[434

13:4). Finally, he expressed his hope that they would repent before his arrival; consequently, both they and Paul would be spared the necessity of severe action (13:5–10).

(1) The basis of his entreaty—his dealings with them had always been in love (12:14–18)

Paul asserted his intention of coming to them for the third time but insisted that he still refused to become a burden to them, appealing to the analogy of the parent and his children (vs. 14). He asserted his willingness to be spent for them and inquired whether his loving them more meant that they loved him less (vs. 15). Verse 16 raises a question concerning Paul's motives, quoting their charge that he had used guile in his dealings with them. Verses 17–18 consist of a series of rhetorical questions in which Paul answered the charges, using argumentation by interrogation.

Verse 14: warns of his coming and insists that he still would refuse to be a burden to them.

Here for the third time I am ready to come to you: should be taken in the natural sense that Paul was about to make a third visit to the church. Some have interpreted the words to mean that he was only making a third preparation to come, that this does not imply that he had made two previous visits. However, such an interpretation strains the Greek and is quite unnecessary. We know of one prior visit of Paul, the one on which he had founded the church at Corinth. He said that he had determined not to make them "another painful visit" (2 Cor. 2:1), which implies that he had made one painful visit already. The best solution to the problem is to suppose that Paul had made a short visit to the church in an attempt to bring peace out of chaos and had failed. Now he intended to make a third visit.

And I will not be a burden: translates a single Greek word which Paul used three times in this section (11:19; 12:13; here). The word has a doubtful meaning, perhaps being a common medical term meaning, "to stupefy." However, the RSV translation seems to be the common meaning. The word seems to have had a bad sound, something like our word "sponge." Paul repeated the word, always with a denial that he did this to the Corinthians and with an implication that the interlopers did do it.

For I seek not what is yours but you: defines the meaning of the previous word to Paul. To *be a burden* would be to seek their possessions. Paul did not want that; he wanted them. Not that he wanted them for his own glory, but that he might present them to Christ (cf. 11:2). He wanted something from them, it is true. He wanted their greatest gift—themselves. The present tense in the verb indicates that this was his habitual motivation.

For children ought not to lay up for their parents: a metaphorical appeal. Paul regarded himself as the father of the Corinthians and so could use the metaphor with meaning. The normal state of affairs in all societies is for the parents to provide the necessities of life for the children, not the contrary. Paul did not, of course, mean that children never had an obligation to support their parents. He appealed only to the normal course of life. *Lay up* is a stronger word than our word "support." It is the same word used by Jesus in the Sermon on the Mount, when he said: "Do not lay up for yourselves treasures on earth" (Matt. 6:19). The Greek means "to lay up treasure" or "to accumulate money." It would be extremely abnormal for a child to do this for his parent, but it is normal for a parent to do this for his child and heir. We need not force the analogy overmuch in speaking of Paul's contacts with his churches. Plummer seems to do this when he remarks that Paul allowed the Macedonians to contribute to his support but did not allow them to "raise a fund" for him. Paul was only using a metaphor to explain why he felt compelled not to ask for money from the Corinthians.

It is worthy of note that this verse speaks with tenderness and affection for the whole church, thus belying the usual contention that this whole section is a diatribe against the church and belongs in another letter. Paul never lost his affection for the church as a whole. His bitterness was evident only when he spoke of the interlopers.

Verse 15: an emphatic iteration of Paul's love for the Corinthians.

I: emphatic in the Greek, meaning "I, for my part." The implied contrast with the attitude of his opponents is clear.

Most gladly: speaks of the willingness of Paul. He was not a reluctant, but a cheerful, giver of himself.

Will . . . spend: verb used for spending money (cf. Mark 5:26). It could also be used, as our English word is, for spending time, energy, and strength. The last meaning is the one Paul had in mind.

And be spent: passive of the same verb with an added preposition which heightens the meaning. This verb means "to be spent completely." Paul was willing to go far beyond the duty of parent to child and to be spent utterly.

For your souls: i.e., for your spiritual good. "Soul" is used in the New Testament for the whole self, but this unusual expression is probably to be taken to mean their spiritual good.

If: a form of the conditional particle which implies the truth of the assumption.

I love you the more: or, "more abundantly." The comparative is for emphasis. If Paul had loved the Corinthians more than he loved his other churches, this would not be strange. Love often grows greater for problem children. However, both the opponents and other churches are forgotten in this tender passage.

Am I to be loved the less: a plaintive question. Is love abundant to be repaid by love weak? This would seem to be the case. However, Paul was probably using the question to chide the Corinthians and call them back to their devotion to him.

Verse 16: turns to a charge against Paul by his opponents.

But granting that I myself did not burden you: It was impossible for his opponents to deny that Paul had refused to accept maintenance from them. He had not been a burden. The words should be taken as an indirect quotation of what others said.

I was crafty, you say: poor translation. *You say* is not expressed in the Greek, but it is implied. Perhaps "they say" would be better. *I was crafty* translates a participial phrase which means "being thoroughly unscrupulous." The expression calls Paul's character into question. His opponents had accused him of having an ulterior motive in his refusal of their money. *Crafty* translates a compound Greek word with two elements: one meaning "all" and the other, "work." The idea of the word is that one is ready to do anything. In a bad sense it means that he is thoroughly unscrupulous, ready to go to any end to attain his ends. This word is found nowhere else in the New Testament, but a cognate word is used often (cf. 4:2; 11:3; 1 Cor. 3:19; Eph. 4:14; Luke 20:23), always in a bad sense—once of the devil's cunning deception of Eve (cf. 2 Cor. 11:3).

Got the better of you by guile: Got the better of you translates a word which means "I took you." The metaphor comes from hunting or fishing. It means that they had accused him of entrapping the Corinthians. *Guile* in this context would mean the bait that one uses to catch fish or to lure game into a trap. Perhaps his opponents had insinuated that Paul had shared in the money that the Corinthians had given his friends, or that some of the money he was collecting for the poor would stick to his fingers. They would hardly have made an open accusation, but Paul brought out the implications of their insinuations.

Verses 17–18: four rapid questions in which Paul asked the Corinthians if they really believed what had been insinuated.

Did I take advantage of you through any of those whom I sent to you: the first rhetorical question demanding a negative answer. *Sent* translates the verbal form of the word from which we get "apostle." It means that Paul had sent his fellow-workers on a definite mission. His question implies that he had been accused of sending emissaries to get money under false pretenses.

Verse 18: I urged Titus to go, and sent the brother with him: reflects the arrangements which Paul had made for the collection of the relief fund for the poor (cf. 8:16–24).[1]

Did Titus take advantage of you: second rhetorical question demanding a negative answer. Of course Titus had not acted dishonestly. Paul knew that the Corinthians could not suspect him of this. Plummer suggests that the fact that Timothy is not mentioned may indicate that he never reached Corinth at all.

Did we not act in the same spirit: a third rhetorical question, but demanding a positive answer. Paul's behavior had been in perfect harmony with Titus.

Did we not take the same steps: another question with the same meaning as the previous one.

(2) The reason for the entreaty—he intended to deal harshly with the unrepentant (12:19—13:4)

This material is divided into two rather well-defined sections. 2 Corinthians 12:19–21 speaks of Paul's fears as he contemplated his return to

---

[1] Allo argues for this, but Hughes thinks it is a general statement including prior missions.

Corinth. He opened this section with a disavowal of any thought of defending himself in his boasting. He had intended, rather, to speak for the edification of the church (vs. 19). Verse 20 expresses his fear that his coming would be marked by disorder caused by further misunderstanding. Verse 21 speaks of a greater fear, the fear that he might be humiliated by finding that they had not repented of their sins at all. Chapter 13:1–4 turns to his intention to be severe with those who remained unrepentant when he returned.

Verse 19: speaks of his fear that they might have misunderstood his intention in writing as he had.

Have you been thinking all along: a good translation. *All along* translates a Greek word which is found only here in the New Testament in this sense, but it commonly meant "for some time past." The verb which is translated *have you been thinking* is a present tense in the Greek, but the combination of words demands the perfect tense in English. Some commentators doubt that this is a question, but to take it as a question seems best. Paul could not have known what they were thinking, but he could surmise.

That we have been defending ourselves before you: i.e., trying to vindicate our apostleship. Many modern commentators have ignored this verse and accused Paul of doing just this in these chapters. We should take him seriously and realize that his words were not spoken with the purpose of self-vindication. *Defending ourselves* is the verbal form of the Greek word *apologia,* from which we get our English word "apology." However, the Greek word had a stronger meaning than the English ordinarily has. It was a technical term for defense in the courtroom and was used in this sense by Paul (cf. 2 Tim. 4:16). Of course the word could indicate any kind of defense, either formal or informal.

In the sight of God: as if God were in the audience. This is not an oath but a guarantee of Paul's truthfulness. He would not lie when God was looking on.

In Christ: i.e., in union with Christ, as one in whom Christ dwells and through whom Christ speaks. This was Paul's deepest expression of his devotion to Christ and his sense of unity with him.

We have been speaking: rather, "We are speaking." The present tense indicates Paul's habitual mode of speaking. He disclaimed any effort to speak in his own name, in his own defense. He spoke as Christ led him to speak.

And all for your upbuilding: i.e., to promote your spiritual growth. The metaphor is a common one with Paul. He thought of Christian character as an edifice that arose on the foundation of surrender to Christ as Lord. The purpose of his writing had been to build that edifice higher.

Beloved: added to remind them of Paul's tender love for them.

Verse 20: speaks of his fears as he faced his coming visit with them. The fears expressed here have to do with a disruption of his personal relations with the Corinthians.

For: is continuative. It introduces the reason why he had felt it necessary to write as he had.

I fear: present tense. This indicates a constant dread that haunted the apostle's mind as he thought of his coming visit.

That perhaps: indicates that his fears were not solidly founded on fact. He could have faced fact with courage, but uncertainty made him fearful.

I may come and find you not what I wish: i.e., repentant of their digressions from true devotion to Christ.

And that you may find me not what you wish: recognizes that he must meet their expectations of an apostle when he came.

That perhaps there may be: again uncertainty is expressed.

Quarreling: the first of eight vices, all of them having to do with personal relationships. The Greek word is *eris*. Eris was the Greek goddess of discord. The primary meaning of the word is that of strife arising from the party spirit.

Jealousy: a twin word with "strife." The Greek word means "zeal," but it is zeal for one's side in a dispute.

Anger: rather, "wrath." The Greek word is the warmer word for *anger*. It does not mean the settled disposition of anger, but the hot, flashing thrust of temper.

Selfishness: i.e., selfish ambition. The word is found only in the writings of Aristotle prior to New Testament times, where it means "a self-seeking pursuit of political office by unfair means." [1] This meaning fits perfectly the situation that Paul might face if the Corinthians still retained respect for the interlopers.

Slander: literally, "speakings against."

Gossip: literally, "whisperings." These two words indicate the kind of speaking which might fill the church if the contention still remained when Paul arrived.

Conceit: literally, "swellings." This word is a participial form of the word which Paul had previously used when he accused some of being "puffed up" (cf. 1 Cor. 4:18). *Conceit* is a good translation of the word, but is perhaps a little weaker than the Greek meaning.

Disorder: regular word for political disturbances and tumults. All of these words speak of the fears that Paul entertained of conditions that might come to pass in his third visit. There is little wonder that he could speak of his feelings as *fear*.

Verse 21: turns to a more dire possibility, that the Corinthians (many of them) might still be practicing the vices against which he had warned them (cf. 1 Cor. 5:1—6:20). Temptation to engage in licentious living is always present with Christians; it was much higher in Corinth, where the Christians had come out of these practices when converted and were surrounded by them in the social life of the community.

I fear: is implied in the verse but not expressed in the Greek.

That when I come again: Of this there was no uncertainty; he was coming.

My God may humble me before you: The RSV omits "again," which is in the Greek text. It speaks of a former visit when Paul had been humbled before them. It was of their sins that Paul spoke, but he looked upon the possibility that they might be continuing in them as an humbling

[1] Arndt, William F. and Gingrich, F. Wilbur, *A Greek-English Lexicon of the New Testament and Other Early Christian Literature* (Chicago: The University of Chicago Press, 1957). Hereafter referred to as Arndt-Gingrich.

of himself. Perhaps his thought was that such a situation would prove that his work among them had after all been in vain.[1]

And I may have to mourn: as a result of their sin. *Mourn* expresses the kind of sorrow that one has over the dead.

Over many of those: not the majority of the church, but not an insignificant minority either.

Who sinned before: probably refers to the chapters in 1 Corinthians where he had dealt with the sins of impurity.

And have not repented: The change of tense in the Greek to the simple past tense is important. *Sinned* is a perfect tense indicating a continuation in a state which was once entered into. *Repented* is the simple past (Greek, aorist) tense, which would indicate a single act of repudiation of former actions. It is impossible to decide whether Paul was thinking of some who might not have been truly converted at all or of Christians who had not repudiated a course of sinful action. In either case he would have spoken thus. It seems to me that he was thinking of the possibility of finding that many of the Corinthians had not had true experiences of conversion. Their persistence in sin would show that their profession of faith was only superficial. If so, one can understand why Paul would think that such a state of affairs would be cause for mourning.

Impurity, immorality, and licentiousness: three words for the sexual sins which were so common in Corinth. *Impurity* is a general word. *Immorality* (literally, "fornication") refers to any kind of unlawful sexual practice. *Licentiousness* adds the dimension of defiance of public decency. The same three words are used in a different order in Galatians 5:19 in speaking of the "works of the flesh." They seem to have formed a sort of unholy trio of words used to describe the kind of behavior that was common in the ancient world and is not unknown in the modern world.

Chapter 13, verses 1–4: contain Paul's warning that he would act severely against those who had sinned and had not repented.

This is the third time I am coming to you: gives the natural meaning of the Greek. Some scholars have understood the expression in other terms, but have had to strain the Greek to do so. The objection here is the same as we noted in our comments on 12:14—the difficulty of fitting a second visit into the known chronology of Paul's movements. However, this should not be a great difficulty. We do not have in the New Testament any attempt to give a day-by-day account of the movements of any man. There must have been many visits and movements of which we know nothing.

Any charge must be sustained by the evidence of two or three witnesses: an abbreviated quotation from Deuteronomy 19:15, which reads: "A single witness shall not prevail against a man for any crime or for any wrong in connection with any offense that he has committed; only on the evidence of two witnesses, or of three witnesses, shall a charge be sustained." This is a strange quotation to insert at this place, and scholars have been hard put to explain the reason for it.

Some have supposed that Paul intended to set up court in Corinth and

---

[1] Thrall comments that this does not mean that Paul would fail to take decisive action.

bring witnesses to testify to the misconduct of those who were to be punished (Lenski). Of course, Paul would not have taken the matter into his own hands, but he would have presided over the congregation as they acted. However, this seems to be a doubtful interpretation, to say the least, for two reasons. One is that facilities were probably not available for such a formal procedure in Corinth. Another is that the sins which would be dealt with were flagrant and well known, and such a formal procedure would be unnecessary to establish guilt.

A second proposal which goes back to early Christian exegesis is that Paul looked upon his third visit as the third witness against the Corinthians. Plummer lists this interpretation as that of Chrysostom and Theodoret as well as Calvin and some modern interpreters. Though the witness would be only one, it would be thrice repeated. Lenski objects to this interpretation, his most cogent suggestion being that Paul's first visit to Corinth took place before the trouble arose in Corinth.

Each of these two interpretations suppose a close connection between 12:21 and 13:1, a connection which may not in reality exist. It is possible that Paul was thinking of charges against himself by his opponents. These chapters are filled with implications that various charges and innuendoes were made against Paul by the interlopers. Perhaps he planned to bring these out in the open and demand that his opponents sustain them by solid evidence or else repudiate them. So far as I know, no interpreter has considered this interpretation. However, it seems to me to be worthy of consideration and to make better sense of the quotation than the other two suggestions.

If this is rejected, we may have to fall back on the suggestion of Strachan that Paul often quoted Old Testament passages, the original meaning of which was not relevant; nevertheless, there was an association of ideas between the Scripture quoted and the situation being discussed. In this case Strachan believes that Paul was being "intentionally whimsical."

Verse 2: Paul's warning of his intended action. The translation of the verse is difficult. The Greek reads literally: "I before said and I before say as when I was present the second time and now being absent to those before sinning and to all the rest, that if I come again I will not spare." Perhaps the connection should be as follows: "I forewarned those who before sinned and the others when I was present on my second visit, and I now forewarn them again being absent, that if I come again, I will not spare." The order of the warnings would thus be: On his second visit he had forewarned them of his intention not to spare them when he came again, if he found them still sinning. Contemplating his third visit, he forewarned them again of the same thing.

Those who sinned before: would be those who had sinned prior to the second visit of Paul. Perhaps these would include the incestuous man of 1 Corinthians 5:1-8 and the immoral Christians mentioned in 1 Corinthians 6:12-20. These are the same ones mentioned in 2 Corinthians 12:21.

All the others: might well be the ringleaders of the opposition, the opponents who had caused the confusion in Corinth. They seem to have received both warnings as well as those who sinned before, and could hardly be "those who had lapsed into sin since that visit" (Plummer). It seems best to suppose that these were the opponents, the Judaizers, whom Paul had forewarned while he was with the church on his second visit.

If I come again: better, "when I come again." It seems that Paul had every intention of returning to see if the church had solved its problems and, if not, to deal with them summarily.

I will not spare: speaks of some kind of action which is left undefined. It may have been public censure or excommunication. It was perhaps better to leave the intended punishment undefined until the exact state of affairs was known.

Verse 3: should be more closely connected with verse 2 than the RSV suggests by inserting a dash between the two verses. Perhaps a semicolon would be better. He would act and thus satisfy their desire for proof that he spoke for Christ.

Since you desire proof that Christ is speaking in me: shows why it was impossible for Paul to spare again those who continued in sin or continued to cause confusion in the church. The church itself had demanded proof, perhaps having in mind some outward miracle that Christ was speaking in Paul. Paul would furnish the proof by refusing to spare the transgressors. Perhaps they themselves were the ones who had demanded proof. "Very well," Paul said, "you shall have it, but you will not like it."

He is not weak . . . but is powerful: words of contrast. Perhaps the Corinthians had thought that Christ was weak; Paul asserted that he was powerful. The Greek word for *powerful* is peculiar to Paul in the New Testament. He always used it for divine power. It is the word from which we get our English words "dynamite, dynamo," etc.

In dealing with you . . . in you: represents two prepositional phrases in the Greek: "unto you . . . in you." Perhaps the first is properly translated by the RSV since the preposition can mean "with reference to." The second phrase should be "among you." Christ had already demonstrated his power with reference to them and among them. The fact that there were saints in Corinth was a power of extreme proportions. The spiritual gifts of which they had boasted came from the one Lord (cf. 1 Cor. 12:5). Scepticism of the power of Christ in Corinth seems to have been willful rather than justified.

Verse 4: continues the thought of verse 3. The verses should not be separated by a period; at most a semicolon should be used.

For: a continuative particle. The fact that Christ had been crucified may point to weakness. "It is true" would be a good translation in this context.

He was crucified in weakness: rather because of weakness. Christ had given up his power to become one with man and assume the weakness that was common to the human race. This weakness is shown by the fact that all men die.

But lives by the power of God: God, by raising Christ from the dead, reversed the judgment of men. One who had overcome death, man's supreme enemy, could hardly be called weak.

For we: emphatic in the Greek, "for even we" or "for we also."

Are weak in him: a play on words. Paul's hesitation in dealing harshly with the Corinthians had been mistaken for weakness. He admitted that this was so. When judged by worldly standards, he had acted weakly. But this was only an evidence of his union with Christ, who dealt tenderly with sinners and sought to win them to repentance by his love.

But: strong adversative particle.

In dealing with you: rather, "with reference to you." The thought is of Paul's proposed action toward those who were still unrepentant.

We shall live . . . by the power of God: The same power that raised Jesus from the dead would be demonstrated in Paul's actions. *We* is either the apostles or Paul and his fellow-workers.

With him: by reason of association with him.

(3) The purpose of the entreaty—Paul hoped they would repent and escape the necessity of harsh severity (13:5–10)

In this final section Paul turned to what he hoped they would do. He called upon them to examine themselves to make sure that they were truly Christians (vs. 5). He expressed his hope that they would find him able to meet the test so that they would be inspired to do the right thing (vss. 6–7). He insisted that he was unable to do anything contrary to the truth (vs. 8) and expressed his prayer for their improvement (vs. 9). Verse 10 is a final statement of his reason for writing as he had.

Verse 5: a call to self-examination.

Examine yourselves: The pronoun is very emphatic. The verb is in the present tense. The idea is that it was themselves that they must continually put to the test. This was the opposite of what they had been doing. They had been trying to judge Paul without considering their own spiritual condition. Paul reminded them that it was not he that they should test but themselves. *Examine* translates the Greek word which can mean either "to tempt" or "to test." The latter translation is the correct one in this verse.

To see whether you are holding to your faith: rather, "to see whether you are in the faith." The idea is that they should examine the very foundations of their Christianity and see if they were secure. Such an examination, if it proved that they were truly Christian, would naturally tend to call them back to Christian action. Their behavior had been following the standards of the world instead of the standards of Christ. Paul wanted them to return to home base and set their compasses in the right direction. He had no fear of judgment on that basis.

Test yourselves: The pronoun is again emphatic. The verb is again present tense of continuous action. The verbal idea is, however, different. The word used here is that for approval after testing. In the spiritual realm it would almost have the sense of reassuring themselves of the reality of their conversion.

Do you not realize that Jesus Christ is in you: a poor translation. The question is rhetorical. Literally, the Greek reads: "Or is it that you do not know with reference to yourselves that Christ Jesus is in you?" Their actions had cast doubt on their conversion. Paul was asking if this was an indication that they did not have full knowledge with reference to themselves (the pronoun is again emphatic) of the fact that Christ dwelt in them. In other words, was their concentration on Paul and others a sign of their own lack of security? We need not suppose that Paul doubted their conversion. He had already said that he was sure of their faith (cf. 1:24). He was calling them to examine themselves, to reassure themselves, to approve themselves as true Christians in the hope that this would lead them to Christian action.

Unless indeed you fail to meet the test: rather, and more forcibly, "unless perhaps you are reprobates." This only makes explicit the meaning implicit in the previous words. The Greek word which is translated "fail to meet the test" comes from the process of testing metals and finding that they are not genuine.

Verse 6: The logical conclusion of their self-testing would be a proper testing of Paul and his fellow-workers. This verse expresses the hope that this would vindicate Paul.

I hope: expresses Paul's confident expectation. *Hope* in the New Testament does not indicate doubt but assurance. We might translate the Greek word "I anticipate."

You will find out that we have not failed: rather, "that you will know that we are not reprobate." "You will know" probably means "you will come to know." Thus, the RSV translation, *you will find out,* is justified. *We have not failed* repeats the same word used in the last part of the previous verse. The outcome of their self-testing would be that both they and Paul would be shown to be genuine—they genuine Christians, he a genuine apostle.

Verse 7: But we pray God that you may not do wrong: Paul had no desire to prove his apostolic power by inflicting punishment. His constant prayer (note the present tense) was that they would not be found doing anything *wrong* (i.e., evil). He would prefer that the genuineness of his apostleship go untested.

Not that we may appear to have met the test: Their doing good might result in this, but this was not Paul's concern.

But that you may do what is right: Their repentance would result in a new kind of life. *Right* translates a word which implies that the good thing done is seen to be morally beautiful.

Though we may seem to have failed: rather, "but we as not genuine may be." If they repented and reformed, the test of genuineness would never be applied to Paul; there would be no need for it. Thus it might seem that he had failed the test. He would not have stood it because it never would really be applied. He could not punish because the need for punishment would be over.

Verse 8: states Paul's principle of life.

For we cannot do anything: is to be given its fullest meaning. Paul meant that he was morally unable to do this; it would be wholly at variance with his character.

Against the truth: i.e., contrary to the gospel truth. They may have thought that his love for them would lead to a compromise of truth on Paul's part. He assured them that this could not be.

But only for the truth: reasserts the same thought in positive terms.

Paul's character was such that he must always be on the side of the gospel, even though it meant turning against his beloved converts in Corinth.

Verse 9: continues the thought of verse 7.

We are glad: Rather than being merely content, we rejoice. Jonah grumbled when God spared the Ninevites from the punishment he had predicted; Paul rejoiced because the Corinthians could be spared his threatened punishment.

When we are weak: not able to manifest power in punishment.

And you are strong: not deserving punishment. Paul preferred to continue to show love and mercy toward the Corinthians (attitudes which the world called weakness) because that would mean that they had mended their ways and no longer deserved severity.

What we pray for is your improvement: This prayer is the positive side of the prayer mentioned in verse 7, but much greater. *Improvement* comes from a Greek word which means "to fit or to equip." The original idea of the word was that of fitting things together, whether of setting bones or reconciling parties (Plummer). The meaning here is that of rectifying or restoring what was wrong among the Corinthians. *Improvement* is a rather insipid word for this idea. Perhaps "perfecting" would be better. The idea is that what was wrong would be rectified, and the Corinthians would again take the path of spiritual growth toward perfection.

Verse 10: states why Paul had written as he had.

I write this: probably encompasses all of chapters 10–13. This whole section of his letter, with its invective against the opponents and its continued appeal to the Corinthians as a whole, is included. It is doubtful that *this* includes the other sections of the letter.

While I am away from you: i.e., being absent.

In order that: particle expressing purpose.

When I come: rather, "being present."

I may not have to be severe: rather, "I may have no need to use sharpness." *Severe* comes from an adverb which means "cut off." "Sharply" would be a better translation. The meaning of the adverb reflects back to the statement, "I write this." In other words, he wrote sharply that he might not have to act sharply.

In my use of the authority which the Lord has given me: i.e., in inflicting punishment and chastisement upon sinners. Paul recognized that he had authority, but it was authority that came as a gift from his Lord.

For building up and not for tearing down: the reason he had been given authority. The Lord never intended that Paul would have to exercise that authority for the purpose of destruction. It had been given for the spiritual edification of people. Throughout this paragraph Paul's emotions hovered between fear and hope: hope that the Corinthians would have solved their problems by the time he arrived, fear that they would not. He had no hatred for them, only love. His great desire is that he may be able to act in love and not with severity toward them.

V. CONCLUSION (13:11–14)

The conclusion of this letter fits the letter itself. There is a final appeal (vs. 11) which reflects the troubles in Corinth. There are greetings of the kind with which Paul usually concluded his letters (vss. 12–13). Finally comes the benediction (vs. 14).

1. Final Appeal (13:11)

Finally: Paul's regular way of introducing what he intended to be the closing words of the letter.

Brethren: reminds them that Paul had written to them in the spirit of brotherhood.

Farewell: regular Greek word for leave-taking or greeting.

Mend your ways: same word as in verse 9. Here the verbal form is used with the meaning "work your way onwards to perfection" (Plummer).[1] The RSV translation probably catches the meaning. There was much that needed to be repaired. It was the responsibility of the Corinthians to see that it was done.

Heed my appeal: probably a good translation in this context of a verb which literally means "be comforted" or "be exhorted." Paul had often used the verb in the letter to introduce his appeals to them. Now he asked them to heed (i.e., obey) his appeal.

Agree with one another: rather, "be of the same mind." The idea is that of harmony of action and purpose.

Live in peace: would be the natural result of being harmonious in action and purpose.

And the God of love and peace will be with you: God's presence depended on their own self-rectification. Their squabbles had shut God out of their midst. If they heeded Paul's appeal, they would open the door for God's return and he would return. *God is love* is a peculiar expression found only here in the New Testament. Possibly Paul wanted to remind the Corinthians that his love reflected the love of God. *God . . . of peace* is a common Pauline expression. It means "the God who gives peace."

---

[1] Lightfoot (*Notes on the Epistles of Paul,* p. 47) speaks of two technical uses of the Greek word: (1) for reconciling factions in a political dispute, and (2) for setting bones by a surgeon. Paul usually used it metaphorically.

2. Salutations (13:12–13)

Salutations were a common feature of ordinary correspondence which Paul adopted in his letter-writing.

Greet one another with a holy kiss: as a sign of agreement and love. The kiss was a custom of the Jews in their synagogue services, and this custom was carried over into the Christian church. Of course, the sexes were divided in the congregation, men kissed men; women kissed women. There was no promiscuous kissing. *Holy* modifies the *kiss* and indicates that it was to be a sign of Christian affection rather than a token of ordinary love. Whether this was to be done in the congregational meeting or not is not said. Probably Paul meant that the completion of the reading of the epistle would be marked by such action.

Verse 13: All the saints greet you: i.e., the Corinthians who were with Paul at the time of the writing, in this case the Christians in Macedonia.

3. Benediction (13:14)

This is the fullest benediction, both in wording and meaning, found in the Pauline epistles. Probably written by his own hand, it embodies the Christian gospel in its essence. This benediction is also the one most commonly used in modern churches.

The grace of our Lord Jesus Christ: i.e., the grace that finds its source in him and comes from him. Note the full title. It should be read, "our Lord, Jesus Christ." *Lord* was Paul's title for Jesus; *Jesus Christ* had come to be a compound name.

The love of God: i.e., love which God inspires.

The fellowship of the Holy Spirit: i.e., the partnership of life which the Holy Spirit imparts. In all three phrases the genitive is subjective.

Be with you all: without exception. Even the opponents were included in the benediction. Though he had said many sharp things about them, Paul wished for them all these blessings from God.

AMEN!

ANNOTATED BIBLIOGRAPHY

1 Corinthians

Books and Commentaries

Allo, Le P. E. -B. *Saint Paul Première Épître aux Corinthiens*. Paris: Libraire LeCoffre, 1956. A thoroughgoing exegetical study based on the Greek text by a Roman Catholic scholar.

Arndt, William F. and Gingrich, F. Wilbur. *A Greek-English Lexicon of the New Testament and Other Early Christian Literature*. Chicago: The University of Chicago Press, 1957. Perhaps the best modern lexicon of New Testament Greek.

Barrett, C. K. *A Commentary on the First Epistle to the Corinthians*. New York and Evanston: Harper and Row, Publishers, 1968. Contains a new translation of the epistle and a discerning commentary on the text.

Craig, Clarence Tucker. "Exegesis of the First Epistle to the Corinthians," *The Interpreter's Bible,* Vol. X. George A. Buttrick, commentary editor. New York: Abingdon-Cokesbury Press, 1956. A brief but scholarly exegesis forming a part of this popular commentary.

Dahl, M. E. *The Resurrection of the Body*. Naperville, Ill.: Alec R. Allenson Inc., 1962. A thorough study of the interpretation of 1 Corinthians 15.

Edwards, Thomas Charles. *A Commentary on the First Epistle to the Corinthians*. London: Hodder and Stoughton, 1903. One of the best commentaries on this epistle, especially valuable in word studies and citations of ancient writers.

Findlay, G. G. "St. Paul's First Epistle to the Corinthians," *The Expositor's Greek Testament,* Vol. II. W. Robertson Nicoll, editor. Grand Rapids, Mich.: Wm. B. Eerdman's Publishing Company. Reprint edition. Part of this classic set of commentaries, usually a rich source of linguistic information.

Fuller, Reginald H. *The New Testament in Current Study*. New York: Charles Scribner's Sons, 1962. Contains a chapter on recent developments in Pauline studies which treats the Corinthian letters briefly.

Goudge, H. L. *The First Epistle to the Corinthians*. London: Methuen & Co, Ltd., 1903. A good commentary based on the English translation. *The Greek New Testament,* edited by: Kurt Aland, Matthew Black, Bruce Metzger, and Allen Wikgren. Published by the American Bible Society, 1966. A critical text with apparatus for those readings which make a difference in the translation of the text.

Grosheide, F. W. *Commentary on the First Epistle to the Corinthians.* Grand Rapids: Wm. B. Eerdmans Publishing Company, 1953. A careful exegesis by a conservative scholar.

Héring, Jean. *The First Epistle of Saint Paul to the Corinthians.* Translated from the second French edition by A. W. Heathcote and P. J. Allcock. London: The Epworth Press, 1962. A good example of Protestant French scholarship.

Hurd, John Coolidge. *The Origin of I Corinthians.* New York: Seabury Press, 1965. A thorough discussion of the historical problems connected with the epistle.

Lenski, R. C. H. *The Interpretation of St. Paul's First and Second Epistles to the Corinthians.* Columbus, Ohio: Wartburg Press, 1946. Combines critical exegetical excellence with popular application.

Lightfoot, J. B. *Notes on the Epistles of St. Paul.* Grand Rapids, Mich.: Zondervan Publishing House, 1895. Notes on various letters of Paul, including all of 1 Corinthians, based on the lectures of Lightfoot and published after his death.

Lockhart, Clinton. *Principles of Interpretation.* Fort Worth, Texas.: S. H. Taylor, printer, 1915 (1901). Used primarily for his discussion of "baptism for the dead."

Moffatt, James. *The First Epistle of Paul to the Corinthians.* New York and London: Harper and Brothers Publishers, n.d. A part of a series edited by Moffatt and based on his translation of the New Testament. Provides excellent background material.

Morgenthaler, Robert. *Statistik Des Neutestamentlichen Wortschaetzes.* Zürich-Frankfurt Am Main: Gotthelf-Verlag, 1958. A meticulous statistical count of the frequency with which New Testament words are used.

Montefiore, Hugh. *A Commentary on the Epistle to the Hebrews.* New York and Evanston: Harper & Row, Publishers, 1964. Thinks Hebrews was written to Corinth by Apollos, thus creating an Apollos party with which Paul was primarily concerned in 1 Corinthians 1—4.

Morris, Leon. *The First Epistle of Paul to the Corinthians.* Grand Rapids, Mich.: Wm. B. Eerdmans Publishing Company, 1958. A brief commentary which collects the scholarly opinions on Corinthians and makes some original contributions to its understanding.

Munck, Johannes. *Paul and the Salvation of Mankind.* Translated by Frank Clarke. Richmond, Va.: John Knox Press, 1959. A treatment of Pauline theology. Two chapters are devoted to Corinthian studies.

Parry, R. St. John. *The First Epistle of Paul the Apostle to the Corinthians.* Cambridge: At the University Press, 1916. An excellent commentary based on the Greek text.

Robertson, Archibald and Plummer, Alfred. *A Critical and Exegetical Commentary on the First Epistle of St. Paul to the Corinthians.* Edinburgh: T. & T. Clark, 1914 (second edition). A classic example of thorough exegesis.

Robertson, A. T., *Word Pictures in the New Testament,* Vol. IV, *The Epistles of Paul.* New York: Harper and Brothers Publishers, 1931. Not a complete commentary but very strong in its treatment of word meanings and grammatical constructions.

Schlatter, D. Adolf. *Die Korintherbriefe.* Stuttgart: Calwer Vereinsbuchhandlung, 1928. Combines scholarly excellence with popular appeal.

Schmithals, Walter. *Paul and Jesus.* Translated by Dorothea M. Barton. Naperville, Ill.: Alec R. Allenson, Inc., 1965. Has incidental but pertinent notes on various passages in Corinthians.

Taylor, Kenneth N. *Living Letters.* Wheaton, Ill.: Tyndale House. Publishers, 1962. A paraphrase of New Testament letters.

Thrall, Margaret E. *The First and Second Letters of Paul to the Corinthians.* Cambridge: At the University Press, 1965. A terse, but often helpful, commentary based on *The New English Bible.*

Wilckens, Ulrich. *Weisheit und Torheit.* Tuebingen: J. C. B. Mohr (Paul Siebeck), 1959. A thorough study of Wisdom and Foolishness in 1 Corinthians 1:10—2:16, both exegetically and from the standpoint of their background in the first century.

Wendland, Heinz-Dietrich. *Die Briefe an die Korinther.* Göttingen: Vandenhoeck & Ruprecht, 1954. Contains a translation and brief explanation of the text.

Articles

Baird, William. "Among the Mature," *Interpretation,* Oct., 1959, pp. 425–432. A study of Paul's idea of wisdom in 1 Corinthians 2:6.

Batey, Richard. "Paul's Interaction with the Corinthians," *Journal of Biblical Literature,* June, 1965, pp. 139–146. Reconstructs the various contacts of Paul with the Corinthians.

Beare, Frank W. "Speaking in Tongues," *Journal of Biblical Literature,* September 1964, pp. 229–246. Critical survey of the evidence in the Gospels, the Book of Acts, the Pauline Epistles, and other New Testament writings.

Boers, H. W. "Apocalyptic Eschatology in I Corinthians 15," *Interpretation,* January 1967, pp. 50–65. A study of contemporary interpretation of the passage.

Caird, George B. "Everything to Everyone," *Interpretation,* October, 1959, pp. 387–408. A study of the theology of the Corinthian letters.

Conzelmann, Hans. "On the Analysis of the Confessional Formula in I Corinthians 15:3–5," translated by Mathias Rissi, *Interpretation,* January 1966, pp. 15–25. Discusses evidence that this is an ancient formula originally written in Greek.

Currie, Stuart D. "Speaking in Tongues," *Interpretation,* July 1965, pp. 274–294. An examination of early evidence outside the New Testament bearing on the subject.

Ellis, E. Earle. "A Note on First Corinthians 10:4," *Journal of Biblical Literature,* March 1957, pp. 53–56. Discusses the rabbinic legends of the Rock following the Israelites and finds it rooted in the Old Testament.

Ford, J. Massingberd. "Levirate Marriage in St. Paul (I Cor. VII),"

New Testament Studies, Vol. 10, pp. 361–365. A discussion of the meaning of "virgin" in 1 Corinthians 7:36–38.

Ford, J. Massingberd. "St. Paul, the Philogamist (I Cor. VII in early Patristic Exegesis)," *New Testament Studies,* Vol. 11, pp. 326–348. A study of the early exegetes' understanding of Paul.

Furnish, Victor Paul. "Fellow Workers in God's Service," *Journal of Biblical Literature,* December 1961. A thorough discussion of the Greek word *sunergos* and the interpretation of it in 1 Corinthians 3:9.

Gilmour, S. MacLean. "The Christophany to More than Five Hundred Brethren," *Journal of Biblical Literature,* September 1961, pp. 248–252. Discusses the meaning of the resurrection faith in the rise of early Christianity.

Hofius, Otfried. " 'Bis Dass Er Kommt' (I Kor. 1:26)," *New Testament Studies,* Vol. 14, pp. 439–441. Discusses the meaning of "until he comes" in this verse.

Hooker, Morna D. "Beyond the Things Which Are Written," *New Testament Studies,* pp. 127–132. An examination of 1 Corinthians 4:6.

Jeremias, Joachim. " 'Flesh and Blood Cannot Inherit the Kingdom of God' (I Cor. XV:50)," *New Testament Studies,* Feb. 1956, pp. 151–158.

Kempthorne, R. "Incest and the Body of Christ: A study of 1 Corinthians vi. 12–20," *New Testament Studies,* Vol. 14, pp. 568–574. Relates this paragraph to the incestuous man and thinks that the body is the corporate group rather than the individual.

Malherbe, Abraham J. "The Beasts at Ephesus," *Journal of Biblical Literature,* March 1968, pp. 71–80. Discusses Paul's statement in 1 Corinthians 15:32.

Moule, C. F. D. "A Reconsideration of the Context of *Maranatha,*" *New Testament Studies,* Vol. 8, pp. 307–310. Believes this was a prayer for the immediate, unseen presence of the Lord.

Petruchowski, Jokob J. " 'Do This in Remembrance of Me' (I Cor. 11:24)," *Journal of Biblical Literature,* December 1957, pp. 293–298. Argues from a *formgeschichtliche* standpoint for a Jewish background for the words.

Richards, J. R. "Romans and I Corinthians: Their Chronological Relationship and Comparative Dates," *New Testament Studies,* Vol. 13, pp. 14–30. A discussion of linguistic, doctrinal, and historical evidence for dating Romans prior to 1 Corinthians.

Sanders, Jack T. "First Corinthians 13," *Interpretation,* April 1966, pp. 159–187.

Sweet, J. P. M. "A Sign for Unbelievers: Paul's Attitude to Glossolalia," *New Testament Studies,* Vol. 13, pp. 240–257. Sweet discusses the phenomena of "tongues" against the background of Peter's activity in Corinth and in relation to the modern Pentecostal phenomena.

2 Corinthians

Books and Commentaries

Note: Refer to the bibliography of 1 Corinthians for data concerning the following authors which were used for both books: Arndt and Gingrich, Greek New Testament, Lenski, Lightfoot, Morgenthaler, Munck, Robertson *(Word Pictures),* Schlatter, Thrall, and Wendland.

Allo, Le P. E. -B. *Saint Paul Seconde Épître aux Corinthiens,* Paris: Librairie LeCoffre, 1956. A good example of painstaking Catholic exegesis.

Barclay, William. *The Letters to the Corinthians.* Philadelphia: The Westminster Press, 1964. A popular treatment of selected passages.

Bernard, J. H. "The Second Epistle to the Corinthians," *The Expositor's Greek Testament,* Vol. III, edited by W. Robertson Nicoll. Grand Rapids, Mich.: Wm. B. Eerdmans Publishing Company, reprint edition. One of the classical commentary sets with special emphasis on grammatical and linguistic exegesis.

Conner, W. T. *The Faith of the New Testament.* Nashville: Broadman Press, 1940. A treatment of New Testament theology. Especially good in dealing with Paul's theology.

Denney, James. *The Second Epistle to the Corinthians.* New York: Eaton & Mains, n.d. This is a part of *The Expositor's Bible* edited by W. Robertson Nicoll. It combines popular exposition with exegetical excellence.

Filson, Floyd V. "Exegesis of the Second Epistle to the Corinthians," *The Interpreter's Bible,* Vol. X., George A. Buttrick, commentary editor. New York: Abingdon-Cokesbury Press, 1956. A brief, but scholarly, exegesis of the epistle.

Héring, Jean. *La Seconde Épître de Saint Paul aux Corinthiens.* Paris: Delachaux & Niestlé, 1958. A good example of French Protestant scholarship.

Hodge, Charles. *An Exposition of the Second Epistle to the Corinthians.* New York: George H. Doran Company, 1859. Expository notes based on solid exegesis.

Hughes, Philip E. *Paul's Second Epistle to the Corinthians.* Grand Rapids, Mich.: Wm. B. Eerdmans Publishing Co., 1962. A painstaking and thorough exegesis of the epistle based on the English translation but with reference to the Greek text.

Plummer, Alfred. *A Critical and Exegetical Commentary on the Second Epistle of St. Paul to the Corinthians.* Edinburgh: T. & T. Clark, 1915. A classic commentary based on the Greek text.

Robertson, A. T. *The Glory of the Ministry.* New York: Fleming H. Revell Company, 1911. A popular exposition of 2 Corinthians 2:12—6:10.

Strachan, R. H. *The Second Epistle of Paul to the Corinthians.* New York and London: Harper and Brothers Publishers, n.d. A part of the Moffatt commentary series. Valuable for background studies.

Tasker, R. V. G. *The Second Epistle of Paul to the Corinthians.* Grand Rapids, Mich.: Wm. B. Eerdmans Publishing Company, 1958. A popular, but scholarly, treatment of the epistle.

Articles

Bahr, Gordon J. "The Subscriptions in the Pauline Letters," *Journal of Biblical Literature,* March 1968, pp. 27–41. A thorough study of the concluding remarks of Paul in his letters. Concludes that Paul began such remarks at 2 Corinthians 10:1.

Baird, William. "Letters of Recommendation," *Journal of Biblical Literature,* June 1961, pp. 166–172. A discussion of the textual problems in 2 Corinthians 3:1–3 and the interpretation of these verses.

Bates, W. H. "The Integrity of II Corinthians," *New Testament Studies,* Vol. 12, pp. 56–69. A defense of the integrity of the letter.

Bornkamm, G. "The History of the Origin of the So-called Second Letter to the Corinthians," *New Testament Studies,* Vol. 8, pp. 258–264. Argues that the letter is not a unity. He adds to the usual arguments a consideration of evidence from the church fathers: Clement, Ignatius, and Polycarp.

Craddock, Fred B. "The Poverty of Christ," *Interpretation,* April 1968, pp. 158–170. An investigation of 2 Corinthians 8:9. Argues that Paul introduced the Christological saying, not to urge the example of Jesus, but to set the offering into the larger context of Christian devotion.

Ellis, E. Earle. "II Cor. V. 1–10 in Pauline Eschatology," *New Testament Studies,* Vol. 6, pp. 211–224. Argues that Paul does not discuss the intermediate state at all but contrasts this age with the age-to-come.

Leivestad, Ragnar. "The Meekness and Gentleness of Christ," *New Testament Studies,* Vol. 13, pp. 156–164. Discusses the meaning of 2 Corinthians 10:1 and Paul's reasons for appealing to the meekness and gentleness of Christ.

Martyn, J. Louis. "Epistemology at the Turn of the Ages: 2 Corinthians 5:16," *Christian History and Interpretation: Studies Presented to John Knox.* Edited by W. R. Farmer, C. F. D. Moule, and R. R. Niebuhr. Cambridge: At the University Press, 1967. Martyn argues that Paul's opponents were Gnostics and that the primary issue was epistemology.

Mullins, Terrence Y. "Paul's Thorn in the Flesh," *Journal of Biblical Literature,* December 1957, pp. 299–303. Seeks to prove by context and Jewish usage that this was a reference to a personal enemy.

Smith, Neil Gregor. "The Thorn That Stayed," *Interpretation,* October 1959, pp. 409–416. A detailed exegesis of 2 Corinthians 12:7–9.

Williamson, Lamar, Jr. "Let in Triumph," *Interpretation,* July 1968, pp. 317–332. A thorough study of the background of and Paul's use of *thriambeuō.*